Acing

Constitutional Law

Third Edition

A Checklist Approach to Solving Constitutional Law Problems

Russell L. Weaver
Professor of Law & Distinguished University Scholar
University of Louisville, Louis D. Brandeis School of Law

Steven I. Friedland
Senior Scholar and Professor of Law
Director, Center for Engaged Learning in Law
Elon University School of Law

Series Editor
A. Benjamin Spencer

ACING SERIES®

WEST ACADEMIC

860 Blue Gentian Road, Suite 350
Eagan, MN 55121
1-877-888-1330

Published in the United States of America

ISBN: 979-8-89209-509-9

To Laurence, Ben and Kate, with love, RLW

For Jen, Adin, and Tylie, with love, SIF

Table of Contents

Acing
Constitutional Law
Third Edition

CHAPTER 1

Judicial Review

The doctrine of judicial review provides the judiciary with the power to interpret the Constitution and invalidate actions of the other branches of government (and, in some instances, the actions of state officials). With the Constitution offering only limited guideposts on the boundaries of the doctrine, the judiciary has been left to chart the nuances of its jurisdiction in constitutional matters.

The Origins. Marbury v. Madison, 5 U.S. (1 Cranch) 137 (1803), is the seminal decision on judicial review. *Marbury* is the foundation for most judicial review issues. The decision by Chief Justice John Marshall established the foundation for judicial review, including the proposition that the U.S. Supreme Court may declare an act of Congress unconstitutional.

Marbury is best viewed in historical context. After John Adams, a Federalist, was defeated in the 1800 presidential election, but before Thomas Jefferson assumed the Presidency, the Federalists attempted to stack the court system with new federal judgeships and fill them with Federalist appointees. One of these appointees was William Marbury, who was confirmed as a magistrate in the District of Columbia. Marbury's commission was signed by President Adams and sealed by the Secretary of State. Unfortunately for Marbury, his commission was not delivered before Jefferson assumed office. When the newly inaugurated President Jefferson ordered his Secretary of State, James Madison, to withhold all undelivered commissions, including Marbury's, Marbury sought a *writ of mandamus* to compel delivery through an original action in the U.S. Supreme Court. The action was based on § 13 of the Judiciary Act of 1789 which gave the Court the "power to issue *writs [of] mandamus*, in cases warranted by the principles and usages of law, to [any] persons holding office, under the authority of the United States."

The *Marbury* Court divided its analysis into several parts. First, the Court decreed that Marbury was entitled to the commission because it became a "vested legal right" when it was signed by the President and sealed by the Secretary of State. Second, the Court held that the law should afford Marbury a remedy for the deprivation of his right. Finally, the Court concluded that ordinarily a *writ of mandamus* (ordering the Executive to deliver the commission) would be an appropriate remedy for the deprivation.

The issue that remained, however, was whether Marbury was entitled to invoke the original jurisdiction of the U.S. Supreme Court. The Court examined the Judiciary Act of 1789 which had been interpreted as authorizing it to issue *writs of mandamus*. Article III of the U.S. Constitution gives the U.S. Supreme Court original jurisdiction only in "cases affecting ambassadors, other public ministers and consuls, and those in which a state shall be a party." In other cases, the Court is only allowed to exercise appellate jurisdiction.

Chief Justice Marshall ruled that the proposed interpretation of Article III (giving the court original jurisdiction over *Marbury's* case, was unconstitutional). He began by declaring that the Constitution is the "fundamental and paramount law of the nation, and consequently that an act of the legislature repugnant to the constitution is void." He also rejected the notion that the judiciary is bound by the legislature's conclusions regarding the legitimacy of a law, stating: "it is emphatically the province and duty of the judicial department to say what the law is. Those who apply the rule to particular cases, must of necessity expound and interpret that rule. If two laws conflict with each other, the courts must decide on the operation of each." Finally, he articulated the concept of judicial review: "if a law be in opposition to the constitution: if both the law and the constitution apply to a particular case, so that the court must either decide that case conformably to the law, disregarding the constitution; or conformably to the constitution, disregarding the law: the court must determine which of these conflicting rules governs the case. This is of the very essence of judicial duty."

Marshall then emphasized that the Constitution requires judges to take an oath to support its provisions and he affirmed the Constitution's supremacy: "The particular phraseology of the Constitution of the United States confirms and strengthens the principle, supposed to be essential to all written constitutions, that a law repugnant to the Constitution is void, and that courts, as well as other departments, are bound by that instrument." Because the Judiciary Act had been interpreted as giving the court jurisdiction in cases not provided for in Article III, the proposed interpretation was invalid.

Over the last two hundred years, the power of judicial review has been broadly used by the courts to invalidate the actions of federal officials as well as of state and local officials. Judicial review is not an unlimited power, however, because the federal courts depend on the willingness of the other branches to voluntarily comply with their orders. Moreover, the executive and legislative branches have various means at their disposal for controlling a wayward judiciary. These means include impeachment, prosecutorial decisions, briefs and arguments before the courts, and executive constructions of texts. The President also can alter the Court's composition and perhaps its decision-making through the appointments power.

Marbury v. Madison's Progeny: Expanding and Reaffirming Judicial Review. Marbury dealt with the limited question of the Court's power to refuse to apply a federal legislative enactment. More difficult questions arose when courts attempted to impose their interpretations of the U.S. Constitution on state officials. *Fletcher v. Peck*, 10 U.S. (6 Cranch) 87 (1810), was the first case in which the Court struck down a state law. In *Fletcher*, the Supreme Court held that the Georgia legislature's attempt to void a Georgia land grant was an unconstitutional attempt to void a valid contract. *Fletcher* was followed by *Martin v. Hunter's Lessee*, 14 U.S. (1 Wheat) 304 (1816). In *Martin*, the Virginia Court of Appeals refused to comply with a mandate of the U.S. Supreme Court. The Court held that it had the power to review a judgment of a Virginia state court when federal constitutional issues are involved. The Court reasoned that the Framers intended for the federal courts to exercise uniform appellate jurisdiction over both federal and state cases.

In another case, *Cooper v. Aaron*, 358 U.S. 1 (1958), the Court dealt with the supremacy issue again. *Cooper* involved resistance to the U.S. Supreme Court's decision in *Brown v. Board of Education*, 347 U.S. 483 (1954), prohibiting the states from segregating public schools. The Governor of Arkansas and state officials took a number of steps to prevent desegregation. When local school board officials continued with their desegregation plans, the Governor dispatched units of the Arkansas National Guard to prevent black children from entering previously white schools. Faced with a confrontation, school board officials filed a petition to delay desegregation noting the "extreme public hostility." *Cooper* rejected the notion that desegregation could be postponed by states or state officials. Relying on the Supremacy Clause, the Court concluded that the Constitution is the "Supreme Law of the Land."

Limits on Supreme Court Jurisdiction. As *Marbury* reveals, the Court's original jurisdiction is limited to cases in which ambassadors or other public ministers or consuls or vice counsels of foreign states are parties; cases between the United States and a state; and cases brought by a state against citizens of another state or aliens. Other cases can only be heard by appeal or arrive at the Court by *certiorari*, a discretionary writ. The Court generally considers only important federal questions that should be decided by the Court, cases that involve conflicts between the federal circuits, or conflicts between state courts of last resort. Also, under the so-called *Rule of Four*, the Court will hear a case only if four justices vote to hear it.

The overwhelming majority of cases arrive at the Court through *certiorari* rather than appeal, leaving the state courts to decide many cases. Note that the only remaining route of "appeal" to the Court is from a three-judge court, and the number of three judge courts has been significantly curtailed.

The Court treats even its "mandatory" appellate jurisdiction as discretionary. For example, whereas there were 51 cases on the Court's docket in 1853, the number rose to 8,000 cases by the mid-1990s. The Court is only able to hear a very small percentage of the cases presented to it, leaving much of the decision-making to the lower federal courts and the state courts. In fact, the number of cases actually heard and decided by the Court on the merits has been declining as evidenced by the fact that the Court issued 145 signed opinions in 1986, it now issues only about 80 decisions per year.

In addition, the justices try to avoid deciding constitutional issues unnecessarily. The Cour sometimes construes ambiguous statutes or other laws in ways that avoid constitutional difficulties, rather than choosing a construction that presents constitutional concerns. Likewise, if a state court has decided a case on federal constitutional grounds, but also has decided it on "adequate and independent" state grounds, the Court might refuse to hear the case on the ground that the state court could have reached the same result on state grounds anyway. As a result, there is no need for the federal courts to resolve the federal constitutional issue, and a federal opinion would constitute nothing more than an advisory opinion.

Congressional Control over Jurisdiction of the Courts. One restraint on federal judicial authority is provided for in the Constitution itself: Congress' right to control the jurisdiction of the U.S. Supreme Court and the lower federal courts. Article III, § 2, cl. 2, gives the Court limited original jurisdiction and appellate jurisdiction "with such Exceptions, and under such Regulations as the Congress shall make." Given that some significant cases arrive at the Court by appeal, Congress' control over the Court's appellate jurisdiction represents a potentially significant restraint on the Court's power.

Given the Court's constitutional role, questions have arisen regarding the scope of Congress' "jurisdiction stripping" power, particularly in controversial subject areas, such as school busing and abortion. In perhaps the most famous case on this subject, *Ex Parte McCardle,* 74 U.S. 506 (1868), the Court upheld Congress' attempt to deprive the Court of jurisdiction. In that case, McCardle was charged with libel for publishing newspaper articles about the post-Civil War military government in Mississippi. After he sought a writ of habeas corpus from a federal court, and the writ was denied, he appealed to the U.S. Supreme Court. While the case was pending, Congress passed an act repealing the Court's jurisdiction to hear the case. In upholding the act and dismissing the appeal, the Court refused to inquire into Congress' motives, emphasizing that "the power to make exceptions to the appellate jurisdiction of this court is given by express words" which must be given effect: "Jurisdiction is power to declare the law, and when it ceases to exist, the only function remaining to the court is that of announcing the fact and dismissing the cause."

McCardle was qualified by the Court's holding in *Ex Parte Yerger,* 75 U.S. (8 Wall.) 85 (1868). In *Yerger,* the Court suggested that the repealing act (at issue in *McCardle*) was intended only to prevent cases from going to the U.S. Supreme Court by appeal, and was not intended to prevent the Court from exercising certiorari jurisdiction. In other words, it was not Congress' intent to prevent both the U.S. Supreme Court and the lower federal courts from hearing the case.

McCardle was further qualified, if not overruled, by the Court's subsequent decision in *United States v. Klein,* 80 U.S. 128 (1871). Congress passed a statute declaring that a presidential pardon shall not be admissible in the Court of Claims to support a claim for recovery and that under certain circumstances appellate jurisdiction in the U.S. Supreme Court shall cease. The Court ruled the statute unconstitutional, stating, "Its great and controlling purpose is to deny to pardons granted by the President the effect which this court had adjudged them to have." In other words, Congress could not meddle with substantive outcomes through its procedural control power.

Today, some read the "exceptions" clause literally, allowing Congress to make those exceptions it wants. Others argue that Congress cannot "destroy the *essential role* of the Supreme Court in the constitutional plan." This issue is unresolved.

Justiciability: The Requirements for Courts Exercising Judicial Power. Justiciability is the term used to describe the prerequisites to a federal court's exercise of judicial power. Since federal courts are courts of limited jurisdiction, with the Constitution requiring that the courts hear only "cases and controversies," plaintiffs are not always granted automatic entry into the judicial system.

Political Questions. The political question doctrine precludes the federal courts from hearing so-called "political questions." The doctrine is applied in instances when the Constitution vests other branches of government with the power to resolve certain issues, as well as when the other branches are more suited for resolving issues than the judiciary. As a result, courts refuse to decide those issues.

The leading political question decision is *Baker v. Carr*, 369 U.S. 186 (1962). In *Baker*, the Tennessee Legislature refused to apportion legislative districts for more than six decades. As a result, Tennessee's electoral districts became severely unbalanced with respect to population. Plaintiffs sued, claiming a violation of equal protection of the laws and seeking reapportionment. The Court concluded that the Tennessee case was justiciable because the subject had not been "committed by the Constitution to another branch of government" and the Court found that "judicially manageable standards" were available under the Equal Protection Clause.

Political question issues have arisen in a variety of other contexts. For example, *Baker* was preceded by what appeared to be a simple trespass action in *Luther v. Borden*, 48 U.S. 1 (1849). Following the American Revolution, Rhode Island continued to function under a royal charter issued by Charles II in 1663. In the 1840s, Rhode Island citizens called a constitutional convention to draft a state constitution. Although the resulting constitution was ratified by the people of Rhode Island, and elections were held, the charter government refused to recognize the constitution or the officials elected under it and instead declared a state of martial law. When the charter government used force to put down the "rebellion," and sent soldiers to search Martin Luther's house, Luther sued for trespass. When the soldiers defended on the basis that they were acting pursuant to governmental authority, the Court held that the Guaranty Clause (guaranteeing the people a republican form of government) did not contain judicially manageable standards and therefore the case presented a political question. The Court also emphasized the need for finality, and the lack of criteria by which the courts could determine which form of government was "republican."

The Court has also refused to hear cases involving political gerrymandering. In *Rucho v. Common Cause*, 588 U.S. 684 (2019), plaintiffs challenged congressional districting maps as unconstitutional partisan gerrymanders. The North Carolina plaintiffs complained that their State's districting plan discriminated against Democrats. The Maryland plaintiffs complained that their

State's plan discriminated against Republicans. The Court concluded that both cases involved political questions, and therefore were not justiciable.

Although the Court has been willing to hear and decide cases involving racial gerrymanders, as well as cases involving departure from the principle of one person, one vote, the Court viewed partisan gerrymanders as different because it could not find a "clear, manageable and politically neutral" test for deciding such cases: "There are no legal standards discernible in the Constitution for making such judgments, let alone limited and precise standards that are clear, manageable, and politically neutral." In addition, the Court emphasized that the Constitution assigns apportionment issues to the states, and therefore to an inherently political process.

In general, the Court has been unwilling to consider the legality or constitutionality of combat operations. The Court has treated such cases as non-justiciable because control over most foreign policy issues is textually committed to Congress and the President.

The judiciary also has been unwilling to involve itself in disputes regarding the recognition of foreign governments, or regarding most foreign affairs issues. *Goldwater v. Carter*, 444 U.S. 996 (1979), concerned President Carter's decision to terminate a treaty with Taiwan and to recognize instead the People's Republic of China. Members of Congress sought declaratory and injunctive relief challenging the President's decision. A divided Court refused to hear the case and remanded the case with directions to dismiss.

Nevertheless, the Court sometimes directly confronts one of the other branches of the federal government. In *Powell v. McCormack*, 395 U.S. 486 (1969), after Adam Clayton Powell, Jr., was duly elected to the United States House of Representatives, the House refused to seat him because he had allegedly engaged in misconduct. The House of Representatives claimed that the question of whether to seat Powell was a political question. In the House's view, the Constitution made a textually demonstrable commitment of the issue to the House, through Art. I, § 5, which provides that "[e]ach House shall be the Judge of the Elections, Returns and Qualifications of its own Members." The Court did *not* find a political question that the House can only exclude based on the grounds set forth in Art. I, § 5. As a result, while Congress is the "Judge" of the qualification of its members," (Art. I, § 5.) those qualifications were set at the time of Mr. Powell's election and could not be changed after the fact.

The Case or Controversy Requirement. Article III, § 2, contains perhaps the most important limitation on the judicial power: the case or controversy requirement. That doctrine provides that the federal courts do not have unlimited jurisdiction, but instead are restricted to hearing "cases" and "controversies," meaning concrete issues only. The case or controversy limitation has produced various doctrines restricting the scope of judicial authority including the prohibition against advisory opinions, the ripeness and mootness doctrines, and the standing requirement.

The Prohibition Against Advisory Opinions. The case or controversy requirement of Article III has led courts to avoid acting as an advisor to the executive or legislative branches. In various cases, courts have dismissed actions that were insufficiently concrete or did not provide redress to the parties involved in the suit.

Ripeness. The "case and controversy" requirement precludes the federal courts from hearing cases that are not ripe for consideration. A case that is brought too early is not "ripe" if it prematurely involves the courts in the adjudication of a matter.

Many ripeness cases arise when an administrative agency threatens to take some action against an individual or company or threatens to withhold governmental benefits. In *United Public Workers of America v. Mitchell*, 330 U.S. 75 (1947), a federal statute (the Hatch Act) made it illegal for federal employees to engage in certain political activities including political campaigns. Appellants, who wished to engage in prohibited activities, sought injunctive relief preventing enforcement of the Act. The Court held that the case was not ripe because plaintiffs had stated their claims in vague terms, and had not clearly indicated what they intended to do. Noting that a "hypothetical threat is not enough" to invoke judicial intervention, the Court refused to "speculate as to the kinds of political activity the appellants desire to engage in or as to the contents of their proposed public statements or the circumstances of their publication."

United Public Workers' narrow view of ripeness is not reflected in the Court's later decisions. For example, *Abbott Laboratories v. Gardner*, 387 U.S. 136 (1967), another administrative case, involved amendments to the Federal Food, Drug, and Cosmetic Act which required manufacturers of prescription drugs to print the "established name" of drugs "prominently and in type at least half as large as that used thereon for any proprietary name or designation for such drug," on labels and other printed material. The Court held that the case was ripe for review. In deciding whether a case is ripe, courts consider two factors: "the fitness of the issues for judicial decision and the hardship to the parties of withholding court consideration." The Court concluded that Abbott Laboratories satisfied this test, noting that the issue was a "purely legal one" and that "the impact of the regulations upon the petitioners is sufficiently direct and immediate as to render the issue appropriate for judicial review at this stage."

In *Trump v. New York*, 592 U.S. 125 (2020), various states sought to challenge then President Donald Trump's decision to exclude aliens from the U.S. who did not have legal immigration status. A number of states sued, claiming that they would be injured by Trump's decision because it could affect the level of their federal funding, as well as the size of their congressional delegations. However, the Court dismissed the case as non-justiciable, concluding that the government had not altered its census calculations in any sort of predictable manner, and it was not clear whether (or if) the President's directive would affect funding or representation:

> The source of any injury to the plaintiffs is the action that the Secretary or President *might* take in the future to exclude unspecified individuals from the apportionment base—not the policy itself "in the abstract," *Summers v. Earth Island Institute*, 555 U.S. 488, 494 (2009). Letting the Executive Branch's decisionmaking process run its course not only brings "more manageable proportions" to the scope of the parties' dispute, but also "ensures that we act *as judges*, and do not engage in policymaking properly left to elected representatives," *Hollingsworth v. Perry*, 570 U.S. 693, 700 (2013). In the meantime the plaintiffs suffer no concrete harm from the challenged policy itself, which does not require them "to do anything or to refrain from doing anything." *Ohio Forestry Assn., Inc. v. Sierra Club*, 523 U.S. 726, 733 (1998).

Mootness. The mootness doctrine involves a claim that may have been ripe at one point, but is now "moot" in that there is no longer an active case or controversy. In essence, the parties are "too late," and the Court again avoids entangling itself in abstract or hypothetical disagreements.

The mootness doctrine is illustrated in *DeFunis v. Odegaard*, 416 U.S. 312 (1974). In that case, DeFunis, who claimed that he had been subjected to reverse racial discrimination, sought and obtained an injunction requiring the University of Washington School of Law to admit him to its entering class. By the time that the case reached the U.S. Supreme Court, DeFunis was in his final term of law school. The Court concluded that the case was moot because DeFunis would receive his diploma regardless of the outcome of the case. As a result, the "controversy between the parties has thus clearly ceased to be 'definite and concrete' and no longer 'touch(es) the legal relations of parties having adverse legal interests.' "

In some instances, when a case is "capable of repetition, but evading review," the Court will hear and decide the case notwithstanding the presence of mootness. In *Roe v. Wade*, 410 U.S. 113 (1973), a Texas statute criminalized abortion. Jane Roe, a single unmarried woman, who was pregnant, claimed that she wished to terminate her pregnancy by an abortion. By the time the case was heard by the Court, Roe was no longer pregnant and the state moved to dismiss her appeal on mootness grounds. The Court held that the case was not moot, noting that the normal pregnancy period is so short (266 days) that it is unlikely that the judicial process will be complete before the pregnancy ends. The Court concluded that the issues raised by the case were "capable of repetition, yet evading review." As a result, the Court did dismiss the case as moot.

In *Susan B. Anthony List v. Driehaus*, 573 U.S. 149 (2014), petitioners challenged an Ohio statute that prohibited certain "false statements" "during the course of any campaign for nomination or election to public office or office of a political party." In particular, the law made it a crime for anyone to "make a false statement concerning the voting record of a candidate or public official," or to "post, publish, circulate, distribute, or otherwise disseminate a false statement concerning a candidate, either knowing the same to be false or with reckless disregard of whether it was false or not." An aggrieved person could file a complaint with the Ohio Elections Commission. If filed within 60 days of a primary election or 90 days of a general election, the complaint was referred to a panel for an expedited hearing, generally within two business days, to determine whether there was probable cause to believe the violation occurred. Upon a finding of probable cause, the full Commission was required to hold a hearing within 10 days. At that hearing, the Commission could subpoena witnesses and compel production of documents. Alternatively, the Commission could issue a reprimand. Violation of the statute is a first-degree misdemeanor punishable by up to six months of imprisonment, a fine up to $5,000, or both. A second conviction was treated as a fourth-degree felony that carries a mandatory penalty of disfranchisement.

The law was challenged by Susan B. Anthony List (SBA), a "pro-life advocacy organization," after it criticized various Members of Congress who voted for the Patient Protection and Affordable Care Act (ACA). The criticism suggested that the members, in voting for the Act, had supported "taxpayer-funded abortion." Then Congressman Steve Driehaus, one of the representatives who was criticized, filed a complaint, claiming that SBA was falsely claiming that he had voted for abortion. Because Driehaus filed his complaint 29 days before the general election, a Commission panel held an expedited hearing and found probable cause that a violation had been committed. SBA filed suit, seeking declaratory and injunctive relief. When Driehaus lost the election, he moved to withdraw his complaint against SBA, and the question was whether the case had become moot. The Court held that a case or controversy continued to exist because SBA had alleged that it intended to make similar statements in future elections. Noting that the SBA was engaged in political speech, and that the SBA had already been prosecuted under the law, the Court found a credible risk of future enforcement: "As long as petitioners continue to engage in comparable electoral speech, that speech will remain arguably proscribed by Ohio's false statement statute," and there may be subsequent attempts to enforce. Indeed, future plaintiffs might be able to "invoke the prior probable-cause finding to prove that SBA knowingly lied." Moreover, since complaints receive expedited consideration during the course of a political campaign, individuals and organizations can use the Act to disrupt opponents and force them to devote time and resources to defending against a complaint, and the complaint may lead the electorate to believe that allegations are false when they might not be.

In *United States v. Juvenile Male*, 564 U.S. 932 (2011), a convicted sex offender challenged a trial court order requiring him to register under the Sex Offender Registration and Notification Act. After he turned 21, and was no longer subject to the jurisdiction of the juvenile court, the special order expired. Since state law would have required him to register as a sex offender anyway, the Court dismissed his challenge to the special order as moot: "When defendant challenges his underlying conviction, this Court's cases have presumed the existence of collateral consequences. But when a defendant challenges only an expired sentence, no such presumption applies and the defendant must bear the burden of identifying some ongoing 'collateral consequence' that is 'traceable' to the challenged portion of the sentence and 'likely to be redressed by a favorable judicial decision.' " The Court found no injury even though state law required him to register since the obligation to register would continue to exist regardless of the outcome in this case.

By contrast, in *United States v. Sanchez-Gomez*, 584 U.S. 38 (2018), the Court refused to conclude that there was a continuing controversy. In that case, four criminal defendants objected to the fact that they were bound in full restraints during their pretrial proceedings. However, by the time that their cases reached the appellate courts defendants had decided to plead guilty. Two defendants, who had been charged with illegal entry into the U.S. claimed that their cases were not moot because their claims were "capable of repetition, yet evading review" because they intended to try to reenter the U.S. The Court rejected the argument, noting that a dispute qualifies for that exception only "if (1) the challenged action is in its duration too short to be fully litigated prior to its cessation or expiration, and (2) there is a reasonable expectation that the same complaining party will be subjected to the same action again." The Court was unwilling to assume jurisdiction based on defendants' claims that they would again violate the law, be apprehended, and be returned to pretrial custody. The Court "assumed that litigants will conduct their activities in compliance with the law and so avoid prosecution and conviction as well as exposure to the challenged course of conduct." The Court rejected the idea that the nature of their offense (illegal entry into the US) made it extremely likely that they would make another illegal entry and again be subjected to pretrial detention.

Standing. The case and controversy requirement also imposes a requirement that the plaintiff have "standing" to bring the case. The question is whether the party bringing the action is suffering sufficient injury to have a meaningful stake in the outcome of the litigation.

Unlike the ripeness and mootness doctrines, both of which focus on whether a suit has been brought in a timely manner (either too soon or too late), standing focuses on whether a plaintiff has a sufficient interest in the litigation to allow her to litigate the issues. In general, the judiciary will not entertain a "generalized grievance against allegedly illegal governmental conduct."

In order to establish standing, plaintiff must allege facts demonstrating that she has been injured and is a proper party to bring the suit. The standing doctrine involves two separate and distinct elements: First, the plaintiff must have suffered an "injury in fact," in the form of an invasion of a legally protected interest, which is both "concrete" and "particularized," and is "actual or imminent, not conjectural or hypothetical." Second, there must be a causal connection between the injury and the defendant's conduct so that the plaintiff's injury will be redressed by a favorable decision. In addition, in cases involving allegations of congressionally authorized standing, plaintiffs must show that they fall within the zone of interest sought to be protected by the congressional authorization.

In addition to serving as a constitutional limitation, standing cases also involve a "prudential" element. In some cases, even though a plaintiff may have sufficient standing to satisfy Article III's case and controversy requirement, the level of injury may be sufficiently low so that the Court deems it prudent to deny standing. In other words, as a matter of discretion, the Court refuses to hear the case.

Taxpayer Standing. In early cases, many plaintiffs attempted to base their standing claims on their status as taxpayers, arguing that taxpayers should have an automatic right to enforce constitutional provisions. However, in *Frothingham v. Mellon*, 262 U.S. 447 (1923), the Court rejected the idea of taxpayer standing. *Frothingham* involved the federal Maternity Act that appropriated money from the federal treasury for the purpose of reducing maternal and infant mortality. Frothingham sued alleging that the statute "took" her property without due process of law. The Court held that Frothingham's claim (that the appropriations would increase her future taxes) was "speculative," that Frothingham was suffering only in "some indefinite way in common with people generally," and therefore the Court declined to hear the case.

The Court allows taxpayer challenges in some instances. For example, in *Baldwin v. G.A.F. Seelig, Inc.*, 294 U.S. 511 (1935), the Court held that a taxpayer always has standing to challenge a tax that he or she is required to pay. In that case, the Court held that a milk distributor could challenge a direct tax on milk. *Baldwin* is distinguishable from *Frothingham* on the basis that *Frothingham* involved a challenge to an *expenditure* (the government's decision to spend money under the Maternity Act) rather than to a tax.

Frothingham did suggest that a municipal taxpayer might have a sufficient interest in the municipality's expenditures to establish standing: "The interest of a taxpayer of a municipality in the application of its moneys is direct and immediate." However, the Court concluded that a taxpayer's interest in the federal treasury was "very different" because municipal monies are "partly realized from taxation and partly from other sources" as well as because the federal taxpayer's interest "is shared with millions of others, [and] is comparatively minute and indeterminable."

The Court expanded the concept of taxpayer standing in *Flast v. Cohen,* 392 U.S. 83 (1968). In that case, the Court held that a federal taxpayer could establish standing to challenge a federal expenditure (as opposed to a tax) that was made under Titles I and II of the Elementary and Secondary Education Act of 1965. The statute was enacted to finance instruction in reading, arithmetic, and other subjects in religious schools, and to provide for the purchase of textbooks and other instructional materials for use in such schools. The *Flast* Court concluded that plaintiff could establish standing if he could show that there is a "logical nexus between the status asserted and the claim sought to be adjudicated" which assures that the plaintiff "is a proper and appropriate party to invoke federal judicial power."

For an Establishment Clause challenge, *Flast* held that a taxpayer might be an appropriate plaintiff if he is challenging an exercise of congressional power under the taxing and spending clause (Art. I, § 8), and is able to show "that the challenged enactment exceeds specific constitutional limitations imposed upon the exercise of the congressional taxing and spending power. It is not enough for a taxpayer to allege that an enactment is generally beyond the powers delegated to Congress by Art. I, § 8." If a taxpayer can satisfy the nexus, then he is "a proper and appropriate party to invoke a federal court's jurisdiction."

Applying the nexus test, the *Flast* Court held that the plaintiffs in that case established standing by challenging a substantial expenditure under Art. I, § 8, and by alleging that the expenditures violated the Establishment and Free Exercise Clauses of the First Amendment. The Court viewed those clauses as providing "a specific constitutional limitation upon the exercise by Congress of the taxing and spending power conferred by Art. I, § 8." The Court distinguished the *Frothingham* plaintiff on the basis that Frothingham's attack was based on an allegation that her tax liability would be increased because of the Maternity Act, and that she would therefore suffer "a deprivation of property without due process of law." The Court concluded that the Due Process Clause did not constitute a specific limitation on the federal spending power.

In subsequent cases, the Court has failed to extend the *Flast* test to other situations. As a result, it is probably limited to its facts. For example, in *United States v. Richardson*, 418 U.S. 166 (1974), a taxpayer challenged the Central Intelligence Agency Act (CIAA) which allowed the government to conceal CIA expenditures from the general public. After unsuccessfully attempting to obtain expenditure information from various governmental agencies, Respondent sued as a citizen and a taxpayer for a detailed statement of CIA expenditures. The Court held that Richardson could not invoke the *Flast* test because he was not alleging that CIA funds were being spent in violation of a "specific constitutional limitation upon the taxing and spending power," but rather was alleging only that he was entitled to information about how CIA funds were being spent so that he could "intelligently follow the actions of Congress or the Executive" and thereby "fulfill his obligations as a member of the electorate in voting for candidates seeking national office." The Court concluded that plaintiff's complaint was a "generalized grievance," and therefore did not involve "any particular concrete injury." The Court suggested that plaintiff must seek remedy through the electoral process rather than the courts.

Flast was also distinguished in *Valley Forge Christian College v. Americans United for Separation of Church and State*, 454 U.S. 464 (1982). In that case, the General Services Administration declared land to be "surplus property," and conveyed it to the Valley Forge Christian College. The purpose of the college was to train laymen and ministers for "Christian service," and the college's faculty members were subject to religious restrictions. Under the terms of the conveyance, the college was required to use the property to make "additions to its offerings in the arts and humanities," and to strengthen its "psychology" and "counseling" courses to provide services in inner-city areas. Americans United for Separation of Church and State, Inc. ("Americans United"), and four of its employees, challenged the conveyance on Establishment Clause grounds, claiming that the conveyance would deprive them "of the fair and constitutional use of [their] tax dollars." The Court held that plaintiffs could not satisfy the *Flast* nexus because they were not challenging a congressional expenditure, but were complaining about the federal agency's decision to transfer federal property, and also were not challenging an expenditure under the Taxing and Spending Clause of Art. I, § 8 (the transfer was made under Congress' power under the Property Clause, Art. IV, § 3, cl. 2).

In *Hein v. Freedom from Religion Foundation, Inc.*, 551 U.S. 587 (2007), the Court suggested that the *Flast* decision would not apply except in cases challenging congressional appropriations. *Hein* involved an Establishment Clause challenge to President George W. Bush's Faith-Based and Community Initiatives program. That program, established by executive order, created Executive Department Centers whose job was to ensure that faith-based community groups were eligible to compete for federal funds without impairing their independence or autonomy. In *Hein*, taxpayers sought to challenge expenditures made by President Bush and Secretary Paige in promoting the program. The Court refused to find taxpayer standing, reiterating the idea that a taxpayer could not (as a general rule) establish injury by showing an unconstitutional federal expenditure, and expressed doubt that the taxpayers could obtain standing by showing that conferences were paid for with money appropriated by Congress. The Court distinguished *Flast* noting that the program challenged in that case was "funded by a specific congressional appropriation" and was "disbursed to private schools (including religiously affiliated schools) pursuant to a direct and unambiguous congressional mandate." By contrast, in *Hein*, respondents were not attempting to "challenge any specific congressional action or appropriation."

Finally, in *Arizona Christian School Tuition Organization v. Winn*, 563 U.S. 125 (2011), the Court refused to allow plaintiffs to use *Flast* to challenge an Arizona law that provided tax credits for scholarships to students attending private schools, including sectarian schools. The Court rejected the idea that taxpayers had standing to challenge the tax credit, as well as the idea that they could establish standing under *Flast*. The Court noted that *Flast* "provides a 'narrow exception' to 'the general rule against taxpayer standing,' " and the Court refused to apply that narrow exception in this case: "The STO tax credit is not tantamount to a religious tax or to a tithe and does not visit the injury identified in *Flast*. It follows that respondents have neither alleged an injury for standing purposes under general rules nor met the *Flast* exception." Justice Scalia argued that *Flast* is an "anomaly" which should be repudiated. Justice Kagan disagreed, arguing that "This novel distinction between appropriations and tax expenditures has as little basis in principle as it has in our precedent. Cash grants and targeted tax breaks are means of accomplishing the same government objective—to provide financial support to select individuals or organizations. From now on, government need follow just one simple rule—subsidize through the tax system—to preclude taxpayer challenges to state funding of religion."

Citizen Standing. As with taxpayer standing, plaintiffs have encountered difficulties establishing standing based on their status as citizens. In *Frothingham*, the Court also held that Frothingham could not establish citizen standing based on her status as a citizen of the United States. A citizen still must show a cognizable "injury," and Frothingham could only show that she was suffering in "some indefinite way in common with people generally." Likewise, in *Schlesinger v. Reservists Committee to Stop the War*, 418 U.S. 208 (1974), the Court held that plaintiffs did not have standing to enforce Article I, § 6, cl. 2 of the U.S. Constitution (a/k/a, the "Incompatibility Clause") which prohibited congresspersons from serving as reservists in the United States armed forces during their terms of office. The Court rejected the proposition that "all constitutional provisions are enforceable by any citizen simply because citizens are the ultimate beneficiaries of those provisions."

Lance v. Coffman, 549 U.S. 437 (2007), involved redistricting by the Colorado legislature following the 2000 census. Colorado citizens sued, claiming that Colorado's Constitution only permits one redistricting per census, and that Colorado had done two (one by the legislature and a second one by the courts). The Court concluded that the plaintiffs lacked standing, noting that: "The only injury plaintiffs allege is that the law, specifically the Elections Clause, has not been followed. This injury is precisely the kind of undifferentiated, generalized grievance about the conduct of government that we have refused to countenance in the past. It is quite different from the sorts of injuries alleged by plaintiffs in voting rights cases where we have found standing."

However, when a citizen can show something more, standing might exist. In *Bond v. United States*, 564 U.S. 211 (2011), a defendant in a criminal case alleged that Congress did not have the power to enact the Chemical Weapons Convention Implementation Act, under which she was being prosecuted. Her argument was based on the Tenth Amendment and the premise that Congress enacted the law in violation of basic federalism principles. The Court held that she had standing to raise the Tenth Amendment claims: "Article III's prerequisites are met. Bond seeks to vindicate her own constitutional interests. The individual, in a proper case, can assert injury from governmental action taken in excess of the authority that federalism defines. Her rights do not belong to a State. Federalism is more than an exercise in setting the boundary between different institutions of government for their own integrity. Federalism also protects the liberty of all persons within a State by ensuring that laws enacted in excess of delegated governmental power cannot direct or control their actions." Justice Ginsburg, joined by Justice Breyer, concurred: "Bond, like any other defendant, has a personal right not to be convicted under a constitutionally invalid law."

Congressional Standing. In some instances, legislators have sought to establish standing based on their status as legislators (a/k/a, legislator standing). In *Raines v. Byrd*, 521 U.S. 811 (1997), the Court rejected an attempt by members of Congress to challenge the Line Item Veto Act. That law gave the President the authority to "cancel" certain spending and tax benefit measures even though they had been signed into law. The congressmen claimed that they had standing because a veto would adversely affect "their constitutionally prescribed lawmaking powers" by allowing the President to rescind a validly enacted appropriation without following prescribed constitutional processes—in particular, passage by both houses of Congress and signature by the President. The Court held that standing did not exist because "the injury claimed by the Members of Congress here is not claimed in any private capacity but solely because they are Members of Congress. The claimed injury thus runs (in a sense) with the Member's seat, a seat which the Member holds (it may quite arguably be said) as trustee for his constituents, not as a prerogative of personal power." The Court held that "individual members of Congress do not have a sufficient 'personal stake' in this dispute and have not alleged a sufficiently concrete injury to have established Article III standing."

Congressionally Authorized Standing. While Congress cannot authorize standing if Article III case or controversy requirements are not met, the Court may be more inclined to hear a case if Congress has invited the Court to hear it and the constitutional minimums are satisfied. The leading decision on congressional authorization is *Association of Data Processing Service Organizations, Inc. v. Camp,* 397 U.S. 150 (1970). In that case, the Court established a two-part test for evaluating claims when Congress seems to have authorized the federal courts to hear a case: plaintiffs must show that they are suffering injury in fact; and they must also show that they fall within the "zone of interest" sought to be protected by the congressional enactment.

Data Processing involved companies that sold data processing services to businesses who challenged a ruling by the Comptroller of the Currency that allowed national banks to make data processing services available to other banks and to bank customers. The Court concluded that plaintiffs were suffering injury in the form of potential pecuniary loss. The Court also found that plaintiffs were "within the zone of interests to be protected or regulated by the statute or constitutional guarantee in question."

The Court noted that the Administrative Procedure Act, in particular 5 U.S.C. § 702, grants standing to a person "aggrieved by agency action within the meaning of a relevant statute." While there has been a tendency to allow statutes to enlarge the class of people who may protest administrative action, since Congress has not prescribed review, the Court held that the association of data processing agencies could establish standing.

The "Injury-in-Fact" Requirement of Standing. The injury-in-fact requirement of standing requires a plaintiff to show that it suffered a legally cognizable injury. It is an essential element in the standing calculus.

The outer limits of "injury" are revealed by the Court's decision in *United States v. SCRAP,* 412 U.S. 669 (1973). That suit was brought by Students Challenging Regulatory Agency Procedures (SCRAP), an unincorporated group of five law students, and the Environmental Defense Fund (EDF), challenging the ICC's failure to suspend a surcharge, that they claimed would cause "economic, recreational and aesthetic harm," especially to recycling efforts. The Court held that plaintiffs should be given the opportunity to prove their allegations, noting that the challenged action was applicable to substantially all railroads, and thus could have an adverse environmental impact on all the natural resources of the country. "To deny standing to persons who are in fact injured simply because many others are also injured, would mean that the most injurious and widespread Government actions could be questioned by nobody."

The Court's current approach to injury is reflected in *Lujan v. Defenders of Wildlife*, 504 U.S. 555 (1992). In that case, plaintiffs sought to challenge the Secretary of the Interior's interpretation of § 7 of the Endangered Species Act of 1973 (ESA). The Secretary construed the ESA as applicable only to actions within the United States or on the high seas, an interpretation that was challenged by individuals concerned about protecting overseas habitats. The Court concluded that the environmental organizations that sought to challenge the rule lacked standing because they were unable to show injury (and redressability). The Court recognized that the "desire to use or observe an animal species, even for purely aesthetic purposes, is undeniably a cognizable interest for purpose of standing," but held that plaintiffs must show that they are "injured" or "directly affected" apart from their "special interest in the subject." The Court held that they could not satisfy these requirements.

The Court did find that standing existed in *Monsanto Co. v. Geerston Seed Farms*, 561 U.S. 139 (2010). That case involved the Animal and Plant Health Inspection Service (APHIS) which decided to deregulate a variety of genetically engineered alfalfa (Roundup Ready Alfalfa (RRA)). That decision was challenged on the basis that APHIS violated the National Environmental Policy Act of 1969 (NEPA), by issuing its deregulation decision without first completing a detailed assessment of the environmental consequences of its proposed course of action. Two different standing issues arose. First, it was contended that Monsanto (who held the patent on RRA) did not have standing. The Court rejected that argument, noting that Monsanto had an interest in marketing its product, and that an adverse judicial decision would harm its ability to sell or license RRA to prospective customers. Second, it was contended that respondents (who challenged the deregulation) lacked standing. The Court rejected that argument as well.

Some of respondents were farmers who "established a 'reasonable probability' that their organic and conventional alfalfa crops will be infected with the engineered gene" if RRA is completely deregulated. A substantial risk of gene flow injured respondents in several ways. For example, respondents represented that, in order to continue marketing their product to consumers who wish to buy non-genetically-engineered alfalfa, respondents would have to conduct testing to find out whether and to what extent their crops have been contaminated. Respondents also alleged that the risk of gene flow would cause them to take measures to minimize the likelihood of potential contamination and to ensure an adequate supply of non-genetically-engineered alfalfa.

In *Summers v. Earth Island Institute*, 555 U.S. 488 (2009), respondent organizations, who were collectively dedicated to protecting the environment, sought to prevent the U.S. Forest Service (USFS) from implementing regulations that exempted small fire-rehabilitation and timber-salvage projects from the notice, comment, and appeal process used by the Forest Service for more significant land management decisions. Although Respondents initially challenged a particular application of the regulations, respondents settled those cases with the USFS. With no pending disputes, the Court concluded that the organizations lacked standing to challenge the regulations. Even though some members of the organizations asserted a desire to go to areas that might be affected by the regulations, the Court held that a "vague desire to return is insufficient to satisfy the requirement of imminent injury." The Court also rejected the idea that Respondents had suffered a "procedural injury" because they will be denied the right to submit comments on future USFS actions. The Court held that those procedural claims could only be asserted against a pending project for which Respondents have been denied the right to comment. In other words, the challenge could not be based on some abstract future injury. Finally, the Court rejected the idea of "statistical injury." Basically, the organizations claimed that they had such a high level of membership that there was a "statistical possibility" that their members would be affected by the regulations in the future. The Court held that a "statistical possibility" of injury was insufficient to establish standing: "The Court has required plaintiffs claiming an organizational standing to identify members who have suffered the requisite harm—surely not a difficult task here, when so many thousands are alleged to have been harmed."

In *California v. Texas*, 593 U.S. 659 (2021), the Court rejected a challenge to the Patient Protection and Affordable Care Act which required most Americans to obtain minimum essential health insurance coverage. Although the Court had upheld the Act under Congress' taxing power in an earlier decision, Congress amended the law to eliminate the tax. At that point, various states sued, claiming that the Act could not be sustained under Congress' Art. I, Sec. 8, powers, since the original reason for upholding the law (that is imposed a tax) no longer existed. The Court concluded that the states could not show the requisite injury to establish a case or controversy because the Act had no enforcement mechanism since all penalties and taxes had been removed from the law.

In *Clapper v. Amnesty International USA*, 568 U.S. 398 (2013), the Court rejected a challenge to the Foreign Intelligence Surveillance Act (FISA) which authorized and regulated governmental electronic surveillance of communications for foreign intelligence purposes. Under FISA, the government was allowed to conduct electronic surveillance operations. Although the focus was on foreign targets, the surveillance could extend to U.S. citizens who communicated with foreign suspects. Respondents, attorneys and human rights, labor, legal, and media organizations whose work allegedly required them to engage in sensitive and sometimes privileged telephone and e-mail communications with colleagues, clients, sources, and other individuals located abroad, challenged the government's surveillance operations. Respondents believed that some of the foreigners with whom they communicated with were likely targets of surveillance under FISA, and they feared that the U.S. government might be monitoring their communications. Although respondents could not prove that they were being surveilled, they argued that there was "an objectively reasonable likelihood that their communications" were being surveilled, and the risk was so substantial that they were forced to take costly and burdensome measures to protect the confidentiality of their international communications.

The Court concluded that respondents could not establish standing. Since the program was secret, respondents could not prove that they actually were the targets of surveillance. The Court concluded that several things need to be shown in order to establish injury, all of which were speculative: "Respondents' argument rests on their highly speculative fear that: (1) the Government will decide to target the communications of non-U.S. persons with whom they communicate; (2) in doing so, the Government will choose to invoke its authority under [FISA] rather than another method of surveillance; (3) the Article III judges who serve on the Foreign Intelligence Surveillance Court will conclude that the Government's proposed surveillance procedures satisfy [the Act's] many safeguards and are consistent with the Fourth Amendment; (4) the Government will succeed in intercepting the communications of respondents' contacts; and (5) respondents will be parties to the communications that the Government intercepts." The Court viewed this as "a highly attenuated chain of possibilities" which was insufficient to prove that the threatened injury was "certainly impending," and the arguments required the government to speculate regarding how governmental officials would choose who to target. Of course, Respondents' task was made more difficult by the fact that the government's surveillance program was secret, and therefore it was difficult or impossible for Respondents to know whether the government was surveilling them.

Two aspects of the *Clapper* decision were particularly interesting. First, the Court rejected the idea that Respondents could establish standing by showing that the fear of surveillance forced them to undertake expensive alternatives to shield their communications: "Respondents cannot manufacture standing by inflicting harm on themselves based on their fears of hypothetical future harm that is not certainly impending." In addition, the Court rejected the argument that the government should be required to inform Respondents whether it was surveilling them.

In *Gill v. Whitford*, 585 U.S. 48 (2018), the Court defined the standing requirements applicable to cases involving claims that political boundaries had been gerrymandered. Some of the plaintiffs alleged that they lived in districts that had been "packed" (packing a party's members into a district that they will win by an overwhelming margin) or "cracked" (splitting a party's members so that they routinely fall just short of a majority in the district), thereby diluting their votes, and they sought to submit a substitute redistricting plan that was perfectly balanced between the political parties. Wisconsin's political geography, particularly the high concentration of Democratic voters in urban centers, afforded the Republican Party a natural, but modest, advantage in the districting process. The Court held that "a plaintiff who alleges that he is the object of a racial gerrymander—a drawing of district lines on the basis of race—has standing to assert only that his own district has been gerrymandered." Of course, *Rucho* later ruled that political gerrymandering cases were not justiciable.

Some cases have dealt with the question of whether so-called "testers" may establish standing to sue. For example, in *Havens Realty Corp. v. Coleman*, 455 U.S. 363 (1982), plaintiffs claimed that defendants had engaged in "racial steering" (steering racial minorities elsewhere) at two apartment complexes in violation of § 804 of the Fair Housing Act of 1968. The complaint identified three plaintiffs: a black man (Coles) who attempted to rent an apartment from Havens and was falsely told that no apartments were available, and two "tester plaintiffs" (Coleman who was black and Willis who was white) who were employed by an independent organization to determine whether Havens practiced racial steering. Coleman was told more than once that no apartments were available while Willis was told that there were vacancies. The two tester plaintiffs alleged that Havens' practices deprived them of the "important social, professional, business and economic, political and aesthetic benefits of interracial associations that arise from living in integrated communities free from discriminatory housing practices." The Court concluded that the alleged injury of an integrated community was "indirect," and that plaintiffs must still establish "injury in fact." The Court remanded to allow plaintiffs to attempt to establish injury, but concluded that it had generally found standing based on the effects of discrimination only within a "relatively compact neighborhood." The Court left open the possibility that the testers could establish standing.

The "Zone of Interest" Test. The zone of interest test (which requires plaintiff to show that he fits within the zone of interest sought to be protected by the statute) has been applied in a variety of cases. In general, the focus is on whether plaintiff falls within the "zone of interest" that Congress or a state legislature sought to protect by the statute. In *Federal Election Commission v. Akins*, 524 U.S. 11 (1998), the Federal Election Commission (FEC) concluded that the American Israel Public Affairs Committee (AIPAC) was not a "political committee" as defined by the Federal Election Campaign Act of 1971 (FECA), and therefore did not have to make disclosures regarding its membership, contributions, and expenditures under federal election laws. A group of voters challenged the FEC's determination, relying on federal election laws which provided that "any party aggrieved by an order of the Commission dismissing a complaint filed by such party may file a petition" in federal court seeking review of that dismissal. The Court held that the voters had standing to challenge the decision. The Court emphasized that Congress specifically provided in FECA that aggrieved individuals could complain, and concluded that plaintiffs fit within the zone of interest protected by the statute because Congress intended "to protect voters such as respondents from suffering the kind of injury here at issue."

In *Winkelman v. Parma City School District*, 550 U.S. 516 (2007), the parents of an autistic child sued under the Individuals with Disabilities Education Act (IDEA), claiming that the child's school was not complying with the IDEA with respect to his education. The Court held that the parents had standing to bring the action on behalf of their child, noting that the statute grants "any party aggrieved by the findings and decision made [by the hearing officer] the right to bring a civil action with respect to the complaint." The Court emphasized that "the Act does not *sub silentio* or by implication bar parents from seeking to vindicate the rights accorded to them once the time comes to file a civil action."

Causation (Redressability). In addition to demonstrating a "concrete and particularized injury," which is "actual or imminent," the Court also requires proof of causation as a prerequisite to standing. Causation requires that there be a correlation between plaintiff's alleged injury and the challenged governmental action such that a judicial order restraining the action will redress the injury. Sometimes, this requirement is also subsumed under the concept of redressability—the idea that he court must be able to redress the plaintiff's grievance if the suit is not to be considered illusory or speculative.

In recent decades, the Court has frequently imposed a causation requirement as a significant limitation on the standing doctrine. In *Allen v. Wright*, 468 U.S. 737 (1984), the parents of African-American children sought to compel the IRS to deny tax-exempt status to racially discriminatory private schools, claiming that the exempt status helped discriminatory schools exist. The Court denied standing on causation grounds, saying the injury was not "fairly traceable" to the tax exemptions and that the "links in the chain of causation between the challenged Government conduct and the asserted injury are far too weak" to establish standing.

In some instances, courts have redefined the injury-in-fact requirement in order to establish causation. For example, in *Heckler v. Mathews*, 465 U.S. 728 (1984), a male brought an equal protection challenge to the Social Security Act which contained a gender based classification that denied him benefits equal to those received by women, and he did so even though the law contained a severability provision which would have prevented plaintiff from obtaining more benefits even if the law was struck down. The Court concluded that, even though plaintiff could not receive more benefits, he still had a redressable injury: "we have never suggested that the injuries caused by a constitutionally underinclusive scheme can be remedied only by extending the program's benefits to the excluded class. Discrimination itself, by perpetuating 'archaic and stereotypic notions' or by stigmatizing members of the disfavored group as 'innately inferior' can cause serious non-economic injuries."

In many cases, the causation requirement is an insurmountable barrier. In *ASARCO, Inc. v. Kadish*, 490 U.S. 605 (1989), an Arizona statute authorized the state land department to lease minerals and school trust lands at a prescribed rate. Individual taxpayers, along with a teacher's association, challenged the statute on the ground that it did not comply with congressionally imposed statutory standards for leasing or selling lands. The Court concluded that none of the plaintiffs could show pecuniary injury because it was "pure speculation" whether, even if more money went to the trust fund, that it would be allocated to education. As a result, the Court concluded that plaintiffs were simply "concerned citizens" bringing "generalized grievances" that are not cognizable in the federal courts.

Jus Tertii (Third Party) Standing. In some instances, third parties have tried to raise the rights and interests of individuals who are not before the court, and courts must decide whether the third parties have standing to assert those rights. This is also referred to as third party or *jus tertii* standing. These third parties, even though they suffer injuries, are generally denied standing.

There are good reasons for denying standing to third parties. As a general rule, the individuals who are affected by a governmental action (rather than third parties) are the best proponents of their own rights. In addition, when a third party is allowed to litigate, there is always the risk that the holder of the right may not wish for the third party to assert the right, or may not wish to assert the right at all.

Exceptions to the general exclusion exist. In deciding whether to recognize third party standing, courts will often focus on the relationship between the third party and the interests he seeks to represent in order to ensure that the third party is likely to be an "effective proponent" of the rights asserted.

Denial of third party standing is particularly appropriate when the third party's interests are not aligned with the interests of the first party. For example, in *Elk Grove Unified School District v. Newdow,* 542 U.S. 1 (2004), the Court rejected a father's attempt to challenge recitation of the Pledge of Allegiance at his daughter's school. The father, an atheist, objected to the Pledge's inclusion of the words "under God" which he viewed as an establishment of religion. When the daughter's mother, the custodial parent, opposed the father's suit, the Court concluded that the father lacked standing to represent his daughter's interest noting that the interested parties were antagonistic, and the father did not have the power to litigate as her "next friend."

In other cases, the third party's intervention is necessary if the right holders' interests are to be vindicated. For example, in *Hamdi v. Rumsfeld*, 542 U.S. 507 (2004), following the 9/11 attack on the World Trade Center in New York City, Hamdi was detained as an enemy combatant. Although he was a U.S. citizen, detained on U.S. soil, he was denied access to an attorney. His father, as next friend, sought a writ of habeas corpus on his behalf. Although the Court devoted little attention to the issue, it allowed the father to pursue the son's interests. Likewise, in *Singleton v. Wulff*, 428 U.S. 106 (1976), the Court held that doctors could establish standing to challenge on constitutional grounds a Missouri statute that excluded abortions that are not "medically indicated" from Medicaid coverage. The doctors who challenged the law performed non-medically indicated abortions, and alleged that they would suffer financial injury (the loss of payment) if the statute remained in effect, and they also sought to assert the rights of their patients. The Court concluded that abortion doctors are "uniquely qualified" to litigate the constitutional claims, and that women seeking abortions might be reluctant to assert their rights for a variety of reasons: they may want to protect the privacy of their decisions, and an individual woman's standing will be lost to mootness relatively quickly.

CHECKLIST

A. **Does judicial review apply?** Predicate questions that might be asked are the following:

1. **Does the issue arise as part of a case or controversy or is it in the posture of an advisory opinion?** *Marbury v. Madison,* 5 U.S. (1 Cranch) 137 (1803), is a good illustration of the concept that federal courts are courts of limited jurisdiction.

2. **Is the court confronted by a potential conflict between a law or executive action and the U.S. Constitution?** If yes, there is a case or controversy that Article III of the Constitution permits courts to resolve.

3. **Could a state court decide the case on state law grounds, rather than applying the U.S. Constitution?** If yes, the federal court might abstain from deciding the case. Note that state courts can interpret their own state constitutions to provide individuals with *greater* rights than are provided for under the United States Constitution.

B. **What limitations apply to the Court's judicial review authority?** A variety of practical considerations limit the power of the federal courts, particularly the United States Supreme Court, to exercise judicial review.

1. **Can the courts exercise prudential self-restraint and refuse to hear a case?** Courts use prudential limits to refuse to hear a case even though technical standing requirements have been met. (This is especially true with third-party standing.) Prudential limits, however, are minimized when Congress authorizes standing. *See, e.g., Association of Data Processing Service Organizations, Inc. v. Camp, supra.*

2. **Are there Congressional limitations on the Supreme Court's authority?** The Court's original jurisdiction is limited and Congress can make "exceptions" to the Court's appellate jurisdiction. Courts are split on the scope of this limit. In *Ex parte McCardle, supra,* the Court upheld

Congress' attempt to deprive the Court of jurisdiction while a case was pending on appeal. In *United States v. Klein, supra,* the Court struck down a jurisdiction stripping statute for going too far.

3. **What is the precedential effect of a denial of certiorari?** Since a writ of certiorari is discretionary, a denial has no precedential effect.

4. **Does the Court sometimes avoid judicial review?** The justices usually state that they have a duty to avoid deciding constitutional issues unnecessarily (*e.g.*, they might adopt a construction of an ambiguous statute or other law that avoids constitutional difficulties). In addition, even if a "case" or "controversy" exists, the Court may decline to hear a case on prudential grounds.

C. **Will the Courts sometimes refuse to hear cases based on the political question doctrine?** The political question doctrine is a well-established limitation on the scope of federal power. A political question may exist when issues are textually committed to another branch of government or there is a lack of judicially manageable standards of review. *Baker v. Carr, supra.* Political questions are frequently found to exist when foreign policy or combat issues are involved.

D. **Courts refuse to hear cases that are brought prematurely and therefore are not ripe?** Cases that are brought too soon, so that the issues are not yet sufficiently sharpened for decision and are speculative, might be dismissed on ripeness grounds. *United Public Workers v. Mitchell, supra.*

E. **Will the courts refuse to hear cases or controversies that are brought after circumstances render a decision in the case moot?** Yes, a court will refuse to hear or decide a moot issue, *e.g.*, *DeFunis v. Odegaard, supra,* unless the issue is "capable of repetition yet evading review," like abortion. *See, e.g., Roe v. Wade, supra.*

F. **In determining whether the plaintiff has standing to bring suit, there are both injury-in-fact and causation requirements.** The injury-in-fact can be pecuniary, a violation of constitutional rights or even an aesthetic injury, but must be personal and not a generalized grievance. *Lujan v. Defenders of Wildlife, supra.* Causation means the issue is redressable by the court so that plaintiff can benefit from a favorable decision. *Heckler v. Mathews, supra.*

G. **Can a plaintiff assert third-party standing?** If a plaintiff is basing a claim on the rights of another, courts will generally be reluctant to find that plaintiff has standing to bring the case. The exception is when there is a nexus between the rights of the first parties and third parties, such that the third parties will represent the rights of the first parties fairly. *See Elk Grove Unified School District v. Newdow, supra.*

H. **Can a Plaintiff claim taxpayer standing?** Generally not. However, the Court has carved out a limited exception for taxpayer standing. Under *Flast v. Cohen, supra,* the taxpayer must be challenging a congressional expenditure, and must be able to show that the expenditures exceeds a specific provision in the Constitution that limits the taxing and spending power.

I. **Can a Plaintiff claim citizen standing?** As a general rule, citizens cannot claim standing in their capacity as citizens. This would count as the type of generalized grievance on which persons cannot base a lawsuit. *Lance v. Coffman, supra.*

J. **Can a legislator claim congressional standing?** The Court has generally refused to grant such standing because legislators lack a personal stake in the outcome.

■ PROBLEMS ■

Problem #1: The National Museum Association in Washington, D.C., (Air and Space, Natural History, etc.), sold soda in nonreturnable low-grade plastic bottles in violation of federal law. Plaintiff, a recycling watchdog organization, brought suit. As the litigation began, the museums voluntarily dropped the sales. Should the federal district court dismiss the suit because it is now moot?

Answer: The answer depends on whether it is clear the conduct will not reoccur. In *Friends of the Earth v. Laidlaw Environmental Services (TOC), Inc.*, 528 U.S. 167 (2000), Friends of the Earth (FOE) and Citizens Local Environmental Action Network, Inc., (CLEAN) sued to prevent a hazardous waste incinerator facility and water treatment plant from discharging waste water in excess of the limits established by its permit. Defendant argued that the case was moot because it had recently closed the facility. The Court disagreed, noting that mootness occurs only if it becomes "absolutely clear that the allegedly wrongful behavior could not reasonably be expected to recur." The Court considered the mootness question as a disputed factual matter.

Problem #2: After Congress bailed out financial institutions in 2009, Congress proposes a constitutional amendment that states: "Any bailout using federal funds must be approved by 2/3 of Congress, unless the President, in writing, declares that an immediate financial emergency justifies the spending." This amendment is voted on by a majority of the states, but is still languishing unapproved three years following its proposal. A Senator files suit, claiming that the amendment proposal has expired and requires a new start. Should a court rule on this claim?

Answer: The general answer is no, the Court has no jurisdiction over such a proceeding, because it presents a political question. There are two reasons for this conclusion—the issue appears to be textually committed to another branch of government, Congress, which can propose amendments, and the states who vote on Congress' proposed amendments and the courts likely will have no standards by which to address the issue. In *Coleman v. Miller*, 307 U.S. 433 (1939), the Court held that "questions of how long a proposed amendment to the Federal Constitution remained open to ratification, and what effect a prior rejection had on a subsequent ratification, were committed to congressional resolution and involved criteria of decision that necessarily escaped the judicial grasp." The Court noted that it was reluctant to inquire whether an enactment had been passed in compliance with necessary formalities. In doing so, the Court emphasized the importance of giving due "respect to coequal and independent departments," and the "need for finality and certainty" which make the courts reluctant to decide whether an amendment has been passed in compliance with constitutional requisites. However, the Court rejected the idea that "courts will never delve into a legislature's records upon such a quest." For example, if "the enrolled statute lacks an effective date, a court will not hesitate to seek it in the legislative journals in order to preserve the enactment. The political question doctrine, a tool for maintenance of governmental order, will not be so applied as to promote only disorder."

Problem #3: Supposed that then President Obama decided to send troops to Pakistan to assist in guarding borders with Afghanistan. When the deployment of troops was imminent, several members of Congress sought to challenge Obama's decision in federal court, claiming that the President's action is unconstitutional. Can a federal district court have heard the case?

Answer: The answer is no, the court should not have heard the case. The ripeness doctrine would have caused the court to refuse to hear the case on the merits (and the political question doctrine would have as well.). For example, in *Dellums v. Bush*, 752 F.Supp. 1141 (D.D.C. 1990), members of Congress sought to challenge President George H.W. Bush's decision to deploy troops in the Persian Gulf region in anticipation of the first Gulf war. The congressional plaintiffs sued claiming that military action was imminent, that such action without a congressional declaration "would deprive the congressional plaintiffs of the voice to which they are entitled under the Constitution." The Court held that the case was not ripe, noting that Congress had not yet declared its intentions on the possible war.

Problem #4: A group of voters in the State of Vermont, "Voters for Fair Counting," challenge a reapportionment by the Vermont state legislature, claiming that the scheme creates racially segregated voting districts and is unconstitutional. Should the Court hear this "racial gerrymandering" claim?

Answer: The short answer is maybe. This case presents a justiciable issue that can result in "racial hostility" and "representational harms." *United States v. Hays*, 515 U.S. 737 (1995), involved a challenge to a reapportionment scheme that plaintiff voters claimed illegally segregated voting districts based on race. The Court noted that segregated districts "threaten to stigmatize individuals by reason of their membership in a racial group." As a result, the Court held, "When a district obviously is created solely to effectuate the perceived common interests of one racial group, elected officials are more likely to believe that their primary obligation is to represent only the members of that group, rather than their constituency as a whole."

Problem #5: Congress wanted to establish a program that promoted Bible-reading by teenagers. It created a special reading tax for this purpose. A group of taxpayers challenged the tax as a violation of the First Amendment to the Constitution. Do the taxpayers have standing?

Answer: The taxpayers likely have standing because they can trace the tax to expenditures that specifically might violate their First Amendment rights. As noted in *Flast v. Cohen, supra*, the Establishment Clause of the First Amendment specifically limits the taxing and spending power conferred on Congress by Art. I, § 8. *Doremus v. Board of Education*, 342 U.S. 429 (1952), is instructive. There, taxpayers and citizens sought to challenge a program of Bible reading in public schools as a violation of the Establishment Clause of the United States Constitution. They sought to establish standing based on the fact that the Bible reading would burden them as taxpayers. Finding that the Bible reading was not supported by a special tax, and that there was no evidence that plaintiffs' taxes had been increased, the Court held that they could not establish standing since there was no "direct dollars-and-cents injury" but rather only a religious difference. Unlike *Doremus*, the tax here involved a "measurable appropriation or disbursement of school-district funds occasioned solely by the activities complained of," which is actionable under *Everson v. Board of Education*, 330 U.S. 1 (1947).

Problem #6: The Sugarloaf Hike and Bike Club regularly hikes on and in the forest surrounding Sugarloaf Mountain in Maine. The U.S. Forest Service decided to build a 40-mile road on and about the mountain. The Hike and Bike Club files suit. What would the Club, an association with 150 members, have to allege to warrant a finding of standing?

Answer: An association such as the Hike and Bike Club would have to demonstrate the two primary requisites, an injury-in-fact and causation. The injury-in-fact would be difficult to show, however, because it must constitute more than just a generalized grievance with specificity. Actual use of the mountain area and damage to the hiking and/or biking would likely be important to the plaintiffs' claimed injury. For example, in *Sierra Club v. Morton*, 405 U.S. 727 (1972), the Sierra Club challenged the U.S. Forest Service's (USFS) decision to build a 20-mile road in the Sierra Nevada Mountains. The Sierra Club, which did not want the area changed, claimed standing based on its "special interest in the conservation and the sound maintenance of the national parks, game refuges and forests of the country." While the Court recognized that "aesthetic and environmental" interests are important enough to confer standing, even though they "are shared by the many rather than the few," the Court concluded that the party seeking review must be "among the injured" in the sense that he/she actually uses the park. Here, the Hike and Bike Club will have to go above and beyond the Sierra Club's allegations. *See also, NAACP v. Alabama*, 357 U.S. 449 (1958).

Problem #7: Several members of Congress filed suit in their capacity as legislators claiming that a proposed constitutional amendment was improperly enacted under Article V. Should the Court hold that the legislators have standing?

Answer: While legislator standing is generally disfavored, this situation presents one of the exceptions to the general rule. The problem parallels *Coleman v. Miller, supra.* There, the Court held that legislators had standing to challenge a constitutional amendment that they claimed was not properly enacted. The Court concluded that the legislators had a "plain, direct and adequate interest in maintaining the effectiveness of their votes" which was sufficient to give them standing: "The twenty senators whose votes would have been sufficient to defeat the resolution ratifying the proposed constitutional amendment, have an interest in the controversy which, treated by the state court as a basis for entertaining and deciding the federal questions, is sufficient to give the Court jurisdiction to review that decision."

Problem #8: A state statute permitted a variety of racially restrictive covenants in various neighborhoods near urban areas in the state. Plaintiffs were beneficiaries of some of these covenants. They brought suit for damages against landowners who sold their land in violation of the covenants. Could the landowner-sellers file counter-claims asserting the rights of the minorities discriminated against in the covenants?

Answer: The short answer is yes, the landowner sellers should be accorded third-party standing. This problem parallels *Barrows v. Jackson,* 346 U.S. 249 (1953), in which a state statute permitted restrictive covenants that exclude covenanted property from being sold to members of specified minority groups. Plaintiffs, beneficiaries of the covenants, sought damages from those who sold real property in violation of their terms. The Court held that the sellers had standing to assert the rights of the minorities, noting that there "is such a close relationship between the restrictive covenant and the sanction of a state court which would punish respondent for not going forward with her covenant, and the purpose of the covenant itself, that relaxation of the rule is called for here. It sufficiently appears that mulcting in damages of respondent will be solely for the purpose of giving vitality to the restrictive covenant, that is to say, to punish respondent for not continuing to discriminate against non-Caucasians in the use of her property." Chief Justice Vinson dissented, arguing that the "majority identifies no non-Caucasian who has been injured or could be injured if damages are assessed against respondent for breaching the promise which she willingly and voluntarily made to petitioners, a promise which neither the federal law nor the Constitution proscribes. Indeed, the non-Caucasian occupants of the property involved in this case will continue their occupancy undisturbed, regardless of the outcome of the suit."

POINTS TO REMEMBER

- Judicial review allocates to the judiciary the power to interpret the Constitution and to review the actions of the legislative and executive branches.
- Federal courts are courts of limited jurisdiction. Their jurisdiction is confined by constitutional limitations set forth in Article III and by prudential limits set by the courts themselves.
- Congress has the constitutional authority to establish federal inferior courts, and to make "exceptions" to the Supreme Court's appellate jurisdiction.

- There are limits on judicial jurisdiction, including the doctrines of ripeness (the case was brought too soon), mootness (the case was brought too late), political questions (cases involve issues that should be decided by the other branches rather than by the courts), and standing (plaintiffs cannot show that they are suffering a redressable injury).
- Standing requires plaintiffs to allege both an injury-in-fact and causation.
- Taxpayers have limited ability to establish standing, and citizens and legislators have little, if any, basis for asserting standing based on their status.
- Third-party standing is disfavored, but can be allowed if the third-party shows the requisite nexus with the first-party's rights.

CHAPTER 2

National Legislative Power

Although some Framers believed that Congress would have limited powers, with the enumeration of powers in Article I of the Constitution serving as both a source of power and as a limitation to what was listed, that has not turned out to be the case. Instead, Congressional power over time has become sweeping in breadth and scope, far beyond what was likely anticipated.

Our First "Constitution:" The Articles of Confederation. As powerful as the U.S. Congress has become over the last two centuries, the Framers did not envision a legislative branch with sweeping powers. Under the Articles of Confederation, the initial governing document that preceded the U.S. Constitution, the states were reluctant to vest broad powers in the federal government.

The Articles, proposed in 1777 and ratified in 1781, did not work well for the new nation. The individual states used their power over commerce to engage in trade battles through tariffs and embargos that made interstate commerce difficult. In addition, the federal government was extremely weak, lacking power over foreign affairs and the nation's defense. The federal government was not given any implied powers, but the Articles provided instead that "everything granted shall be expressly and minutely described without such implied powers, the new government lacked a significant source of authority." Despite only having been enacted in 1781, by the mid-1780s, many in the nation had had enough. A convention was called to "amend" the Articles of Confederation, leading to the constitutional convention that began in 1787 and then to a completely redrawn governing document, the United States Constitution.

The Constitutional Convention. During the Constitutional Convention in Philadelphia in the summer of 1787, Alexander Hamilton, a so-called "federalist," pushed for a broad federal power, arguing that Congress should be given the "power to pass all laws which [it] shall judge necessary to the common defense and general welfare of the Union." Others argued for more limited federal powers.

During these debates, the two sovereigns, the federal and state governments, each sought to extend their respective authority.

In the Constitution that was ultimately developed, the Framers created a government of limited, enumerated powers that were often shared or checked by powers held by the other branches. Many of the enumerated powers were located in Article I, Section 8, which provides that this section gives Congress "[a]ll legislative powers herein granted. . . ." Another set of limits was reflected in the Bill of Rights which reflected the vast distrust of concentrated powers by the nascent nation.

Judicial Interpretation of the Legislative Powers. The courts have the responsibility of interpreting the Constitution, including the scope of Congress' powers. The Constitution omits, however, any description of how this interpretation should occur. While just about everyone agrees that the starting point ought to be the language of the Constitution, the interpretation of that language has been subject to considerable debate. Many judges and commentators believe that, after reviewing the Constitution's language, the next step is to ascertain the Framers' intent regarding the meaning of the words. This has often been a difficult if not impossible task. In deciding *McCulloch v. Maryland*, 17 U.S. (4 Wheat.) 316 (1819), Chief Justice Marshall uttered his now famous statement: "[In] considering this question, then, we must never forget that it is a *Constitution* we are expounding." Marshall's language suggests that the Constitution was intended to be a living, breathing thing and to change over time.

The Legislative Powers Framework. Article 1, Section 8, provided Congress with a variety of explicit powers (powers specifically listed in the Constitution itself). Included among the eighteen paragraphs of enumerated powers are the right to borrow money, to establish uniform rules on naturalization and bankruptcy, to coin money, to provide punishment for counterfeiting, to establish post offices and roads, to regulate commerce among the several states, as well as with foreign nations and Indian tribes, to provide for the protection of scientists and artists through rules governing rights to writings and discoveries, to provide and maintain a navy, to raise and support armies, and to define and punish piracies. Other provisions of the Constitution grant other powers to Congress, including the power to create lower federal courts, (Art. III, Sec. 1, U S Const.), to regulate the appellate jurisdiction of the Supreme Court, (Art. III, Sec. 2, U.S. Const.), to define the crime of treason (Art. III, Sec. 3, U.S. Const.), to stipulate the procedures for providing full faith and credit to the laws and judgments of the states (Art. IV, Sec. 1, U.S. Const.), to admit new states to the Union (Art. IV, Sec. 3, U.S. Const.), to regulate U.S. territories and properties (Art. IV, Sec. 3,

U.S. Const.). In addition, various amendments gave Congress the power to abolish slavery, (Amendment 13, Sec. 5, U.S. Const.), to prohibit discrimination on the basis of race in voting (Amendment 15, Sec. 2, U.S. Const.), as well as to do other things. (*See, e.g.*, Amendment 16 and the imposition of an income tax and Amendment 24, Sec. 2 and the abolition of poll taxes.)

Under this framework, when Congress acts, the first issue is whether it has the power to do so. Congress cannot pass legislation simply to promote the health, safety, welfare and morals of the public. Those are considered the "police" powers of the state, and Congress is constrained by the fact that it is limited to its enumerated powers. Even if Congress has the power to enact legislation, if the law or action is prohibited by one of the limits or rights also contained in the Constitution, such as the Bill of Rights, the law will be unconstitutional. This two-step analysis offers a routine for approaching constitutional questions about Congressional action.

The Necessary and Proper Clause. One of the most important enumerated powers is found in Article I, Section 8, clause 18. It provides that Congress shall have the power to "make all Laws which shall be necessary and proper for carrying into Execution the foregoing Powers, and all other Powers vested by this Constitution in the Government of the United States, or in any Department of Officer thereof."

The Necessary and Proper Clause expands and relates to the enumerated powers. For example, since Article I, Section 8, explicitly gives Congress the power to "provide and maintain a Navy," paragraph eighteen allows Congress to do those things that are "necessary and proper" to maintain a Navy.

The meaning of the Necessary and Proper Clause has been subject to considerable debate. Thomas Jefferson, for example, advocated a narrow interpretation of the clause, saying it should mean that Congress is only authorized to do those things that are "absolutely necessary" to the enumerated powers. Alexander Hamilton, on the other hand, argued for a broader interpretation, giving Congress the power to do all things that are "helpful" or "convenient" to the enumerated powers.

In *McCulloch v. Maryland,* the Court offered a broad view of the necessary and proper clause. The case involved a Maryland statute that taxed the operations of all banks that had not been chartered by the state itself. The Bank of the United States, which had been chartered by Congress and was owned by the federal government, refused to pay the tax, arguing that the state did not have the power to tax an instrumentality of the federal government. In a landmark decision by Chief Justice Marshall, the Court agreed with Congress and struck down the tax.

In *McCulloch*, Chief Justice Marshall adopted a broad view of constitutional authority, emphasizing the difference between a detailed code and a constitution. He said that the nature of a constitution "requires, that only its great outlines should be marked, its important objects designated, and the minor ingredients which compose those objects, be deduced from the nature of the objects themselves."

Consequently, the Court concluded that Congress had the power to create a bank. The Court held that "a government, entrusted with such ample powers, on the due execution of which the happiness and prosperity of the nation so vitally depends, must also be entrusted with ample means for their execution." Not surprisingly, Marshall rejected a narrow interpretation of the necessary and proper clause. Instead of requiring that a proposed governmental action be "indispensable" to the express powers, he adopted a construction which required that a proposed action be merely "convenient, or useful, or essential" to an enumerated power.

Marshall then laid down a general framework for when Congress can legitimately act, including creating a bank to carry out its enumerated powers. He wrote, "Let the end be legitimate, let it be within the scope of the constitution, and all means which are appropriate, which are plainly adapted to that end, which are not prohibited, but consist with the letter and spirit of the constitution, are constitutional."

The expansive *McCulloch* approach became the accepted interpretation over time. For example, in *United States v. Comstock*, 560 U.S. 126 (2010), the Court upheld a federal civil commitment statute under the Necessary and Proper Clause. The law authorized the U.S. Department of Justice to detain a mentally ill, sexually dangerous federal prisoner beyond the date the prisoner would otherwise be released. The Court rejected a challenge to the law, noting that "the Constitution grants Congress the authority to enact § 4248 as 'necessary and proper for carrying into Execution' the powers 'vested by' the 'Constitution in the Government of the United States.' Art. I, § 8, cl. 18." The Court construed the clause broadly, noting that "the Constitution's grants of specific federal legislative authority are accompanied by broad power to enact laws that are 'convenient, or useful' or 'conducive' to the authority's 'beneficial exercise.' The word 'necessary' does not mean 'absolutely necessary.' " The question is whether the law "constitutes a means that is rationally related to the implementation of a constitutionally enumerated power." The Court emphasized that "Congress routinely exercises its authority to enact criminal laws in furtherance of its enumerated powers to regulate interstate and foreign commerce, to enforce civil rights, to spend funds for the general welfare, to establish federal courts, to establish post offices, to regulate bankruptcy, to regulate naturalization, and so forth. Similarly, Congress, in order to ensure the enforcement of federal criminal laws enacted in furtherance of its enumerated powers, can cause a prison to be erected within the jurisdiction of the United States, and direct that all persons sentenced to imprisonment under the laws of the United States shall be confined there. Moreover, Congress, having established a prison system, can enact laws that ensure that system's safe and responsible administration." As a result, the Court concluded that the statute was a "necessary and proper" means of exercising the federal authority that permits Congress to create federal criminal laws, to punish their violation, to imprison violators, to provide appropriately for those imprisoned, and to maintain the security of those who are not imprisoned but who may be affected by the federal imprisonment of others.

Despite the Court's generally expansive approach to the Clause, the Court has periodically retrenched, focusing on the fact that Congress was accorded only enumerated powers. For example, in *Kansas v. Colorado*, 206 U.S. 46 (1907), Congress sought to divert water from the Arkansas River at a point where it was not navigable. The Court held that Congress had exceeded its authority which extended only to navigable waterways. Likewise, in *National Federation of Independent Business v. Sebelius*, 567 U.S. 519 (2012), after the Court held that the "individual mandate" (a provision that requires individuals to purchase health insurance) could not be upheld under the Commerce Clause (see discussion, *infra*), the Court examined whether it could be upheld under the Necessary and Proper Clause. In its decision, discussed more fully in the Commerce Clause section, the Court held that the individual mandate could not be justified under the Necessary and Proper Clause.

The Commerce Clause. Article I, Section 8, clause 3, contains perhaps the most important and elastic congressional power, the Commerce Clause. It states: "The Congress shall have Power . . . to regulate Commerce with foreign Nations, and among the several States, and with the Indian Tribes."

Under the Articles of Confederation, the states gave control over commerce to themselves and deprived the federal legislature of that power. The absence of central control often led to state opposing state through taxes and tariffs, among other trade impositions. The fighting among the states led to significant economic woes. By 1785–76, the nation was mired in a recession caused by "a high national debt, increasing trade deficits, and economic infighting." DANIEL A. FARBER & SUZANNA SHERRY, A HISTORY OF THE AMERICAN CONSTITUTION 25 (1990).

With the adoption of the U.S. Constitution, the center of commerce power tilted significantly toward Congress. The tilt was not so far that Congress was given a general police power which would have allowed it to pass any legislation appropriate for the health, safety and welfare of the nation. Two areas of commerce power, though, have been firmly established. Congress' power over commerce with foreign nations has always been regarded as broad and plenary, and its power over commerce with Indian tribes has been regarded as similarly broad. *See Cherokee Nation v. Georgia*, 30 U.S. (5 Pet.) 1 (1831).

Early Commerce Clause Cases: Defining Terms. In their early cases, the Justices were tasked with providing an initial definition of the Commerce Clause. At the time of the adoption of the Constitution, interstate commerce concerned goods that crossed state lines, as distinguished from manufacturing or agricultural processes. Early decisions reflected this distinction but soon recognized that even the internal commerce of a state could have a substantial effect on interstate commerce.

Gibbons v. Ogden, 22 U.S. 1 (1824), offered the Court's first authoritative interpretation of the commerce clause. There, the New York legislature granted Livingston a long-term monopoly to operate steamboats in New York waters. Livingston subsequently assigned part of the monopoly to Ogden to run steamships between New York City and Elizabethtown, New Jersey. When Gibbons was granted a federal license to operate steamboats along a similar route, Ogden sued, claiming that the federal license was invalid. The Court found that the federal law was valid and supreme under the Supremacy Clause and therefore the state law and its monopoly holder (Ogden) must give way to federal license holder (Gibbons).

Chief Justice Marshall concluded that the term "commerce" was not limited to "the interchange of commodities," but instead extended to "intercourse between nations, and parts of nations, in all its branches." The commerce power extends to commerce "among the several States" which "cannot stop at the external boundary line of each State, but may be introduced into the interior" even though it cannot extend to the "exclusively internal commerce of a State." "The power of Congress, then, whatever it may be, must be exercised within the territorial jurisdiction of the several States."

Gibbons recognized that states had the possibility of sharing some of the commerce power, and having sole domain over such things as "inspection laws, quarantine laws, health laws of every description, as well as laws for regulating the internal commerce of a State, and those which respect turnpike roads, ferries".

Gibbons illustrates several important points. First, the federal commerce power, when interpreted broadly, could shape the way the country and its markets develop. Second, the Supremacy Clause could play a large role in settling federal-state conflicts. Third, judicial review would be necessary to interpret Commerce Clause conflicts. Fourth, the Court tried to design formalistic categories, including "before" and "during" commerce, to create a predictable framework of analysis.

While the broad interpretation of the Commerce Clause in *Gibbons* became one of John Marshall's lasting legacies, subsequent cases were not always in lock step. *Paul v. Virginia,* 75 U.S. (8 Wall.) 168 (1868), for example, involved a Virginia statute that discriminated against insurance companies incorporated in other states. In an opinion by Justice Field, the Court rejected the challenge by concluding that an insurance policy is not "a transaction of commerce." Similarly, in *Kidd v. Pearson*, 128 U.S. 1 (1888), the Court upheld an Iowa statute that prohibited the manufacture of liquor as applied to an Iowa company that sold its products in other states, concluding that Congress' power does not extend to "the purely internal domestic commerce of a state, which is carried on between man and man within a state or between different parts of the same state."

Twentieth Century Case Law. The roller coaster of judicial twists and turns in Commerce Clause analysis continued in the Twentieth Century. By the end of the Nineteenth Century, the economy was in a period of rapid transition, shifting from a largely agrarian society to an industrial one. Industrialization produced profound changes. Railroads and cars increased commerce exponentially and people and goods began to move more freely across state borders. The increasing ease and proliferation of transportation shattered traditional conceptions of what were "national" as compared to "local" matters. Congress began to assume a more active regulatory role, passing the Interstate Commerce Act of 1887 to oversee the burgeoning railroad industry. The Sherman Antitrust Act, first passed in 1890 by an overwhelming vote, was intended to prohibit certain trusts.

Basic principles were developed to deal with these changes. In the early 20th Century, the Court supported Congress' power to ban items completely from interstate commerce. In *Champion v. Ames*, 188 U.S. 321 (1903) (called the "*Lottery Case*"), a federal statute made it illegal to transport lottery tickets across state lines. The Court held that Congress' power to "regulate" commerce included the power to prohibit items from commerce because of the plenary nature of the power.

The Court also held that the federal power reached the internal commerce of a state when there is a "close and substantial relationship" to interstate commerce. In *Houston, East & West Texas Railway Company v. United States*, (The *Shreveport Rate Case*), 234 U.S. 342 (1914), the Court upheld an Interstate Commerce Commission (ICC) decision which had found interstate railroad rates from Shreveport to named Texas points to be unreasonable, especially in relation to the intrastate rates. The Court essentially upheld Congress' power to enact "all appropriate legislation" for the "protection and advancement" of interstate commerce, and to control intrastate commerce that has "such a close and substantial relation to interstate traffic that the control is essential or appropriate to the security of that traffic, to the efficiency of the interstate service."

Houston, East and West Texas Railway Co., was a significant break with prior judicial reasoning about the Commerce Clause. After that decision, Congress had the Court-sanctioned power to regulate the internal commerce of a state when the item being regulated had a "close and substantial" relationship to interstate commerce—a significant opportunity for additional regulation.

Not all decisions followed the lead of *Champion* and *Houston, East and West Texas Railway Co.* in expanding federal power. One well-known case was *Hammer v. Dagenhart,* 247 U.S. 251 (1918). In *Hammer,* Congress attempted to prohibit the interstate shipment of goods produced within the prior thirty days by children under the age of fourteen, or by children working long days or hours. The Court rejected Congress' claim that it possessed the power to regulate, viewing the regulation as an attempt "to standardize the ages at which children may be employed in mining and manufacturing within the states." Further, the goods produced by the child labor were "themselves harmless," and the production by children was over before the goods were shipped. The Court regarded "production" as a matter for local regulation, and the power to regulate child labor as within the auspices of the states under the "police power" of the Tenth Amendment.

The Twentieth Century, Phase II: The "New Deal" and New Constitutionalism. This constitutional period was characterized by significant economic, social and political upheaval. Following the stock market crash of 1929, the country settled into a prolonged period of economic depression. When President Franklin Roosevelt was elected in 1932, the country was experiencing troubled times. In 1931 alone, the year before he was elected, more than 2,000 banks had failed. ROBERT S. MCELVAINE, THE GREAT DEPRESSION 137

(1984). By the winter of 1932–33, shortly before FDR assumed office, "one-fourth of the nation's work force was unemployed" and the price of wheat had dropped by "nearly 90 percent." Industrial output had fallen by 60 percent.

FDR took office on the rallying cry of a "New Deal." One of his first acts was to call an extraordinary session of Congress to begin five days after his inauguration. During this session, the House passed eleven major bills after only forty hours of debate. In his first hundred days, Roosevelt managed to push through Congress numerous bills regulating financial markets, creating federal work programs, and regulating prices and wages. Included were the Agricultural Adjustment Act, the Bituminous Coal Act, the Farm Relief Act, the Emergency Farm Mortgage Act, the National Industrial Recovery Act, the Railway Pension Act, & the Truth-in-Securities Act.

The courts, however, were not on board with the President's aggressive agenda. A heavyweight square-off between the President, Congress and the Judiciary commenced in 1936, with *Carter v. Carter Coal Co.*, 298 U.S. 238 (1936). This 5–4 decision was a suit brought by a stockholder against his own company seeking to have the company avoid paying the Act's excise tax. The case presented a direct challenge to one New Deal statute, the Bituminous Coal Conservation Act of 1935. That Act, designed to stabilize the coal-mining industry, imposed a 15% excise tax on the sale of coal from a mine not operated in compliance with the Act, and the Act contained minimum price provisions. In striking down the Act, the Court found that Congress was trying to regulate the purely internal commerce of a state. The Court regarded the "manufacture" of goods as a "purely local" activity. The Court drew a line between activities that have a direct effect on commerce and those having an indirect effect, with indirect effects beyond federal legislative control. The Court, in part, was worried about a possible slippery slope, allowing Congress unchecked power to regulate.

Carter was but one of many setbacks for FDR's "New Deal." The Court also struck down the Railroad Retirement Act of 1934, *Railroad Retirement Board v. Alton Railroad Co.*, 295 U.S. 330 (1935), and the National Industrial Recovery Act. *A.L.A. Schechter Poultry Corp. v. United States*, 295 U.S. 495 (1935). *Schechter Poultry* continued the indirect-direct analysis of the Court and yielded the concept of "chickens at rest"—post-commerce—that were beyond the regulatory reach of Congress. The Court also struck down the Agricultural Adjustment Act of 1933 in *United States v. Butler*, 297 U.S. 1 (1936). The Court found that the government exceeded its taxing and spending powers, focusing on the limits of federalism and the powers granted by the Constitution.

In addition to viewing the commerce clause restrictively, the Court also struck laws down based on the unlawful delegation doctrine. In *Panama Refining Co. v. Ryan*, 293 U.S. 388 (1935), the Court struck down Section 9(c) of the National Industrial Recovery Act (NIRA) of 1933 because it did not provide defined standards by which the President was expected to exercise his discretion to prohibit so-called "hot" oil. The Court concluded that Congress had improperly delegated its legislative authority. Likewise, in *A.L.A. Schechter Poultry Corp. v. United States*, the Court struck down other sections of the NIRA on unlawful delegation grounds, stating that Section 3 of the NIRA was "without precedent." The New Deal was being pummeled. Even though not all decisions during these years restricted the scope of congressional power, the Court struck down four major pieces of federal legislation in only two years and the federal courts issued hundreds of injunctions against New Deal legislation. In sum, by the mid-1930s, Congress still retained some commerce power despite the Court's restrictive interpretation. Congress could regulate interstate commerce, streams of commerce and intrastate activities that directly affect interstate commerce. States, on the other hand, had an area carved out of their own, allowing them to regulate purely intrastate matters, the means of production ("before" interstate commerce), sometimes the streams of commerce, and activities that indirectly affect interstate commerce.

Roosevelt was reelected by a huge majority in 1936 and quickly focused his attention on the Supreme Court with his now infamous Court Packing Plan. The Plan provided that, when a judge or justice of any federal court reached the age of seventy without retiring, a new member could be appointed by the President. If the plan had passed, since six justices were age 70 or older, the Court's membership would have expanded to a maximum of fifteen members giving Roosevelt the chance to obtain a majority of members sympathetic to his position.

The plan was constitutionally permissible. Congress controls the number of justices on the Supreme Court and had allocated varying numbers between five and the current nine over the years. Despite the fact that the number of justices could have been changed if Congress so desired, the plan met with significant resistance because of its overt attempt to influence the judicial branch.

The court-packing plan never came to a vote in Congress. While the legislation was pending, the Court decided *West Coast Hotel Co. v. Parrish*, 300 U.S. 379 (1937), and *NLRB v. Jones & Laughlin Steel Corp*, 301 U.S. 1 (1937). *Jones & Laughlin Steel Corp.* was a 5–4 decision like many cases that preceded it in the 1930s. Only this time, Justice Roberts voted with the group upholding federal power. Justice Roberts' switch has been called "the switch in time that saved nine," referring of course to President Roosevelt's court-packing plan.

Jones & Laughlin Steel Corp. involved the NLRB's holding that a company had engaged in an unfair labor practice. The Court found that Congress has the power to regulate intrastate activities that "have such a close and substantial relation to interstate commerce that their control is essential or appropriate to protect that commerce from burdens and obstructions." While the court concluded that Congress could not reach intrastate activities that were so "indirect and remote" as to "effectually obliterate the distinction between what is national and what is local and create a completely centralized government," the Court found that the question was one of degree. The Court noted that a labor stoppage in the coal industry "would have a most serious effect upon interstate commerce" and the Court considered it "idle to say that the effect would be indirect or remote" because the coal industry was organized on a national scale, and its relationship to interstate commerce is a dominant factor in its activities.

The Commerce Clause in the Latter Part of the 20th Century. Jones and Laughlin Steel Corp. ushered in a half-century of case law during which the Court effectively validated every commerce clause power claim by Congress, accepting claims on several different grounds. First, the Court routinely held that Congress has the power to "regulate the channels of interstate commerce." *United States v. Lopez,* 514 U.S. 549, 558 (1995). Second, it allowed Congress to regulate the instrumentalities of interstate commerce. *See The Shreveport Rate Case,* 234 U.S. 342 (1914). Third, and finally, the Court recognized that Congress could regulate intrastate activities that have a "substantial effect" on interstate commerce. *NLRB v. Jones & Laughlin Steel Corp.*, 301 U.S. 1, 37 (1937).

Instead of actively policing federal Commerce Clause claims, the Court adopted a deferential approach, applying weak "rational basis," the Court's minimum level of scrutiny, generally serving as a rubber stamp for challenged legislation. The Tenth Amendment became more or less a truism in the Court's view, providing no real substantive check on federal legislation.

The Court's post-1936 approach is illustrated by *United States v. Darby,* 312 U.S. 100 (1941). In that case, the Court upheld a statute prohibiting the interstate shipment of lumber manufactured by employees whose wages were less than a prescribed minimum or whose weekly hours of labor at that wage were greater than a prescribed maximum. The law was similar to others that had been invalidated prior to 1936. Yet, the Court held that Congress could indirectly regulate the wages of employees who manufactured lumber. The Court deferred to Congress' determinations and expressly repudiated *Hammer v. Dagenhart*, noting that its holding "was a departure from the principles which have prevailed in the interpretation of the commerce clause both before and since the decision." As for the Tenth Amendment, the Court treated it as a mere "truism," without any protective power against federal enactments.

Wickard v. Filburn, 317 U.S. 111 (1942), was arguably the high-water mark in federal Commerce Clause power. In the Agricultural Adjustment Act of 1938, Congress authorized the Secretary of Agriculture to apportion allotments of wheat among states and counties, and individual farms to maximize stability in the marketplace. The government attempted to apply the Act to a small Ohio farm that produced a small crop of winter wheat, part of which was used for home consumption. When plaintiff produced wheat in excess of his allotment, he was subjected to a penalty of 49 cents a bushel. Plaintiff claimed that Congress did not have the power to regulate wheat raised on his own farm for home consumption. In a unanimous decision, the Court disagreed, concluding that plaintiff's activities had a "close and substantial relation to interstate traffic." Noting that homegrown wheat production could affect the overall market, the Court concluded that, while plaintiff's contribution to the demand for wheat might be regarded as "trivial," Congress could regulate his production because "his contribution, taken together with that of others similarly situated, is far from trivial." Thus, an individual's home consumption affected the market by withdrawing from that market and was not viewed in isolation, but with all other persons growing and consuming their own wheat.

Civil Rights Legislation and the Commerce Clause. Early decisions, such as The *Civil Rights Cases*, 109 U.S. 3 (1883), have had a lasting impact on the scope of Congress' powers to enforce the Reconstruction Amendments. In the earlier disputes, the Court had rebuffed Congress' attempts to enact civil rights legislation based on the Fourteenth Amendment to the U.S. Constitution. After 1936, however, the Court used the Commerce Clause to uphold various statutes that included anti-discrimination provisions. These statutes, most notably the Civil Rights Act of 1964, served as landmark legislation in the fight for equal treatment. In *Heart of Atlanta Motel, Inc. v. United States*, 379 U.S. 241 (1964), the Court upheld Title II of the Civil Rights Act of 1964. That Title prohibited discrimination on the basis of race, color, religion, or national origin in the use of goods, services, facilities, privileges, advantages, and accommodations. The law was applied to a hotel located in downtown Atlanta near two major interstates. Approximately 75 percent of the hotel's guests came from out-of-state, and the hotel advertised on in-state billboards and highway signs and in national magazines. The Court held that Congress did not exceed the scope of its commerce clause power, noting that racial discrimination places "burdens on interstate commerce" by making it difficult for affected individuals to find transient accommodations and that the discrimination might have "a substantial and harmful effect upon that commerce."

In *Katzenbach v. McClung*, 379 U.S. 294 (1964), the Court shifted its focus from hotels to restaurants, upholding the Civil Rights Act of 1964 as applied to a family-owned restaurant in Alabama, Ollie's BBQ, a well-known local eatery. The restaurant served barbecued meats and homemade pies with more than 200 seats—but only offered take-out service to African-Americans. The business employed 36 persons, two-thirds of whom were African-American. The Court used a rational basis standard in concluding, "racial discrimination in restaurants had a direct and adverse effect on the free flow of interstate commerce."

Areas of Expansive Regulation Under the Commerce Clause. One area of expansive regulation after the *Jones & Laughlin Steel Corp.* shift in approach involved federal criminal law. Federal laws expanded both in number and nature. For example, *Perez v. United States*, 402 U.S. 146 (1971), upheld the Consumer Credit Protection Act, criminalizing "extortionate credit transactions," defined as deals characterized by the use or threat of the use of "violence or other criminal means" in enforcement. A "loan shark," charged with violating the Act claimed that Congress had exceeded its power under the commerce clause. Relying on *Darby* and *Wickard*, the Court upheld the law noting that purely intrastate extortionate transactions "may in the judgment of Congress affect interstate commerce." The evidence showed that extortion was a $350 million per year business, and that "loan sharks serve as a source of funds to bookmakers, narcotics dealers, and other racketeers."

Likewise, in *Taylor v. United States*, 579 U.S. 301 (2016), defendant was charged with violating the Hobbs Act for breaking into the homes of two drug dealers. The question was whether the conduct had a sufficient relationship to interstate commerce to justify the federal law. In both cases, Taylor and other gang members broke into the homes, confronted the residents, demanded the location of drugs and money, found neither, and left relatively empty handed. Nevertheless, the Court held "that the Commerce Clause gives Congress authority to regulate the national market for marijuana, including the authority to proscribe the purely intrastate production, possession, and sale of this controlled substance. Because Congress may regulate these intrastate activities based on their aggregate effect on interstate commerce, it follows that Congress may also regulate intrastate drug *theft*. Since the Hobbs Act criminalizes robberies and attempted robberies that affect any commerce 'over which the United States has jurisdiction,' § 1951(b)(3), the prosecution in a Hobbs Act robbery case satisfies the Act's commerce element if it shows that the defendant robbed or attempted to rob a drug dealer of drugs or drug proceeds. By targeting a drug dealer in this way, a robber necessarily affects or attempts to affect commerce over which the United States has jurisdiction."

Another area of legislative expansion involved environmental and regulatory laws. *Hodel v. Virginia Surface Mining and Reclamation Association, Inc.*, 452 U.S. 264 (1981), involved the Surface Mining Control and Reclamation Act (SMCRA), a comprehensive statute designed to "establish a nationwide program to protect society and the environment from the adverse effects of surface coal mining operations." In reviewing the SMCRA, the Court held that it would defer to Congress' finding that a regulated activity affects interstate commerce if there is a "rational basis for such a finding," and if the means of regulation chosen by Congress "are reasonably adapted to the end permitted by the Constitution." In upholding the statute, the Court noted that Congress had found that many surface mining operations disturb surface areas, and "adversely affect commerce and the public welfare by destroying or diminishing the utility of land for commercial, industrial, residential, recreational, agricultural, and forestry purposes."

Another noteworthy area of expansion was in the area of administrative regulations, causing the federal government to augment its size significantly. This expansion was due to the Court pulling back on its vigorous review not only in the Commerce Clause arena, but in parallel arenas as well, allowing the Congress to continue making new claims to power on different fronts. In particular, the Court relaxed its vigilant approach to delegation in the non-delegation doctrine. Decisions during the 1930s, in particular *Panama Refining* and *Schechter*, limited Congress' authority to delegate power to administrative agencies. In the post-1930s era, *Panama Refining* and *Schechter* were effectively overruled. As a result, the Court began to sustain increasingly broad assertions of power. For example, in *INS v. Chadha*, 462 U.S. 919, 985 (1983), the Court recognized that "restrictions on the scope of the power that could be delegated diminished and all but disappeared." While delegations were required to be made pursuant to an "intelligible principle" designed to restrict the delegation, decisions like *Chadha* upheld delegations based on ambiguous formulations including phrases such as "just and reasonable," in the "*public interest*," "public convenience, interest, or necessity," and "unfair methods of competition." The relaxed enforcement of the non-delegation doctrine has led to an explosion of administrative agency regulations. As one court observed, "administrative agencies may well have a more far-reaching effect on the daily lives of all citizens than do the combined actions of the executive, legislative and judicial branches." *Ballerina Pen Co. v. Kunzig*, 433 F.2d 1204, 1207–08 (D.C. Cir. 1970), *cert. denied*, 401 U.S. 950 (1971).

The Attempt to Limit Congress' Commerce Clause Power: Lopez. The Court signaled it was ready to end (or at least slow down) the half-century of untrammeled expansion of federal commerce clause power in *United States v. Lopez*, 514 U.S. 549 (1995). In *Lopez*, the Court struck down the Gun-Free School Zones Act of 1990. That Act made it a federal offense "for any individual knowingly to possess a firearm at a place that the individual knows, or has reasonable cause to believe, is a school zone." Because the Act did not purport to regulate a commercial activity, or contain a requirement that the possession be connected in any way to interstate commerce, the Court held that Congress exceeded its power under the commerce clause. *Lopez* recognized that Congress could establish jurisdiction over commerce under any of three theories. First, Congress has the power to "regulate the use of the channels of interstate commerce." Second, Congress may "regulate and protect the instrumentalities of interstate commerce, or persons or things in interstate commerce, even though the threat may come only from intrastate activities." Third, Congress can regulate activities that have a "substantial relation to interstate commerce" if they "substantially affect interstate commerce."

Lopez departed from its post-1937 jurisprudence by holding that none of the three bases of regulation applied. In a significant departure from prior rulings, the Court doubted that the activities being regulated "substantially affected interstate commerce." Moreover, Congress did not provide findings demonstrating a link to interstate commerce. Chief Justice Rehnquist, for the Court, rejected the dissent's "costs of crime" argument that guns in school zones affect the national economy by increasing insurance costs, limiting the willingness of individuals to travel in areas deemed to be unsafe, and posing a substantial risk to "the educational process by threatening the learning environment" which would result in a less productive citizenry. The Court essentially utilized the slippery slope, noting that if the government's "costs of crime" and "national productivity" analysis prevailed, Congress could justifiably "regulate any activity that it found was related to the economic productivity of individual citizens" (*e.g.*, family law, including marriage, divorce, and child custody), and it would be "difficult to perceive any limitation on federal power, even in areas such as criminal law enforcement or education where States historically have been sovereign."

While *Lopez appeared* to put the brakes on congressional overreaching, Congress still was able to pass a wide variety of laws in its aftermath. For example, in *Reno v. Condon*, 528 U.S. 141 (2000), the Court upheld the Privacy Protection Act, which prohibited state governments from selling information that they received from driver's license applicants absent consent or an exemption. The focal point was not the information, but rather its sale, which constituted commerce and was within Congress' authority to regulate. In *United States v. Robertson*, 514 U.S. 669 (1995)(*per curiam*), the Court upheld the Racketeer Influenced and Corrupt Organizations Act (RICO) as applied to an individual who invested the proceeds of illegal narcotics offenses in an Alaskan gold mine. The Court found a relationship to interstate commerce because the mine's activities were commercial and they crossed state lines.

Despite these decisions, the Court was not finished stunting Congress' Commerce Clause reach. In *United States v. Morrison,* 529 U.S. 598 (2000), the Court struck down a portion of the Violence Against Women Act of 1994. The Act provided a federal civil remedy for the victims of gender-motivated violence as applied to a university student who filed a civil suit for rape. The Court refused to apply a *Wickard*-type aggregate effects analysis because the underlying activity was not economic in nature. The Court also rejected the argument that Congress could regulate under its Fourteenth Amendment remedial powers because of the absence of state action.

Those who wished to see *Lopez*'s limits advance even further in the next big case were disappointed. The Court instead returned to its reliance on *Wickard* to resolve *Gonzales v. Raich*, 545 U.S. 1 (2005). That case involved a California statute authorizing the use of marijuana for medicinal purposes. Two women, who used marijuana in treating serious medical conditions, challenged the federal Controlled Substances Act's (CSA) provisions that prohibited individuals from possessing, obtaining, or manufacturing cannabis for their personal medical use. The Court relied on *Wickard* and its aggregate effects analysis, as well as on rational basis analysis, in concluding that marijuana use has a "substantial effect" on interstate commerce. Using this analysis, the Court found that leaving home-consumed marijuana unregulated would affect the price and market conditions of the product. In addition, the Court found that there was a risk that high demand in the interstate market would draw home grown marijuana into the market. Unlike the holdings in *Lopez* and *Morrison*, the Court was deferential to Congress, concluding that it need only find that Congress had a "rational basis" for its conclusions.

The Affordable Care Act and the Commerce Clause. In the Affordable Care Act of 2010, Congress imposed a mandate that all citizens were required to purchase health insurance. One way that Congress sought to justify the legislation was under the commerce clause. However, in *National Federation of Independent Business v. Sebelius*, 567 U.S. 519 (2012), the Court rejected that argument. The Court emphasized that the Constitution does not grant Congress the power "to perform all conceivable functions of government," but rather only limited and enumerated powers: "If no enumerated power authorizes Congress to pass a certain law, that law may not be enacted, even if it would not violate any of the express prohibitions in the Bill of Rights or elsewhere in the Constitution." Since Congress was given the commerce power, and that power is expanded and enhanced by the Necessary and Proper Clause, it argued that Congress may order individuals to buy health insurance because the failure to do so affects interstate commerce, and could undercut the ACA's other reforms. In particular, it argued that the failure to purchase insurance "has a substantial and deleterious effect on interstate commerce" by creating a cost-shifting problem.

The Court rejected that argument, noting that "Congress has never attempted to rely on that power to compel individuals not engaged in commerce to purchase an unwanted product." The Court concluded that the "individual mandate does not regulate existing commercial activity, but instead compels individuals to become active in commerce by purchasing a product, on the ground that their failure to do so affects interstate commerce." The Court rejected this argument, noting that construing "the Commerce Clause to permit Congress to regulate individuals because they are doing nothing would open a new and potentially vast domain to congressional authority. Every day individuals do not do an infinite number of things. Allowing Congress to justify federal regulation by pointing to the effect of inaction on commerce would bring countless decisions an individual could potentially make within the scope of federal regulation, and empower Congress to make those decisions for him." The Court concluded that the "individual mandate's regulation of the uninsured as a class is divorced from any link to existing commercial activity."

The Taxing Power. Article I, Section 8, provides Congress with another important power, the power to tax: "The Congress shall have Power To lay and collect Taxes, Duties, Imposes and Excises. . . ." This power also has constitutionally explicit limits, namely that "direct Taxes shall be apportioned among the several States," (Art. I, Sec. 2, Cl. 3, U.S. Const.) and that all "Duties, Imposts and Excises shall be uniform throughout the United States." (Art. I, Sec. 8, Cl. 1, U.S. Const.) In *Pollock v. Farmers' Loan & Trust Co.*, 157 U.S. 429 (1895) the Court used these sections of the Constitution to conclude that Congress could not impose a federal income tax. Since direct taxes must be imposed in proportion to population, the income tax was found to be invalid because it imposed taxes on the basis of income. *Pollock,* however, was effectively overruled by the Sixteenth Amendment to the Constitution. The Amendment states, "The Congress shall have power to lay and collect taxes on incomes, from whatever source derived, without apportionment among the several States . . . ." The Court recorded this change in *New York ex rel. Cohn v. Graves*, 300 U.S. 308 (1937).

Congress has used the taxing power as both a tool to raise money and as a method of coercion. Both of these objectives have been subjected to a variety of challenges. In *Bailey v. Drexel Furniture Co.*, 259 U.S. 20 (1922), also known as the *Child Labor Tax Case*, the Court struck down the Child Labor Tax Law. That law involved Congress' attempt to use its taxing power to enforce child labor regulations that were struck down in *Hammer v. Dagenhart*. The Court struck down this law as well, holding that "where the sovereign enacting the law has power to impose both a tax and penalty, the difference between revenue production and mere regulation may be immaterial." However, when the federal government only has the power to tax, and the power of regulation lies in another arena, a different analysis arises. The Court focused on motive, stating a tax is permissible when Congress' primary motive is to raise revenue. Thus, a tax used to penalize—and regulate—was unconstitutional.

In later cases, however, following the Court's post-1937 shift, the Court was much more likely to uphold laws that had the effect of raising revenue, regardless of the actual motive of the legislature in enacting the statute. Thus, *Bailey* probably would not be followed today. *See, e.g., Sonzinsky v. United States*, 300 U.S. 506 (1937) (tax on wagering).

In *National Federation of Independent Business v. Sebelius*, 567 U.S. 519 (2012), although the Court held that the Affordable Care Act of 2010 could not be upheld under the spending power or the commerce power, it did uphold the "individual mandate" to purchase health insurance under Congress' power to tax. The Act imposed a "shared responsibility payment" on those who failed to purchase insurance, and the Court described that payment as a "penalty" which was payable to the Internal Revenue Service as part of an individual's annual tax filing. As a result, the Court upheld the individual mandate as a tax: "The 'shared responsibility payment' is paid into the Treasury by 'taxpayers' when they file their tax returns. It does not apply to individuals who do not pay income taxes because their household income is less than the filing threshold. For taxpayers who owe the payment, its amount is determined by such familiar factors as taxable income, number of dependents, and joint filing status. The requirement to pay is found in the Internal Revenue Code and enforced by the IRS, which must assess and collect it 'in the same manner as taxes.' This process yields the essential feature of any tax: it produces at least some revenue for the Government." The Court went on to note that the tax was expected to raise about $4 billion per year. "Although the payment will raise considerable revenue, it is designed to expand health insurance coverage. But taxes that seek to influence conduct are nothing new. Some of our earliest federal taxes sought to deter the purchase of imported manufactured goods in order to foster the growth of domestic industry." Subsequent to the decision in *Sebelius*, Congress eliminated the "tax" imposed as part of the ACA mandate. Subsequently, individuals and some states sued seeking to invalidate the ACA. The Court upheld the ACA again.

The Spending Power. The same area of the Constitution that sets forth the power to tax and regulate commerce also contains the spending power, Article I, Section 8, gives Congress the power to spend for the general welfare: "The Congress shall have Power To lay and collect Taxes, Duties, Imposes and Excises, to pay the Debts and provide for the common Defense and general Welfare of the United States."

The meaning of spending for "the general welfare" was initially debated. At one point, Madison argued for a narrow interpretation, such that "the grant of power to tax and spend for the general national welfare must be confined to the enumerated legislative fields committed to the Congress." In contrast, Hamilton argued for a much broader view, that the purpose must be "general, and not local." Hamilton's broader view won out.

For example, in *South Dakota v. Dole,* 483 U.S. 203 (1987), involved a federal statute that directed the Secretary of Transportation to withhold a percentage of federal highway funds from any state that allowed individuals less than twenty-one years of age to purchase alcoholic beverages. While the Court noted that the spending power is not "unlimited," in that any spending must be in pursuit of the "general welfare," any conditions imposed on the funds must be unambiguous so that states can knowingly decide whether to accept or reject the conditions, and the spending provision must be related "to the federal interest in particular national projects or programs." In *Dole*, the Court upheld the statute, noting that Congress could appropriate money with reasonable conditions.

The Court reaffirmed the principle that Congress controls the purse strings and how it distributes money in *Pennhurst State School & Hospital v. Halderman,* 451 U.S. 1 (1981). *Pennhurst State School* involved the Developmentally Disabled Assistance and Bill of Rights Act of 1975, providing financial assistance to participating states to aid them in creating programs to care for and treat the developmentally disabled. States were free to choose whether to voluntarily comply with the Act, but faced a loss of federal funding if they declined. The Court upheld Congress' power to condition its spending under the spending clause, noting that Congress has the authority to decide the terms on which it will disburse money to the states, and that the states are free to choose whether to accept or reject the federally-imposed conditions. The Court concluded that Pennsylvania "voluntarily and knowingly" accepted the terms that were imposed, but concluded that the Act did not require the States to assume the high cost of providing appropriate treatment in the least restrictive environment to their mentally disabled citizens.

However, there are limits that Congress cannot transcend. Another aspect of the Affordable Care Act that drew litigation was the Medicaid expansion. Under that expansion, in exchange for federal Medicaid funding, states were required to provide health care to all citizens whose income falls below a certain threshold. That marked a significant expansion of the Medicaid program at significant cost to the states. The Medicaid expansion was challenged in *National Federation of Independent Business v. Sebelius*, 567 U.S. 519 (2012), on the basis that it increased the costs to all states. In *Seberlius*, the Court concluded that Congress could not force states to comply with the Medicaid expansion. States must either be given the choice to accept federal funding or decline it so that they retain political accountability for the decisions they make. Thus, although Congress can condition the receipt of federal funds on the States' willingness to comply with restrictions on the use of those funds, thereby encouraging and pressuring states to take certain actions, those conditions cannot be so coercive as to pass the point at which 'pressure turns into compulsion.' " In *Sebelius*, the Court concluded that the Affordable Care Act's requirement was so coercive as to constitute "a gun to the head." If a state did not comply, it would have lost all Medicaid funding which was approximately 20% of an average state's budget. Moreover, the Medicaid expansion went far beyond the scope of the original Medicaid program (which was designed to help four needy groups (the disabled, the blind, the elderly, and needy families with dependent children) to a program that extends to the entire non-elderly population with income below 133 percent of the poverty level). As a result, the Court regarded the "expansion" as an entirely new program and held that states must be given the choice whether to stick with the old program or adopt the new one. Thus, the Court effectively rewrote the Act by giving states the choice between remaining in the old Medicaid program (which had seemingly been abolished) or opting into the new program.

Foreign Powers. The Power to Declare War and Regulate Foreign Affairs. Article I gives Congress a role in international matters, including the power to declare war. The President, as Commander-in-Chief of the Army and Navy under Article II, Section 2, also has powers in this area, and uses that power to protect and defend the country, often in concert with Congress. Yet, the two branches often are uneasy bedfellows in the foreign powers arena, particularly when it comes to armed conflict and committing troops abroad. In recent years, the President has acted sometimes unilaterally in engaging troops in armed conflict without a declaration of war. Included here are conflicts in Korea and Vietnam as well as in Grenada and Iraq. However, Congress has additional foreign powers in the Constitution, including the general power to "regulate foreign affairs." To illustrate, in *Perez v. Brownell*, 356 U.S. 44 (1958), the Court upheld a congressional enactment that mandated a loss of U.S. citizenship for "voting in a political election in a foreign state."

The Treaty Power. While the President has the power to make treaties under Article II, Section 2 of the Constitution, the legislative branch is made a partner of sorts by requiring a two-thirds vote of the Senate for ratification.

While the constitutional interdependence of the Executive and Legislative branches is clear, the scope and power of treaties have been contested over the years. An initial issue involved the status of treaties that conflicted with the Constitution. Although there was some thought that treaties were extra-constitutional and not restrained by the Constitution's individual provisions, the Court rejected this approach. In *Missouri v. Holland*, 252 U.S. 416 (1920), the Court upheld the Migratory Bird Treaty after examining whether the treaty contravened "any prohibitory words to be found in the Constitution." Similarly, in *Reid v. Covert*, 354 U.S. 1 (1957), the Court recognized that "no agreement with a foreign nation can confer power on the Congress, or on any other branch of Government, which is free from the restraints of the Constitution."

Another disputed area involves treaties that conflict with federal statutes, raising the question of which controls. The Court answered this question by viewing the two types of enactments as relative equals, yielding the general rule, the last enactment in time prevails. In *Whitney v. Robertson,* 124 U.S. 190 (1888), merchants who imported sugar claimed that a treaty required that their sugar be admitted on the same basis as similar items produced in Hawaii. After the treaty was signed, Congress passed an inconsistent statute. The Court held that the statute enacted after the treaty controlled, essentially viewing the statute as a controlling modification.

The first step in the analysis for the Court explored an important issue regarding the scope of treaties—whether the treaty was self-executing and applied domestically at all. The Court reasoned that, "When the stipulations are not self-executing, they can only be enforced pursuant to legislation to carry them into effect, and such legislation is as much subject to modification and repeal by Congress as legislation upon any other subject." If a treaty is self-executing, in that it requires no legislation to render its provisions effective, the treaty has the "force and effect of a legislative enactment."

A third question involves the relative status of treaties as they relates to state laws. *Missouri v. Holland*, 252 U.S. 416 (1920), dealt with that issue as well. In that case, the Court upheld the Migratory Bird Treaty against a Tenth Amendment challenge by the State of Missouri. Could international treaties enter into the local sphere of states? The Court answered in the affirmative, noting that "there may be matters of the sharpest exigency for the national well being that an act of Congress could not deal with but that a treaty followed by such an act could, and it is not lightly to be assumed that, in matters requiring national action, "a power which must belong to and somewhere reside in every civilized government is not to be found."

Congressional Enforcement of Civil Rights. The aftermath of the Civil War led to significant constitutional changes, primarily in the adoption of the "Reconstruction Amendments," the Thirteenth, Fourteenth and Fifteenth Amendments. The Reconstruction Amendments tilted the responsibility for protecting individual rights, which were almost entirely left to the states prior to the War. The Reconstruction Amendments modified the governmental responsibilities. Almost immediately, the Amendments supported a series of post-Civil War legislation enacted by Congress, namely the Civil Rights Acts of 1866, 1870, 1871 and 1875, which still exist in some form today. In particular, the Reconstruction Amendments focused the federal government on granting and protecting the citizenship of former slaves. *See* the *Slaughter-House Cases*, 83 U.S. (16 Wall.) 36 (1872). To reflect this power shift, each Amendment was embedded with an enforcement provision—Section 2 of the 13th and 15th Amendments and Section 5 of the 14th Amendment. These provisions gave Congress "the power to enforce, by appropriate legislation, the provisions of this article."

While the abolition of slavery and the reconstruction of the country after the Civil War offered an immediate application for the Amendments, the overall reach of the Amendments and the intent of those who framed them remained unclear. In fact, the first test of the scope of post-civil war federal power, the *Slaughter-House Cases,* had nothing to do with race.

The *Civil Rights Cases of 1883*, 109 U.S. 3 (1883), was the first case testing the scope of congressional authority to enforce civil rights. These consolidated cases challenged the constitutionality of the Civil Rights Act of 1875, and Congress' authority to use the 13th and 14th Amendments and the Commerce Clause to enact legislation that prohibited private businesses from discriminating on the basis of race. The Court's construction of the enforcement clauses resonates to this day. There were four holdings:

> First, Section 5 of the 14th Amendment did not give Congress affirmative authority, but rather only the remedial power "to enforce the prohibition" against state laws that violate the equal protection clause, as interpreted by judicial decision. Congress does not have plenary power to legislate in areas that the Court determines are not within the domain of national regulation.
>
> Second, Section 5 of the 14th Amendment does not give Congress the power to legislate in areas within the domain of state regulation. Congress can only provide redress against the operation of state laws and the actions of state officials that are subversive of the fundamental rights specified in Section 1.
>
> Third, the Court limited the scope of the Fourteenth Amendments to "state action.". . . "[U]ntil some State law has been passed, or some State action through its officers or agents has been taken, adverse to the rights of citizens sought to be protected by the Fourteenth Amendment, no legislation of the United States under said amendment, nor any proceeding under such legislation, can be called into activity: for the prohibitions of the amendment are against State laws and acts done under State authority."
>
> Fourth, the scope of congressional action is limited to the wrong that the 14th Amendment was intended to protect against. Congress could not redress other wrongs unconnected to the 14th Amendment.

The Court did not reach the issue of whether the Commerce Clause empowered Congress to legislate in the field of civil rights. Nevertheless, the decision chilled major federal civil rights legislation until 1957, when Congress enacted the Civil Rights Act of 1957. That Act was followed by the enactment of the Civil Rights Act of 1960. Significantly, on June 19, 1963, the late President Kennedy called for even more extensive civil rights legislation in a message to Congress. Its stated purpose was "to promote the general welfare by eliminating discrimination based on race, color, religion, or national origin in . . . public accommodations through the exercise by Congress of the powers conferred upon it . . . to enforce the provisions of the fourteenth and fifteenth amendments, to regulate commerce among the several States, and to make laws necessary and proper to execute the powers conferred upon it by the Constitution." It was not until July 2, 1964, however, with President Johnson presiding, that the Civil Rights Act of 1964 finally passed.

Modern Protection of Civil Rights. In more recent times, Congress has turned to the Commerce Clause to justify civil rights legislation in recent decades because of the restrictive interpretation of the Reconstruction Amendments in the *Civil Rights Cases* and the Court's expansive view of its Commerce Clause powers after the 1930s. Congress took exactly that approach in enacting the Civil Rights Act of 1964.

In *Heart of Atlanta Motel v. United States,* 379 U.S. 241 (1964), discussed in the Commerce Clause section above, the Court upheld the constitutionality of Title II of the Civil Rights Act of 1964. Congress had premised the law on evidence that hotels and restaurants nationwide refused to serve African American patrons, with the result that discrimination "interferes significantly with interstate travel." The Court ruled that the commerce power alone provided sufficient authority to enact the legislation. The Court reasserted that Congress' power extends to those intrastate activities that so affect interstate commerce that they are appropriate means to the attainment of a legitimate end. (This approach originated in *McCulloch v. Maryland, supra.*) The test was: (1) whether Congress had a rational basis for finding that racial discrimination by motels affected commerce; and (2) if it had such a basis, whether the means it selected to eliminate that evil are reasonable and appropriate.

As discussed earlier, the *Civil Rights Cases* dealt a serious blow to the federal defense of civil rights through the Reconstruction Amendments) (the 13th, 14th and 15th Amendments to the Constitution) which were adopted following the Civil War. The Warren Court sought briefly to expand the potential for enforcement under the Reconstruction Amendments in *Katzenbach v. Morgan,* 384 U.S. 641 (1966). In *Morgan,* the State of New York challenged the federal government's power to prohibit state laws requiring voters to be able to read and write as a prerequisite to voting pursuant to the Voting Rights Act of 1965. The Court rejected the State's argument that there had to have been a prior judicial finding that one of the Amendments had been violated in order for Congress to exercise congressional power under Section 5 of the Fourteenth Amendment.

This glimmer of broader federal enforcement power was brief. During the Rehnquist era, the Court again adopted a narrower view of *The Civil Rights Cases,* in which Congress' power was remedial in scope only. The power to determine whether a constitutional violation occurred again lay firmly within the jurisdiction of the courts, not the Congress. *City of Boerne v. Flores,* 521 U.S. 507 (1997).

In addition to narrowing judicial constructions of the Reconstruction Amendments, there are other limits on the congressional enforcement power. In particular, Congress goes beyond its bounds under the Tenth Amendment when its legislation strips the states of their power of self-governance. Some of these excessive federal laws involved the Voting Rights Act of 1965. In *Oregon v. Mitchell,* 400 U.S. 112 (1970), the Court declared unconstitutional a 1970 amendment to the Voting Rights Act. The amendment lowered the voting age to eighteen in state and local elections. The majority held that the federal government was constitutionally empowered to regulate federal elections, but that the states are free to determine within the limits of the Constitution the qualification for voters in state and local elections, subject to the Reconstruction Amendments' prohibition against racial discrimination.

The holding in the *Civil Rights Cases of 1883,* limiting the reach of Congress under section 5 to "state action," has lost some of its vitality. In the Court's decision in *United States v. Guest,* 383 U.S. 745 (1966), it threatened to expand the applicability of Section 5 of the 14th Amendment. While the *Civil Rights Cases of 1883* require "state action" and that was the basis for *Guest,* a majority of the justices were ready to extend Section 5 to even private actors, in this case White Supremacists who conspired to deprive African Americans of their civil rights.

United States v. Morrison, 529 U.S. 598 (2000), indicated that preparation for such an expansion was premature. A female student sued Virginia Polytechnic Institute and two male football players who she alleged had raped her while they had been attending the university. She sued under the Violence Against Women Act. (42 U.S.C. Sec. 13981.) The Act provided a federal civil remedy for the victims of gender-motivated violence. The Court dismissed the expansive parts of *United States v. Guest* as "naked dicta" and upheld the *Civil Rights Cases of 1883* prohibition against congressional legislation under Section 5 against private conduct. The section of the VAWA in question was struck down because Congress had exceeded its powers under both the Commerce Clause and the Fourteenth Amendment.

The limitation of congressional regulation to state action also applied to the Fifteenth Amendment. The Court treated the Thirteenth Amendment differently, however, finding in *Jones v. Alfred H. Mayer Co.,* 392 U.S. 409 (1968), that Congress could enforce the 13th Amendment against private actors.

While the harm the Reconstruction Amendments were intended to address clearly covered race discrimination, the Court extended the scope of Congress' Article 5 powers to include prohibitions against sex discrimination, age discrimination, discrimination based on disability, religious practices, and violence against women. Congress can act to enforce the explicit constitutional guarantees of equal protection and due process in Section 1, as well as those incorporated into the fourteenth amendment, including the liberties guaranteed by the First Amendment and other provisions of the Bill of Rights. *See, e.g., United States v. Georgia,* 546 U.S. 151 (2006). However, Section 5 legislation that reaches beyond the scope of Section 1's guarantees of due process and equal protection must exhibit "congruency and proportionality" between the injury to be prevented or remedied and the means adopted by Congress to that end. In *City of Boerne,* the Court articulated and applied this test because protection of religious freedom is outside the scope of Section 1's actual guarantees. The Court found the evidence of injury by the States' to religious liberties was not congruent with or proportionate to the sweeping legislation embodied in the Religious Freedom Restoration Act.

The "congruence and proportionality" test provides a check on Congress to determine if it has gone too far in enforcing civil rights. The little guidance given by the Court to determine if Congress had crossed the "remedial" line into making "substantive changes" can be found in *Kimel v. Florida Board of Regents,* 528 U.S. 62 (2000)(concerning the ADEA) and *Board of Trustees of the University of Alabama v. Garrett,* 531 U.S. 356 (2001)(concerning the ADA). The Court applied the congruency and proportionality test in each case and held that the Age Discrimination in Employment Act and Title I of the Americans with Disabilities Act were not appropriate remedial legislation under Section 5 of the 14th Amendment. For that reason, both Acts were also deemed an unconstitutional abrogation of the States' sovereign immunity.

CHECKLIST

A. **Necessary and Proper Clause**—Is Congress' action supported by an enumerated power or is it "necessary and proper" in support of those powers? While Congress is purportedly constrained by enumerated powers, these powers have been expansively interpreted and are supported by an expansive "Necessary and Proper" clause promoting implied powers.

B. **Commerce Clause I**—Is Congress regulating within states? If yes, that regulation is permitted if the intrastate activity is protecting, advancing or sufficiently affecting interstate commerce.

C. **Commerce Clause II**—Is Congress' regulation under the Commerce Clause post-*Lopez* supported by one of three grounds? If Congress is regulating a *channel* of commerce, an *instrumentality* of commerce or the activity *substantially affects* interstate commerce, the regulation likely will be upheld.

D. **Commerce Clause III**—What does a "substantial effect" mean? First, if Congress has a rational basis for concluding that the subject of regulation substantially affects interstate commerce, it will be upheld. Activities that have a substantial *economic* effect on interstate commerce are almost always considered to have a substantial effect on interstate commerce because it affects the marketplace of commerce. In addition, if a law requires proof of a sufficient nexus to interstate commerce, that proof can meet the constitutional requirement on a case-by-case basis.

E. **Taxing Power**—Can Congress levy a tax that penalizes the taxpayer? Congress is permitted to raise revenue through taxing, despite incidental penalties that might occur, so long as the tax is uniform.

F. **Spending Power**—Can Congress attach strings or conditions to the funds it disburses under its spending power? Congress can spend for the "general welfare" using reasonable conditions.

G. **Foreign Affairs Power**—Does Congress have plenary power over foreign affairs? No, the power is shared with the President, but Congress has substantial powers nonetheless, including international commerce power, shared treaty power, the power to declare war, and more.

H. **Treaty Power**—Has the Senate approved a treaty by a $2/3$-majority vote? If not, the treaty is not valid. Even if the Senate has given its approval, a later federal law generally controls, because treaties are generally accorded the same status a federal statute. If a treaty is not self-executing and it was not intended to apply domestically, it may not have domestic applicability.

I. **Enforcement of Civil Rights Power**—Is the Congress relying on its enforcement powers in the Reconstruction Amendments (the Thirteenth, Fourteenth and Fifteenth) or on its Commerce Clause power to enforce civil rights? After the *Civil Rights Cases* of 1883, Congress' powers under the Reconstruction Amendments have been limited to remedial action, whereas its powers under the Commerce Clause have been broader and more fluent.

■ PROBLEMS ■

Problem #1: A ferryboat regularly plied the waters of Lake Norman in the late 1800s. The lake was located entirely within the State of North Carolina. The boat traveled all around the lake, especially in the summer, transporting people and food from nearby states, such as South Carolina, to people who lived on the lake. Congress enacted a regulation that required all boats such as the Lake Norman ferry to carry a certain number and type of life jackets, among other limitations. Is the federal law constitutional?

Answer: Even in the late 1800s, the law likely would be upheld as within the Commerce Clause power of Congress, despite the fact that in the 19th Century, the Commerce Clause power was not interpreted to be as extensive as it is today, and that the boat was located entirely within a single state. *The Daniel Ball*, 77 U.S. 557 (1870), is illustrative. That case involved a steamer that traveled routes wholly within the State of Michigan, but which carried merchandise being transported to, or from, other states, and a federal safety regulation that applied to the steamer. In an opinion by Justice Field, the Court concluded that Congress possessed the requisite power to impose the regulation: "[W]e are unable to draw any clear and distinct line between the authority of Congress to regulate an agency employed in commerce between the States, when that agency extends through two or more States, and when it is confined in its action entirely within the limits of a single State."

Problem #2: In 1910, Congress banned the transportation in interstate commerce of all soft drinks containing cocaine. A soft drink manufacturer, *Cola Cola*, Co., claims Congress exceeded its power to regulate. Will a court side with *Cola Cola* in this case?

Answer: *Cola Cola*, Co. will lose its case. The Congress had and still retains the power to ban items from interstate commerce, including noxious articles such as cocaine, marijuana or heroin. *Champion v. Ames*, 188 U.S. 321 (1903), the "*Lottery Case*," teaches that Congress has plenary power over the channels of interstate commerce, even if items are not being bought or sold at that time. (*See Champion v. Ames, supra.*) Thus, Congress could regulate to ban such transportation of a noxious article.

Problem #3: In 1960, Congress enacts a law prohibiting companies from selling fire insurance without a five-day opt-out period. This law was opposed by a Delaware company that claimed insurance does not move across state lines, does not affect interstate commerce and only has an indirect impact on commerce at best. Should the Delaware insurance company, Good Hands Insurance, Inc., prevail?

Answer: The insurance company will lose in the year 1960. Under the expansive interpretation of the Commerce Clause in the modern era, such a regulation will be upheld. In one of its early cases, *Paul v. Virginia*, 75 U.S. (8 Wall.) 168 (1868), the Court found that insurance policies are not commerce and not properly regulated by Congress under the Commerce Clause. Later, in *United States v. South-Eastern Underwriters Ass'n*, 322 U.S. 533 (1944), the Court overturned *Paul,* stating: "[I]t would indeed be difficult now to hold that no activities of any insurance company can ever constitute interstate commerce so as to make it subject to such regulation;— activities which, as part of the conduct of a legitimate and useful commercial enterprise, may embrace integrated operations in many states and involve the transmission of great quantities of money, documents, and communications across dozens of state lines."

Problem #4: Congress enacts a tax law in the year 2000 that imposes a tax on butter at 4 cents a pound and 14 cents a pound on margarine. The largest oleomargarine manufacturer in the country challenges the law, claiming the tax is a penalty and inconsistent with Article I, Section 8 of the Constitution. How should the Supreme Court rule?

Answer: The Court should uphold the tax as within Congress' taxing power. Illustrative of the Court's modern approach is the holding in *United States v. Sanchez*, 340 U.S. 42 (1950). In that case, the Court upheld the Marihuana Tax Act against claims that Congress was imposing a penalty rather than a tax. Congress had two primary motives in passing the legislation: raising revenue and promoting its efforts to control illegal narcotics. The Act required that all transfers be recorded on forms issued by the Secretary of the Treasury, and provided for a tax of $1 per ounce on all sales that are registered and taxed, or $100 per ounce on sales that are not registered and on which no tax is paid. The Court upheld the tax "despite the regulatory effect and the close resemblance to a penalty." The Court noted, "a tax does not cease to be valid merely because it regulates, discourages, or even definitely deters the activities taxed," and even though "the revenue obtained is obviously negligible, or the revenue purpose of the tax may be secondary." In addition, the Court concluded that a tax statute does not "necessarily fall because it touches on activities which Congress might not otherwise regulate."

Problem #5: The President, with the approval of the Senate, enters into a treaty with Italy, permitting citizens of either country to inherit property in the other country. The treaty was self-executing in its effect and intended to apply to the entire United States. A longstanding California law prohibits non-U.S. Citizens from inheriting property in the state. When Sheila Lupino's great aunt passed away in Los Angeles, the aunt left property to Sheila, a citizen and resident of Italy. Sheila sued to take lawful possession of the property. Will Sheila win?

Answer: Sheila will win. Essentially, a lawfully enacted self-executing treaty will take precedence over conflicting state laws. Here, the California law would give way in favor of the federal treaty. This result mirrors the case of *Hauenstein v. Lynham*, 100 U.S. 483 (1879). There, a federal treaty was held to control over a Virginia law that prohibited aliens from taking by descent or inheritance in the state. The Court relied on the Supremacy Clause in holding: "It is the declared will of the people of the United States that every treaty made by the authority of the United States shall be superior to the laws of any individual State. . . ."

Problem #6: Congress enacts a law prohibiting "any false information to be distributed by states or local governments about when and under what circumstances voting will take place for public elections." The law follows congressional hearings which concluded several states deterred minorities from voting through the distribution of disinformation about times and places of election voting. The law provided $1 million fines for every incidence of discrimination and allowed private suits to enforce voting rights. Is the law Constitutional?

Answer: If the law is based on the enforcement power of the Fourteenth and Fifteenth Amendments, the law must not only be remedial—remedying state discrimination—but also congruent and proportional to the remedy allotted. The Court applies a congruence and proportionality test when Congress uses its Section 5 power to reach conduct beyond the scope of the actual guarantees of due process and equal protection found in Section 1. In order to authorize private individuals to recover money damages against the States, there are several requirements. There must be a pattern of discrimination by the States which violates the Fourteenth Amendment, and the remedy imposed by Congress must be "congruent and proportional" to the targeted violation. The Court determines proportionality in several steps. First, the Court identifies, with some precision the scope of the constitutional right in issue to determine whether Section 1 places any limitations upon the States' treatment of the class of people claiming a constitutional violation. Then, the Court looks at the conduct that Congress considers unconstitutional. Congress must do due diligence and provide a legislative record that affirmatively identifies irrational discrimination by the States towards the class. In the Voting Rights cases, the unconstitutional conduct was flagrant, pervasive, and widespread and subject to correction based on the actual guarantees of Section 1.

POINTS TO REMEMBER

- Congress's powers are enumerated in the Constitution and ostensibly are limited as a result. Broad interpretations of the enumerated powers, however, often extend the scope of those powers considerably.
- The necessary and proper clause is less a limit on Congress than an affirmation that Congress can engage in nonenumerated activities in support of its enumerated powers.
- The Commerce Clause is one of Congress' broadest powers and permits Congress to regulate within states as well as items that cross state lines. When in doubt, the Commerce Clause is a good place to begin to determine if Congress has the power to act.
- Congress can regulate the channels and instrumentalities of commerce, as well as anything that has a "substantial relation to interstate commerce" or that which may "substantially affect interstate commerce."
- The "substantial affects" test is limited, but allows for substantial economic affects as well as some non-economic affects and movement of people, particularly if Congress has a rational basis for its conclusion that interstate commerce is affected.

CHAPTER 3

Federal Executive Powers

The Executive branch is one-third of the triumvirate holding federal powers, which also includes the Legislature and the Judicial branch. The states and the federal government have Executive branches. This duality of sovereign Executive branches is a product of the system we call federalism. The powers of these branches often mirror each other, although differences arise from federal to state.

EXECUTIVE POWER REVIEW

The federal Executive branch's constitutional powers are generally located in Article II of the Constitution. The express powers are wide-ranging and are also referred to as enumerated powers. These powers include faithfully executing the law, appointing and removing government officers, participating in the legislative process by approving or vetoing legislative enactments, acting as the Commander-in-Chief of the armed forces, serving as the country's chief diplomat in relations with foreign entities, entering into treaties with other countries, and more. These powers are vested entirely in the President of the United States, although the President's support "team" includes several hundred high-ranking officers and many more staff members. The Executive branch has implied powers, such as the power to implement the express powers enumerated in the Constitution. One implied power is to protect members of the government, such as for the Supreme Court and its justices. *See, e.g.*, *In re Neagle*, 135 U.S. 1 (1890).

The scope and application of these Executive powers have evolved over time. In a post 9/11 world, the powers used to fight terrorism have garnered the most attention, but the other powers still exist and are implemented regularly.

I. The Power to Execute the Law. The obligation to faithfully execute the law occurs in a variety of contexts. The Executive branch serves as the government's lawyer in the criminal and civil legal systems, for example. Executive branch lawyers try federal crimes and advocate for government plaintiffs and defendants in civil lawsuits. The United States Attorney offices, led by lawyers appointed by the President, are scattered throughout the country. In addition, the Executive branch utilizes and enforces many administrative regulations to help effectuate the goals of legislation. These regulations occur with a wide range of subjects, from the Internal Regulatory Service tax code to the Food and Drug Administration rules about various foods, such as what qualifies as "organic."

Note that one way the president executes the law is through Executive Orders. Every president has issued executive orders. The use of such orders does not change the constitutional separation of powers, but can appear to reorder the way laws are applied.

For example, in April of 2024, Congress enacted the Protecting Americans From Foreign Adversary Controlled Applications Act, banning operations in the United States of Internet apps controlled by a "foreign adversary," including the People Republic of China. ByteDance, the owner of TikTok and a Chinese company, was included in the ban. President Trump, after one day of self-imposed shut down of the TikTok app, delayed the application of the law in an executive order, which states the order is based on the Constitution and the laws of the United States. Several other executive orders by President Trump have subsequently delayed the enforcement of this particular law until an agreement was apparently reached in September of 2025.

One focal point within this area of Executive powers is immigration. Can a president restrict the entry of non-citizens from certain countries on a finding that their entry would be "detrimental to the interests of the United States" in accord with federal law? This question was answered in *Trump v. Hawaii*, 585 U.S. 667 (2018). In that case, President Trump restricted entry into the United States of citizens of seven other countries—Iran, Iraq, Libya, Somalia, Sudan, Syria, and Yemen. The Supreme Court found that the President acted within his power to enforce the law.

In recent times, the president has used his powers to detain persons in the country unlawfully, either by overstaying a visa or not having the appropriate authorization in the first place. The president's policies are being enforced by an administrative agency, the United States Immigration and Customs Enforcement.

While the President is in charge of the branch that prosecutes the federal criminal laws, the President also has the corollary power to issue pardons, which in a way can be seen as exceptions to carrying out the law. Presidential pardons are considered unreviewable by the other branches of government and thus need not be justified (except perhaps in the court of public opinion) or based on any particular standards. Pardons can occur for people facing or convicted of criminal charges and can halt an entire prosecution or simply involve a commutation of a sentence. For example, President Trump's pardons before leaving office included Joe Arpaio, convicted of Criminal Contempt, and Dinesh D'Souza, convicted of campaign contribution fraud. He also commuted the sentence of Rod Blagojevich, the former governor of Illinois. Other presidents have used their pardon power liberally.

II. The Powers to Appoint and Remove. The President has the powers to appoint and remove some government officials. The powers of appointment and removal are distinguishable and should be dealt with separately. The Constitution divides the appointment of government employees into two broad categories—Officers of the United States and inferior officers. Officers of the United States refers to the highest-ranking officials, although the term is not defined in the Constitution. These Officers have come to include ambassadors, federal judges, and the heads of departments, such as the Secretary of State. Inferior officers means all remaining officials, generally those persons holding lesser amounts of responsibility. The distinction between Officers of the United States and inferior officers matters. For the high-ranking Officers of the United States, often called principal officers, the President has the power to appoint only in conjunction with the "advice and consent" of the Senate. Supreme Court justices, such as Sonja Sotomayor, as well as other federal judges, are nominated by the President, but then go through confirmation hearings by the Senate Judiciary Committee and confirmation by the full Senate. As for "inferior" officers, the Appointments Clause gives Congress the power to vest their appointment in the Executive, the courts, or heads of departments. *See, e.g.*, *Morrison v. Olson*, 487 U.S. 654 (1988). Thus, inter-branch appointments are not unusual and are constitutional.

The Supreme Court has explored the nuances of the appointments doctrine in the past decade. In *Lucia v. Securities and Exchange Commission (SEC)*, 585 U.S. 237 (2018), for example, the Court analyzed whether administrative law judges (ALJs) of the SEC were Officers of the United States requiring the advice and consent of the Senate for their appointment. The Court used the "significant authority" test to decide which category in which the ALJs fell and found that the ALJs were almost "carbon-copies" of the special trial judges of the United States Tax Court who were found to be principal officers in a prior case, *Freytag v. Commissioner*, 501 U.S. 868 (1991).

In *United States v. Arthrex*, 594 U.S. 1 (2021), the Court considered whether judges on the Patent Trial and Appeal Board

(PTAB), established to review the validity of challenged patents, were ministerial and inferior officers or principal officers requiring the advice and consent of the Senate for their appointment. While appointed by the Secretary of Commerce, the appellate patent judges render a final decision for the Executive branch. The lack of accountability and Executive oversight of the patent judges which occurred by giving them the last word in the appeals process led the Court to find that the structure violated the Appointments Clause.

The theory of the unitary executive suggests that the president alone has the power over the Executive Branch, including the firing Executive Branch employees. In *Trump v. Wilcox*, 606 U.S. ___ (2025), the President wanted to fire a member of the National Labor Relations Board (NLRB) and a member of the Merit Systems Protection Board (MSPB). The Supreme Court observed that officials exercising executive powers may be removed without cause by the President, who is alone vested with the Executive Powers by Article II of the Constitution. In the case at hand, the Court remanded for a full determination of whether the two boards in question exercise considerable executive power and lie within the "without cause" category.

The Constitution provides virtually no guidance concerning the power to remove government officials, other than requiring impeachment for some, such as the President and federal judges. The impeachment requirement has led to some interesting and awkward situations, including a federal judge attempting to retain his job after a conviction for lying to a grand jury because he believed the conviction was unjust. Because the federal judge, Walter Nixon, could not simply be fired, he retained his job after his conviction, until, finally, the Senate voted unanimously to impeach him. *Nixon v. United States*, 506 U.S. 224 (1993).

It has been assumed that if the President has the power to appoint, there is also an associated power to discharge. That is not always true in a system characterized by its interdependence. Instead, the Supreme Court has tended toward a shared responsibility for firing between Congress and the President, particularly for officials who are "hybrid," in that they have some judicial responsibilities. These officials generally do not serve "at the pleasure of the President."

III. The President's Legislative Role. The President and members of the Executive branch generally have no law-making ability. That job is allocated to the legislature in Article I of the Constitution. Yet, there is one important potential exception. In *Youngstown Sheet and Tube Co. v. Sawyer*, 343 U.S. 579 (1952), commonly called "the Steel Seizure" case, the Supreme Court concluded that President Truman exceeded the powers of the President when he ordered steel workers to end their strike and report to work. Of particular note in the case was Justice Jackson's concurrence, illustrating that concurrences sometimes matter a lot. Jackson's concurrence has provided a lasting framework for evaluating the President's potential legislative role through the creation of three categories. The Jackson trilogy divided up the world of domestic President action into: (1) the strongest basis for domestic actions, when Congress approves the Executive activity; (2) the chewy middle, when Congress is silent about the conduct in question; and (3) the weakest basis for Presidential action, when Congress disapproves; and

In addition to the small possibility of direct law-making, the Constitution still gives the President a role to play in the legislative process. Pursuant to the "presentment clauses" of Article I, Section 7, Clauses 2 and 3, the President must approve or disapprove of a legislative bill before the bill becomes law. If the President approves, the bill becomes law. (Many a photo opportunity has arisen at the signing of legislation.) If the President refuses to approve the bill, this is known as a veto, and Congress can override the veto only on a two-thirds vote. The veto is a stand-alone power, in that it is not associated with any of the other powers, but it certainly reflects the Separation of Powers and the interdependence of the three branches when exercising power.

There are several forms of vetoes, some of which have been found unconstitutional. The line-item veto, for example, was one form used by presidents to disapprove of a single line item of an overall bill. This form, as applied in the Line Item Veto Act of 1996, was found to exceed the scope of the veto power—an all-or-nothing power, essentially—by the Supreme Court in *Clinton v. New York,* 524 U.S. 417 (1998). A legislative veto also was created to provide a check on the way the Executive carried out the law. This type of veto was held by one branch of Congress and was used to nullify some Executive action. It was found to be unconstitutional in *Immigration and Naturalization Service v. Chadha,* 462 U.S. 919 (1983). Another form of veto is the "pocket veto." Here, the President can indirectly veto legislation by failing to approve a bill submitted within 10 days of legislative adjournment. Instead, the President simply waits until the legislature has adjourned, leaving the bill in "the pocket."

In recent decades, presidents also have adopted a strategy that permits them to voice their opposition to or give their interpretation of a bill, short of a veto. The Executive's views are given in documents called signing statements. While this practice has become fairly common in recent years, these signing statements are not directly supported by the Constitution and are thus of questionable constitutional significance. *See* Phillip Cooper, *By Order of the President: the Use and Abuse of Direct Presidential Action* (University Press of Kansas 2002)(describing a variety of tools used by presidents to wield power, from executive orders to signing statements).

IV. Foreign Affairs Powers. The President, by virtue of the job title and responsibilities, is the leading representative of the United States in relations with foreign governments and entities. The job of diplomacy is firmly rooted in the Executive branch, extending beyond the President, as exemplified by the State Department and its titular head, the Secretary of State.

A significant foreign power involves treaties, which under Article II, Section 2, is granted to the President, subject to the power-sharing "Advice and Consent" of the Senate. A two-thirds Senate vote is required for approval, indicating the Framers were serious about having multi-branch participation in this area. One of the most famous early treaties, the so-called "Jay Treaty," suggests that the treaty process can be both collaborative and contentious at the same time. In 1795, the then Chief Justice, John Jay, was sent by President George Washington to help negotiate various issues with Great Britain. Despite objections, the resulting treaty was approved by the Senate. It laid the foundation for the significance of treaties in both the political and legal realms.

Treaties can have far-ranging legal impact. Treaties take precedence over existing federal law and can be binding domestic law if Congress has enacted implementing statutes or intended the domestic application to be self-executing. *See Medellin v. Texas*, 552 U.S. 491 (2008). For example, a self-executing treaty relating to migratory birds supersedes conflicting state law concerning those birds. *See Missouri v. Holland*, 252 U.S. 416 (1920) (involving a federal treaty with Great Britain that conflicted with claims by the State of Missouri to migratory birds.)

A special kind of foreign policy instrument is the Executive Agreement. This tool allows the President to enter into agreements with foreign nations without the express consent of the Senate. Executive agreements usually involve lesser issues, such as the protocols to be followed in a visit by a head of state, but can involve more significant matters, such as the release of hostages negotiated in 1980–1981 with Iran that led to the Supreme Court case, *Dames & Moore v. Regan*, 453 U.S. 654 (1981). The case concerned the constitutionality of executive agreements and orders associated with the release. President Jimmy Carter had frozen some Iranian assets in the United States after Iran took 53 Americans from the American Embassy in Iran hostage for 444 days, starting in 1979 through 1981.

The release of the hostages was predicated in part on releasing attachments to Iranian property and funds as well as ending some legal proceedings. The Supreme Court, in *Dames & Moore*, affirmed these actions as constitutional.

V. Commander-in-Chief Power. The President is the Commander-in-Chief of the armed forces. Art. II, Sec. 2. This power allows the President to defend Americans on American soil or abroad. Based in large part on this power, the President has become the face of the military and national security. While Congress shares national defense powers in several ways, it has become the President who takes the initiative in this area over the past half-century. In recent decades, the President has engaged the United States in military actions in various countries, including Korea, Vietnam, and Iraq. In reaction to presidential use of this power, the Congress enacted the War Powers Resolution of 1973, attempting to prescribe limits on the unilateral deployment of troops. To date, the Resolution has not been subject to thorough judicial scrutiny and as a result has been more ceremonial than anything else.

The President has created a Sixth Branch of the Armed Forces, the space force. This group was formed in 2018 to prevent satellite collisions, monitor debris in space and promote spaceflight safety.

The area where the Commander-in-Chief power has been the most controversial relates to its use in deterring and prosecuting terrorism. After the attacks on the United States on September 11, 2001, the Executive branch instituted a variety of responses, involving surveillance, interrogation and detention, both unilaterally and in conjunction with laws enacted by Congress. Shortly after the attacks Congress enacted The Authorization for Use of Military Force (AUMF), to provide "necessary and appropriate force against those nations, organizations or persons" that planned, authorized or harbored persons who committed the attacks. As a result of the AUMF, the President issued an executive order directing the detention of any persons who were part of terrorist organizations or aided those organizations. Persons detained under this order were often sent to the American naval base in Guantanamo Bay, Cuba, and were held indefinitely without charges. This process brought several high-profile lawsuits testing the scope of the President's and Congress' powers.

The case of *Hamdi v. Rumsfeld*, 542 U.S. 507 (2004), for example, involved a United States citizen, Yaser Esam Hamdi, who was captured in Afghanistan. He was imprisoned as an "enemy combatant," a fighter not aligned with any particular nation. (The "enemy combatant" description has been dropped by the Administration of President Obama, although many people still use the term.) The Supreme Court was faced with the question of whether these detainees, generally held at the American naval base in Guantanamo Bay, had any due process rights. Justice O'Connor, writing for a plurality of the Court, held that such prisoners had the right to challenge their status as enemy combatants, including advancing Habeas Corpus claims, under the auspices of Due Process of law. Justice O'Connor included the admonition, "a state of war is not a blank check for the President when it comes to the rights of the Nation's citizens." *Hamdan v. Rumsfeld,* 548 U.S. 557 (2006), presented a different but equally significant issue. Hamdan involved a non-citizen, Osama Bin Laden's alleged former driver. The issue before the Supreme Court was whether trying enemy combatants by special Military Tribunal was permissible. The Court held that the trials, as conceived, violated both the Uniform Code of Military Justice and the Geneva Conventions.

In the face of creating bad precedent, one government strategy has been to release the prisoner or formally charge him, rather than maintaining the detainee as an enemy combatant. In *Padilla v. Hanft,* 547 U.S. 1062 (2006), for example, Jose Padilla allegedly intended to detonate a "dirty" bomb—an explosive device containing nuclear material—on United States soil. He was detained in Chicago and imprisoned. Padilla sought to be charged or released and filed a habeas corpus petition. He was eventually charged with a variety of crimes and the constitutional issues he presented were mooted.

In a more recent case in 2009, detainee Ali al-Marri's lawsuit was mooted when he was charged with crimes under federal law. Mr. al-Marri was the last remaining "enemy combatant" detainee at the time on American soil, located in the Charleston Naval Base Brig.

These cases illustrate the on-going evolution of critical questions, such as what constitutes war, who is a soldier, and what remedies can be taken to detain people involved in or suspected of being involved in terrorist activities against the United States, particularly whether indefinite Executive detention is legal. In this new era, the one rule that has emerged is that the old definitions do not fit.

VI. Protection from Other Branches. The Constitution gives the Executive branch two primary protections from the other branches: immunity from suit; and privilege from disclosure. Immunity from suit is a partial "castle wall" against lawsuits, promoting the separation of powers and the ability to act freely in executing the law. This partial immunity still permits the Executive and those in the Executive Branch to be sued under certain circumstances, however. The Executive branch's amenability to suit was affirmed early in our history in the famous case of *Marbury v. Madison,* 5 U.S. 137 (1803), where the Court permitted a claimant, William Marbury, to sue the Secretary of State, James Madison, for failing to deliver a judicial commission. While immunity from suit centers around official acts while the Executive is in office, the Supreme Court has refused to broadly extend the immunity to conduct taking place prior to serving as Chief Executive. In *Clinton v. Jones*, 520 U.S. 681 (1997), the Supreme Court allowed a civil suit against President Clinton to proceed after balancing the interests at hand. The suit was based on alleged acts occurring prior to the time Mr. Clinton became President.

In 2024, the Supreme Court examined the scope of a president's immunity from criminal prosecution in *Trump v. United States*, 604 U.S. ___ (2024). The case involved the indictment of a former president for acts taken by the president during his presidency, specifically acts leading up to January 6, 2021. The indictment alleged a conspiracy to overturn the 2020 election through knowingly false claims of election fraud. The Court held that the separation of powers doctrine requires a former president to have absolute immunity for official acts relating to the exercise of core constitutional powers. Regarding the exercise of official acts not within core constitutional powers, the court found that there is a presumptive presidential immunity. Unofficial acts of a president are different; there could be a prosecution of a president for unofficial acts during a presidency.

The dissenting justices, including Justices Sotomayor, Kagan, and Jackson, argued that the decision creates a profound change in the institution of the presidency. They claimed the decision makes a mockery of the principle that no person is above the law. Also, they argued the Court did not clearly define what was an official as compared to an unofficial act.

A related protection is Executive privilege, which is different from immunity in that it involves the non-disclosure of information. In *United States v. Nixon*, 418 U.S. 683 (1974), involving President Richard Nixon and the secret tapes he made in the Oval Office concerning the infamous Watergate burglary, the Supreme Court held there was an implied constitutional Executive privilege from disclosure, but that the privilege would be determined by balancing the competing interests involved. The President's initial refusal to turn over secret oval office tapes based on Executive privilege was rebuffed by the trial judge, Judge Sirica, and the Supreme Court. These events eventually led to the resignation of the President.

In another illustration, *Cheney v. United States District Court*, 542 U.S. 367 (2004), the Supreme Court reaffirmed a partial Executive privilege. This case involved a civil suit against then Vice

President Cheney, seeking the disclosure of information about several meetings the Vice President had which included members of private industry. The Supreme Court remanded, permitting the lower court to rule on the discovery requests after balancing the interests involved.

VII. Limits on Power-Impeachment. The removal of a President, Vice President and "civil officers of the United States" can occur through the impeachment process included in Article I, Sections 2 and 3, of the Constitution. This extreme measure requires the participation of both houses of Congress—the House of Representatives votes to impeach and the Senate tries the impeachment—and provides an example of intrabranch checks and balances. Presidents Andrew Johnson and Bill Clinton were both impeached by the House of Representatives and then acquitted in the Senate. President Donald Trump was impeached by the House twice and then acquitted by the Senate twice. The second impeachment occurred after President Trump was defeated by Joseph Biden and was based on the claim that the President incited the January 6, 2020, Capitol riot.

CHECKLIST

A. **Challenge to Executive Action**—Is the challenged governmental action attributable to the President or the Executive branch? Look for actors in agencies that appear to have enforcement powers, distinguishing pure and hybrid actors—those solely with enforcement powers versus those with powers overlapping other branches.

B. **Faithfully Executing the Law.**

1. **Carrying out the Law**—Is the Executive carrying out (executing) or making the law? The Executive can fill in the outlines of government action under the "delegation doctrine," so long as Congress enacts laws with an "intelligible" principle.

2. **Pardons**—Is there a pardon or clemency granted by the President? If yes, the actual pardon or clemency is a nonjusticiable political question, beyond the review of the courts.

C. **Powers to Appoint and Remove.**

1. **Appointment**—Is the officer to be appointed a high-ranking "officer of the United States," such as a federal judge? If yes, then the President nominates the officer with the advice and consent of the Senate. If no, then the Executive receives direction from Congress about its role in the hiring process.

2. **Removal**—What is the nature of the job responsibilities of the person to be removed? The President's powers are greater with respect to those officials whose jobs are solely executive in nature and not hybrid, containing some judicial function as well.

D. **Legislative Role.**

1. **Presentment Clause**—Has the bill ratified by both houses of Congress been properly presented to the President for approval?

2. **Veto**—Has the President approved or disapproved of a bill presented to him or taken no action within 10 days of receipt?

E. **Foreign Affairs.**

1. **Chief Diplomat**—Is the Executive acting as a representative of the United States in relations with foreign countries or governments?

2. **Treaties**—Has the President entered into an agreement with a foreign country or government with the advice and consent of the Senate after a two-thirds vote? Is the law self-executing domestically or has the Congress enacted enabling legislation?

3. **Executive Agreements**—Has the President entered into an agreement with a foreign country or government with the implied authorization of Congress?

F. **Commander-in-Chief**—Is the President detaining a person for actual or suspected terrorist activities? If so, what due process rights has the person been accorded? *See Hamdan v. Rumsfeld*, 548 U.S. 557 (2006). Is the Executive engaged in secret surveillance of individuals? If so, is the surveillance supported by Congressional enactment or justified by the Executive's own power?

G. Protection from Other Branches.

1. **Separation of Powers**—Is one of the other branches encroaching on the Executive's job responsibilities?

2. **Immunity from Suit**—Does the President have immunity from suit? Acts occurring prior to the President taking office generally do not get immunity.

3. **Executive Privilege**—Can the Executive branch claim this implied constitutional privilege? Balance the competing interests involved, particularly examining whether the context is a civil or criminal case.

H. Limits-Impeachment

Limits-Impeachment—Has the President committed an impeachable offense included in "high crimes and misdemeanors?" These offenses are not spelled out by the Constitution, but apparently include perjury and other serious criminal offenses. *See Nixon v. United States*, 506 U.S. 224 (1993).

■ PROBLEMS ■

Problem #1: A computer hacker opposed to the success of social networking sites on the World Wide Web jams several of the major sites, including Facebook, Instagram, and X, until they are so overloaded, the sites crash. Congress, in recess at the time of the overload, has not created legislation for monitoring and preventing such crashes. Congress had been considering a bill just before the recess that would have given the President a variety of powers to prevent interruption of the World Wide Web through the creation of a new Computer Security Department, authorizing immediate action if the Web had been interrupted. The bill had grown to more than 1,000 pages and Congress was simply trying to stop unrelated additions and get it ready for passage. Through an executive order, the President does not wait for Congress to return to consider the passage of the law, but instead creates a new department, the Department of Internet Security, with the power to confiscate domestic computers involved in or suspected to be involved in debilitating transmissions. Are the President's actions constitutional?

Answer: The President's powers generally do not support actions that equate to domestic legislation. Evaluating the constitutionality of the President's domestic action is not entirely transparent, however, and depends on Justice Jackson's concurrence in the Steel Seizure Case, *Youngstown Sheet and Tube Co. v. Sawyer*, 343 U.S. 579 (1952). That concurrence set up the trilogy of categories into which a President's actions are considered to fall. The category determines the strength of the President's action, with Congressional approval serving as the strongest basis for a President's domestic conduct, Congressional disapproval the weakest, and Congressional silence somewhere in the middle. Here, there are several facts that are relevant to the analysis. With Congress in recess, the President can argue the legislature is not available to do its job of legislating. Further, there is evidence of how Congress wants this question decided. Unlike the Steel Seizure case, there has been no disapproval of Presidential action through the rejection of Presidential participation. To the contrary, Congress was at the time considering a bill that would give the President the power to act in such a situation. Thus, the President can readily argue here that his conduct falls at least in the middle category, the "twilight zone," where Congress has been silent, trending toward the category of Congressional approval. In light of this classification and the two weeks required before Congressional action, the President's actions are probably constitutional.

Problem #2: The President recognizes there is a shortage of certain types of medical equipment in the United States that will merely grow over the years if not dealt with immediately. As a result, the President, in conjunction with a two-thirds approving vote of the Senate, enters into a treaty with China. The treaty included a purchase of a wide variety of health care equipment for government hospitals for the reasonable sum of $50 million dollars. This money was to be paid by the government in four installments as the equipment was delivered. If the House of Representatives objects, arguing that it also must approve any appropriations of federal money, what should be the result?

Answer: This problem illustrates what happens when two different constitutional powers conflict. The President has treaty power, with the advice and consent of the Senate. A lawful treaty does not need House of Representatives participation in any fashion. The appropriation of funds, however, does need House of Representative approval under Article I of the Constitution. Thus, the President cannot use one power to circumvent another. While the treaty is beneficial for the country, a cost-benefit analysis does not overcome the Separation of Powers dividers erected in the Constitution.

Problem #3: Congress enacts the "Legitimate Medical Practice" Act, 21 U.S.C. §§ 801, et seq., a law that dictates the general scope of permissible medical practices in a variety of contexts, including insurance reimbursement, research and "alternative" forms of treatment practices. The State of Vermont enacts a subsequent law prohibiting "all futile treatment," including resuscitation of terminally ill patients in the final states of death under certain circumstances. An exception is if the patient requests resuscitation. The Attorney General of the United States interprets the federal law, the Legitimate Medical Practice Act, to prohibit "do not resuscitate" orders unless the patient specifically requests it, reversing the Vermont law. The Attorney General then threatened to prosecute any Vermont doctor or hospital that followed the Vermont law. A physician who works in the Emergency room of a big Vermont hospital files suit for a declaratory judgment of her rights. How should the court rule?

Answer: The initial question is whether the Executive has the power to interpret lawful legislation. Here, the law is likely firmly grounded on Congress' Commerce Clause power, among other powers. The real issue is whether the Executive's interpretation of the law is permissible. When the text of the law does not expressly indicate its parameters, some interpretation may be required. That interpretation must be consistent with the intent of Congress. Here, there is no indication that Congress intended to reach the Vermont law and no indication that if it was reached, it would legislate consistent with the Attorney General's position. Given that, this appears to be Executive legislation, a violation of the doctrine of Separation of Powers. *See Gonzales v. Oregon*, 546 U.S. 243 (2006) (a 6–3 decision by Justice Kennedy).

Problem #4: Asan Mandi was captured in Afghanistan, designated an "enemy combatant" and detained indefinitely without charges at the American naval base in Guantanamo Bay, Cuba. In the preceding years, Congress had enacted the Military Commissions Act (MCA) and the Detainee Treatment Act (DTA). The combined effect of the two Acts suspended the privilege to assert the writ of Habeas Corpus, a writ that asks a court to literally "release the body." While the writ of Habeas Corpus is protected by the Constitution, its withdrawal is allowed under certain circumstances through the Suspension Clause of Article I, Section 9, Clause 2. Mandi wishes to challenge his status as an "enemy combatant" through the writ of habeas corpus. Can non-citizen prisoners on foreign soil claim the privilege?

Answer: The Constitution states, "The Privilege of the Writ of Habeas Corpus shall not be suspended, unless when in Cases of Rebellion or Invasion the public Safety may require it." Art. I, Section 9, Cl. 2. This provision recognizes the importance of the writ and creates a significant and lasting barrier to its revocation for all but extreme circumstances. For example, President Lincoln suspended the writ in 1861. Which detained persons are entitled to assert the writ is a more difficult issue. The clause does not expressly bar habeas corpus claims by non-citizens or those persons located on foreign soil. While a strict territorial test for which detainees can assert the writ is more predictable than a balancing approach, such a test does not account for American control over foreign soil, as exemplified by the American control over Guantanamo Bay for more than 100 years. The Supreme Court, in *Boumediene v. Bush*, 553 U.S. 723 (2008), found that three factors are relevant in determining whether the Suspension Clause applies: "(1) the citizenship and status of the detainee... (2) the nature of the sites where apprehension and then detention took place; and (3) the practical obstacles." In applying these factors, the extraterritoriality of Guantanamo Bay does not outweigh the intervention of judicial process here through habeas corpus, particularly when Mandi claims his designation is incorrect and he is located in a place Americans appear to have indefinite and long-lasting control. *See Boumediene* for an elaboration on this analysis.

POINTS TO REMEMBER

- If the Executive Branch is acting, the powers are generally greater in foreign, rather than purely domestic, arenas.
- The Executive executes the law domestically, unless exercising powers to pardon or veto, which are effectively law-stoppers.
- The President's power to enter treaties and executive agreements depends on express or implied Congressional approval.
- The President's power to protect Americans at home and abroad as Commander-in-Chief is one of the President's broadest powers and is asserted in many national security issues, particularly with terrorism. This power is limited, however, by Due Process of law.
- Presidential protections from the Judicial and Legislative branches, primarily meaning immunity from suit and privilege from disclosure, are generally only partial and often may be overcome by a balancing of interests.

CHAPTER 4

State Power to Regulate Commerce

While Congress clearly has the power to regulate commerce under the Commerce Clause, which is found in Article I, Section 8, Clause 3, of the Constitution, whether states could do so was not as clear. Further, numerous issues have arisen about the circumstances in which states could exercise such a power if one was granted by the Constitution. These issues follow a long and winding road of case law, with more than a century of lineage filled with contortions and contradictions, often dependent on the social and economic times. State regulation of commerce remains an important and action-filled constitutional area to this day, with an entirely new front created by the expansion of technology, the internet in particular, and new forms of trade.

In the twentieth century, the U.S. Supreme Court retooled its commerce regulation framework. During the first third of the twentieth century, the Court construed the Tenth Amendment to give states the power to regulate "purely local" commerce. During this time, most commerce cases involved claims that the federal government was violating the states' reserved power.

The constitutional shift of 1937, following the New Deal and the so-called "Court-Packing Plan," affected commerce as well. Following that shift, the distinction between "purely internal" intrastate commerce and commerce "among" the states was no longer adhered to vigorously by the Court. As a result, the power of the federal government to regulate commerce grew and the Tenth Amendment, the early protector of state regulation, was relegated to the status of a truism. While the battle still persists between the scope of federal and state power, the federal power retains the strong upper hand and usually wins any conflict, express or implied.

State power to regulate commerce is often denoted as the "Dormant" Commerce Clause or "Negative Implications" of the Commerce Clause to reflect the implied nature of the state power. It also identifies the source of many of the issues. For many, however, the appellations "dormant" and "negative" are the opposite of the intricate and interesting questions presented about the scope of state power and its interface with one of Congress' strongest powers.

The Early Years. The Constitution provides little guidance about the regulation of commerce other than to explicitly give Congress the power to regulate commerce in Article I, Section 8. It is silent on the states' powers to regulate commerce.

The closest the Commerce Clause comes to discussing state regulation is its description of the scope of Congress' power to regulate commerce "among the several states." The issue of state power was consequently left to the courts. Several early cases asked whether the federal government's authority over commerce was exclusive or whether the states had concurrent authority. *Gibbons v. Ogden*, 22 U.S. (9 Wheat) 1 (1824), one of the early decisions, was another seminal decision by Chief Justice John Marshall. In *Gibbons*, the Court adopted an expansive view of federal power, limiting state power in the process. There, a New York statute had given Messrs. Livingston and Fulton the "exclusive" right to navigate steamboats in certain state waters, but they had assigned the route between New York and New Jersey to Ogden. Gibbons, acting pursuant to a federal license, wished to operate ships along the same New York and New Jersey route. In resolving the conflict between the federal license and the state license, the U.S. Supreme Court ruled in favor of Gibbons and his federal license on Supremacy Clause grounds, thus starting a long string of victories for the federal government when a conflict between federal and state powers arose. However, *Gibbons* did not resolve the question of whether states still retained the power to regulate navigation if no conflict existed. In *dicta*, the Court foreshadowed the possibility of concurrent commerce regulation by both federal and state sovereigns, using the taxing power as an example of a power which, "in its own nature, is capable of residing in, and being exercised by, different authorities at the same time."

The Court did establish a limit on federal power in the form of inspection laws, and of items "before commerce," as well as other similar regulations in a category of completely internal commerce that were for the state alone to regulate. The Court explained that this category was exclusively for the states because such regulations "act upon the subject before it becomes an article of foreign commerce, or of commerce among the States, and prepare it for that purpose" and "can be most advantageously exercised by the States themselves." Despite the creation of this protected state zone of regulation, if federal regulatory power was proper in an area, then the Court seemed inclined to grant "full power over the thing to be regulated,"—although it did not decide that question in a definitive manner.

An Initial Framework of Analysis: "National Versus Local." Subsequent Courts modified the *Gibbons* approach. A framework of "national versus local" activities was created by the Court to help determine whether the states can regulate commerce as an initial matter. Two main categories were created. If the subject of the regulation was considered to be a national issue, then it was left for Congress to regulate exclusively, unless Congress consented to state regulation. In *Leisy v. Hardin*, 135 U.S. 100 (1890), for example, the Court agreed that congressional consent to regulation in the national arena is important: "as the grant of the power to regulate commerce among the states, so far as one system is required, is exclusive, the states cannot exercise that power without the assent of Congress."

If the regulation involved a local issue, then states were permitted to regulate subject to several prohibitions. The framework was established out in the famous case of *Cooley v. Board of Wardens*, 53 U.S. 299 (1851). In *Cooley,* a Pennsylvania law required ships to use local pilots when navigating in the Delaware River. Plaintiff did not want to use a local pilot and claimed the law was unconstitutional because it impeded Congress' power to regulate commerce. Also in the mix was a 1789 federal law that appeared to give the states authority to enact local pilot laws. In resolving the dispute, the Court delineated two main categories of regulatory power, reasoning that commerce is a "vast field" such that some subjects required a "single uniform rule, operating equally on the commerce of the United States in every port;" but that other subjects required diversity to "meet the local necessities of navigation." In determining which activities went into which category, the Court focused on whether the subject is by its "nature national, and therefore requires 'exclusive legislation by Congress,' or local, allowing for states to regulate sometimes as well."

The Court in *Cooley* applied this framework to uphold the state pilot law, reasoning that the issue "is local and not national; to be the best provided for, not by one system, or plan of regulations, but by as many as the legislative discretion of the several states should deem applicable to the local peculiarities of the ports within their limits." Although the Court found that Congress had legislated on the subject, "its legislation manifests an intention, with a single exception, not to regulate this subject, but to leave its regulation to the several states."

Neither *Cooley* nor subsequent cases provided definitive definitions for "national" and "local." The Court left these issues for future definition. Further, later courts had to determine whether Congress had authorized states to regulate in "national" arenas. In

Prudential Ins. Co. v. Benjamin, 328 U.S. 408 (1946), for example, the Court upheld a South Carolina tax imposed on foreign insurance companies as a condition of doing business in the state. The Court concluded that a federal law authorized the tax because Congress "expressly and affirmatively" declared that "continued state regulation and taxation of this business is in the public interest and that the business and all who engage in it 'shall be subject to' the laws of the several states in these respects."

Preemption by Congress. While federal law operates exclusively in national matters as a general rule, otherwise valid "local" state regulations that conflict with a valid federal law also are unconstitutional. The determination is often readily observable if the conflict is express. More nuanced and complex questions arise with preemption, especially when there is no explicit conflict between federal or state laws and the federal laws do not explicitly preempt state law.

If the federal government has regulated in a subject area within the scope of its authority, and a state law conflicts, as in *Gibbons*, the state law is invalid under the Supremacy Clause. Congress' broad Commerce Clause powers combined with the Supremacy Clause are virtually an unbeatable combination, particularly for conflicting state regulations. Preemption can be either express or implied. In some instances, Congress provides its express desire to "preempt" a field and preclude state regulation. In other instances, the Court implies preemption when Congress enacts a "scheme of federal regulation so pervasive as to create a reasonable the inference that Congress left no room to supplement it." Preemption also might occur "because the Act of Congress may touch a field in which the federal interest is so dominant that the federal system will be assumed to preclude enforcement of state laws on the same subject." *Fidelity Federal Savings & Loan Ass'n v. de la Cuesta*, 458 U.S. 141 (1982). Preemption further can occur because "compliance with both federal and state regulations is a physical impossibility," or where state law "stands as an obstacle to the accomplishment and execution of the full purposes and objectives of Congress." While these examples illustrate several of the judicial roads leading to a finding that the federal law impliedly preempts state law in the area, it is important to point out that just because the federal government is regulating in an area does not mean it intends to preempt state law as well. For example, in *Pacific Gas and Electric Co. v. State Energy Resources Conservation and Development Commission*, 461 U.S. 190 (1983), the Court rejected a preemption claim despite the fact that the federal government had regulated in the same area as the State of California. Specifically, Congress regulated some aspects of nuclear energy under the Atomic Energy Act of 1954 (AEA), while California enacted a statute that conditioned the right to build nuclear power plants on evidence that the project included adequate means for storage and disposal of nuclear waste. California's "spent fuel" law did not directly conflict with the federal law and was upheld by the Court. There was no preemption because there was no "clear and manifest purpose of Congress" to supersede any state laws. Instead, Congress "preserved the dual regulation of nuclear-powered electricity generation: the federal government maintains complete control of the safety and 'nuclear' aspects of energy generation; the states exercise their traditional authority over the need for additional generating capacity, the type of generating facilities to be licensed, land use, ratemaking, and the like." In essence, Congress did not intend to occupy the entire field.

Federal Opt-Out Schemes and Preemption. In some instances, Congress provides states with an opportunity for dual legislation that creates partial preemption. A prime illustration of this duality is *Gade v. National Solid Wastes Management Association,* 505 U.S. 88 (1992), where Congress created a comprehensive regulatory scheme, but gave the states the ability to "opt out" by creating their own consistent regulatory schemes. *Gade* involved Illinois' Hazardous Waste Crane and Hoisting Equipment Operators Licensing Act and Hazardous Waste Laborers Licensing Act. The two state acts were designed "to promote job safety" and "protect life, limb and property." The Court held that both acts were preempted by the federal Occupational Safety and Health Act of 1970 (OSHA), and the regulations promulgated under that act by the Occupational Safety and Health Administration (OSHA). Although Congress authorized the Secretary of Labor to set mandatory occupational safety and health standards applicable to all businesses affecting interstate commerce, Congress also reserved certain areas to state regulation (*e.g.*, state workers' compensation laws), and gave the States the option of opting out of the federal regulation entirely. However, Illinois chose not to exercise this option. The Court concluded that "nonapproved state regulation of occupational safety and health issues for which a federal standard is in effect is impliedly preempted by the federal statute." The law allowed a state to create its own plan, but only if the plan was approved by the federal government: "The unavoidable implication of this provision is that a State may not enforce its own occupational safety and health standards without obtaining the Secretary's approval." The Court also implied preemption from the fact that the Secretary was given the power to withdraw her approval of a state plan, finding that "Congress sought to promote occupational safety and health while at the same time avoiding duplicative, and possibly counterproductive, regulation."

The cases lead to an important conclusion: when Congress creates an opt-out scheme for the states, the Court is more likely to find preemption for states that fail to exercise their right to "opt out."

While a detailed federal law often connotes an intent to occupy the field, that is not always the case. For example, in *Askew v. American Waterways Operators, Inc.*, 411 U.S. 325 (1973), the Court upheld Florida's Oil Spill Prevention and Pollution Control Act (Act) that imposed strict liability for any damage incurred by the State or private persons as a result of an oil spill in the State's territorial waters, despite a federal law on the same subject. Congress enacted the Water Quality Improvement Act of 1970 just prior to the Florida law. The federal law subjected ship owners and terminal facilities to liability without fault up to $14,000,000 and $8,000,000, respectively, for cleanup costs incurred by the Federal Government as a result of oil spills. It also authorized the President to promulgate regulations requiring ships and terminal facilities to maintain equipment for the prevention of oil spills. Although the federal law imposed a "pervasive system of federal control over discharges of oil", (the Court refused to find preemption) noting that, "there was 'no conflict' between the Florida statute when it comes to damages to property interests, for the Federal Act reaches only costs of cleaning up." Moreover, "while the Federal Act determines damages measured by the cost to the United States for cleaning up oil spills, the damages specified in the Florida Act relate in part to the cost to the State of Florida in cleaning up the spillage." As a result, the Court regarded the acts as "harmonious parts of an integrated whole. While the Federal Act was concerned only with actual cleanup costs incurred by the Federal Government, the State of Florida was concerned with its own cleanup costs." Hence there need be no collision between the Federal Act and the Florida Act because, as noted, the Federal Act presupposes a coordinated effort with the States, and any federal limitation of liability runs to "vessels," not to shore "facilities." Moreover, since Congress dealt only with "cleanup" costs, it left the States free to impose "liability" in damages for losses suffered both by the States and by private interests.

State Regulations that Discriminate Against Interstate Commerce. When a state uses its regulatory power in a "local," area of regulation, and the federal government has no conflicting law or has not preempted regulation in the area, the state's enactment still might be unconstitutional if it discriminates against interstate commerce on its face or in its objectives. Discrimination on its face is generally explicit and discrimination in its objectives is generally implicit, despite facially neutral language.

The underlying purpose of prohibiting states from discriminating against interstate commerce was historical. Trade wars during the time of the Articles of Confederation helped lead to the passage of the Constitution and to Congress being accorded the power to regulate commerce by the Framers. The distrust of states to regulate fairly and evenly with other states continued the keen judicial oversight in the area. Consequently, statutes that discriminate against interstate commerce are considered to be presumptively unconstitutional and the statutes survive only if there are no less restrictive methods of achieving the statute's objectives.

To determine which statutes offend these proscriptions, the courts generally look at the language of the state statutes first. If the language or "text" of the statute is unclear or otherwise ambiguous, the courts seek the legislative intent. If the intent was unavailable, policy might on occasion enter into the analysis.

Discrimination on the Face of the Law. Laws that expressly favor a regulating state (or likewise disfavor non-regulating states) provide the clearest type of discrimination and seldom survive close judicial scrutiny. *Baldwin v. G.A.F. Seelig, Inc.,* 294 U.S. 511 (1935), for example, involved a New York law that set minimum prices for milk. There, a dealer who purchased its product for less than the minimum price from out-of-state producers was denied a license to do business in New York. The Court struck down the law as beyond the power of the State of New York, asserting that New York did not have the power to regulate the price of milk in nearby states or to prohibit the introduction of "milk of wholesome quality" acquired in other states at lower prices. The Court likened the New York law to the imposition of a customs duty which the Constitution prohibits: "If New York, in order to promote the economic welfare of her farmers, may guard them against competition with the cheaper prices of Vermont, the door has been opened to rivalries and reprisals that were meant to be averted by subjecting commerce between the states to the power of the nation."

The Court affirmed a constitutional vision of "national solidarity," effectively advancing the idea that "the peoples of the several states must sink or swim together, and that in the long run prosperity and salvation are in union and not division." This solidarity idea prohibits states from regulating so as to give economic advantages over to their businesses or citizens, thereby placing themselves "in a position of economic isolation" by imposing minimum prices which establish "an economic barrier against competition with the products of another state or the labor of its residents." Along these lines, the Court has struck down differential licensing requirements as discriminating against out-of-state interests. In *Crutcher v. Kentucky*, 141 U.S. 47 (1891), for example, the Court invalidated a Kentucky law that required agents of express companies not incorporated in Kentucky to obtain a license before conducting business in the state. Before obtaining a license, the company had to prove it had a minimum amount of capitalization. The Court concluded that this statutory scheme violated the Constitution by effectively abandoning the non-discrimination rule, which was a right of the people, not a privilege handed down from the states.

Proving Discrimination. The Court wrestled with the question of when a law ought to be considered discriminatory, particularly when the law does not appear to discriminate on its face. The Court confronted this issue in *Hughes v. Oklahoma*, 441 U.S. 322 (1979). There, an Oklahoma law made it illegal to "transport or ship minnows for sale outside the state which were seized or procured within the waters of this state." The Court first held that the party challenging the statute has the burden of showing discrimination. If the party meets that burden, the burden then shifts to the state to demonstrate "the unavailability of nondiscriminatory alternatives adequate to preserve the local interests at stake." The Court again did not accept the natural resource protection argument, because, "far from choosing the least discriminatory alternative, Oklahoma has chosen to 'conserve' its minnows in the way that most overtly discriminates against interstate commerce." Thus, discrimination trumped claims of conservation of state resources.

Exxon Corporation v. Maryland, 437 U.S. 117 (1978), illustrates the difficulty for courts in assessing whether there is actionable discrimination. There, the Court upheld a Maryland statute that prohibited producers or refiners of petroleum products from operating a retail service station within the State. Maryland enacted the law as a result of evidence that gasoline stations operated by producers or refiners received preferential treatment during a prior gasoline shortage. The Court concluded that the law did not favor local producers and refiners since Maryland's entire gasoline supply flowed in interstate commerce, and there were no Maryland producers and refiners. In addition, competition was preserved because there were several major interstate marketers of petroleum that own and operate their own retail gasoline stations (and which were not precluded from operating retail stations in the state since they did not refine or produce gasoline), and these interstate dealers competed directly with Maryland's independent dealers: "The fact that the burden of a state regulation falls on some interstate companies [*e.g.*, refiners] does not, by itself, establish a claim of discrimination against interstate commerce."

Analyzing Facially Neutral Statutes for Discrimination. One of the most difficult issues for courts lies in analyzing facially neutral statutes to determine if there is implicit discrimination in the statutes' purposes or effects. States are usually good at declaring a virtuous objective for the statutes they pass, thereby hiding their true intentions. For example, when the State of New York imposed minimum milk prices in *Baldwin*, it proclaimed that the "end to be served is the maintenance of a regular and adequate supply of pure and wholesome milk; the supply being put in jeopardy when the farmers of the state are unable to earn a living income." The Court pierced through the state's analysis and concluded that the state's real objective was economic isolation.

Permissible State Discrimination: Quarantine Laws. One area where the states have been allowed to discriminate against interstate commerce is in imposing quarantine laws designed to prohibit the importation of such things as diseased livestock. In those cases, the Court has characterized quarantine laws as police measures designed to protect the public's health and safety. Such laws, however, must be narrowly drawn and not be a protectionist law in disguise. The Court has used the same analysis in reviewing state efforts to ban harmful "products." *City of Philadelphia v. New Jersey*, 437 U.S. 617 (1978), is illustrative. There, the Court struck down a New Jersey law that prohibited the importation into New Jersey of most "solid or liquid waste that originated or was collected outside the territorial limits of the State." The Court concluded that even the movement of waste is protected under the Commerce Clause, and the Court found that New Jersey was discriminating against it. The Court observed that the "evil of protectionism can reside in legislative means as well as legislative ends" and held that "discrimination against articles of commerce coming from outside the State is prohibited unless there is some reason, apart from their origin, to treat them differently." The Court distinguished New Jersey's blanket prohibition from legitimate quarantine laws, noting that those other laws "banned the importation of articles such as diseased livestock that required destruction as soon as possible because their very movement risked contagion and other evils." The Court's ruling did not strip New Jersey from all self-help methods, however. New Jersey and other states still could impose reasonable neutral regulations on garbage transportation and landfill drop-offs within the State.

Permissible State Discrimination: Surviving Strict Scrutiny. In a small number of cases, a state's interests will be sufficiently important to justify some discrimination against interstate commerce. These cases survive a very close analysis of the state's claims, often denoted as strict scrutiny. Perhaps the most widely used illustration of a case that survived judicial Everest is *Maine v. Taylor*, 477 U.S. 131 (1986). There, the Court upheld a Maine statute banning the importation of live baitfish into the state. The Court rejected the constitutional challenge to the statute despite its blatant discrimination against interstate commerce. The Court held that the statute satisfied the test used to determine if a discriminatory statute was still allowed, strict scrutiny. It found that the state's asserted purpose, the protection of Maine's "unique and ecologically fragile" fisheries, could not be protected by a less burdensome method. The Court concluded that less-restrictive inspection methods, such as testing imported baitfish for parasites, would not reliably produce disease free shipments.

Generally Impermissible State Justifications for Discrimination: Natural Resource Protection; Health and Safety.

Natural Resource Protection. States often want to protect their own natural resources from other states and try to do so by enacting laws that insulate their resources from other states and their citizens. The Court has generally disapproved of this practice, finding that it violated the non-discrimination rule. In *Pennsylvania v. West Virginia*, 262 U.S. 553 (1923), the Court struck down a West Virginia law that prohibited the interstate shipment of natural gas produced in the state unless and until the state's internal needs had been met. The law was passed after a cold winter in which gas supplies were inadequate. The Court struck down the law anyway. The Court noted in justifying its decision, "we are a single nation—one and the same people." Since the Court regarded natural gas as an article of commerce, and its transmission from one state to another for sale and consumption as interstate commerce, the Court held that a state law "which by its necessary operation prevents, obstructs or burdens such transmission is a regulation of interstate commerce—a prohibited interference." Indeed, the Court noted that, if "the states have such power a singular situation might result. Pennsylvania might keep its coal, the Northwest its timber, the mining states their minerals. And why may not the products of the field be brought within the principle?" This "slippery slope" argument is prevalent in court cases involving discrimination against interstate commerce.

Health and Safety. In most cases when states claim their discrimination is justified because of a local health or safety interest, the Court disagrees. For example, in *Dean Milk Co. v. City of Madison*, 340 U.S. 349 (1951), a Madison, Wisconsin ordinance prohibited the sale of milk processed and bottled at an unapproved pasteurization plant outside of a five-mile radius from the city. The ordinance also prohibited the sale of milk in Madison without an inspection permit, which could be granted a maximum of twenty-five miles from the city center. An Illinois milk distributor, who obtained milk from farms in Illinois and Wisconsin outside of the twenty five mile limit from Madison, successfully challenged the regulations. In holding for the distributor, whose plants were licensed in Chicago and whose milk qualified as "Grade A" under a Chicago ordinance modeled after the federal standards, the Court found that "reasonable nondiscriminatory alternatives, adequate to conserve legitimate local interests" were available. The Court noted that if Madison wanted to rely upon its own officials to inspect distant milk sources, it could do so by charging the actual and reasonable cost of such inspection to the out-of-state producers and processors. However, Madison could not simply prohibit out-of-state milk without "placing a discriminatory burden on interstate commerce" and inviting "a multiplication of preferential trade areas destructive of the very purpose of the Commerce Clause." The Court again decried any movement toward "economic isolation."

New Energy Co. of Indiana v. Limbach, 486 U.S. 269 (1988), provides another illustration of the problem. In that case, the Court struck down an Ohio statute that appeared to favor the regulating state in its competition against other states. Ohio had awarded a tax credit against its motor vehicle fuel sales tax for every gallon of the alternative gas fuel ethanol sold by fuel dealers, but only if the ethanol was produced in Ohio or in a state offering reciprocal tax advantages to ethanol produced in Ohio. The tax credit was intended to promote the use of ethanol, especially since it was more costly than regular gasoline. In evaluating the Ohio tax credit's constitutionality, the Court first observed that the law "on its face appears to violate the cardinal requirement of nondiscrimination." While facial discrimination usually is "fatal in fact," the Court then applied strict scrutiny to determine if the law survived close scrutiny. The Court held that the law did not survive because although "reciprocity requirements are not *per se* unlawful," the Court found that Ohio could not use a threat to Indiana's acceptance by taxing a product made by out-of-state "manufacturers at a rate higher than the same product made by Ohio manufacturers, without justification for the disparity." Once again the Court sounded a familiar theme, stating that a state may "not use the threat of economic isolation as a weapon to force sister states to enter into even a desirable reciprocity agreement."

The Modern Trend in Discrimination Cases. Under modern precedent, the Court continues to strike down legislation that discriminates against interstate commerce. For example, in *West Lynn Creamery, Inc. v. Healy*, 512 U.S. 186 (1994), the Court struck down a Massachusetts tax and subsidy scheme that required extra payments on all fluid milk sold by dealers (who were mostly based out-of-state) to Massachusetts retailers. The extra payments would be deposited into a "Massachusetts Dairy Equalization Fund" for distribution to Massachusetts's producers. Two-thirds of the milk sold by dealers was produced out of state. The Court concluded that the law unconstitutionally discriminated against interstate commerce because its real objective was to protect Massachusetts's dairy farms against extremely low prices by requiring mostly out-of-state dealers to make extra payments. The Court viewed the law as a "paradigmatic example of a protective tariff or customs duty, both of which have historically been regarded as attractive because they raise revenue, benefit local producers, and burden out-of-state competitors, and artificially encourage in-state production even though the same goods can be produced more cheaply." The Court held that, when "a nondiscriminatory tax is coupled with a subsidy to one of the groups hurt by the tax, a state's political processes can no longer be relied upon to prevent legislative abuse, because one of the in-state interests which would otherwise lobby against the tax has been mollified by the subsidy."

State Regulations Placing Non-Discriminatory Burdens on Interstate Commerce. Even if a state law does not discriminate against interstate commerce, the law may still affect commerce and be circumscribed through judicial review. The key to judicial scrutiny is the extent of the burden the law places on interstate commerce when compared to its anticipated benefits.

The Early Approach to Non-Discriminatory Legislation: Judicial Deference. Courts at one time were extremely deferential to non-discriminatory state legislation that affected interstate commerce. A case in point is the well-known *South Carolina State Highway Department v. Barnwell Brothers,* 303 U.S. 177 (1938), in which the Court upheld a South Carolina law prohibiting motor trucks and semi-trailer trucks from using state highways if they exceeded 90 inches in width and weighed more than 20,000 pounds. The Court found these questions to be "matters of local concern, the regulation of which unavoidably involves some regulation of interstate commerce but which, because of their local character and their number and diversity, may never be fully dealt with by Congress." The Court focused on the State interest in safety and the evenhanded nature of the regulation, which differed greatly from discrimination against interstate commerce and laws conflicting with federal regulations. The Court noted that if Congress objected to the way the states use their discretion to promote safety, Congress could always jump in and legislate.

This limited role for courts suggested a restrained approach to judicial competence. This notion is captured in the Court's pronouncement that federal "courts do not sit as Legislatures, either state or national," and a reviewing court is "not called upon to determine what, in its judgment, is the most suitable restriction to be applied of those that are possible, or to choose that one which in its opinion is best adapted to all the diverse interests affected." On the contrary, when "the action of a Legislature is within the scope of its power, fairly debatable questions as to its reasonableness, wisdom, and propriety are not for the determination of courts, but for the legislative body, on which rests the duty and responsibility of decision."

The Modern Approach: No More Deference. The Court departed from *Barnwell's* holding in *Southern Pacific Co. v. Arizona*, 325 U.S. 761 (1945), and effectively abandoned its deferential posture to non-discriminatory state regulation. *Southern Pacific* involved an Arizona statute that prohibited railroad trains with more than fourteen passenger cars or seventy freight cars from passing through Arizona. The Court struck a very different tone in asserting that, when "Congress has not acted, this Court, and not the state legislature, is under the commerce clause the final arbiter of the competing demands of state and national interests." While acknowledging that states have some discretion to regulate "matters of local concern," even though those matters affect interstate commerce, they may not "materially restrict the free flow of commerce across state lines, or interfere with it in matters with respect to which uniformity of regulation is of predominant national concern." The new operative question is "whether the relative weights of the state and national interests involved are such as to make inapplicable the rule, generally observed, that the free flow of interstate commerce and its freedom from local restraints in matters requiring uniformity of regulation are interests safeguarded by the commerce clause from state interference."

This transformation in judicial approach had many pragmatic effects, including how trial courts approached constitutional cases. Courts now took elaborate testimony to affix the relative interests so they could be balanced. In *South Pacific Co.*, for example, the trial court took months of testimony about train lengths and standard train practices.

In subsequent cases, the Court has followed the *Southern Pacific Co.* hands-on approach rather than *Barnwell's* deference. For example, in *Bibb v. Navajo Freight Lines, Inc.*, 359 U.S. 520 (1959), the Court struck down an Illinois statute requiring the use of contoured rear fender mudguards on trucks and trailers operated in the state. The new mudguard differed from the mudguard permitted in 45 other states, including those states nearby. The Illinois legislature had relied on evidence showing that contour flaps promote safety by preventing trucks from throwing debris onto the windshields of surrounding vehicles. While a state's safety measures might come with a "strong presumption of validity," the presumption did not cause the Court to adopt a passive role. Instead, it conducted its own analysis and found that the contoured mudguards had no safety advantages, and further, that Illinois' law imposed a significant burden on interstate commerce. If a trailer is to be operated in both Illinois and Arkansas, states which have different mud flap rules, "mudguards would have to be interchanged, causing a significant delay" of two to four hours. The Court left the door open for innovation, saying that sometimes new safety devices that are inconsistent with the requirements of other States may be so compelling that they should be permitted. The Court added, "But the present showing—balanced against the clear burden on commerce—is far too inconclusive to make this mudguard meet that test."

Of course, even though a court conducts its own review of the competing interests, the result is not necessarily fatal to the local law. Illustrative of this point is *Minnesota v. Clover Leaf Creamery Co.*, 449 U.S. 456 (1981), which upheld a Minnesota statute that banned the retail sale of milk in plastic nonreturnable, nonrefillable containers, but permitted sales in other types of nonreturnable, nonrefillable containers, such as paperboard milk cartons. The law was enacted to deal with the solid waste management problem of nonreturnables. Given the "substantial state purposes," and the non-discriminatory nature of law, the Court concluded that the law should not be struck down simply because it caused some business "to shift from a predominantly out-of-state industry to a predominantly in-state industry."

Another Discrimination Exception: The State as a Market Participant. In some instances, instead of regulating private markets involving interstate commerce, the states enter those markets as participants, meaning buyers, sellers or barterers. When states decide to enter a market, courts often apply different rules to determine the validity of state actions. *Reeves, Inc. v. Stake*, 447 U.S. 429 (1980), is illustrative. That case involved South Dakota's decision to allocate cement from a state-owned plant to residents, excluding non-residents, some of whom had historically purchased almost all of their cement from the plant. The Court upheld the state's action because the state was a market participant, not a regulator. The

Court reasoned that based on state sovereignty, each state has the right to act "as guardian and trustee for its people." In addition, when acting as a business owner, states have the right to exercise discretion about with whom they will deal. The Court noted that states can limit "the enjoyment of state educational institutions, energy generated by a state-run plant, police and fire protection, and agricultural improvement and business development programs" to citizens because those activities "reflect the essential and patently unobjectionable purpose of state government—to serve the citizens of the State." The Court distinguished its prior holdings in *Baldwin*, *Hughes*, and *Philadelphia v. New Jersey,* saying the state can limit "benefits generated by a state program," while leaving access to the marketplace by private companies. Thus, over dissent, the court found that this kind of conduct was not impermissible "economic Balkanization."

The Court has also utilized the "market participant" doctrine in evaluating state government contracts and the hiring of residents. In *White v. Massachusetts Council of Construction Employers, Inc.*, 460 U.S. 204 (1983), the Court rejected a commerce clause attack on an executive order by Boston's Mayor requiring at least 50 percent of the persons hired to work on construction projects supported by city funds to be city residents. The key to upholding what otherwise appeared to be protectionist or discriminatory action was that all persons "affected by the order were, in a substantial if informal sense, 'working for the city.' "

Simply because the government is functioning as a market participant does not mean that it is free to impose whatever limits it desires on the marketplace, particularly restrictions that are considered to be "downstream." In *South-Central Timber Development, Inc. v. Wunnicke*, 467 U.S. 82 (1984), the Court struck down an Alaska law that required timber taken from state lands to be processed within the State prior to export. The Court held that *Reeves'* market participant doctrine did not insulate the state here because Alaska was attempting to impose "downstream" conditions in the timber-processing market. Although Alaska, as a state, could directly subsidize the timber-processing industry, such as funding some of the timber processing in the state, Alaska was not free to regulate in a discriminatory manner once the timber was no longer owned by the state. Alaska had crossed over from being a participant, a tree grower, to a regulator of tree processing, and would be judged based on the rules of discriminatory regulation.

South-Central Timber Development, Inc. also teaches that if a state enters the marketplace as a processor, its processing actions will be reviewed as a participant and the market participant doctrine of *Reeves* applies. This was the case in *United Haulers Association, Inc. v. Oneida-Herkimer Solid Waste Management Authority*, 550 U.S. 330 (2007). There, a county adopted a "flow control" ordinance that required all trash haulers to deliver solid waste to a particular waste public processing facility. Unlike the ruling in *C & A Carbone, Inc. v. Clarkstown*, 511 U.S. 383 (1994), which struck down a flow control ordinance as a violation of the Commerce Clause because the law required haulers to deliver waste to a particular *private* processing facility, the flow control ordinance in *United Haulers Association* requiring delivery to a *public* processing facility was upheld. Several critical distinctions from *Carbone* existed, including that the ordinance required delivery to a state-created public benefit corporation, that trash disposal had "been a traditional government activity for years," and that "laws that favor the government in such areas—but treat every private business, whether in-state or out-of-state, exactly the same—do not discriminate against interstate commerce for purposes of the Commerce Clause." As a result, the Court upheld the flow control ordinance.

The Interstate Privileges and Immunities Clause. The interstate Privileges and Immunities Clause of Article IV, § 2 states: "The Citizens of each State shall be entitled to all Privileges and Immunities of Citizens in the several States." This clause is a form of comity or equal protection clause, protecting out-of-state citizens from protective legislation by other states. While several exceptions exist, just like the framework of most other constitutional prohibitions, the Clause penetrates the interstate commerce area. The trick is understanding when and how the Clause applies.

In *Toomer v. Witsell*, 334 U.S. 385 (1948), the Court held that the Privileges and Immunities Clause would be used to protect out-of-state residents from economic discrimination. There, the Court struck down a South Carolina law that imposed a $2,500 per boat fee on non-resident commercial shrimpers while imposing only a $25 fee on resident shrimpers. The Court noted that nothing "indicates that non-residents use larger boats or different fishing methods than residents, that the cost of enforcing the laws against them is appreciably greater, or that any substantial amount of the State's general funds is devoted to shrimp conservation." The Court specifically rejected South Carolina's "ownership theory" which suggests that states have "power to preserve and regulate the exploitation of an important resource." Thus, while South Carolina could regulate its fisheries through such means as what types of boats or safety equipment would be required, it could not charge non-residents extra fees unrelated to the "added enforcement burden they may impose or for any conservation expenditures from taxes which only residents pay."

Continuing this theme, the Court in *Hicklin v. Orbeck*, 437 U.S. 518 (1978), struck down Alaska's "Local Hire Under State Leases" Act. That Act required that "all oil and gas leases," and other such interests "to which the state is a party", contain a provision requiring the employment of qualified Alaska residents in preference to nonresidents. As part of that program, Alaskans were given certificates of residence that they could present to their private employers. In applying the Privileges and Immunities Clause, the Court held there must be a "reasonable relationship between the danger represented by non-citizens, as a class, and the discrimination practiced upon them." The Court found that Alaska was unable to show that nonresidents were "a peculiar source of the evil" that "Alaska Hire was enacted to remedy, namely, Alaska's 'uniquely high unemployment.' " Consequently, the Court struck down the law as an unconstitutional preference of residents (citizens) over non-residents. A common analogy was utilized, but one not usually found in constitutional analysis, namely the Constitution "was framed upon the theory that the peoples of the several states must sink or swim together, and that in the long run prosperity and salvation are in union and not division."

Another case along the same lines is *Supreme Court of New Hampshire v. Piper*, 470 U.S. 274 (1985). There, the Court struck down a New Hampshire law with a restrictive legal theme—nonresidents were prohibited from becoming attorneys. (The Court voted 8–1 in holding the law unconstitutional.) The law was challenged by a Vermont resident who had passed the New Hampshire bar and had already been vetted and found to be of good moral character. Further, the challenger lived only 400 yards from the New Hampshire border. The Court emphasized that the Privileges and Immunities Clause was intended to create a "national economic union" and to guarantee citizens the opportunity to do business in other states on a basis of "substantial equality with the citizens of that State." This right extends to the practice of law which the Court regarded as important to the national economy and therefore a "fundamental right," in part because "out-of-state lawyers may—and often do—represent persons who raise unpopular federal claims," and provide "the only means available for the vindication of federal rights." This fundamental rights analysis was expansive, broadly construed to include property and vocations, not just fundamental rights reflected in the Constitution.

The Court concluded the New Hampshire law could be saved only if it met the elements of an exception drawn by prior precedent in the area: (i) there is a substantial reason for the difference in treatment; and (ii) the discrimination practiced against nonresidents bears a substantial relationship to the State's objective." The State could not meet these elements because out-of-state attorneys could prepare and learn as much as in-state attorneys.

Baldwin v. Fish and Game Commission of Montana, 436 U.S. 371 (1978), offers a second exception to application of the Privileges and Immunities Clause. There, the Court rejected a privileges and immunities challenge to a Montana law which charged non-residents 7½ times more than residents were charged to purchase a license to hunt elk in combination with other game, and 25 times more than residents were charged to hunt only elk. The Court viewed the Privileges and Immunities Clause as prohibiting the states "from imposing unreasonable burdens on citizens of other States in their pursuit of common callings within the State, in the ownership and disposition of privately held property within the State, and in access to the courts of the State." There were exceptions to this rule though. The Court noted, "No one would suggest that the Privileges and Immunities Clause requires a State to open its polls to a person who declines to assert that the State is the only one where he claims a right to vote. The same is true as to qualification for an elective office of the State." Indeed, some "distinctions between residents and nonresidents merely reflect the fact that this is a Nation composed of individual States, and are permitted; other distinctions are prohibited because they hinder the formation, the purpose, or the development of a single Union of those States." The key question is whether the "privileges" and "immunities" bear "upon the vitality of the Nation" so that the state must "treat all citizens, resident and nonresident, equally." For example, the "states may not interfere with the 'right of a citizen of one state to pass through, or to reside in any other state, for purposes of trade, agriculture, professional pursuits, or otherwise; to claim the benefit of the writ of habeas corpus; to institute and maintain actions of any kind in the courts of the state; to take, hold and dispose of property, either real or personal.' " The Court found recreation to be quite different, however, and permitted distinctions such as the one drawn by Montana. For nonresidents such as Lester Baldwin, elk hunting was "merely a recreation and a sport" and not a "means to the nonresident's livelihood." While the Court stated it would prohibit discrimination based on "fundamental" rights and activities, "elk hunting by nonresidents in Montana is not one of them."

Another avenue for states to engage in differential treatment of out-of-state citizens occurs when there is a substantial state interest in doing so and the law crafted to meet this objective is substantially related to that interest. This equal protection-like test permits differential treatment based on the circumstances.

CHECKLIST

A. **Is there a direct conflict with a valid federal law?** If yes, the state law will be found unconstitutional.

B. **Is a state law or activity expressly or impliedly pre-empted by federal law?** If yes, even if the area of regulation is considered "local," because of the extent of the federal Commerce Clause power and the Supremacy Clause, the state law will be unconstitutional.

C. **If there is no express or implied conflict between federal and state law (and no preemption of state law), is the state law considered "national" or "local"?** If it is a "national" matter requiring uniformity, the state law generally will be unconstitutional because it lies in the forbidden zone of regulation.

D. **If the states are regulating in the "national" zone, has the Congress assented to state regulation?** If yes, the state laws likely will be found constitutional.

E. **If a state law is local in nature, requiring diversity, does the law discriminate against interstate commerce?** If yes, the law generally will be struck down.

F. **If the state law discriminates against interstate commerce, can it meet strict judicial scrutiny?** If yes, the law will be constitutional.

G. **If the state law discriminates against interstate commerce, is the state a market participant?** If the state is acting as a buyer or seller, and not as a regulator, the law might survive a constitutional challenge. If the state is a market participant but is regulating "downstream," the state has switched roles and the laws are evaluated with the state acting in its capacity as regulator.

H. **If a state law is local and nondiscriminatory in nature, does the law impose a burden on interstate commerce?** If yes, the benefits to the state and burdens on interstate commerce will be balanced and if the burdens are undue, the law will be struck down.

I. **If the state law discriminates against out-of-state citizens or residents, what constitutional analysis is most appropriate?** If these circumstances exist, the interstate Privileges and Immunities Clause of Article IV, Section 2, should be utilized.

■ PROBLEMS ■

Problem #1: The State of Alabama enacts a law requiring non-citizens over the age of 18 to register with the State, fill out a lengthy form with background information and pay a registration fee. One year later, Congress enacts a law requiring non-citizens over the age of 14 to register, but not fill out a form or carry a registration card. If Alex, a 19-year-old student at the University of Alabama and a citizen of Canada, refuses to fill out the form in Alabama, must he do so pursuant to the Alabama law?

Answer: This problem poses an issue of preemption. There are two laws, one federal and one state. The order in which they were enacted is not constitutionally significant. There are differences in the laws that suggest a conflict might occur, but not express statements in the federal law indicating an intent by Congress to preempt and occupy the registration field. The facts of this problem were drawn from *Hines v. Davidowitz*, 312 U.S. 52 (1941), and likely would be analyzed in a similar fashion. In that case, the Court struck down a Pennsylvania law that required all non-citizens 18 years of age or over to register with the state, pay a $1 annual registration fee, and carry an identification card indicating citizenship status. Following passage of the Pennsylvania law, Congress enacted its own law in the area, the Alien Registration Act, requiring a single registration of non-citizens 14 years of age and over. The federal law required detailed information, but did not contained a card-carrying mandate like the state law. In striking down the Pennsylvania law, the Court offered several factors that augured in favor of striking down the law—the purpose of both the federal and state law was identical (registration of non-citizens as a distinct group), the federal law is supreme in the area of immigration, naturalization and deportation, state authority in this subject area is limited, and the Pennsylvania law stood as an obstacle to accomplishing Congress' objectives. The Court noted the inconsistency in the two laws, saying that Congress had rejected many provisions included in the Pennsylvania law, and that the purpose of this federal system was to create "one uniform national registration system," and to otherwise leave aliens "free from the possibility of inquisitorial practices and police surveillance."

Problem #2: The State of Delaware enacts a law in 1890 prohibiting the sale of adulterated food of any kind. Cali owned a small food store in Delaware that sold milk, butter and various other items. Cali was prosecuted and convicted for selling adulterated butter in 1894. She appealed her conviction, claiming, among other things, that the Delaware law constituted an unconstitutional usurpation by the state of the power to regulate commerce. Is Cali correct?

Answer: Cali likely would lose her constitutional claim even in the 1890s. Early cases provided for state regulation of some subjects that otherwise could have been considered commerce. In *Plumley v. Commonwealth of Massachusetts,* 155 U.S. 461 (1894), Plumley was convicted of violating a Massachusetts law prohibiting the sale of adulterated oleomargarine. Plumley promptly challenged the law's constitutionality. The Court upheld the Massachusetts law, finding it did not violate Congress' commerce power: "If there be any subject over which it would seem the states ought to have plenary control, and the power to legislate, it is the protection of the people against fraud and deception in the sale of food products."

Problem #3: The State of Oklahoma enacts the following law: "There shall be no sale of goods in this state that were manufactured out-of-state without a license." Is the Oklahoma law constitutional?

Answer: This problem offers another state licensing scheme that treats the regulating state differently than other states. Generally, these laws discriminate against interstate commerce and will be struck down by courts. In *Welton v. Missouri*, 91 U.S. (1 Otto) 275 (1875), for example, the Court struck down a state statute that prohibited the sale of out-of-state goods by peddlers without a license. The Court observed that the subject matter was proper for state regulation, but it objected to the differential manner in which the regulation was implemented. Far from evenhanded, the Court saw this license as a tax on out-of-state goods: "the commercial power continues until the commodity has ceased to be the subject of discriminating legislation by reason of its foreign character. That power protects it, even after it has entered the State, from any burdens imposed by reason of its foreign origin."

Problem #4: The State of North Carolina enacts a law prohibiting 65-foot "double" trucks on any North Carolina highways, including all interstate roads, with the exceptions of roads in border cities with 20,000 or more residents, such as Charlotte or Asheville. Many commercial trucks, particularly those traveling cross-country, utilize the 65-foot double trailer. A study of these trucks found that they are about as safe and reliable as a single large truck that is slightly smaller, but also wider and taller. North Carolina received anecdotal information that these trucks are more dangerous than the alternatives. Shortly after the law was enacted, a trucker bringing in

30,000 pounds of bananas to Raleigh filed suit after being ticketed for violating this law while driving on I-40. Is the law constitutional?

Answer: This law is a state regulation affecting interstate commerce. A court could evaluate it in one of two ways—as a non-discriminatory law that burdens interstate commerce or as a law that discriminates against interstate commerce. In finding discrimination, the Court searches for some evidence that the state is trying to advantage local interests to the detriment of interstate interests. Here, the border city exception appears to be local favoritism suggesting discrimination. Even if it was not, the law likely would be struck down because it places an undue burden on interstate commerce. For example, in *Kassel v. Consolidated Freightways Corp.*, 450 U.S. 662 (1981), the Court struck down an Iowa statute that prohibited 65-foot trucks on Iowa highways, but allowed 65-foot mobile homes if they were traveling to or from an Iowa location, and also allowed longer trucks in "border cities" if the other city permitted longer trucks. The border exemption suggested that the state legislature was not as focused on safety considerations. Indeed, if the legislature was really concerned about the fact that longer trucks were dangerous, it might have precluded longer trucks even in border cities. Of course, even if the court does not conclude that a statute is protectionist, the court might strike it down if it involves an undue burden on interstate commerce.

Problem #5: The State of Texas, fearing an influx of H1N1 influenza, often called "the swine flu," prohibited the importation of pigs, pig parts or any animal that has come in contact with pigs from any state having any outbreak of H1N1 influenza in the past 24 months, unless the pigs brought into Texas are first quarantined in Texas at the owner's expense for at least 2 months. A farmer from Iowa bringing pigs to market in Texas is stopped because of the law. The farmer challenges the law as unconstitutional. Will the farmer win?

Answer: The farmer likely will win, but it will depend on whether the Court considers this law to be sufficiently narrowly drawn to qualify as a legitimate quarantine law. In *Railroad Co. v. Husen*, 95 U.S. 465 (1877), for example, the Court struck down a Missouri statute banning the importation of Texas, Mexican or Indian cattle between March 1 and November 1. The Court declined to characterize the law as a valid quarantine measure due to its categorical nature (*i.e.*, not banning importation of just diseased cattle, but rather cattle from a certain origin). If the state had enacted a law that restricted a type of diseased cattle, the Court likely would have upheld the law.

Problem #6: A Utah law required in breach of contract actions that the parties be "present" in the state as a prerequisite to the statute of limitations running. If the party was not "present," then the statute would be tolled until it was. Presence for a foreign corporation was indicated by the appointment of an agent for service of process. In essence, this requirement mandated that a foreign corporation consent to be sued in Utah if it wanted to take advantage of any statute of limitations. A Delaware corporation wanted to do a deal in Utah, but not appoint such an agent. Must an agent be appointed?

Answer: The short answer to this question is that an agent need not be appointed because the law is an unconstitutional imposition on interstate commerce. In the case on point, *Bendix Autolite Corp. v. Midwesco Enterprises, Inc.*, 486 U.S. 888 (1988), the Court struck down an Ohio law that tolled the statute of limitations in actions for breach of contract or fraud actions for any period that a person or corporation is not "present" in the State. To be present for the purposes of the law, a foreign corporation must appoint an agent for service of process, which operates as consent to be sued. While the law operated evenhandedly and did not discriminate against out-of-state commerce, the Court found that the burden on interstate commerce outweighed the local interest. The burden was great because the law required foreign corporation to appoint an agent for service of process in all cases, including those in which there is insufficient connection between the state and the action to otherwise permit the assertion of jurisdiction. While the Court recognized that "serving foreign corporate defendants may be more arduous than serving domestic corporations or foreign corporations with a designated agent for service, and we have held for equal protection purposes that a State rationally may make adjustments for this difference by curtailing limitations protection for absent foreign corporations," the Court noted that Midwesco could have been served through the limitation period under Ohio's long-arm statute. "The Ohio statute of limitations is tolled only for those foreign corporations that do not subject themselves to the general jurisdiction of Ohio courts. In this manner the Ohio statute imposes a greater burden on out-of-state companies than it does on Ohio companies, subjecting the activities of foreign and domestic corporations to inconsistent regulations."

Problem #7: The State of Maine provides the following in its state code: "All residents of the State shall have a special discounted tuition of 50 percent when compared to any full tuition paid by out-of-state residents." Josie, a resident of the State of New Hampshire, is admitted to the University of Maine at Oreno but must pay full tuition. She sues, claiming the law is unconstitutional. Will she win?

Answer: The answer is no, Josie will lose. While Josie can state a claim under the Privileges and Immunities Clause (Article IV, Section 2) because the law is discriminating on its face against out-of-state residents, an exception to the non-discrimination principle applies. The state will be able to show the law is based on a substantial state interest in educating its own residents and that the law is substantially related to that interest by providing for lower tuition. These differential tuition rates are not so much a penalty for out-of-state residents as a way of compensating in-state residents for the fair share of tax money they have paid to fund the state schools.

POINTS TO REMEMBER

- States have some implied concurrent power to regulate commerce with Congress, particularly if the issue is considered "local."
- Congress holds the upper hand and if there is an express or implied conflict, Congress usually wins because of the strength of the Commerce Clause coupled with the Supremacy Clause.
- Courts determine whether there is implied preemption by evaluating whether Congress intended to occupy the field, were in fact the dominant participant in that field or whether compliance with state law would impede federal law or objectives.
- If there is no conflict, states cannot discriminate against interstate commerce, unless they can meet strict scrutiny or if they are a market participant and not a market regulator.
- Even if state laws are not discriminatory, courts still require those laws not to be an undue burden on interstate commerce, as determined by balancing the benefits to the state regulator against the burdens to interstate commerce.
- The Privileges and Immunities Clause of Article IV, Section 2, governs state laws that discriminate against out-of-state citizens, and should precede a "dormant" commerce clause analysis in these circumstances.

CHAPTER 5

Intergovernmental Immunities

The Constitution creates a system of dual sovereignty that allocates some powers to the federal government and the remaining powers to state governments or to the people. The intergovernmental immunity doctrine is an offshoot of the dual sovereignty system and embodies the notion that one government (federal or state) has the right to be free from regulation or taxes by the other government.

State Power to Tax the Federal Government. Taxation is a major source of revenue for both federal and state governments. The power to tax can turn burdensome, however, particularly when it is used as a tool by one sovereign government against the other. In *McCulloch v. Maryland*, 17 U.S. (4 Wheat.) 316 (1819), a landmark opinion by Chief Justice John Marshall, the Court held that the states did not have the power to tax the federal government. That case involved a Maryland statute, which provided that all banks not established under state law must choose between paying an annual fee to the state, or issuing notes only on stamped paper supplied (and taxed) by the state. After holding that the federal government has the power to establish a national bank, the Court struck down the Maryland tax. While the Court recognized that states have the power to impose taxes, it held that the state tax could not be imposed on the federal bank. The Court observed that under the Supremacy Clause, the Constitution and laws of the United States are supreme, and, in a famous phrase, that the "power to create implies a power to preserve" and a power to tax involves a power to destroy, leading to the conclusion that a state power to tax the federal government is dangerous and unconstitutional.

Taxing Federal Property. The holding of *McCulloch* was extended in later cases to the taxation of federal property. In *Van Brocklin v. Anderson*, 117 U.S. 151 (1886), for example, the Court struck down a state tax on federal property. The Court noted that there was a debate about whether a neutral tax, applied to all property and not just to federal property, might be sustainable.

However, in *Van Brocklin* the Court held that "no state can tax the property of the United States without their consent."

Taxing Interest on Federal Bonds. It is generally unconstitutional for states to tax the interest on federal bonds. In *Weston v. City Council of Charleston*, 27 U.S. 449 (1829), the Court struck down a state tax on federal bonds. The Court observed that allowing such a tax would lead down a slippery slope that could be ruinous to the federal government because of the importance "of borrowing money on the credit of the nation." In addition, the states have not been allowed to tax federal sales without Congress' consent. For example, the states cannot tax the sale of liquor sold at United States military installations.

Taxing Federal Employee Salaries. A ray of light shines on states, however, when they tax the salaries of federal employees. While allowing such taxes might allow states to start down a slippery slope, in *Graves v. New York,* 306 U.S. 466 (1939), the Court overruled *Dobbins v. Commissioners of Erie County,* 41 U.S. 435 (1842), and upheld a general state income tax as applied to the salaries of federal employees. The Court concluded that there is a logical distinction between taxing the government and taxing the salaries of government employees. So long as the state tax is neutral, in that it is applied to the salaries of all employees (federal, state or private), then the tax is permissible notwithstanding the possible economic burden of the tax on the federal government.

Tax Exemptions for State Employees but Not Federal Employees. Yet, the ray of light for state taxation falters when states decide to give a tax exemption for state law enforcement employees but not federal law enforcement officers essentially performing the same job in the same state. In *Dawson v. Steager*, 586 U.S. 171 (2019), the Court considered whether it was constitutional for West Virginia to give retired state law enforcement officers a tax exemption on their pensions when equivalent federal law enforcement officers were taxed on their pensions by the state. The Court held that West Virginia unconstitutionally discriminated in creating these classifications, regardless of motive.

Federal Power to Tax the State Governments. A different analysis applies to the federal government taxing states indirectly or directly. This analysis offers the federal government various avenues of taxation, as well as limitations on those roads to revenue.

Taxing Interest on State Bonds. As a general matter, the federal government can impose a tax on the interest received by private parties on state and local bonds. In *Willcuts v. Bunn,* 282 U.S. 216 (1931), the Court held that Congress could exercise discretion regarding whether to tax the interest on state and local bonds as a matter of governmental policy. The Court noted that the burdens of such taxes are not so great as to render the taxes unconstitutional, unless it clearly appears "that a substantial burden upon the borrowing power of the State would actually be imposed."

The federal government mostly has chosen not to tax the interest on state bonds. This means that the bonds are more attractive to investors because it increases their returns.

Taxing State Employee Salaries. While the Court in several early cases wavered in allocating the federal government this power, later cases dating from the 1930s permitted such federal taxes of state employees. In *Helvering v. Gerhardt,* 304 U.S. 405 (1938), for example, the Court overruled an earlier case, *Collector v. Day,* 78 U.S. 113 (1870), and held that the salaries of state employees were subject to a nondiscriminatory tax applied to both publicly and privately employed individuals. The Court found that while a tax on the salary paid to key state officers could increase the cost of governing, it would not stop the States from performing their traditional government functions.

Direct Federal Taxation of States. The more perplexing question is whether the federal government can impose a tax directly on the states. Some early cases distinguished federal interference with "traditional state functions" from interference with nonessential government activities equivalent to those of a private business. *See, e.g., Collector v. Day,* 78 U.S. 113 (1870).

Later decisions have rejected the distinction between a state's proprietary functions (when the government is operating a business in a manner similar to an ordinary business), and essential governmental activities (*e.g.*, taxing and regulating). These decisions have instead concluded that the federal government might be free to tax both activities. *See Collector v. Day*, in *Massachusetts v. United States*, 435 U.S. 444 (1978). In *Massachusetts,* the Court upheld an annual registration tax on civil aircraft applied to a State of Massachusetts helicopter used to patrol highways and engage in other police functions. The Court found that the tax was non-discriminatory (in that it applied to all aircraft and not just state-owned aircraft), and indeed was structured to favor the states that were exempt from the 7-cent-per-gallon fuel tax applied to private noncommercial general aviation. Consequently, the tax fairly approximated the cost of the benefits civil aircraft receive from the federal activities.

The power of the federal government to tax the states is not without limits. In addition to certain types of state immunities, federal taxation is permissible only so far as the tax is calibrated to recover the actual costs of the federal program.

State Immunity from Federal Regulation. Prior to the 1930s, the question of state immunity from federal regulation was not an operative one. Instead, courts used the Tenth Amendment to reign in federal action, construing federal power narrowly, such as with the Commerce Clause. *See, e.g., Hammer v. Dagenhart,* 247 U.S. 251 (1918).

Things changed dramatically in the era ushered in after 1937, an era characterized by great judicial deference to Congress in the exercise of its commerce power. As a result, federal authority expanded significantly. *See, e.g., United States v. Darby Lumber Co.,* 312 U.S. 100 (1941), where the Court upheld wage and hour restrictions on employees. *See also, Crosby v. Nat'l Foreign Trade Council,* 530 U.S. 363 (2000), where the Court found that a Massachusetts law prohibiting state entities from purchasing goods and services from businesses doing business with Myanmar (then Burma) was a violation of the Preemption Doctrine and the Supremacy Clause and consequently unconstitutional.

Because of the Court's shift in position, Congress was free to impose more restrictions on wages and hours and directly regulate the wages and hours of state employees. The Court apparently was not ready to let Congress have total control, however. In *National League of Cities v. Usery,* 426 U.S. 833 (1976), the Court held that Congress could not apply the Fair Labor Standards Act (FLSA) to state employees, and thereby require states to pay their employees a minimum hourly wage and overtime for hours worked. The Act did make some exceptions for public employment relationships that were without counterpart in the private sector (*e.g.*, fire protection and law enforcement personnel). In striking down the Act, the Court found there are attributes of state sovereignty that may not be impaired by Congress, and that the states' right to determine the wages and hours of governmental employees who are carrying out governmental functions is one of those attributes. These determinations are "essential" to the states' "separate and independent existence," and their regulation would "impermissibly interfere with the integral governmental functions of these bodies."

In subsequent cases, the Court struggled to apply *Usery* with any degree of predictability. Nine years after *Usery*, the Court gave up its effort to draw clear distinctions. In *Garcia v. San Antonio Metropolitan Transit Authority,* 469 U.S. 528 (1985), the Court overruled *Usery* and held that Congress could apply the FLSA to a city-owned bus line. *Garcia* noted that the third *Usury* factor (traditional governmental functions) had proven hard to apply and that it was "difficult, if not impossible, to identify an organizing principle that places each of the cases in the first group on one side of a line and each of the cases in the second group on the other side." The Court left protections against federal overreaching to the democratic process: "The genius of our government provides that, within the sphere of constitutional action, the people—acting not through the courts but through their elected legislative representatives—have the power to determine as conditions demand, what services and functions the public welfare requires."

The Tenth Amendment and the Federal Commandeering of States. In addition to questions about the federal taxation and regulation of states, another related issue was whether Congress could use its regulatory power to commandeer the states to enact laws on Congress' behalf. The Court eventually pared down Congress' power in this area. In *New York v. United States*, 505 U.S. 144 (1992), the Court struck down portions of the Low-Level Radioactive Waste Policy Amendments Act of 1985. The Court found that Congress had impermissibly sought to compel the states to provide for the disposal of radioactive waste generated within their borders. The Act provided for three types of incentives to encourage the States to comply with their statutory obligations. First, the law imposed surcharges to provide monetary incentives to states that did not take control of radioactive waste within their borders. Second, the Act imposed "access incentives" constituting additional surcharges or a denial of access to states to disposal sites if they failed to meet required deadlines. Finally, the Act imposed a "take title" provision on any state that failed to provide for the disposal of all such waste generated within the State.

While upholding the first two provisions as permissible encouragement, the Court struck down the "take title" provision as a form of impermissible coercion or commandeering in violation of the Tenth Amendment. The Court concluded that federal control of state regulatory processes would diminish the accountability of both state and federal officials and the ability of voters to control governmental officials through the political process. Voters would have a difficult time distinguishing between whether the regulation was attributable to the federal or state government.

The Court upheld the monetary incentives program as a conditional exercise of Congress' authority under the Spending Clause. The Court also held the denial of access provisions as "within the power of Congress to authorize the States to discriminate against interstate commerce," and concluded that Congress may "offer States the choice of regulating that activity according to federal standards or having state law preempted by federal regulation." Thus, the

Court delineated between the states being forced to act and the states being given a choice, either through the federal government offering to be a substitute or through monetary encouragement.

The Court struck down the "take title" provision because it "commandeers the legislative processes of the States by directly compelling them to enact and enforce a federal regulatory program." The Court emphasized that the states "are not mere political subdivisions of the United States," and that they retain "a residuary and inviolable sovereignty" that is "reserved explicitly to the States by the Tenth Amendment." "Whatever the outer limits of that sovereignty may be, one thing is clear: The Federal Government may not compel the States to enact or administer a federal regulatory program."

In *Printz v. United States*, 521 U.S. 898 (1997), the Court struck down portions of the Brady Handgun Violence Prevention Act that required state and local law enforcement officers to conduct background checks on prospective handgun purchasers and to perform certain related tasks. Although the local officials (referred to as "CLEOs") were required to make a "reasonable effort to ascertain within 5 business days whether receipt or possession would be in violation of the law," the Act did not require the official to take any particular action. In striking down the Act, the Court did not regard as controlling historical evidence suggesting that the federal government passed early statutes pressing state courts into service for various purposes. Even though the states had surrendered various powers to the federal government under the Constitution, the Court concluded that they retained "a residuary and inviolable sovereignty" and could not be pressed into service on behalf of the federal government.

Printz reflected the view that the United States was not based on a system of a central government that would "act upon and through the States." Instead, the Framers envisioned a system of independent state governments that were accountable to their own citizens, and that created a structural protection for liberty that reduced "the risk of tyranny and abuse from either front." By remaining independent, the states prevented the federal government from becoming too powerful.

The "no commandeering or coercion" principle is not without limits. For example, in *South Carolina v. Baker,* 485 U.S. 505 (1988), the Court upheld the Tax Equity and Fiscal Responsibility Act of 1982 (TEFRA) that denied federal tax-exempt status to state and local bonds that were issued in unregistered forms. The states challenged the Act on the basis that the federal government was effectively forcing them to issue bonds only in registered form. The

Court disagreed, holding that a state could choose to issue bonds in either format, and that states were only affected if they wanted to claim tax exempt status for their bonds. The Court did not regard this requirement as a "constitutional defect" and found no violation of the Tenth Amendment. Justice O'Connor dissented: "I would invalidate Congress' attempt to regulate the sovereign States by threatening to deprive them of this tax immunity, which would increase their dependence on the National Government."

Thus, the Court drew a line between commandeering and coercion, on the one hand, and encouragement on the other hand. As a result, Congress could entice states to act through conditional spending, such as providing funds if states regulated their speed limits.

In *Murphy v. National Collegiate Athletic Association (NCAA)*, 584 U.S. 453 (2018), the Supreme Court considered the constitutionality of a federal law, the Professional and Amateur Sports Protection Act (PASPA), prohibiting the states from allowing sports gambling. New Jersey voters had approved a state constitutional amendment authorizing the state legislature to legalize sports gambling, which the legislature did in 2012. While there was a conflict between the federal and state laws, the Court found that the federal law violated the anticommandeering principle; the Congress could regulate sports gambling directly but could not order the states to not regulate it.

Successive Federal and State Prosecutions for the Same Crime. In *Gamble v. United States*, 587 U.S. 678 (2019), the Supreme Court considered whether to upend the well-established rule that because the federal and state governments are two different sovereigns, the Double Jeopardy Clause does not apply to successive prosecutions in state and federal courts for the same conduct. The Court upheld the long-standing rule and permitted such prosecutions precisely because of the dual sovereignty principle.

The Legality of Marijuana Use in the States. In a majority of states, marijuana is not legal in some form, either for medicinal purposes or for broader recreational use. Yet, under federal law, marijuana remains illegal, a Schedule I drug under the Controlled Substances Act, 21 U.S.C. §§ 801, et seq., "with a high potential for abuse." Thus, it is in error to say that marijuana use is "legal" in light of the federal law, since the state laws are preempted by the federal law under the Supremacy Clause. What has allowed usage in those states that have permitted it is the non-enforcement of the federal law.

Who Controls the Primary Ballot for President? Several Colorado voters brought suit to exclude former president Donald Trump from the state's Republican primary ballot for president. The Colorado Supreme Court subsequently agreed with the exclusion. The Supreme Court of the United States, in *Trump v. Anderson*, 601 U.S. 100 (2024), disagreed, finding that it was not the states' job to determine who shall be the candidates for federal office. The Court stated in a per curiam decision,: "Because the Constitution makes Congress, rather than the States, responsible for enforcing Section 3 against federal officeholders and candidates, we reverse."

CHECKLIST

A. **State Power to Tax the Federal Government**—Are the states taxing a federal agency, federal property or interest on a federal bond? If the answer is yes, the tax is likely unconstitutional. If the state is taxing federal employee salaries, is the tax nondiscriminatory, meaning it is applicable to federal, state and private employees? It is this neutrality that is critical.

B. **Federal Power to Tax the State Government**—Is the taxation direct or indirect? Both might be permissible. If direct, the key question is whether the tax is commensurate with the costs of federal services or programs and not excessive. If indirect, the question becomes what kind of tax is it? Is the federal government taxing the interest on state bonds or state employee salaries? If the answer is yes to either, it is probably constitutional.

C. **State Immunity from Federal Regulation**—Is the state claiming it is immune from federal regulation? This claim is generally without merit after *Garcia*, whether the regulation is for a traditional government function or a proprietary one.

D. **Federal Commandeering of State Resources**—Is Congress commandeering the states to regulate on Congress' behalf or is Congress merely encouraging the states through monetary incentives or a choice of regulatory schemes? While commandeering is considered unconstitutional coercion, the other forms of incentives are considered constitutional.

■ PROBLEMS ■

Problem #1: Contractor Carol contracted with the federal government to remodel several government buildings. Carol refused to pay a state occupation tax that was measured from gross receipts, as compared to net income. Carol based her objection on intergovernmental immunity. Will Carol have to pay the tax?

Answer: Carol likely will have to pay the tax. While some taxes cannot be collected by the states involving the federal government, it appears that a nondiscriminatory tax to be paid by all, not just federal government contractors, would be upheld. In *James v. Dravo Contracting Co.*, 302 U.S. 134 (1937), the Supreme Court rejected a contractor's claim that it was immune from a state occupation tax. The Court held that a nondiscriminatory tax is permissible until Congress declares otherwise. Likewise, in *City of Detroit v. Murray Corp.*, 355 U.S. 489 (1958), the Court upheld use taxes on machinery and other property used by private companies in conjunction with cost-plus contracts that required the Government to reimburse them for state taxes paid by them, stating that the tax is not unconstitutional provided that the tax is imposed equally on similarly situated constituents of the State.

Problem #2: A federal law taxed mineral water sold by public and private organizations. New York Water was a state-run company that bottled and sold stream water owned by the State of New York. The company objected to the tax, claiming it violated intergovernmental immunity under the Constitution. Must New York Water pay the tax?

Answer: The state company most likely will have to pay the tax. The old distinctions, such as whether the activity is "proprietary" or "governmental," or whether the activity is "historically sanctioned" or "profit-making," are no longer applied by courts to determine whether a tax is proper. *New York v. United States,* 326 U.S. 572 (1946), is controlling. There, the Court upheld a tax on mineral waters sold by a state-owned entity. In upholding the tax, the Court again rejected distinctions based on whether a state government is engaged in "proprietary" as opposed to "governmental" activities, or whether it is simply involved in "historically sanctioned" versus "profit-making" activities. The Court found "no restriction" against including the States in "a tax exacted equally from private persons upon the same subject matter."

Problem #3: Congress enacts a law "prohibiting states from paying overtime to employees in excess of 30 hours without some form of extra pay for those hours." Is this law constitutional?

Answer: While such a law likely would have been unconstitutional under *National League of Cities*, it is equally likely to be found constitutional under *Garcia*. The distinction between traditional government functions reserved for states alone and other functions properly subject to federal regulation disappeared with *Garcia*. *Garcia* strips the 10th Amendment of some of its teeth and forces the states to contemplate tough economic decisions—if states are faced with greater payments to employees, they will either have to raise taxes or hire fewer workers. Either way, it is not the best scenario for the states.

Problem #4: Congress enacts a law to promote energy conservation. The law says that "any state that engages in wind power production or research will be compensated by the federal government of up to $200 million per state, depending on the production or research." Most states will not be able to pass up this amount of money, no matter what the states' position is on this alternative energy source. Is this law constitutional?

Answer: The short answer is yes. While Congress cannot order states to engage in wind power operation or research because of the states' independent sovereignty, *New York* permits alternative methods of persuasion that do not cross the line of unconstitutionality. These methods include offering monetary incentives through the Congress' spending power and offering a choice, including the federal government substituting for state activity. Perhaps the most well known example of such Congressional persuasion involved federal incentives offered to states in the past several decades to keep speed limits at 55 m.p.h.

POINTS TO REMEMBER

- The Federal Government generally has greater latitude in taxing states than the states have freedom to tax the federal government. A significant illustration is the seminal case of *McCulloch v. Maryland,* 17 U.S. (4 Wheat.) 316 (1819).
- Since *Garcia* overturned *National League of Cities,* state immunity from regulation is generally left to the political process and not the Tenth Amendment.
- The Tenth Amendment does have some teeth insofar as it protects states from the federal government compelling them to regulate. The federal government is permitted to encourage states to act, through the spending power or by offering a choice.

CHAPTER 6

Procedural Due Process

Due process of law is one of the more important rights in the Constitution. There are two separate due process clauses in the Amendments to the Constitution with the same language. This is not a typo. One clause is located in the Fifth Amendment to the Constitution and limits only the federal government. The other clause is located in the Fourteenth Amendment and limits the states. Each clause prohibits the government from depriving individuals of life, liberty, or property without due process of law. The due process clauses have been the source of multiple doctrines, each with their own tests and formulas. These include procedural due process, and much more. The other doctrines include substantive due process, which has led to the creation of a family of rights, the incorporation doctrine, which incorporates those fundamental rights to the American scheme of ordered liberty in the Bill of Rights (first ten amendments), void for vagueness, which finds that a law that is so vague reasonable people must guess as to its meaning and fails to provide reasonable notice is unconstitutional, and basic due process, requiring laws at a minimum to be reasonable.

Procedural due process means that the government must follow appropriate procedures before depriving persons of their lives, liberty, or property. Thus, the limitation does not prevent the government from taking someone's life, liberty or property, but it does require the government to adhere to appropriate processes when it does so. The goal of the procedural framework is to promote fairness and transparency.

In theory, procedural due process applies only in a narrow category of cases involving "life," "liberty," and "property." However, the Court has defined these terms broadly, particularly the terms "liberty" and "property," so that they apply in a variety of contexts involving such things as government benefits and employment, thereby expanding the traditional notions of liberty and property.

The Court could have applied a single test to all deprivations in sort of a "one size fits all" approach. Instead, the Court decided to apply the procedural due process limit in a flexible way, requiring different levels of process for different types of deprivations. In a given case, one must first focus on the nature of the interest that is being infringed, and then inquire how much process is due for a deprivation of that interest. As a general rule, the more severe the deprivation, the more process is due.

Legislative Versus Adjudicative Determinations. An initial fork in the road in evaluating procedural due process claims is whether the government has made a "legislative" determination or an "adjudicative" determination. A legislative determination involves a broad statement of policy by Congress, a state legislature, municipal subdivision, or an administrative agency when it adopts a rule or regulation. An adjudicative determination usually involves the application of some broad rule to a specific set of facts such as when government enforces a law, an administrative rule, or an agency decision.

Legislative determinations generally fall outside of procedural due process. Thus, legislatures (and even agencies) are usually not constitutionally required to permit input from the public or to hold hearings prior to enacting general legislation or rules. Congress can choose to require agencies to provide an opportunity for input, though, and sometimes Congress requires agencies to allow comment or utilize trial-like procedures. *See* Administrative Procedure Act, 5 U.S.C. §§ 553, 554, 556 & 557. Despite the fact that agencies usually offer some form of hearing or process prior to adopting new rules, this process might not be constitutionally required for regulated entities affected by the rule or the law.

Adjudicative determinations are different and generally fall within the constraints of procedural due process. If, for example, an individual is sanctioned for violating a statute or regulation, those sanctions might constitute a deprivation of property that requires procedural due process. Such an individualized sanction differs from a law or regulation that enacts a general deprivation, such as an increase in tax or decrease in benefits. This distinction is evident in the holding in *Bi-Metallic Investment Co. v. State Board of Equalization*, 239 U.S. 441 (1915). In that case, the Court rejected the argument that persons subject to an increase in the valuation of taxable property were entitled to due process protection. The Court noted that when "a rule of conduct applies to more than a few people, it is impracticable that everyone should have a direct voice in its adoption" and that individual recourse from general statutes must come through the political process through "the right to vote and the right to choose one's representatives."

The Procedural Due Process Test. The Court uses a two-step analysis in applying procedural due process principles. The first step is to categorize the governmental action to determine whether procedural due process principles apply. The second step involves a flexible analysis which focuses on the type of process that is due under the circumstances.

Step #1: The first step asks whether a person has been deprived of an interest that can be characterized as life, liberty, or property within the meaning of the due process clause. A liberty interest is defined not only as a deprivation of freedom (*e.g.*, incarceration), but encompasses some government action that imposes a stigma on a person's reputation, plus an additional harm, like an inability to obtain gainful employment. *See generally, Paul v. Davis*, 424 U.S. 693 (1976) (exploring the limits of the "liberty" interest definition, with the Court observing that mere harm to reputational interests were insufficient to assert a violation of procedural due process interests). A property interest is defined by state law and includes not only traditional notions of personal property, but also legitimate expectations of "entitlement," such as the continuation of government employment or the receipt of government benefits. The seminal case of *Goldberg v. Kelly*, 397 U.S. 254 (1970), recognized a procedural due process claim for the termination of welfare benefits.

Step #2: If a property, liberty, or life interest is to be deprived by the government, the second step is to determine what process is due. In *Mathews v. Eldridge*, 424 U.S. 319 (1976), the Court articulated the concept of flexible due process and factors that courts should consider in determining what process is due. In assessing the level of process that is due, a court must focus on the nature of the infringement. In making that assessment, the court should consider three factors: "First, the private interest that will be affected by the official action; second, the risk of erroneous deprivation of such interest through the procedure used, and the probable value, if any, of additional safeguards; and finally, the Government's interest, including fiscal and administrative burdens." Thus, the balancing test yields different results depending on the nature of the deprivation. The test places trust in the ability of the courts to apply the test in a way that will be predictable and fair.

In certain contexts, a full-scale hearing is required. For example, in criminal proceedings when the individual is threatened with the possibility of imprisonment or something worse (*e.g.*, capital punishment), a high level of process is due. Generally, the defendant will have the right to fair notice of the allegations against him/her, the right to counsel, and the right to present evidence and witnesses, and cross-examine opposing witnesses.

In other contexts, much less process may be required. For example, when the government seeks to cut-off welfare benefits, nothing more than a "fair hearing" may be required. In other words, the recipient may not be entitled to counsel, but may be entitled to present witnesses and to cross-examine opposing witnesses. When a student is expelled from school for behavioral misconduct, the principal might be required to do no more than talk to the student about the situation and given the student an opportunity to explain. The same is true when a tenured professor is terminated for incompetence or misbehavior. By contrast, when a contract professor is not renewed, a formal hearing might not be required.

One question that has arisen is whether there must be a pre-termination hearing, or whether the hearing can be held post-termination. In the case of welfare benefits, the Court has held that the hearing must be held pre-termination. Likewise with the informal hearing required for a school suspension. However, pre-termination hearings are not always required. For example, the Court has held that a pre-termination hearing is not required before the termination of disability payments.

One issue concerning due process hearings involved the civil forfeiture of vehicles that were used to commit a drug offense. The Supreme Court found that a timely hearing is necessary before forfeiture occurs, but that a separate preliminary hearing is not required. *Culley v. Marshall*, 601 U.S. 377 (2024)(Kavanaugh, J.).

The balancing process usually considers two types of process—notice and a hearing. There are a variety of forms of notice and there different types of hearings ranging from informal meetings to full-blown trials with witnesses, lawyers and argument.

The context of deportation has raised procedural due process issues. For example, in *Trump v. J.G.G.*, 604 U.S. 670 (2025), the Supreme Court held that due process considerations applied and mandated that detainees could not be summarily removed from the U.S. without being given "reasonable notice" and an opportunity to challenge the government's attempt to remove them.

CHECKLIST

A. **Did federal or state action create a deprivation?** Is it a federal or state action being challenged? If federal, the Fifth Amendment procedural due process applies. If state or a subdivision, it is the Fourteenth Amendment procedural due process that applies.

B. **Was a deprivation the result of a legislative or adjudicative determination?** Is it a legislative determination, where procedural due process likely does not attach or is it an adjudicative determination, where it likely does attach?

C. **If it was a legislative determination, use step #1 of the procedural due process test.** If it is a legislative determination, ask if the government deprived the plaintiff of a life, liberty, or property interest. *See, e.g., Goldberg v. Kelly*, 397 U.S. 254 (1970).

D. **Then apply step #2 of the test.** If the answer is "yes" in Step #1, proceed to step #2, which examines the process that is due. The answer depends on the *Mathews v. Eldridge*, 424 U.S. 319 (1976), balancing test.

E. **How much process is due?** The more severe the deprivation, the more process likely will be due. This means that the more severe deprivations will be accorded greater notice and more formal hearings.

■ PROBLEMS ■

Problem #1: A concerned parent sought to civilly commit her 11-year-old son due to his troubling behavior. The behavior included hallucinations, severe bouts of depression, and manic phases where the child would sit and sing and yell for hours on end. The state law permitted immediate commitment by parents for up to 6 months, with medical reviews and informal hearings every six months thereafter. The son, through a guardian appointed by the court, challenged the law. Is the law constitutional?

Answer: This commitment is subject to procedural due process safeguards. Since a state is acting, the Fourteenth Amendment due process clause applies. Step #1 asks whether a life, liberty, or property interest has been deprived. Here, the child has been deprived of his freedom, a liberty interest, since he was involuntarily committed. (There are also voluntary commitments. These commitments do not garner the same safeguards.) Step #2 asks what process is due. Applying the *Mathews* balancing test, the child's interests, the state's interests and the likelihood of error need to be weighed against each other. In the Supreme Court case based on similar facts, *Parham v. J.R.*, 442 U.S. 584 (1979), the Court held that an independent and neutral fact-finder was required to evaluate the child's mental and emotional condition, the need for treatment and whether the statutory admission requirements have been met. The Court further required an interview with the child.

Problem #2: Arnold separated from his wife and both moved out of their marital home. Arnold kept the house in the settlement, paid off the mortgage, and rented it. The renters left after one year. Arnold then paid off the mortgage. The taxes were no longer being paid, however, and the city sent a certified letter saying the property was going to be sold in a tax sale. The letter was returned "unclaimed" because no one was at the house to sign for it and no one picked it up at the post office within two weeks. If the city proceeds with the sale, and Arnold sues the city, claiming his property was being taken without due process of law, should Arnold win?

Answer: Arnold is complaining about a state actor, thus the Fourteenth Amendment due process clause applies. Step #1 is not the pivotal question, because it is clear that the state is depriving Arnold of his property interest in his house. The real issue lies in Step #2, which asks the question, what process is due? The initial inquiry here, whether there was sufficient notice, was the focus of the Supreme Court case based loosely on these same facts, *Jones v. Flowers*, 547 U.S. 220 (2006). In *Jones*, the Court stated that notice is sufficient for the purposes of procedural due process if it is reasonably calculated to reach the intended recipient. A returned letter could simply be due to bad timing and the state can use other forms of notice, such as signage, reasonably calculated to give actual notice. Thus, a state generally must go further when a mailed notice of a tax sale is returned unclaimed. But note that the additional reasonable steps are tempered by what is practicable.

Problem #3: Shakira Sandoval, a 7th grade student at Parton Public School in Los Angeles, was suspended for 9 days for talking back to a teacher. The procedure at the school was to permit immediate suspension, "followed by a mailed statement of the reasons to the student's parents." After half of the suspension has been served, the student can seek to have the remainder voided through a conference with the principal or assistant principal." Is this procedural scheme constitutional?

Answer: When a school suspends students, procedural due process issues are raised. Because the suspension here was in a state school, the 14th Amendment due process clause applies. Step #1 asks whether the government has deprived a person of a life, liberty, or property interest. Here, the student Shakira was deprived of a property interest because, as the Supreme Court in *Goss v. Lopez*, 419 U.S. 565 (1975), held, students have a legitimate claim of entitlement to a public school education. Thus, suspensions or expulsions trigger due process. Step #2 asks what process is due. The Court in *Goss* found that oral or written notice of the specific grounds are required, and must occur relatively quickly. If the student denies the school's contentions, the student will then have the opportunity to present her side of the story in what might be called an informal hearing setting. This opportunity need not be accorded any time for preparation, but just must offer a fair opportunity for rebuttal. In this case, because of the delay, the officials probably violated the student's due process rights.

POINTS TO REMEMBER

- There are two due process clauses, one in the Fifth Amendment that limits the federal government and one in the Fourteenth Amendment that limits states.
- The two clauses are identical and operate in the same way.
- The procedural due process limit applies mostly to adjudicative determinations and not broad legislative determinations.
- The test for procedural due process has two analytical steps, whether there is a government deprivation of life, liberty, or property and, if so, what process is due.
- The process that is due is determined by a balancing test and is usually some form of notice and/or a hearing.

CHAPTER 7

Substantive Protection of Economic Rights

Over the course of the nation's history, there has been much debate about whether, and to what extent, economic interests warrant constitutional protection. *See Calder v. Bull*, 3 U.S. (3 Dall.) 386 (1798). Nevertheless, during the early years, the Court rarely overturned governmental actions on economic grounds. During the period before the Bill of Rights applied to the states, review came, if at all, through the contract clause. It was not until the Court's holding in *Dred Scott v. Sandford*, 60 U.S. (19 How.) 393 (1856), that the Court applied substantive due process to issues involving economic rights and liberties. As Chief Justice Roger B. Taney said, "the right of property in a slave is distinctly and expressly affirmed in the Constitution. And, federal legislation depriving a citizen of 'his property in[ ] a particular Territory . . . could hardly be dignified with the name due process of law."

With the eventual rejection of *Dred Scott* by war, economic rights theory gained increasing currency as the latter half of the nineteenth century progressed. In the *Slaughter-House Cases*, 83 U.S. (16 Wall.) 36 (1872), Justice Field did not command a majority of the Court, but argued that "the right to acquire and possess property of every kind" was a matter which "of right belong[s] to the citizens of all free governments." Nevertheless, in *Allgeyer v. Louisiana*, 165 U.S. 578 (1897), the Court embraced the due process clause as the basis for: "the right of the citizen to be free in the enjoyment of all his faculties; to be free to use them in all lawful ways; to live and work where he will; to earn his livelihood by any lawful calling; to pursue any livelihood or avocation; and for that purpose to enter into all contracts which may be proper, necessary and essential to his carrying out to a successful conclusion the purposes above mentioned."

There has always been tension between the right to economic freedom and the police powers possessed by state and federal governments. These "police power" regulations (a/k/a "health and welfare regulations") are imposed to protect the health, welfare, safety, and morals of society. For example, a legislature might limit the number of hours that employees can work or mandate minimum compensation for employees. Alternatively, a legislature might place conditions on the ability of out-of-state companies to do business within the state, or choose to prohibit certain types of businesses (*e.g.*, gambling establishments).

Regulations enacted under the police power might be challenged on any number of constitutional grounds including the contract clause, the protection for liberty contained in the Fourteenth Amendment, the equal protection clause, and sometimes the privileges and immunities clause. For example, in *Allgeyer*, the Court struck down a state law that prohibited foreign insurance companies from doing business in the state without a license and without retaining an agent authorized to conduct business on its behalf: "[T]he statute is a violation of the fourteenth amendment of the federal constitution, in that it deprives the defendants of their liberty without due process of law. . . . The 'liberty' mentioned in that amendment means, not only the right of the citizen to be free from the mere physical restraint of his person, as by incarceration, but the term is deemed to embrace the right of the citizen to be free in the enjoyment of all his faculties; to be free to use them in all lawful ways; to live and work where he will; to earn his livelihood by any lawful calling; to pursue any livelihood or avocation; and for that purpose to enter into all contracts which may be proper, necessary, and essential to his carrying out to a successful conclusion the purposes above mentioned."

Inevitably, substantive due process cases raise questions regarding the scope of judicial review, especially regarding whether the judiciary should be deferential to legislative judgments or should engage in a more independent review process. Ordinarily, in reviewing legislation under the due process clause, the Court invokes means-ends analysis which requires a reviewing court to examine the "end" that the legislature is seeking to accomplish, and the "means" by which the legislature is seeking to accomplish it. At times, the Court has reviewed the means and ends of legislation more closely than at other times.

The high-point of substantive due process review, as applied to economic regulation, involved the Court's decision in *Lochner v. New York*, 198 U.S. 45 (1905). In that case, the Court struck down a New York law that prohibited bakers from working more than sixty hours in a single week. In what is regarded as a classic example of the Court substituting its judgment for that of the legislature, the Court said the law was an infringement of the bakers' right to contract. The Court rejected the notion that the law could be sustained as a "fair, reasonable, and appropriate exercise of the police power of the state," noting that the legislature had "no reasonable ground for interfering with the liberty of person or the right of free contract, by determining the hours of labor, in the occupation of a baker." The Court regarded statutes of this nature as "mere meddlesome interferences with the rights of the individual, and they are not saved from condemnation by the claim that they are passed in the exercise of the police power and upon the subject of the health of the individual whose rights are interfered with, unless there be some fair ground, reasonable in and of itself, to say that there is material danger to the public health, or to the health of the employees, if the hours of labor are not curtailed." In *Lochner*, the Court took the right to contract much more seriously, and was less willing to allow the government to interfere with that right. The Court had much more of a *laissez faire* philosophy regarding government's relationship with the individual.

By the mid-1930s, the Courts approach to substantive due process as applied to economic regulations was beginning to change. For example, in *Nebbia v. New York*, 291 U.S. 502 (1934), the Court upheld a New York law that established a milk control board with the power to establish minimum and maximum retail prices for milk as applied to Nebbia who sold below the stated price. In doing so, the Court recognized that contract rights are not absolute and can be regulated to further the common interest. Instead of the searching scrutiny involved in *Lochner*, the Court asked only whether the "end" to be accomplished was "unreasonable, arbitrary, or capricious," and whether the "means" used to achieve that objective bore "a real and substantial relation to the object sought to be attained." The Court held that the law "appears not to be unreasonable or arbitrary, or without relation to the purpose to prevent ruthless competition from destroying the wholesale price structure on which the farmer depends for his livelihood, and the community for an assured supply of milk." Ultimately, the Court was deferential to the legislative judgment.

This analysis of "means" and "ends" continues to be used today. In other words, the Court examines the "end" or "objective" that the legislature is seeking to accomplish, and also the "means" that it is using to accomplish that objective. However, the Court applies differing tests in this means-ends analysis depending on what it is reviewing. The three levels of review can be characterized as strict, intermediate, and low (generally called rational basis scrutiny). The Court applies the highest standard of review (*e.g.*, strict scrutiny) to only a limited number of situations. When strict scrutiny is applied, the governmental enactment is more likely to be struck down. On the other hand, the Court applies a "rational basis" test to most situations and the Court is more likely to sustain the enactment when using this test.

By the 1930s, following the constitutional crisis related to President Roosevelt's so-called Court-packing plan, the Court moved to a more deferential approach towards economic regulation. In *West Coast Hotel Co. v. Parrish*, 300 U.S. 379 (1937), the Court upheld a State of Washington law stipulating minimum wages for women and minors rejecting a contract clause claim. Likewise, in *Williamson v. Lee Optical*, 348 U.S. 483 (1955), the Court upheld an Oklahoma law that made it illegal for anyone except a licensed optometrist or ophthalmologist to fit lenses or to duplicate or replace frames lenses or other optical appliances, except upon written prescriptive authority of an Oklahoma licensed ophthalmologist or optometrist.

By 1938, the Court had adopted a very deferential approach to economic regulation. In *United States v. Carolene Products Co.*, 304 U.S. 144 (1938), the Court held that economic legislation should be upheld if "any state of facts either known or which could reasonably be assumed affords support for it." In deciding that case, the Court held that decisions about whether milk "should be left unregulated, or in some measure restricted, or wholly prohibited," was a "decision . . . for Congress, neither the finding of a court arrived at by weighing the evidence, nor the verdict of a jury can be substituted for it." However, the Court distinguished between economic rights and other rights, suggesting that it might apply a more rigorous review standard to some constitutional rights: "There may be narrower scope for operation of the presumption of constitutionality when legislation appears on its face to be within a specific prohibition of the Constitution, such as those of the first ten Amendments, which are deemed equally specific when held to be embraced within the Fourteenth." The Court went on to state that:

> It is unnecessary to consider now whether legislation which restricts those political processes which can ordinarily be expected to bring about repeal of undesirable legislation, is to be subjected to more exacting judicial scrutiny under the general prohibitions of the Fourteenth Amendment than are most other types of legislation. On restrictions upon the right to vote, on restraints upon the dissemination of information, on interferences with political organizations.
>
> Nor need we enquire whether similar considerations enter into the review of statutes directed at particular religious, or national, or racial minorities, whether prejudice against discrete and insular minorities may be a special condition, which tends seriously to curtail the operation of those political processes ordinarily to be relied upon to protect

minorities, and which may call for a correspondingly more searching judicial inquiry.

In subsequent cases, the Court has continued to state that it distinguishes between economic regulation, and legislation affecting such matters as the right to free speech, or equal protection claims involving denial of certain rights. As a result, in modern decisions, the Court has been less willing (than in *Lochner*) to use the Contract Clause to strike down general economic legislation, and has provided much greater protection for rights like the First Amendment right to freedom of speech.

The Takings Clause. The Fifth Amendment Takings Clause prohibits the government from taking private property for a public purpose without providing "just compensation." Two major issues arise under the Takings Clause. First, some litigants question whether their property is being taken for a "public purpose" (as opposed to a private purpose) and therefore argue that the taking is impermissible. Second, at times, there are disputes about whether there is a "taking" at all.

The Requirement of a "Public Use." In general, when litigants claim that a taking is not for a "public purpose," the Court resolves that issue in favor of the government. For example, in *Hawaii Housing Authority v. Midkiff,* 467 U.S. 229 (1984), the State of Hawaii condemned private land to redistribute it. The Court sustained the law because its goal was to reduce the concentration of land ownership in Hawaii, and the Court found a "public use" in the purpose of eliminating the "social and economic evils of a land oligopoly." Likewise, in *Berman v. Parker*, 348 U.S. 26 (1954), the Court upheld a Washington, D.C., redevelopment plan that took property for redevelopment, and ultimately transferred it to other private interests. When a department store owner challenged the condemnation of its property, noting that his property was not blighted, and claiming that the goal of creating a "better balanced, more attractive community' was not a 'valid public use,' " the Court disagreed noting that the redevelopment plan was designed to serve the public good, and that the plan must include the entire area to achieve its objectives.

One of the more controversial decisions in modern times is *Kelo v. City of New London*, 545 U.S. 469 (2005), which involved a city's redevelopment plan that took private property (houses) in order to redevelop and eliminate blight in particular parts of the city. A homeowner whose property was not blighted sought to challenge the taking as not for a private purpose. The Court disagreed and upheld the government's power to take one person's private property and transfer it to another private person in pursuit of the public interest.

Although *Kelo* rejected the challenge, it restated the fundamental proposition that the government may not take property, solely for the purpose of transferring it to another private party, even if the government is willing to pay just compensation for the property. But, since the New London development plan focused on "redevelopment," the Court found a "public purpose" even though the entire piece of property would not be open to the general public. The Court also suggested that it normally gives deference to legislative judgments on takings issues.

The Definition of a "Taking." A taking clearly occurs when the government condemns a person's property and assumes title to it, as well as when the government occupies the property for its own purposes (whether temporarily or permanently). As the Court stated in *Pennsylvania Coal Co. v. Mahon,* 260 U.S. 393 (1922), a taking occurs "when the state makes a 'direct appropriation' of property, or the functional equivalent of a '*practical ouster* of [the owner's] possession.'" In *United States v. Causby*, 328 U.S. 256 (1946), the Court held that flights over the claimant's land constituted a taking because the government essentially appropriated the land as a flight path and destroyed the present use of the land as a chicken farm.

Many Takings Clause cases do not involve a literal "taking" in the sense of an acquisition, but instead involve land use or zoning restrictions imposed by government for the greater public good. As a result, many cases involve whether government can regulate property use without paying the property owner for any diminution in property value resulting from the regulation. In *Goldblatt v. Hempstead*, 369 U.S. 590 (1962), the Court held that no taking occurred when a city safety ordinance banned excavations below the level of the water table because the taking was designed to effect a "substantial public purpose" (protection of surrounding properties). Further, the city ordinance did not have an unduly harsh impact upon the value of the property (even though the regulation effectively terminated claimant's sand and gravel mining business that had been in operation for forty years), and did not prevent other reasonable uses of the property. In *Pennsylvania Coal Co. v. Mahon,* 260 U.S. 393 (1922), the Court held that a state statute that substantially furthers important public policies may so frustrate distinct investment-backed expectations as to amount to a "taking." In that case, the claimant sold the surface rights to particular parcels of property, but reserved the right to remove coal underneath the land. When Pennsylvania passed a law that prohibited the mining of coal that would cause the subsidence of a house not owned by the owner of the underlying coal, thereby making it commercially impracticable to mine the coal, the Court concluded that the law effectively destroyed the "rights claimant had reserved from the owners of the surface land" and therefore involved a taking which required compensation.

In some cases, even though there is a significant impact on property, no compensation is required. In *Miller v. Schoene*, 276 U.S. 272 (1928), the Court held that a state statute providing for the destruction of cedar trees infected with blight did not require compensation. The Court held that "the state does not exceed its constitutional powers by deciding upon the destruction of one class of property in order to save another which, in the judgment of the legislature, is of greater value to the public." Likewise, in *Block v. Hirsh,* 256 U.S. 135 (1921), the Court upheld a Washington, D.C., rent control law that limited the amount that landlords could charge tenants. The Court concluded a "public exigency" could justify restricting property rights in land to a certain extent without compensation.

In other decisions, the Court has broadly construed the concept of a taking. In *United States v. General Motors Corp.*, 323 U.S. 373 (1945), the Court indicated that the concept of "property" should be broadly defined: property refers to the entire "group of rights inhering in the citizen's relation to the physical thing, as the right to possess, use and dispose of it. . . . The constitutional provision is addressed to every sort of interest the citizen may possess."

In *Penn Central Transportation Company v. City of New York*, 438 U.S. 104 (1978), the Court provided guidance regarding the scope of permissible regulatory takings. In its decision, the Court upheld a New York law designed to protect historic landmarks. Under the law, the City did not acquire the landmarks, but did prohibit modifications without governmental approval. When the law was applied to prevent the owners of the Grand Central Terminal from constructing a multi-story office tower over the station, the owners sued, claiming that their property had been taken without compensation. The Court disagreed, emphasizing that the objective of the takings clause was to ensure that the government did not force "some people alone to bear public burdens which, in all fairness and justice, should be borne by the public as a whole." In determining whether there was a taking, the Court indicated that it would consider various factors, including the economic impact of the regulation on the claimant, the extent to which the regulation interferes with distinct investment-backed expectations, and the character of the governmental action with a "physical invasion" more likely to be considered a taking than an "interference [that] arises from some public program adjusting the benefits and burdens of economic life to promote the common good." But the Court recognized that government could not function if it were required to pay compensation every time it made a change in its general regulatory law, and the Court held that government could promote "the health, safety, morals, or general welfare" by prohibiting particular uses of land even though those regulations destroy or adversely affect recognized real property interests. The Court offered the example of local zoning laws which are permissible even though they may prohibit "the most beneficial use of the property."

After the *Penn Central* decision, questions remained about the nature and extent of limits to the government's authority to regulate land use. At some point, would a regulation be deemed to have gone too far so that compensation would be required? The Court provided a partial answer to this question in *Lucas v. South Carolina Coastal Council*, 505 U.S. 1003 (1992), in which the Court held that a regulation which deprives a landowner of all "economically beneficial uses" of his property qualifies as a taking. In evaluating whether a property owner has been deprived of all economically beneficial uses, so that there has been a "total taking," courts should consider a variety of factors including the following: "the degree of harm to public lands and resources, or adjacent private property, posed by the claimant's proposed activities, the social value of the claimant's activities and their suitability to the locality in question, and the relative ease with which the alleged harm can be avoided through measures taken by the claimant and the government (or adjacent private landowners) alike." In general, if a use has been permitted for a long time, and especially if it is engaged in by similarly situated landowners, it must generally be considered permissible absent changed circumstances. Moreover, the Court concluded that South Carolina could not prevail merely by showing that "the uses Lucas desires are inconsistent with the public interest." The state must, instead, prove that Lucas' activity was enjoinable in a common-law action for public nuisance.

The *Lucas* Court qualified its holding by suggesting that a taking does not occur, even when all economically beneficial uses are prohibited, if "the nature of the owner's estate shows that the proscribed use interests were not part of his title to begin with." In other words, the governmentally imposed limitation "must inhere in the title itself, in the restrictions that background principles of the State's law of property and nuisance already place upon land ownership." If the regulation is one that could have been imposed anyway, for example under nuisance laws, then no compensation is required. The Court offered the example of a lake-bed owner who could be denied a permit to fill-in the lake on the ground that nearby landowners would suffer flooding. Likewise, the owner of a nuclear generating plant could be ordered to cease operations "upon discovery that the plant sits astride an earthquake fault." In such situations, even if a regulation prohibits all economically productive uses, they do "not proscribe a productive use that was previously permissible under relevant property and nuisance principles."

The Court distinguished *Lucas* in *Tahoe-Sierra Preservation Council v. Tahoe Regional Planning Agency*, 535 U.S. 302 (2002), in upholding a moratorium on land development during the creation of a master land use plan. Even though the moratorium arguably imposed a denial of all economically beneficial uses during the period of the moratorium, and even though the moratorium lasted for a considerable period of time, the Court held that there was no taking. The Court suggested that a temporary denial of use might not constitute a taking because property "cannot be rendered valueless by a temporary prohibition on economic use," because "the property will recover value as soon as the prohibition is lifted." In addition, the Court was reluctant to find a taking from the "normal delays in obtaining building permits, changes in zoning ordinances, variances, and the like," or from "orders temporarily prohibiting access to crime scenes, businesses that violate health codes, fire-damaged buildings." If these actions were construed as takings, the Court feared that it might render "routine government processes prohibitively expensive or encourag[ing] hasty decision-making." Moreover, the Court emphasized that moratoria are widely used by land-use planners to preserve the status quo while formulating comprehensive development plans. In *Tahoe-Sierra Preservation Council*, the Court held that the government can impose a moratorium as a "tool" in the planning process, but the Court also emphasized that the moratorium was imposed for a limited period of time. Despite the holding, a number of justices would have required compensation even for a moratorium.

The Supreme Court has wrestled with the question of what constitutes a taking over the past century and still does not have clarity today on what constitutes a taking under the Fifth and Fourteenth Amendments. In *Murr v. Wisconsin*, 582 U.S. 383 (2017), the Supreme Court considered whether a state law limiting the sale or improvement of a 'substandard' sized lot—and effectively merging two lots into one—constitutes a regulatory taking. The Court focused on what ought to be considered the proper 'denominator,' meaning the land serving as the basis for comparison against what was alleged to have been taken by the government. In the end, the Court reasoned it was appropriate to merge the two lots and treat them as one. It then concluded that the law as applied to petitioner's vacant residential lot was a reasonable regulation and thus not a taking.

The opaqueness of the Court's approach extends to the question of when to apply a Penn Central "multi-factorial" analysis for a regulatory taking or a bright line test for a per se physical taking. In *Cedar Point Nursery v. Hassid,* 594 U.S. 139 (2021), the Court addressed a California law providing unions with access to an employer's land at certain times and days during the year. The Court held that the law constituted a per se physical taking requiring compensation.

Some regulatory takings litigation has focused on whether the government can impose restrictions as part of the process for obtaining permits. For example, in *Nollan v. California Coastal Commission,* 483 U.S. 825 (1987), the Court found a taking when California's Coastal Commission approved an application to demolish a small old oceanfront home and build a new one on condition that the owners create a public easement across their oceanfront property. Although a land-use regulation does not involve a taking if it "substantially advance[s] legitimate state interests" and does not "den[y] an owner economically viable use of his land," the Court found that the Commission's asserted purposes (protecting the public's ability to see the beach, assisting the public in overcoming the "psychological barrier" to using the beach created by a developed shorefront, and preventing congestion on the public beaches) were valid, but that the condition must be related to those objectives. Likewise, in *Dolan v. Tigard,* 512 U.S. 374 (1994), the Court struck down a requirement that the plaintiff must dedicate portions of her property for a public greenway as a condition of obtaining a building permit.

Procedural Issues. Other Takings litigation has focused on procedural issues. In *Knick v. Township of Scott, Pennsylvania,* 588 U.S. 180 (2019), for example, the court considered the validity of a requirement that a takings claimant first litigate in state court, despite the fact that if the claimant loses, they are precluded from bringing a claim thereafter in federal court. The Supreme Court found that such a litigative requirement "imposes an unjustifiable burden on takings plaintiffs, conflicts with the rest of our takings jurisprudence, and must be overruled." Notably, the Court held that a property owner has a takings claim and can sue at the time the government takes his property without paying for it, regardless of the post-taking remedies available. In essence, compensation for a taking can be given after the fact, not necessarily at that exact time of the taking.

Another procedural issue is whether the Takings Clause is self-effectuating or needs state law to provide a remedy. In *Deviller v. Texas*, 601 U.S. 285 (2024), petitioner claimed there was no Takings cause of action authorized in Texas, and argued that the Constitution itself authorized suit. The Court did not have to reach the issue, however, finding instead that Texas did in fact authorize a Takings cause of action. The Court consequently remanded the case to allow the litigants to proceed under the state law.

The Contracts Clause. Prior to *Lochner*, which articulated the concept of substantive due process as applied to contracts, constitutional protection of contractual interests was grounded in the contracts clause which prohibits states from enacting any "Law impairing the Obligation of Contracts."

The contracts clause specifically applies only to existing (rather than future) contracts. The clause was a response to a history of debtors seeking legislative relief from their debts despite existing contractual obligations. There was a concern that these legislative relief provisions undermined the "confidence essential to prosperous trade" and threatened the "utter destruction of credit." *Home Building & Loan Association v. Blaisdell*, 290 U.S. 398, 427 (1934).

In *Fletcher v. Peck*, 10 U.S. (6 Cranch) 87 (1810), the Court overturned the Georgia legislature's rescission of a land grant that had been tainted by bribery and fraud. When the law was challenged by persons who acquired land in the aftermarket, and claimed they were purchasers in due course, the Court relied on the contracts clause and principles of natural law to overturn the rescission. In later cases, the Court has upheld state prohibitions on the sale of beer or lottery tickets even though both activities were previously valid.

The Court's present interpretation of the Contracts Clause is reflected in *Home Building & Loan Association v. Blaisdell*, 290 U.S. 398 (1934). In that case, the Court upheld Minnesota's Mortgage Moratorium Law which gave Minnesota courts the power to impose moratoria on mortgage foreclosures provided that the mortgagor paid the reasonable rental value of the property. After concluding that the contracts clause does not impose an absolute ban on impairments of contractual obligations, the Court held that impairments should be evaluated in light of "whether the legislation is addressed to a legitimate end and the measures taken are reasonable and appropriate to that end." In upholding the Minnesota act, the Court noted that the legislation was motivated by a desire to provide temporary relief in order "to protect the vital interests of the community" during a period of economic distress, and that the relief was appropriate to the emergency. "[T]he integrity of the mortgage indebtedness is not impaired; interest continues to run; the validity of the sale and the right of a mortgagee-purchaser to title or to obtain a deficiency judgment, if the mortgagor fails to redeem within the extended period, are maintained; and the conditions of redemption, if redemption there be, stand as they were under the prior law." Although the mortgagor could keep possession of the property during the moratorium, he was required to pay the rental value of the premises as determined by a judge. The Court also noted that the mortgagees were primarily corporations, rather than small investors, whose principal interest was in the "reasonable protection of their investment security." The Court felt that this interest was reasonably protected. In addition, the relief was temporary.

Nevertheless, there are limits to the scope of legislative authority to impair contracts. In *Allied Structural Steel Company v. Spannaus,* 438 U.S. 234 (1978), the Court struck down a state's attempt to alter a company's pension obligations. Prior to the passage of the Act, Allied Structural Steel Co. (Allied) created a pension plan for its salaried employees, and made annual contributions to the fund. Although the contributions were not revocable, the plan did not require the company to make specific contributions or impose any sanction for failing to adequately fund the plan. An employee who did not die, quit or be fired prior to meeting the plan requirements would receive a fixed pension at age 65 if the company remained in business and elected to continue the pension plan in its existing form. The Act altered the company's obligations by providing that a private employer with 100 or more employees (and at least one Minnesota resident) who provided a qualified pension plan was subject to a "pension funding charge" if it terminated the plan or closed a Minnesota office. The charge was assessed if the pension funds were not sufficient to cover full pensions for all employees who had worked at least 10 years. The State sought to apply the charge to Allied when it closed its plant and there were unvested employees. The Court found that this "severe disruption of contractual expectations was necessary to meet an important general social problem" akin to the "broad and desperate emergency economic conditions of the early 1930's." In concluding that the contracts clause prohibited the charge, the Court focused on whether the PPBPA "operated as a substantial impairment of a contractual relationship," and was troubled by the Act because Allied set aside the amount required each year for its plan, as required by the plan and by the federal tax laws, and it did not expect that employee's rights would "vest" except in accordance with the plan. The Act had a "severe impact" because it altered a "basic term of the pension contract" and required a substantial infusion of cash ($185,000) on the closing of Allied's offices. This liability was completely unexpected.

In evaluating contractual impairments, the Court balances the severity of the impairment against the governmental interest. In *Exxon Corp. v. Eagerton,* 462 U.S. 176 (1983), the Court upheld a state law that prohibited oil and gas producers from passing severance taxes on to customers. The law was applied to contracts entered into before the Act even though those contracts required reimbursement for severance taxes. The Court held that the Contracts Clause is not violated simply because a statute restricts, or even bars, the performance of duties created by contracts entered into prior to its enactment. Despite the "broad societal interest" in protecting consumers from excessive prices, the Court concluded that the anti-pass through law was distinguishable from the law struck down in *Spannaus*. In *Block v. Hirsh*, 256 U.S. 135 (1921), the Court upheld a Washington, D.C., rent control law despite claims that tenants were allowed to remain in possession at the same rent that they had been paying, thereby interfering with the landlord's right "to do what he will with his own and to make what contracts he pleases." In upholding the law, the Court noted that it was a temporary measure, designed to deal with a passing emergency, and that landlords were assured of a "reasonable rent" considering the large influx of potential tenants into the market and the government's desire to prevent "unjust profits."

CHECKLIST

A. There has been much debate about whether, and to what extent, economic interests warrant constitutional protection.

   1. There has always been tension between the right to economic freedom and the police powers possessed by state and federal governments.

   2. These "police power" regulations (a/k/a "health and welfare regulations") are imposed to protect the health, welfare, safety, and morals of society.

   3. Regulations enacted under the police power might be challenged on any number of constitutional grounds including the contracts clause, the protection for liberty contained in the Fourteenth Amendment, the equal protection clause, and sometimes the privileges and immunities clause.

   4. Substantive due process cases raise questions regarding the scope of judicial review, especially regarding whether the judiciary should be deferential to legislative judgments or should engage in a more independent review process.

5. Ordinarily, in reviewing legislation under the due process clause, the Court invokes means-ends analysis which requires a reviewing court to examine the "end" that the legislature is seeking to accomplish, and the "means" by which the legislature is seeking to accomplish it. At times, the Court has reviewed the means and ends of legislation more closely than at other times.

B. The high-point of substantive due process review, as applied to economic regulation, is reflected in the decision in *Lochner v. New York*, 198 U.S. 45 (1905).

C. By the mid-1930s, the Courts approach to substantive due process as applied to economic regulations was beginning to change.

1. By 1938, the Court had adopted a very deferential approach to economic regulation.

2. In *United States v. Carolene Products Co.*, 304 U.S. 144 (1938), the Court held that economic legislation should be upheld if "any state of facts either known or which could reasonably be assumed affords support for it."

3. *Carolene* distinguished between economic rights and other rights, suggesting that the Court might apply a more rigorous review standard to some constitutional rights such as the Bill of Rights, those included in the first ten Amendments, which are deemed equally specific when held to be embraced within the Fourteenth.

4. As a result, in modern decisions, the Court has been less willing (than in *Lochner*) to use the Contract Clause to strike down general economic legislation. The Court has provided much greater protection for rights like the First Amendment right to freedom of speech.

D. The Fifth Amendment Takings Clause prohibits the government from taking private property for a public purpose without providing "just compensation."

1. In general, when litigants claim that a taking is not for a "public purpose," the Court resolves that issue in favor of the government.

2. The Court has even allowed governments to take private property for redevelopment, and to transfer it to private parties.

3. A taking clearly occurs when the government condemns a person's property and assumes title to it, as well as when

the government occupies the property for its own purposes (whether temporarily or permanently).

4. Many taking cases do not involve a literal "taking" in the sense of an acquisition, but instead involve land use or zoning restrictions that are imposed for the greater public good.

5. Many cases involve the question of whether the government can regulate property use without paying the property owner for the diminished value of the property.

6. In *Penn Central Transportation Company v. City of New York*, 438 U.S. 104 (1978), the Court recognized that government could not function if it were required to pay compensation every time it made a change in its general regulatory law, and the Court held that government could promote "the health, safety, morals, or general welfare" by prohibiting particular uses of land even though those regulations adversely affect recognized real property interests.

7. In *Lucas v. South Carolina Coastal Council*, 505 U.S. 1003 (1992), the Court held that a regulation which deprives a landowner of all "economically beneficial uses" of his property qualifies as a taking.

8. The *Lucas* Court qualified its holding by suggesting that a taking does not occur, even when all economically beneficial uses are prohibited, if "the nature of the owner's estate shows that the proscribed use interests were not part of his title to begin with." In other words, the governmentally imposed limitation "must inhere in the title itself, in the restrictions that background principles of the State's law of property and nuisance already place upon land ownership."

9. In *Tahoe-Sierra Preservation Council v. Tahoe Regional Planning Agency*, 535 U.S. 302 (2002), the Court upheld a moratorium on land development during the creation of a master land use plan.

10. In *Nollan v. California Coastal Commission*, 483 U.S. 825 (1987), the Court found a taking when California's Coastal Commission approved an application to demolish a small old oceanfront home and build a new one on condition that the owners create a public easement across their oceanfront property.

E. Constitutional protection of contractual interests is grounded in the contracts clause which prohibits states from enacting any "Law impairing the Obligation of Contracts."

1. The clause specifically applies only to existing (rather than future) contracts.
2. The clause was a response to a history of debtors seeking legislative relief from their debts despite existing contractual obligations. There was a concern that these legislative relief provisions undermined the "confidence essential to prosperous trade" and threatened the "utter destruction of credit." *Home Building & Loan Association v. Blaisdell*, 290 U.S. 398, 427 (1934).
3. In resolving contracts clause cases, the Court evaluates impairments in light of "whether the legislation is addressed to a legitimate end and the measures taken are reasonable and appropriate to that end."
4. In *Allied Structural Steel Company v. Spannaus,* 438 U.S. 234 (1978), the Court struck down a state's attempt to alter a company's pension obligations that interfered with settled expectations.

■ PROBLEMS ■

Problem #1: The nation enters a severe economic downturn with lots of people out of work and unable to make their mortgage payments. As a result, foreclosure rates spike to near those of the Depression Era. Congress and the states pass economic stimulus packages, all to no avail. In an effort to relieve the burden on society, the Commonwealth of Kentucky passes a law providing for debtor relief. Under the terms of the law, all debtors are granted a one year moratorium on the payment of their mortgages. During this time, no interest will accrue on the principal balance, and the mortgages will be treated as if the payments had been made. Is the Kentucky law constitutional?

Answer: No. Although the Court upheld a "mortgage moratorium" in *Blaisdell*, the Court emphasized several things about the moratorium. First, the debtors were required to pay rent during the period of the moratorium. Second, mortgage interest continued to accrue. Third, the principal balance of the mortgage was not adversely affected (in the long run). The Kentucky law is more objectionable because the debtors are not required to pay rent, interest does not accrue, and the creditors never receive the payments for the moratorium year. Under the rule of reasonableness, this law is probably unconstitutional.

Problem #2: The Louisville International Airport (LIA) recently built a new runway that has planes taking off and landing directly over plaintiff's property. Because LIA has a United Parcel Service distribution center, planes take off and land at all hours of the night (UPS provides an overnight service and planes are landing and taking off in early morning hours). Because of the flights, plaintiff and his family are unable to sleep as planes rumble over their house all night long. Indeed, the roar is deafening. Plaintiff claims that LIA has taken his property and demands compensation. LIA defends on the theory that it has not "taken" anything since plaintiff remains in possession of the property. Is there a taking?

Answer: Yes. A taking, for due process purposes, can be actual or constructive. Had LIA decided to condemn the property and take title to it, there would clearly have been a taking. A taking can also occur when someone is constructively evicted from property, or the government creates a substantial interference. In this case, the interference is so substantial as to be regarded as a taking for purposes of the takings clause.

POINTS TO REMEMBER

- There has been much debate about whether, and to what extent, economic interests warrant constitutional protection.
- There has always been tension between the right to economic freedom and the powers possessed by state and federal governments. The state "police power" regulations (a/k/a "health and welfare regulations"), in particular, are imposed to protect the health, welfare, safety, and morals of society.
- The high-point of substantive due process review, as applied to economic regulation, involved the Court's decision in *Lochner v. New York*.
- In evaluating the constitutionality of an enactment, the Court considers both the "means" and the "ends." In other words, the Court examines the "end" or "objective" that the legislature is seeking to accomplish, and the "means" that it is using to accomplish that objective.
- However, the Court applies differing levels of review to this means-ends analysis depending on the nature of the interest involved.

- Since the 1930s, the Court has used a very deferential approach to laws imposing economic regulation (as contrasted with fundamental rights such as free speech).
- The Fifth Amendment Takings Clause prohibits the government from taking private property for a public purpose without providing "just compensation."
- In general, when litigants claim that a taking is not for a "public purpose," the Court resolves that issue in favor of the government.
- A taking clearly occurs when the government condemns a person's property and assumes title to it, as well as when the government occupies the property for its own purposes (whether temporarily or permanently).
- Many taking cases do not involve a literal "taking" in the sense of an acquisition, but instead involve land use or zoning restrictions that are imposed for the greater public good.
- In general, governmental attempts to regulate property do not require the payment of compensation.
- A regulation that deprives a landowner of all "economically beneficial uses" of his property qualifies as a taking.
- However, a state can impose a moratorium on development (for planning purposes) without creating a taking.
- Government does not have unfettered discretion to impose restrictions or exactions as part of its permitting process.
- The Contracts Clause specifically applies only to existing (rather than future) contracts.
- The Contracts Clause does not prohibit all impairments of contract, but only unreasonable impairments.
- Impairments are more likely to be invalid when they upset settled expectations.

CHAPTER 8

Substantive Due Process: Modern Fundamental Rights

Despite its controversial history, the due process clause emerged in the final decades of the twentieth century as the basis for the right of privacy. This right has several dimensions to it, including a woman's liberty to elect an abortion, the right to marry, the right of a family to live together, the right to refuse medical treatment necessary to sustain life, and aspects of reproductive autonomy.

In *United States v. Carolene Products Co.*, 304 U.S. 144, 154 n. 4 (1938), the Court appeared to back off its use of the due process clause as a source of fundamental rights. Several decades later, however, it announced that a woman's liberty to elect an abortion was grounded in that provision. This development reignited the debate over the role of the judiciary, as critics maintain such decision-making is anti-democratic. Proponents maintain that the Bill of Rights is not an exhaustive listing of fundamental rights, and that substantive due process review thus is a legitimate exercise of judicial power.

The Court's decision-making reflects sensitivity to the negative legacy of early fundamental rights doctrine and an effort to control the risk of subjectivism. Modern exponents argue that the analytical process is tighter and better controlled. In this regard, identification of a fundamental right hinges upon whether it is perceived as "implicit in the concept of ordered liberty" or "rooted in the Nation's traditions and history." Detractors, however, maintain that these guidelines are too loose to protect against subjective outcomes.

Incorporation. The due process clause is the means by which provisions of the Bill of Rights are applied to the states. The Bill of Rights, as originally structured and construed, operated only against the federal government. *Barron v. Baltimore,* 32 U.S. 243 (1833). Adoption of the Fourteenth Amendment altered this understanding.

The path toward the due process clause as the basis for identifying fundamental rights, however, was somewhat convoluted. Incorporation initially was proposed through the privileges and immunities clause of the Fourteenth Amendment. The Court foreclosed this possibility in the *Slaughter-House Cases,* 83 U.S. (16 Wall.) 36 (1872). Although the privileges and immunities clause may have been the more logical basis for fundamental rights development, the Court eventually embraced the due process clause for this purpose. Early due process review regarded the "liberty" component of the due process clause as an independent source of fundamental rights and liberties. Many of these judicially identified rights and liberties paralleled provisions of the Bill of Rights and thus their identification had the same effect as incorporation.

The incorporation model was heralded in *United States v. Carolene Products Co.,* 304 U.S. 144, 154 n. 4 (1938), when the Court held that the Fourteenth Amendment was not an independent source of rights or liberties but a channel through which provisions of the Bill of Rights might be incorporated. Using this premise in *Palko v. Connecticut,* 302 U.S. 319 (1937), the Court found that the double jeopardy clause was not incorporated through the Fourteenth Amendment. In so doing, it introduced two key incorporation criteria. Determination of whether a right is fundamental thus turned upon whether (1) it was "of the very essence of a scheme of ordered liberty" and (2) its denial would violate a "principle of justice so rooted in the traditions and conscience of our people as to be ranked as fundamental."

In *Adamson v. California,* 332 U.S. 46 (1947), the Court embraced the principle of selective incorporation of the Bill of Rights, and rejected the idea of total incorporation. Pursuant to the selective incorporation model, the Court must determine on a clause-by-clause basis whether a proposed right or liberty applies to the states. The Court thus rejected the concept of total incorporation that was grounded in an understanding that the Fourteenth Amendment made the entire Bill of Rights applicable to the states.

The incorporation process represented a major restructuring of constitutional doctrine. Insofar as most provisions of the Bill of Rights have been incorporated on a case-by-case basis, however, there are not many opportunities for future debate. The Court has determined that the Fifth Amendment grand jury clause and the Seventh Amendment guarantee of a jury trial in civil cases are not incorporated through the Fourteenth Amendment. The Court has decided that the Second Amendment guarantee of the right to bear arms is incorporated, but has not ruled on whether the Third Amendment prohibition against quartering soldiers in private homes is incorporated. The Court has held that incorporated provisions of the Bill of Rights apply with equal force to federal and state government.

The Right of Privacy—Seminal Developments. The text of the Constitution makes no reference to a general right of privacy. The Court has noted, however, that a "right of personal privacy, or a guarantee of certain areas or zones of privacy does exist under the Constitution" and traces back "perhaps as far as" late 19th Century case law. *Roe v. Wade,* 410 U.S. 113, 152 (1973). In this regard, the Court has referenced *Union Pacific R. Co. v. Botsford,* 141 U.S. 250, 251 (1891), which announced that "the right to one's person may be said to be a right of complete immunity: to be let alone." Harbingers of a broad privacy right also were present in *Meyer v. Nebraska,* 262 U.S. 390 (1923), when the Court struck down a state law requiring the use of English for instruction in public and private schools. Liberty as set forth in the due process clause thus included:

> not merely freedom from bodily restraint but also the right of the individual to contract, to engage in any of the common occupations of life, to acquire useful knowledge, to marry, establish a home and bring up children, to worship God according to the dictates of his own conscience, and generally to enjoy those privileges long recognized at common law as essential to the orderly pursuit of happiness by free men.

Similar reasoning guided the Court's decision in *Pierce v. Society of Sisters,* 268 U.S. 510 (1925), which struck down a state law requiring parents to send their children to public schools.

Development of fundamental rights as an incident of judicial review took a significant step forward in *Skinner v. Oklahoma,* 316 U.S. 535 (1942). The Court in that case invalidated a state law that mandated sterilization for habitual felons on grounds it burdened fundamental liberties of marriage and procreation. Although the decision was grounded in equal protection rather than due process, the analysis and outcome evidenced the Court's willingness to expand fundamental rights and liberties beyond specific constitutional enumerations.

Reproductive Freedom. The modern right of privacy emerged more clearly in *Griswold v. Connecticut,* 381 U.S. 479 (1965). That case involved a state law that criminalized the distribution of contraceptives. In striking down the enactment, the Court found that several provisions of the Bill of Rights established a protected zone of privacy. These provisions, created what the Court referred to as "penumbras" which included the First Amendment right of association, the Third Amendment guarantee forbidding government from quartering soldiers in private homes, the Fourth Amendment protection against unreasonable searches and seizures, the Fifth Amendment safeguard against self-incrimination, and the Ninth Amendment which reserves for the people rights that are not specifically enumerated by the Constitution. The resulting right of privacy thus extended to the "marriage relationship."

The ruling resurrected debate over the legitimacy of fundamental rights development by the Court. Justice Douglas maintained that the Court was not reverting back to the largely discredited economic rights model of the early twentieth century. Justice Black saw it differently, however, noting that neither the due process clause nor any other constitutional provision empowers the judiciary to substitute its opinion for that of the legislature merely because it disagrees with its wisdom. Justice Goldberg concurred with the majority but argued for basing the decision upon the Ninth Amendment. Justice Harlan favored using the due process clause.

In *Eisenstadt v. Baird,* 405 U.S. 438 (1972), the Court extended the right to use contraceptives to unmarried persons. That decision was based upon the equal protection clause. In *Carey v. Population Services International,* 431 U.S. 678 (1977), the Court invalidated a state law that prohibited the sale of contraceptives to persons under the age of 16 and allowed only pharmacists to sell them. It attributed to *Griswold* the notion "that the Constitution protects individual decisions in matters of childbearing from unjustified intrusion by the State."

Abortion. In 2022, the Supreme Court overturned the seminal abortion case, *Roe v. Wade,* 410 U.S. 113 (1973). While the fundamental right to choose to have an abortion first recognized in Roe had been narrowed over time since its recognition in 1973, *Dobbs v. Jackson's Women's Health Organization,* 597 U.S. 215 (2022) overruled both *Roe v. Wade* and its major progeny, *Planned Parenthood of Southeastern Pa. v. Casey,* 505 U.S. 883 (1992). It is important to observe that *Dobbs* did not outlaw abortion, but left abortion to be regulated by the states. On the federal and state levels after *Dobbs,* abortion regulations must be justified by rational basis scrutiny, the same scrutiny applied to other non-fundamental government regulation.

The 49-Year History of Roe *Leading up to* Dobbs.

At issue in *Roe* was a Texas law banning abortion unless the mother's life was in danger. The state viewed the fetus as a person and thus protected as a "life" interest under the due process clause of the Fourteenth Amendment. The Court, in an opinion authored by

Justice Blackmun, refused to embrace this premise for constitutional purposes and determined that the interest in electing an abortion was "implicit in the concept of ordered liberty." It acknowledged, however, that the right was not unqualified and must be balanced when the state identified sufficiently importance reasons for regulating the procedure. A state, for instance, might have legitimate interests in protecting a woman's health and the potential for life. Regulation for either of these purposes, however, must serve a compelling governmental interest and be narrowly tailored to the achievement of that objective.

The signature aspect of *Roe v. Wade* was the trimester framework that the Court created for balancing the competing concerns. During the first three months of pregnancy, when abortion is less risky to a woman's health than childbirth, the Court held that a state may not prohibit the procedure, but can regulate only to protect the mother's health. A state thus might impose a licensing requirement for abortion facilities or personnel. A woman's freedom over the course of the second trimester was left largely unrestricted. Beginning with the third trimester, the point at which the Court found that viability commenced, the state's interest in prohibiting abortion became compelling. Justice Rehnquist in dissent argued that, because most states banned abortion, the nation's traditions and history provided no support for the liberty. Justice White maintained that abortion was not within the Constitution's ambit of concern but a matter for the political process to resolve.

Through the late 1980s, and although divided, the Court held fast to *Roe v. Wade* and consistently struck down laws that imposed a significant burden upon this protected liberty interest. In *Doe v. Bolton,* 410 U.S. 179 (1973), it struck down provisions of a state law that created unique accreditation, authorization, and examination requirements as a prerequisite for performing abortions. The Court, in *Planned Parenthood v. Danforth,* 428 U.S. 52 (1976), rejected spousal consent and parental consent requirements for unmarried women under the age of 18. This outcome was driven by the understanding that, among all stakeholders, pregnancy most impacts the woman. The Court noted, however, that some minor children might not be able to provide effective consent. In *Planned Parenthood v. Ashcroft*, 462 U.S. 476 (1983), the Court thus upheld a parental consent or notification requirement provided that there was a judicial bypass option for the minor. If a minor seeks to bypass her parents, a court must determine that she is sufficiently mature to make the decision herself or that an abortion is in her best interest.

In *Akron v. Akron Center for Reproductive Health*, 462 U.S. 416 (1983), the Court viewed a panoply of limitations as impermissible roadblocks to a woman's freedom. At issue were provisions requiring physicians to provide information concerning the medical risks and morality of abortion, imposing a 24-hour waiting period, and requiring abortions after the first trimester to be performed in hospitals. The Court determined that these restrictions were unnecessarily and unduly burdensome. For similar reasons, the Court in *Thornburgh v. American College of Obstetricians and Gynecologists,* 476 U.S. 747 (1986), struck down a law requiring disclosure of referring and performing physicians and the patient and compelling the use of post-viability abortion procedures that maximized the possibility of fetal survival.

In *Webster v. Reproductive Health Services,* 492 U.S. 490 (1989), the Department of Justice joined with anti-abortion advocates and argued that *Roe v. Wade* created "an unworkable framework" and usurped the role of the legislature. At issue was a Missouri law that prohibited abortion in state-funded hospitals and required fetal viability testing after 20 weeks. The preamble to this enactment announced that life begins at conception and the unborn have constitutionally protected interests in life and liberty. Although acknowledging that the preamble made "a value judgment favoring childbirth over abortion," the Court determined that the state was not precluded from expressing this preference. It also determined that, because the pronouncement imposed no substantive restrictions on abortions, it had no constitutional significance.

With respect to the prohibition against abortions in public hospitals, the Court cited to case law which upheld restrictions on public funding. A decade earlier, the Court had held in *Harris v. McRae,* 448 U.S. 297 (1980) and *Maher v. Roe,* 432 U.S. 464 (1977), that neither federal nor state government respectively was obligated to fund abortion for an indigent woman. These decisions reflected the sense that, if a woman could not afford an abortion, the impediment was her economic condition rather than government. With respect to viability testing, the Court determined that the procedure properly reflected and accounted for advances in medical technology. This determination essentially undid the trimester model. The Court, however, refused to abandon *Roe v. Wade* altogether. Justice O'Connor, in a concurring opinion, maintained that the Missouri law did not present the right case for overruling *Roe v. Wade.* Justice Scalia argued that the Court should overrule *Roe v. Wade* on the ground that it was erroneously decided. Justice Blackmun expressed concern that the Court had relaxed the standard for reviewing abortion regulation by asking not whether the reason for it was compelling but whether it was legitimate. Although the Court did not abandon *Roe,* Blackmun thought that the indications of *Webster* were "very ominous."

The Court's abortion jurisprudence continued to be a source of polarization in the following years and decades. Justice Scalia, concurring in *Webster v. Reproductive Health Services,* referenced public demonstrations outside the Court as an indication that the matter should be resolved through the political process. Three years later, in *Planned Parenthood of Southeastern Pennsylvania v. Casey,* 505 U.S. 833 (1992), the Court reaffirmed the central meaning of *Roe v. Wade.* At issue was a state law that (1) required abortion providers to give women information identifying the physical and psychological risks of abortion; (2) prohibited abortion pending a 24-hour waiting period; (3) required minors to obtain the consent of a parent or judge; (4) required a married women to notify her spouse; and (5) obligated physicians to file reports showing compliance with the law for every abortion they performed. Except for the reporting requirement, each provision allowed an exception in the event of a medical emergency.

Justices Sandra Day O'Connor, Anthony Kennedy and David Souter, in a plurality opinion, maintained that a state generally cannot deny an abortion prior to fetal viability. The plurality, however, determined that the trimester framework was too "rigid." It thus proposed that abortion regulations should be assessed on the basis of whether they "unduly burden" a woman's freedom prior to viability. Using this standard, the plurality found that the spousal notification requirement constituted an undue burden (because it transferred decision-making power from the woman to a third party).

The plurality found no other provision of the law to be unduly burdensome. Disclosure of the physical and psychological risks of abortion was viewed as an appropriate means for ensuring an informed decision by the woman. Without evidence indicating that the 24-hour waiting period would interfere unreasonably with a woman's freedom to choose, and although it might increase the cost of an abortion, the plurality was satisfied that the waiting period also advanced the objective of informed judgment.

Although the "undue burden" test had not captured a clear majority, the Court deployed it in *Mazurek v. Armstrong,* 520 U.S. 968 (1997). That case concerned a state law permitting only licensed physicians to perform abortions. From the Court's perspective, the law did not impose a substantial impediment to securing an abortion A majority of the Court also used the test in *Stenberg v. Carhart,* 530 U.S. 914 (2000), in finding that a state law prohibiting partial birth abortions created substantial obstacles to a woman's freedom.

In *Gonzales v. Carhart,* the Court revisited the issue of partial birth abortions. At issue was the Partial Birth Abortion Act of 2007 (which Congress enacted in response to *Stenberg v. Carhart*). The specific procedure at issue, used when the physician is concerned with bleeding, infection, or injury, entails partial delivery of the fetus and crushing of the skull to facilitate removal. Historically, the Court had required restrictions on abortion to provide exceptions when the mother's health was at risk. The Court noted the disagreement among medical experts on this point but, in an opinion by Justice Kennedy, determined that this uncertainty did not prevent Congress from enacting the law. Rather, it concluded that it could use its legislative authority on behalf of "the life within the woman." Although the law mirrored the enactment struck down in *Stenberg*, the Court differentiated it on grounds the federal regulation provided more specific guidance and applied only when the procedure was "deliberately and intentionally" performed. Because the Court for the first time upheld a restriction regardless of the mother's health interests, Justice Ginsburg described the outcome as "alarming." From her perspective, it represented growing "hostility" toward *Roe* and *Casey*.

There has been much litigation related to abortion issues over the years. In *Box v. Planned Parenthood of Indiana and Kentucky, Inc.,* 587 U.S. 490 (2019), for example, the Court upheld an Indiana law that excluded fetal remains from the definition of "infectious and pathological waste," thereby preventing incineration of fetal remains along with surgical byproducts, and requiring "humane and dignified disposal." Since there was no claim that the law implicated a fundamental right, the Court applied a rational basis standard, and concluded that Indiana had a "legitimate interest in the proper disposal of fetal remains."

A number of cases were percolating in the lower courts before and after *Dobbs* was decided, and some still might need judicial intervention. For example, the issues included whether a state can prohibit dilation and extraction abortions, *see Bernard v. Individual Members of Indiana Licensing Board,* 392 F.Supp.3d 935 (S.D. Ind. 2019), whether a state can require health care providers that prescribe abortion-inducing medications to also have a contract with a physician with admitting privileges at a local hospital, whether states can prohibit abortions that are based on sex, race or disability, whether a state can impose a 72 hour waiting period for an abortion, and whether a minor's parents must be informed prior to a court-authorized abortion.

Dobbs involved a Mississippi law, the Gestational Age Act, that banned abortion after gestation of 15 weeks. The case swept away the framework, structure, and holding of *Roe* and its progeny. *Dobbs* found that the legal history did not support an implied fundamental right to abortion. Instead, abortion could be protected, but it would left to the states to decide how abortion should be protected, if at all.

In *Dobbs*, Justice Alito, joined by Justices Thomas, Gorsuch, Kavanaugh, and Barrett, found that the right to an abortion is not "deeply rooted in the nation's history," nor is it an essential part of "ordered liberty." The Court found that the five factors to consider in determining whether to overturn precedent in light of the *stare decisis* doctrine—"the nature of their error, the quality of their reasoning, the "workability" of the rules they imposed on the country, their disruptive effect on other areas of the law, and the absence of concrete reliance"—weighed strongly in favor of overruling both *Roe* and *Casey*.

While Justices Thomas, Kavanaugh, and Roberts concurred, Justices Breyer, Sotomayor and Kagan dissented. The dissent claimed that overturning Roe was not justifiable based on history or precedent and that the case was relied on by many over the 50 years of its existence.

Of significance for the future is whether the decision in *Dobbs* will lead to the elimination or minimization of the other implied rights within the right to privacy discussed below, such as family life and marriage.

Family Life and Marriage. Even before the Court recognized a formal right of privacy, it protected personal choices in the context of family life and marriage. Modern case law accounts for these interests as incidents of the right of privacy. It is not always clear, however, where the boundaries of the protected interest are located. The Court in *Village of Belle Terre v. Boraas,* 416 U.S. 1 (1974), for instance, upheld a zoning ordinance that limited multiple occupancy of single-family dwellings to blood relatives. In *Moore v. City of East Cleveland,* 431 U.S. 494 (1977), however, it refused to differentiate between nuclear and extended families. Although acknowledging that the city had a legitimate interest in managing traffic and parking congestion, avoiding financial burdens on the school system, and preventing overcrowding, the Court determined that the regulation only served these interests marginally. Because these risks could be presented by nuclear as well as extended families, a four-justice plurality of the Court determined that the regulation had a tenuous relation to the city's objective and thus was invalid. This outcome was achieved pursuant to a standard of review that, although not strict, was heightened.

Although finding that the regulation could not stand, the plurality acknowledged the risks of substantive due process review. It noted that historical experience supported concern that judicial review of the political process may veer toward subjectivism. The Court thus stressed the importance of learning from experience and being sensitive to basic societal values. Justice Stewart, joined by Justice Rehnquist, dissented on grounds the interest in shared living space was not "implicit in the concept of ordered liberty." Justice White agreed with this assessment and made an observation that was predictive of future substantive due process review. His point was that the Court risks illegitimacy when it makes law with little or no discernible grounding in constitutional text or design. He thus maintained that the Court should be "extremely reluctant" to use the due process clause to invalidate decisions made through the political process. White also was skeptical of inquiries into what is deeply rooted in the nation's traditions. From his perspective, traditions are debatable and a process for discerning them invites rather than avoids subjectivism.

The right to marry was one of the principles that the Court referenced in *Loving v. Virginia,* 388 U.S. 1 (1967), to strike down anti-miscegenation laws. Although this right stood on its own for many decades, the Court in *Zablocki v. Redhail,* 434 U.S. 374 (1978) determined that it was a dimension of the right to privacy. At issue in *Zablocki* was a state law that prohibited marriage by residents who were in arrears on their child support and unable to prove their children would not end up on welfare. The Court employed a strict scrutiny standard of review, determined that the law interfered directly and substantially with the right to marry, and noted that there were less constitutionally burdensome means of achieving the state's goals. Justice Rehnquist dissented, arguing that no fundamental right was at stake, and viewing the enactment as a legitimate exercise of the state's power to regulate family life and ensure payment of child support.

The dissenting concerns in the *Moore* and *Zablocki* cases became the dominant influence in *Michael H. v. Gerald D.,* 491 U.S. 110 (1989). At issue in that case was whether a natural father could be denied visitation rights with a daughter who was conceived in an extra-marital affair. The Court rejected the argument that biological fatherhood alone established a protected liberty interest. In a four-justice opinion authored by Justice Scalia, the plurality maintained that the critical factor was the respect given to relationships within a unitary family. The adulterous backdrop to the father-daughter relationship, from the plurality's perspective, was "not the stuff of which fundamental rights qualifying as liberty interests are made."

Justice Scalia, writing for himself, proposed an analytical model that would constrain and perhaps even preclude fundamental rights development through the due process clause. He maintained that an inquiry into whether a right or liberty is fundamental must begin by defining the interest at a high level of specificity. Rather than describing a general parental right, a higher level of specificity would depict the right under review as that of a father whose child was conceived in an adulterous relationship. The higher the level of specificity, therefore, the less likely that the proposed right will be denominated fundamental.

Justice Brennan, in a dissenting opinion joined by Justices Marshall and Blackmun, criticized the plurality for employing a "misguided" standard of review. By focusing upon whether an interest historically and traditionally was "protected," rather than "important," the court from their perspective merely confirmed the importance of interests already protected by the political process. Countering the plurality's concern with the risk of due process review. Brennan contended that it was essential that the Constitution not become a static document bound by prejudices and dated assumptions.

The Court revisited the issue of parental liberty in *Troxel v. Granville*, 530 U.S. 57 (2000), when it invalidated a state law that gave grandparents the right to visit the children of a sole surviving parent. Justice O'Connor, writing for a four-justice plurality, found that the state had no grounds to inject itself into the family domain. The result might be different if there was evidence suggesting that a parent was not providing adequate care. Justices Thomas and Scalia separately raised concern that the Court was protecting a right that was not constitutionally enumerated.

Sexual Orientation. Although the right of privacy has been a source of persisting controversy, its development has been incremental. In *Whalen v. Roe*, 429 U.S. 589 (1977), the Court noted that "state legislation which has some effect on individual liberty or privacy may not be held unconstitutional simply because a court finds it unnecessary, in whole or in part." Reticence to push boundaries was a consistent theme in dissenting opinions challenging extension of the right of privacy to abortion, family life, and marriage cases. This disposition reflected majority sentiment when, in *Bowers v. Hardwick,* 478 U.S. 186 (1986), the Court first considered the matter of sexual orientation. *Bowers* involved the prosecution of two men charged with violating a law prohibiting oral or anal sex by persons of the same gender. Although the law did not differentiate between homosexual and heterosexual relationships, the Court focused on (and rejected) what it described as a proposed "constitutional right of homosexuals to engage in acts of sodomy." In an opinion authored by Justice White, the Court held that this proposed right had no resemblance to those interests such as family relationships, marriage, procreation, abortion, and child-rearing that it historically had protected.

Reflecting its cautious approach to due process review, the Court stressed the importance of ensuring that rights not enumerated by the Constitution are not merely imposed pursuant to the justices' personal values. The critical inquiry thus was whether the proposed liberty interest was "implicit in the concept of ordered liberty" or "deeply rooted in this Nation's history and traditions." From its perspective, and citing the history and pervasiveness of anti-sodomy laws, the Court found that the proposed right met neither of these criteria. The outcome reflected further the concern that the judiciary becomes "most vulnerable and comes nearest to illegitimacy when it deals with judge-made constitutional law having little or no cognizable roots in the language or design of the Constitution."

Justice Blackmun, joined by three of his colleagues, disagreed with the majority's characterization of the issue. Instead of concerning "a fundamental right to engage in homosexual sodomy," the issue from his perspective involved " 'the most comprehensive of rights and the right most valued by civilized men,' namely, 'the right to be let alone.' " Even if sodomy had been widely condemned for centuries, Blackmun argued that long history and strong feelings should not shield a law from constitutional review. He further noted that freedom to differ meant little if it covered only "things that do not matter much."

In *Romer v. Evans*, 517 U.S. 620 (1996), the Court struck down a Colorado constitutional amendment prohibiting state and municipal governments from extending the protection of anti-discrimination laws to homosexuals. From the Court's perspective, the law was so unrelated to a legitimate state interest that it could be understood only as a reflection of "animus" toward homosexuals. The Court did not indicate whether sexual orientation provided the basis for a heightened standard of review.

In *Lawrence v. Texas*, 539 U.S. 558 (2003), the Court revisited the premise of *Bowers v. Hardwick* and concluded that it had misapprehended the liberty interest there. At issue was the conviction of two adult men under a state law that prohibited "deviate sexual intercourse, namely anal sex, with a member of the same sex." The Court found no legitimate governmental interest, absent physical or mental harm, in prohibiting private sexual activity between consenting adults. It extended the liberty interest, moreover, beyond the privacy of the home, noting that "there are other spheres of our lives and existence, outside the home, where the State should not be a dominant presence. Freedom extends beyond spatial bounds. Liberty presumes an autonomy of self that includes freedom of thought, belief, expression, and certain intimate contact." The boundaries of personal liberty thus extended to the "spatial" and the "transcendent."

Although abandoning its decision in *Bowers v. Hardwick*, the Court did not establish same-sex relationships as a fundamental right. It simply held that the state had presented no legitimate interest in support of its prohibition, and thus failed the rational basis test. The Court reserved the possibility of a different outcome if a case arose concerning a minor, coercion, public activity, or prostitution. It nonetheless suggested an expansive and flexible understanding of constitutional liberty, which it described as not being locked into any time in history and available so that "persons in every generation can invoke its principles in their own search for greater freedom."

Justice O'Connor concurred in the judgment but disagreed with the majority's overruling of *Bowers*. Because the state criminalized "deviate sexual intercourse" in the context of same-sex relationships, but not opposite-sex relationships, she maintained that there was an equal protection violation. Her approach would have enabled the state to enact an anti-sodomy law that applied both to heterosexual and homosexual relationships. In a dissenting opinion joined by two other justices, Justice Scalia challenged the majority's opinion as hypocritical, driven by irrelevant considerations, and the product of a "law-professor culture, that has largely signed on to the homosexual agenda." Scalia also criticized the Court for departing from norms that establish fundamental rights only on the basis of what is "deeply rooted in this Nation's history and tradition." Without the power to enact legislation based upon moral choices, he maintained, state laws against a range of behavior including incest, prostitution, bestiality, and obscenity could be called into doubt. Justice Scalia thus viewed the decision as a potential source of "massive disruption of the current social order." To find that the state has no legitimate interest that justifies intrusion into personal and private lives, as Justice Scalia saw it, would "decree the end of all morals legislation." He also accused the Court of "taking sides in the culture war, departing from its role of assuring, as neutral observer, that the democratic rules of engagement are observed." Justice Thomas characterized the law as "silly" and, if a member of the legislature, would have voted to repeal it. He found, however, no constitutional provision that established a "general right of privacy" and thus no basis for invalidating it.

Recent cases have also established a right to same-sex marriage. These cases are discussed in the chapter on equal protection.

Right to Refuse Medical Treatment. Case law concerning a person's right to decline medical treatment relates back to the early twentieth century. The Court, in *Jacobson v. Massachusetts*, 197 U.S. 11 (1905), held that the government's interest in disease prevention outweighed an individual's freedom to refuse a smallpox vaccination. Cases concerning patient rights and state interests in this context reflect a conflict between personal autonomy and societal norms that disfavor suicide or assisting it. In *Cruzan v. Director, Missouri Department of Health*, 497 U.S. 261 (1990), the Court held that refusal of medical treatment was within the ambit of the right of privacy. That case concerned a woman on long-term life support pursuant to severe brain damage suffered in an automobile accident. Based upon medical evaluations determining that her vegetative condition was permanent, the parents asked for a court order taking her off life support. They maintained that this outcome was consistent with their daughter's wishes. The Court upheld the decision of the Missouri Supreme Court that, absent "clear and convincing evidence" of the daughter's intent, the parents could not make the decision for their daughter.

Although identifying a right to refuse medical treatment, the Court differentiated between competent and incompetent people. When competence is lacking, a person is unable to make an informed and voluntary decision. If the right is to be exercised, therefore, it must be by a surrogate. Because a choice between life and death is "a deeply personal decision of obvious and overwhelming finality," the Court concluded that the state has a legitimate concern with the decision's integrity. The state's insistence on "clear and convincing" evidence reflects a valid concern with protecting human life and ensuring the integrity of a decision to starve oneself to death. In this regard, the Court noted that a third-party's (even a family member's) decision would not necessarily be the same as the patient's.

Justice Scalia, concurring, agreed with the outcome but objected to the Court's reliance on the due process clause. He maintained that the issue was beyond the competency of the judiciary and should be resolved by the political process. Justice Brennan, dissenting joined by two other justices, argued that the patient had a fundamental right that was not outweighed by the state's interests. From his perspective, medical technology created a condition in which death had commenced but life existed only in a formalistic sense. He maintained that the state's only interest is in ensuring and protecting the integrity of the patient's wishes. The key question for him was whether an incompetent person would want to exist in a permanent vegetative condition sustained only by life support. Instead of requiring clear and convincing evidence, he would have deferred to the person to whom the decision most likely would have been delegated.

Cruzan did hold that a competent person has a protected liberty interest in refusing medical treatment. The next question, addressed in *Washington v. Glucksberg,* 521 U.S. 702 (1997), was whether assisted suicide was constitutionally protected. For this proposition, the Court found no support in the nation's history and traditions. In deciding the case, the Court expounded on how fundamental rights and liberties are to be identified. It noted first that they must be not only "deeply" but "objectively rooted in this Nation's history and tradition." The Court also observed that, using the nation's "history, traditions, and practices" as reference points, a fundamental right must be "carefully described." Pursuant to those criteria, it held that the state had a valid interest in protecting human life, particularly for those in a vulnerable state, and safeguarding the integrity and ethics of the medical profession. Absent a constitutionally protected interest, the Court used a rational basis standard of review. Finding that the law was reasonably related to important and legitimate state interests, the Court found no basis for invalidating the state law. Justice O'Connor, joined by two other justices in a concurring opinion, maintained that the decision failed to resolve whether a person in pain might have a constitutional interest in ending his or her life.

Consistent with the holding in *Glucksberg,* the Court in *Vacco v. Quill,* 521 U.S. 793 (1997), rejected an equal protection challenge to a state law prohibiting physician-assisted suicide and held that there was no fundamental right at stake. The Court also found that the state made a legitimate distinction between permitting persons to decline unwanted medical treatment and enabling assisted suicide. In that regard, the Court noted that refusal of medical treatment results in death from the underlying disease. The cause of death by means of assisted suicide, however, is not the disease.

Postlude. Substantive due process review is a continuing source of constitutional controversy. Detractors maintain that the Court, when it develops fundamental rights not explicitly set forth by the Constitution, trumps the will of people as expressed through the representative process. To the extent the due process clause is used to assess the constitutionality of legislation, they maintain that it should be used sparingly and narrowly cabined. Justice Harlan, in *Poe v. Ullman,* 367 U.S. 497 (1961) (Harlan, J., dissenting), offered a more tolerant perspective in observing that "due process has not been reduced to any formula; its content cannot be determined by reference to any code. The best that can be said is that through the course of this Court's decisions it has represented the balance which our Nation, built upon postulates of respect for the liberty of the individual, has struck between that liberty and the demands of organized society. If the supplying of content to this Constitutional concept has of necessity been a rational process, it certainly has not been one where judges have felt free to roam where unguided speculation might take them. The balance of which I speak is the balance struck by this country, having regard to what history teaches are the traditions from which it developed as well as the traditions from which it broke. That tradition is a living thing. A decision of this Court which radically departs from it would not long survive, while a decision which builds on what has survived is likely to be sound. No formula could serve as a substitute, in this area, for judgment and restraint."

The sourcing of fundamental but textually unenumerated rights is not restricted to the due process clause. The Court, for instance, has recognized interstate travel and voting as rights that are fundamental. These guarantees, although not textually enumerated, have been inferred from the structure of the Constitution and representative nature of the political process it creates. These rights, as discussed in the next chapter, typically are analyzed within the context of the equal protection guarantee.

CHECKLIST

A. Provisions of the Bill of Rights have been selectively incorporated into the Fourteenth Amendment due process clause.

1. The test for incorporation is whether the relevant provision of the Bill of Rights is "implicit in the concept of ordered liberty" or is so deeply rooted in history and tradition "as to be ranked fundamental."

2. Nearly all provisions of the Bill of Rights have been incorporated.

   a. Exceptions are the Fifth Amendment guarantee conditioning criminal trials upon a grand jury indictment and the Seventh Amendment right to a jury trial.

b. When a right or liberty is incorporated, it applies with the same force (i.e., jot-for-jot) against the states as it does with the federal government.

B. Fundamental Rights Generally.

1. A fundamental right is identified when the pertinent interest is found to be "implicit in the concept of ordered liberty" or "deeply rooted in this Nation's history and traditions."

2. The standard of review, when government action burdens a fundamental right, is strict scrutiny.

   a. Pursuant to this criterion, a court will assess whether the regulatory goal is supported by a compelling interest, and the regulatory means necessarily is related to, and narrowly tailored to that purpose.

C. Non-Fundamental Rights.

1. Non-fundamental rights, pursuant to modern case law, are those that fall outside the ambit of the right of privacy (discussed below).

2. Economic rights such as liberty of contract, which during the first few decades of the twentieth century were deemed fundamental, are no longer regarded as fundamental.

3. The standard of review, when a non-fundamental right is burdened by government action, is the rational basis test.

   a. Pursuant to this standard, a court will assess whether the regulation advances a legitimate government interest and is rationally related to the objective.

      1.) This standard's hallmark is its laxity. The lines of inquiry, when the rational basis test is utilized, are whether government is acting (i) within the scope of its power and (ii) whether it acted arbitrarily or irrationally. Since 1937, no economic regulation has been invalidated pursuant to the due process clause.

D. Right of Privacy Precursors.

1. Early cases reference a right "to be let alone," which encompasses freedom from bodily restraint, and the right to contract, engage in occupation, acquire useful knowledge, marry, establish a home, raise children, worship the God of one's choice, and enjoy privileges recognized by common law

as essential to the orderly pursuit of happiness. *Union Pacific R. Co. v. Botsford; Meyer v. Nebraska.*

2. Freedom to procreate and marry were recognized in the context of equal protection as the basis for striking down a mandatory sterilization law. *Skinner v. Oklahoma.*

3. The right of privacy originally was grounded in "penumbras" that the Court constructed from the First, Third, Fourth, Fifth, and Ninth Amendments. *Griswold v. Connecticut.*

4. Modern case law recognizes the right of privacy as an incident of liberty protected by the due process clause of the Fourteenth Amendment (with respect to the states) and Fifth Amendment (with respect to the federal government).

E. Reproductive Freedom.

1. There is a fundamental right for adults to use birth control, a right that protects both suppliers and users.

    a. This right originally was recognized in the context of marriage. *Griswold v. Connecticut.*

    b. The right was extended to unmarried persons pursuant to the equal protection clause. *Eisenstadt v. Baird.*

    c. It is uncertain whether this right extends to minors.

F. Abortion.

1. Liberty to elect an abortion initially was established in *Roe v. Wade,* which constructed a trimester framework that provided for the balancing of the right to have an abortion against state interests according to the stage of pregnancy. *Roe* held that:

    a. During the first trimester, government had minimal grounds for burdening a woman's liberty to obtain an abortion.

    b. During the second trimester, government could regulate to protect the mother's health (but not that of the fetus).

    c. During the third trimester, the government's interest in protecting the fetus became compelling pursuant to an understanding that it had achieved viability.

2. Subsequent case law has reaffirmed the right to secure an abortion prior to viability but has expanded the range of

state interests that may trump the right—including protection of potential life. *Planned Parenthood of Southeastern Pennsylvania v. Casey.*

a. The primary point of inquiry is whether regulation imposes an "undue burden" and thus creates a "substantial obstacle" to obtaining a pre-viability abortion.

   1.) The Court has determined that informed consent (*Casey*) and restrictions on partial birth abortions (*Gonzales v. Carhart*) are not undue burdens.

b. Consent

   1.) Spousal consent (*Planned Parenthood of Central Missouri v. Danforth*) and notification (*Casey*) provisions are impermissible.

   2.) Parental consent is permissible provided that there is a judicial bypass procedure.

      a.) A judicial bypass hearing focuses upon whether the minor is sufficiently mature to make the decision for herself.

c. Public financing and facilities

   1.) Government may deny public funding (*Maher v. Roe; Harris v. McRae*) and the use of public facilities (*Casey*) for the performance of abortions.

   2.) Government may condition funding of family-planning clinics on the basis of compliance with rules that prohibit counseling for abortion or referral to a provider.

d. Abortion procedure

   1.) Government may prohibit partial birth abortions even if the provider believes it is necessary to ensure the woman's health. *Gonzales v. Carhart.*

      a.) This determination reflects the Court's deference to congressional findings that partial birth abortions are never necessary to protect the woman's health and thus do not constitute an undue burden.

      b.) The Court found the prohibition against partial birth abortions reasonably related to the state's interest in protecting potential life and the mother from subsequent regret of her decision. This analysis reflects a more relaxed standard of review than strict scrutiny.

e. A number of challenges to Roe are currently percolating in the courts, including a Mississippi law which bans abortion prior to viability, and a Texas law which bans abortion once a fetal heartbeat can be detected.

G. Family Life and Marriage.

1. Parents have a fundamental right to rear their children and determine how they will be educated. *Pierce v. Society of Sisters.*

   a. They also have the right to determine who will have access to their children. *Troxel v. Granville.* A state thus may not provide visitation rights to grandparents without first giving special weight to the parents' concerns.

2. The right of a family (nuclear or extended) to live together is a constitutionally protected liberty interest. *Moore v. City of East Cleveland.*

3. There is no fundamental right for persons unlinked by blood or marriage to live together. *Village of Belle Terre v. Boraas.*

4. A state cannot condition marriage upon payment of child support in connection with a prior relationship. *Zablocki v. Redhail.*

H. Sexual Orientation.

1. The Court has not recognized sexual orientation as a fundamental liberty.

   a. It nonetheless has invalidated laws that criminalize homosexual sodomy. *Lawrence v. Texas.*

   b. This outcome was achieved pursuant to the rational basis test, as the Court determined that the law "demean[ed]" homosexuals and was entirely irrational.

I. Right to Refuse Medical Treatment.

1. A competent adult cannot be required to receive unwanted medical treatment, including life support. *Cruzan v. Missouri.*

   a. The state has an important interest in preserving life.

b. A state may condition termination of life support upon clear and convincing evidence that this outcome is consistent with the patient's wishes.

J. Right to Commit Suicide.

1. There is no constitutional right to take one's life either directly or with the assistance of a third-person. *Washington v. Glucksberg.*

■ PROBLEMS ■

Problems: The State of Unity has enacted a law that is designed to secure what the legislature has characterized as "founding societal values." Toward this end the enactment declares in its preamble that "Life, Liberty, and the Pursuit of Happiness are inalienable rights. The state embraces the premise that life begins at the age of conception, the traditional family unit should be preserved, and it is to be protected against alternative models of group living."

This preamble precedes a law that is subdivided into three sections as follows:

Abortion. No medical facility receiving state funding may provide abortions under any circumstance. Private medical facilities may provide abortions only to the extent that the father (spouse or otherwise) has consented, and it is certified that the woman has received 30 days of counseling to ensure her consent is informed.

Family Unit. A family under state law consists of a mother, father, grandparents, and any direct offspring. All other individuals, whether or not related by blood, are considered to be outside the family unit. No student may enroll in a primary or secondary public school without proof that he or she is living with a member of an approved family unit.

Marriage. Marriage is a privilege that may be granted in the state's discretion. Pursuant to the state's interest in an intelligent and mentally healthy citizenry, it may deny a license upon determination that either applicant is intellectually inferior or emotionally unstable.

Please analyze and assess how this enactment would be reviewed, what results would be achieved, and why.

Answers: Preamble. The preamble to the enactment articulates specific and precise value judgments with respect to abortion and family life. The Constitution does not prohibit the state from expressing its preferences in this manner. By itself, the preamble also does not impose restrictions upon any protected rights. It thus violates no constitutional right or liberty.

Abortion. The Court has recognized that the right of privacy comprehends a woman's freedom to elect an abortion. This liberty, however, is not absolute. The standard for determining the constitutionality of a pre-viability restriction on abortion is whether it "unduly burdens" the mother's freedom. The Court has determined that preclusion of government funding and facilities does not impose an unreasonable impediment. A spousal consent requirement creates such a burden, however, because it transfers decision-making power from the woman to a third party. It also is unreasonable for the woman's freedom to be held hostage in instances when the father may be difficult to locate or identify. Although the Court has upheld a short waiting period to ensure informed judgment, a 30-day waiting period would be unreasonable. For many women, it would eliminate the option of a pre-viability abortion.

Family Unit. The right to have and raise a family is within the scope of the right of privacy. Case law establishes that a state may differentiate, for regulatory purposes, according to whether persons are related by blood or not. The Court has scrutinized regulation that differentiates between nuclear and extended families. In so doing, it has required at least an important state interest and substantial relationship between the regulatory means and end. Especially because extended families are well-grounded in the nation's history and traditions, it is difficult to see how a restriction on them could substantially advance the state's objectives. Although education is not a fundamental right, the Court has noted that total deprivation of basic education may be unconstitutional. Such a denial likely would be deemed irrational insofar as there would be no clear relationship between the regulatory means and objective.

Marriage. The right to marry has been recognized as an aspect of the right of privacy. The state thus may not restrict it as a matter of discretion. To the extent it imposes limitations upon marriage, they will be subject to strict scrutiny. Screening for intelligence and emotional stability is unlikely to be recognized as a compelling interest—and probably will be viewed as invidious. Denial of a marriage license also would not prevent persons within these categories from living together. Without a sufficient justification, therefore, the provision is destined to fail under the Constitution.

POINTS TO REMEMBER

- Most provisions of the Bill of Rights have been incorporated selectively through the due process clause of the Fourteenth Amendment and thus made applicable to the states.
- The test for determining whether a right is fundamental is whether it is "implicit in the concept of ordered liberty" or "deeply rooted in this Nation's history and traditions."
- Official action that burdens a fundamental right is subject to strict scrutiny.
- Official action that burdens a non-fundamental right is subject to rational basis review.
- Modern fundamental rights are aspects of the right of privacy.
- The right of privacy includes reproductive freedom, a woman's liberty to elect an abortion, the right of a family to live together, the right to marry, and the right to refuse unwanted medical treatment.
- Laws that limit the right to secure an abortion prior to fetal viability are assessed for purposes of determining whether they impose an undue burden and create a substantial obstacle.
- Spousal consent or notification as a condition for obtaining an abortion is impermissible.
- Parental consent as a condition for obtaining an abortion is permissible, provided that there is a judicial bypass procedure.
- Government is not obligated to subsidize or provide facilities for an abortion.
- Partial birth abortions may be prohibited even if the provider believes that the mother's health is endangered.
- A family has a right to live together, but persons unrelated by blood or marriage do not.
- Sexual orientation has not been recognized as a fundamental liberty.
- Laws criminalizing homosexual sodomy have been invalidated pursuant to the rational basis test.
- A competent adult has the right to refuse unwanted medical treatment.
- Termination of life support may be conditioned upon clear and convincing evidence that of the patient's desire.

- There is no right to take one's life directly or with the assistance of a third party.

CHAPTER 9

Equal Protection

The Equal Protection Clause can be found in the Fourteenth Amendment. While there are two due process clauses, there is only one equal protection clause, and it only applies to the states. When the Court is confronted by federal action challenged as a violation of equal protection, the Court relies on an implied version of the doctrine within the Fifth Amendment due process clause. *See, e.g., Bolling v. Sharpe,* 347 U.S. 497 (1954).

The guarantee's primary accomplishments include ending official racial segregation and eliminating various types of discrimination. Government's power to classify persons for regulatory persons is constitutionally permissible except when certain groups are targeted or excluded. For most purposes, classifications (*e.g.*, tax rates based upon income, driver license requirements based upon age) are constitutionally inconsequential and thus subject to a rational basis standard of review. Heightened standards of review operate when classifications differentiate on the basis of race, gender, alienage, illegitimacy, or selectively deny a fundamental right. Within the equal protection context, the standards of review are strict, intermediate, or rational basis. The elements of these tests are set forth in the following table.

Standard of Review	**Quality of Government Interest**	**Relationship Between Means and Ends**
Strict Scrutiny	Compelling	Narrowly Tailored
Intermediate Scrutiny	Important	Substantially Related
Rational Basis Review	Legitimate	Rationally Related

The Equal Protection Clause of the Fourteenth Amendment emerged from the reconstruction process following the Civil War. Read in conjunction with the Citizenship Clause of the same amendment, it prohibits states from denying "any person within its jurisdiction the equal protection of the laws." Until the middle of the twentieth century, the Equal Protection Clause had minimal consequence. The Court in the *Slaughter-House Cases*, 83 U.S. 36 (1872), upon first interpreting the Fourteenth Amendment, determined that the equal protection guarantee was concerned exclusively with state laws that discriminated against "the newly emancipated negroes." These enactments were the Black Codes, which southern states adopted after abolition to maintain the subordinate status of former slaves. Despite this concern, the equal protection clause over its first several decades had minimal significance. Justice Holmes characterized its vitality, when he referred to it in *Buck v. Bell*, 274 U.S. 200, 208 (1927) as "the usual last resort of constitutional arguments."

Modern equal protection review as it relates to general economic or social regulation is highly deferential toward the political process. The Court thus operates on the premise, articulated in *Lindsley v. Natural Carbonic Gas Co.*, 220 U.S. 61 (1911), that "if any state of facts reasonably can be conceived that would sustain the classification, the existence of that state of facts at the time the law was enacted must be assumed." This standard typically is referred to as the "rational basis test." When measured against this criterion, the challenged law almost invariably is upheld. The rare exceptions include a state constitutional amendment prohibiting legislation against discrimination on the basis of sexual orientation, *Romer v. Evans,* 517 U.S. 620 (1996), and a municipality's denial of a special use permit for a group home for mentally disabled children. *City of Cleburne v. Cleburne Living Center*, 473 U.S. 432 (1985).

Economic and Social Classifications. The deferential nature of the rational basis test is evidenced by the Court's decision in *Railway Express Agency v. New York,* 336 U.S. 106 (1949). This case concerned a local ordinance that prohibited display advertising on motor vehicles except those that were owner operated. The enactment was presented as a traffic safety measure. Although the risk of motorist distraction would not seem to hinge upon whether the advertising was on an owned or hired vehicle, the Court indicated that it did not have sufficient expertise to make this determination. The Court also found that the discrimination was not of a type relevant to the equal protection clause and, in any event, it was not obligated to choose between eliminating all hazards or none. It is noteworthy that, if the regulation were to be reviewed today, it would be susceptible to a First Amendment challenge. Commercial speech at the time of the case, unlike now, was not constitutionally protected.

The term rational basis, as it has evolved, provides wide latitude for legislative judgment. Even if legislation does not identify a clear objective, this purpose may be established on the basis of legal arguments of what is "conceivable" when a regulation's constitutionality is litigated. Two key incidents of a classification are over-inclusiveness and under-inclusiveness, either of which may be constitutionally significant. In the *Railway Express Agency* case, the burden was over-inclusive (for-hire advertising was no less distracting than owner advertising) and under-inclusive (owner advertising was equally distracting). For the same reasons, the benefit also was over-inclusive and under-inclusive.

Among the classifications that the Court has placed in the economic or social category, and thus subject to rational basis review, are wealth, age, mental retardation, and sexual orientation.

Although the rational basis test generally is renowned for its deference to the political process, there are instances when the Court employs a higher intensity version of rational basis review. Although a classification may not be "facially invidious," it nonetheless may reflect a "recurring constitutional difficulty." The Court thus may insist that the "classification reflects a reasoned judgment" and advance substantial state interests. *Plyler v. Doe*, 457 U.S. 202 (1982). This enhanced version of rational basis review has been evidenced in decisions invalidating laws that discriminated against persons on the basis of mental retardation, *City of Cleburne v. Cleburne Living Center*, 473 U.S. 432 (1985); sexual orientation, *Romer v. Evans*, 517 U.S. 620 (1996); and children of undocumented aliens.

Racial Classifications.

Race and the Nation's Founding. The primary challenge of the Constitutional Convention, as noted by James Madison, was to reconcile the positions of Northern and Southern states on slavery. The union's founding was predicated upon the principle of federal neutrality with respect to slavery and the understanding that each state would decide the issue for itself. This premise instead of achieving resolution prefaced several decades of mounting tension, periodic compromise, and rising stakes. Westward expansion, controversy over the status of fugitive slaves, and escalating sectional mistrust ultimately pushed the issue of slavery beyond the competency of the political process.

By the late 1850s, with the political system gridlocked, the Supreme Court emerged as a potential source of resolution. Case law until then generally had accommodated slavery consistent with the principle of federal neutrality. In *Dred Scott v. Sandford*, 60 U.S. 393 (1856), the Court abandoned this premise in favor of an understanding that the Constitution actually supported slavery.

Based upon Chief Justice Taney's belief that African-Americans were inferior by nature, he determined that they neither could be citizens of the United States nor have rights under the federal constitution. Noting specific constitutional references to slavery, he maintained that "the right of property in a slave is distinctly and expressly affirmed in the Constitution."

Instead of resolving the controversy, the decision further exacerbated sectional tensions. Some northern courts disregarded the ruling. President Lincoln ignored it and eventually issued the Emancipation Proclamation. Slavery by the end of the Civil War had become a focal point of the conflict. The Thirteenth Amendment abolished slavery in 1865. Immediately thereafter, the former slave states adopted laws (the Black Codes) which limited economic opportunity, residence, travel, assembly, voting, and other activities. The Civil Rights Act of 1866 aimed to prohibit these enactments—a purpose that became a key driver of the Fourteenth Amendment.

The Court in *Strauder v. West Virginia*, 100 U.S. 303 (1879), offered its first important response to a claim of racial discrimination. At issue was a state law excluding African-Americans from juries, which it found unconstitutional. The Court characterized the Fourteenth Amendment as a guarantee against official discrimination that implied racial inferiority. It further noted that the equal protection guarantee specifically required that state laws must be the same for all persons regardless of race. Notwithstanding the *Strauder* ruling, the Court for the next several decades interpreted the equal protection clause in a manner that accommodated systematic differentiation on the basis of race.

Separate but Equal. Official segregation, secured by laws designed to protect racial integrity and preserve white supremacy, became a dominant feature of the civil landscape during the late nineteenth century. Although invented in the north prior to the Civil War, segregation was evolved further in the south pursuant to comprehensive and prescriptive legislation. In *Plessy v. Ferguson*, 163 U.S. 537 (1896), the Court determined that segregation on the basis of race was a permissible exercise of state police power. At issue in *Plessy* was a state law requiring "equal but separate accommodations for the white and colored races" on passenger trains. The Court restated the premise of *Strauder v. West Virginia*, that the Fourteenth Amendment established "the absolute equality of the two races before the law." It noted that the Constitution did not prohibit racial distinctions that resulted in social (as opposed to political) inequalities and could not compel "commingling of the two races upon terms unsatisfactory to either." This differentiation was critical for purposes of reconciling the decision with *Strauder's* prohibition of discriminations that imply racial inferiority. As the Court saw it, the law made no implication to this effect.

The constitutionality of official segregation rested in significant part upon the premise that it did not impact civil or political rights. Insofar as one race was seen as inferior to another socially, the Court determined that this condition was beyond the purview of the Constitution. Justice Harlan, in a dissenting opinion, maintained that this characterization evaded the real issue. He argued that the law was grounded in the premise that African-Americans were inferior and at odds with a Constitution that is color-blind.

The separate but equal doctrine, despite its rhetorical nod to equality, primarily was about separation. Through the 1930s, scant attention was paid to funding and other inequalities associated with racial segregation. In *Cumming v. Richmond County Board of Education*, 175 U.S. 528 (1899), for instance, the Court upheld a school board's decision to close an African-American high school due to a purported lack of financial resources. Despite the unequal outcome, the Court determined that closing the all-white school would create an additional burden without ameliorating the other. The Court, in *Berea College v. Kentucky*, 211 U.S. 45 (1908), upheld a law that prohibited voluntary integration in higher education. In *McCabe v. Atchison, Topeka & Santa Fe Railway Co.*, 235 U.S. 151 (1914), the Court determined that railroads must provide separate accommodations regardless of demand or usage. In *Gong Lum v. Rice*, 275 U.S. 78 (1927), the Court upheld a state's decision to place a student of Chinese descent in a "colored" school.

The demise of official segregation began with the implementation of a litigation strategy developed by the National Association for the Advancement of Colored People (NAACP) in the 1930s. Its early achievements included a victory in *Missouri ex rel. Gaines v. Canada*, 305 U.S. 337 (1938), when the Court determined that a state must create a law school for nonwhites if it wished to maintain a racially exclusive institution. As the NAACP strategy unfolded, two important doctrinal developments helped clear the path for constitutional change. In *United States v. Carolene Products Co.*, 304 U.S. 144, 154 n.4 (1938), a case about the Filled Milk Act of 1923, the Court noted in its now famous Footnote 4, that "prejudice against discrete and insular minorities may be a special condition, which tends seriously to curtail the operation of th[e] political processes ordinarily relied upon to protect minorities, and which may call for a correspondingly more searching inquiry." This observation indicated the Court's readiness to scrutinize more closely laws that imposed disadvantages on groups excluded from the political process. In so doing, the Court was willing to restrict the extent to which there would be a presumption of constitutionality attached to government classifications. The significance of *Carolene Products* was heightened by *Korematsu v. United States*, 323 U.S. 214 (1944), a case concerning the federal government's relocation of more than 100,000 Japanese-Americans from the West Coast to detention camps during World War II. Although upholding the program on national security grounds, the Court adopted a more rigorous standard of review for racial classifications. As the Court put it, "all legal restrictions which curtail the civil rights of a single racial group are immediately suspect [and] courts must subject them to the most rigid scrutiny."

The *Korematsu* decision thus introduced the contemporary standard of review for racial classifications—strict scrutiny. Although many states tried to save segregation in its final years, by increasing funding for minority schools and creating parallel universities and colleges, the Court expanded its focus beyond financial considerations. In *Sweatt v. Painter*, 339 U.S. 629 (1950), it ordered the University of Texas to desegregate its school of law. This decision reflected the realization that factors other than money, such as institutional prestige, faculty qualifications, extracurricular activities, alumni influence, facilities, and linkage to professional opportunities, bear upon the quality of professional education.

Desegregation. The Court in *Brown v. Board of Education,* 347 U.S. 483 (1954), declared that racially segregated education is "inherently unequal." Notwithstanding historical indications that segregation was consistent with the framers' and ratifiers' view of the Fourteenth Amendment, the Court refused "to turn the clock back to 1868 when the Amendment was adopted, or even to 1896 when *Plessy v. Ferguson* was adopted." To support this position, the Court noted that public education had become such a significant function of local government and so key to personal development and success that it must be assessed with an appreciation of its evolved utility. The Court also cited psychological data indicating that segregation has "a detrimental effect upon the colored children . . . [and] is usually interpreted as denoting the inferiority of the negro group."

The *Brown* decision thus found that official segregation of public schools violated the equal protection clause. Reaching the same result in the District of Columbia was more problematic, insofar as the Fourteenth Amendment applies only to the states. In *Bolling v. Sharpe*, 347 U.S. 497 (1954), the Court determined that segregation had no reasonable relationship to a legitimate government objective and thus constituted an arbitrary deprivation of liberty under the Fifth Amendment due process clause. It thereby read equal protection into the due process clause.

In an effort to defuse and overcome anticipated resistance to its ruling, the Court attempted to engage local authorities in the process of framing and implementing remedies. In *Brown v. Board of Education (II)*, 349 U.S. 294 (1955), it announced that racial segregation in public schools must be eliminated with "all deliberate speed." Federal district courts were given the responsibility of determining whether compliance efforts were being undertaken in good faith. Typically, however, they proved to be sympathetic toward local authorities and interests. Consequently, there was little progress with respect to desegregation in the decade following the *Brown* decision. This period was defined primarily by a contest of wills between the Court and the states.

Resistance to the desegregation mandate was at the center of *Cooper v. Aaron*, 358 U.S. 1 (1958), the first major test of the Court's resolve. At issue was the Little Rock, Arkansas school board's request to delay implementation of a desegregation plan pursuant to intense resistance and threats of violence. When the governor dispatched the National Guard to prevent African-American students from enrolling at the city's all-white high school, President Eisenhower responded by sending federal troops to enforce desegregation. Despite the intensity of the circumstances, the Court unanimously rejected the school board's request for a delay. Citing to *Marbury v. Madison*, the Court reaffirmed its power "to say what the law is"—and that desegregation was the law of the land. The ruling sent a clear message that desegregation would not be impeded by violence and disorder, and that maintenance of law and order would not be at the cost of equal protection.

The circumstances of *Cooper v. Aaron* were reflective of the widespread resistance to the desegregation mandate. Not until Congress enacted the Civil Rights Act of 1964 did the political system become fully engaged with the desegregation process. This enactment authorized the attorney general to sue school districts and for the executive branch to withhold federal funds from systems that refused to desegregate. At the same time, the Court ratcheted compliance standards up from "all deliberate speed" to plans that "promise[d] realistically to work now." Segregated school systems thus were required to take whatever steps were necessary to achieve racially unitary status. By "racially unitary," the Court meant that all vestiges of discrimination had been eliminated "root and branch."

These developments resulted in significant gains in desegregation. In the 1970s, the desegregation process peaked. The Court, in *Swann v. Charlotte-Mecklenburg Board of Education*, 402 U.S. 1 (1971), provided a detailed rendition of the federal judiciary's role in the desegregation process. It cited traditional equitable powers as the basis for authority to make pupil assignments according to race and transport students to as a means of effecting these placements. Busing was permissible so long as time or distance did not create health risks or negatively impact the educational process. The Court also approved fixed ratios for faculty assignments as a starting point for achieving racial balance. This determination represented a rare deviation from increasingly normative understandings that quotas are constitutionally impermissible. Although having defined federal judicial power expansively, the Court indicated that desegregation duties were neither limitless nor endless. It noted that, when unitary status was achieved and minus evidence that any resegregation was caused by official action, there were no further desegregative responsibilities. The *Swann* ruling thus set the stage for key limiting principles that emerged soon thereafter.

The first significant limitation of the desegregation mandate was announced in *Keyes v. School District No. 1*, 413 U.S. 189 (1973), when the Court differentiated between *de jure segregation* and *de facto segregation*. By requiring proof that segregation was the function of intentional government action, the Court narrowed the potential of *Brown* to impact parts of the country (primarily in the north and west) where segregation had not been officially prescribed. Outside the South, segregation often (but not always) was an incident of residential demographics rather than formal prescription. The *de jure-de facto* distinction is not as precise as it may seem at first blush. In those communities where segregation was not mandated specifically by law, government nonetheless had a hand in facilitating it pursuant to the enforcement of restrictive racial covenants, location of public housing, and red-lining of neighborhoods pursuant to federal home loan policies.

The Court in *Milliken v. Bradley*, 418 U.S. 717 (1974), introduced another constraint upon desegregation when it reversed a lower court decision requiring inter-district busing of students. Specifically at issue was the inclusion of suburban school districts in a plan designed to desegregate Detroit public schools. "White flight" had resulted in a predominantly African-American student population in Detroit, to the point that meaningful integration was impossible without suburban participation. After rejecting the trial court's findings that the state had played a significant role in the segregation of city schools, the Court stated that the scope of the remedy could not exceed the extent of the constitutional violation. A court thus could order an inter-district remedy only when one district's intentional actions contributed significantly to segregation in the other district. This application of the *de jure* principle, in a context where suburbs largely were a post-segregation phenomenon, meant that metropolitan desegregation plans would be a rarity. In *Milliken v. Bradley II*, 433 U.S. 267 (1977), the Court reaffirmed the finding of a constitutional violation. Because any semblance of a meaningful racial balance was impossible, the remedy was limited to state funding of compensatory and remedial education programs.

In *Pasadena City Board of Education v. Spangler*, 427 U.S. 424 (1976), the Court reiterated its message in *Swann* that the duty to desegregate ended once racially unitary status was achieved. In the event segregation recurred, any duty to desegregate was conditioned on proof of official intent.

In each of these cases, Justice Marshall (who had been a primary architect of the NAACP's challenge to segregation) authored sharp critiques. With respect to the Court's decision in *Milliken v. Bradley*, he maintained that the Court provided "no remedy at all . . . guaranteeing that Negro children . . . will receive the same separate and inherently unequal education in the future as they have been unconstitutionally afforded in the past." Marshall especially objected to the determination that "white flight" was constitutionally insignificant, noting that it was driven by reaction to the undoing of segregated systems. The outcomes reflected the Court's growing reservations about the ability of courts to effect meaningful and lasting change. This reorientation was reflected further by case law in the 1990s, which emphasized the importance of reducing the federal judiciary's role and reverting control to local school officials. In *Oklahoma City Board of Education v. Dowell*, 498 U.S. 237 (1991), the Court relaxed the standard for compliance with a desegregation order. Instead of requiring school boards to show they had eliminated the vestiges of discrimination "root and branch," it required only that they had been redacted "to the extent practicable."

The Court sent a similar message in *Freeman v. Pitts,* 503 U.S. 467 (1992), when it determined that courts could restore local authority on an incremental basis. Although the district at issue had not achieved unitary status in all respects, the Court allowed school officials to regain control over those areas where desegregation goals had been achieved. The factors it identified for determining whether a court should exit included whether full compliance has been achieved, judicial control is necessary to achieve compliance, and the school system has demonstrated good-faith efforts to comply.

Using the standards set forth in *Freeman v. Pitts,* the Court in *Missouri v. Jenkins*, 495 U.S. 33 (1990), reviewed a court order requiring the state to fund magnet programs and teacher salary increases in Kansas City schools until student achievement levels approached national norms. The Court determined that these scores were irrelevant to whether the school system had achieved unitary status, and the question of judicial control should be settled pursuant to the criteria set forth in *Freeman*. Applying the principle of *Milliken v. Bradley*, the Court also determined that the lower court had exceeded its authority by adopting an inter-district remedy for an intra-district violation.

Some school systems by the turn of the century, either to maintain desegregation gains or achieve the values attributed to a diverse student body, adopted desegregation maintenance or diversification plans. In *Parents Involved in Community Schools v. Seattle School District No. 1,* 551 U.S. 701 (2007), a case concerning diversity enhancement plans in Seattle and Louisville, the Court divided over their permissibility. Noting that racial classifications are subject to "strict scrutiny," the Court observed that government is required to show that they are narrowly tailored to achieve a compelling government interest. Although noting that remedying the effects of past intentional discrimination is a compelling interest, the Court found no evidence of wrongdoing in these cases. The Court distinguished the prohibition of race in primary and secondary school from higher education, where it may be a nonexclusive factor in the admission process. Minus any evidence that school officials had considered other methods to attain their goals, the Court determined that they had failed to meet the narrow tailoring requirement of "serious, good faith consideration of workable race-neutral alternatives." Justice Kennedy, in a concurring opinion, maintained that a school district may account for diversity—provided no individual is burdened or rewarded because of race. Kennedy's position, combined with the arguments of four dissenting justices who would have upheld the programs, left open the possibility that race may be factored to some extent. The ruling also did not preclude the use of income and other social factors to achieve a diverse student-body composition. Nor did it address the permissibility of diversification or integration maintenance plans pursuant to state constitutions.

The Discriminatory Purpose Requirement. The official systems of racial discrimination maintained during the separate but equal era largely vanished over the course of the late 20th Century. Although public schools were the primary focus of desegregation case law, the logic of these decisions extended to other venues and practices. In *McLaughlin v. Florida*, 379 U.S. 184 (1964), the Court invalidated a law that barred interracial cohabitation by persons of opposite sexes. The Court, in *Loving v. Virginia*, 388 U.S. 1 (1967), struck down a law prohibiting interracial marriage. Although racially symmetrical in their application, such laws reflected the ideology of racial superiority. In addition to finding an equal protection violation, the Court found that the enactment abridged the "freedom to marry" and thus violated due process.

The *de jure* requirement set forth in the desegregation context, conditioning an equal protection violation upon proof of segregative intent, introduced what became a prerequisite for establishing any equal protection claim. In a series of cases beginning with *Washington v. Davis*, 426 U.S. 229 (1976), the Court reviewed policies and programs challenged on grounds they had a racially disproportionate impact. Its conclusion in each instance was that, minus proof a discriminatory intent, there was no constitutional violation. At issue in *Washington v. Davis* was a test used to screen police officer candidates and upon which white applicants performed significantly better. The Court determined that statistical evidence by itself was insufficient and, to establish a *prima facie* case, the plaintiffs were required to prove a discriminatory purpose. It adopted this standard, among reasons, out of concern that a wide range of laws and regulations otherwise would be subject to constitutional challenge.

Proving a discriminatory motive was easy when formal segregation was the issue, because the illegal purpose was overt. When intent is not evident on the face of the law, proving its existence is more challenging. Laws that may appear racially neutral nonetheless may be discriminatory in their application. The Court recognized this possibility, in *Yick Wo v. Hopkins*, 118 U.S. 356 (1886), when it invalidated a city ordinance that prohibited laundries from operating in wooden buildings unless they applied for and received an exemption. Although neutral on its face, the law was applied in a discriminatory fashion. All applications for exemptions were granted, except for those by persons of Chinese descent.

Once discrimination was declared illegal, proof of wrongful motive became more challenging and dependent upon circumstantial evidence. In *Arlington Heights v. Metropolitan Housing Development Corp.*, 429 U.S. 252 (1977), the Court identified some factors that might support a finding of discriminatory intent. At issue was a zoning ordinance that did not target but effectively precluded development of racially integrated and low-income housing. Although reaffirming the discriminatory purpose requirement, the Court indicated that circumstantial evidence could establish an unconstitutional motive. In this regard, it referenced the utility of statistical disparities, patterns or effects that are inexplicable except on grounds of race, legislative history, and departures from normal procedures.

The Court, in *McCleskey v. Kemp*, 481 U.S. 279 (1987), upheld Georgia's death penalty law despite a showing that it disproportionately impacted African-Americans both at the prosecution and conviction levels. Referencing the state's history of a dual system of criminal justice, Justice Brennan noted that defense lawyers invariably (and pursuant to their ethical obligations) would factor race into the advice they gave clients with respect to accepting or rejecting a plea agreement. The Court was unmoved by statistical disparities that, in its words, "appear[ ] to correlate to race."

Other contexts in which the discriminatory purpose issue has arisen include the jury selection process and electoral redistricting. In *Batson v. Kentucky,* 476 U.S. 79 (1986), the Court determined that discriminatory purpose is established when it is shown that peremptory challenges were used to exclude persons on the basis of race. The Court, in *Shaw v. Reno,* 509 U.S. 630 (1993), found that an oddly configured congressional district could be understood only as the function of a racial motive.

In *United States v. O'Brien,* 391 U.S. 367 (1968), the Court observed that legislative motive is difficult to discern and thus should not be a part of First Amendment analysis. It has not explained why this concern is less in the equal protection context.

Affirmative Action. Case law concerning affirmative action typically relates to government policies or programs that establish preferences on the basis of race. Such classifications have been described as "benign" insofar as they are justified on grounds of remedying past discrimination or facilitating diversification. Standards of review in this area have evolved toward strict scrutiny, pursuant to the notion that all racial classifications are suspect. Contemporary equal protection principles allow race to be taken into account only in limited instances (i.e., to remedy a proven instance of discrimination or as one of multiple factors to achieve diversity in a higher education setting).

Remedial Classifications. Affirmative action decisions typically have been the work of a divided Court. This phenomenon commenced in *Regents of the University of California v. Bakke,* 438 U.S. 265 (1978), when the Court struck down a medical school admissions program that set aside seats for minority applicants. Four justices found that the program violated Title VI of the Civil Rights Act of 1964 and thus refused to address the constitutional issue. Four other justices determined that the program violated neither Title VI nor the equal protection guarantee. The outcome turned upon the opinion of Justice Powell, who found an equal protection and Title VI violation. He maintained that race could be a factor in the admission process, however, provided it was not an exclusive consideration.

Justice Powell's opinion was highly influential with respect to the Court's ultimate position on affirmative action. Key points that emanated from his opinion are that racial preferences should be strictly scrutinized and cannot be justified on the basis of societal discrimination. The university identified four key points in support of its preferential admissions policy, which included (1) ensuring that the school enrolled a minimum number of minority students, (2) eliminating discrimination, (3) improving health care in disadvantaged communities, and (4) maintaining a diverse student body. Responding to these rationales, Powell maintained that fixed racial goals were facially invalid. Although acknowledging that remedying past discrimination represented a valid interest, he believed that such action required specific legislative or judicial findings of wrongdoing by the institution itself. Powell saw no correlation between the goal of improved health care in disadvantaged communities and increased numbers of minority graduates. The one compelling interest he identified was diversification of the student body. In this regard, he observed that a diverse student body enriches the educational experience. Justice Brennan, joined by three other justices, advocated an intermediate standard of review that differentiated the law's good intentions from traditionally invidious racial classifications. Justice Blackmun, also dissenting, reasoned that "to get beyond racism, we must first take account of race."

For the next decade, the Court was divided over the appropriate standard of review for affirmative action cases. In *Fullilove v. Klutznick*, 448 U.S. 448 (1980), the Court upheld a federal set-aside program for minority contractors in public works projects. In an opinion authored by Chief Justice Burger, a three-justice plurality referenced Congress's power to enforce the Fourteenth Amendment as a key consideration. The Court, in *Wygant v. Jackson Board of Education,* 476 U.S. 267 (1986), struck down a collectively-bargained layoff plan that gave a preference to recently hired minorities. Writing for a four-justice plurality, Justice Powell used strict scrutiny to invalidate the plan. Pursuant to this standard of review, the plurality concluded that a general legacy of societal discrimination by itself was "too amorphous a basis" for a remedial racial preference. The Court, in *United States v. Paradise*, 480 U.S. 149 (1987), upheld a court order setting aside 50 percent of promotions to the rank of corporal for qualified African American state troopers in Alabama. This outcome, which included the use of quotas, was influenced by the state's intransigence toward rectifying its discriminatory practice. Although not embracing strict scrutiny, Justice Brennan maintained that the court order would meet this standard.

In *Richmond v. J. A. Croson Co.*, 488 U.S. 469 (1989), a majority of the Court adopted strict scrutiny as the standard of review for all racial classifications. This case concerned a municipal government's set-aside program for minority business enterprises that paralleled the federal plan upheld in *Fullilove v. Klutznick*. Writing for a four-justice plurality, Justice O'Connor determined that racial classifications regardless of their nature should be strictly scrutinized. The reason for this standard, from her perspective, was that remedial classifications had the capacity to stigmatize, reinforce racial stereotypes, and maintain the relevance of race throughout society. Without strict scrutiny, she maintained that there was no way to discern whether a classification was the function of a permissible purpose or unacceptable prejudice or stereotype.

In a concurring opinion, Justice Scalia maintained that race could be taken into account only to undo unlawful discrimination. Justice Marshall, in a dissenting opinion joined by Justices Brennan and Blackmun, argued for a lesser (intermediate) standard of review. The difference between strict and intermediate scrutiny is a matter of degree, evidenced by the intensity of terminology associated with each standard. Strict scrutiny assesses whether the government regulatory interest is "compelling" and the regulatory means are "narrowly tailored" toward the regulatory objective. An intermediate standard of review considers whether the regulatory interest is "important" and the regulatory means are "substantially related" to the regulatory objective. Both standards denote modalities of review that are more rigorous than the highly deferential rational basis test, which is used when the challenged government action does not implicate a constitutional interest. Although their operative terminology is less than precise, strict and intermediate standards of review imply a differentiation with respect to their level of intensity. Laws are at a higher constitutional risk when reviewed pursuant to a strict or intermediate standard of review (as opposed to a rational basis standard). The risk is greater when the review is based on strict rather than intermediate scrutiny.

Left open by the *Croson* decision was whether federal set aside programs, such as those upheld in *Fullilove v. Klutznick*, had been placed in jeopardy. In *Metro Broadcasting, Inc. v. Federal Communications Commission*, 497 U.S. 547 (1990), the Court employed an intermediate standard of review for purposes of evaluating racial preferences in the broadcast licensing process. This decision, like the ruling in *Fullilove v. Klutznick*, reflected deference to Congress. A less rigorous standard for federal programs bowed to Congress' authority, through the reconstruction amendments, the necessary and proper clause, and commerce clause, to enact enabling legislation. The Court ended this duality in *Adarand Constructors, Inc. v. Pena,* 515 U.S. 200 (1995), when it determined that federal affirmative action programs (like state programs) should be strictly scrutinized. Any such program thus must be justified by a compelling reason and narrowly tailored toward its purpose. The relevant governmental unit also must identify some instance of past racial discrimination, for which it is responsible, as a basis for taking race-conscious remedial action.

Diversity as a Compelling Interest. Affirmative action cases in the early twenty-first century have focused primarily upon diversification policies in higher education. As noted previously in connection with *Regents of the University of California v. Bakke,* Justice Powell endorsed the use of race as a nonexclusive factor in a university medical school's admission process. A majority of the Court, in *Grutter v. Bollinger,* 539 U.S. 306 (2003), embraced the premise that a diverse student body constitutes a compelling interest. It determined that diversity facilitates readiness for a multicultural life experience, cross-racial understanding, and dissipation of stereotypes. At issue in *Grutter* was the University of Michigan Law School's admission policy, which was structured to ensure a "critical mass" of students from designated historically disadvantaged groups. Consistent with Powell's admonition in *Bakke,* the university did not restrict the concept of diversity to race or ethnicity. The critical mass factor was important, from the school's perspective, because it improved minority student engagement. In assessing whether the policy was narrowly tailored, the Court determined that each candidate was individually evaluated without regard to race and assessed on how he or she might contribute to a diverse environment. Such individualized review, as opposed to a quota system, satisfied the Court that the process was narrowly tailored. Although upholding the program, the Court noted that the Fourteenth Amendment aimed to eliminate all official discrimination on the basis of race. It thus emphasized that policies that factor race must be limited in duration. The Court also anticipated that racial preferences would no longer be necessary in 25 years. Chief Justice Rehnquist, in a dissenting opinion joined by Justices Scalia, Kennedy, and Thomas, maintained that admission data over a period of several years indicated a fixed quota system.

In *Gratz v. Bollinger,* 539 U.S. 244 (2003), the Court reviewed the University of Michigan's undergraduate admission policy (which awarded 20 extra points to admission scores for applicants from designated minority groups). Although acknowledging that diversity could be a compelling interest, the Court determined that the challenged policy was not narrowly tailored toward this end. Chief

Justice Rehnquist, writing for the majority, maintained that the undergraduate process (unlike that of the law school) did not consider each student individually. The automatic boost in scores virtually guaranteed admission for minorities who met minimum standards. Individualized review of all applicants may be impossible for many schools, but the Court found this irrelevant. Justice O'Connor, joined by Justice Kennedy, concurred on grounds the points system amounted to a quota. Justice Thomas also concurred and emphasized that racial classifications in higher education categorically are impermissible. Justice Ginsburg, joined by Justice Souter, argued that a diverse student body was a narrowly tailored remedy for undoing the effects of racial discrimination.

In *Fisher v. University of Texas at Austin*, 570 U.S. 297 (2013) *Fisher I*, the Court, in a 7–1 decision, affirmed the central precepts of *Bakke*, *Gratz*, and *Grutter*, holding that institutions of higher education could seek to achieve the educational benefits of diversity, so long as their policies met judicial standards under strict scrutiny. The Court vacated the decision and remanded the case to the Court of Appeals to determine if the University had met its heavy evidentiary burden under strict scrutiny. Justice Ginsburg dissented, finding that the Court of Appeals had applied the proper analysis. Going forward, it appears a majority of the Court will reject the use of race in higher education admissions policies, unless the government can meet rigorous narrow-tailoring analysis, including proof that the government could not achieve its compelling purpose using race-neutral alternatives. The majority wrote: "The reviewing court must ultimately be satisfied that no workable race-neutral alternatives would produce the educational benefits of diversity."

In *Schuette v. Coalition to Defend Affirmative Action, Integration, Immigrant Rights and Fight for Equality by any Means Necessary*, 572 U.S. 291 (2014), the Court was confronted by a state constitutional amendment that banned affirmative action. The amendment was offered following the Court's decision in the University of Michigan's undergraduate affirmative action plan in *Gratz v. Bollinger*, 539 U.S. 244 (2003), and the Court's decision to uphold a law school admission plan that was presented in *Grutter v. Bollinger*, 539 U.S. 306 (2003). Although both admissions plans permitted the explicit consideration of an applicant's race, *Gratz* invalidated the undergraduate plan, and *Grutter* upheld the law school admission plan's more limited use of race-based preferences. In response to *Gratz*, the university revised its undergraduate admissions process in a way that still allowed a limited use of race-based preferences. Thereafter, Michigan voters adopted the constitutional amendment which prohibited state and other governmental entities in Michigan from granting race-based preferences in a wide range of actions and decisions. Noting that the case was not about the permissibility of race-conscious admissions policies in higher education, the Court upheld the constitutional amendment: "The question is whether, and in what manner, voters in the States may choose to prohibit the consideration of racial preferences in governmental decisions, in particular with respect to school admissions." Noting that the Amendment "reflects in part the national dialogue regarding the wisdom and practicality of race-conscious admissions policies in higher education," the Court upheld the Amendment: "there was no infliction of a specific injury of the kind at issue in *Mulkey* and *Hunter*," the Court refused to restrict "the right of Michigan voters to determine that race-based preferences granted by Michigan governmental entities should be ended." "Here Michigan voters acted in concert and statewide to seek consensus and adopt a policy on a difficult subject against a historical background of race in America that has been a source of tragedy and persisting injustice. Were the Court to rule that the question addressed by Michigan voters is too sensitive or complex to be within the grasp of the electorate; or that the policies at issue remain too delicate to be resolved save by university officials or faculties, acting at some remove from immediate public scrutiny and control; or that these matters are so arcane that the electorate's power must be limited because the people cannot prudently exercise that power even after a full debate, that holding would be an unprecedented restriction on the exercise of a fundamental right held not just by one person but by all in common. It is the right to speak and debate and learn and then, as a matter of political will, to act through a lawful electoral process."

Gender Classifications. The Supreme Court invented the "intermediate" standard of judicial scrutiny in a decision involving gender classification. *Craig v. Boren*, 429 U.S. 190 (1976). The Court's opinions before 1971 upheld gender classifications in cases where state interests reflected stereotyped distinctions between the sexes. A state law excluding women from the practice of law was upheld in *Bradwell v. Illinois*, 83 U.S. (16 Wall.) 130 (1872), on the grounds that "the female sex" are unfit for "many of the occupations of civil life", that the "domestic sphere" is "that which properly belongs to the domain and functions of womanhood", and that "the idea of a woman adopting a distinct and independent career from that of her husband" is "repugnant". More than 90 years later, the Court upheld a statute that exempted women from jury duty in *Hoyt v. Florida*, 368 U.S. 57 (1961), on the theory that women serve as "the center of home and family life". Court, in *Reed v. Reed*, 404 U.S. 71 (1971), indicated the potential for more meaningful review of gender classifications.

The *Reed* Court rejected the state law's implicit reliance on stereotyped assumptions that, because they are not as "conversant with business affairs" women as a class are less qualified than men to act as the administrators of estates. The state law in *Reed* provided that when two persons seek appointment to serve as the administrator of an decedent's estate, and when each person is equally entitled to this appointment under state law, the probate judge must select a male applicant over a female applicant. The plaintiff in *Reed* was the mother of a child who had died intestate, and given the fact that she and the child's father were equally entitled to appointment as administrators, the state law required the probate judge to select the father. The *Reed* Court recognized that there was "some legitimacy" in the state's purported interest in reducing the workload of probate courts through the adoption of rules that would eliminate disputes between persons seeking appointment as administrators. But the Court ruled unanimously that the establishment of a "mandatory preference for either sex" was an arbitrary legislative choice. Thus, the law was not "reasonable" and did not "rest upon some ground of difference having a fair and substantial relation" to the state's interest.

Soon after *Reed*, the Court invalidated a federal law that automatically granted medical benefits and a housing allowance to wives of men in the armed services, but denied such benefits to husbands unless such women could show that he depended upon her for more than 50% of his support. The law in *Frontiero v. Richardson*, 411 U.S. 677 (1973), thus discriminated against men because only the benefits of husbands were restricted (and discriminated against women because the proof requirement imposed upon female service members was not imposed on their male colleagues). The government argued that administrative convenience justified the federal law, since the armed services included 99% male members and 1% female members. A plurality of four justices proposed that strict scrutiny should be used to invalidate the law in *Frontiero*, but Justice Rehnquist provided the fifth vote for this result. He noted that the *Reed* Court's analysis supplied "abundant" support for the *Frontiero* Court's result and, because of the "far-reaching implications" of such a decision, he saw no reason to add gender to the list of suspect classifications.

Three years later, the *Craig* majority endorsed an analytical compromise between the strict scrutiny standard and the rational basis standard, a criterion which came to be described as "intermediate scrutiny". The *Craig* Court declared that the use of gender classifications should serve "important governmental objectives" and that such classifications "must be substantially related to the achievement of these objectives". The law in *Craig* discriminated against men between 18 and 21, who could not purchase low-alcohol beer even though women of the same age could do so. The Court accepted the state's interest in traffic safety as "important" in *Craig*, but rejected the use of this gender classification as an "administratively convenient" method for achieving that interest. The state's classification was not based on empirical evidence that young men drove drunk more often than young women, but only on "archaic and overbroad" generalizations about each sex.

In later cases, the Court sometimes upheld gender classifications under the intermediate scrutiny standard. In *Califano v. Webster*, 430 U.S. 313 (1977), the Court upheld a federal law that gave women higher social security benefits. The Court recognized the importance of the government interest in compensating women as a class for having been "unfairly hindered from earning as much as men" and for having received lower retirement benefits on the average than men. The Court accepted the idea that such class-based remedial treatment was "substantially related to the achievement of the government interest." If the Court had applied strict scrutiny, however, narrow tailoring of the law arguably would have required the law to grant the higher social security benefits only to women who had low retirement benefits. In *Rostker v. Goldberg*, 453 U.S. 57 (1981), the Court upheld the federal law that required only men but not women to register for the draft, determining that this exclusion of women was substantially related to the federal exclusion of women from combat. If the Court had applied strict scrutiny, the law arguably would have been invalidated because of the lack of narrow tailoring, given the fact that women could be drafted to serve in non-combat positions.

The Court's modern interpretation of intermediate scrutiny was exhibited in *United States v. Virginia*, 518 U.S. 515 (1996). In this case, which concerned an all male military academy, the Court reiterated the language of earlier opinions which declared that gender classifications require "an exceedingly persuasive justification." In pairing that phrase with the *Craig* formula, the Court emphasized that it would exercise "skeptical scrutiny of official action" to support gender classifications because of "volumes of history" concerning the prevalence of sex discrimination. The Court held that the government failed to provide the required justification for the exclusion of women from the state military college, notwithstanding the effort to show that only men could be expected to possess the physical and mental stamina required to cope with its rigors. The Court viewed the state's gender-exclusion policy as embedded in arbitrary and stereotyped judgments about men and women, a promise that had been condemned in every Equal Protection decision since *Reed*.

Alienage Classifications. Modern Supreme Court decisions apply strict judicial scrutiny to most state laws that treat citizens and non-citizens differently. This standard was adopted for alienage classifications in *Graham v. Richardson*, 403 U.S. 365 (1971). Strict scrutiny also applies to classifications which treat citizens or non-citizens differently according to the national origins of their ancestors. Some classifications discriminate in both ways, like the invalidated state law in *Takahashi v. Fish & Game Commission*, 334 U.S. 410 (1948), which prohibited the issuance of a commercial fishing license to any alien Japanese (including all foreign-born persons of Japanese ancestry).

The *Takahashi* decision predated *Brown v. Board of Education*, 347 U.S. 483 (1954), and so the Court did not employ the *Brown*-based formulas that would be used in *Graham* and later cases. However, the *Takahashi* Court did establish an important concept—the so-called "right of abode" for aliens, which the Court found to be embodied in the Equal Protection Clause, in the federal civil rights laws, and in the federal immigration laws. This right encompassed that of any lawful resident alien to enter any state and settle there, the right to seek employment and earn a living there, and the right to "abide in any state" on "an equality of legal privileges with all citizens under non-discriminatory laws".

The Court's recognition of the right of abode for aliens produced two rules that laid the foundation for modern Equal Protection analysis. First, the *Takahashi* Court held that state alienage classifications cannot conflict with federal immigration law under the Supremacy Clause. Only Congress has the federal constitutional power to regulate the admission, naturalization, and residence of aliens. States cannot impair the rights of aliens that are recognized implicitly in federal law, such as the right to earn a living as residents of any state. Second, the Court held that the state interest in the preservation of resources is not weighty enough alone to justify the denial of the right of abode to aliens. This holding pushed the deferential "special public interest" doctrine aside, and served as the first sign of its decline and ultimate demise. The *Takahashi* decision implicitly recognized that all state residents, citizens and non-citizens alike, share a community interest in state resources.

Following the *Brown* ruling, the Court's analysis of alienage classifications began to fortify Equal Protection doctrine as it related to aliens. The *Graham* Court recognized that strict scrutiny is appropriate for such classifications because aliens as a class comprise a "discrete and insular minority" and alienage classifications are "inherently suspect". In the 1970s, the Court's alienage decisions required state laws to advance a "substantial" state interest, achieved by means that are "necessary and precisely drawn." By the mid-1980s, the alienage opinions echoed the familiar strict-scrutiny formula for racial classifications, including the requirements of a "compelling state interest" achieved through narrow legislative tailoring by the "least restrictive means".

The *Graham* decision illustrates the operation of modern analysis for alienage classifications. One state law in *Graham* denied welfare benefits to aliens who became indigent after admission to the United States. Another state's law granted such benefits only to aliens who were long-term residents of the state before their indigency occurred. In effect, these laws meant that aliens would have no money for food, clothing, or shelter, when they lost their jobs due to disability or illness. As in *Takahashi,* the *Graham* Court rejected the argument that such laws could be defended based on a "special public interest" in preserving state benefits for others by depriving aliens of access to them. This state interest was too insubstantial to justify the denial of the Equal Protection right of abode to aliens. The *Graham* Court also held that these laws encroached upon federal immigration policy by deterring aliens from seeking admission to the country and settling in any state.

The new element of the *Graham* analysis included the Court's emphasis on the fact that aliens and citizens make equal contributions to the state and national communities, through their payment of federal and state taxes, their service in the armed forces, and their contributions to local economies from working and spending their incomes in the state. Indigent aliens and indigent citizens thus deserve to have equal access to tax-revenue-funded programs, based on their fulfillment of shared obligations to their state communities. The *Graham* Court also made use of a classic *Brown* concept in declaring that states may not preserve the fiscal integrity of any program through the use of "invidious" classifications.

In post-*Graham* cases, the Court invalidated other state laws using strict scrutiny. In *Nyquist v. Mauclet,* 432 U.S. 1 (1977), the state law made resident aliens ineligible to apply for state-funded college scholarships, based on the state interest in enhancing the education of the electorate. Given the insignificant impact that alien scholarships would have on the funds available for all scholarship awards, the Court held that the state interest was too insubstantial to justify the alien-exclusion law. In *Application of Griffiths,* 413 U.S. 717 (1973), the Court reviewed a law that barred all aliens from the practice of law on the theory that they might allow loyalty to a "foreign power" to supercede other duties held that the law was not narrowly tailored to achieve the state's interest in insuring attorney loyalty towards clients and courts, because the law. It rejected the state's unsubstantiated assumption that aliens performing the traditional work of attorneys would be subjected to such loyalty conflicts.

In later cases, the Court continued to validate the broad principles of *Takahashi* and *Graham* by invalidating state laws that imposed discriminatory burdens on aliens that conflicted with Congressional policy. For example, in *Toll v. Moreno*, 458 U.S. 1 (1982), the Court invalidated a state law that disqualified state-domiciled aliens from receiving the benefit of discounted college tuition for "in-state" residents. It noted that federal law treated such aliens as eligible for state domiciles and for tax exemptions that gave them incentives to settle in the United States. By contrast, in *DeCanas v. Bica*, 424 U.S. 351 (1976), the Court upheld a state law that did not conflict with federal immigration policy by penalizing employers who hired non-lawful-resident aliens as defined by federal law.

The Court's modern alienage decisions recognize three exceptions to strict scrutiny. The first two allow the Court to use a "rational basis" level of judicial review. The "political function" exception allows a state to exclude aliens from eligibility for particular civil service jobs. Specifically, the Court has upheld the exclusion of aliens from employment as public school teachers and police or probation officers. These jobs require the performance of a basic government function by a civil servant who must exercise discretionary power in a position of authority over others. Therefore, the Court has found that the exclusion of aliens from these jobs serves "legitimate political ends." Only citizens possess the right to vote, and under the "political function" exception, only they may be declared eligible for government jobs that "substantially" affect other citizens and involve the execution of public policy in a democracy.

However, the law in *Sugarman v. Dougall*, 413 U.S. 634 (1973), serves as an example of a classification that cannot qualify for the "political function" exception. That law barred aliens from all competitive civil services jobs. It was overinclusive because it covered office worker jobs who had no duties or discretionary power to make or implement "policy". The Court found the law was not narrowly tailored. Given the insufficient showing of a nexus between the attribute of alien status, and the state interest in saving the costs of training new civil servants, it invalidated the enactment.

The second exception to strict scrutiny allows the Court to use "rational basis" scrutiny for federal alienage classifications. The

Court justifies this deferential type of scrutiny based on the importance of federal lawmaking on issues of immigration and naturalization. As a result, the Court's decisions have upheld federal alien-exclusion laws that would fail the strict scrutiny standard if enacted by state legislatures. For example, even though *Sugarman* invalidated a state law excluding aliens from all civil service jobs, the federal courts upheld a similar federal ban that was established by an executive order.

The third exception to strict scrutiny applies to state classifications of non-lawful-resident aliens, which classifications receive "intermediate" judicial scrutiny. The Court invalidated a law that excluded non-lawful-resident child aliens from public schools in *Plyler v. Doe*, 457 U.S. 202 (1982), because the government could not make an adequate showing that the law furthered a "substantial" state interest. The state's interests bore some resemblance to the old "special public interests" in preserving resources for citizens. Its evidence was insufficient to show that the exclusion of illegal-alien children would reduce the failure of non-excluded children to put their education to use within the state, or improve the quality of public education in the state, or lift a significant burden from the state's economy.

Classifications Involving Unmarried Parents and Their Children. The Supreme Court adopted the intermediate scrutiny standard in *Clark v. Jeter*, 486 U.S. 456 (1988), for the assessment of Equal Protection challenges to classifications that restrict the rights of unmarried parents and their children. This doctrinal step came after twenty years of litigation, during which time the Court decided cases involving a variety of such classifications (many of which were designed to deter fraudulent claims of paternity). The *Clark* Court recognized that the advent of DNA testing cast doubt upon the need for such laws, however, because it is possible to determine paternity as a matter of almost virtual certainty using the DNA parentage test.

The *Clark* Court invalidated a six-year time limit on support suits by non-marital children, a provision which did not apply to the children of married parents. Even though the *Clark* Court recognized that this objective of the state was "important," the Court held that it could not show that the six-year time limit was "substantially related to the achievement" of this objective. The law was overinclusive because DNA testing provided a better means of discovering and eliminating false paternity claims. The law was underinclusive because the state did not apply the six-year time limit to all suits raising paternity issues.

In the pre-*Clark* era, dissenting justices argued repeatedly for an intermediate scrutiny standard as a replacement for the rational basis test. The results in several cases thus were undermined by the Court's decision to embrace the intermediate standard. For example, the Court upheld statutes which provided that a non-marital child could not inherit from a father who died intestate unless the child had obtained a notarized document expressing the father's desire to "legitimate" the child (or obtained a court order of "filiation" during the father's lifetime). *See Labine v. Vincent*, 401 U.S. 532 (1971); *Lalli v. Lalli*, 439 U.S. 259 (1978). In *Mathews v. Lucas*, 427 U.S. 495 (1976), a provision of the Social Security Act allowed a non-marital child to receive surviving-child-insurance benefits only by providing proof that the deceased father supported the child at the time of his death. The *Mathews* Court upheld this law based on "administrative convenience", even though this state interest was rejected in the early gender classification cases that relied on rational basis review. Finally, in *Parham v. Hughes*, 441 U.S. 347 (1979), the Court upheld a law that barred an unmarried father from bringing a wrongful death suit against the tortfeasor responsible for his child's death—unless the father had filed a petition for a court order of legitimation when the child was alive. The soundness of each of these rulings is suspect today, in light of the ready availability of DNA testing, and in light of the difficulty of defending these laws as being "substantially related to the achievement" of the state objectives at issue.

The Court has used the pre-*Clark* rational basis test to invalidate a variety of laws that prohibited non-marital children and their parents from receiving legal benefits that granted to married parents and their children. For example, in *Gomez v. Perez*, 409 U.S. 535 (1973), the Court struck down a law that barred non-marital children from seeking orders of support from their parents. In *Trimble v. Gordon*, 430 U.S. 762 (1977), the Court invalidated a law that barred non-marital children from sharing in the intestate estate of their father. In *Weber v. Aetna Casualty & Surety Co.*, 406 U.S. 164 (1972), the Court held that "unacknowleged" non-marital children could not be deprived of worker's compensation benefits. In some of these cases, the Court viewed the laws as examples of "invidious discrimination" that penalized non-marital children for a status beyond their control. The rational basis test could be used to invalidate these laws because of the obvious lack of "some ground of difference" between non-marital and marital children which had "a fair and substantial relation" to the state's interest.

In other cases in the pre-*Clark* era, the Court invalidated laws that deprived unmarried fathers of their rights to custody of their children. For example, in *Stanley v. Illinois*, 405 U.S. 645 (1972), the Court relied on Due Process as well as Equal Protection to strike down a law that automatically cut off an unmarried father's right to the custody of his child when the child's mother died. Similarly, in *Caban v. Mohammed*, 441 U.S. 380 (1979), the Court used Equal Protection to invalidate a law that granted the right to block an adoption only to unmarried mothers and not to unmarried fathers.

In the post-*Clark* era, the Court has upheld laws that involve the intertwined classifications of gender, non-marital children and their parents, and immigration. The Court purports to rely on intermediate scrutiny in cases involving these intertwined classifications, rather than the rational basis standard that is used for evaluating federal immigration classifications. The pro-government results in these decisions may be ascribed, in part, to judicial deference that derives from the immigration context. For example, under the naturalization law, a non-marital child of a citizen mother will be granted citizenship automatically when born outside the U.S., but a citizen father of the same child would not be able to obtain citizenship for his non-marital child without taking additional steps to demonstrate paternity. This different treatment was upheld in *Tuan Anh Nguyen v. Immigration and Naturalization Service*, 533 U.S. 53 (2001). The Court reasoned that the intermediate scrutiny standard was satisfied because Congress justifiably recognized the significant differences with respect to the relationship of each parent to a non-marital child at the time of birth. The different treatment of citizen mothers and citizen fathers could be upheld because they "substantially relate" to the important state interest in assuring that a biological relationship exists between parent and child. There is an additional important interest of insuring that an opportunity exists for the development of real ties between the child, the parent, and the United States.

Classifications of Persons with Mental Disabilities. The Supreme Court decided to evaluate classifications of persons with mental disabilities under a rational basis standard in *City of Cleburne v. Cleburne Living Center*, 473 U.S. 432 (1985), rather than the intermediate scrutiny standard advocated by a plurality of three justices. It nonetheless invalidated a city ordinance that required the plaintiff to obtain a special use permit for the operation of a group home for mentally disabled persons.

In explaining why the intermediate scrutiny standard was not appropriate for classifications based on mental disability, the Court reasoned that the adoption of this standard could create a "floodgates" problem. The same level of scrutiny would have to be adopted for other groups with a history of discrimination and immutable disabilities, such as aged persons and persons with physical disabilities. The Court also opined that modern laws do not usually create arbitrary restrictions on the rights of the mentally disabled without a valid interest, and reasoned that the rational basis test would provide sufficient protection for the civil rights of mentally disabled people.

Based on the record in *City of Cleburne*, the Court articulated two rationales for its determination that the denial of the permit was based on invidious discrimination. First, the city defended the denial of the permit based on the potential hostility of neighbors, and the Court rejected this government interest as an illegitimate endorsement of private bias. Second, all the other justifications for the permit denial could have been used to deny permits to other facilities with no mentally disabled inhabitants, but such justifications never produced denials of other permits for other group home applicants.

A second example of the operation of the rational basis test is illustrated by *Heller v. Doe*, 509 U.S. 312 (1993). The *Heller* Court upheld a classification that provided more limited rights for mentally disabled persons than for mentally ill people. Specifically, mentally disabled people could be committed based on a lesser proof standard (clear and convincing evidence) and their relatives could supply evidence as parties in commitment proceedings. By contrast, mentally ill people received the protections of a higher proof standard (beyond a reasonable doubt) and prohibition upon their relatives acting as parties. The Court found that the state had a rational basis for creating these different procedures based, in part, on the more serious consequences that follow from commitment of mentally ill people (including treatment for mental illness).

Classifications Based on Sexual Orientation. The Supreme Court precedents of *Bowers v. Hardwick,* 478 U.S. 186 (1986) and *Lawrence v. Texas*, 539 U.S. 558 (2003) are discussed in the chapter on Substantive Due Process and Fundamental Rights, in the section on Sexual Orientation.

After the *Bowers* Court used rational basis scrutiny to hold that the Due Process right of privacy did not encompass a "constitutional right to engage in sodomy," the Court turned to Equal Protection doctrine when it addressed sexual orientation in *Romer v. Evans*, 517 U.S. 620 (1996). The *Romer* Court invalidated a state constitutional amendment that repealed state and local anti-discrimination laws provide protections for "homosexual, lesbian or bisexual orientation, conduct, practices or relationships" and prohibited the future enactment of such laws. The Court reasoned that this classification lacked any rational relationship to a legitimate state interest. In effect, this amendment denied to a class of persons the right to seek the enactment of laws to protect themselves from discrimination. It thus violated the Equal Protection Clause.

In *Lawrence*, the Court overruled *Bowers* and invalidated a state statute that made it a crime to engage in sodomy with a person of the same sex, reasoning that the rational basis standard of review required the Court to find that this ban on same-sex private conduct was inconsistent with the Due Process privacy right. The *Lawrence* Court expressly declined to base its ruling on Equal Protection, as advocated by Justice O'Connor's concurrence. In relying on Due Process, the Court made it clear that the constitutional defect of the law could not be cured by redrafting it with narrower tailoring.

The next area of litigation focused on the right to same-sex marriage. In 2013, in *Hollingsworth v. Perry*, 570 U.S. 693 (2013), the Court struck down Section 3 of the Defense of Marriage Act (DOMA), 110 Stat. 2419. That section provided a federal definition of "marriage" and "spouse": "In determining the meaning of any Act of Congress, or of any ruling, regulation, or interpretation of the various administrative bureaus and agencies of the United States, the word 'marriage' means only a legal union between one man and one woman as husband and wife, and the word 'spouse' refers only to a person of the opposite sex who is a husband or a wife." In rejecting DOMA, the Court emphasized that "the definition and regulation of marriage has been treated as being within the authority and realm of the separate States," that the federal government has historically "deferred to state-law policy decisions with respect to domestic relations," and that an individual state's decision to give a class of citizens the right to marry confers "upon them a dignity and status of immense import." In striking down the law, the Court noted that DOMA departs from the "history and tradition of reliance on state law to define marriage," and "violates basic due process and equal protection principles applicable to the Federal Government."

At the same time, the Court decided *Hollingsworth v. Perry*, 570 U.S. 693 (2013), in which the Court refused to decide the question of whether the Equal Protection Clause "prohibits the State of California from defining marriage as a union between a man and a woman." The Court held that a challenge by same-sex couples was not justiciable. The case arose in 2008 after the California Supreme Court held that the equal protection clause of the California Constitution prohibited the state from limiting the official designation of marriage to opposite-sex couples. California voters responded by passing a ballot initiative (Proposition 8) that amended California's Constitution to provide that "only marriage between a man and a woman is valid or recognized in California." Cal. Const., Art. I, § 7.5. Respondents, two same-sex couples who wished to marry, challenged Proposition 8 in federal court based on the Due Process and Equal Protection Clauses of the Fourteenth Amendment to the Federal Constitution. The District Court declared Proposition 8 unconstitutional, permanently enjoined the California officials from enforcing the law. When California officials decided not to appeal the order, the proponents of the ballot initiative attempted to do so. The Court concluded that they lacked standing.

The most important decision regarding same-sex marriage was rendered in *Obergefell v. Hodges*, 576 U.S. 644 (2015). In that case, same-sex couples sued, claiming that state laws defining marriage as a union between a man and a woman violated both the Equal Protection Clause and the Fourteenth Amendment by denying them the right to marry or to have their marriages, lawfully performed in another State, given full recognition. The Court agreed. The Court held that the Constitution protects certain "fundamental liberties" including "personal choices central to individual dignity and autonomy, including intimate choices that define personal identity and beliefs." And the Court regarded the right to marry as one of those fundamental rights, noting that it had struck down laws prohibiting interracial unions, a law prohibiting fathers who were behind on child support from marrying, and a law prohibiting prison inmates from marrying. The Court based its decision on several factors. First, the Court held that "the right to personal choice regarding marriage is inherent in the concept of individual autonomy. Like choices concerning contraception, family relationships, procreation, and child-rearing, all of which are protected by the Constitution, decisions concerning marriage are among the most intimate that an individual can make." Second, the right to marry supports a two-person union: "Marriage offers the hope of companionship and understanding and assurance that while both still live there will be someone to care for the other. Same-sex couples have the same right as opposite-sex couples to enjoy intimate association." Third, "the right to marry safeguards children and families. Marriage affords the permanency and stability important to children's best interests. Without the recognition, stability, and predictability marriage offers, the children of same-sex couples suffer the stigma of knowing their families are somehow lesser." Finally, the Court emphasized that "marriage is a keystone of our social order. Just as a couple vows to support each other, so does society pledge to support the couple, offering symbolic recognition and material benefits to protect and nourish the union." In particular, married receive benefits related to taxation; inheritance and property rights; rules of intestate succession; spousal privilege in the law of evidence; hospital access; medical decisionmaking authority; adoption rights; the rights and benefits of survivors; birth and death certificates; professional ethics rules; campaign finance restrictions; workers' compensation benefits; health insurance; and child custody, support, and visitation rules." In addition, the Court expressed concern that, by excluding same-sex couples from the right to marry, there is the "effect of teaching that gays and lesbians are unequal in important respects." As a result, laws "excluding same-sex couples from the marriage right impose stigma and injury of the kind prohibited by our basic charter." Therefore, the Court concluded that the same-sex marriage ban burdens "the liberty of same-sex couples," and "abridge central precepts of equality." The "right to marry is a fundamental right inherent in the liberty of the person, and under the Due Process and Equal Protection Clauses of the Fourteenth Amendment couples of the same-sex may not be deprived of that right and that liberty," and "the State laws challenged in these cases are invalid to the extent they exclude same-sex couples from civil marriage on the same terms and conditions as opposite-sex couples." The Court flatly rejected the idea that "allowing same-sex couples to wed will harm marriage as an institution."

Equal Protection and Fundamental Rights. Two types of discrimination count for equal protection purposes. The first category includes classifications on the basis of group status. The second category consists of selective denials of fundamental rights, regardless of the claimant's group status. Such a deprivation triggers a heightened standard of review. Equal protection review of a fundamental rights deprivation generally mirrors due process analysis. Many cases concerning fundamental rights implicate both the due process and equal protection clauses. Government action that abridges liberty on a wholesale basis gives rise to a due process claim. Equal protection claims arise when a liberty is denied selectively. The due process clause thus prohibits government action altogether insofar as it burdens a fundamental right. The equal protection guarantee precludes government action only to the extent it classifies impermissibly. The law may be allowable to the extent it can be structured in a manner that it is not inappropriately exclusionary.

Equal Protection and Enumerated Rights. Regardless of whether a constitutional right is enumerated or not, equal protection is implicated when it is denied on a selective basis. When government controls access to a public forum on the basis of preferred viewpoints, for instance, it violates not only the First Amendment but the equal protection guarantee. The Court in *Police Department of Chicago v. Mosley*, 408 U.S. 92 (1972), thus observed that government must give all points of view an equal opportunity to be heard.

Limitations on access to the criminal justice system raise both Sixth Amendment (which provides for "Assistance of Counsel" to persons accused of a crime) and equal protection concerns. In *Griffin v. Illinois*, Justice Black made the point that equal justice is impossible when the quality of a trial depends on the defendant's wealth. The Court, in *Douglas v. California*, 368 U.S. 815 (1961), relied on the equal protection guarantee in support of its determination that counsel must be provided to indigent appellants pursuing a first appeal as a matter of right. This right was extended to discretionary appeals in *Ross v. Moffitt*, 417 U.S. 600 (1974).

The Court, in *Bearden v. Georgia*, 461 U.S. 660 (1983), differentiated the focal points of due process and equal protection analysis. In this regard, it explained that due process review is concerned with the fairness of the relationship between the defendant and criminal justice process. Equal protection review is concerned with whether the defendant has been denied an important benefit available to other classes of defendants.

Equal Protection and Unenumerated Rights.

The Right to Interstate Travel. The Constitution does not indicate specifically a right to interstate travel. Because a viable political and economic union depends upon the right to travel freely across state lines, there is not much debate over its constitutional validity (unlike, for instance, the textually unenumerated right of privacy). In *Saenz v. Roe*, 526 U.S. 489 (1999), the Court noted that the right to travel has three separate and distinct components. It "protects the right of a citizen of one State to enter and to leave another State, the right to be treated as a welcome visitor rather than an unfriendly alien when temporarily present in the second State, and for those travelers who elect to become permanent residents, the right to be treated like other citizens of that State."

The right to travel cases primarily concern the constitutionality of residence-based requirements which establish eligibility for various types of state benefits. The issue in these cases is not the legitimacy of the state's interest in setting *bona fide* residence requirements. This concern is acknowledged as reasonable and would be reviewed pursuant to a rational basis standard. The key question centers upon the length of the pre-eligibility period. The permissible duration generally depends upon the significance of the interest at stake. In this regard, it is useful to focus upon whether it represents a "basic necessity" of life.

The seminal right to travel decision, for equal protection purposes, is *Shapiro v. Thompson*, 394 U.S. 618 (1969). At issue in this case was a one-year residence requirement to establish eligibility for welfare benefits. The state justified the waiting period on grounds it was necessary to protect the fiscal integrity of its public assistance programs. Although noting that the state's concern with fiscal integrity was valid, the Court determined that the requirement unconstitutionally burdened interstate migration. It also rejected arguments that residents should be treated differently based upon the length of their relationship with the state and corresponding tax contributions. This outcome was reached pursuant to a strict scrutiny standard of review.

The same standard was used in *Memorial Hospital v. Maricopa County*, 415 U.S. 250 (1974), when the Court struck down a one-year residence requirement for county-subsidized non-emergency medical care. The Court noted that residence requirements and waiting periods are not *per se* unconstitutional and indicated that use of strict scrutiny is reserved for instances when a necessity of life is at stake.

Consistent with this understanding the Court in *Sosna v. Iowa*, 419 U.S. 393 (1975), upheld a one-year residency requirement for seeking a divorce. Likewise, in *Vlandis v. Kline*, 412 U.S. 441 (1973), it upheld a one-year residency requirement to qualify for in-state tuition at a public university. Rational basis review, because of its deferential nature, typically favors the challenged government policy. The opposite occurred in *Zobel v. Williams,* 457 U.S. 55 (1982), however, when the Court struck down an Alaska program that distributed oil production royalties to citizens on the basis of length of residence in the state. It found no rational basis for the state's arguments that the program created a financial incentive for persons to establish and maintain residence in Alaska, encouraged prudent management of the fund, and apportioned benefits on the basis of contributions made by residents over the years. None of these rationales, from the Court's perspective, supported the validity of a residence requirement. In this regard, the Court was concerned with the possibility that other rights, benefits, and services might be conditioned upon length of residence.

Residence requirements for veteran benefits have been subject to different levels of review. The Court in *Hooper v. Bernalillo County Assessor*, 472 U.S. 612 (1985), invalidated a tax exemption for Vietnam veterans who resided in the state prior to a designated date. Although the state viewed the exemption as a means of recognizing its citizens' military contributions, the Court found no reasonable relationship between this interest and the classification. The use of the rational basis test contrasts with the invalidation of a hiring preference for veterans who lived in the state at the time they joined the military. In *Attorney General of New York v. Soto-Lopez*, 476 U.S. 898 (1986), a plurality of the Court used strict scrutiny to achieve this result. The more exacting standard of review reflected the perceived importance of the interest. The plurality maintained that the state's desire to recognize military contributions could have been achieved constitutionally by extending the preference to all veterans living in the state.

Voting. The right to vote in federal elections is conferred by Art. I, sec. 2 of the Constitution. Although the right to vote in state elections is not mentioned by the federal constitution, the Court has described it as "fundamental" to a "free and democratic society." *Harper v. Virginia Board of Elections,* 383 U.S. 663, 665 (1966). This understanding derives from the sense that the right to vote is preservative of basic civil and political rights. In *Baker v. Carr,* 369 U.S. 186 (1962), the Court declared voting a fundamental right and announced that state legislative districts must reflect the principle of "one man, one vote." The significance of the right to vote is evidenced by several constitutional provisions that limit governmental power to regulate it. The Fifteenth Amendment prohibits denial of the right to vote "on account of race, color, or previous condition of servitude." The Nineteenth Amendment prohibits abridgment of the right to vote "on account of sex." The Twenty-fourth Amendment prohibits poll taxes. The Twenty-sixth Amendment extends the right to vote to citizens who are 18 years or older. Equal protection cases concerning the right to vote fall into two categories, which relate respectively to denial and dilution of the right to vote.

Voter eligibility requirements, unrelated to age, citizenship, or residence, typically draw close attention. The most commonly reviewed tools for limiting eligibility have been poll taxes and special purpose districts.

Poll Taxes. Throughout the South, poll taxes were a common tool for denying African-Americans the right to vote. In *Harper v. Virginia State Board of Elections,* the Court determined that wealth was not relevant to a person's ability to participate intelligently in the electoral process. It further found that imposing a tax on the right to vote constituted an "invidious" discrimination that violated the equal protection guarantee. The Twenty-fourth Amendment prohibited poll taxes.

Special Purpose Districts. Limitations on the right to vote in special purpose elections typically are subject to "close and exacting" review. Consistent with this standard, the Court in *Kramer v. Union Free School District,* 395 U.S. 621 (1969), invalidated a state law that restricted voting in school board elections to persons who owned or leased property or had children enrolled in the district's schools. The enactment aimed to limit voting to those citizens who had a primary interest in decisions concerning the schools. The Court determined that the law excluded some persons with a direct interest in school matters and included others whose concern was indirect or remote. Based upon this assessment, it concluded that the restriction was not sufficiently precise.

The Court, in *Salyer Land Co. v. Tulare Lake Basin Water Storage District,* 410 U.S. 719 (1973), upheld a law limiting participation in water storage district elections to land owners. Although absentee land owners could vote, persons who lived in the district but did not own land were excluded from the electoral process. This outcome reflected the Court's understanding that the district disproportionately affected landowners and was not a traditional government authority. The Court reached its result pursuant to rational basis review rather than the strict scrutiny standard used in *Kramer*. Taken together, these cases indicate that eligibility requirements for a special purpose district will be a function of how narrow the scope of governmental authority (i.e., the narrower the purpose, the more restrictively voter participation may be defined). Absent a special interest election, as the Court noted in *Hill v. Stone,* 421 U.S. 289 (1975), classifications restricting the right to vote are impermissible unless the state demonstrates they account for a compelling interest.

Voter Identification Requirements. In recent years, a number of states have enacted voter identification laws. Basically, these laws provide that voters must produce a valid photo identification in order to vote in state and federal elections. States defend these laws on the basis that they help prevent voter fraud by ensuring that only eligible individuals vote in elections. Representatives of minority groups claim that African-Americans and Hispanics are disproportionately unable to obtain valid photo identifications. In general, these laws have been upheld. *See Veasey v. Abbott*, 888 F.3d 792 (5th Cir. 2018); *Lee v. Virginia State Board of Elections*, 2016 WL 6921611 (E.D. Va.); *Greater Birmingham Ministries v. Merrill*, 284 F.Supp.3d 1253 (N.D. Ala. 2018); *Gentges v. Oklahoma State Election Board*, 419 P.3d 224 (Okla. 2018). A Kansas law requiring a voter to provide proof of citizenship was struck down in *Fish v. Schwab*, 957 F.3d 1105 (10th Cir. 2020). Among other things, the court held that the Kansas law was preempted by the National Voting Rights Act.

During the COVID-19 pandemic, there was much litigation regarding the right to vote. In *Texas Democratic Party v. Abbott*, 961 F.3d 389 (5th Cir. 2020), the court stayed a trial court order requiring Texas to allow mail-in voting because of the pandemic. In *Thomas v. Andino*, 613 F.Supp.3d 926 (D. S.C. 2020), the court stayed a requirement that an absentee ballot contain a witness' signature. At the same time, the South Carolina Supreme Court was confronted by a request to require the state to expand the use of absentee ballots.

See Bailey v. South Carolina State Election Commission, 844 S.E.2d 390 (S.C. 2020). In *Gottlieb v. Lamont*, 465 F.Supp.3d 41 (D. Conn. 2020), plaintiffs sought unsuccessfully to have Connecticut's petition signature requirements relaxed because of the pandemic. A similar decision was rendered in *Arizonans for Fair Election v. Hobbs*, 454 F.Supp.3d 910 (Ariz. 2020). In *Gottlieb v. Lamont*, 465 F.Supp.3d 41 (D. Conn. 2020), the court held that Connecticut's ballot access rules (which required independent candidates to obtain signatures from 5% of the population o the district were unconstitutional given the pandemic. In *People First of Alabama v. Merrill*, 467 F.Supp.3d 1179 (N.D. Ala. 2020), two individuals who were at higher risk from COVID-19 challenged Alabama's absentee process which required proof of identity plus a witness signature, and obtained a preliminary injunction against enforcement. However, the U.S. Supreme Court, in *Merrill v. People First of Alabama*, 141 S.Ct. 190 (2020), stayed the order.

Early Voting Periods. Previously, Ohio had a 35-day early voting period (allowing voters to vote prior to election day). However, Ohio decided to reduce the early voting period from 35 days to 29 days. In the process, it also eliminated the "Golden Week" (the early voting days that were eliminated) during which voters could both register and vote at the same time. The law was challenged on the basis that it imposed an undue burden on the voting rights of African-Americans. In *Ohio Democratic Party v. Husted*, 834 F.3d 620 (6th Cir. 2016), the court upheld the law on the basis that it imposed a "minimal burden," as well as because there is no constitutional right to an early voting period, and (in any event) the Court regarded a 29 day early voting period as ample.

Voter Removal. In *Husted v. A. Philip Randolph Institute*, 584 U.S. 756 (2018), the Court upheld an Ohio law that allowed removal of voters from the voting rolls. Basically, if a voter failed to vote in two straight elections, Ohio would send a preaddressed, postage prepaid card to the individual. Only if the individual did not return the card, or otherwise notify the state that he had not moved, could the voter be removed from the voting rolls. The case involved an interpretation of the National Voter Registration Act, and the Court held that the Ohio law was consistent with that Act.

Dilution of the Right to Vote. Methods for diluting the right to vote include apportionment processes, restrictions on ballot access, and processes for recording and counting votes. Legislative districting generally is governed by the principle of one-person, one-vote, although some deviation may be permitted especially for state processes. With respect to ballot access, the focus is on the severity of the burden imposed by the restriction.

The Voting Rights Act. In *Shelby County v. Holder*, 570 U.S. 529 (2013), the Court found Section 4(b) of the Voting Rights Act unconstitutional. The Court held that the Act's coverage formula, which determined which jurisdictions would be required to preclear any changes in voting procedures with the Attorney General or D.C. District Court, was based on vastly outdated information. Writing for the majority, Chief Justice John Roberts Jr. found that, "It would have been irrational for Congress to distinguish between States in such a fundamental way based on 40-year-old data, when today's statistics tell an entirely different story." The Court left it to Congress to draft another formula, while leaving the actual preclearance requirement in Section 5 intact—although it will be without operative power until Congress revises Section 4's coverage formula. A core component of the decision involved federalism. The case served to further delineate the long and winding dividing line between the federal and state governments on voting rights.

Apportionment. Apart from slavery, a formula for congressional representation was the thorniest issue for the Constitutional Convention. The debate between large and small states was resolved by establishing a bicameral legislature that correlated representation in the House to state population and gave every state two senators. Although most states have adopted a bicameral legislative model, counties and districts are units of state government rather than independent sovereigns. The Court in *Reynolds v. Sims*, 377 U.S. 533 (1964), thus determined that state legislative districts must be proportional. At issue in this case was a districting plan weighted heavily in favor of rural interests to the point that 25% of the population could elect a house and senate majority. The Court stressed that weighting a citizen's vote on the basis of where he or she lives undermines a basic principle of representative governance. It noted that population was both the "starting point" and "controlling criterion" for purposes of reviewing an apportionment plan. In this regard, the Court determined that the equal protection guarantee requires both houses of a state legislature to be apportioned on the basis of population.

For practical purposes, precise equality may be impossible. In acknowledging this point, the Court noted that there must be "an honest and good faith effort" to achieve equality of population to the extent possible. For example, in *Harris v. Arizona Independent Redistricting Commission*, 578 U.S. 253 (2016), the Court rejected a challenge to a state legislature redistricting plan despite a claim that the districts were insufficiently equal in population. The Court held that, because the maximum population deviation between the largest and the smallest district was less than 10%, appellants could not simply rely upon the numbers to show that the plan violated the Constitution. The Court went on to hold that appellants provided insufficient other evidence of disparity. *Reynolds* specifically excluded history, economic interests, and group identity or concerns as grounds for justifying deviations from population-based representation. Given the possibility of demographic change, the Court required a reasonable plan for periodic reapportionment and indicated that decennial review would meet the minimal requirements of that standard.

Political Gerrymandering. The principle of one-person, one-vote operates in conjunction with other legitimate apportionment factors. Among these valid concerns, as indicated by the Court in *Karcher v. Daggett* are the desire for compact districts, respect for municipal boundaries, maintaining the core of private districts, and avoiding contests between incumbents. State districting may deviate more from the equality principle than is permissible with respect to congressional districting. Despite the greater tolerance, state apportionment processes must reflect a good-faith effort to achieve equality of representation. The Court has noted that there are no "specialized calipers" that enable it to determine what range of deviation is permissible. A 16.4 percent deviation thus was allowed in Virginia and an 89 percent underrepresentation factor permitted in Wyoming, where a legislative seat was created for the state's least populated county.

Multi-member districts have been used to dilute voting rights, especially those of minorities. In *Rogers v. Lodge,* 458 U.S. 613 (1982), the Court found that an at-large system for electing the city council discriminated on the basis of race. The success of such claims is dependent upon establishing a discriminatory motive.

Legislative reapportionment presents an opportunity to secure a partisan advantage for whichever party is dominant at the time. In an early decision in *Davis v. Bandemer*, 478 U.S. 109 (1986), a four-justice plurality determined that a constitutional violation hinges upon proof of intentional discrimination against an identifiable group and a discriminatory effect. Although Democrats received 52% of a statewide vote, but won only 43% of the legislative seats, the plurality determined that this variance did not establish intentional discrimination. Proof of intentional discrimination could be made, according to the plurality, only when apportionment consistently "degrades" a voter's or a group of voters' influence in the political process taken as a whole.

However, for many years, the Court struggled to find an appropriate way to resolve political gerrymanders. For example, in *Vieth v. Jubelirer,* 541 U.S. 267 (2004), a four-justice plurality concluded that a claim of political gerrymandering is non-justiciable and should be resolved through the political process. However, in *League of United Latin American Citizens v. Perry*, 548 U.S. 399 (2006), affirmed that political gerrymandering cases or controversies are justiciable under the equal protection guarantee. It also noted continuing disagreement among the justices with respect to an appropriate standard of review.

In *Gill v. Whitford*, 585 U.S. 48 (2018), the Court seemed close to asserting jurisdiction over political gerrymandering cases. Although the Court concluded in that case that a partisan gerrymandering case was not justiciable because plaintiffs lacked standing, the Court remanded the case to the lower courts to give plaintiffs a chance to formulate their standing allegations differently. In *Gil*, plaintiffs claimed that Wisconsin had "packed" and "cracked" voters in an effort to give Republicans an electoral advantage. Cracking involves dividing a party's supporters among multiple districts so that they lack a majority in each one, and packing involves concentrating one party's backers in a few districts that they win by overwhelming margins. As a result, even if Republicans received less than a majority of the votes, their chances of controlling the state legislature were high. The Court held that plaintiffs lacked standing to bring the suit. The Court reiterated that standing in partisan gerrymandering cases requires plaintiffs to show that they have: (1) suffered an injury in fact, (2) that is fairly traceable to the challenged conduct of the defendant, and (3) that is likely to be redressed by a favorable judicial decision." In order to do that, voters must make district specific allegations of injury, and argue that the remedy lies in revising the boundaries of the district to eliminate the injury. Thus, they cannot sue to invalidate the whole State's legislative districting map; such complaints must proceed "district-by-district." The Court rejected plaintiff's argument that their injury extends to the statewide harm to their interest "in their collective representation in the legislature," and in influencing the legislature's overall "composition and policymaking." Our cases to date have not found that this presents an individual and personal injury of the kind required for Article III standing. Justice Kagen filed a lengthy dissent offering suggestions about how plaintiffs might be able to establish standing for a statewide claim.

However, in *Rucho v. Common Cause*, 588 U.S. 684 (2019), the Court slammed the door on its willingness to decide political gerrymandering cases. The case involved challenges to districting maps in Maryland (where Democrats had disadvantaged Republicans) and North Carolina (where Republicans had disadvantaged Democrats). The lopsided maps meant that the disadvantaged party would not receive seats equivalent to the votes it received. Nevertheless, the Court concluded that the cases involved non-justiciable political questions because the Framers assigned redistricting power to the state legislatures, and there was no "suggestion that the federal courts had a role to play." The Court viewed it's one person, one vote, cases as different because courts could apply a relatively simple mathematical calculus. Likewise, the Court regarded racial gerrymandering cases as different because laws "that explicitly discriminate on the basis of race, as well as those that are race neutral on their face but are unexplainable on grounds other than race, are presumptively invalid." Partisan gerrymandering cases are more difficult because districting was inherently partisan because the Framers entrusted districting to political entities.

While the Court suggested that it might have been inclined to intervene when a state legislature had created an unduly partisan map, the Court struggled to find a test for determining whether a particular "political gerrymandering has gone too far." The Court emphasized that any "standard for resolving such claims must be grounded in a 'limited and precise rationale' and be 'clear, manageable, and politically neutral' " so that courts do not unduly intervene in the political process. In regard to partisan gerrymandering claims, the Court concluded that the "federal courts are not equipped to apportion political power as a matter of fairness, nor is there any basis for concluding that they were authorized to do so":

> The difficulty in settling on a "clear, manageable and politically neutral" test for fairness is that it is not clear what fairness looks like. There is "unfairness" in any winner-take-all system. Fairness may mean a greater number of competitive districts. Such a claim seeks to undo packing and cracking so that supporters of the disadvantaged party have a better shot at electing their preferred candidates. But making as many districts as possible competitive could be a disaster for the disadvantaged party. "A narrow statewide preference for either party would produce an overwhelming majority for the winning party in the state legislature." *Bandemer*, 478 U.S. at 130 (plurality). Perhaps the ultimate objective of a "fairer" share of seats in the congressional delegation is most readily achieved by yielding to the gravitational pull of proportionality and engaging in cracking and packing, to ensure each party its "appropriate" share of "safe" seats. Such an approach comes at the expense of competitive

districts and of individuals in districts allocated to the opposing party. Or perhaps fairness should be measured by adherence to "traditional" districting criteria, such as maintaining political subdivisions, keeping communities of interest together, and protecting incumbents. But protecting incumbents enshrines a particular partisan distribution. And the "natural political geography" of a State—such as the fact that urban electoral districts are often dominated by one political party—can itself lead to inherently packed districts. Traditional criteria such as line compactness and contiguity "cannot promise political neutrality. A decision under these standards would unavoidably have significant political effect, whether intended or not." *Vieth*, 541 U.S. at 308 (Kennedy concurring). There are no legal standards discernible in the Constitution for making such judgments, let alone limited and precise standards that are clear, manageable, and politically neutral. Any judicial decision on what is "fair" in this context would be an "unmoored determination" of the sort characteristic of a political question beyond the competence of the federal courts.

Only after determining how to define fairness can [one] begin to answer the determinative question: "How much is too much?" If compliance with traditional districting criteria is the touchstone, how much deviation from those criteria is constitutionally acceptable and how should mapdrawers prioritize competing criteria? Should a court "reverse gerrymander" other parts of a State to counteract "natural" gerrymandering caused by the urban concentration of one party? If a districting plan protected half of the incumbents but redistricted the rest into head to head races, would that be constitutional? A court would have to rank the relative importance of traditional criteria and weigh how much deviation to allow. If a court focused on the respective number of seats in the legislature, it would have to decide the ideal number of seats for each party and determine at what point deviation from that balance went too far. If a 5–3 allocation corresponds most closely to statewide vote totals, is a 6–2 allocation permissible, given that legislatures have the authority to engage in a degree of partisan gerrymandering? Which seats should be packed and which cracked? Or if the goal is as many competitive districts as possible, how close does the split need to be for the district to be considered competitive? Even assuming the court knew which version of fairness to

> be looking for, there are no discernible and manageable standards for deciding whether there has been a violation. The questions are "unguided and ill suited to the development of judicial standards," *Vieth*, 541 U.S. at 296 (plurality opinion), and "results from one gerrymandering case to the next would likely be disparate and inconsistent."

Although the parties proposed a number of "tests" for evaluating partisan gerrymandering claims, the Court concluded that none of them provided "a limited and precise standard that is judicially discernible and manageable. And none provides a solid grounding for judges to take the extraordinary step of reallocating power and influence between political parties. Determining that lines were drawn on the basis of partisanship does not indicate that the districting was improper. A permissible intent—securing partisan advantage—does not become constitutionally impermissible, like racial discrimination, when that permissible intent 'predominates.' " The Court concluded: "We have no commission to allocate political power and influence in the absence of a constitutional directive or legal standards to guide us in the exercise of such authority."

Racial Gerrymandering. Racial politics is a long-standing phenomenon that, among other things, has been manifested by bloc voting. In *Shaw v. Reno*, 509 U.S. 630 (1993), the Court determined that race was not to be included among the factors tolerated in the context of political gerrymandering. Consistent with its affirmative action decisions, the Court determined that strict scrutiny applies to race-conscious districting plans. At issue in *Shaw* was an irregularly configured and predominantly African-American congressional district in North Carolina. The state maintained that it was structured to achieve compliance with the Voting Rights Act of 1965. The Court found that it was so oddly configured, however, that there could have been no motive other than race for its creation. After remand, the Court in *Shaw v. Hunt*, 517 U.S. 899 (1996), determined that race was the predominant factor in configuring the congressional district. To reach this outcome, the Court applied strict scrutiny. Although acknowledging that compliance with the Voting Rights Act of 1965 might be regarded as a compelling state interest, the Court held that the plan was not narrowly tailored. In *Hunt v. Cromartie*, 526 U.S. 541 (1999), the Court reversed a lower court finding that race was a factor in the district's reconfiguration. It noted the "sensitive nature" of the process and the need to presume that legislation was enacted in "good faith."

The Court also applied strict scrutiny in *Miller v. Johnson*, 515 U.S. 900 (1995), a case concerning a Georgia redistricting plan that created three predominantly African American districts. These districts resulted from the Justice Department's requirement of majority-minority districts to eradicate the effects of past discrimination. Although acknowledging that remedying past discrimination is a compelling governmental interest, the Court indicated that it would strike down reapportionment plans that reflect racial stereotypes. However, a revised districting plan which included one majority-minority district was upheld in *Abrams v. Johnson,* 521 U.S. 74 (1997).

The Court in *Bush v. Vera,* 517 U.S. 952 (1996), indicated that the use of strict scrutiny depends on whether race is a predominant factor in development of the plan. That case concerned a congressional districting plan that created three majority-minority districts. Because race was the predominant (albeit not exclusive) consideration, the court applied strict scrutiny. Although the Court held that compliance with the Voting Rights Act of 1965 might be regarded as a compelling interest, the plan must not exceed the scope of the enactment's requirements.

In *Bethune-Hill v. Virginia State Board of Elections,* 580 U.S. 178 (2017), the Court adjudicated challenges to the State of Virginia's redistricting plan, and provided further guidance regarding how to resolve racial gerrymandering claims. The case arose after the Court held that § 4(b) of the Voting Rights Act could no longer be used to require preclearance under § 5 of the Voting Rights Act. *See Shelby County v. Holder,* 570 U.S. 529 (2013). Because many of the minority-majority districts were underpopulated, the legislature was required to move non-minority voters into some of those districts. Nevertheless, the legislature sought to achieve a 55% majority-minority balance in certain districts.

In deciding the case, the Court explained that a plaintiff might establish that race played a predominant role in redistricting by showing "that the legislature subordinated traditional race-neutral districting principles to racial considerations." The Court rejected the idea that race did not have a "prohibited effect on a district's lines if the legislature could have drawn the same lines in accordance with traditional criteria," noting that the "racial predominance inquiry concerns the actual considerations that provided the essential basis for the lines drawn, not *post hoc* justifications the legislature in theory could have used but in reality did not." The Court concluded that a state "could construct a plethora of potential maps that look consistent with traditional, race-neutral principles" so the question is whether "race for its own sake" was "the overriding reason for choosing one map over others." Although a "conflict or inconsistency between the enacted plan and traditional redistricting criteria is not a threshold requirement or a mandatory precondition in order for a challenger to establish a claim of racial gerrymandering," a "conflict or inconsistency may be persuasive circumstantial evidence tending to show racial predomination." So, the Court focused on whether "the enacted plan conflicts with traditional redistricting criteria." Indeed, "in the absence of a conflict with traditional principles, it may be difficult for challengers to find other evidence sufficient to show that race was the overriding factor causing neutral considerations to be cast aside." However, the Court recognized that "there may be cases where challengers will be able to establish racial predominance by presenting direct evidence of the legislative purpose and intent or other compelling circumstantial evidence." "A court faced with a racial gerrymandering claim therefore must consider all of the lines of the district at issue; any explanation for a particular portion of the lines must take account of the district wide context." In fact, a holistic analysis is necessary.

In *Cooper v. Harris*, 581 U.S. 285 (2017), the Court reaffirmed the principle that a state may not use race as the predominant factor in drawing district lines unless it has a compelling reason to do so, and unless it can show that the means used are narrowly tailored. While the Court again emphasized that compliance with the Voting Rights Act of 1965 constitutes a compelling governmental interest, but also emphasized that the remedy must be narrowly tailored. In analyzing the case, North Carolina's redrew two congressional districts, both of which had long included substantial populations of black voters. The Court struck down one district because it concluded that the design of that "serpentine" district was race-centric, and could not be justified as a reasonable attempt to comply with the VRA. The next year, the State responded with a new districting plan, including a new District 12—and residents brought another lawsuit alleging an impermissible racial gerrymander. Racial considerations did not predominate in designing the revised District 12. Rather, that district was the result of a political gerrymander—an effort to engineer, mostly "without regard to race," a safe Democratic seat. The State had redrawn its congressional districts in 2001, to account for population changes revealed in the prior year's census. Under the 2001 map, which went unchallenged, neither District 1 nor District 12 had a black voting-age population (a "BVAP") that was a majority of the whole: The former had a BVAP of around 48%, the latter a BVAP of around 43%. Nonetheless, in five successive general elections conducted in those reconfigured districts, all the candidates preferred by most African-American voters won their contests—and by handy margins. The Court concluded that race furnished the predominant rationale for the district's redesign, and held that the State's interest in complying with the VRA could not justify the consideration of race. The Court emphasized that the State's mapmakers had "purposefully established a racial target: African-Americans should make up no less than a majority of the voting-age population," and that this decision "had a direct and significant impact" on the district's configuration.

Vote Recording and Counting. Voting methodology and procedures vary among jurisdictions, but factors like voting instructions, equipment, and tabulation can have a bearing on whether the right to vote is denied or diluted. In *Bush v. Gore*, 531 U.S. 98 (2000), the Court cited data indicating that approximately two percent of votes cast in presidential elections are not counted due to voter error or defects in counting technology. At issue in that case was a Florida Supreme Court order which required the recounting of ballots that appeared to have been punched, but were not entirely perforated," and required the counters to try to discern the "intent of the voter." The Court found no problem with this objective. However, the Court struck down the order because the Florida court did not establish a uniform standard for the recount and that they would be given equal weight. Although seven justices agreed that the original counting problem warranted a remedy, a majority refused to permit further recount procedures because of an impending deadline for the state to choose its electors.

Access to the Ballot. Cases concerning restrictions on candidate access to ballots turn upon the degree of burden imposed. Significant impediments are evaluated more carefully that those which impose lesser restrictions. The Court, in *American Party of Texas v. White*, 415 U.S. 767 (1974), upheld a provision requiring parties receiving less than 2 percent of the gubernatorial vote in the prior election to obtain signatures of at least 1 percent of those who voted. This requirement, from the Court's perspective, was not excessively burdensome. In *Lubin v. Panish*, 415 U.S. 709 (1974), the Court struck down a law requiring candidates to pay a filing fee, totaling 2 percent of the annual salary of the office they sought. The Court determined that the restriction unduly burdened the ability of indigent candidates to secure a position on the ballot.

Education. The idea of a fundamental right to education relates back to the 1920s when, in *Pierce v. Society of Sisters*, 268 U.S. 510 (1925), the Court struck down a state law requiring parents to send their children to public schools. In so doing, the Court determined that the enactment unreasonably interfered with a parental liberty interest in how their children are raised and educated. In *Brown v. Board of Education*, the Court highlighted the importance of education as "perhaps the most important function of state and local government, . . . the very foundation of good citizenship, [and] . . . a principal instrument in awakening the child to cultural values, in preparing him for later professional training, and in helping him to adjust normally to his environment." The *Brown* Court further observed that when the state provides for public education, it is "a right that must be made available to all on equal terms." In *Bolling v. Sharpe*, the Court found that segregated public education constituted a denial of "liberty under the Due Process Clause".

Despite a backdrop that may seem suggestive of a fundamental right, the Court eventually determined that there is no general fundamental right to education. This point was made in *San Antonio Independent School District v. Rodriguez,* 411 U.S. 1 (1973), when the Court upheld a state funding plan that relied on local property taxes to finance public education and thus was characterized by substantial funding disparities. Although acknowledging that education constitutes an important interest, the Court determined that it was not a fundamental right. Funding varied on the basis of local wealth, but the Court found that the resulting differences did not create a suspect classification. Without a fundamental right or suspect classification at stake, there was no basis for strict scrutiny. Using the rational basis test, the Court found a reasonable relationship existed between the funding model and state's interest in facilitating local control of schooling.

The *Rodriguez* decision is a primary example of the Court's reluctance to use the equal protection clause as a means for redistributing wealth. It left open the possibility of a different result, however, in the event that the state denied educational opportunity altogether. In *Plyler v. Doe,* 457 U.S. 202 (1982), the Court determined that a state's refusal to provide public education to the children of illegal aliens violated the equal protection clause. Although reaffirming that neither a fundamental right nor suspect classification was at issue, the Court found that the classification was not supported by a "substantial state interest." This terminology typically is utilized in connection with intermediate scrutiny, but the Court did not explicitly indicate that it was using a heightened standard of review. It characterized children of illegal aliens as "a permanent caste" and "discrete class," however, who were not responsible for their condition.

The decision in *Plyler v. Doe* is unique both with respect to standard of review and outcome. In *Kadrmas v. Dickinson Public Schools,* 487 U.S. 450 (1988), the Court restated that education is not a fundamental right and used a traditional rational basis standard of review. At issue was a state law that allowed school districts to charge students a school bus transportation fee. The Court determined that, although some indigent children could not afford the cost, there was no constitutional violation.

CHECKLIST

A. Nature and Scope of Equal Protection.

1. The equal protection clause of the Fourteenth Amendment was a key element of Reconstruction designed to achieve equal status under the law for former slaves.

    a. Until the mid-twentieth century, its role was constitutionally inconsequential as standards of review (even in the context of race) were lax.

    b. During the latter part of the twentieth century, the guarantee evolved to include alienage, gender, illegitimacy, and fundamental rights (as well as race) within its ambit.

2. Government regulation frequently classifies on the basis of individual or group status. For instance, tax rates are established on the basis of wealth. Eligibility for welfare benefits is determined on the basis of economic need.

    a. Most classifications are permissible and thus subject to a rational basis standard of review.

    b. Classifications on the basis of race, alienage, gender, and illegitimacy are subject to a higher level of scrutiny.

        1.) Racial classifications and some alienage classifications are suspect.

        2.) Gender and some illegitimacy classifications are subject to intermediate review.

        3.) Some alienage and illegitimacy classifications are subject to a rational basis standard of review.

3. Classifications that burden a fundamental right tend to be strictly scrutinized.

B. Economic and social classifications that are not suspect and do not burden a fundamental right are subject to rational basis review.

1. The rational basis test is highly deferential and merely requires a legitimate governmental objective and rational relationship between the regulatory means and regulatory objective.

2. If the legislature is not clear in its purpose, the legitimacy of a challenged regulation's objective may be established in court by a conceivable or arguable reason.

3. Classifications on the basis of wealth, age, mental retardation, and sexual orientation are not suspect and thus are subject to rational basis review.

   a. Laws discriminating on the basis of sexual orientation and mental retardation have been invalidated pursuant to rational basis review.

C. **Race and the Nation's Founding. The primary challenge of the Constitutional Convention was to reconcile Northern and Southern positions on slavery.**

1. Compromise by both sides established the principle of federal neutrality on slavery.

2. Westward expansion and fugitive slave issues resulted in escalating tension between North and South and eventual gridlock of the political process.

3. The Court eventually determined that African-Americans were an inferior class and could not be citizens of the United States.

D. **Reconstruction: the Thirteenth Amendment abolished slavery.**

1. The Black Codes limited its impact by imposing extensive restrictions on the civil and political freedom of former slaves.

2. The Civil Rights Act of 1866 aimed to negate the Black Codes and was the precursor for the Fourteenth Amendment.

3. The equal protection clause was designed to secure equal standing under the law for former slaves.

   a. The Court initially described the Fourteenth Amendment as a guarantee against official discrimination that implied racial inferiority. *Strauder v. West Virginia.*

E. **Separate but Equal: racial segregation was pervasive in the South from the late nineteenth century through the mid-twentieth century.**

1. The Court viewed segregation as a reasonable exercise of state police power and differentiated *Strauder v. West*

Virginia on grounds it did not imply the inferiority of any race.

a. The Court in *Plessy v. Ferguson* determined that the Constitution did not prohibit racial distinctions that resulted in social inequality and could not compel interaction among races that was unwanted by either.

2. Justice Harlan, in a dissenting opinion, maintained that segregation in fact implied inferiority, and that the Constitution mandated color blindness.

3. Case law through the 1930s emphasized racial separation and paid little attention to the equality factor of the "separate but equal"" doctrine.

4. The first significant challenge to the separate but equal doctrine arose in the context of higher education.

5. The Court determined that a state must provide a law school for non-whites if it wanted to maintain a school exclusively for whites. *Missouri ex rel. Gaines v. Canada.*

6. The Court eventually found that equal protection was not satisfied merely by funding parity. *Sweatt v. Painter.*

   a. Relevant factors, in determining compliance with the equal protection guarantee during segregation's final years, included institutional prestige, faculty qualifications, extracurricular activities, alumni influence, facilities, and linkage to professional opportunities, bear upon the quality of professional education.

7. Two doctrinal developments were instrumental for purposes signaled the eventual demise of the separate but equal doctrine.

   a. The Court (in a case that narrowed the judiciary's role in developing fundamental rights, as discussed in Chapter 7) indicated that it might employ more searching inquiry when prejudice impacted discrete and insular minorities and denied them the opportunity to protect themselves through the political process. *United States v. Carolene Products Co.*

   b. The Court subsequently announced that all legal restrictions which curtail civil rights on the basis of race are suspect and subject to strict scrutiny. *Korematsu v. United States.*

F. Desegregation: the Court in 1954 declared that racially segregated public education was "inherently unequal" and thus violated the equal protection guarantee. *Brown v. Board of Education.*

1. The *Brown* decision was grounded in the premises that public education had become a critical facilitator of personal development and good citizenship, and segregation had a detrimental effect on minority children.

    a. Contrary to its rationale in *Plessy v. Ferguson,* the Court determined that segregation typically was understood as denoting the inferiority of non-whites.

    b. The Court relied upon the due process clause of the Fifth Amendment to strike down segregation of District of Columbia schools as an arbitrary deprivation of liberty. *Bolling v. Sharpe.*

    c. The initial standard for compliance with the *Brown* decision was to desegregate "with all deliberate speed." *Brown v. Board of Education II.*

2. Response to the desegregation mandate was characterized by widespread resistance and delay until the mid-1960s. *Cooper v. Aaron.*

    a. Progress toward meaningful desegregation was spurred by enactment of the Civil Rights Act of 1964 and conditioning of federal education funds upon compliance with *Brown.*

    b. The "all deliberate speed" standard was superseded by insistence upon elimination of the vestiges of racial discrimination "root and branch" and implementation of remedies that realistically promised to work immediately. *Green v. County School Board.*

3. Remedies for achieving desegregation are consistent with the judiciary's traditional equitable powers. *Swann v. Charlotte-Mecklenburg County Board of Education.*

    a. These powers in the desegregation context include authority to make pupil assignments on the basis of race, transport students, and establish fixed ratios as a starting point for achieving a racially balanced faculty.

4. Limiting Principles

    a. A constitutional violation is conditioned upon a showing of *de jure* segregation (i.e., segregation that was intentionally established by government policy or action). *Keyes v. School District No. 1.*

1.) *De jure* segregation is viewed as an intended outcome of government policy or action, and *de facto* segregation is understood as an unintended effect.

b. Consistent with the *de jure-de facto* distinction, the Court determined that an inter-district remedy is permissible only when the intentional actions of one district contribute to segregation in another district. *Milliken v. Bradley.*

c. Desegregation responsibilities end once a district achieves racially unitary status. *Pasadena City Board of Education v. Spangler.*

1.) In the event that segregation recurs, any duty to desegregate is dependent upon showing it is a function of official intent.

d. Control over schools may revert back to local officials when the vestiges of discrimination are eliminated to the extent practicable. *Oklahoma City Board of Education v. Dowell.*

1.) This standard relaxes the above-referenced requirement of *Green v. County School Board,* which demanded elimination of the vestiges of discrimination "root and branch."

e. Courts may restore local authority over schools on an incremental basis rather than awaiting their achievement of unitary status. *Freeman v. Pitts.*

1.) Local officials may regain control of contexts in which goals have been achieved.

a.) Relevant factors in deciding whether to return control include whether and to what extent compliance has been achieved, judicial control is necessary to achieve compliance, and the school system has demonstrated good-faith efforts to comply.

f. Student achievement levels are irrelevant for purposes of determining whether schools have achieved unitary status. *Missouri v. Jenkins.*

g. Integration maintenance and diversity policies.

1.) The constitutionality of efforts to remedy the effects of past discrimination is dependent upon evidence of intentional wrongdoing. *Parents Involved in Community Schools v. Seattle School District No. 1.*

a.) Racial classifications in the desegregation or integration context are subject to strict scrutiny (and thus must be supported by a compelling interest and narrowly tailored).

i.) Remedying the effects of past intentional discrimination is a compelling government interest.

ii.) The narrow tailoring requirement is unmet absent serious and, good faith consideration of racially neutral options.

2.) Income and other social factors may be used to achieve a diverse student-body composition.

3.) The Court has not foreclosed (nor considered) reliance upon state constitutions to maintain integration gains or achieve diversification.

G. The Discriminatory Purpose Requirement: an equal protection violation is dependent upon proof of an official intent to discriminate. *Washington v. Davis.*

1. The discriminatory purpose requirement reflects a concern that, if a racially disparate effect was sufficient, a wide range of social and economic regulations would be constitutionally imperiled.

2. Discerning a discriminatory motive is an uncomplicated task when it is overt, as it was in the context of official segregation.

3. Discriminatory purpose is more difficult to identify when evidence is circumstantial.

a. A law that prohibited interracial marriage violated the equal protection clause (and the right to marry and travel interstate), even though no race was singled out. *Loving v. Virginia.*

b. A law that is neutral on its face may be intentionally discriminatory in its application. *Yick Wo v. Hopkins.*

c. Relevant circumstantial evidence includes statistical disparities, patterns or effects that are inexplicable except on grounds of race, legislative history, and departures from normal procedures. *Arlington Heights v. Metropolitan Housing Development Corp.*

d. Statistical disparities or disproportionalities alone do not establish a discriminatory purpose. *McCleskey v. Kemp.*

4. The discriminatory intent requirement in the context of equal protection contrasts with the repudiation of motive-based inquiry in the First Amendment setting, where the Court finds evidence of wrongful purpose difficult to discern. *United States v. O'Brien.*

H. Affirmative Action.

1. "Affirmative action," in the constitutional law context, typically refers to government policies or programs that establish preferences on the basis of race.

   a. Such classifications are permissible on a limited basis to (1) remedy past discrimination or (2) achieve the benefits of diversity in higher education.

   b. The standard of review for affirmative action is the same as for any racial classification—strict scrutiny.

      1.) The rationale for strict scrutiny is that remedial classifications, even if well-intended, may stigmatize, reinforce stereotypes, promote notions of racial inferiority and perpetuate racial politics.

         a.) Strict scrutiny enables a court to determine whether a classification is the function of a permissible purpose or unacceptable prejudice or stereotype.

         b.) Critics maintain that these risks can be identified pursuant to intermediate scrutiny.

2. Remedying Past Discrimination

   a. The remedying of past intentional discrimination constitutes a compelling interest.

      1.) The constitutionality of a race-conscious remedy hinges upon proof that a person or entity has discriminated against an identifiable individual or group.

a.) An employer who discharges a worker because of race, for instance, may be ordered to rehire the employee.

b.) A person or entity that has violated the law may be required to provide a remedy that benefits the group which suffered discrimination, even if the individual beneficiaries were not directly impacted. *United States v. Paradise.*

c.) The nation's general legacy of societal discrimination has been found "too amorphous" to be a basis for race-conscious remedies. *Wygant v. Jackson Board of Education.*

3. An affirmative action policy must be narrowly tailored to its purpose.

   a. Quotas, goals, targets, or racial balancing typically are impermissible, insofar as there are more flexible and less burdensome means of achieving the desired goal.

   b. Racially neutral policies and programs, which may establish a preference on the basis of economic or other disadvantage (but may disproportionately benefit minorities) are a first line of preference.

I. Promoting Diversity.

1. Diversity constitutes a compelling interest in the context of student admissions in higher education, insofar as it facilitates multicultural competency, cross-racial understanding, and dissipation of stereotypes. *Grutter v. Bollinger.*

   a. Race may be factored into the student admission process so long as it is not an exclusive factor.

   b. A university admission process meets the narrowly tailored requirement insofar as each applicant is assessed, without regard to race, on how he or she might contribute to a diverse environment.

      1.) A quota or specific goal typically would not be narrowly tailored.

2. Race may not be taken into account in determining pupil assignments at the elementary or high school level. *Parents Involved in Community Schools v. Seattle School District No. 1.*

a. Race may be factored into student assignment decisions, at the elementary and secondary school level, unless it is established that the school system intentionally had segregated its schools.

J. Gender Discrimination.

1. The Court's decisions before 1971 upheld gender classifications in cases where state interests reflected judgments based on stereotyped views about differences between men and women.

   a. In *Bradwell v. Illinois*, 83 U.S. (16 Wall.) 130 (1872), the Court upheld a law excluding women from the practice of law, reasoning that women were "unfit" for this profession and that women should not seek careers but devote their energies to the "domestic sphere".

   b. In *Hoyt v. Florida*, 368 U.S. 57 (1961), the Court upheld a statute that exempted women from jury duty on the grounds that their duties in the "domestic sphere" justified this exemption.

2. In *Reed v. Reed*, 404 U.S. 71 (1971), the Court invalidated a law that required a probate judge to appoint a man to be the administrator of an estate whenever a man and a woman applied for this position and were equally qualified under state law to perform this function as a relative of the decedent.

   a. In relying on the rational basis standard of scrutiny, the Court found that the purported state interest had "some legitimacy" because of the value of reducing the workload of probate courts (by eliminating competing claims to receive an appointment as an estate administrator).

   b. However, the Court held that the state law was not reasonable in establishing an "arbitrary" mandatory preference for one sex (men), which preference did not "rest upon some ground of difference" between men and women that had any "fair and substantial relation" to the interest in reducing the workload of the probate court.

3. In *Frontiero v. Richardson*, 411 U.S. 677 (1973), the Court invalidated a federal law that denied benefits to husbands of female members of the armed services which benefits were automatically granted to wives of male service members.

a. The Court rejected the government's argument that administrative convenience justified the gender classification, which discriminated both against men as husbands and against female service members as women.

b. A plurality of the *Frontiero* Court advocated the use of strict scrutiny for gender classifications but a majority never endorsed that proposition.

4. In *Craig v. Boren*, 429 U.S. 190 (1976), the Court invented a new type of scrutiny for gender classifications, which requires that the classification must serve an "important government objective" and that the law "must be substantially related to the achievement of this objective".

a. The *Craig* Court invalidated a law that allowed women between the ages of 18 to 21 to purchase low-alcohol beer but not men of the same age.

b. The Court recognized the importance of the state's interest in traffic safety, but rejected the argument that administrative convenience justified the gender classification, which was not based on empirical evidence but only on stereotyped judgments about each sex.

5. Some gender classification cases illustrate how intermediate scrutiny is easier for the government to satisfy than strict scrutiny.

a. In *Califano v. Webster*, 430 U.S. 313 (1977), the Court upheld a federal law granting women more money than men in social security benefits. The *Califano* Court recognized the importance of the state's interest in compensating women for discrimination in employment that resulted in low retirement benefits, and also held that the class-based benefit of providing more money to all women was "substantially related to the achievement of this objective." Strict scrutiny of the law would have required a more narrowly tailored means for providing this benefit.

b. In *Rostker v. Goldberg*, 453 U.S. 57 (1981), the Court upheld a federal law exempting women from the draft, on the theory that this exclusion was substantially related to another law excluding women from combat positions. Strict scrutiny of the draft exemption law would have allowed the Court to invalidate the draft exclusion law on the grounds that women could be drafted for non-combat positions.

6. In *United States v. Virginia*, 518 U.S. 515 (1996), known as the *VMI* case, the Court emphasized that gender classifications require "an exceedingly persuasive justification" because "volumes of history" concerning the prevalence of sex discrimination should make courts engage in "skeptical scrutiny of official action."

   a. The Court invalidated the exclusion of women from the VMI state military college based on the stereotyped judgments about the abilities of women and men.

K. Alienage Classifications.

1. In *Graham v. Richardson*, 403 U.S. 365 (1971), the Court largely adopted the strict scrutiny standard for classifications based on alienage and national origins. The Court's earlier decision in *Takahashi v. Fish & Game Commission*, 334 U.S. 410 (1948), established the building blocks for the analysis used in *Graham*.

   a. The *Takahashi* Court recognized the "right of abode" for aliens, embedded in the Equal Protection Clause, the federal civil rights laws, and the federal immigration laws. This right was a critical concept that enabled the Court to invalidate a state law that prohibited the issuance of a commercial fishing license to any alien Japanese.

   b. The Court relied on the right of abode in holding that the state law conflicted with federal immigration law. It also relied on the right of abode in rejecting the state's argument that the "special public interest" in preserving the resource of fishing stock for its citizens justified the alien exclusion law. The Court found that this interest was too insubstantial to justify the denial of the right of abode to aliens.

2. The *Graham* Court invalidated state laws that denied welfare benefits to aliens who became indigent after they arrived in the U.S. because they lost their jobs due to disability or illness. The Court rejected the state's "special public interest" in preserving welfare funds for its own citizens or for alien residents of longstanding, because this interest was too insubstantial to justify the denial of the right of abode to aliens.

a. The *Graham* Court also reasoned that the state's denial of welfare benefits was an "invidious classification," and emphasized that aliens and citizens make equal contributions to federal and state taxes, serve equally in the armed forces, and contribute equally to state economies. Thus, indigent aliens and indigent citizens deserve to share in the tax-funded programs of the state communities.

b. By the 1980s, the Court had transformed the *Graham* version of strict scrutiny into the recognizable strict scrutiny test used for racial classifications (which requires a compelling state interest that is achieved by the least restrictive means).

3. In the post-*Graham* era, the Court invalidated other state laws using strict scrutiny, including laws that made resident aliens ineligible for state-funded college scholarships and "in-state" discounted college tuition rates, and that barred aliens from the practice of law.

4. The Court established three exceptions to strict scrutiny of alienage classifications and classifications based on national origin.

a. The Court uses rational basis for laws that exclude aliens from civil service jobs that require the exercise of discretionary power in a position of authority over others, specifically including the jobs of public school teacher, police officer, and probation officer. This "political function" exception does not apply to jobs that do not involve the implementation of policy. The exclusion of aliens from all civil service jobs would not qualify for this narrow exception. The Court held that such a state ban did not satisfy strict scrutiny. *Sugarman v. Dougall*, 413 U.S. 634 (1973).

b. The Court uses rational basis for federal alienage classifications, based on the importance of federal lawmaking on issues of immigration and naturalization. This standard allowed the federal courts to uphold the validity of a federal ban on aliens from civil service jobs that would not have been upheld using strict scrutiny.

c. The Court uses intermediate scrutiny for state classifications of non-lawful-resident aliens. In *Plyler v. Doe*, 457 U.S. 202 (1982), the Court invalidated a law that excluded non-lawful-resident child aliens from public schools, because the government could not make a showing that the law furthered a "substantial" state interest.

L. Classifications of Unmarried Parents and Their Children.

1. In *Clark v. Jeter*, 486 U.S. 456 (1988), the Court adopted the intermediate scrutiny standard for classifications based on the non-marital status of parents and their children.

    a. The Court invalidated a six-year time limit on support suits by non-marital children, finding that although it was an "important objective" for the state to deter fraudulent paternity claims, the means of the time limit was not "substantially related" to this interest because DNA parentage testing provided a more accurate means for achieving this objective.

2. Some of the Court's precedents upheld classifications under the rational basis test during the era before *Clark* adopted the intermediate scrutiny test. The results in these cases should no longer be regarded as sound, especially because DNA testing was not available when these cases were decided.

    a. These precedents include cases in which the Court upheld laws that required onerous proofs of paternity that excluded some or many non-marital children from the right to obtain a share of an intestate father's estate, and excluded some or many unmarried fathers from bringing a wrongful death suit against the tortfeasor who cause his child's death.

    b. These precedents also include a case in which the Court upheld a federal classification based on administrative convenience that required onerous proof of dependency that excluded some or many non-marital children from obtaining surviving-child-insurance benefits.

3. During the era before the adoption of intermediate scrutiny, the Court used rational basis scrutiny to invalidate laws that completely barred non-marital children or unmarried parents from obtaining access to rights granted to married parents and their children.

    a. The Court invalidated laws that barred non-marital children from seeking orders of support from parents, from sharing in the intestate estate of a father, and from receiving worker's compensation benefits.

b. The Court also invalidated laws that deprived unmarried fathers of the right to custody of their children after the death of the child's mother, and deprived such fathers of the right to block an adoption.

4. The Court uses intermediate scrutiny for evaluating a classification that is based on immigration status as well as non-marital status and gender. However, some deference to the government's means for achieving important objectives appears in these decisions.

   a. In *Tuan Anh Nguyen v. Immigration and Naturalization Service*, 533 U.S. 53 (2001), the Court upheld a federal naturalization law that granted citizenship automatically to a non-marital child of a citizen mother when that child is born outside the U.S., but required proofs of paternity from a similarly situated citizen father.

   b. The Court held that the classification was substantially related to the achievement of important interests in proving a biological relationship and insuring the development of the child's ties to the United States.

M. Mental Disabilities.

1. In *City of Cleburne v. Cleburne Living Center*, 473 U.S. 432 (1985), the Court decided not to use intermediate scrutiny to evaluate classifications of people with mental disabilities but to use the rational basis standard instead.

   a. One reason that the Court preferred to use the rational basis standard was in order to avoid a "floodgates" problem, given the fact that if intermediate scrutiny were used for people with mental disabilities, then other groups with immutable disabilities and a history of discrimination would argue that classifications concerning their group should receive the same type of scrutiny.

   b. The City of *Cleburne* Court invalidated the city decision to deny a permit to the applicant who wanted to establish a group home for mentally disabled people.

   c. The Court reasoned that the city's decision was based on private bias exemplified in the hostility of neighbors, and that all of the justifications used for denying the permit were not used to deny permits to other similar institutions, even though the justifications for denial applied equally to their permit applications.

2. In *Heller v. Doe*, 509 U.S. 312 (1993), the Court upheld a state law that granted greater procedural protections in commitment hearings to mentally ill persons than were granted to persons with mental disabilities, including a higher standard of proof and a prohibition on the participation of relatives as parties.

   a. The *Heller* Court relied on the more serious consequences of a commitment hearing for mentally ill people in finding a rational basis for the greater procedural protections at such a hearing.

N. Sexual Orientation.

1. In *Romer v. Evans*, 517 U.S. 620 (1996), the Court invalidated a state constitutional amendment that repealed state and local anti-discrimination laws which provided protections for "homosexual, lesbian or bisexual orientation, conduct, practices or relationships."

   a. The Court found that this classification lacked any rational relationship to a legitimate state interest, as it prohibited one class of persons from seeking to persuade legislatures to enact legislation to protect their civil rights, while allowing all other persons and groups to engage in this political activity.

2. When *Lawrence* overruled *Bowers*, as described in the chapter on Substantive Due Process, the Court recognized that the Due Process right of privacy covers consensual same-sex private conduct, and declined to rely on Equal Protection so as to make it clear that the invalidated sodomy law could not be saved by more narrow tailoring.

3. State court decisions and legislation in a handful of states have recognized the legality of gay marriage, but some new laws or constitutional amendments have overturned these decisions and statutes by popular vote. These new laws and amendments are now the subject of litigation based on Due Process and Equal Protection challenges.

O. Equal Protection and Fundamental Rights.

1. Selective deprivation of a constitutionally enumerated right triggers strict scrutiny regardless of whether the classification itself is suspect.

   a. Viewpoint discrimination that resulted in the exclusion of speech from a public forum has been found impermissible pursuant to the First Amendment and equal protection guarantee. *Police Department of Chicago v. Mosley.*

   b. The Sixth Amendment guarantee of assistance of counsel must be provided to indigent defendants both for appeals as a matter of right and those that are discretionary. *Douglas v. California; Ross v. Moffit.*

2. A classification that selectively denies a fundamental right, regardless of whether it is suspect, triggers strict scrutiny.

P. Right to Travel.

1. Waiting periods for new residents to qualify for a basic necessity of life (*e.g.*, welfare or health care) are strictly scrutinized. *Shapiro v. Thompson; Memorial Hospital v. Maricopa County.*

2. One-year residence requirements for obtaining a divorce or receiving in-state tuition were upheld pursuant to a rational basis standard of review. *Sosna v. Iowa; Vlandis v. Kline.*

Q. Voting.

1. Denial of right to vote

2. Poll taxes selectively deny the right to vote, without any reasonable relationship to voter qualification, and thus have been strictly scrutinized and invalidated. *Harper v. Virginia Board of Elections.*

3. A requirement for voters to own property or have a particular interest in the election is strictly scrutinized.

4. A school district requiring voters either to own or lease property in the district or have children enrolled in its schools did not serve a compelling state interest and thus was invalidated. *Kramer v. Union Free School District No. 15.*

5. Voting may be limited to a particularly group that is disproportionately affected by a special district's policies.

Salyer Land Co. v. Tulare Lake Basin Water Storage District.

6. Dilution of right to vote

   a. Electoral districts must be apportioned in a manner that generally equalizes voting power (i.e., one person, one vote). *Reynolds v. Sims.*

   b. Political gerrymandering

      1.) Partisan claims of gerrymandering are generally regarded as unjusticiable.

      2.) To the extent race is the dominant factor in drawing electoral districts, the Court will strictly scrutinize the plan.

7. Access to the ballot

   a. Significant restrictions on third parties or that impose barriers on the basis of wealth are strictly scrutinized.

R. Education.

1. There is no fundamental right to a public education.

2. A system of public financing that favored districts with high property tax bases did not create a suspect classification or burden a fundamental right and thus was upheld pursuant to the rational basis test. *San Antonio Independent School District v. Rodriguez.*

3. Denial of public education altogether to a particular group may give rise to an equal protection violation.

■ PROBLEMS ■

Problem #1: The State of Columbia has enacted a statute that increases the minimum age for a driver's license from 16 to 18. This law reflects the legislature's sense that younger drivers have more traffic accidents than the general population. The legislative record contains no specific evidence that supports this premise. Does the law violate the equal protection guarantee? If so, why? If not, why not?

Answer: Classifications on the basis of age are subject to rational basis review. Pursuant to this standard, a court must determine whether the classification (1) reflects a valid regulatory purpose and (2) is rationally related to that objective. Highway safety is a legitimate state concern, and regulation that promotes this interest represents a legitimate exercise of the state's police power. It is immaterial whether the legislature has grounded the law in hard data. So long as a credible argument can be made that there is a linkage between age and highway safety risk, the law will survive constitutional review. Given the state's valid regulatory concern and the rational relationship between the classification and the regulatory objective, the age classification is compatible with the equal protection guarantee.

Problem #2: The City of Hearts is a community where schools historically were segregated by law. This condition resulted from a state law that required all school systems to separate white students from non-white students. After the Supreme Court in 1954 declared segregation unconstitutional, the city school board in that same year determined that it would resist rather than comply. When the Civil Rights Act of 1964 was enacted and federal funding was conditioned upon desegregation, however, school officials adopted a rule providing that all future pupil assignment policies should be racially neutral. They thus adopted a policy giving parents freedom of choice with respect to where their students attended school. Because the racial composition of the schools remained unchanged, a federal district court in 1985 determined that the city must take steps that immediately would end all vestiges of racial segregation. The city did not appeal this ruling and adopted a desegregation plan. Over the course of the next decade, the racial identity of city schools diminished but did not disappear. The court in 1998 determined that the city had made a good faith effort to desegregate but, because of the extensive migration of white families from the city to the suburbs, could achieve only so much with respect to altering the schools' racial composition. It thus declared the schools unitary and reverted control to local authorities. By 2010, demographics had evolved to the point that for practical purposes city schools were non-white and suburban schools were all-white. In response to this condition, a group of parents from the city and suburbs brought an action in which it asked a federal district court to order an inter-district desegregation plan. Pursuant to this request, the court ordered the city and suburban districts to implement a plan that would ensure all schools had the same racial composition.

Please (1) identify any equal protection claims that might have been brought against the city since 1954, (2) explain how they would have been resolved, and (3) indicate whether the federal district court's rulings in 1985, 1998, and 2010 were correct.

Answer: The Supreme Court's determination that prescriptive segregation of public schools was unconstitutional imposed a responsibility on the city to desegregate. Initial resistance to the desegregation mandate would have warranted a lawsuit against the city on grounds that it was defying the Court and continuing to violate the Constitution. *See Cooper v. Aaron.*

An equal protection claim also could have been made when the city adopted its freedom of choice plan. This policy hedged on the obligation to implement effective desegregation remedies (ones that realistically promised to work "now") and eliminate the vestiges of racial segregation "root and branch." *See Green v. County School Board.*

Based upon the city's failure to take affirmative and effective action to undo its legacy of formal segregation, the federal court's decision in 1985 to mandate desegregation was appropriate. The limited achievements of desegregation appear attributable to the exodus of white families rather than the absence of good faith on the part of city officials. It thus appears that desegregation was achieved to the extent practicable. *Oklahoma City Board of Education v. Dowell.* Under these circumstances, the court should terminate the desegregation order and return control to local authorities. The 1998 order thus appears sound.

The court order for cross-district relief appears to exceed the scope of any violation. There is no evidence of any action by the suburban districts intended to cause segregation in the city. Racial segregation is unconstitutional only if it is *de jure*—that is, if segregation is the result of intentional government policy or action. The population shift from the city to the suburbs is a function of private action rather than government action. To the extent that there was a history of segregation in the City of Commerce, it appears to have been eliminated when the court declared schools racially unitary. It is unlikely that the 2010 order will survive appellate review.

Problem #3: The City of Harmony is a suburban community that was developed in the 1970s. Prior to its creation, the area was ranch and farm land. The sparse population of farmers and ranchers was entirely white. At the area grew during the 1980s and 1990s, the population became more diverse. Census data indicate that, in 2000, the population of Harmony was 12% African-American and 9% Hispanic. The Harmony City Council beginning in 2003 enacted some measures that had racial implications. They included provisions that (1) required all candidates for promotion to supervisory positions in city government to achieve a minimum score on the Scholastic Aptitude Test; (2) set aside 10% of the seats at the city university for African-Americans and Hispanics; (3) identified racial diversity as one of several factors that could justify admission of designated minorities who met minimum qualification standards but had lesser

SAT scores than some whites; and (4) established racial diversity as a basis for assigning students to city primary and secondary schools.

A group of employees, each of whom is African-American or Hispanic and did not achieve the minimum score on the SAT, has claimed that the test discriminates on the basis of race. The aggrieved employees' evidence consists of data showing that, since the city began administering the test, whites have been successful in achieving the minimum score 48% of the time. African-Americans and Hispanics have been successful 31% of the time. A total of 38 persons have taken the examination over the course of its utilization. The city maintains that the examination, although typically used in educational settings, is a valid means of identifying persons who (even if they have not attended college) can evidence the talent level that college admission confirms.

The city maintains that the university enrollment targets reflect its interest in contributing to remediation of the nation's history of discrimination. For those students that are admitted beyond the 10% set aside, it has provided evidence that the decision to admit them is made in a process that gives individualized attention to all applications and considers a range of diversity factors (*e.g.*, economic disadvantage, special skills, accomplishments, place of residence). The city justifies the diversification policies for admission to the university and assignment to primary and secondary schools on grounds that diversity in the classroom provides an important educational benefit.

Please assess each of these provisions and indicate whether and how you think they would be analyzed and assessed for constitutional purposes.

Answer: (1) An equal protection claim cannot be established minus proof of discriminatory purpose. Statistical evidence by itself is insufficient to establish such motive. Absent evidence of official intent, the rational basis test will be used to assess the test's constitutionality. Because the city has a legitimate interest in establishing qualifications for supervisors, and setting the standard at a level that is indicative of college admissibility, there is a rational basis for the testing requirement.

(2) Set-asides constitute an intentional racial classification and will be strictly scrutinized. Societal discrimination is too amorphous a basis for a remedial classification. To establish a racial preference, the city at least must show a specific act of intentional discrimination for which it is responsible. This requirement cannot be met in an environment that is bereft of any history of racial discrimination.

Even if the city has a compelling interest, the city must exhaust racially neutral alternatives.

(3) The use of race as one of several factors considered in the university admission process also will be strictly scrutinized. A diverse student body constitutes a compelling interest. So long as race is not the exclusive consideration and all applications for admission receive individualized review, it is not necessary for the policy to be entirely race-neutral.

(4) Although diversity has been recognized as a compelling interest in post-secondary education, it has yet to be acknowledged as such in the primary and secondary context. In this setting, the city would be prohibited from factoring race into its pupil assignment process.

Problem #4: The State of Hermosa in the past decade has become an increasingly popular relocation destination. This attraction owes to relatively low taxes, balmy year-round climate, mainstream family values, and affordable real estate. The influx of new residents has imposed significant burdens upon the state's infrastructure and services. Governing officials realize that raising taxes would be politically impossible, given the mind of the electorate. To optimize cost efficiencies, the state has adopted a series of residence and other requirements that determine when a person may qualify for a service, benefit, or right. Each of the requirements, as set forth below, is justified on the basis of cost minimization or efficiency or preservation of traditional family values.

Education. Enrollment in Hermosa's elementary schools is limited to children who have been born in or lived in the state for at least five years.

Welfare Benefits. Assistance for needy families is restricted to persons who have been born in or lived in the state for at least five years.

Medical Care. Access to emergency medical care for indigent persons varies depending upon the length of residence. Consistent with the varying sums of tax contributions to the state, each individual is entitled to one free emergency room visit per year of residence.

Marriage. To ensure the sanctity of the traditional family unit, no marriage license will be issued to anyone who has been in a previous marriage and divorced.

Voting. Eligibility to vote is conditioned upon the registrant's paying $100 per election. This fee is designed to cover the cost of the election process and reflects an understanding that persons with this amount of money to spare are likely to be more intelligent and informed.

Please assess analyze and assess the constitutionality of each of the provisions and provide your reasoning with respect to whether each should be upheld or invalidated.

Answer: Each of these provisions impacts a right that, although no enumerated by the Constitution, has been recognized as fundamental. To the extent these rights have been selectively burdened, they raise questions of equal protection.

The residence requirement for elementary schooling implicates the right to travel. The standard of review in right to travel cases depends upon whether the interest being burdened is a basic necessity of life. Although education is not a fundamental right, it is an important interest. Insofar as a state law denies educational opportunity altogether, it may be invalid even pursuant to rational basis review. Although cost efficiency is a valid government interest, the five-year waiting period effectively precludes persons not born in the state from enrolling in public grade schools. The relationship between the regulatory purpose and means, therefore, is likely to be found unreasonable.

The five-year waiting period to obtain welfare benefits also implicates the right to travel. Insofar as a residence requirement burdens a basic necessity of life, it will be strictly scrutinized. Effective management of the public treasury is a compelling interest. The five-year waiting period exceeds even the one-year waiting period that the Court has found excessive. This provision will not withstand strict scrutiny.

The correlation of emergency medical care availability to time in residence, like the education and welfare provisions, impacts the right to travel. Because the state is rationing a basic necessity, the regulation is subject to strict scrutiny. Cost management is a valid and compelling interest. The state may not treat residents differently, however, based upon the length of their relationship with the state and corresponding tax contributions.

Marriage is an incident of the right to privacy. Restrictions on it are subject to strict scrutiny. Although the state may have a legitimate and even compelling interest in public morals, denying divorcees the right to marry is likely to be found unduly burdensome. Divorce is a legal means of dissolving a relationship pursuant to reasons that the state has approved. The dissolution process actually may reflect respect for the family unit, as in cases of adultery. Allowing persons to remarry also may restore family units, insofar as the alternative would be a single-parent household. The regulatory means in this instance thus would not advance the regulatory purpose.

The $100 fee on voting constitutes a poll tax. It is prohibited by the Twenty-Fourth Amendment. The Court has determined, moreover, that wealth is not a determinant of voter qualification. Even if the funding interest is compelling, as a cost management tool, the regulatory means thus does not necessarily achieve the regulatory objective.

Problem #5: A man was denied admission to School of Nursing at a state-supported university because the School of Nursing program was limited to female applicants. The university was founded as a school for women in 1884. The state defended the School of Nursing's gender-based exclusion policy on the grounds that it served as a type of affirmative action for women to compensate them for past discrimination in education. As the second state interest offered in support of this exclusionary policy, the state argued that the presence of men in nursing program's classes would serve to distract the women students from their studies. What standard of judicial scrutiny will be used to evaluate the male plaintiff's challenge to this law based on Equal Protection? How will the Court analyze the two state interests? Will the law be upheld or invalidated?

Answer: In *Mississippi University for Women (MUW) v. Hogan*, 458 U.S. 718 (1982), the Court used the intermediate scrutiny standard to invalidate the gender-exclusion policy that discriminated against men, and also emphasized that the state failed to show the "exceedingly persuasive justification" necessary to defend this policy. The *MUW* Court reasoned that instead of serving "to compensate for discriminatory barriers faced by women", the policy "perpetuates the stereotyped view of nursing as exclusively a women's job". In fact, the profession of nursing was predominantly female at the time of the *MUW* decision, with 94% of nursing degrees being earned by women. Therefore, the state could not show that women actually suffer a disadvantage that required compensation through the gender-exclusion policy of the nursing program. The Court held that the state could not meet its burden under *Craig* of showing how the "important" government objective was "substantially related to the achievement" of that objective. As for the second interest, the facts showed that MUW allowed men to audit the nursing classes, and so the exclusion of male students from the nursing program did not prevent women students from being distracted by men in the classroom. But even without such evidence of male student auditors, the state's second interest could have been dismissed by the Court as insufficiently important to justify the result of the gender discrimination against men that perpetuated harmful stereotypes about women. Even when a state law is not defended explicitly on the basis of arbitrary and stereotyped judgments about men and women, the Court has condemned the state's use of gender classifications that implicitly reflect such judgments.

Problem #6: A state law prohibits aliens from obtaining a license to be a notary public. The state argues that the "public function" exception should apply, based on the fact that notaries are designated as "public officers" under the state constitution. The duties of notaries include the authentication of witnesses, the administration of oaths, and the taking of out-of-state depositions. With regard to the state's interests, the government argues that aliens are not sufficiently familiar with Texas law to serve as notaries, and that alien notaries are not likely to be available as witnesses of their acts in later years. However, the state does not administer a test to notary applicants to determine their knowledge of state law. What standard of judicial scrutiny will be used to evaluate a challenge to this law based on Equal Protection? How will the Court analyze the two state interests? Will the law be upheld or invalidated?

Answer: In *Bernal v. Fainter*, 467 U.S. 216 (1984), the Court rejected the state's argument that the "political function" exception should be applied to the law excluding aliens from the notary public position. The fact that the state constitution designates notaries as "public officers" was not relevant because the function of the position is what must be examined to determine whether the "political function" exception applies. The Court determined that the actual duties involved in serving as a notary are mainly "clerical" and "ministerial" ones. Notaries do not have the discretion to execute public policy and do not routinely exercise their authority over others. Therefore the Court did not use "rational basis" review and instead subjected the law to strict scrutiny as in *Sugarman*. With regard to the first state interest, the Court reasoned that the state's absolute class-wide exclusion was overinclusive because aliens can acquire familiarity with Texas law, and the state's failure to require a test for notaries suggested that the state's interest was less than compelling. The Court treated the second state interest as speculative, in the absence of any showing by the state that alien notaries would create a real problem of unavailability, based on the hypothesis that they would be likely to leave the state and move to locations where they could not be contacted.

Problem #7: Bobby is the non-marital child of Fred, who is Bobby's sole source of support. Bobby has lived with his father since birth. Several years *after* Bobby was born, Fred became disabled and could not work. One year *after* Fred became disabled, Bobby's sister Amy was born. Amy is also the non-marital child of Fred. Like Bobby, Amy has lived with Fred since she was born, and Fred is her sole source of support. Under the Social Security Act, the dependents of a disabled wage earner are entitled to receive "child-of-wage-earner" disability benefits. However, when Fred applied for these benefits for Bobby and Amy, Bobby's application was granted but Amy's was denied, because the law provides that a non-marital child can qualify for benefits only if the disabled parent "contributed to the child's support *or* lived with the child *prior* to the parent's disability". When Fred files a lawsuit on Amy's behalf and challenges the Act as a violation of Equal Protection, the government defends the Act by arguing that non-marital children like Amy "are not likely to possess the requisite economic dependency on the wage earner that would entitle them to the benefits", and because granting benefits to children in this class "would open the door to spurious claims". What standard of judicial scrutiny will be used to evaluate a challenge to this law based on Equal Protection? How will the Court analyze the two state interests? Will the law be upheld or invalidated?

Answer: In *Jimenez v. Weinberger*, 417 U.S. 628 (1974), the Court held that the law violated Equal Protection, relying on the reasoning of *Weber v. Aetna Casualty & Surety Co.*, 406 U.S. 164 (1972). Today the Court would apply the intermediate scrutiny standard as required by *Clark*. The *Jimenez* Court determined that the main purpose of the law was to provide present and future support to all the dependents of a disabled wage earner like Bobby and Amy, not merely to replace the financial support that a child like Bobby received before the disability of the wage-earning parent occurred. Therefore, an "afterborn" child like Amy should be entitled to the benefits for the same reason that Bobby is entitled to them, as both children are Fred's dependents. Even though the prevention of spurious claims of dependence is an important government objective, the "blanket exclusion" of children like Amy is not "substantially related to the achievement" of that objective. The *Jimenez* Court noted that the potential for spurious claims actually is the same for non-marital and marital children born *after* the onset of a parent's disability. Thus, the Act is overinclusive with respect to the benefits granted automatically to marital afterborn children and underinclusive with respect to the benefits that are denied automatically to non-marital afterborn children. If Fred had been married to Amy's mother when Amy was born, Amy would be entitled to benefits, and the different treatment of Amy cannot be justified under intermediate scrutiny. More narrow tailoring of the Act is required, so at the very least, children like Amy must be given the opportunity to make a showing of proof of their dependency. As in *Gomez*, *Trimble*, and *Weber*, the government's complete denial of rights to non-marital children must be invalidated here.

POINTS TO REMEMBER

- Most classifications are subject to rational basis review and are constitutional.
- Classifications on the basis of race, gender, alienage, and illegitimacy generate more rigorous review.
- Racial and some alienage classifications are subject to strict scrutiny.
- Classifications based on gender and non-marital status of children and their parents are subject to intermediate review.
- General economic and social classifications are subject to rational basis review.
- A more intense version of rational basis review may be employed for classifications that burden certain groups in a way that presents a "recurring constitutional difficulty."
- The Constitutional Convention's compromise on slavery established the principle of federal neutrality that eventually broke down as a prelude to civil war.
- The Court, in *Dred Scott v. Sandford,* determined that African-Americans were inferior and could not be citizens of the United States.
- The equal protection clause of the Fourteenth Amendment aimed to secure equal status under the law for former slaves.
- Laws that imply racial inferiority are impermissible under the equal protection guarantee.
- Racial segregation initially was upheld as a reasonable exercise of state power and pursuant to the premise that it did not imply racial inferiority.
- Racial classifications since the 1940s have been viewed as suspect and subject to strict scrutiny.
- Racial segregation eventually was invalidated on grounds it was inherently unequal.
- The Civil Rights Act of 1964 was the primary impetus for meaningful desegregation.
- A court's power to desegregate a school district includes authority to order busing, assign pupils on the basis of race, and establish fixed ratios to achieve a racially balanced faculty.
- Segregation is unconstitutional only if it is *de jure* (intentional).

- Inter-district desegregation remedies are permissible only if intentional actions of one district caused segregation in another.
- The duty to desegregate ends when a school district achieves racially unitary status, which occurs when the vestiges of discrimination have been eliminated to the extent practicable.
- School districts may be relieved of the duty to desegregate on an incremental basis.
- An equal protection violation is dependent upon proof of intentional discrimination.
- Discriminatory intent may be discerned from circumstantial evidence, but such a showing is difficult.
- Statistical disparities by themselves do not establish discriminatory intent.
- Affirmative action policies may be permissible to the extent they remedy past discrimination or (at least in higher education) facilitate diversity.
- Affirmative action, like any other racial classification, is subject to strict scrutiny.
- Societal discrimination is not a permissible basis for affirmative action.
- Quotas, goals, targets, or racial balancing (except as noted in the desegregation context) typically are impermissible.
- Student diversity is a compelling interest in the higher education setting.
- Race may be factored into the admissions process provided it is not the exclusive factor and evaluation of applicants is individualized.
- The Court's precedents before 1971 relied on gender stereotypes to uphold statutory exclusions of women from the legal profession and to exempt women from jury service.
- The Court's first decision invalidating a gender classification relied on rational basis review and held that it was arbitrary to mandate that men should be appointed as estate administrators rather than women (when both candidates for appointment were equally qualified for the appointment as relatives of the decedent).
- Although a Court plurality advocated the use of strict scrutiny for gender classifications, the Court ultimately decided to invent

a new standard, which became known as "intermediate scrutiny" and was later adopted for other classifications as well.

- In the Court's first decision to apply intermediate scrutiny, the Court invalidated a law that prohibited men between 18 and 21 from buying low-alcohol beer, but allowed women of the same age to do so.
- The Court used intermediate scrutiny to uphold a law that gave women more money than men in social security benefits so as to compensate them for discrimination in employment and for receiving lower retirement benefits.
- The Court used intermediate scrutiny to uphold a law that excluded women from registration for the draft.
- The Court emphasized the need for "an exceedingly persuasive justification" in striking down the exclusion of women from the VMI state military college.
- The Court's modern precedents mostly use strict scrutiny for state-law classifications based on alienage or national origins.
- An alienage classification treats citizens differently from non-citizens.
- A classification based on national origins treats people differently depending on the national origin of their ancestors.
- The Court relied on the "special public interest doctrine" before 1948 to uphold state laws that classified aliens as persons who could not own property, qualify for job licenses, or obtain access to natural resources.
- In 1948, the Supreme Court recognized the Equal Protection "right to abode" of aliens, which protects their rights to reside and earn a living in any state, and to enjoy the same legal privileges as citizens residing in any state.
- The Court has used strict scrutiny since 1970 to invalidate laws restricting the rights of aliens to obtain a license to practice law, to obtain a civil service job, and to obtain state welfare benefits and financial aid for education.
- The Court uses rational basis scrutiny for state laws that fit the "political function exception", which does not covers civil service jobs requiring the performance of basic government functions and the exercise of discretionary power in a position of authority.
- The Court upheld restrictions under the "political function exception" upon the right of aliens to obtain jobs as public school teachers, state troopers, and state probation officers.

- The Court uses rational basis scrutiny for federal laws that are enacted pursuant to the Congressional power to regulate immigration and naturalization. For example, courts have upheld an executive order excluding aliens from competitive civil service jobs.
- The Court uses intermediate scrutiny for state laws that restrict the rights of non-lawful-resident aliens.
- The Court used intermediate scrutiny to invalidate a state law that excluded non-lawful-resident-alien children from public schools.
- The Court uses intermediate scrutiny to assess classifications that restrict the rights of non-marital children and their parents.
- The Court used intermediate scrutiny to invalidate a six-year time limit on support suits by non-marital children because DNA testing is a more effective means of eliminating false paternity claims.
- The Court's earlier decisions relied on rational basis to invalidate laws that established complete prohibitions on the access of non-marital children and their parents to legal rights available to married parents and their children, such as orders of support sought by children from parents, shares of the intestate estate of a father, and worker's compensation benefits.
- The Court invalidated laws that prohibited an unmarried father from obtaining custody of his child after the death of the mother, and that granted the right to block an adoption only to unmarried mothers and not unmarried fathers.
- The Court upheld a federal law that granted citizenship automatically to the non-marital child, born outside the U.S. to a citizen mother, but not to a non-marital child of a citizen father who must take additional steps to demonstrate paternity.
- The Court uses the rational basis standard to evaluate classifications of persons with mental disabilities.
- The Court used the rational basis standard to invalidate a city decision to deny a permit for a group home for persons with mental disabilities, where that decision was based on the private bias of hostile neighbors, and where the justifications to deny the permit applied equally to applicants whose permit requests were not denied.
- The Court used the rational basis standard to uphold a state law that classified persons with mental disabilities differently from

persons with mental illness, and provided greater procedural protections for the latter group in commitment proceedings.

- Selective deprivation of a fundamental right is subject to strict scrutiny.
- State laws establishing residence minimums as a condition of qualifying for a basic necessity are subject to strict scrutiny.
- Residence requirements for interests that are not fundamental are subject to the rational basis test.
- Electoral districts must be apportioned so as generally to achieve one-person, one-vote.
- Limitations on the right to vote in a special purpose election are subject to "close and exacting" review.
- Limitations on voting in a special purpose district depend upon the significance and directness of the interest and the scope of government authority at stake.
- Unless a group consistently has been excluded from the political process, political gerrymandering is unlikely to be invalidated.
- Racial gerrymandering is subject to strict scrutiny, but political gerrymandering claims are regarded as non-justiciable.
- Significant barriers to securing space on a ballot are strictly scrutinized.
- Education is not a fundamental right.

CHAPTER 10

Freedom of Expression

The First Amendment to the United States Constitution guarantees citizens the right to engage in freedom of expression. Recognition of this right did not come easily or quickly. Prior to the late Seventeenth Century, governments imposed various types of restrictions on free speech. Most governments were headed by kings, who were presumed to have been divinely appointed and to be effectuating God's will, and therefore it was considered inappropriate (and, in many cases, illegal) for an ordinary person to criticize the king or the King's government. As a result, governments imposed various types of restrictions on freedom of expression. For example, at one point, the English government imposed licensing requirements. In other words, in order to print something, an individual must obtain a license from the government, and the English government (in particular) would refuse licenses for works that it deemed objectionable. In addition, England used the crime of seditious libel to prosecute those who criticized government (on the theory that the King could do no wrong and thus could not be criticized), and it did not regard truth as a defense. Some of these restrictions (particularly, seditious libel) were imposed in the American colonies.

When the United States Constitution did not include a bill of rights (including protections for freedom of expression), it rapidly became clear that the Constitution would not be ratified. In order to obtain ratification, it was agreed that the First Congress would adopt a Bill of Rights that would include protections for expressive freedom. The First Amendment provided that "Congress shall make no law . . . abridging the freedom of speech, or of the press." Although the First Amendment was explicitly applicable only to Congress, it was eventually interpreted as applying to all of the federal government as well as to the actions of state and local governments.

Because there was such widespread support for protecting freedom of expression, there was little explanation for why speech should receive special protection. Over the ensuing centuries, courts and commentators have offered various justifications for according freedom of expression a preferred position in the constitutional structure. For example, in *Abrams v. United States*, 250 U.S. 616, 630 (1919) (Holmes, J., dissenting), Justice Holmes embraced the "marketplace of ideas" theory which provides that "the ultimate good is better reached by free trade in ideas and the best test of truth is the power of thought to get itself accepted in the marketplace of ideas." However, the Court has articulated other justifications for protecting freedom of speech, including the notion that speech helps facilitate personal development and self-fulfillment, has inherent value for purposes of promoting participatory decision-making in a democracy, as well as for providing a social safety value (a way to let off steam and advance one's ideas and agenda) through speech rather than through violence. *See* Alexander Meiklejohn, *The First Amendment Is an Absolute*, 1961 SUP. CT. REV. 245 (1961); *see also Whitney v. California*, 274 U.S. 357 (1927) (Whitney, J., concurring).

Although Congress phrased the First Amendment in broad and absolute terms ("Congress shall make *no law* . . ."), the U.S. Supreme Court has not interpreted the First Amendment as providing absolute protection for free expression. As Justice Holmes stated, the right to freedom of expression does not protect someone who yells "fire" in a crowded theater.

Nonetheless, the Court has accorded free speech a "preferred" position in the constitutional structure, and free speech interests frequently prevail against competing interests. Indeed, as a general rule, when a speech restriction is content-based or viewpoint-based, the Court generally applies "strict scrutiny." As a result, the restriction must be supported by a "compelling" or "overriding" governmental interest, and must be the least restrictive means for accomplishing that interest. However, there are a number of different categories of speech (*e.g.*, fighting words and true threats) that do not receive constitutional protection.

Speech Advocating Violent or Illegal Action. There has been considerable litigation regarding whether the government (federal, state or local) can prohibit speech that advocates violent or illegal action. For much of the nation's history, the Court interpreted the First Amendment as providing only limited protection for expression, and therefore as providing very limited protection for speech advocating violence or illegal action.

Advocacy cases came to the forefront during World War I, following the Russian Revolution, when there were fears that Communism would spread to other countries, and possibly sweep the world. Congress responded by enacting the Espionage Act and the Sedition Act of 1918, and many states passed criminal syndicalism laws that were the functional equivalent of seditious libel laws, and which allowed government to prosecute individuals who advocated communism or espoused anarchic or revolutionary doctrine. In *Schenck v. United States*, 249 U.S. 47 (1919), the Court upheld the convictions of protesters for disseminating leaflets calling on draft eligible men to resist military service. Justice Holmes, writing for the majority, decreed that the critical issue was "whether the words are used in such circumstances and are of such a nature as to create a clear and present danger that they will bring about the substantive degree of evils the Congress has a right to prevent." Even though there was no evidence that anyone had actually resisted the draft, the Court found a clear and present danger because of the defendants' motives. In two other cases decided about the same time, *Frohwerk v. United States*, 249 U.S. 204 (1919), and *Debs v. United States,* 249 U.S. 211 (1919), the Court upheld convictions of antiwar protesters under the Espionage Act. Instead of applying clear and present danger principles, the Court focused upon the speech and its "natural tendency and reasonably probable effect."

The foundation of the modern approach to illegal advocacy speech was articulated in a dissent by Justice Holmes in *Abrams v. United States*, 250 U.S. 616 (1919). In that case, in which the Court upheld convictions under the Espionage Act, Holmes argued that illegal advocacy should not be punished unless it "so imminently threaten[s] immediate interference with the lawful and pressing purpose of the law that an immediate check is required to save the country." The dissent is also famous for introducing the marketplace of ideas metaphor.

Despite Holmes' dissent, some subsequent cases applied the "bad tendency" test to uphold convictions. For example, in *Gitlow v. New York,* 268 U.S. 652 (1925), the Court upheld convictions under a criminal anarchy statute of individuals who printed and distributed a manifesto advocating class struggle and mass political strikes. *Gitlow* held that when the legislature had specifically identified the type of speech to be prohibited, there was no room for judicial inquiry. Likewise, in *Whitney v. California,* 274 U.S. 357 (1927), the Court affirmed the conviction of an individual who helped organize a Marxist-oriented group in violation of a state criminal syndicalism statute. The Court followed this concurrence in a couple of subsequent cases. *See Herndon v. Lowry,* 301 U.S. 242 (1937); *DeJonge v. Oregon,* 299 U.S. 353 (1937). Nevertheless, in some subsequent cases, the Court revived older jurisprudence in cases arising during the Cold War era and the McCarthy era. *See Dennis v. United States*, 341 U.S. 494 (1951) (plurality opinion).

The Court's current approach to subversive advocacy draws heavily upon the Brandeis-Holmes model of analysis. In

Brandenburg v. Ohio, 395 U.S. 444 (1969), the Court reversed convictions of Ku Klux Klan members under the state's criminal syndicalism statute. The case involved a cross burning and claims that the KKK might need to take "revengeance" (sic). In overturning the convictions, the Court held that a conviction cannot be sustained unless it "is directed to inciting or producing imminent lawless action and is likely to incite or produce such action." *Brandenburg* was based on the marketplace of ideas theory, and suggests that governmental suppression of speech is inappropriate so long as time exists for the "marketplace of ideas" to respond to speech with dangerous tendencies.

Whether *Brandenburg's* test will be faithfully applied during periods of ferment and turmoil, when the nation is under threat, is far from clear. Indeed, the Court departed from the *Brandenburg* formula in *Holder v. Humanitarian Law Project,* 561 U.S. 1 (2010), a case involving a federal law that prohibited individuals or groups from providing "material support" to any group that the Secretary of State had designated as a "foreign terrorist organization." Humanitarian organizations, which provided training in peaceful dispute resolution and other non-violent methods, maintained that the law chilled their freedoms of speech and association. In *Holder,* the Court held that the First Amendment did not preclude Congress from barring aid even if the aid has a speech component. In reaching that result, the Court employed strict scrutiny. Although there was no disagreement that combating terrorism constitutes a compelling interest, the Court fractured over whether the regulatory means were narrowly tailored. The majority concluded that government reasonably could conclude that the assistance provided by the groups, even if designed to advance peaceful outcomes, likely would promote terrorist goals. The Court noted that providing aid to a group's humanitarian activities could free up resources for terrorist activities.

Justice Breyer's dissent emphasized *Brandenburg,* and the idea that "the First Amendment protects advocacy even of unlawful action so long as that advocacy is not 'directed to inciting or producing imminent lawless action and likely to incite or produce such action.' " He noted that, in the facts before the Court, the groups sought to advocate peaceful, lawful action to secure political ends.

The Categorical Approach to Speech. In *Chaplinsky v. New Hampshire,* 315 U.S. 568 (1942), the Court made clear that there are certain categories of speech that are not protected under the First Amendment. The Court stated that there are "certain well-defined and narrowly limited classes of speech, the prevention and punishment of which have never been thought to raise any Constitutional problem." The Court included within these categories, the lewd and obscene, the profane, the libelous, and insulting or "fighting words."

The idea of a "categorical" approach to speech is somewhat misleading. In fact, the Court has frequently made statements which reject the idea of a categorical approach. For example, the Court has indicated that both content-based restrictions on speech, and viewpoint-based restrictions on speech are presumptively unconstitutional and must be subjected to strict scrutiny. Illustrative is the holding in *Matal v. Tam*, 582 U.S. 218 (2017), a trademark case in which petitioner tried to trademark his band's name, "The Slants." The Patent and Trademark Office (PTO) declined to register the name, relying on a provision of federal law that allowed the PTO to reject a trademark that might "disparage or bring into contempt or disrepute" any "persons living or dead." The Court struck down the law on the basis that it violated the Free Speech Clause because it offended a "bedrock First Amendment principle": "The government may not prohibit the expression of an idea simply because society finds the idea itself offensive or disagreeable." *Texas v. Johnson*, 491 U.S. 397, 414 (1989). The Court explained: "We have said time and again that 'the public expression of ideas may not be prohibited merely because the ideas are themselves offensive to some of their hearers.'" *Street v. New York*, 394 U.S. 576, 592 (1969). Justice Kennedy, joined by three other justices, authored a concurring opinion: "The viewpoint discrimination rationale renders unnecessary any extended treatment of other questions raised by the parties. It is a fundamental principle of the First Amendment that the government may not punish or suppress speech based on disapproval of the ideas or perspectives the speech conveys. An applicant may register a positive or benign mark but not a derogatory one. The law thus reflects the Government's disapproval of a subset of messages it finds offensive. This is the essence of viewpoint discrimination."

Likewise, in *Iancu v. Brunetti*, 588 U.S. 388 (2019), the Court invalidated a U.S. Patent & Trademark Office (PTO) decision involving the word "FUCT." Brunetti, an artist and entrepreneur, founded a clothing line that used the trademark "FUCT," which functioned as the clothing's brand name, but which was pronounced as four letters, one after the other: F-U-C-T. When Brunetti tried to register his trademark with the PTO, his application was denied based on a prohibition against "immoral or scandalous matter." According to the PTO, the question was whether a "substantial composite of the general public" would find the mark "shocking to the sense of truth, decency, or propriety"; as "giving offense to the conscience or moral feelings"; as "calling out for condemnation";

"disgraceful"; "offensive"; "disreputable"; or as "vulgar." Finding that Brunetti's trademark flunked that test, his application for a trademark was denied. The Court overturned the PTO decision which it regarded as "viewpoint discrimination": "The Lanham Act permits registration of marks that champion society's sense of rectitude and morality, but not marks that denigrate those concepts." Finding the law substantially overbroad, the Court invalidated the relevant provisions of the Lanham Act.

Similarly, in *Reed v. Town of Gilbert*, 576 U.S. 155 (2015), the Court struck down a sign ordinance because it applied different rules to different types of signs based on the content of the speech. In particular, the ordinance distinguished between "political" signs, "ideological" signs and "directional" signs: "The Town's Sign Code singles out specific subject matter for differential treatment, even if it does not target viewpoints within that subject matter. Ideological messages are given more favorable treatment than messages concerning a political candidate, which are themselves given more favorable treatment than messages announcing an assembly of like-minded individuals. That is a paradigmatic example of content-based discrimination." Noting that government "has no power to restrict expression because of its message, its ideas, its subject matter, or its content," the Court applied strict scrutiny in evaluating the ordinance. The Town asserted only two interests in support of the provision: preserving the Town's aesthetic appeal and traffic safety. The Court found those asserted justifications inadequate: "The Town cannot claim that placing strict limits on temporary directional signs is necessary to beautify the Town while at the same time allowing unlimited numbers of other types of signs that create the same problem. The Town similarly has not shown that limiting temporary directional signs is necessary to eliminate threats to traffic safety, but that limiting other types of signs is not." Accordingly, the Court struck the ordinance down.

Despite the Court's hesitancy to sustain content-based and viewpoint-based restrictions on speech, the Court has carved out certain categories of speech as "unprotected." In other words, strict scrutiny does not apply.

Fighting Words. One category of speech that is unprotected is so-called "fighting words"—words "which by their very utterance inflict injury or tend to incite an immediate breach of the peace." *Chaplinsky* involved a Jehovah's Witness who gave a speech and distributed literature on the streets of Rochester on a Saturday afternoon, and who was arrested when he refused to stop after the crowd became restless. On the way to the police station for booking, when Chaplinsky encountered the City Marshall, he stated: "You are a God damned racketeer" and "a damned Fascist and the whole government of Rochester are Fascists or agents of Fascists." Chaplinsky was convicted under a New Hampshire law that prohibited anyone from addressing "any offensive, derisive or annoying word to any other person who is lawfully in any street or other public place" and also prohibited anyone from calling such person by any "offensive or derisive name." In upholding the conviction, the Court concluded that such "utterances are no essential part of any exposition of ideas, and are of such slight social value as a step to truth that any benefit that may be derived from them is clearly outweighed by the social interest in order and morality. Resort to epithets or personal abuse is not in any proper sense communication of information or opinion safeguarded by the Constitution, and its punishment as a criminal act would raise no question under that instrument." The Court defined the term fighting words as involving words that "men of common intelligence would understand would be words likely to cause an average addressee to fight."

Many "fighting words" convictions are reversed on vagueness and overbreadth grounds. The statutes and ordinances on which these convictions are based are frequently phrased in very broad terms, or use terms that suffer from vagueness or ambiguity (*e.g.*, prohibiting the use of "opprobrious" or "abusive" language. *See, e.g., City of Houston v. Hill*, 482 U.S. 451 (1987)). As a result, it is relatively rare for a fighting words conviction to be sustained.

Defamatory Speech. Among the categories of speech that *Chaplinsky* identified as unprotected was defamatory speech. The tort of defamation provides individuals with an action for reputational injury that is caused by written or spoken falsehoods (libel and slander, respectively). Until the 1960s, the Court regarded libelous speech as unprotected under the First Amendment. However, the Court dramatically altered its approach, and provided defamatory speech with constitutional protection, in its landmark decision in *New York Times Co. v. Sullivan*, 376 U.S. 254 (1964). In that case, the Court recognized the citizenry's interest in governmental processes in a democracy, as well as the potential chilling effect of defamation judgments, and held that a public official cannot recover for defamation unless he can prove by clear and convincing evidence that the defendant made the defamatory statements with "actual malice." The term "actual malice" requires that defendant must have acted with "knowledge that [the allegedly defamatory statement] was false or in reckless disregard of whether it was false or malicious." In other words, public officials cannot recover simply by showing that they were defamed by incorrect statements, or that the publisher was negligent. Actual malice is a constitutional question and thus will be reviewed independently by an appeals court. The practical effect of the actual malice standard is that governmental officials are essentially precluded from recovering for defamation.

In later cases, the Court extended the actual malice standard to defamation suits brought by so-called "public figures." *See Curtis Publishing Co. v. Butts*, 388 U.S. 130 (1967). Like public officials, public figures are "intimately involved in the resolution of important public questions or, by reason of their fame, shape events in areas of concern to society at large." However, the Court has refused to extend the actual malice standard to defamation actions brought by private individuals. In *Gertz v. Robert Welch, Inc.*, 418 U.S. 323 (1974), the Court differentiated private individuals on the basis that they do not invite public attention to themselves, have not voluntarily exposed themselves to a higher risk of reputational harm, and do not command access to the media and possess an ability to undo or mitigate reputational injury. The Court held that, in a suit by a private individual, a state could not subject the defendant to strict liability, and could not impose presumed or punitive damages absent a showing of actual malice. Such plaintiffs could only recover for "out-of-pocket loss" or such things as "impairment of reputation and standing in the community, personal humiliation, and mental anguish and suffering." This standard thus factors into actual damages at least some of the considerations that traditionally have been referenced in connection with presumed damages.

Gertz also provided some definition of the term "public figure." The Court held that individuals can become public figures when they "occupy positions of such pervasive power and influence that they are deemed public figures for all purposes," they "have thrust themselves to the forefront of particular public controversies in order to influence the resolution of the issues involved," or have become immersed in public events. However, a lawyer who merely represents a client in a high-profile case will not necessarily be regarded as a public figure.

Over time, the Court began to distinguish between private individuals based on whether their cases involved the public interest. For example, in *Dun & Bradstreet, Inc. v. Greenmoss Builders, Inc.*, 472 U.S. 749 (1985), the Court held that a private individual who was involved in a matter of purely private interest could recover based on a lesser standard. In *Dun*, plaintiff was a private individual who sued over an inaccurate credit report. The Court concluded that the states have broader authority to impose liability in cases involving private individuals involved in matters of purely private interest.

Intentional Infliction of Emotional Distress. Chaplinsky did not address the question of whether speech that inflicts mental or emotional distress is a category of speech that receives no First Amendment protection. However, in *Hustler Magazine v. Falwell*, 485 U.S. 46 (1988), the Court placed constitutional restrictions on the ability of plaintiffs to recover for the tort of intentional infliction of emotional distress. In a satirical parody, Hustler magazine depicted the Reverend Jerry Falwell, a televangelist who was involved in politics and public affairs, as having engaged in a lewd incestuous relationship with his mother. The Court held that the parody was entitled to First Amendment protection, noting that even depictions that cause distress can have speech value, and noting further that political cartoonists and satirists often make insulting or upsetting commentary. The Court dismissed Falwell's contention that Hustler's parody of him was "outrageous," noting that the Court could not draw a "principled standard" separating the Hustler parody from traditional political cartoons. As a result, since Falwell was a public figure, he was required to show that Hustler ran the parody with actual malice (as defined in the *New York Times* case). Since Hustler's depiction involved a parody, with no suggestion that the allegations were true, Falwell could not recover for defamation or intentional infliction of mental and emotional distress.

The Court's most recent intentional infliction of emotional distress decision was rendered in *Snyder v. Phelps*, 562 U.S. 443 (2011). That case involved the Westboro Baptist Church (and its pastor Fred Phelps) whose members believe that God hates and punishes the United States for its tolerance of homosexuality, particularly in the military. In an effort to publicize their views, church members frequently picketed at military funerals, having picketed at nearly 600 funerals over a twenty year period. After Marine Lance Corporal Matthew Snyder was killed in Iraq in the line of duty, six Westboro parishioners decided to protest his funeral. They did so on public land adjacent to public streets near the Maryland State House, the United States Naval Academy, and Matthew Snyder's funeral (although they were distanced from the funeral so that the mourners could not see them), and carried signs with messages such as "God Hates the USA/Thank God for 9/11," "America is Doomed," "Don't Pray for the USA," "Thank God for IEDs," "Thank God for Dead Soldiers," "Pope in Hell," "Priests Rape Boys," "God Hates Fags," "You're Going to Hell," and "God Hates You." The Westboro picketers displayed their signs for about 30 minutes prior to the funeral, and they also sang hymns and recited Bible verses. However, the picketers did not enter church property or go to the cemetery or the grave site.

Snyder's father could not read the signs at the time of the funeral, because the protest was set back 200 to 300 feet from the funeral, but he could see the tops of the picket signs. He did see the signs later that evening while watching a news broadcast. In addition, while doing an Internet search, he came across a Web posting (referred to by the Court as the "epic") that was posted several weeks after the funeral which contained religiously oriented denunciations of the Snyders interspersed among lengthy Bible quotations. Snyder filed suit against Phelps, his daughters, and the Westboro Baptist Church, alleging defamation, publicity of private life, intentional infliction of emotional distress, intrusion upon seclusion, and civil conspiracy. Although the trial court rendered judgment against Snyder on the defamation and publicity claims, the remaining claims went to trial where Snyder testified that he was "unable to separate the thought of his dead son from his thoughts of Westboro's picketing, and he testified that he often becomes tearful, angry, and physically ill when he thinks about it." Expert witnesses testified that Snyder had suffered "emotional anguish" and "severe depression" which exacerbated his pre-existing health conditions. Snyder prevailed in the trial court on the intentional infliction of emotional distress, intrusion upon seclusion, and civil conspiracy claims, and obtained judgments against Westboro liable for $2.9 million in compensatory damages and $8 million in punitive damages. However, the punitive damages were remitted to $2.1 million.

The U.S. Supreme Court reversed the judgment, refusing to consider the epic because it was not submitted to the jury and was not mentioned in Snyder's petition for certiorari. In regard to the picketing, the Court emphasized that it related to a matter of public concern (Westboro's views regarding the U.S. position on homosexuality), rather than to matters of purely private concern, and therefore was entitled to First Amendment protection because "speech concerning public affairs is more than self-expression; it is the essence of self-government." Indeed, the Court emphasized that "speech on public issues occupies the highest rung of the hierarchy of First Amendment values, and is entitled to special protection."

The Court did suggest that states might have greater leeway to impose liability for the tort of intentional infliction of emotional distress when speech relates to "matters of purely private significance" (as in defamation, specifically, the *Dun & Bradstreet* case, which involved a private credit report). When private speech is involved, there "is no threat to the free and robust debate of public issues; there is no potential interference with a meaningful dialogue of ideas"; and the "threat of liability" does not pose the risk of "a reaction of self-censorship" on matters of public import. The dividing line between the two types of speech focuses on whether the speech relates to matters of "political, social, or other concern to the community," as well as on whether it involves "a subject of legitimate news interest; that is, a subject of general interest and of value and concern to the public." The mere fact that the method or style of speech is inappropriate does not deprive it of First Amendment protection when a matter of public interest is involved.

Despite the offensiveness of the signs, the Court viewed the signs as conveying messages related to matters of public interest because they highlighted "the political and moral conduct of the United States and its citizens, the fate of our Nation, homosexuality in the military, and scandals involving the Catholic clergy." In addition, by focusing on military funerals, Westboro was trying to reach a broader audience. Even though a few of the signs focused on Matthew Snyder himself (*e.g.*, signs which stated "You're Going to Hell" and "God Hates You"), the overall thrust of the picketing was on American policy rather than on Snyder himself. The Court noted that "Westboro had been actively engaged in speaking on the subjects addressed in its picketing long before it became aware of Matthew Snyder, and there can be no serious claim that Westboro's picketing did not represent its 'honestly believed' views on public issues." In addition, since there was no pre-existing relationship or conflict between Westboro and Snyder, there was no indication that Westboro's speech was a thinly veiled attempt to attack Snyder. Moreover, even though Westboro chose to use Snyder's funeral as a way to communicate its views, a choice that was particularly hurtful to Snyder's father, that fact did not deprive the protest of First Amendment protection.

An important factor in the case was the fact that the protest was held in a public place, a venue which occupies a "special position in terms of First Amendment protection." Over the decades, the Court has "repeatedly referred to public streets as the archetype of a traditional public forum," and concluded that " 'time out of mind' public streets and sidewalks have been used for public assembly and debate." Of course, the state was free to impose reasonable time, place, and manner restrictions on the protests as it had done (requiring that the protest be set back from the grave site).

The problem for Snyder was that the distress caused by the picketing did not relate to the time, place and manner of the demonstration, but rather to the content and the viewpoint of the message. As a result, the Court held that the government could not prohibit Westboro's message: "If there is a bedrock principle underlying the First Amendment, it is that the government may not prohibit the expression of an idea simply because society finds the idea itself offensive or disagreeable." The Court rejected the trial court's conclusion that Westboro could be held liable simply because the jury viewed the picketing as "outrageous" which might allow a juror to punish statements that they dislike. The Court worried that such a standard might pose "a real danger of becoming an instrument for the suppression of 'vehement, caustic, and sometimes unpleasant' expression. In public debate we must tolerate insulting, and even outrageous, speech in order to provide adequate 'breathing space' to the freedoms protected by the First Amendment."

The Court also rejected the trial court's holding that Westboro could be held liable for intrusion upon seclusion and civil conspiracy on the basis that Snyder was an unwilling listener or viewer of the protests: "the Constitution does not permit the government to decide which types of otherwise protected speech are sufficiently offensive to require protection for the unwilling listener or viewer. Rather, the burden normally falls upon the viewer to avoid further bombardment of his sensibilities simply by averting his eyes." Since Westboro stayed away from the memorial service, and Snyder could see no more than the tops of the signs, "there is no indication that the picketing in any way interfered with the funeral service itself." As a result, the Court refused to extend the captive audience doctrine to the case, emphasizing that "Westboro addressed matters of public import on public property, in a peaceful manner, in full compliance with the guidance of local officials. The speech was indeed planned to coincide with Matthew Snyder's funeral, but did not itself disrupt that funeral, and Westboro's choice to conduct its picketing at that time and place did not alter the nature of its speech."

Justice Alito, the lone dissenter, argued that the nation's "profound national commitment to free and open debate is not a license for the vicious verbal assault that occurred in this case." He also argued that Snyder was entitled to "bury his son in peace," but was deprived of that right because of a "malevolent verbal attack on Matthew and his family at a time of acute emotional vulnerability" that caused the father "severe and lasting emotional injury." He concluded that Westboro had no "right to brutalize Mr. Snyder."

The *Phelps* decision is broadly consistent with U.S. First Amendment jurisprudence. While the views of Westboro Baptist Church, as well its tactics, might be regarded as offensive by many, the Westboro protestors had a constitutional right to express those views. In some respects, Westboro Baptist Church is no different than other dissident or minority views that have received constitutional protection. During the Civil Rights Era, might Southern officials might have regarded the demands of African-American protestors for equal rights as "extremist"? Likewise, at the turn of the last century, when women demanded the right to vote, might some officials might have regarded those views as "extremist" as well? Nevertheless, these views were entitled to constitutional protection.

In recent years, intentional infliction issues have arisen in new contexts that have not yet been resolved by the U.S. Supreme Court. For example, some individuals have published so-called "revenge porn." For example, following the breakup of a relationship, a boyfriend published sexually explicit pictures of his former girlfriend on a "revenge porn" site. In addition, some legislators have attempted to pass laws prohibiting so-called "cyber bullying." These laws have not yet made it to the Court.

Privacy. The tort of invasion of privacy can also have constitutional dimensions and implications. The Fifth and Fourteenth Amendments have been construed as protecting the right to make personal choices in certain settings, and the Fourth Amendment protects individuals against unreasonable searches and seizures.

In general, the Court has been reluctant to impose liability for publication of lawfully obtained truthful information even when there are privacy implications. For example, in *Cox Broadcasting Corp. v. Cohn*, 420 U.S. 469 (1975), the Court refused to uphold a damages claim premised upon a state law prohibiting publication of a rape victim's name because the victim's identity had been obtained legally from a public record. Likewise, in *Landmark Communications, Inc. v. Virginia*, 435 U.S. 829 (1978), the Court held that liability could not be imposed for a newspaper report regarding a confidential judicial disciplinary proceeding because the information was not only truthful but lawfully obtained. In *Smith v. Daily Mail Publishing Co.*, 443 U.S. 97 (1979), although the Court refused to establish an absolute privilege for disclosure of truthful private information, it held that liability for publishing accurate information on an issue of "public significance" (a child murderer's name) could not be established minus "a state interest of the highest order." Finally, in *The Florida Star v. B.J.F.*, 491 U.S. 524 (1989), the Court held that a newspaper could not be liable in damages for an inadvertent publication of the name of a rape victim in violation of state law.

The Court has also imposed constitutional limitations on recovery in false light privacy actions. Like defamation cases, false light claims involve false statements or suggestions that can cause injury. However, unlike defamation cases, the false light information does not necessarily cause reputational injury. The most important false light case is *Time, Inc. v. Hill*, 385 U.S. 374 (1967), which arose when a magazine misrepresented a family's hostage experience. In deciding the case, the Court overrode state law by imposing the *New York Times* actual malice standard in false light privacy cases. In other words, absent proof that defendant published the false light information with knowledge of falsehood or reckless disregard of the truth, plaintiff could not recover.

An overlay has also been imposed on the right of privacy that protects an individual's economic interest in the use of name, image, talent. The plaintiffs in this branch of the tort are commonly athletes, entertainers, and performers. For example, in *Zacchini v. Scripps-Howard Broadcasting Co.,* 433 U.S. 562 (1977), the Court sustained a recovery vindicating an entertainer's right to publicity in a case involving a television station's broadcast of a human cannonball entertainer's performance. In protecting the entertainer's interest, the Court emphasized the entertainer's right to profit from his talents, as well as society's interest in facilitating and rewarding an entertainer for his creative energy. Although the Court recognized the importance of news gathering to the media, the Court concluded that the media could be required to account to plaintiff without incurring a significant burden. If the public desired access to the performance, it could gain access for the required admission price. On the other hand, if the entertainer were not compensated, he would be deprived of the incentive to produce the performance, and the public might be deprived of the opportunity to view it. Under the First Amendment, the Court has also placed restrictions on the ability of plaintiffs to recover for the tort of invasion of privacy.

Obscenity. In *Chaplinsky v. New Hampshire,* 315 U.S. 568, 572 (1942), in dicta, the Court suggested that obscenity is another category of speech that is not protected under the First Amendment, noting that obscenity plays "no essential part of any exposition of ideas, and has slight social value as a step to the truth." In *Roth v. United States,* 354 U.S. 476, 484 (1957), the Court reinforced that idea by stating that obscenity is "utterly without redeeming social importance." In *Roth v. United States,* 354 U.S. 476 (1957), the Court acknowledged that sex and obscenity are not synonymous terms, and suggested that obscenity involves material that "deals with sex in a manner appealing to the *prurient interest.*" An obscenity determination must involve work that "the average person, applying contemporary community standards, [would find that] the dominant theme of the material taken as a whole appeals to prurient interest." *Roth* focused on "contemporary community standards," thereby precluding a finding of obscenity based upon a particularly sensitive group's response to sexually explicit publication, and the decision required consideration of the work "as a whole."

The *Roth* decision did not produce a workable definition of obscenity, ultimately prompting Justice Potter Stewart's observation that while he could not define obscenity, he knows it when he sees it. *Jacobellis v. Ohio*, 378 U.S. 184 (1964). Indeed, through the 1960s and the early 1970s, the Court struggled to establish a viable definition of obscenity as applied in various contexts. In subsequent decisions, the Court held that obscenity prosecutions can implicate constitutional rights, and therefore the Court must independently assess whether a given publication is in fact obscene. Of course, without a clear definition of obscenity, the Court was forced to deal with each publication on a case-by-case basis.

In *Miller v. California*, 413 U.S. 15 (1973), the Court finally agreed upon a variant of the three-prong test for evaluating obscenity cases. Under that test, a court should ask: "(1) whether the average person applying contemporary community standards would find that the work, taken as a whole, appeals to the prurient interest, (2) whether it depicts or describes, in a patently offensive way, sexual conduct specifically defined by the applicable state law, and (3) whether the work taken as a whole, lacks serious literary, artistic, political, or scientific value." In *Miller*, the Court rejected the requirement of a national standard, in favor of a local standard. While a local standard could be out of the mainstream, the Court held in *Jenkins v. Georgia*, 418 U.S. 153 (1974), that any potential harshness was softened by the fact that appellate courts must independently review constitutional claims in obscenity cases.

An important aspect of the *Miller* decision was its alteration of the "utterly" lacks social value requirement to require that the work must have "serious" literary, artistic, political, or scientific value. In other words, the decision made it easier to find that a particular publication is obscene. Unlike the prurient interest and patent offensiveness standards, courts were required to use "contemporary community standards" to assess whether material lacks the required social value. In *Pope v. Illinois*, 481 U.S. 497 (1987), the Court held that the focus should be on the "reasonable person". Nevertheless, even following *Miller*, the Court has sometimes invoked overbreadth and vagueness principles to strike down obscenity convictions.

While *Miller* created the possibility that a local jury's standards could be out of the mainstream, the Court ameliorated this problem by holding in *Jenkins v. Georgia*, 418 U.S. 153, that appellate courts must independently review constitutional claims in obscenity cases. Although the Court reaffirmed the notion that questions of pruriency and patent offensiveness are jury questions, jury findings cannot be sustained unless the publication involves "patently offensive 'hard core' sexual conduct." As a result, even if a jury concludes that a publication is inconsistent with contemporary community standards, the Court can review and reverse for constitutional deficiencies.

Even though obscenity receives no constitutional protection, the Court has held that citizens have the right to possess obscene materials in the privacy of their homes. *See Stanley v. Georgia*, 394 U.S. 557 (1969) (overturning a homeowner's conviction for possession of obscene material in his own home). However, the Court has declined to hold that individuals have the right to sell obscenity, or to purchase obscenity (even to take it to their homes), or to view it outside of the home. *See Paris Adult Theatre I v. Slaton*, 413 U.S. 49 (1973).

New Categories of Unprotected Speech? In general, the Court has been reluctant to create new categories of unprotected speech. For example, *United States v. Alvarez*, 567 U.S. 709 (2012), involved a man who falsely claimed to have won the Congressional Medal of Honor when he introduced himself at a district water board meeting. The man was criminally charged with violating the Stolen Valor Act of 2005, 18 U.S.C. § 704, which made it a crime for anyone to falsely claim to have won the medal. Since the Act imposed a content-based restriction on speech, the Court applied strict scrutiny, emphasizing that, as "a general matter, the First Amendment means that government has no power to restrict expression because of its message, its ideas, its subject matter, or its content." The Court also rejected the idea that it should create new categories of unprotected speech based on a "free-floating test" for First Amendment coverage involving a simple "balancing of relative social costs and benefits" related to the speech. Emphasizing that content-based restrictions on speech are allowed only when they involve one of a few "historic and traditional categories of expression long familiar to the bar" (*e.g.*, advocacy intended, and likely, to incite imminent lawless action, speech integral to criminal conduct, so-called "fighting words," child pornography, fraud, true threats, and speech presenting some grave and imminent threat the government has the power to prevent). The Court concluded that these categories of speech "have a historical foundation in the Court's free speech tradition," but do not unduly intrude upon the "vast realm of free speech and thought always protected in our tradition."

In particular, the Court refused to recognize any general exception to the First Amendment for false speech. Relying on *New York Times v. Sullivan*, the Court emphasized "that some false statements are inevitable if there is to be an open and vigorous expression of views in public and private conversation, expression the First Amendment seeks to guarantee." While there have been some limitations on false speech in cases involving "defamation, fraud, or some other legally cognizable harm associated with a false statement, such as an invasion of privacy or the costs of vexatious litigation, in those decisions the falsity of the speech at issue was not irrelevant to the Court's analysis, but neither was it determinative." Of course, as the Court recognized, there are instances when the government can prohibit lies: "first, the criminal prohibition of a false statement made to a Government official, 18 U.S.C. § 1001; second, laws punishing perjury; and third, prohibitions on the false representation that one is speaking as a Government official or on behalf of the Government, *see, e.g.*, § 912; § 709." However, the Court did not view these exceptions as creating a broad "principle that all proscriptions of false statements are exempt from exacting First Amendment scrutiny." Rather, the Court viewed those examples as involving more limited prohibitions relating to the functioning of government. For example, the Court viewed perjury as "at war with justice" because perjury "undermines the function and province of the law and threatens the integrity of judgments that are the basis of the legal system." Likewise, "Statutes that prohibit falsely representing that one is speaking on behalf of the Government, or that prohibit impersonating a Government officer, also protect the integrity of Government processes, quite apart from merely restricting false speech."

Turning specifically to the Stolen Valor Act, while the Court emphasized that the First Amendment deprives government of any "freewheeling authority to declare new categories of speech outside the scope of the First Amendment," the Court recognized that there may exist "some categories of speech that have been historically unprotected but have not yet been specifically identified or discussed in our case law." But the Court indicated that it would not recognize a new category of exempted speech without being presented with "persuasive evidence that a novel restriction on content is part of a long (if heretofore unrecognized) tradition of proscription," and the Court concluded that there was insufficient evidence that "false statements generally should constitute a new category of unprotected speech on this basis." The Court emphasized that the Act could have been applied to "personal, whispered conversations within a home," and that it seeks to control and suppress false statements of this type "in almost limitless times and settings." Moreover, the Court expressed concern that, if the government were allowed to prohibit this lie, there might emerge a general principle suggesting a general governmental authority "to compile a list of subjects about which false statements are punishable." The Court rejected this idea, noting that, were "this law to be sustained, there could be an endless list of subjects the National Government or the States could single out." The court did recognize that false claims can be restricted when they are designed to "effect a fraud or secure moneys or other valuable considerations." But the Court viewed the Act as creating a "broad censorial power unprecedented in this Court's cases or in our constitutional tradition," and noted that this power would create "a chill, a chill the First Amendment cannot permit if free speech, thought, and discourse are to remain a foundation of our freedom."

Since the Act imposed a content-based restriction on speech, the Court concluded that it must apply the "most exacting scrutiny." Although the Court agreed that military medals "serve the important public function of recognizing and expressing gratitude for acts of heroism and sacrifice in military service," and admitted that the "Government's interest in protecting the integrity of the Medal of Honor is beyond question," the Court held that the law could not survive strict scrutiny which requires that the Act be "actually necessary" to achieve the governmental interest. In the *Alvarez* case, the Court concluded that "the dynamics of free speech, of counter speech, of refutation, can overcome the lie. Respondent lied at a public meeting." Indeed, after Alvarez's lie was exposed, he "was ridiculed online, his actions were reported in the press, and a fellow board member called for his resignation." "It is a fair assumption that any true holders of the Medal who had heard of Alvarez's false claims would have been fully vindicated by the community's expression of outrage, showing as it did the Nation's high regard for the Medal." The government nonetheless argued that counterspeech will not necessarily be effective because some military records have been lost or are unverifiable. The Court rejected this argument, noting that "in cases where public refutation will not serve the Government's interest, the Act will not either." In addition, the Court concluded that the Act is not the "least restrictive means among available, effective alternatives." In particular, Government could create a database of Congressional Medal of Honor Award winners.

There has also been litigation regarding whether the Court should create a new category of excluded speech for so-called "crush videos." *United States v. Stevens*, 559 U.S. 460 (2010), involved a federal law that imposed criminal penalties on anyone who knowingly "creates, sells, or possesses a depiction of animal cruelty," if done "for commercial gain" in interstate or foreign commerce. 18 U.S.C. § 48(a). The law defined "animal cruelty" as a depiction "in which a living animal is intentionally maimed, mutilated, tortured, wounded, or killed," if that conduct violates federal or state law where "the creation, sale, or possession takes place." The law created an exception for any depiction "that has serious religious, political, scientific, educational, journalistic, historical, or artistic value."

In enacting the law, Congress was concerned about the interstate market for so-called "crush videos" which feature the torture and killing of helpless animals, including cats, dogs, monkeys, mice, and hamsters by women who slowly crush the animals to death "with their bare feet or while wearing high heeled shoes." In some of the videos, the women are shown "talking to the animals in a kind of dominatrix patter" which is heard above "the cries and squeals of the animals, who are obviously in great pain." Such videos are purchased by individuals with a sexual fetish for such activities. The acts in question were prohibited by the animal cruelty laws of all 50 states and the District of Columbia. In most instances, the crush videos did not disclose the participants' identities, thereby making it difficult for the government to prosecute the underlying conduct.

The law was challenged by Stevens who was indicted for selling videos depicting fights between dogs and other animals. Among other things, the government argued that depictions of animal cruelty are not entitled to First Amendment protection. The Court disagreed, noting that government may not "restrict expression because of its message, its ideas, its subject matter, or its content," and rejected the law because it explicitly regulated content: "The statute restricts 'visual and auditory depictions,' such as photographs, videos, or sound recordings, depending on whether they depict conduct in which a living animal is intentionally harmed." As a result, the Court held that the law was subject to strict scrutiny, meaning that it would be regarded as "presumptively invalid" and that the government would bear the burden of proving constitutionality. In other words, the Court declined to create a new category of speech that was beyond the scope of First Amendment protection. It preferred to limit excepted speech to areas that had traditionally been excepted.

The Court also rejected the argument that animal cruelty videos have "minimal redeeming value" that they are not entitled to First Amendment protection. Even though most First Amendment exceptions involve balancing, in the sense that restricted speech involves "such slight social value as a step to truth that any benefit that may be derived from them is clearly outweighed by the social interest in order and morality," the Court rejected the idea that speech was subject to a simple cost-benefit analysis, and holding that even recent free speech exceptions (*e.g.*, child pornography) were based on a showing of a compelling governmental interest (in the case of child pornography in protecting children against abuse), and the speech had *de minimis* value.

In addition, the Court was concerned that the statute suffered from overbreadth. The law was so broadly written that it might have prohibited such things as shows on fishing and hunting (which some regard as "cruel").

Likewise, in *Brown v. Entertainment Merchants Association*, 564 U.S. 786 (2011), the Court struck down a California statute that prohibited the sale or rental of "violent video games" to minors, and also required that their packaging be labeled "18." The Act applied to games which allow a player to engage in "killing, maiming, dismembering, or sexually assaulting an image of a human being, if those acts are depicted" in a manner that "a reasonable person, considering the game as a whole, would find appeals to a deviant or morbid interest of minors," that is "patently offensive to prevailing standards in the community as to what is suitable for minors," and that "causes the game, as a whole, to lack serious literary, artistic, political, or scientific value for minors." The statute was enforceable by civil fines of up to $1,000.

In a challenge brought by video game and software industry companies, the Court struck the law down, concluding that the "Free Speech Clause exists principally to protect discourse on public matters," but "that it is difficult to distinguish politics from entertainment, and dangerous to try." The Court concluded that video games "communicate ideas—and even social messages—through many familiar literary devices (such as characters, dialogue, plot, and music) and through features distinctive to the medium (such as the player's interaction with the virtual world)." As a result, the Court held that video games are entitled to First Amendment protection, and it affirmed the idea that government may not "restrict expression because of its message, its ideas, its subject matter, or its content" unless speech fits within one of the categories of excepted speech (*e.g.*, fighting words, obscenity, child pornography). However, the Court regarded those exceptions as "well-defined and narrowly limited classes of speech, the prevention and punishment of which have never been thought to raise any Constitutional problem."

The California statute was interesting because it tracked the Court's obscenity jurisprudence as reflected in *Ginsberg v. New York*, 390 U.S. 629 (1968). Under that jurisprudence, states could prohibit the sale to minors of sexual material that would be obscene from the perspective of a child, and therefore harmful to children. In an attempt to track *Ginsberg*, the California statute made it illegal to sell videos that might be harmful to children. The Court rejected the analogy: "No doubt a State possesses legitimate power to protect children from harm, but that does not include a free-floating power to restrict the ideas to which children may be exposed." In other words, when speech is not obscene as to children, Congress cannot suppress it merely "from ideas or images that a legislative body thinks unsuitable for them." Moreover, the Court noted that the nation had rarely taken steps to insulate children from depictions of violence: "Certainly the books we give children to read—or read to them when they are younger—contain no shortage of gore. Grimm's Fairy Tales, for example, are grim indeed. As her just deserts for trying to poison Snow White, the wicked queen is made to dance in red hot slippers 'till she fell dead on the floor, a sad example of envy and jealousy.' THE COMPLETE BROTHERS GRIMM FAIRY TALES 198 (2006 ed.). Cinderella's evil stepsisters have their eyes pecked out by doves. And Hansel and Gretel (children!) kill their captor by baking her in an oven."

The Court also rejected California's claim that video games are "of special concern because they are 'interactive,' in that the player participates in the violent action on screen and determines its outcome." The Court noted that interactive games had existed since 1969, and that the current games are different only as "a matter of degree than of kind." Even if the games contain disgusting levels of violence, or violence directed at particular ethnic groups, the Court concluded that "disgust is not a valid basis for restricting expression" and government's objection to particular messages cannot provide the basis for repression. Because the statute was content based, the Court concluded that the statute could only be upheld if it could survive strict scrutiny in the sense that "it is justified by a compelling government interest and is narrowly drawn to serve that interest." The Court held that California could not satisfy this standard because California could not "show a direct causal link between violent video games and harm to minors." Although California submitted various psychological studies in an attempt to show the casual link, the Court found that the studies were not compelling, noting that they had been "rejected by every court to consider them," and did not "prove that violent video games cause minors to act aggressively." Also, the Court found "significant, admitted flaws in methodology." Even if the studies showed "some effect on children's feelings of aggression," the Court found that "those effects are both small and indistinguishable from effects produced by other media."

The Court also held that the California statute was underinclusive as well as overinclusive. It was underinclusive because it failed to restrict other depictions of violence. As a result, the Court raised questions about whether the government's asserted justification for the video game ban was the real justification for the law: "California has singled out the purveyors of video games for disfavored treatment—at least when compared to booksellers, cartoonists, and movie producers—and has given no persuasive reason why." In any event, parents could use the industry's voluntary rating system to control their children's use of inappropriate video games if they chose to do so. The statute was overinclusive because the statute prohibited children from purchasing video games on their own even when the parents did not object.

Near Obscene Speech. The Court has also held that local governments may create zoning laws that restrict the location of adult entertainment enterprises based on the secondary effects of those businesses. *See City of Renton v. Playtime Theatres, Inc.*, 475 U.S. 41 (1986) (upholding ordinance that prohibited adult businesses from operating within 1,000 feet of any residential zone, church, park, or school). In upholding these laws, the Court has generally focused on local efforts to control the "secondary effects" of crime and neighborhood decline, and has held that the governmental interest is "substantial." The Court also upheld an ordinance prohibiting clubs from knowingly or intentionally displaying nudity. *See City of Erie v. Pap's A.M.*, 528 U.S. 962 (1999). The ordinance involved an effort to improve neighborhood quality and abate crime. Although the Court has upheld these "secondary effects" ordinances, courts require proof of a substantial governmental interest. *See City of Los Angeles v. Alameda Books, Inc.*, 535 U.S. 425 (2002).

"Offensive" Speech. In general, the Court has been reluctant to hold that speech can be banned simply because it is "offensive." Even though it may be possible for someone to state a given protest less offensively (*e.g.*, in *Cohen v. California*, 403 U.S. 15 (1971), Cohen wore a jacket with the statement "Fuck the Draft" rather than using the less offensive "I oppose the draft."), government cannot generally force people to say things in inoffensive ways. Indeed, in some instances, emotive language is more powerful, and speakers have the option to use the more offensive language unless the speech fits within some other unprotected category (*e.g.*, fighting words) which Cohen's speech did not. The Court noted that those offended by Cohen's jacket could simply avert their eyes.

In many offensive speech cases, the Court applies "vagueness" and "overbreadth" principles to overturn convictions. *See Gooding v. Wilson*, 405 U.S. 518 (1972). Likewise, in *Collin v. Smith*, 578 F.2d 1197 (7th Cir. 1978), the Seventh Circuit held that the state could not prohibit the American Nazi party from holding a march in Skokie, Illinois, despite the presence of several thousand survivors of the Nazi holocaust in that city. Since the marchers intended to carry Nazi flags and display swastikas, a lower court had enjoined the march. Even though the courts ultimately upheld the Nazi's right to march, they decided to hold their parade elsewhere.

In a few (limited) contexts, offensive speech is subject to governmental regulation. For example, in *FCC v. Pacifica Foundation*, 438 U.S. 726 (1978), the Court upheld the FCC's decision to place restrictions on offensive speech (the seven "filthy" words) by limiting such broadcasts to late night hours when children would be less likely to be listening. However, the decision was premised upon the idea that broadcasters are subject to special rules, that do not apply to other speech, and the Court emphasized that radio broadcasts can intrude into the home.

The Court has also upheld limitations on offensive speech when the government is financing the speech. *National Endowment for the Arts v. Finley*, 524 U.S. 569 (1998), involved a congressional statute requiring the National Endowment for the Arts (NEA) to consider "general standards of decency and respect for the diverse beliefs and values of the American public" in making art awards. The Court upheld the statute, noting that the law only required the NEA to take "decency and respect" into consideration in making grants, and therefore did not require the NEA to engage in "invidious viewpoint discrimination" against offensive speech. However, in *Erznoznik v. City of Jacksonville*, 422 U.S. 205 (1975), the Court struck down a local ordinance that prohibited the showing of films containing nudity by a drive-in movie theater when its screen was visible from a public street. The Court found that the ordinance was overbroad because it swept in more than just explicit nudity to include depictions of a "baby's buttocks, the nude body of a war victim, or scenes from a culture in which nudity is indigenous." The Court rejected the state's attempt to justify the ordinance as a "traffic regulation" (on the theory that nudity on a drive-in movie screen might distract passing motorists) because a variety of other types of scenes that could also distract motorists were not prohibited.

Child Pornography. Child pornography is a category of speech that the Court has recently recognized is unprotected. *See New York v. Ferber*, 458 U.S. 747 (1982). In placing depictions of child sexuality as outside of constitutional protection, the Court emphasized that the state has a compelling interest in protecting the physical and psychological well-being of minors, that depictions of child sex abuse creates a permanent record of a child's participation, and that the state can dry up the market for child pornography only by imposing criminal penalties on those who sell, advertise or promote it. In addition, the Court regarded the speech value of child pornography as "exceedingly modest, if not *de minimis*." The Court offered several justifications for giving states greater leeway to ban child pornography. First, the Court held that New York had a "compelling" interest in "safeguarding the physical and psychological well-being" of minors, and the Court was deferential to the legislature's conclusion that suppression of child pornography was necessary to achieve that objective. Second, the Court held that the distribution of photographs and films depicting sexual activity by juveniles was intrinsically related to the sexual abuse of children because it created a permanent record of a child's participation and that harm was reinforced by circulation of the materials. Moreover, the Court concluded that the most effective means of "drying up the market" for child pornography was to impose severe criminal penalties on those who sell, advertise or promote it. Third, the Court found that the advertising and selling of child pornography provided an "economic motive" for the production of such materials. Fourth, the Court expressed doubt about whether "visual depictions of children performing sexual acts or lewdly exhibiting their genitals would often constitute an important and necessary part of a literary performance or scientific or educational work." Fifth, even though the child pornography restrictions were content related, the Court held that New York's law was so closely related to the welfare of children that "the balance of competing interests" was "clearly struck" so that the materials were not entitled to First Amendment protection.

Unlike obscenity, which individuals may possess in the privacy of their homes (even if they cannot make, buy or distribute it), the Court has held that individuals do not have a constitutional right to possess child pornography in their homes. *See Osborne v. Ohio*, 495 U.S. 103 (1990). Noting that child pornography has minimal speech value, the Court held that given the "market for the exploitative use of children," it is "surely reasonable for the State to conclude that it will decrease the production of child pornography if it penalizes those who possess and view the product, thereby decreasing demand." Moreover, the Court noted that child pornography "permanently records the victim's abuse," and "causes continuing harm to the child victims by haunting the children in years to come," so that a ban on possession and viewing encourages the possessors of these materials to destroy them. Finally, the Court worried that such materials might be abused by pedophiles.

Nevertheless, the Court has held that government cannot prohibit virtual (as opposed to actual) depictions of child pornography. *See Ashcroft v. The Free Speech Coalition*, 535 U.S. 234 (2002). Virtual child pornography generally involves computer generated images that appear to involve a minor engaged in sexual conduct. In *Ashcroft*, the Court concluded that a law prohibiting virtual depictions was so broad that it could apply to a broad range of pictures, including pictures in psychology manuals, as well as images that were not "patently offensive," that did not "contravene community standards," and that might have "serious literary, artistic, political, or scientific value."

In rendering its decision, the Court emphasized that youth sexuality has been a theme in art and literature "throughout the ages" in such works as Romeo and Juliet (in which one of the lovers was only 13 years old), as well as in recent prominent movies. The Court also rejected the argument that virtual child pornography might lead to actual child abuse. Even though pedophiles could use virtual child pornography to seduce children, the Court noted that many "innocent" things can be abused—including cartoons, video games, and candy—but government cannot prohibit such items merely because of the possibility of misuse. The Court concluded that government should deal with this problem by punishing adults who provide unsuitable materials to children, and by enforcing criminal penalties for unlawful solicitation. The Court rejected the argument that virtual child pornography "whets the appetites of pedophiles and encourages them to engage in illegal conduct." The "mere tendency of speech to encourage unlawful acts is not a sufficient reason for banning it." Finally, the Court rejected the argument that virtual child pornography could be prohibited in order to help eliminate the market for pornography that uses real children, noting that pornographers would be more likely to use virtual images than real ones if there were no criminal penalties for using virtual pictures. The Court left open the question of whether the state might (one day) prohibit virtual child pornography if technology advances to the point where it is impossible to distinguish virtual child pornography from actual child pornography.

In recent years, some prosecutors have charged teens who send text messages that show nude photos of themselves or other minors, with child pornography. *See* Chana Joffe-Walt, *"Sexting": A Disturbing New Teen Trend?*, National Public Radio broadcast (Mar. 12, 2009). They have also charged minors who received the text message photos, but did not delete them from their phones.

Pornography as Discrimination Against Women. The only court to consider the issue rejected the idea that non-obscene pornography is deprived of constitutional protection, and can be prohibited if it conveys negative images regarding women. In doing so, the court rejected the arguments of scholars who have argued in favor of the validity of such prohibitions. *See* Catherine MacKinnon, *Pornography, Civil Rights and Speech*, 20 HARV. C.R.-C.L. L. REV. 1 (1985); Andrea Dworkin, *Against the Male Flood: Censorship, Pornography and Equality*, 8 HARV. WOMEN'S L.J. 1 (1985).

The issue arose in the context of an Indianapolis ordinance that portrayed women in certain ways (*e.g.*, as subordinated, as enjoying pain or humiliation, or as sexual objects who enjoy pain or humiliation). The ordinance applied to obscene pornography, as defined by *Miller*, as well as to non-obscene pornography. Indianapolis attempted to defend the ordinance on the basis that "pornography influences attitudes" and that "the statute was a way to alter the socialization of men and women rather than to vindicate community standards of offensiveness." It was also argued that the ordinance would "play an important role in reducing the tendency of men to view women as sexual objects, a tendency that leads to both unacceptable attitudes and discrimination in the workplace and violence away from it."

In *American Booksellers Association, Inc. v. Hudnut*, 771 F.2d 323 (7th Cir. 1985), in an opinion by Judge Easterbrook, the Ninth Circuit struck down the law because it involved a viewpoint-based restriction on speech. Speech which refers to women in the "approved way" (*e.g.*, in positions of equality) is permissible, but speech that portrays women in a "disapproved way" is prohibited without regard to "how significant the literary, artistic, or political qualities of the work taken as a whole." Judge Easterbrook concluded that the state "may not ordain preferred viewpoints" and may not "declare one perspective right and silence opponents." "If there is any fixed star in our constitutional constellation, it is that no official, high or petty, can prescribe what shall be orthodox in politics, nationalism, religion, or other matters of opinion or force citizens to confess by word or act their faith therein."

In the course of his opinion, Judge Easterbrook rejected various arguments. For example, defenders of the ordinance argued that some pornographers depict torture of women, and some pornographers use fraud, trickery, or force to compel women to perform in pornographic films. Judge Easterbrook emphasized that the state is free to prohibit such conduct, but that it can do so without prohibiting the ideas conveyed by the pornographers. Indianapolis argued that the "marketplace of ideas" metaphor was inapplicable to the prohibited speech which is, by its nature, "unanswerable." Judge Easterbrook responded that "the Constitution does not make the dominance of truth a necessary condition of freedom of speech," and he rejected the argument that government has the power to declare "truth." Finally, he rejected the argument that pornography is "low value" speech. He noted that, even with low value speech, the government is not allowed to choose among viewpoints. Moreover, he questioned whether pornography is low value speech since Indianapolis chose to prohibit this speech because it "influences social relations and politics on a grand scale, that it controls attitudes at home and in the legislature," and he found that Indianapolis' view "precludes a characterization of the speech as low value." Indeed, he noted that free speech has generally "been on balance an ally of those seeking change."

"Hate" Speech. "Hate speech" refers to expression that derogatorily targets individuals or groups by reason of their race, ethnicity, sex, or sexual preference. In an early decision, the Court uphold an Illinois criminal statute which made it a crime to portray "depravity, criminality, unchastity, or lack of virtue of a class of citizens, of any race, color, creed or religion which said publication or exhibition exposes the citizens of any race, color, creed or religion to contempt, derision, or obloquy or which is productive of breach of the peace or riots" because they tend to promote strife and obstruct society. *See Beauharnais v. Illinois,* 343 U.S. 250 (1952). However, in later decisions, the Court has suggested that government does not have the power to prohibit hate speech (assuming, of course, that it does not fit into an unprotected category of speech such as fighting words). *See R.A.V. v. City of St. Paul,* 505 U.S. 377 (1992). The Court has generally concluded that such statutes contain "content discrimination" or "viewpoint discrimination," and the Court has rejected the idea that government may "regulate speech based on hostility—or favoritism—towards the underlying message." The Court also rejected the idea that hate speech ordinances can be upheld as a way of ensuring the "basic human rights of members of groups that have historically been subjected to discrimination, including the right of such group members to live in peace where they wish." Note that the Court has not held that government is precluded from imposing any content-based restrictions on speech. Indeed, as we have seen, the Court's First Amendment jurisprudence is based on the notion that certain categories of speech may be treated differently than other categories (*e.g.*, obscenity is not constitutionally protected). However, the Court has held that political ideas cannot be prohibited based simply on their content or viewpoint.

For these same reasons, courts have generally struck down campus speech codes designed to limit so-called "hate speech." *See Doe v. University of Michigan,* 721 F.Supp. 852 (E.D. Mich. 1989). Almost invariably, these codes suffer from vagueness and overbreadth. In addition, the codes usually involve "content based" or "viewpoint based" restrictions on speech.

The Court has also rejected the idea that one's ideas can be considered in a sentencing hearing when they bear no relationship to the crime, and are introduced simply to prejudice the defendant. *See Dawson v. Delaware,* 503 U.S. 159 (1992) (reversing a sentence of capital punishment against an individual who belonged to a white supremacist organization). However, when there is a correlation between the crime and the belief, and the racial belief motivated the crime, the Court has held that the belief can be considered for sentence enhancement purposes on the theory that judges have historically considered a range of factors in deciding on the appropriate punishment. *Wisconsin v. Mitchell*, 508 U.S. 476 (1993). The Court has noted that "bias-inspired conduct" is "thought to inflict greater individual and societal harm" because such conduct is "more likely to provoke retaliatory crimes, inflict distinct emotional harms on their victims, and incite community unrest."

True Threats. In one decision, the Court struck down a cross burning ordinance because it involved content-based and viewpoint-based discrimination against speech. *See R.A.V. v. City of St. Paul*, 505 U.S. 377 (1992). However, in *Virginia v. Black*, 538 U.S. 343 (2003), the Court suggested that it might uphold a cross burning statute when the cross is burned with the intent to intimidate another person or group of persons. In other words, the burning involved a "true threat" to subject another to death or physical violence.

In suggesting that a cross-burning statute could be valid, *Black* reviewed the history of cross-burning, and concluded that cross burning in the United States has been used by the Ku Klux Klan (KKK) as a "tool of intimidation and as a threat of impending violence" against the targets of the cross-burning. Because of this history, the Court concluded that a burning cross can convey a very serious threat of future bodily harm. Moreover, given the KKK's history, the Court found that this threat (of possible injury or death) should not be regarded as purely "hypothetical" because the cross itself involves "a serious threat, meant to coerce the victim to comply with the Klan's wishes unless the victim is willing to risk the wrath of the Klan." As a result, the cross burning could be regarded as a "true threat" which the Court defined as "those statements where the speaker means to communicate a serious expression of an intent to commit an act of unlawful violence to a particular individual or group of individuals." The Court held that such threats could be prohibited whether or not the speaker actually intends to carry out the threat, because the doctrine is designed to protect individuals from the fear of violence as well as the possibility of violence.

Even though Virginia could prohibit true threats, the Court concluded that the statute was unconstitutional because it contained a prima facie evidence provision which allowed the trial court to presume that a cross burning was undertaken with the intent to intimidate. As a result, a conviction could be obtained under the statute without any showing of intimidation or a threat. In other words, a conviction might be based solely "on the fact of cross burning itself, and therefore created an "unacceptable risk of the suppression of ideas" without regard to whether there was intimidation." The Court noted that "[b]urning a cross at a political rally would almost certainly be protected expression" and might not involve an attempt at intimidation.

In *Elonis v. United States*, 575 U.S. 723 (2015), the Court refused to definitively define the mental state required for a "true threat" under the First Amendment. 18 U.S.C. § 875(c), prohibits "any communication containing any threat to injure the person of another." The defendant posted rap lyrics on Facebook that contained violent language and imagery, along with disclaimers that his lyrics depicted real persons, and claims that he was simply exercising his First Amendment rights. However, the lyrics were viewed as threatening by his estranged wife, his co-workers, and the FBI agents who arrested him. At trial, although the defense sought a jury instruction that required proof of an "intent to communicate a true threat," the trial judge gave the jury the following instruction: "A statement is a true threat when a defendant intentionally makes a statement in a context or under such circumstances wherein a reasonable person would foresee that the statement would be interpreted by those to whom the maker communicates the statement as a serious expression of an intention to inflict bodily injury or take the life of an individual."

The Court reversed, holding that as a matter of statutory interpretation, when a statute is silent regarding the required mental state, a court must imply a mental state that "is necessary to separate wrongful conduct from otherwise innocent conduct." With regard to the threat statute, the Court believed that " 'the crucial element separating legal innocence from wrongful conduct' is the threatening nature of the communication," which is why "the mental state requirement must apply to the fact that the communication contains a threat." Thus, the Court regarded the "reasonable person" or negligence standard argued for by the government as "inconsistent with 'the conventional requirement for criminal conduct—awareness of some wrongdoing." "If the defendant transmits a communication for the purpose of issuing a threat, or with knowledge that the communication will be viewed as a threat," then "the mental state requirement of § 875(c) is satisfied." The Court refused to decide whether recklessness would be sufficient under the statute because that issue was not briefed or argued by either party.

On remand, Elonis' conviction was reinstated. *See United States v. Elonis*, 841 F.3d 589 (3rd Cir. 2016). The court held that, if "a defendant transmits a communication for the purpose of issuing a threat or with knowledge that the recipient will view it as a threat, and a jury determines that communication is objectively threatening, then the defendant has violated Section 875(c) whether or not he agrees the communication was objectively threatening." Given the overwhelming evidence that this standard was satisfied, the Third Circuit concluded that the error in the original jury instruction was "harmless." The Court refused to hear the case a second time.

In *Counterman v. Colorado*, 600 U.S. 66 (2023), the Court finally defined the *mens rea* for true threats. The case involved Billy Counterman who sent hundreds of Facebook messages to C. W., a local singer and musician, over a two year period. Some of the messages were harmless ("Good morning sweetheart"; "I am going to the store would you like anything?"), but others suggested that Counterman might be surveilling C. W. ("was that you in the white Jeep?", "a fine display with your partner"), and a few suggested anger and envisaged harm befalling her ("Fuck off permanently." "Staying in cyber life is going to kill you." "You're not being good for human relations. Die."). C. W. claimed that the messages put her in fear that Counterman was "threatening her life," and that Counterman was following her and might hurt her. As a result, she had "a lot of trouble sleeping," suffered severe anxiety, declined social engagements, and canceled performances.

The Court worried that true threat prosecutions might chill protected speech: "Prohibitions on speech have the potential to chill, or deter, speech outside their boundaries. A speaker may be unsure about the side of a line on which his speech falls. Or he may worry that the legal system will err, and count speech that is permissible as instead not." As a result, the Court held that the First Amendment requires some proof that the defendant had a subjective understanding of the threatening nature of his statements, but that the *mens rea* of "recklessness" was sufficient, meaning that the state must prove that defendant consciously disregarded a substantial risk that his communications would be viewed as threatening violence. The Court remanded the case for consideration under a recklessness standard.

Commercial Speech. Historically, the Court has not protected so-called "commercial expression" (speech that proposes an economic transaction or that pertains "solely to the economic interests of the speaker and audience"). However, the Court reversed its earlier precedent in *Virginia State Board of Pharmacy v. Virginia Citizens Consumer Council*, 425 U.S. 748 (1976), and extended constitutional protection to commercial speech in striking down a Virginia law that banned the advertisement of prescription drugs. The Court concluded that advertising has speech value because it provides increased information to the public, thereby facilitating competition and informed consumer choices. Rejecting Virginia's claim that it has the right to protect consumers against advertising, the Court concluded that the public interest is better served when consumers have the information they need to make intelligent and informed decisions.

Even though commercial speech is constitutionally protected, the Court has accorded commercial speech much less protection than it gives to political speech, and has suggested that such speech could be subjected to prior restraints, as well as disclaimers, disclosures, and warnings. The Court's current approach to commercial speech was articulated in *Central Hudson Gas & Electric Co. v. Public Service Commission*, 447 U.S. 557 (1980). While that decision held that commercial speech is protected under the First Amendment, the Court concluded that commercial speech is sufficiently different from political speech so that it is not entitled to the same level of protection. The Court then articulated a four-part test for evaluating commercial speech regulations: 1) whether the regulated speech is misleading or related to an unlawful transaction in which case regulation is permissible; 2) if the speech is not misleading or related to an unlawful activity, whether the regulation is supported by a substantial government interest; 3) whether the regulation directly advances the interest; 4) whether the governmental interest can be achieved by a more limited restriction on commercial speech.

In recent years, the justices have sometimes disagreed regarding the standard of review to be applied in commercial speech cases. For example, in *44 Liquormart, Inc. v. Rhode Island*, 517 U.S. 484 (1996), the Court struck down a law that banned retail liquor advertising with a plurality of the Court stating that the Court should apply a "rigorous" standard of review for total bans on "truthful nonmisleading commercial messages for reasons unrelated to the preservation of a fair bargaining process." However, the Court continued to apply the *Central Hudson* test in *Thompson v. Western States Medical Center*, 535 U.S. 357 (2002), to invalidate a federal law that prohibited manufacturers of compounded drugs (drugs tailored to the needs of a particular patient as opposed to mass produced drugs) from advertising or promoting their drugs.

In recent years, the Court has begun to apply the prohibition against content-based and viewpoint-based restrictions to commercial speech. For example, in *Barr v. American Association of Political Consultants, Inc.*, 591 U.S. 610 (2020), the Court extended its prohibition against content-based speech restrictions to the commercial speech area. That case involved the Telephone Consumer Protection Act of 1991, known as the TCPA, which generally prohibited robocalls to cell phones and home phones. However, a

2015 amendment authorized robocalls that were made to collect debts owed to or guaranteed by the Federal Government, including robocalls made to collect student loan and mortgage debts. The law was challenged by organizations that wanted to make political robocalls to cell phones in order to discuss candidates and issues, solicit donations, conduct polls, and get out the vote, but could not do so because of the law. Emphasizing that government generally "has no power to restrict expression because of its message, its ideas, its subject matter, or its content," the Court held that government may not discriminate "in the regulation of expression on the basis of the content of that expression." A law is deemed to be content based if it "draws distinctions based on the message a speaker conveys." The Court concluded that the TCPA was content based because it favored speech made for collecting government debt over political and other speech, and indeed over other types of debt collection. In applying strict scrutiny, the Court emphasized that, while governmental debt collection is a worthy goal, the government failed to sufficiently justify "the differentiation between government-debt collection speech and other important categories of robocall speech, such as political speech, charitable fundraising, issue advocacy, commercial advertising, and the like." Rather than strike down the entire law, the Court invalidated only the amendment allowing calls to collect government debt.

Likewise, in *Sorrell v. IMS Health, Inc.*, 564 U.S. 552 (2011), the Court invalidated a state law that prohibited: 1) the sale of "prescriber-identifying information" by pharmacies; 2) the disclosure by pharmacies of such information for marketing purposes; and 3) the use of such information by pharmaceutical manufacturers. Before the law was enacted, a pharmacy could sell such information to "data miners," who would produce reports about prescriber behavior that would be leased to drug companies, which would, in turn, employ "detailers," who would seek to improve marketing strategies and increase sales of the companies' brand-name drugs to doctors. The Court held that the law was not narrowly drawn to advance the State's governmental interest in protecting the confidentiality of prescriber information. Such an interest might have been used to justify a law that provided only limited disclosure exceptions, but the law in question disallowed only disclosures for marketing purposes, and therefore limited speech "for a narrow class of disfavored speakers" while allowing the information to be made widely available otherwise. Second, the Court found that the law did not advance the interests of lowering medical costs and promoting public health "in a permissible way." Instead, the law relied on "the indirect means of restraining certain speech by certain speakers" in order to diminish the influence of the detailers to promote brand-name drugs. The

Court noted that the State may not create burdens for protected speech "in order to tilt public debate in a preferred direction." In response to the State's claim that the law protected doctors from "harassing sales behaviors," the Court pointed out that doctors "can simply decline to meet with detailers," and the State provided no explanation why similar remedies other than the content-based law were not adequate. As for the State's argument that the detailers' use of prescriber information "undermines the doctor-patient relationship," the Court noted that if the detailers' "marketing affects treatment decisions," then "it does so because doctors find it persuasive," and "the fear that speech might persuade provides no lawful basis for quieting it."

A number of commercial speech cases have focused on whether the First Amendment protects the advertising of professional services against governmental regulation and restrictions. In *Bates v. State Bar of Arizona*, 433 U.S. 350 (1977), the Court struck down a disciplinary decision prohibiting a newspaper from carrying an advertisement listing a law clinic's fees, and from making representations regarding the quality of the clinic's service or the results it could achieve. The Court focused on the public's interest in receiving truthful information that might facilitate informed consumer decisions, and left open the possibility that a more narrowly tailored regulation (as opposed to a total ban) might survive constitutional scrutiny if it were directed at particularly objectionable perils (*e.g.*, predatory behavior) of lawyer advertising. In *Ohralik v. Ohio State Bar Association*, 436 U.S. 447 (1978), the Court emphasized the potential for "fraud, undue influence, intimidation, overreaching, and other forms of 'vexatious conduct' " when lawyers solicit clients, as well as the state's interest in protecting the public against those harms. However, in *In re Primus*, 436 U.S. 412 (1978), the Court distinguished ordinary lawyer solicitation for personal gain from solicitation by not-for-profit organizations that litigate to promote political or social agendas. In *Edenfield v. Fane*, 507 U.S. 761 (1993), the Court struck down a state law banning personal solicitation of clients by accountants. However, in *Tennessee Secondary School Athletic Association v. Brentwood Academy*, 551 U.S. 291 (2007), the Court held that a state athletic association could limit a high school football coach's recruitment of prospective athletes without infringing the First Amendment.

The Court has dealt with lawyers' claims of competence as well. In *In re R.M.J.*, 455 U.S. 191 (1982), the Court held that a lawyer was improperly disciplined for advertising areas of practice and qualifications not permitted under state rules, noting that the advertisement was not deceptive, and that the state had offered no substantial justification for limiting the content of the advertisement. Similarly, in *Peel v. Attorney Registration and Disciplinary Commission of Illinois*, 496 U.S. 91 (1990), the Court struck down a disciplinary rule that prohibited attorneys from representing themselves as "certified" or "specialists" in particular areas notwithstanding a state supreme court's finding that such designations can be misleading. In *Zauderer v. Office of Disciplinary Counsel*, 471 U.S. 626 (1985), the Court struck down a restriction that prohibited a newspaper advertisement, directed at women injured by a contraceptive device, which stated that legal services would be provided without charge unless damages were recovered. The Court held that any restriction on advertising should be no greater than necessary to prevent consumer deception, and that the advertisement was potentially deceptive because it did not mention the possibility of liability for court charges.

Overbreadth. As previously noted, the Court frequently uses the overbreadth and vagueness doctrines in the First Amendment area to protect free speech interests. In overbreadth cases, plaintiffs claim that an overbroad law "chills" expression by causing "persons whose expression is constitutionally protected to refrain from exercising their rights for fear of criminal sanctions by a statute susceptible of application to protected expression." Because of this chilling effect, the Court has allowed individuals to attack overbroad laws, even though the conduct of those individuals is clearly unprotected by the First Amendment, and even though their conduct could have been proscribed by a narrowly drawn law.

Both the vagueness and overbreadth doctrines can involve either a "facial" challenge to a law (a suit which alleges that a law is facially unconstitutional and should be struck down in its entirety) or an "as applied" challenge (alleging that the law is invalid as applied to the facts of a particular case). Facial challenges are controversial because the party before the court may not be arguing that a particular law is "vague" or "overbroad" as to her (or her conduct), but instead may be asking the court to strike down a law because it is overbroad or vague as applied to others. In other words, the party may be seeking to raise the rights of others not before the court. In general, courts are hesitant to allow individuals to assert the rights of others, and have generally required plaintiffs to establish "standing" in their own right. Nevertheless, in the First Amendment area, the courts have sometimes been willing to consider facial challenges because of the chilling effect of speech regulations.

Even in the First Amendment area, the Court tends to be restrictive in its application of the vagueness and overbreadth doctrines. The Court has stated that facial challenges involve "strong medicine" because they allow "a defendant whose speech may be outside the scope of constitutional protection to escape punishment because the state failed to draft its law with sufficient precision." *Gooding v. Wilson,* 405 U.S. 518 (1972). In addition, the Court has argued that it is better for a reviewing court to work from a developed record that provides the "facts needed for an informed judgment." *Broadrick v. Oklahoma,* 413 U.S. 601, 610 (1973). By using this approach, the Court is better able to decide whether a law can be narrowly construed to avoid constitutional infirmities. Sometimes, in the face of an overbreadth claim, the Court will adopt a limiting construction that saves the law. As a result, the Court has tended to apply the overbreadth doctrine "only as a last resort," and has generally required that the overbreadth be "substantial" before a law will be invalidated on its face.

Vagueness. The "vagueness" doctrine is grounded in the due process clause. As the Court stated in *Connally v. General Construction Co.*, 269 U.S. 385, 391 (1926), "a statute which either forbids or requires the doing of an act in terms so vague that men of common intelligence must necessarily guess at its meaning and differ as to its application violates the first essential of due process of law." There are various justifications underlying the vagueness doctrine. "First, vague laws may trap the innocent by not providing fair warning. Second, if arbitrary and discriminatory enforcement is to be prevented, laws must provide explicit standards for those who apply them. A vague law impermissibly delegates basic policy matters to policemen, judges, and juries for resolution on an *ad hoc* and subjective basis, with the attendant dangers of arbitrary and discriminatory application." In addition, as the Court noted in *Grayned v. City of Rockford,* "uncertain meanings inevitably lead citizens to steer far wider of the unlawful zone than if the boundaries of the forbidden areas were clearly marked." This so-called "chilling effect" is particularly objectionable when citizen's speech rights are implicated.

Prior Restraints—Licensing. In general, the First Amendment imposes a very strong presumption against the validity of "prior restraints"—restrictions on speech that are imposed prior to its dissemination. In its landmark decision in *Lovell v. City of Griffin,* 303 U.S. 444 (1938), the Court struck down a local ordinance that prohibited the distribution of circulars, handbooks, advertising or literature within the city limits of Griffin, Georgia, without permission, on pain of criminal sanction. The Court emphasized that the "struggle for the freedom of the press was primarily directed against the power of the licensor" and was a primary motivation for adoption of the First Amendment. Since the ordinance was "void on its face," the Court held that Lovell was not required to seek a permit before distributing literature.

The Court has been more lax in applying the prohibition against prior restraints to motion picture licensing schemes. For example, in *Times Film Corp. v. City of Chicago*, 365 U.S. 43 (1961), the Court upheld a City of Chicago ordinance which required that all motion pictures be licensed (after submission and review) before they could be shown. In *Freedman v. Maryland*, 380 U.S. 51 (1965), the Court struck down a Maryland statute that prohibited the exhibition of films that had not been submitted to the State Board of Censors because of concerns about delays, as well as because of the lack of prompt judicial participation. In doing so, the Court reiterated the presumption against prior restraints and recognized that any "censorship system for motion pictures presents peculiar dangers to constitutionally protected speech." In addition, the Court concluded that a valid motion picture licensing scheme must contain a number of components: 1) the burden of proving that a film is unprotected expression must rest on the censor; 2) while the State may require advance submission of a films, the censor must, within a specified brief period, either issue a license or go to court to restrain showing the film; 3) the procedure must also assure a prompt final judicial decision, to minimize the deterrent effect of an interim and possibly erroneous denial of a license."

The courts have also allowed the federal government to require pre-publication review of books or articles that implicate national security interests, and that current or former intelligence officials wish to publish. As part of that process, the government reserves the right to require redaction or modification of information that might damage national security or intelligence interests. Despite the general prohibition against pre-publication review systems, courts have upheld restrictions in these areas provided that they are reasonable. *See Edgar v. Coats*, 454 F.Supp.3d 502 (D. Md. 2020).

Courts have also upheld content neutral time, place, and manner licensing requirements for parades and other public events. *See Cox v. New Hampshire*, 312 U.S. 569 (1941). Such restrictions are deemed essential to "prevent confusion by overlapping parades or processions, to secure convenient use of the streets by other travelers, and to minimize the risk of disorder."

Injunctions. The rule against prior restraints has also been applied to injunctions against expression. In *Near v. State of Minnesota*, 283 U.S. 697 (1931), the Court struck down a Minnesota statute that provided for abatement as a public nuisance of any "malicious, scandalous and defamatory newspaper, magazine or other periodical." Under this statute, the county attorney obtained an injunction against The Saturday Press for publishing articles that he regarded as "malicious, scandalous and defamatory." Even though the Court acknowledged the seriousness of the accusations, the Court struck down the injunctions and held that defamed individuals had their sole recourse (if at all) through civil damage actions. The Court emphasized that "for approximately one hundred and fifty years there has been almost an entire absence of attempts to impose previous restraints upon publications relating to the malfeasance of public officers is significant of the deep-seated conviction that such restraints would violate constitutional rights." The Court rejected the idea that an injunction could be justified by the fact some members of the press may abuse their position by making unfair allegations of scandal. The Court found that it made no difference that the press had charged the plaintiffs with "derelictions which constitute crimes."

In *New York Times Co. v. United States*, 403 U.S. 713 (1971), also known as the *Pentagon Papers* case, the Court extended the prohibition against prior restraints to publications that implicate national security interests. In that case, the United States sought to prohibit newspapers from publishing classified documents (the "Pentagon Papers") entitled "History of U.S. Decision—Making Process on Viet Nam Policy" that had been stolen from the Pentagon. Although some lower courts refused to enjoin publication, the Second Circuit did issue an injunction. In a *per curiam* opinion, the U.S. Supreme Court vacated the injunction reaffirming the prohibition against prior restraints which it concluded come with a "heavy presumption" against "constitutional validity" and require "a heavy burden of showing justification for the imposition of such a restraint." The decision produced a number of concurrences and dissents. Daniel Ellsberg, the Pentagon employee who stole the documents, was criminally prosecuted.

In recent years, similar controversies have arisen regarding "leaked" documents. For example, U.S. Army Pfc. Bradley Manning (now Chelsea Manning) was convicted of multiple counts of violating the Espionage Act for stealing classified documents. However, unlike the *Pentagon Papers* case, in which the government did not seek to bring criminal charges against either the Washington Post or the New York Times, the government aggressively sought to determine whether WikiLeaks had collaborated with Manning in stealing the documents, and eventually brought criminal charges against WikiLeaks' founder, Julian Assange.

In June 2013, Edward Snowden, a contractor for the National Security Agency (NSA), leaked documents to the media showing that the government was collecting extensive amounts of data from phone and internet companies. The government was collecting those documents entirely in secret, and everyone (including contractors like Snowden, as well as the phone and internet companies subject to the collection process) was ordered to be secret about the program. Although President Obama claimed that the program did not target the communications of U.S. citizens, he admitted that it could target U.S. citizens who were communicating with foreigners. Snowden felt that the U.S. people had the right to be informed regarding the existence of the program so he leaked secret NSA documents revealing the substance of the collection program. The government, believing that national security had been compromised, indicated its intent to prosecute Snowden under the Espionage Act for revealing the existence of the NSA program. Snowden fled and sought refuge in Russia.

In a similar vein, there has been much litigation regarding the government's attempt to enjoin Simon & Schuster from publishing THE ROOM WHERE IT HAPPENED, a memoir by former National Security Advisor John Bolton about his eighteen months working for the Trump administration. The DOJ argued that the content of the book included classified information that would harm national security, and that Bolton violated non-disclosure agreements by failing to obtain final approval from the National Security Council before publication. The federal district court judge found that since the book had been printed and shipped to a national audience, with advance copies in the possession of reviewers, it was too late to stop the publication and an injunction was no longer an appropriate remedy. However, the judge noted that the release of Bolton's book "may indeed have caused the country irreparable harm," especially if it contained classified information, and therefore Bolton "stands to lose his profits from the book deal, exposes himself to criminal liability, and imperils national security." Harper Neidig & Jesse Byrnes, *Judge Denies Request to Block Bolton Book*, THE HILL, June 20, 2010, https://thehill.com/regulation/court-battles/503695-judge-denies-request-to-block-bolton-book.

The Court did sustain a prior restraint in *Madsen v. Women's Health Center, Inc.*, 512 U.S. 753 (1994). That case involved the constitutionality of an injunction entered by a state court that imposed various restrictions against abortion protest activities. Even though the restrictions were imposed on abortion protestors, the Court concluded that they did not involve "content based" or "viewpoint based" restrictions on speech. The injunction was not viewpoint-based, even though it restricted only abortion protestors and not those who protested in favor of abortion, because of the "lack of any similar demonstrations by those in favor of abortion, and of any consequent request that their demonstrations be regulated by injunction." Nevertheless, the Court decided that a simple rational basis standard was too low, and that injunctions should still be subject to a "more stringent" standard of review that focuses on whether there is a "fit between the objectives of an injunction and the restrictions it imposes on speech" so that the relief is "no more burdensome to the defendants than necessary to provide complete relief to the plaintiffs." In applying the "significant government interest" test, the Court upheld some of the provisions of the injunction and struck down others.

"Symbolic" Speech. The Court has also held that "symbolic speech" (speech that expresses ideas through symbols rather than spoken or written words) is protected under the First Amendment. However, symbolic speech can involve either pure speech (as when an individual wears a black arm band to protest a war), or can involve conduct (the burning of a draft card). When conduct is involved, the Court has been less inclined to provide as much protection as it does for pure speech.

The Court's current approach to symbolic speech was articulated in *United States v. O'Brien,* 391 U.S. 367 (1968), which involved a criminal conviction for burning a draft card, and a challenge to the federal law (prohibiting the knowing destruction of a draft card) on which the conviction was based. The Court held that, when speech and non-speech elements are intertwined (such as when O'Brien burnt his draft card to express opposition to the draft), incidental restrictions on First Amendment freedoms might be permissible. The Court then articulated a four-part test for evaluating restrictions on symbolic speech. In general, such restrictions are permissible provided that four requirements are met: 1) the government must have the power to regulate in the field; 2) the regulation must advance a substantial or important governmental interest; 3) the interest must be unrelated to the suppression of free expression; & 4) the incidental burden on speech must be no greater than necessary to achieve the governmental interest.

If the government has targeted the symbolic speech because of its content, and assuming that the speech is not low or no value speech (*e.g.*, obscenity), the *O'Brien* test will not apply (because part three of the test is not satisfied) and the Court will instead apply strict scrutiny. Illustrative are the holdings in *United States v. Eichman*, 496 U.S. 310 (1990), and *Texas v. Johnson*, 491 U.S. 397 (1989), in which the Court struck down flag desecration statutes. The statutes were content based because the focus of the legislation was on whether the flag destruction was "respectful." The Court concluded that the government could not articulate a compelling governmental interest for prohibiting desecration. Even though Eichman & Johnson could not be prosecuted under flag burning statutes, they might have been subject to prosecution under content-neutral and viewpoint-neutral statutes prohibiting other criminal acts (*e.g.*, arson or theft (since Johnson had stolen the flag that he burned). Following the decision in *Texas v. Johnson*, there were numerous attempts to amend the United States Constitution to allow the government to prohibit flag burning. All of these efforts failed.

Public Forum Doctrine. The Court has applied special rules when individuals attempt to use public places for speech purposes. Historically, certain public venues (*e.g.*, streets, sidewalks and parks) have been available for expressive activity. These are so-called "traditional public fora." By contrast, there are also "designated public fora" which are places that have not traditionally been made available for expressive activities, but which the state has chosen to make available for those purposes. For example, a school may choose to make its auditorium available to public organizations, or a university activity fund may provide financial support for the publications of student groups, thereby creating public fora. Of course, some venues (*e.g.*, jails and defense facilities) are treated as "nonpublic" in the sense that they have traditionally been closed to most expressive activities.

Modern public forum doctrine recognizes that governments may have legitimate non-content-based reasons for restricting access to fora based on the time, place and manner of the expression. These reasons include the protection of governmental property, the management of competing uses, efficient traffic flow, public safety, and other considerations. As a result, the courts have upheld content-neutral restrictions that relate to the time, place, or manner of expression. For example, government might justifiably require those who wish to hold a parade to obtain a permit so that government can anticipate and deal with possible traffic disruptions.

In traditional public fora, government may impose content-based restrictions on speech only if it can satisfy strict scrutiny. *Perry Education Association v. Perry Local Educators' Association*, 460 U.S. 37 (1983). By contrast, the government may impose content-neutral regulations if they are narrowly tailored to serve a significant government interest and leave open ample alternative channels of communication. Because of the higher level of scrutiny, content-based restrictions on public fora have generally been struck down unless they are supported by a compelling or overriding governmental interest, are "narrowly tailored," and impose the least restrictive imposition on speech. In *Carey v. Brown*, 447 U.S. 455 (1980), the Court struck down a law that prohibited the picketing of dwellings, but excepted places of employment implicated in a labor dispute. However, in *Frisby v. Schultz*, 487 U.S. 474 (1988), the Court upheld a restriction on residential picketing directed toward a particular household finding that the stated interests in the "well-being, tranquility, and privacy of the home" were of the "highest order." Because the law did not ban all picketing in a neighborhood, but only focused picketing aimed at a particular household, the Court concluded that the restriction was narrowly tailored. The Court left open the possibility that focused picketing might be permissible if it was directed at a house being used as a place of business or for a public meeting.

Even when a restriction is content-neutral, the Court will examine it to see whether it is narrowly tailored. In *McCullen v. Coakley*, 573 U.S. 464 (2014), the Court considered the constitutionality of the Massachusetts Reproductive Health Care Facilities Act. That law created an 18-foot zone around abortion clinics in order to establish a buffer between abortion opponents and advocates of abortion rights. Anyone could enter the area, but once within it, no one (other than certain exempt individuals) could knowingly approach within six feet of another person—unless that person consented—"for the purpose of passing a leaflet or handbill to, displaying a sign to, or engaging in oral protest, education, or counseling with such other person." A separate provision imposed criminal sanctions on anyone who "knowingly obstructs, detains, hinders, impedes or blocks another person's entry to or exit from a reproductive health care facility." The law was modeled on a law that the Court had previously upheld. Later, Massachusetts amended its law to extend the buffer zone to 35 feet from which individuals were categorically excluded. The 35-foot buffer zone applied only "during a facility's business hours," and was required to be "clearly marked and posted." The Act exempted four classes of individuals: (1) "persons entering or leaving such facility"; (2) "employees or agents of such facility acting within the scope of their employment"; (3) "law enforcement, ambulance, firefighting, construction, utilities, public works and other municipal agents acting within the scope of their employment"; and (4) "persons using the public sidewalk or street right-of-way adjacent to such facility solely for the purpose of reaching a destination other than such facility."

In evaluating the validity of the expanded buffer zone, the Court emphasized that public streets and sidewalks are regarded "as venues for the exchange of ideas" and have historically been open to the public for speech activities. As a result, the government's ability to restrict speech in such locations is "very limited." In particular, the "government has no power to restrict expression because of its message, its ideas, its subject matter, or its content" in traditional public fora. However, the Court rejected the idea that the law drew content-based distinctions: "Whether petitioners violate the Act 'depends' not 'on what they say,' but simply on where they say it." The law was regarded as content-neutral even though it had the "inevitable effect" of restricting abortion-related speech more than speech on other subjects." The Court held that "a facially neutral law does not become content based simply because it may disproportionately affect speech on certain topics." This was true even though the law applied only to abortion clinics and not to all government buildings. The Court concluded that a distinction between abortion clinics and other government buildings was permissible because there "were apparently no similar recurring problems associated with other kinds of healthcare facilities, let alone with every building in the State that hosts any activity that might occasion protest or comment."

The Court also rejected the argument that the law was content based because it exempted four classes of individuals, including "employees or agents of a reproductive healthcare facility acting within the scope of their employment." Although "an exemption from an otherwise permissible regulation of speech may represent a governmental 'attempt to give one side of a debatable public question an advantage in expressing its views to the people,' " the Court held that the "statutory exemption for clinic employees and agents acting within the scope of their employment does not appear to be such an attempt." "Given the need for an exemption for clinic employees, the 'scope of their employment' qualification simply ensures that the exemption is limited to its purpose of allowing the employees to do their jobs." Moreover, the Court found that there "is no suggestion that any of the clinics authorize their employees to speak about abortion in the buffer zones," and the Court indicated that it would view the situation differently if they did: "The Act's exemption for clinic employees would then facilitate speech on only one side of the abortion debate—a clear form of viewpoint discrimination that would support an as-applied challenge to the buffer zone at that clinic."

However, the Court ultimately struck the law down because it was not "narrowly tailored to serve a significant governmental interest." "By demanding a close fit between ends and means, the tailoring requirement prevents the government from too readily 'sacrificing speech for efficiency.' " In order to be narrowly tailored, a restriction must not "burden substantially more speech than is necessary to further the government's legitimate interests." Although the law was enacted to promote "public safety, patient access to healthcare, and the unobstructed use of public sidewalks and roadways," interests which the Court recognized as legitimate, the Court concluded that the law "impose[d] serious burdens on petitioners' speech" by pushing the protestors "well back from the clinics' entrances and driveways" and make it very difficult for them to "initiate the close, personal conversations that they view as essential to 'sidewalk counseling.' " As a result, protestors found it very difficult to communicate with women and protestor success rates had plummeted. The buffer zones also made it substantially more difficult for petitioners to distribute literature to arriving patients. As a result, the Court concluded that the Act deprived the protestors of their two primary methods of communicating with patients.

Government ownership of property by itself does not give the public a right to access the property for speech and assembly purposes. Like a private property owner, federal, state and local governments have an interest in using the property under their control for the uses to which they are lawfully dedicated. As a result, in *Perry Education Association v. Perry Local Educators' Association*, 460 U.S. 37 (1983), the Court held that a collective bargaining agreement that gave teachers' elected bargaining agent a right of access to teacher mailboxes did not create a public forum. Likewise, in *International Society for Krishna Consciousness, Inc. v. Lee,* 505 U.S. 672 (1992), the Court refused to treat airports as traditional public fora. Unlike public streets and parks, airports have not been used since time "immemorial" for expressive purposes, and they are dedicated primarily to travel rather than to speech and assembly purposes. The Court rejected arguments that airports are variable use facilities that are adapted to speech and assembly. Likewise, in *United States v. American Library Association*, 539 U.S. 194 (2003), the Court held that Internet terminals in libraries should not be treated as forums for public speech.

In non-public areas, the government has greater authority to limit speech, but its choices must still be reasoned. For example, *Minnesota Voters Alliance v. Mansky*, 585 U.S. 1 (2018), involved a Minnesota law that purported to restrict speech in polling places. There were three prohibitions contained in the law, but the main challenge was to the political apparel ban which stated that a "political badge, political button, or other political insignia may not be worn at or about the polling place." The political apparel ban only applied within the polling place, and it banned articles of clothing and accessories with "political insignia" upon them. The law was supplemented by an "Election Day Policy" which provided guidance on enforcement of the ban. The Policy specified that examples of apparel falling within the ban "include, but are not limited to", "any item including the name of a political party in Minnesota, such as the Republican, Democratic-Farmer-Labor, Independence, Green or Libertarian parties. Any item including the name of a candidate at any election. Any item in support of or opposition to a ballot question at any election. Issue oriented material designed to influence or impact voting (including specifically the 'Please I.D. Me' buttons). Material promoting a group with recognizable political views (such as the Tea Party, MoveOn.org, and so on)." Some voters associated with EIW ran into trouble with the ban on Election Day. One individual was asked to cover up his Tea Party shirt. Another refused to conceal his "Please I.D. Me" button, and an election judge recorded his name and address for possible referral. Petitioner Cilek—who was wearing the same button and a T-shirt with the words "Don't Tread on Me" and the Tea Party Patriots logo—was twice turned away from the polls, then finally permitted to vote after an election judge recorded his information.

The Court struck the law down, emphasizing that the law's ban on wearing any "political badge, political button, or other political insignia" plainly restricts a form of expression within the protection of the First Amendment." The Court emphasized that there are three types of speech fora, including traditional public fora, designated public forums, and nonpublic forums. Viewing a polling place as a nonpublic forum, a space that "is not by tradition or designation a forum for public communication," the Court concluded that the government has greater latitude to limit speech. The government may reserve such a forum "for its intended purposes, communicative or otherwise, as long as the regulation on speech is reasonable and not an effort to suppress expression merely because public officials oppose the speaker's view." These restrictions can include content-based restrictions, "including restrictions that exclude political advocates and forms of political advocacy." Indeed, the Court had upheld a ban on campaigning within a restricted zone near polling places as a way of dealing with fraud, voter intimidation, confusion, and general disorder that had plagued polling places in the past. And the Court did not object to Minnesota's conclusion that a polling place should be set aside as "an island of calm in which voters can peacefully contemplate their choices."

But, while the State "may reasonably take steps to ensure that partisan discord not follow the voter up to the voting booth, and distract from a sense of shared civic obligation at the moment it counts the most," the Court concluded that there were limits on the state's authority in the sense that the state must draw a reasonable line. In that case, the state interpreted the ban to proscribe "only words and symbols that an objectively reasonable observer would perceive as conveying a message about the electoral choices at issue in the polling place." But the limitation was not focused only on campaign apparel, and extended to any "electoral choices." The Court viewed that restriction as unduly vague. The Court recognized that the state could prohibit a voter from displaying the name of a political party, items displaying the name of a candidate, and items demonstrating "support of or opposition to a ballot question." But the Court concluded that the ban on "issue oriented material designed to influence or impact voting," raised more questions than it answered:

> What qualifies as an "issue"? The answer, as far as we can tell is any subject on which a political candidate or party has taken a stance. For instance, the Election Day Policy notes that the "Please I.D. Me" buttons are prohibited. But a voter identification requirement was not on the ballot in 2010, so a Minnesotan would have had no explicit "electoral choice" to make in that respect. The buttons were nonetheless covered because the Republican candidates for Governor and Secretary of State had staked out positions on whether photo identification should be required. A rule whose fair enforcement requires an election judge to maintain a mental index of the platforms and positions of every candidate and party on the ballot is not reasonable. Candidates for statewide and federal office and major political parties can take positions on a wide array of subjects of local and national import. Would a "Support Our Troops" shirt be banned, if one of the candidates or parties had expressed a view on military funding or aid for veterans? What about a "#MeToo" shirt, referencing the movement to increase awareness of sexual harassment and assault? The State indicated that the ban would cover such an item if a candidate had "brought up" the topic.

In addition, the law sought to prohibit any item "promoting a group with recognizable political views," which the State construed as limited to groups with "views" about "the issues confronting voters in a given election." But that prohibition was also vague because the State did not confine the ban to groups that have endorsed a candidate or taken a position on a ballot question, and any number of associations, educational institutions, businesses, and religious organizations could have an opinion on an "issue confronting voters in a given election."

While the Court recognized that the legislature was not required to draft the law with perfect clarity, it expressed concern that a vague prohibition could carry with it "the opportunity for abuse, especially where it has received a virtually open-ended interpretation." The

Court concluded that, "if a State wishes to set its polling places apart as areas free of partisan discord, it must employ a more discernible approach than the one Minnesota has offered here. Minnesota has not supported its good intentions with a law capable of reasoned application."

The Court has rejected the idea that public access television channels constitute public fora. *Manhattan Community Access Corp. v. Halleck*, 587 U.S. 802 (2019), involved a New York cable operator that was required by its contract (and by government regulation) to create public access channels. The operator decided to ban two producers from those channels because of their viewpoints (they were critical of the operator). Applying the state action doctrine, the Court held that the cable operator was a private actor, rather than a state actor, because it did not perform a function "traditionally exclusively reserved to the State." "A private entity who opens its property for speech by others is not transformed by that fact alone into a state actor. In operating the public access channels, MNN is a private actor, not a state actor, and MNN therefore is not subject to First Amendment constraints on its editorial discretion." The Court rejected the idea that public access channels create a public forum for speech: "The Constitution does not disable private property owners and private lessees from exercising editorial discretion over speech and speakers on their property." Justice Sotomayor, joined by three other justices, dissented: "This is a case about an organization appointed by the government to administer a constitutional public forum. New York City secured a property interest in public-access television channels when it granted a cable franchise to a cable company. State regulations require those public-access channels to be open to the public on terms that render them a public forum. The City contracted out the administration of that forum to a private organization, Manhattan Community Access Corporation (MNN). By accepting that agency relationship, MNN stepped into the City's shoes and thus qualifies as a state actor, subject to the First Amendment."

The mere fact that a city permits private individuals to erect monuments on its lands does not necessarily mean that the government has created a public forum. In *Pleasant Grove City, Utah v. Summum*, 555 U.S. 460 (2009), even though a city had already allowed for the erection of 15 permanent displays, it did not have to permit erection of an additional stone display by a religious group (which would have stated the fundamental beliefs of that group). The Court concluded that the existing monuments did not involve creation of a free speech forum, and the Court treated the monuments as government speech: "Just as government-commissioned and government-financed monuments speak for the government, so do privately financed and donated monuments that the government accepts and displays to the public on government land."

Summum was followed and reinforced by the holding in *Walker v. Texas Division Sons of Confederate Veterans, Inc.*, 576 U.S. 200 (2015). In that case, the Court held that a state's specialty license plate program involved government speech even though the design for the plate may have been submitted, and paid for, by a private party. The Texas Division of the Sons of Confederate Veterans, Inc. (SCV), viewed the plates as private speech and argued that the state was prohibited from engaging in content-based or viewpoint-based discrimination against that speech. SCV specifically objected to the Texas Department of Motor Vehicle Board's rejection of its proposed plate on the basis that it contained a copy of the Confederate battle flag, which some found offensive. The Court disagreed, concluding that the plates constituted government speech.

In rejecting the SCV's challenge, the Court held that specialty license plates "issued pursuant to Texas's statutory scheme convey government speech." The Court relied heavily on *Summum* and offered several justifications for its decision: license plates have historically communicated messages from the States (*e.g.*, New Hampshire plates have featured the profile of the "Old Man of the Mountain," Massachusetts plates have included a representation of the Commonwealth's famous codfish, and Wyoming plates have displayed a rider atop a bucking bronco), each plate is a government article serving the governmental purposes of vehicle registration and identification and each contains the state identification, and the states own the designs of the plates even if they have been created by private individuals. Although individuals could simply display their messages on bumper stickers, they prefer license plates because they suggest "government agreement with the message displayed." In addition, the State of Texas maintained control over the messages conveyed on its specialty plates, and its Board must approve every specialty plate design.

As a result, the Court concluded that license plates (like the monuments at issue in *Summun*) constitute governmental speech. Governmental entities must be allowed to formulate governmental speech in the way that they prefer, and need not include opposing or dissenting viewpoints. As a result, the Court has refused "to hold that the Government unconstitutionally discriminates on the basis of viewpoint when it chooses to fund a program dedicated to advance certain permissible goals, because the program in advancing those goals discourages alternative goals. When the government speaks, it is entitled to promote a program, to espouse a policy, or to take a position." In addition, the Court rejected the idea that specialty license plate designs are not government speech because they are sometimes provided by private parties. The Court held that "the State did not intend to use its specialty license plate program to create a public forum: "First, the State exercises final authority over each specialty plate design. This authority militates against a determination that Texas created a public forum. Second, Texas takes ownership of each specialty plate design, making it untenable that the State intended specialty plates to serve as a forum for public discourse. Finally, Texas license plates have traditionally been used for government speech, are primarily used as a form of government ID, and bear the State's name. These features of Texas license plates indicate that Texas explicitly associates itself with the speech on its plates."

Justice Alito, joined by three other justices, strongly dissented. He questioned the validity of the Court's assumption that Texas was engaged in speech through its specialty license plate program: "Suppose you sat by the side of a Texas highway and studied the license plates on the vehicles passing by. You would see, in addition to the standard Texas plates, an impressive array of specialty plates. (more than 350 varieties.) Would you really think that the sentiments reflected in these specialty plates are the views of the State of Texas and not those of the owners of the cars? If a car with a plate that says 'Rather Be Golfing' passed by on a Monday morning, would you think: 'This is the official policy of the State—better to golf than to work?' If you did your viewing at the start of the college football season and you saw Texas plates with the names of the University of Texas's out-of-state competitors in upcoming games—Notre Dame, the University of Oklahoma—would you assume that the State was officially (and perhaps treasonously) rooting for the Longhorns' opponents? When a car zipped by with a plate that reads 'NASCAR—24 Jeff Gordon,' would you think that Gordon (born in California, raised in Indiana, resides in North Carolina) is the official favorite of the State?" While Justice Alito agreed that specialty plates convey "some government speech (*e.g.*, the name of the State and the numbers and/or letters identifying the vehicle)," he argued that "the State of Texas has converted the remaining space on its specialty plates into mobile billboards on which motorists can display their own messages." Indeed, the program was not highly selective. As a result, Justice Alito argued that Texas had created a "limited public forum" through its specialty license plate program, and he argued that the state should not be allowed to "discriminate on the basis of viewpoint," and he concluded that the Board rejected Texas SCV's design because public comments have shown that members of the general public find the design offensive. He concluded that Texas cannot forbid private speech based on its viewpoint.

In *Ysura v. Pocatello Education, Association*, 555 U.S. 353 (2009), the Court upheld a state law that allowed a public employee to elect to have a portion of his wages deducted by his employer and remitted to his union to pay union dues, but did not allow the employee to choose to have an amount deducted and remitted to the union's political action committee: "The First Amendment prohibits government from 'abridging the freedom of speech'; it does not confer an affirmative right to use government payroll mechanisms for the purpose of obtaining funds for expression. Idaho's law does not restrict political speech, but rather declines to promote that speech by allowing public employee checkoffs for political activities."

Religious Speech: Establishment Clause-Free Speech Tension. Although the First Amendment's speech clause gives all citizens the right to free expression, that amendment also prohibits the government from "establishing" religion. Some have argued that the Establishment Clause is violated when religious groups use governmental facilities or seek governmental funding for their speech. However, the Court has held that government cannot discriminate against religious speech in public forums, and must (in some instances) allow religious groups to use school premises on the same basis as other groups. In *Rosenberger v. Rector and Visitors of the University of Virginia*, 515 U.S. 819 (1995), the Court struck down a university policy that funded the publications of registered student organizations, but specifically excluded the publications of religious groups. The Court viewed the funding mechanism as a limited public forum, and held that the government may not discriminate against speech based on its viewpoint. Content discrimination is permitted, but only if it serves the purposes of the limited forum. Since the program was broadly defined to include "student news, information, opinion, entertainment, or academic communications media groups," and the religious group's speech fit within the parameters of the permissible discussion, the University was not allowed to discriminate against the religious group.

Campaign Finance Laws. The Court has also held that campaign finance—the raising and spending of money for political campaign purposes—is entitled to constitutional protection. The most famous campaign finance decision is *Buckley v. Valeo*, 424 U.S. 1 (1976), which involved a challenge to the Federal Election Campaign Act of 1971 (FECA), and related provisions of the Internal Revenue Code of 1954, all as amended in 1974. FECA imposed limits on the amount of money or services that individuals could raise to support their campaigns, and also imposed spending restrictions (*e.g.*, on millionaires who decided to finance their own campaigns). In *Buckley*, the Court held that both campaign donations and campaign expenditures constitute protected speech because they involve discussions regarding public issues and the qualifications of candidates. Although the Court held that campaign contributions were entitled to protection, the Court viewed contribution limitations as having less impact on free expression. Although a contribution reflects support for a candidate, it does not convey the underlying basis for support. In any event, the Court suggested that restrictions on campaign contributions could be justified by the interest in prohibiting corruption or the appearance of corruption.

However, the Court rejected the idea that the state has the right to equalize the resources of individuals and groups and their ability "to influence the outcome of elections." In addition, the Court struck down the limitation on expenditures by candidates from personal or family resources, holding that a candidate has the right to "vigorously and tirelessly to advocate his own election and the election of other candidates. By relying on personal funds, candidates reduce their reliance on "outside contributions and thereby counteract the coercive pressures and attendant risks of abuse to which the Act's contribution limitations are directed."

The *Buckley* Court upheld FECA's disclosure provisions that required candidates to publicly disclose the names of their donors because such information provides the electorate with information as to the places and groups from which political campaigns are receiving their money, and provides an indication of the interests to which a candidate is likely to be responsive. Finding "substantial governmental interests" supporting the disclosure requirements, the Court then balanced those interests against the "burden" that disclosure requirements impose on individual rights. The Court recognized that, by requiring public disclosure of contributions to candidates and political parties, the Act would "deter some individuals who otherwise might contribute" for fear of harassment or retaliation. Nevertheless, the Court found that the disclosure provisions constituted the least restrictive means of curbing the evils of campaign ignorance and corruption.

The Court also upheld provisions providing for public financing of presidential election campaigns. Section 9006 established a Presidential Election Campaign Fund (Fund), financed from general revenues based on designations by individual taxpayers, to finance (1) party nominating conventions, (2) general election campaigns, and (3) primary campaigns. The Court upheld the public financing provisions finding that public financing provides a "means of eliminating the improper influence of large private contributions" and furthers a "significant governmental interest." In regard to the claim that the law discriminated against candidates nominated by "minor" parties, the Court found that "Congress' interest in not funding hopeless candidacies with large sums of public money, necessarily justifies the withholding of public assistance from candidates without significant public support."

Regulating Corporate Campaign Expenditures. In *Austin v. Michigan Chamber of Commerce*, 494 U.S. 652 (1990), the Court held that the states could treat corporations differently than individuals for purposes of campaign finance. The case involved the Michigan Campaign Finance Act that prohibited corporations from making contributions and "independent expenditures" in connection with state candidate elections. The Act exempted any expenditure from a "segregated" fund (in other words, a fund separate and segregated from the corporation's general funds), and corporations could solicit contributions for these segregated funds only from an enumerated list of persons associated with the corporation. In upholding the law, the Court referenced its prior decision in *FEC v. Massachusetts Citizens for Life, Inc.* (*MCFL*), 479 U.S. 238 (1986), which held that a statute requiring corporations to make independent political expenditures only through "special segregated funds" burdened corporate freedom of expression. The Court reasoned that small nonprofit corporations would face "organizational and financial hurdles" in establishing and administering segregated political funds (*e.g.*, the corporation would be forced to appoint a treasurer, maintain records of all contributions, file a statement of organization, and submit updated financial statements periodically), and that these hurdles might disincentivize them to engage in political speech.

In *Austin*, even though the Court found that Michigan's segregated fund requirement was similar to the Massachusetts requirement considered in *MCFL*, the Court upheld the law finding a compelling state interest in the fact that state law grants corporations "special advantages (*e.g.*, limited liability, perpetual life, and favorable treatment of the accumulation and distribution of assets) that help them attract capital and allow them to obtain "an unfair advantage in the political marketplace." The Court concluded that this advantage can be unfair because: "the resources in the treasury of a business corporation are not an indication of popular support for the corporation's political ideas. They reflect instead the economically motivated decisions of investors and customers. The availability of these resources may make a corporation a formidable political presence, even though the power of the corporation may be no reflection of the power of its ideas." Whereas *Buckley* had focused on the danger of "financial *quid pro quo*" corruption, *Austin* relied on what it referred to as "the corrosive and distorting effects of immense aggregations of wealth that are accumulated with the help of the corporate form and that have little or no correlation to the public's support for the corporation's political ideas."

Despite *Austin's* holding, *First National Bank of Boston v. Bellotti*, 435 U.S. 765 (1978), struck down a criminal statute that prohibited expenditures by banks and business corporations for the purpose of influencing the vote on referendum proposals except for matters "materially affecting any of the property, business or assets of the corporation." The Court concluded that the law implicated speech designed to inform and enlighten the public, and held that "the legislature is constitutionally disqualified from dictating the subjects about which persons may speak and the speakers who may address a public issue." The Court found that the "risk of corruption" so inherent in candidate elections was "not present in a popular vote on a public issue." Although corporate advertising could "influence the outcome of the vote," "the fact that advocacy may persuade the electorate is hardly a reason to suppress it."

The Court has also considered the constitutionality of independent expenditures by political action committees. In *FEC v. National Conservative Political Action Committee*, 470 U.S. 480 (1985), the Court struck down portions of the Presidential Election Campaign Fund Act (PECFA), 26 U.S.C. § 9001 et seq., which gave Presidential candidates of major political parties the option of receiving public financing for their general election campaigns, but made it a crime for independent "political committees" to spend more than $1,000 in support of a candidate who accepted the financing. The Court found that the expenditures involved "speech at the core of the First Amendment," and that the Act's $1,000 limitation was equivalent "to allowing a speaker in a public hall to express his views while denying him the use of an amplifying system." The Court rejected the notion that the political action committees in question were not engaged in "individual speech, but merely 'speech by proxy.' because the contributors did not control or decide upon the use of the funds by the PACs or the specific content of the PACs' advertisements and other speech." Moreover, the Court found that "contributors obviously like the message they are hearing from these organizations and want to add their voices to that message; otherwise they would not part with their money." The Court emphasized that *Buckley* had held that preventing corruption or the appearance of corruption were the only legitimate and compelling government interests for restricting campaign finance, and that the Act's limitation on independent expenditures by political committees was unconstitutional because it was not designed to prevent corruption or the appearance of corruption.

The Court then distinguished its decision in *FEC v. National Right to Work Committee*, 459 U.S. 197 (1982). (NRWC). The Court noted that NRWC "turned on the special treatment historically accorded corporations. In return for the special advantages that the State confers on the corporate form, individuals acting jointly through corporations forgo some of the rights they have as individuals." Although the political action committees in question were incorporated, the Court found that § 9012(f) applied "not just to corporations but [to] an informal neighborhood group that solicits contributions and spends money on a Presidential election as to the wealthy and professionally managed PACs involved in these cases."

The Court again shifted direction in *Citizens United v. Federal Elections Commission*, 558 U.S. 310 (2010). *Citizens United* involved a documentary that was critical of Hillary Clinton, produced and paid for by a conservative nonprofit organization. In January 2008, Citizens United released a film titled *Hillary: The Movie*. It was a 90-minute documentary about then Senator Hillary Clinton, who was a candidate in the Democratic Party's 2008 presidential primary elections. *Hillary* depicted interviews with political commentators and other persons, most of whom were quite critical of Senator Clinton. *Hillary* was released in theatres and on DVD, but Citizens United wanted to increase distribution by making it available through video-on-demand.

In holding that government may not restrict spending by corporations and unions during the campaign process, the decision overruled *Austin* and that part of *McConnell v. Federal Election Commission* that had upheld limitations on corporate or union campaign spending. Before the Bipartisan Campaign Reform Act of 2002 (BCRA), federal law had prohibited—and still does prohibit—corporations and unions from using general treasury funds to make direct contributions to candidates or independent expenditures that expressly advocate the election or defeat of a candidate, through any form of media, in connection with certain qualified federal elections. BCRA § 203 amended 2 U.S.C. § 441b to prohibit any "electioneering communication," which is defined as "any broadcast, cable or satellite communication" that "refers to a clearly identified candidate for Federal office" and is made within 30 days of a primary or 60 days of a general election. Corporations and unions were barred from using their general treasury funds for express advocacy or electioneering communications. Corporations were permitted to establish a "separate segregated fund" (known as a political action committee, or PAC) for these purposes. The monies received by the segregated funds were limited to donations from stockholders and employees of the corporation or, in the case of unions, members of the union.

Writing for the majority, Justice Kennedy observed that "if the First Amendment has any force, it prohibits Congress from fining or jailing citizens, or associations of citizens, for simply engaging in political speech." Although BCRA exempted broadcasters from the restrictions, the Court maintained that there was no effective way to differentiate media corporations from other corporations. From the majority's perspective, the law thus represented a potential threat to political expression through mainstream and other media. The Court believed that the option to form segregated funds did "not alleviate the First Amendment problems" because such funds "are burdensome alternatives; they are expensive to administer and subject to extensive regulations." The law "necessarily reduces the quantity of expression by restricting the number of issues discussed, the depth of their exploration, and the size of the audience reached." The Court doubted whether government should have the power to silence "certain voices at any of the various points in the speech process."

Viewing the "right of citizens to inquire, to hear, to speak, and to use information to reach consensus" as "a pre-condition to enlightened self-government and a necessary means to protect it," the Court applied strict scrutiny and doubted whether government should be allowed to restrict corporate speech: "By taking the right to speak from some and giving it to others, the Government deprives the disadvantaged person or class of the right to use speech to strive to establish worth, standing, and respect for the speaker's voice. The Government may not by these means deprive the public of the right and privilege to determine for itself what speech and speakers are worthy of consideration. The First Amendment protects speech and speaker, and the ideas that flow from each. We find no basis for the proposition that, in the context of political speech, the Government may impose restrictions on certain disfavored speakers. Both history and logic lead us to this conclusion."

The Court then addressed *Austin's* anti-distortion rationale for restricting corporate speech—that corporations have "an unfair advantage in the political marketplace" because they can use "resources amassed in the economic marketplace." The Court noted that *Buckley* rejected the premise that the Government has an interest "in equalizing the relative ability of individuals and groups to influence the outcome of elections," despite "the skyrocketing cost of political campaigns." The Court emphasized that the First Amendment's protections do not depend on the speaker's "financial ability to engage in public discussion," noting that *Austin* distinguished corporations on the ground that "state law grants corporations special advantages such as limited liability, perpetual life, and favorable treatment of the accumulation and distribution of assets." *Citizens United* rejected that rationale for restricting corporate speech: "It is rudimentary that the State cannot exact as the price of those special advantages the forfeiture of First Amendment rights." Moreover, the Court rejected the idea that corporate funds may "have little or no correlation to the public's support for the corporation's political ideas." The Court noted that all "speakers, including individuals and the media, use money amassed from the economic marketplace to fund their speech. The First Amendment protects the resulting speech, even if it was enabled by economic transactions with persons or entities who disagree with the speaker's ideas." Indeed, the Court concluded that this antidistortion rationale "would produce the dangerous, and unacceptable, consequence that Congress could ban political speech of media corporations. They are now exempt from § 441b's ban on corporate expenditures. Yet media corporations accumulate wealth with the help of the corporate form, the largest media corporations have 'immense aggregations of wealth,' and the views expressed by media corporations often 'have little or no correlation to the public's support' for those views." The Court expressed concern because the "purpose and effect of this law is to prevent corporations, including small and nonprofit corporations, from presenting both facts and opinions to the public." And the Court rejected the idea that the restrictions could be imposed "in order to prevent corruption or its appearance." The Court emphasized that *Buckley* was focused on *quid pro quo* corruption. The fact that speakers may have influence over or access to elected officials does not mean that these officials are corrupt. Therefore, the Court concluded: "*McConnell* relied on the antidistortion interest recognized in *Austin* to uphold a greater restriction on speech than the restriction upheld in *Austin*, and we have found this interest unconvincing and insufficient. This part of *McConnell* is now overruled."

An important aspect of the *Citizens United* decision was its recognition that BCRA exempted media organizations from many of its prohibitions. The Court noted that there "is no precedent supporting laws that attempt to distinguish between corporations which are deemed to be exempt as media corporations and those which are not, especially in an Internet era. So the exemption would allow a conglomerate that owns both a media business and an unrelated business to influence or control the media in order to advance its overall business interest. Some other corporation, with no media outlet in its ownership structure, would be forbidden to speak or inform the public about the same issue. This differential treatment cannot be squared with the First Amendment." Moreover, the ban extends not only to large corporations, but also to "small corporations without large amounts of wealth."

Justice Stevens, joined by three justices, concurred in part and dissented in part. He argued that the idea "that corporations must be treated identically to natural persons in the political sphere is not only inaccurate but also inadequate to justify the Court's disposition of this case. Today's ruling makes a hash out of BCRA's 'delicate and interconnected regulatory scheme.' " He argued that, going forward, "corporations and unions will be free to spend as much general treasury money as they wish on ads that support or attack specific candidates, whereas national parties will not be able to spend a dime of soft money on ads of any kind. The Court's ruling thus dramatically enhances the role of corporations and unions—and the narrow interests they represent—vis-a-vis the role of political parties—and the broad coalitions they represent—in determining who will hold public office."

Stevens also questioned the majority's conclusion that the only "sufficiently important governmental interest in preventing corruption or the appearance of corruption" is "limited to *quid pro quo* corruption." Indeed, he noted that, as corporations grow more and more adept at crafting "issue ads" to help or harm a particular candidate, these nominally independent expenditures would "corrupt the political process in a very direct sense. The sponsors of these ads were routinely granted special access after the campaign was over. Many corporate independent expenditures had become essentially interchangeable with direct contributions in their capacity to generate *quid pro quo* arrangements. In an age in which money and television ads are the coin of the campaign realm, it is hardly surprising that corporations deployed these ads to curry favor with, and to gain influence over, public officials."

Stevens also emphasized the "antidistortion rationale" which he viewed as tied to the special concerns raised by corporations. He believed that the focus should be on improper "influences on officeholders that debilitate the democratic process" rather than simply an "equalizing" idea in disguise. He noted that there are major differences between corporations and people: "Unlike natural persons, corporations have 'limited liability' for their owners and managers, 'perpetual life,' separation of ownership and control, 'and favorable treatment of the accumulation and distribution of assets that enhance their ability to attract capital and to deploy their resources in ways that maximize the return on their shareholders' investments.' " In addition, corporations may be foreign controlled. "The resources in the treasury of a business corporation may make a corporation a formidable political presence, even though the power of the corporation may be no reflection of the power of its ideas." "When corporations grab up the prime broadcasting slots on the eve of an election, they can flood the market with advocacy that bears 'little or no correlation' to the ideas of natural persons or to any broader notion of the public good. The opinions of real people may be marginalized."

He believed that § 203 functions as a time, place, and manner restriction. He noted that Citizens United could have broadcast *Hillary* right before the primary provided that it refused to take business contributions or it used funds from its PAC. He doubted that the law created a situation where Citizens United would be silenced.

BCRA and McConnell. In an effort to address continuing problems in the campaign finance system, and to close loopholes in those laws, Congress enacted the Bipartisan Campaign Finance Reform Act of 2002 (BCRA). BCRA was challenged in *McConnell v. Federal Election Commission,* 540 U.S. 93 (2003). In the first majority opinion, the Court upheld Section I and Section II of BCRA. The Court viewed BCRA as designed to deal with flaws in the prior campaign finance scheme. First, the prior scheme created a distinction between "hard money" and "soft money" contributions to federal campaigns. Although "hard money" was subject to FECA's disclosure requirements as well as to its source and amount limits, corporations, unions and individuals could also contribute "soft money" in an effort to influence state and local elections, and political parties could use that money to fund various activities (*e.g.*, get-out-the-vote drives and generic party advertising), as well as the costs of "legislative advocacy media advertisements" (as long as the advertisements did not expressly advocate for a particular candidate's election or defeat). The Court took notice of the fact that the amount of soft money had expanded dramatically since the decision in *Buckley*, and that national parties were transferring ever larger amounts of soft money to state parties. Under FECA, "hard money" was money raised in accordance with FECA's contribution limits. In other words, a given individual could contribute only in accordance with FECA's limits. "Soft money" was money that was not raised in compliance with FECA's limits.

Second, the Court believed that *Buckley* had made what the Court regarded as an unjustified distinction between communications that "expressly advocate the election or defeat of a clearly identified candidate," which were subject to FECA's limitations and could only be financed with hard money, and "issue ads" (designed to state positions on "issues" and perhaps influence the legislative agenda on those issues) which could be financed with "soft money." The Court found that the distinction between the two types of ads was illusory because little practical difference existed between "an ad that urged viewers to 'vote against Jane Doe' and one that condemned Jane Doe's record on a particular issue before exhorting viewers to 'call Jane Doe and tell her what you think.' " In fact, if anything, the Court felt that issue ads were more effective than those that targeted a particular candidate.

Third, the Court was concerned about what it perceived as a "meltdown" of the campaign finance system. Relying on a congressional report, the Court noted that both political parties were promising special access to candidates and senior governmental officials in an effort to attract soft-money donations. In addition, both political parties were using large amounts of soft money to pay for issue advertising in an effort to influence federal elections.

The Court rejected the argument that BCRA was impermissibly overbroad because it subjected *all* funds raised and spent by national parties to FECA's hard-money source and amount limits, including funds spent on purely state and local elections in which no federal office was at stake. The Court concluded that the government's interest in preventing corruption and the appearance of corruption justified subjecting all donations to national parties to the source, amount, and disclosure limitations of FECA. Relying on *Buckley*, the Court upheld the first section of Title II, § 201, which required political committees to file detailed periodic financial reports with the FEC for "electioneering communications" referring to any "broadcast, cable, or satellite communication." The Court found that the "important state interests that prompted the *Buckley* Court to uphold FECA's disclosure requirements—providing the electorate with information, deterring actual corruption and avoiding any appearance thereof, and gathering the data necessary to enforce more substantive electioneering restrictions—apply in full to BCRA." The Court also upheld Section 202 of BCRA which amended FECA § 315(a)(7) to provide that disbursements for "electioneering communications" that are coordinated with a candidate or party will be treated as contributions to, and expenditures by, that candidate or party. The Court held that there "is no reason why Congress may not treat coordinated disbursements for electioneering communications in the same way it treats all other coordinated expenditures." Finally, the Court upheld a provision which prohibited corporations and unions from using funds in their treasuries to finance advertisements expressly advocating the election or defeat of candidates in federal elections.

The Court also rejected a challenge to Section 204 of BCRA which applied the prohibition on the use of general treasury funds to pay for electioneering communications by not-for-profit corporations.

The Court noted that its recent decision in *Federal Election Comm'n v. Beaumont*, 539 U.S. 146 (2003), confirmed that the requirement was valid except [as] it applied to a sub-category of corporations described as "*MCFL* organizations," as defined [by] *MCFL*. The characteristics of these corporations involved several criteria, including the fact that they were "formed for the express purpose of promoting political ideas, and cannot engage in business activities [so that] requests for contributions that will be used for political purposes [reflect] political support"; . . . have no shareholders or other persons who have a claim on their assets or earnings; . . . was not established by a business corporation or a labor union, and it is its policy not to accept contributions from such entities [so that the organization is not a conduit for] the type of direct spending that creates a threat to the political marketplace."

In a second majority opinion by Chief Justice Rehnquist, the Court upheld BCRA § 311 which required that "electioneering communications" clearly identify the candidate or committee or, if not so authorized, identify the payor and announce the lack of authorization. The Court found that the law bore "a sufficient relationship to the important governmental interest of '[shedding] the light of publicity' on campaign financing." However, the Rehnquist opinion struck down BCRA § 318 which added a provision prohibiting individuals "17 years old or younger" from contributing to candidates or political parties. The Court held that minors are protected by the First Amendment, and that the asserted governmental interest (protecting against corruption, by preventing parents from circumventing contribution limitations by channeling money through their children) was too attenuated to "withstand heightened scrutiny."

In a third majority opinion by Justice Breyer, the Court upheld BCRA § 504's "candidate request" provisions that required broadcast licensees to "keep" a publicly available file "of all requests for broadcast time made by or on behalf of a candidate for public office," along with a notation showing whether the request was granted, and (if granted) a history that includes "classes of time," "rates charged," and when the "spots actually aired." The Court concluded that all of these record keeping requirements helped the FCC determine whether broadcasters are carrying out their statutory obligations. The Court doubted that the provision infringed the requestor's rights by requiring "premature disclosure of campaign strategy" because the information requested (*e.g.*, names, addresses, and the fact of a request) did not require disclosure of substantive campaign content.

Buckley was followed by the holding in *Randall v. Sorrell*, 548 U.S. 230 (2006), which involved a Vermont campaign finance statute, and in which the Court struck down the law that controlled the total amount a candidate for state office could raise and spend during a "two-year general election cycle" that included the primary election and the general election. The limits were slightly adjusted to favor challengers over incumbents. The Court concluded that the *Buckley* Court was aware of the connection between expenditure limits and a reduction in fund raising time, but found this connection insufficient to sustain expenditure limitations. In regard to the contribution limits, the Court reaffirmed *Buckley's* holding that contribution limits, like expenditure limits, "implicate fundamental First Amendment interests," namely, the freedoms of "political expression" and "political association." The Court concluded that contribution limitations are permissible as long as the Government demonstrates that the limits are "closely drawn" to match a "sufficiently important interest." It found that the interest advanced in the case, "prevent[ing] corruption" and its "appearance," was "sufficiently important" to justify the statute's contribution limits. Nevertheless, the Court struck down Vermont's limits expressing concern that they were so low as to prevent candidates from "amassing the resources necessary for effective [campaign] advocacy" and thereby placed challengers (who may need to raise and spend more money) at a significant disadvantage.

Portions of the *McConnell* decision were effectively overruled only three years later in *Federal Election Commission v. Wisconsin Right to Life, Inc.*, 551 U.S. 449 (2007). In that case, the Court rejected *McConnell's* notion of "sham" issue ads and struck down portions of BCRA as applied. The Court upheld BCRA to the extent that it prohibited express advocacy or its functional equivalent, but the Chief Justice rejected *McConnell's* notion of "sham" issue ads, and the idea that such ads are the " 'functional equivalent' of speech expressly advocating the election or defeat of a candidate for federal office." The Court noted that candidates, "especially incumbents, are intimately tied to public issues involving legislative proposals and governmental actions." As applied to Wisconsin Right to Life's advertisement (questioning the Senate filibusters designed to prevent confirmation votes on judicial nominees), the Chief Justice held that it was protected under the First Amendment. "[A] court should find that an ad is the functional equivalent of express advocacy only if the ad is susceptible of no reasonable interpretation other than as an appeal to vote for or against a specific candidate."

Campaign Contributions and Judicial Disqualification. In *Caperton v. Massey*, 556 U.S. 868 (2009), the Court found that a state supreme court justice who received substantial campaign contributions from a corporate executive should have recused himself from a lawsuit concerning his company. The justice, who had received $3 million in contributions from the donor, voted to overturn a $50 million jury verdict against the corporation. The Court determined that the "extreme facts" of the case established a sufficient possibility of "actual bias or prejudgment" and thus rose to the level of a due process clause violation. Although finding a constitutional violation in what it characterized as "an exceptional case," the Court noted that not all campaign contributions create a probability of bias sufficient to warrant recusal, but that the facts of that case gave rise to objective and reasonable perceptions of risk.

The Right to Associate. Even though the First Amendment does not explicitly mention the right to associate, it does contain a number of rights that are associational in nature, including the right to peacefully assemble. In addition, since the Constitution protects "speech," it implicitly protects the right of association since people can speak more effectively when they join together to speak with a common voice.

NAACP v. Alabama, 357 U.S. 449 (1958), is the seminal freedom of association case. That case involved an effort by the State of Alabama to prohibit the National Association for the Advancement of Colored People (NAACP) from conducting business in the state because it failed to produce records and papers showing the names and addresses of its Alabama members and agents. The U.S. Supreme Court held that the right to associate is constitutionally protected on the theory that "[effective advocacy of both public and private points of view, particularly controversial ones, is undeniably enhanced by group association,]" and the Court held that the right could be used to shield the NAACP's membership lists from disclosure. The Alabama order imposed a "substantial restraint" upon the NAACP's members' right of association because known members were subject to "economic reprisal, loss of employment, threat of physical coercion, and other manifestations of public hostility," as well as because disclosure might preclude the NAACP from obtaining or retaining members. The Court held that the interest in association requires that any significant restriction must be supported by a compelling governmental interest. The Court found that Alabama's asserted interest (in determining whether petitioner was conducting intrastate business in violation of the Alabama foreign corporation registration statute) was not compelling. The NAACP had already admitted that it was conducting activities in the state, and had offered to comply with the state's qualification statute.

Despite the *NAACP* holding, the Court rejected an associational claim the following year in *Barenblatt v. United States*, 360 U.S. 109 (1959). In that case, petitioner was convicted of refusing to answer questions put to him by a Subcommittee of the House Committee on Un-American Activities during the course of an inquiry into alleged Communist infiltration into the field of education. The questions all related to his membership in, or knowledge of, the Communist Party. In rejecting Barenblatt's associational claims, the Court concluded that the balance of interests favored the government. Congress was seeking information pursuant to its power to legislate, and the Court emphasized the "close nexus" between the Communist Party and violent overthrow of government, and the Court was unwilling to treat the Communist Party as an "ordinary political party from the standpoint of national security." As a result, the Court was deferential to Congress.

NAACP v. Alabama's holding was reaffirmed in *Americans for Prosperity Foundation v. Bonta,* 594 U.S. 595 (2021). That case involved a California law which required charitable organizations to disclose to the state the identities of their major donors to facilitate the state's monitoring of possible misconduct by charities. One of the petitioners, Americans for Prosperity Foundation, was a public charity that was "devoted to education and training about the principles of a free and open society, including free markets, civil liberties, immigration reform, and constitutionally limited government." A second petitioner, Thomas More Law Center, was a public interest law firm whose mission was "to protect religious freedom, free speech, family values, and the sanctity of human life." Both petitioners alleged that disclosure of their donor information would make donors less likely to contribute, and would subject donors to a risk of reprisal.

In its decision, the Court reaffirmed the right of association, citing *NAACP v. Alabama,* and it also reaffirmed the idea that forced "disclosure of affiliation with groups engaged in advocacy may constitute as effective a restraint on freedom of association as other forms of governmental action." Applying "exacting scrutiny," which requires "a substantial relation between the disclosure requirement and a sufficiently important governmental interest" which is narrowly tailored, the Court struck down the California law. While the Court did not doubt that "California has an important interest in preventing wrongdoing by charitable organizations," the Court found a "dramatic mismatch between the interest that the Attorney General seeks to promote and the disclosure regime." There was little evidence indicating that California had made use of the donor information in its enforcement efforts, and the Court concluded that the state had alternate methods (subpoenas and audit letters) for obtaining comparable information.

The interesting aspect of the decision was that the Court sustained a facial challenge to the law rather than simply striking it down "as applied." The Court did so because it found that the law suffered from substantial overbreadth. The Court emphasized that the disclosure requirement "creates an unnecessary risk of chilling" in violation of the First Amendment indiscriminately sweeping up the information of *every* major donor with reason to remain anonymous. In *Bonta*, petitioners offered evidence showing that they and their supporters had been subjected to bomb threats, protests, stalking, and physical violence, and numerous amici made similar claims. As a result, the Court concluded that the "disclosure requirement imposes a widespread burden on donors' associational rights which could not be justified on the ground that the regime was justified as a way of investigating charitable wrongdoing, or based on the State's argument of administrative convenience."

Conflicts with Laws Prohibiting Discrimination. Many freedom of association cases focus not on whether the government can compel an organization to disclose the names of its members, but on whether government can force organizations to accept members that they do not want. In *Roberts v. United States Jaycees*, 468 U.S. 609 (1984), the Court held that Minnesota could force the United States Jaycees to admit women as regular members. The Jaycees were founded to promote the interests of young men, and regular membership was limited to men between the ages of 18 and 35. Women could be associate members, but could not vote, hold office, or participate in certain leadership training and awards programs.

In upholding the Minnesota law, which was construed as requiring the Jaycees to admit women, the Court noted that there are different prongs of the right to associate, including the right to engage in "intimate human relationships" and the right to associate for expressive purposes. The Court held that the Jaycees were not engaged in association of an "intimate nature" which involves "highly personal relationships" such as the "creation and sustenance of a family," including marriage, childbirth, the raising and education of children, and cohabitation with one's relatives. These "relationships, by their nature, involve deep attachments and commitments to the necessarily few other individuals with whom one shares not only a special community of thoughts, experiences, and beliefs but also distinctively personal aspects of one's life. These relationships are distinguished by relative smallness, a high degree of selectivity in decisions to begin and maintain the affiliation, and seclusion from others in critical aspects of the relationship." The Court found that such "intimate" relationships "must be secured against undue intrusion by the State because of the role of such relationships in safeguarding the individual freedom that is central to our constitutional scheme" and which are "a fundamental element of personal liberty." The Court recognized that large business associations could not qualify for protection under this prong of the right to associate. In particular, the Jaycees could not qualify because the organization was "large and basically unselective" and therefore did not fall within the constitutional protection for "intimate relationships."

The Court also recognized that "associational relationships" can help further speech and expression interests because the right to speak, to worship, and to petition the government for the redress of grievances "could not be vigorously protected from interference by the State unless a correlative freedom to engage in group effort toward those ends were not also guaranteed." Applying strict scrutiny, the Court upheld the law even though the law forced the Jaycees to admit members that it did not wish to admit. The Court held that Minnesota's law was supported by a compelling interest in "eradicating discrimination against its female citizens." After finding a compelling governmental interest, the Court concluded that the Jaycees could be forced to admit women because the Jaycees were more involved in commercial or quasi-commercial conduct than pure speech. Although the Court agreed that the Jaycees were engaged in expression, it held that the admission of women as full voting members would not "impede the organization's ability to engage in these protected activities or to disseminate its preferred views." The Jaycees could continue to adhere to their creed of promoting the interests of young men, and the organization was allowed to exclude any person (male or female) whose ideologies or philosophies were inconsistent with that objective.

Roberts was followed by *New York State Club Association, Inc. v. City of New York,* 487 U.S. 1 (1988), which involved a New York City law that prohibited discrimination by any "place of public accommodation, resort or amusement" in an effort to ensure that all people have the opportunity to "participate in the business and professional life of the city." The law's passage was prompted by "the discriminatory practices of certain membership organizations where business deals are often made and personal contacts valuable for business purposes, employment and professional advancement are formed." The Court upheld the law because it did not affect "in any significant way" the ability of individuals to associate to advocate their views. The Court suggested that, if a club was organized to promote "specific expressive purposes," and could show that the law would affect its ability to express its desired positions, it might be constitutionally entitled to an exemption. However, the Court found that most large clubs subject to the law were "not of this kind."

In yet another case limiting the right to associate, *Christian Legal Society Chapter of the University of California v. Martinez*, 561 U.S. 661 (2010), involved Hastings School of Law which created a "Registered Student Organization" (RSO) program under which it granted official recognition to student groups. Approved groups were eligible to do a variety of things: seek financial assistance from the Law School (which subsidizes their events using funds from a mandatory student-activity fee imposed on all students); allows RSOs to use Law School channels to communicate with students; place announcements in a weekly Office-of-Student-Services newsletter; advertise events on designated bulletin boards; send e-mails using a Hastings-organization address; participate in an annual Student Organizations Fair designed to advance recruitment efforts; apply for permission to use the Law School's facilities for meetings and office space; and use the Hastings name and logo. In exchange for these benefits, RSOs must abide by certain conditions, including compliance with the law school's Policy on Nondiscrimination. Hastings interpreted the Nondiscrimination Policy, as it relates to RSOs program, as mandating acceptance of all comers: School-approved groups must "allow any student to participate, become a member, or seek leadership positions in the organization, regardless of her status or beliefs."

Christian Legal Society (CLS) required members and officers to sign a "Statement of Faith" and to conduct their lives in accord with prescribed principles. Among those tenets was the belief that sexual activity should not occur outside of marriage between a man and a woman, and excluded from affiliation anyone who engages in "unrepentant homosexual conduct." CLS also excluded students who held religious convictions different from those in the Statement of Faith. Hastings declined to grant CLS an exemption to the all-comers policy. If CLS chose to operate outside the RSO program, the school "would provide CLS the use of Hastings facilities for its meetings and activities." CLS would also have access to chalkboards and generally available campus bulletin boards to announce its events. In other words, Hastings would do nothing to suppress CLS's endeavors, but neither would it lend RSO-level support for them. CLS sought to challenge Hasting's all-comers policy as a violation of its right to freedom of association.

In upholding the all-comers policy, the Court concluded that CLS was not forced to accept unwanted members. However, since Hastings had created a "limited public forum," RSOs could gain access to that forum (*e.g.*, receive state subsidies) only if they agreed to modify their membership policies. If they choose to opt out, and forego the benefits of the program, they retained the right to "exclude any person for any reason if it forgoes the benefits of official recognition." According to the Court, Hastings was essentially "dangling the carrot of subsidy, not wielding the stick of prohibition." The Court distinguished *Rosenberger* on the basis that the school in that case had selected "for disfavored treatment those student journalistic efforts with religious editorial viewpoints," thereby engaging in impermissible "viewpoint discrimination."

In deciding the case, the Court considered whether Hastings' policy was "reasonable taking into account the RSO forum's function and 'all the surrounding circumstances.' " In deciding that issue, the Court emphasized "that judges lack the on-the-ground expertise and experience of school administrators," and noted that courts should resist "substituting their own notions of sound educational policy for those of the school authorities which they review." The Court noted that the open-access policy "ensures that the leadership, educational, and social opportunities afforded by RSOs are available to all students." Moreover, the policy "encourages tolerance, cooperation, and learning among students," and "subsumes state-law proscriptions on discrimination, conveys the Law School's decision 'to decline to subsidize with public monies and benefits conduct of which the people of California disapprove.' " Finally, under the policy, "substantial alternative channels remained open for CLS-student communication to take place." Indeed, Hastings still offered CLS "access to school facilities to conduct meetings and the use of chalkboards and generally available bulletin boards to advertise events."

Interestingly, the Court rejected CLS's argument that Hastings' all-comers policy was inconsistent with the concept of diverse viewpoints: "there can be no diversity of viewpoints in a forum if groups are not permitted to form around viewpoints." Indeed, CLS argued that the policy would "facilitate hostile takeovers because saboteurs will infiltrate groups to subvert their mission and message." The Court viewed this possibility as "more hypothetical than real," and concluded that if "students begin to exploit an all-comers policy by hijacking organizations to distort or destroy their missions, Hastings presumably would revisit and revise its policy. Justice Alito, joined by three other justices, dissented, arguing that Hastings failed to maintain viewpoint neutrality: "When Hastings refused to register CLS, it claimed that CLS bylaws impermissibly discriminated on the basis of religion and sexual orientation." In his view, both of these grounds constituted impermissible viewpoint discrimination.

In *Boy Scouts of America v. Dale*, 530 U.S. 640 (2000), the Court held that the Boy Scouts could exclude individuals based on their sexual orientation despite a local law requiring non-discrimination. The Boy Scouts were dedicated to instilling values in young people, and regarded homosexual conduct as inconsistent with its message. The Court held that the New Jersey law could not be applied to the Boy Scouts without significantly burdening their right of expressive association which includes the right to express their views regarding homosexual conduct, and to exclude views with which they disagree.

The Right to Association and the Electoral Process. In some instances, government has tried to impose restrictions on the right to associate in the context of the electoral process. For example, in *Timmons v. Twin Cities Area New Party,* 520 U.S. 351 (1997), the Court upheld a Minnesota law that prohibited "fusion" candidates (candidates that appear on election ballots as the nominee of more than one party) against a political party's claim that it had an associational right to list the candidate of its choice as its nominee regardless of whether that candidate appeared as the nominee of another party. The Court disagreed, noting that the law did not prevent any party from endorsing, supporting, or voting for the candidate of its choice, and did not affect or control any party's internal structure, governance or policy making. Although the law might prevent a party from listing a particular candidate as its nominee, the Court found that this burden was not "severe" and was outweighed by the state's interest "in protecting the integrity, fairness, and efficiency of their ballots and election processes as means for electing public officials." The Court found that the states have a "strong interest in the stability of their political systems."

In *Clingman v. Beaver,* 544 U.S. 581 (2005), the Court upheld a semi-closed primary system under which a political party could invite only its registered members and independents to vote in its primary. The Court held that the semi-closed system did not violate the right to political association because it imposed only a minor burden on the associational rights of the state's citizenry, and advanced important regulatory interests in preserving political parties as viable and identifiable interest groups (*e.g.*, it aided parties' electioneering and party-building efforts, and prevented party raiding).

The Right "Not to Speak." One component of the right to associate is the right not to be forced to be associated with ideas or principles with which one disagrees. In *West Virginia State Board of Education v. Barnette,* 319 U.S. 624 (1943), the Court struck down a state law that required students to salute the United States flag as a way of "honoring the Nation" and further providing that any "refusal to salute the Flag be regarded as an Act of insubordination" that shall be dealt with accordingly. The Court held that a flag salute is a "form of utterance" and that the First Amendment protects an individual from being forced to "utter what is not in his mind." "If there is any fixed star in our constitutional constellation, it is that no official, high or petty, can prescribe what shall be orthodox in politics, nationalism, religion, or other matters of opinion or force citizens to confess by word or act their faith therein."

Likewise, in *Wooley v. Maynard*, 430 U.S. 705 (1977), the Court struck down a state law that required motor vehicle owners to display license plates with the motto "Live Free or Die." The case was brought by a Jehovah's Witness who found the motto morally and religiously objectionable. The Court concluded that neither the state's interest in mandating uniform license plates, nor its interest in promoting state history and its pride in individualism, was sufficient to sustain the law. The Court applied strict scrutiny, and concluded that the state's interests could be fostered by less drastic means, and were outweighed by the individual interest.

The Court qualified *Barnette* and *Wooley* in *Rumsfeld v. Forum for Academic and Institutional Rights, Inc.*, 547 U.S. 47 (2006), in upholding the Solomon Amendment against freedom of association claims. Although the military discriminates on the basis of sexual orientation, some law schools had policies that excluded employers from interviewing who discriminated on the basis of sexual orientation. The Solomon Amendment required these law schools to admit military recruiters on the same basis as other employers on pain of losing federal funding. *Rumsfeld* rejected the law schools' argument that the statute forced them to engage in speech in violation of the compelled speech doctrine, holding that the statute did not require law schools to express any ideas, and instead required them only to allow military recruiters onto campus and to post notices regarding the place and time. The Court concluded that the Solomon Amendment did not affect the law schools' speech since the schools were not speaking when they hosted interviews and recruiting receptions. The Court also rejected the argument that, if law schools are required to give military recruiters equal access, the public might perceive that the law schools do not object to the military's policies. The Solomon Amendment did not preclude law schools and law students from protesting the presence of the military, or expressing disagreement with its policies, so long as the schools provide access.

By contrast, in *Hurley v. Irish-American Gay, Lesbian and Bisexual Group of Boston*, 515 U.S. 557 (1995), the Court held that parade organizers could not be forced to include a message that they did not want to convey in a St. Patrick's day/Evacuation day (which marked the date when royal troops and loyalists "evacuated" from the city) parade. The parade was sponsored by the South Boston Allied War Veterans Council. GLIB, a group of gay, lesbian and bisexual descendants of the Irish immigrants, sought to march in the parade as a way of expressing "pride in their Irish heritage as openly gay, lesbian, and bisexual individuals, to demonstrate that there are such men and women among those so descended, and to express their solidarity with like individuals who sought to march in New York's St. Patrick's Day Parade." The Council denied the request and the Court rejected GLIB's challenge, noting that parades are often organized for expressive purposes, that there were multiple messages behind this parade (*e.g.*, "England get out of Ireland," "Say no to drugs"), and that the organizers did not forfeit the right to control their "message" even though they allowed "multifarious voices" to participate. More to the point, the organizers could exclude voices with which they did not wish to associate.

The Court also struck down a compelled speech requirement in *National Institute of Family and Life Advocates v. Becerra*, 585 U.S. 755 (2018), a case that involved California's FACT Act which required crisis pregnancy centers to inform women that "California has public programs that provide immediate free or low-cost access to comprehensive family planning services (including all FDA-approved methods of contraception), prenatal care, and abortion for eligible women. To determine whether you qualify, contact the county social services office at [insert telephone number]." The centers, which were generally pro-life, objected to the idea of being required to inform women about abortion options. The Court struck the law down, viewing the notice as a content-based restriction on speech, requiring the application of strict scrutiny, because it altered the content of the centers' speech.

In deciding the case, the Court rejected the idea that the speech was subject to regulation because its speech constituted nothing more than "professional speech": "Speech is not unprotected merely because it is uttered by "professionals." The Court noted that it had afforded less protection to professional speech in two circumstances—neither of which turned on the fact that professionals were speaking. "First, our precedents have applied more deferential review to laws that require professionals to disclose factual, noncontroversial information in their 'commercial speech.' Second, States may regulate professional conduct even though that conduct incidentally involves speech." However, the Court viewed both of those lines of precedent as inapplicable because the subject matter was highly controversial.

The Court recognized that it had applied a lower level of scrutiny to laws that compel disclosures in certain contexts. For example, the Court had upheld a rule requiring lawyers who advertised their services on a contingency-fee basis to disclose that clients might be required to pay some fees and costs. However, the Court viewed that line of cases as inapplicable because the required notice was not limited to "purely factual and uncontroversial information about the terms under which services will be available." Indeed, the notice did not even relate to the services that the clinics provided, but instead required them to disclose information about state-sponsored services. In addition, the Court recognized that it had upheld regulations of professional conduct that incidentally burdened speech. For example, in *Planned Parenthood of Southeastern Pa. v. Casey*, this Court upheld a law requiring physicians to obtain informed consent before they could perform an abortion. 505 U.S., at 884. But the Court viewed the California law as going well beyond the *Casey* law because it was not designed to facilitate informed consent to a medical procedure. And the Court viewed the California act as involving viewpoint discrimination: regulating the content of professionals' speech "poses the inherent risk that the Government seeks not to advance a legitimate regulatory goal, but to suppress unpopular ideas or information." *Turner Broadcasting*, 512 U.S., at 641.

The Court concluded that the "licensed notice cannot survive even intermediate scrutiny." The Court emphasized that California asserted an interest in providing low-income women with information about state-sponsored services. However, California did not require all clinics to provide women with such information. It only required clinics that have a "primary purpose" of "providing family planning or pregnancy-related services" and that provide two of six categories of specific services, to do so. As a result, most clinics were not required to give patients the information. In the Court's view, such "underinclusiveness raises serious doubts about whether the government is in fact pursuing the interest it invokes, rather than disfavoring a particular speaker or viewpoint." Further, the Court noted that California could inform low-income women about its services "without burdening a speaker with unwanted speech." For example, California could inform the women itself with a public-information campaign. Indeed, California could even post the information on public property near crisis pregnancy centers.

The Court also rejected the idea that unlicensed facilities could be required to post the notices. The notice requirement only applied to facilities that primarily provide "pregnancy-related" services, but facilities that advertise and provide nonprescription contraceptives were excluded—even though the latter were no less likely to make women think they are licensed. Moreover, the requirement applied to all advertisements and was quite burdensome. An unlicensed facility was required to call attention to the notice, instead of its own message, by some method such as larger text or contrasting type or color. This scripted language had to be posted in English and other languages. Thus, a billboard for an unlicensed facility that says "Choose Life" would have to surround that two-word statement with a 29-word statement from the government, in as many as 13 different languages. As a result, the notice requirement would have drowned out the facility's own message effectively squelching the desirability of having such a billboard.

Compelled Contributions. There has been considerable litigation regarding whether government can compel individuals or groups to provide financial support for messages with which they disagree. The seminal decision is *Abood v. Detroit Board of Education*, 431 U.S. 209 (1977), which involved non-union public school teachers who challenged a collective bargaining agreement that required them to pay a "service fee," as a condition of their employment, that was equivalent to the cost of union dues. The teachers complained that the union was using a portion of their dues to engage in political speech to which they objected, and sought on freedom of association grounds to withhold the portion of dues attributable to the speech. The Court held that an objecting teacher could prevent the Union from using that portion of their required service fee to support political candidates to which they objected, and from expressing objectionable political views unrelated to the union's duties as exclusive bargaining representative.

Abood was followed and reinforced by the holding in *Keller v. State Bar of California*, 496 U.S. 1 (1990), in which lawyers admitted to practice in California were required to join the state bar association and to fund activities "germane" to the association's mission of "regulating the legal profession and improving the quality of legal services." The Court held that, while the state could require the lawyers to join the association as a condition of practicing law, it could not require them to fund the bar association's political expression.

However, the Court limited the scope of *Abood* and *Keller* in a number of later decisions. For example, in *Board of Regents of the University of Wisconsin System v. Southworth*, 529 U.S. 217 (2000), in upholding the University of Wisconsin's student activity fee that supported student organizations (RSOs). Students could apply for funds, which were provided on a viewpoint neutral basis, or they could seek funding through a student referendum which could also be used to deny funding to RSOs. Relying on *Abood* and *Keller*, students challenged the activity fee claiming that it required them to contribute to the speech activities of organizations with which they disagreed. In upholding the fee, the Court noted that it would be "impractical" to allow each student to list those causes which he or she will or will not support without creating a system that was disruptive and expensive. Moreover, the University could choose to provide "the means to engage in dynamic discussions of philosophical, religious, scientific, social, and political subjects in their extracurricular campus life outside the lecture hall," and could impose a mandatory fee to finance the dialogue. However, the Court made clear that it would sustain only a "viewpoint" neutral fee, expressed concern that the program provided for a referendum in which students could decide which speech to fund or defund, and remanded for further hearings on whether the referendum could result in discrimination against minority viewpoints.

Likewise, in *Locke v. Karass*, 555 U.S. 207 (2009), the Court dealt with the permissibility of allowing a local union to charge nonmembers a service fee that (among other things) reflected an affiliation fee that the local union paid to its national union organization. The Court upheld the fee even though it was used to pay for litigation expenses incurred in large part on behalf of *other* local units. The Court held that the fee was permissible provided that the subject matter of the (extra-local) fees were of a kind that would be chargeable if the litigation were local (*e.g.*, litigation appropriately related to collective bargaining rather than political activities, and the litigation charge is reciprocal in nature) and the contributing local reasonably expects other locals to contribute similarly to the national's resources used for costs of similar litigation on behalf of the contributing local if and when it takes place.

Abood was partially overruled in *Janus v. American Federation of State, County, and Municipal Employees*, 585 U.S. 878 (2018). In *Janus*, the Court held that objecting employees could not be required to pay for union representation. Janus, who dissented from the Union's position on bargaining issues, claimed that he would not be a free rider if he did not pay union fees. Rather, if required to pay, he would be "more like a person shanghaied for an unwanted voyage." In other words, he would be required to subsidize bargaining positions that he found objectionable. The Court held that avoiding free riders did not qualify as a "compelling governmental interest," emphasizing that many "private groups speak with the objective of obtaining government action that will benefit nonmembers. Suppose that a group lobbies or speaks out on behalf of senior citizens or veterans or physicians. Could the government require that all seniors, veterans, or doctors pay for that service even if they object?"

Janus has turned out to be a very consequential decision. In 2018, the year the decision was rendered, nearly 210,000 individuals stopped paying agency fees to unions. The hardest hit was the American Federation of State, County, and Municipal Employees (AFSCME) which saw a 98 percent drop in agency payers (leaving a total of 2,200 payers) followed by the Service Employees International Union (SEIU) which lost 94 percent of its agency payers (leaving a total of 5,800). Some teachers' unions were also hard hit. In terms of membership (members are required to pay dues), AFSCME showed a nine percent increase in membership, but the SEIU showed only a 0.3 percent decline. *Janus* also generated a series of other legal challenges, including challenges to requirements that all lawyers belong to state bar associations, and industry groups who sought to challenge required contributions to advertising for their products. Individuals have also challenged whether unions can act as the "exclusive representative" for workers or impose conditions on when individuals can stop paying dues.

In *Glickman v. Wileman Brothers & Elliott, Inc.*, 521 U.S. 457 (1997), the Court upheld a Department of Agriculture rule that imposed generic advertising costs for California tree fruit upon the state's tree fruit growers, holding that the rule did not compel speech in a way that implicated the First Amendment. The Court emphasized that no fruit grower was forced to speak against his or her will or to embrace any objectionable political or ideological message. However, in *United States v. United Foods, Inc.*, 533 U.S. 405 (2001), the Court distinguished *Glickman* in a case involving mushroom growers. The Court noted that *Glickman* involved cooperative advertising as part of a broader collective enterprise in which freedom already was constrained by a general regulatory scheme. In *United Foods*, because the assessment for promotional advertising was not ancillary to a comprehensive regulatory scheme, but the principal object of it, the Court concluded that First Amendment interests against compelled speech and association should prevail.

In *Davenport v. Washington Education Association*, 551 U.S. 177 (2007), the Court upheld a Washington statute that prohibited public sector labor unions from using the agency-shop fees of a non-member for election-related purposes unless the nonmember affirmatively consents. The Court found that the First Amendment was not violated by a law requiring explicit consent: "We do not believe that the voters of Washington impermissibly distorted the marketplace of ideas when they placed a reasonable, viewpoint-neutral limitation on the State's general authorization allowing public-sector unions to acquire and spend the money of government employees. Quite obviously, no suppression of ideas is afoot, since the union remains as free as any other entity to participate in the electoral process with all available funds other than the state-coerced agency fees lacking affirmative permission." However, the Court limited its holding to public sector unions.

In *Johanns v. Livestock Marking Association,* 544 U.S. 550 (2005), the Court upheld the Beef Promotion and Research Act of 1985 (Act) that was designed to promote the marketing and consumption of "beef and beef products" by using funds raised by an assessment on cattle sales and importation. The statute authorized the Secretary of Agriculture to impose a $1-per-head assessment (or "checkoff") on all sales or importation of cattle and a comparable assessment on imported beef products. The assessment was used to fund beef-related projects, including promotional campaigns. The Secretary or his designee were required to approve each project and, in the case of promotional materials, the content of each communication. Much of the money was spent on advertising with the trademarked slogan "Beef. It's What's for Dinner." Some of the advertising included the notation "Funded by America's Beef Producers" or the Beef Board logo "BEEF." The Act was challenged by two associations, both of whom were required to pay the checkoff, but who complained that the advertising promoted beef as a generic commodity in contravention of their efforts to promote the superiority of American beef, grain-fed beef, or certified Angus or Hereford beef. Although the Court had struck down laws requiring individuals to fund speech programs, the Court emphasized that all of these laws involved speech that "was, or was presumed to be, that of an entity other than the government itself." The Court concluded that individuals could not object to compelled support of government speech even if the governmental program involved speech to which the individual objected. In *Johanns,* the Court suggested that the message in question might be attributable to the government so that listeners might not attribute the government's message to the beef producers. The Court emphasized that Department of Agriculture officials review all advertisements and the Secretary exercises final approval authority. However, the Court remanded for consideration of whether the reference to "America's Beef Producers" suggested that the advertisements were attributable to respondents.

Unconstitutional Conditions. Ordinarily, when government attempts to regulate or control speech, it does so directly. However, government can also try to regulate or control expressive liberty through encouragement or financial incentives. The "unconstitutional conditions" doctrine suggests that, in some instances, the nature or level of governmental encouragement or incentives transcends constitutional bounds. Government has the right to express itself and to promote policies and programs in ways that are consistent with its preferred ideology or agenda, and it can provide funds to convey a particular message while at the same time imposing requirements designed to ensure that the government's message is not undermined. Nevertheless, while government may set policy, implement programs necessary to effectuate its goals, and establish conditions upon distribution of resources, government must operate within constitutional limits, including those imposed by the First Amendment. Consistent with this premise, while government may distribute benefits, it may not condition their receipt upon waiver of a basic right or liberty.

The framing and development of government policy typically reflects value judgments and involves choices, priorities, and standards. For example, the federal tax code distributes burdens and benefits on the basis of legislative policy considerations. In *Regan v. Taxation with Representation of Washington*, 461 U.S. 540 (1983), the Court held that Congress may choose to make contributions to nonprofit organizations deductible only if those organizations do not engage in lobbying activities. The Court emphasized that Congress was not discriminating on the basis of viewpoint, and did not require lobbying organizations to forego their speech rights. Congress had simply decided that it would not subsidize lobbying activities by making contributions to lobbyists tax deductible.

In *Federal Communications Commission v. League of Women Voters,* 468 U.S. 364 (1984), the Court struck down a federal law which denied federal funding to public broadcasting stations that editorialized on the air. Even though the law was designed to insulate public broadcasters from the possibility that their funding would be jeopardized by the airing of unpopular views, the Court was concerned because the restriction implicated political speech which is ordinarily accorded high value under the First Amendment. The Court inquired whether the government regulation was supported by a substantial or important government interest, that was narrowly tailored to achieve its purpose, and found such an interest in the government's goal of ensuring balanced coverage of public issues. Nevertheless, the Court found that an editorial ban under-served this interest.

League of Women Voters was distinguished in *Rust v. Sullivan,* 500 U.S. 173 (1991), a case that upheld federal rules that denied federal funds to family planning clinics that counseled abortion or made abortion referrals. In upholding the condition on funding, the Court held that government is free to use private speakers to transmit information pertaining to its own program, and may take reasonable steps to ensure that its message is clear and not distorted.

The unconstitutional conditions issue has also arisen in the context of federal arts funding. In *National Endowment for the Arts v. Finley*, 524 U.S. 569 (1998), the Court upheld a federal law which required that the National Endowment for Arts consider general standards of "decency" and "respect" for the nation's diverse values and beliefs, in making decisions about whether to award arts grants. In upholding the restriction, the Court emphasized that, although the Endowment was required to take the listed factors into account, it retained discretion to make awards for contrary projects. The Court held that the decency and respect requirements did not involve viewpoint discrimination.

The government's ability to impose restrictions on speech funding is not without limits. In *Rosenberger v. University of Virginia*, 515 U.S. 819 (1995), the Court invalidated a government funding program's decision to deny funding to a group because the decision involved viewpoint discrimination. The Court held that a university could not choose to fund most publications, but exclude publications by religious groups. In reaching its conclusion, the Court concluded that viewpoint discrimination is impermissible when, instead of conveying its own message, government has chosen to expend "to encourage a diversity of views from private speakers."

Rosenberger's holding was followed in *Legal Services Corp. v. Velazquez*, 531 U.S. 533 (2001), in which the Court struck down a federal law that prohibited federally funded legal services offices from challenging the constitutional or statutory validity of welfare laws. The Court concluded that Congress was not obligated to fund legal services or to fund the entire range of legal claims. However, to the extent that Congress precluded legal services offices from pursuing theories that may be critical to effective litigation, the law was invalid. Congress could not insulate the government's interpretation of the Constitution from challenge by legal services attorneys. Because the case involved only private speech (involving the developing and presenting of legal theories), as opposed to government expression through an agent, the Court found the government's analogy to *Rust* inapt. The funding condition thus was declared invalid to the extent it was aimed to suppress ideas considered inimical to government's interests.

Another decision that limited government's ability to place restrictions on funding was rendered in *Agency for International Development v. Alliance for Open Society International, Inc.*, 570 U.S. 205 (2013). In that case, the Court struck down a provision in The United States Leadership Against HIV/AIDS, Tuberculosis, and

Malaria Act of 2003, 22 U.S.C. § 7601 *et seq.* which detailed a comprehensive strategy for combatting the spread of HIV/AIDS around the world. Under the Act, Congress appropriated billions of dollars to fund efforts by nongovernmental organizations to assist in the effort, and directed the President to establish a "comprehensive, integrated" strategy for combatting HIV/AIDS." The Act provided that the strategy must include, *inter alia,* plans to increase the availability of treatment for infected individuals, prevent new infections, support the care of those affected by the disease, promote training for physicians and other health care workers, and accelerate research on HIV/AIDS prevention methods, all the while providing a framework for cooperation with international organizations and partner countries. The Act also made "the reduction of HIV/AIDS behavioral risks a priority of prevention efforts" which must promote abstinence, encourage monogamy, increase the availability of condoms, promote voluntary counseling and treatment for drug users, and "educate men and boys about the risks of procuring sex commercially" as well as "promote alternative livelihoods, safety, and social reintegration strategies for commercial sex workers." Congress found that the "sex industry, the trafficking of individuals into such industry, and sexual violence" were factors in the spread of the HIV/AIDS epidemic, and determined that "it should be the policy of the United States to eradicate" prostitution and "other sexual victimization."

The U.S. enlisted the help of non-governmental organizations to help achieve the goals of the program. However, it attached two conditions on their funding: no funds made available to carry out the Leadership Act "may be used to promote or advocate the legalization or practice of prostitution or sex trafficking"; & no funds may "provide assistance to any group or organization that does not have a policy explicitly opposing prostitution and sex trafficking, except to the Global Fund to Fight AIDS, Tuberculosis and Malaria, the World Health Organization, the International AIDS Vaccine Initiative or to any United Nations agency." In order to enforce the conditions, the Department of Health and Human Services (HHS) and the United States Agency for International Development (USAID), the federal agencies primarily responsible for overseeing implementation of the Leadership Act, required the recipients to agree in the award document that they were opposed to "prostitution and sex trafficking because of the psychological and physical risks they pose for women, men, and children." Plaintiffs feared that adoption of a policy explicitly opposing prostitution might alienate certain host governments, and might diminish the effectiveness of some of their programs by making it more difficult to work with prostitutes in the fight against HIV/AIDS. They were also concerned that the Policy

Requirement might require them to censor their privately funded discussions in publications, at conferences, and in other forums about how best to prevent the spread of HIV/AIDS among prostitutes.

In striking down the conditions, the Court began by emphasizing the basic proposition that "freedom of speech prohibits the government from telling people what they must say," but the Court recognized that Congress has broad discretion to tax and spend for the "general Welfare," as well as to impose limits to ensure that funds are used in the manner Congress intends. If a party objects to a condition on federal funding, its recourse is to decline the funds. However, the Court distinguished between conditions that "define the limits of a government spending program—those that specify the activities Congress wants to subsidize—and conditions that seek to leverage funding to regulate speech outside the contours of the program itself." The Court concluded that the Act fell into the latter category: "The Government is not simply seeking organizations that oppose prostitution. Congress has expressed its purpose 'to eradicate' prostitution and sex trafficking, and it wants recipients *to adopt* a similar stance." As a result, the Court concluded that the Act effectively compelled "a grant recipient to adopt a particular belief as a condition of funding," and therefore extended to "protected conduct outside the scope of the federally funded program. A recipient cannot avow the belief dictated by the Policy Requirement when spending Leadership Act funds, and then turn around and assert a contrary belief, or claim neutrality, when participating in activities on its own time and dime. By requiring recipients to profess a specific belief, the Policy Requirement goes beyond defining the limits of the federally funded program to defining the recipient."

The Government argued that the program guidelines were constitutional because they allowed grantee organizations to either: (1) accept Leadership Act funding and comply with the Policy Requirement, but establish affiliates to communicate contrary views on prostitution; or (2) decline funding themselves (thus remaining free to express their own views or remain neutral), while creating affiliates whose sole purpose is to receive and administer Leadership Act funds. However, the Court rejected those arguments, noting that "Affiliates cannot serve that purpose when the condition is that a funding recipient espouse a specific belief as its own. If the affiliate is distinct from the recipient, the arrangement does not afford a means for the *recipient* to express *its* beliefs. If the affiliate is clearly identified with the recipient, the recipient can express those beliefs only at the price of evident hypocrisy."

The Court also rejected the argument that the program was constitutional because, absent the Policy Requirement, "the grant of federal funds could free a recipient's private funds 'to be used to promote prostitution or sex trafficking.'" Although the Court was unwilling to assume "that federal funding will simply supplant private funding, rather than pay for new programs or expand existing ones," it concluded that the requirement went "beyond preventing recipients from using private funds in a way that would undermine the federal program. It requires them to pledge allegiance to the Government's policy of eradicating prostitution." The Court then quoted from *Barnette* for the proposition that: "If there is any fixed star in our constitutional constellation, it is that no official, high or petty, can prescribe what shall be orthodox in politics, nationalism, religion, or other matters of opinion or force citizens to confess by word or act their faith therein." Justice Scalia, joined by Justice Thomas, dissented, arguing that the "Policy Requirement is a means of selecting suitable agents to implement the Government's chosen strategy to eradicate HIV/AIDS," and he concluded that it "is perfectly permissible under the Constitution."

Following the holding in the *Agency for International Development* case, the Court was confronted by follow-up litigation in *Agency for International Development v. Alliance for Open Society International, Inc.*, 591 U.S. 430 (2020). That case dealt with the issue of whether participating foreign organizations were also exempt from having a "policy explicitly opposing prostitution and sex trafficking." § 7631(f). The Court held that foreign organizations could be subjected to the requirement, emphasizing that foreign citizens outside the U.S. do not possess the same rights under the Constitution as U.S. citizens, and that separately incorporated entities and organizations can be treated as separate legal units with distinct rights and obligations. Moreover, the Court viewed foreign policy decisions, including foreign aid decisions, as peculiarly within congressional authority: "Congress may condition funding on a foreign organization's ideological commitments—for example, pro-democracy, pro-women's rights, anti-terrorism, pro-religious freedom, anti-sex trafficking, or the like. Doing so helps ensure that U.S. foreign aid serves U.S. interests." The Court rejected plaintiffs' argument that foreign entities must be treated like U.S. entities: "We see no constitutional justification for the Federal Judiciary to interfere with American foreign policy and American aid to foreign organizations. In short, plaintiffs' foreign affiliates are foreign organizations, and foreign organizations operating abroad have no First Amendment rights." The Court also rejected the argument that "the foreign affiliates' required statement of policy against prostitution and sex trafficking might be incorrectly attributed to the American organizations," and that "the American organizations themselves possess a First Amendment right against imposition of the Policy Requirement on their foreign affiliates."

In an earlier case, *Rumsfeld v. Forum for Academic and Institutional Rights, Inc.*, 547 U.S. 47 (2006), discussed earlier in connection with the right of association, involved a federal statute requiring law schools to admit military recruiters on the same basis as other recruiters on pain of losing federal funds. The Court upheld the law, noting that Congress has a constitutional right to provide for the common defense, which includes the power to require colleges and law schools to provide campus access to military recruiters. The Court rejected the notion that the "unconstitutional conditions" doctrine would limit Congress' authority to require law schools to provide access to military recruiters. The Court noted that the Solomon Amendment left colleges and law schools free to exercise their First Amendment rights because the Amendment "neither limits what law schools may say nor requires them to say anything. Law schools remain free under the statute to express whatever views they may have on the military's congressionally mandated employment policy, all the while retaining eligibility for federal funds." In addition, the Court viewed the Solomon Amendment as a regulation of conduct rather than a regulation of speech: "It affects what law schools must *do*—afford equal access to military recruiters—not what they may or may not *say*."

First Amendment Rights of Public Employees. A simmering debate has existed regarding whether, and to what extent, governmental employees may be treated differently than other citizens for First Amendment purposes. In some instances, they can be treated quite differently.

Political Activities. One context in which the Court has treated governmental employees differently is in regard to their ability to engage in partisan political practices. In *United Public Workers of America v. Mitchell*, 330 U.S. 75 (1947), the Court upheld § 9(a) of the Hatch Act which prohibited federal employees from taking "any active part in political management or in political campaigns." The Court applied a limited standard of review (whether Congress acted "within reasonable limits"), and the Court was deferential to Congress. In addition, the Court balanced the rights of employees to engage in free speech against the "evil of political partisanship by classified employees of government," and concluded that an "actively partisan governmental personnel threatens good administration" in that "political rather than official effort may earn advancement and to the public in that governmental favor may be channeled through political connections." The Court emphasized that Congress did not prohibit federal employees from voting in elections, and the law prohibited "only the partisan activity of federal personnel deemed offensive to efficiency. With that limitation only, employees may make their contributions to public affairs or protect their own interests, as before the passage of the act." The Court emphasized that the Hatch Act did not prohibit employees from exercising their First Amendment rights in other ways (*e.g.*, expressing their opinions on public affairs, personalities or matters of public interest). Moreover, the Court concluded that the restrictions could be applied even if an individual employee's job was not connected to the public. For example, the Court held that the Act could be applied to a "roller" at the Mint who was performing essentially mechanical skills: "Evidently what Congress feared was the cumulative effect on employee morale of political activity by all employees who could be induced to participate actively. It does not seem to us an unconstitutional basis for legislation."

In *United States Civil Service Commission v. National Association of Letter Carriers, AFL-CIO*, 413 U.S. 548 (1973), the Court reaffirmed *Mitchell*, and offered several justifications for the Hatch Act. In particular, the Court noted that a prohibition on partisan political activities reduces "the hazards to fair and effective government" by removing actual improprieties as well as the appearance of impropriety. In addition, the prohibition avoids the risk that the government work force might be used "to build a powerful, invincible, and perhaps corrupt political machine." Finally, as the Court recognized in *Mitchell*, one's career in government service should not depend on political performance, and government employees "should be free from pressure and from express or tacit invitation to vote in a certain way or perform political chores in order to curry favor with their superiors rather than to act out their own beliefs."

Honoraria. Despite the holding in *Mitchell*, not all restrictions on the expressive activities of governmental employees have been upheld. In *United States v. National Treasury Employees Union*, 513 U.S. 454 (1995), the Court struck down a criminal statute that prohibited federal employees from accepting any compensation for making speeches or writing articles which applied whether or not the subject had any relationship to the employee's official duties. In its decision, the Court recognized that a number of "literary giants" (*e.g.*, Nathaniel Hawthorne and Herman Melville) had been government employees, and that the law imposed a significant burden on expressive activity by taking away the financial incentive for more expression. Although the law was rooted in problems related to a small group of employees, the breadth of the law threatened to create a "large-scale disincentive to Government employees' expression" that would impose "a significant burden on the public's right to read and hear what the employees would otherwise have written and said." In addition, since the speech does not relate to the employee's jobs, and takes place off the job, the law could not be justified as a means of preventing "workplace disruption." "One can envision scant harm, or appearance of harm, resulting from the same employee's accepting pay to lecture on the Quaker religion or to write dance reviews."

Other Public Employee Free Speech Rights. Beginning in the 1950s, the Court rendered a number of decisions on public employees' right to free expression in other contexts both on and off the job. For example, in *Wieman v. Updegraff,* 344 U.S. 183 (1952), the Court held that public school teachers could not be required to swear an oath of loyalty to the state and to reveal the groups with which were they associated. In *Pickering v. Board of Education,* 391 U.S. 563 (1968), the Court held that governmental employees do not relinquish their right to comment on matters of public interest simply because of their status as government employees. In that case, the Court overturned the dismissal of a high school teacher who criticized a board of education's allocation of funds between athletics and education, as well as its methods of informing taxpayers about the need for additional revenue. While recognizing that the state has a greater interest in regulating the speech of its employees, the Court tried to strike a balance "between the interests of the employee, as a citizen, in commenting upon matters of public concern and the interest of the State, as an employer, in promoting the efficiency of the public services it performs through its employees." This balance has subsequently been referred to as the *Pickering* balancing test. In overturning the dismissal, the Court concluded that Pickering's speech involved "a matter of legitimate public concern" upon which "free and open debate is vital to informed decision-making by the electorate."

The *Pickering* test was applied in *Connick v. Myers,* 461 U.S. 138 (1983) in which the Court sustained a district attorney's decision to dismiss an assistant district attorney for intra-office speech. The assistant, who was upset about a transfer, prepared a questionnaire on various office-related topics (transfer policy, morale, the need for a grievance committee, the level of confidence in supervisors, and whether employees felt pressured to work in political campaigns), and distributed the questionnaire to fellow assistants. When the district attorney learned about the questionnaire, he terminated Myers for refusing to accept the transfer and for insubordination in distributing the questionnaire. The Court held that "government officials should enjoy wide latitude in managing their offices, without intrusive oversight by the judiciary in the name of the First Amendment," and that employee "speech on private matters falls into one of the narrow and well-defined classes of expression which carries so little social value, such as obscenity, that the state can prohibit and punish such expression by all persons in its jurisdiction." In this context, "a federal court is not the appropriate forum in which to review the wisdom of a personnel decision taken by a public agency allegedly in reaction to the employee's behavior."

In applying these principles to the assistant's speech, the Court concluded that the assistant's questionnaire did not relate to matters of "public concern." The Court viewed the questionnaire as focusing on questions relating to discipline and morale in the workplace, and as an attempt to "gather ammunition for another round of controversy with her superiors." The Court did hold that one of Myers' questions, which focused on whether employees had ever been pressured to work in political campaigns, did touch upon a matter of public concern because of the risk that such pressure could involve "a coercion of belief in violation of fundamental constitutional rights," as well as because the public has an interest in making sure that government employees should be evaluated based "upon meritorious performance rather than political service." Despite the public importance of one of the questions, the Court upheld the dismissal based on the governmental interest in "the effective and efficient fulfillment of its responsibilities to the public." While the questionnaire did not impede Myers' ability to perform her own duties, it did cause a "mini-insurrection" in the office and interfered with working relationships, and the Court deferred to the employer's conclusions regarding the need to fire Myers. In addition, although the survey involved matters of public concern in a limited sense, the Court held the questionnaire concerned "internal office policy," and the Court concluded that the First Amendment did not require the District Attorney to "tolerate action which he reasonably believed would disrupt the office, undermine his authority, and destroy close working relationships." In conclusion, the Court emphasized that it was seeking a balance between the "First Amendment's primary aim" which the Court regarded as "the full protection of speech upon issues of public concern" and the "practical realities involved in the administration of a government office."

In *Waters v. Churchill*, 511 U.S. 661 (1994), the Court also upheld a discharge for speech. *Waters* involved a nurse in an obstetrics department who was terminated for talking about "how bad things are in [obstetrics] in general," as well as for criticizing a supervisor. The nurse denied making the statements, claimed that she actually supported the supervisor and did not complain about obstetrics, but admitted that she complained about the hospital's "cross-training" policy (under which nurses from one department could work in another department when their usual location was overstaffed). In upholding the discharge, the Court concluded that, if the supervisors really believed the stories about the discharged employee's criticisms, based on their investigation, the discharge was reasonable.

Even though the Court gave deference to the employer in *Myers*, the same is not true of the holding in *Rankin v. McPherson*, 483 U.S. 378 (1987). That case involved a deputy (McPherson) in a constable's office who was discharged during her probationary period. Although the Constable's office performed law enforcement functions, McPherson was not a commissioned peace officer, did not wear a uniform, was not authorized to make arrests or allowed to carry a gun, and performed only clerical duties. The case arose when McPherson and some fellow employees heard on the radio that there had been an attempt to assassinate President Reagan. McPherson then told a co-worker, her boyfriend, "shoot, if they go for him again, I hope they get him." McPherson was fired for the remark.

In overturning the discharge, the Court again focused on the "balance" between the employee's interest in commenting on matters of public concern, and the state's interest "in promoting the efficiency of the public services it performs through its employees." The Court found that McPherson's comment dealt with a "matter of public concern" because it concerned the policies of the President's administration, and was made in response to an attempt on the President's life. In balancing McPherson's interest in making the statement against "the interest of the State, as an employer, in promoting the efficiency of the public services it performs through its employees," the Court concluded that the employer could not justify the discharge given that there was no evidence that McPherson's statement interfered with the efficient functioning of the office, that it disturbed or interrupted other employees, or even that anyone else heard the remark. In addition, the statement did not discredit the office (because it was made in a private conversation with another employee), and did not reflect "a character trait that made respondent unfit to perform her work." The Court also expressed concern that McPherson may have been discharged because of the content of her speech.

Ultimately, each employee speech case must be evaluated on its own facts weighing the public and private components. For example, in the Court's earlier decision in *Mt. Healthy City School District v. Doyle*, 429 U.S. 274 (1977), after a principal issued a directive on teacher dress and appearance, one teacher leaked a copy of the directive to a local disc jockey who announced it as a news item. A month later, the principal recommended that Doyle not be rehired for the following year because of "a notable lack of tact in handling professional matters which leaves much doubt as to your sincerity in establishing good school relationships." The principal's recommendation referred to the radio station incident and to an obscene gesture that Doyle had made. The Court held that the dismissal was actionable if it was based on Doyle's communication with the radio station. Having shown that his speech was a "substantial factor" or a "motivating factor" in the Board's decision not to rehire, the Board was required to prove that it would have reached the same result even in the absence of Doyle's communication with the station.

However, there are a number of instances when the Court has concluded that the speech rights of governmental employees are trumped by the employer's needs. For example, in *City of San Diego v. Roe*, 543 U.S. 77 (2004), a police officer was terminated for off-duty speech (selling videotapes depicting himself engaged in sexually explicit acts while wearing a police uniform, including one video which depicted a police officer engaged in sex acts while issuing a citation). The department concluded that the officer had violated specific police department policies, including engaging in conduct unbecoming of an officer and immoral conduct. In evaluating the case, the Court indicated that it would balance the competing interests except when the employee's speech could compromise the proper functioning of government offices. In applying these principles, the Court noted that the: "debased parody of an officer performing indecent acts while in the course of official duties brought the mission of the employer and the professionalism of its officers into serious disrepute." In addition, Roe's expression did not "implicate the public interest because Roe was not attempting to inform the public regarding any aspect of the department's functioning or operation."

Speech Pursuant to Duties. In *Garcetti v. Ceballos*, 547 U.S. 410 (2006), the Court imposed an important new qualification on its precedents relating to the free speech rights of public employees. Ceballos was a deputy district attorney who was involved in a "heated exchange" regarding the handling of a case, and who was subsequently subjected to a series of retaliatory employment actions. The Court held that the First Amendment does not protect a government employee from discipline based on speech made pursuant to the employee's official duties. Relying on *Pickering*, the Court rejected Ceballos' First Amendment claim because his expressions were made "pursuant to his duties" as a prosecutor. In addition, the Court noted that employers "have heightened interests in controlling speech made by an employee in his or her professional capacity." The Court noted that the memo "demanded the attention of his supervisors and led to a heated meeting with employees from the sheriff's department. If Ceballos' superiors thought his memo was inflammatory or misguided, they had the authority to take proper corrective action." The Court concluded that there were other means available for dealing with corruption. As a result, the Court rejected the notion "of a constitutional cause of action behind every statement a public employee makes in the course of doing his or her job."

In *Lane v. Franks*, 573 U.S. 228 (2014), the Court held that the *Pickering* test protected an employee who provided truthful testimony in response to a subpoena regarding matters that he discovered in the course of his employment. According to the Court, the question is whether the government has "an adequate justification for treating the employee differently from any other member of the public" based on the government's needs as an employer. In particular, the Court cited the employer's legitimate "interests in the effective and efficient fulfillment of their responsibilities to the public," including "promoting efficiency and integrity in the discharge of official duties," and "maintaining proper discipline in public service." In that case, the Court noted that the employer's side of the *Pickering* scale was "entirely empty" because the government did not "assert, and cannot demonstrate, any government interest that tips the balance in their favor. There is no evidence that Lane's testimony at Schmitz' trials was false or erroneous or that Lane unnecessarily disclosed any sensitive, confidential, or privileged information while testifying." As a result, the Court concluded that "Lane's speech is entitled to protection under the First Amendment."

Associational Rights. Even though a number of cases have suggested that governmental employees have limited expressive freedom rights, some cases have recognized that they do have associational rights. For example, in *Wieman v. Updegraff*, 344 U.S. 183 (1952), the Court held that a State could not force its employees to recite a loyalty oath denying their past affiliation with Communists. Likewise, in *Keyishian v. Board of Regents*, 385 U.S. 589 (1967), the Court invalidated New York statutes barring employment on the basis of membership in "subversive" organizations on the basis that political associations, by themselves, do not constitute an adequate ground for denying public employment.

In *United States v. Robel*, 389 U.S. 258 (1967), the Court invalidated portions of the Subversive Activities Control Act of 1950, which provided that, when a Communist-action organization is under a final order to register, it shall be unlawful for any member of the organization to work at a defense facility. The law was passed to protect security and prevent sabotage at defense facilities. *Robel* held that the Act violated the right to associate as applied to a member of the Communist Party who was employed as a machinist at a shipyard designated as a "defense facility." In striking down the Act, the Court held that "The operative fact upon which the job disability depends is the exercise of an individual's right of association, which is protected by the provisions of the First Amendment."

In *Elrod v. Burns*, 427 U.S. 347 (1976), the Court held that an employee had been improperly discharged because of his party affiliation. Although the employee was not in a merit system job, he could not dismissed solely because of his political affiliations. The Court rejected the argument that the law was supported by the need to make sure that the workforce supported the administration in power, noting that when large numbers of public employees are replaced each time the government changes hands, there is considerable inefficiency. In any event, the Court found that there were other means for ensuring employee effectiveness and efficiency, including dismissal for insubordination or poor job performance. The Court noted that it might be permissible to dismiss those in "policymaking" positions, but the Court noted that even individuals with substantial responsibilities (*e.g.*, supervisors) may not have "policymaking" responsibilities. The Court remanded for a determination of whether the government could show an "overriding interest" in support of the dismissals.

In *Branti v. Finkel*, 445 U.S. 507 (1980), the Court defined the term "policymaking" when it overturned the dismissal of an assistant public defender solely because he was a Republican. The Court emphasized that the "primary, if not the only, responsibility of an assistant public defender is to represent individual citizens in controversy with the State," and therefore any "policymaking" that the defender exercises "must relate to the needs of individual clients and not to any partisan political interests."

In *Minnesota State Board for Community Colleges v. Knight*, 465 U.S. 271 (1984), the Court upheld a Minnesota law that authorized public employees to select an exclusive representative to bargain collectively over the terms and conditions of their employment, but provided that a government employer could only exchange views on nonmandatory subjects with the exclusive representative. The law was challenged by faculty at one college who claimed a violation of their constitutional rights. In upholding the restriction, the Court concluded that members of the public do not generally have a right to be heard by public bodies engaged in policymaking, and held therefore that employees' speech and associational rights were not therefore infringed: "The state has in no way restrained appellees' freedom to speak on any education-related issue or their freedom to associate or not to associate with whom they please, including the exclusive representative. Nor has the state attempted to suppress any ideas."

Student Free Speech Rights. There has been considerable litigation regarding the expressive rights of students in public schools. While the Court has recognized in a number of cases that students do not relinquish their First Amendment rights at the schoolhouse door, the Court has been reluctant to hold that student speech rights are co-extensive with those of adults.

In *Tinker v. Des Moines Independent School District*, 393 U.S. 503 (1969), the Court recognized that high school students have a First Amendment right of expression. That case involved two high school students and a junior high school student who wore black armbands to demonstrate their opposition to the Vietnam War in violation of a newly adopted policy providing for the suspension of any student who refused to remove an armband. The Court recognized that the wearing of armbands is "symbolic speech," protected by the First Amendment, and is "closely akin to 'pure speech.'" While the Court noted that the free speech rights of teachers and students are tempered by the "special characteristics of the school environment," and the need to "prescribe and control conduct in the schools," the Court held that school officials could not discipline students "for a silent, passive expression of opinion." In order to discipline, school officials must show that the students' conduct "materially and substantially interfere with the requirements of appropriate discipline in the operation of the school." The Court found that school officials could not meet the required burden because there was no indication of any disruption attributable to the armbands.

Because of the special characteristics of the school environment, the Court has upheld some restrictions on student speech. For example, in *Bethel School District No. 403 v. Fraser*, 478 U.S. 675 (1986), the Court upheld a disciplinary action against a high school student who delivered a sexually explicit speech at a school assembly during which he nominated a fellow student for student elective office. The Court distinguished *Tinker* on the basis that the sanctions were not viewpoint based, as well as on the basis that school officials might legitimately conclude that the student's "vulgar and lewd speech" might "undermine the school's basic educational mission." Likewise, in *Morse v. Frederick,* 551 U.S. 393 (2007), the Court upheld a principal's decision to suspend a student who displayed a banner with the words "Bong Hits for Jesus" at a school event (students had gone outside of the school, during the school day, to witness a runner bearing the Olympic torch go by). The Court held that "schools may take steps to safeguard those entrusted to their care from speech that can reasonably be regarded as encouraging illegal drug use." The Court emphasized the important governmental interest in deterring drug use by schoolchildren, and the strong interest of schools in educating students regarding the dangers of drug use.

In *Hazelwood School District v. Kuhlmeier*, 484 U.S. 260 (1988), the Court upheld a high school principal's decision to require students to delete two pages from the school's newspaper. The pages dealt with students' experiences with pregnancy and the impact of divorce on students at the school. In rejecting the students' First Amendment claims, the Court held that a "school need not tolerate student speech that is inconsistent with its 'basic educational mission,' " and that school officials should be given deference in determining what speech is inappropriate. Moreover, the Court refused to hold that the newspaper was a forum for public expression concluding, instead, that it was "a supervised learning experience for journalism students." As a result, the Court held that school officials could impose reasonable regulations on the content of the newspaper, especially since students, parents, and members of the public might reasonably perceive the paper to bear the imprimatur of the school. In upholding the action, the Court focused on the nature of the topics being discussed and the way in which they were discussed, noting that student' identities were not adequately protected, and that "the article was not sufficiently sensitive to the privacy interests of the students' boyfriends and parents, who were discussed in the article but who were given no opportunity to consent to its publication or to offer a response." In addition, one student made critical comments about her father which the "principal could reasonably have concluded that an individual publicly identified as an inattentive parent was entitled to an opportunity to defend himself as a matter of journalistic fairness."

But there are limits to the ability of school officials to suppress expression even in the school environment. For example, in *Board of Education v. Pico*, 457 U.S. 853 (1982), a local school board ordered the removal of certain books from high school and junior high school libraries on the basis that they were "anti-American, anti-Christian, anti-Semitic, and just plain filthy." The Board stated that "it is our duty, our moral obligation, to protect the children in our schools from this moral danger as surely as from physical and medical dangers." Five students sued the school district, alleging that the board had ordered the removal "because particular passages in the books offended their social, political and moral tastes and not because the books, taken as a whole, were lacking in educational value," and arguing that the board's actions violated their rights under the First Amendment. A plurality of the Court held that while school officials have "significant discretion to determine the content of their school libraries," they may not exercise their discretion "in a narrowly partisan or political manner." Moreover, the "Constitution does not permit the official suppression of *ideas*." As a result, if "petitioners *intended* by their removal decision to deny respondents access to ideas with which petitioners disagreed, and if this intent was the decisive factor in petitioners' decision, then petitioners have exercised their discretion in violation of the Constitution."

A school's attempt to regulate student speech becomes more problematic when the speech occurs off-campus. The school may still have some justification for limiting student speech in that context, but courts will examine the school's actions much more closely. For example, in *Mahanoy Area School District v. B.L.*, 594 U.S. 180 (2021), after a young woman was denied her preferred position on the school's softball team, and was also relegated to the junior varsity cheerleading squad, she created vulgar Snapchat posts (which disappear within a 24-hour period) and distributed them to about 250 "friends," including schoolmates The first post showed B. L. and a friend with middle fingers raised and it bore the caption: "Fuck school fuck softball fuck cheer fuck everything." The second image was blank but for a caption, which read: "Love how me and another student get told we need a year of jv before we make varsity but that doesn't matter to anyone else?" The caption also contained an upside-down smiley-face emoji. The images were shared with other members of the cheerleading squad and eventually came to the attention of school officials. Because the posts used profanity in connection with a school extracurricular activity, school officials decided that they violated team and school rules, and suspended B. L. from the junior varsity cheerleading squad for the upcoming year.

The Court held that school officials had violated B. L.'s First Amendment rights. The Court reaffirmed earlier decisions, suggesting that school officials may regulate student speech in several different situations, involving (1) "indecent," "lewd," or "vulgar" speech uttered during a school assembly on school grounds; (2) speech, uttered during a class trip, that promotes "illegal drug use"; and (3) speech that others may reasonably perceive as "bearing the imprimatur of the school," such as that appearing in a school-sponsored newspaper. Although the Court viewed off-campus speech as less subject to regulation, it recognized that school officials may have an interest in regulating off-campus speech in some contexts (*e.g.*, when there is serious or severe bullying or harassment targeting particular individuals; threats aimed at teachers or other students; the failure to follow rules concerning lessons, the writing of papers, the use of computers, or participation in other online school activities; and breaches of school security devices, including material maintained within school computers). In addition, the Court hypothesized that school authorities might be able to exercise control in other situations "when the school is responsible for the student; the school's immediate surroundings; travel en route to and from the school; all speech taking place over school laptops or on a school's website; speech taking place during remote learning; activities taken for school credit; and communications to school e-mail accounts or phones."

Nevertheless, the Court distinguished a school's regulation of off-campus speech from its regulation of in-school speech. The Court saw three main differences: "*First*, the doctrine of *in loco parentis* treats school administrators as standing in the place of students' parents under circumstances where the children's actual parents cannot protect, guide, and discipline them. Geographically speaking, off-campus speech will normally fall within the zone of parental, rather than school-related, responsibility. *Second*, regulations of off-campus speech, when coupled with regulations of on-campus speech, include all the speech a student utters during the full 24-hour day. Courts must be skeptical of a school's efforts to regulate off-campus speech, for doing so may mean the student cannot engage in that kind of speech at all. When it comes to political or religious speech that occurs outside school or a school program or activity, the school will have a heavy burden to justify intervention. *Third*, the school has an interest in protecting a student's unpopular expression, especially when the expression takes place off campus. "America's public schools are the nurseries of democracy. Our representative democracy only works if we protect the "marketplace of ideas." This free exchange facilitates an informed public opinion, which, when transmitted to lawmakers, helps produce laws that reflect the People's will. That protection must include the protection of unpopular ideas, for popular ideas have less need for protection."

Applying these principles, the Court concluded that B. L.'s speech was entitled to First Amendment protection. The Court recognized that her speech was vulgar and involved "criticism, of the team, the team's coaches, and the school—in a word or two, criticism of the rules of a community of which B. L. forms a part." However, the Court emphasized that the speech was not obscene and would generally be regarded as "the kind of pure speech to which, were she an adult, the First Amendment would provide strong protection," and was made outside of school hours from a non-school location. Finally, B. L. "did not identify the school in her posts or target any member of the school community with vulgar or abusive language," and she "transmitted her speech through a personal cellphone, to an audience consisting of her private circle of Snapchat friends." As a result, the Court held that the school had a diminished interest in punishing B. L.'s utterance.

While the Court recognized that the school might have an interest in prohibiting students from using vulgar language to criticize a school team or its coaches, the Court held that the "strength of this anti-vulgarity interest is weakened considerably by the fact that B. L. spoke outside the school on her own time" so that "there is no reason to believe B. L.'s parents had delegated to school officials their control of B. L.'s behavior" at that time. Moreover, the school was unable to show that it had otherwise acted to control student vulgarity outside the school environment. Also, referencing *Tinker*, the Court emphasized that there was no "no evidence of 'substantial disruption' of a school activity or a threatened harm to the rights of others that might justify the school's action." At most, a small amount of time (5 to 10 minutes) was spent discussing the matter in a class, and some members of the cheerleading squad were upset. Finally, the Court concluded that there was "little to suggest any serious decline in team morale—to the point where it could create a substantial interference in, or disruption of, the school's efforts to maintain team cohesion."

Government Financed Speech. In some instances, the government provides financial support for speech, and questions have arisen regarding the government's right to dictate the message for which it pays. In some instances, these issues arise under the unconstitutional conditions doctrine discussed earlier.

When the government is financing speech, the Court has been more willing to allow the government to impose restrictions. Illustrative is *Rust v. Sullivan*, 500 U.S. 173 (1991), in which a federal statute provided funding for "preventive family planning services, population research, infertility services, and other related medical, informational, and educational activities," but specifically precluded the use of funds for "programs where abortion is a method of family planning." In addition, the Secretary promulgated regulations imposing three additional restrictions: First, a "Title X project may not provide counseling concerning the use of abortion as a method of family planning or provide referral for abortion as a method of family planning." Second, the regulations broadly prohibited a Title X project from engaging in activities that "encourage, promote or advocate abortion as a method of family planning." Third, the regulations required that Title X projects be organized so that they are "physically and financially separate" from prohibited abortion activities.

The regulations were challenged by a group of Title X grantees, and doctors who supervised Title X funds, who claimed that the regulations violated the rights of Title X clients and the First Amendment rights of Title X health providers. The Court rejected the argument that the regulations imposed "viewpoint" based restrictions on speech, holding that the government may "selectively fund a program to encourage certain activities it believes to be in the public interest, without at the same time funding an alternative program which seeks to deal with the problem in another way." In other words, the regulatory restrictions are simply "designed to ensure that the limits of the federal program are observed." "This is not a case of the Government 'suppressing a dangerous idea,' " but of a prohibition on a project grantee or its employees from engaging in activities outside of the project's scope." The Court also found that the regulations did not significantly impinge the doctor-patient relationship because they did not require doctors to make statements that they did not believe to be true, and the program was not so "all encompassing" as to make patients believe that they were receiving comprehensive medical advice. Indeed, the program did not provide post-conception medical care, and therefore a doctor's silence with regard to abortion cannot reasonably be thought to mislead a client into thinking that the doctor does not consider abortion an appropriate option for her. In any event, the doctor was free to state that abortion alternatives are beyond the program's scope. *Rust* also rejected the argument that the government had imposed an unconstitutional condition by conditioning Title X funding on the relinquishment of speech rights.

There has been considerable litigation regarding funding by the National Endowment for the Arts. There was controversy over a grant that funded a retrospective on photographer Robert Mapplethorpe's *The Perfect Moment*, which included homoerotic photographs that some condemned as pornographic, and further controversy over Andres Serrano's work *Piss Christ*, which involved a photograph of a crucifix immersed in urine. Because of the controversy, Congress amended the statute governing NEA grants to require the Chairperson of the National Endowment for the Arts (NEA) to ensure that "artistic excellence and artistic merit are the criteria by which [grant] applications are judged, taking into consideration general standards of decency and respect for the diverse beliefs and values of the American public." 20 U.S.C. § 954(d)(1).

In *National Endowment for the Arts v. Finley*, 524 U.S. 569 (1998), the Court upheld the amendments, rejecting claims of viewpoint discrimination. The Court noted that the law imposed no categorical prohibition against any type of speech other than obscenity, and simply admonished the NEA to take factors like "decency and respect" into consideration. As a result, the Court rejected the argument that the criteria were sufficiently "subjective" that they could be used to engage in viewpoint discrimination: "The NEA has limited resources and it must deny the majority of the grant applications that it receives, including many that propose 'artistically excellent' projects. Absolute neutrality is simply 'inconceivable.' "

Despite the holdings in *Rust* and *Finley*, the government does not have unfettered discretion when it decides to fund speech. As noted earlier in *Legal Services Corp. v. Velazquez,* 531 U.S. 533 (2001), the Court struck down restrictions imposed on governmentally funded lawyers that prevented them from raising constitutional issues on behalf of their clients.

The Press Clause. Since the press clause specifically mentions the press, some have argued that the Framers intended to distinguish it from the speech clause. Justice Stewart referred to the press clause as a "*structural* provision" that "extends protection to an institution." Potter Stewart, *Of the Press*, 26 HASTINGS L.J. 631, 633–34 (1975). Under this view, the press clause provides the basis for giving different and special protections to the media, including protections against being forced to give grand jury testimony, protections against newsroom searches, access to prison facilities, and access to judicial proceedings. Chief Justice Burger disagreed, arguing that the press clause provides the press with no special rights. He perceived "no difference between the right of those who seek to disseminate ideas by way of a newspaper and those who give lectures or speeches and seek to enlarge the audience by publication and wide dissemination." *First National Bank of Boston v. Bellotti*, 435 U.S. 765, 801–02 (1978) (Burger, C.J., concurring). As a result, he did not view the press as some special preserve of a "definable category of persons or entities." In general, the Court has rejected the notion that the press has a special status that provides it with special rights over and above the speech rights of other citizens. Case law suggests that the Court does not view the press as an institution, but as simply part of an overall process that is critical to informed self-governance.

Even if the press is not accorded special privileges, the press has historically performed a unique and important role in enlightening and educating the public. During the colonial period, newspapers and pamphleteers were active in the revolutionary discourse. Since the nation's founding, the press has continued to play a crucial role in informing the public. In construing the press clause, the Court has tended to focus on function rather than institutional structure. As a result, the press clause provides as much protection to the producers of pamphlets and circulars as it does to a "large metropolitan publisher."

Reporter's Privilege. In the process of investigating and reporting, the press sometimes acquires information that may be of interest to governmental officials, especially the police. However, in some instances, reporters may have obtained this information by making a promise of confidentiality. In *Branzburg v. Hayes*, 408 U.S. 665, 704 (1972), the Court rejected the notion that reporters have a First Amendment privilege that shields them from being forced to testify before grand juries regarding their sources. Despite arguments that reporters must be able to protect the confidentiality of their sources, for fear that they will have less information available to them, the Court has held that the press has the same obligation as anyone else to provide testimony before a grand jury. Because the press flourished without a privilege in the past, the Court questioned whether it was needed for the press to perform its function. Following *Branzburg*, some states have legislatively provided reporters with a shield that protects their sources. The nature and scope of these legislated privileges vary, as do the levels of protection. In some instances, courts have subordinated even seemingly absolute privileges to a defendant's right to a fair trial.

Given the holding in *Branzburg*, there is a risk that a reporter may breach a promise of confidentiality. In *Cohen v. Cowles Media Co.*, 501 U.S. 663 (1991), the Court held that the First Amendment permitted a breach of contract claim against a reporter who obtained information from a political campaign aide in exchange for a promise of confidentiality, but who later breached that promise. In imposing liability, the Court held that the First Amendment protects the right to publish lawfully acquired information, but that the promise of confidentiality creates an enforceable contractual obligation. The Court also rejected a newsworthiness defense premised on the idea that the breach provided the public (and, more particularly, voters) with relevant and important information.

Newsroom Searches. Just as reporters can be subpoenaed to appear and testify before grand juries, prosecutors sometimes obtain warrants to search newsrooms. In *Zurcher v. Stanford Daily*, 436 U.S. 547 (1978), the Court held that a newsroom search did not violate the First Amendment. It noted that news organizations have no special immunity against search warrants. The Court also held that a prosecutor is not required to proceed by subpoena in seeking information from a newspaper, provided that Fourth Amendment requirements are observed with "scrupulous exactitude" when First Amendment interests are implicated. Congress responded to *Zurcher* by enacting the Privacy Protection Act of 1980, 42 U.S.C. §§ 2000aa–1–2000aa–12 (1980), which established a preference for subpoenas as a means for obtaining evidence from news organizations. The Act created exceptions for situations when the information holder is suspected of a crime, as well as when there are exigent circumstances relating to life, serious injury or loss of evidence.

Access to Prisons. In *Pell v. Procunier*, 417 U.S. 817 (1974), and *Saxbe v. Washington Post Co.*, 417 U.S. 843 (1974), the Court upheld state and federal prison regulations prohibiting media interviews with inmates. The Court emphasized that the prisoners themselves have reduced First Amendment rights, that prisons have a need for increased security, and that courts should not second guess prison administrators. Likewise, in *Beard v. Banks*, 548 U.S. 521 (2006), the Court upheld a prison policy that denied newspapers and magazines access to a group of especially dangerous and recalcitrant inmates. The Court emphasized the importance of deferring to prison officials, especially in cases involving inmates who have been "continually disruptive, violent, dangerous or a threat to the orderly operation of their assigned facility." Finally, in *Houchins v. KQED, Inc.*, 438 U.S. 1 (1978), the Court upheld a decision to deny access to the part of a jail where a prisoner had committed suicide. A plurality concluded that the First Amendment provides the press with no greater right of access than is available to the public.

Access to Judicial Proceedings. Generally, the courts have held that the public has a right to information regarding judicial proceedings, especially criminal proceedings, and that the press and the public have a right of access to such proceedings. This right was first recognized in *Richmond Newspapers, Inc. v. Virginia*, 448 U.S. 555 (1980), when the Court invalidated an order that closed a trial to the press and the public. Likewise, in *Globe Newspapers, Inc. v. Superior Court*, 457 U.S. 596 (1982), the Court struck down a state law that required the closure of judicial proceedings in cases involving a juvenile victim of a sex offense. The Court emphasized that such proceedings had traditionally been open to the public, and noted that public access and openness provide a safeguard against judicial abuse. The Court rejected the state's argument that closure was necessary to protect minors from further harm or embarrassment, as well as to encourage them to freely testify. The Court applied strict scrutiny, noting that closure must be supported by a compelling governmental interest that is narrowly tailored to serve that interest. Although the protection of minor sex offense victims was a compelling interest, the Court held that it did not justify mandatory closure.

The Court has extended access rights to other judicial proceedings. In *Press-Enterprise v. Superior Court*, 464 U.S. 501 (1984), it held that a court could not close a *voir dire* proceeding absent an "overriding governmental interest" and a finding "that closure is necessary to ensure higher values and is narrowly tailored to serve that interest." Likewise, in *Waller v. Georgia*, 467 U.S. 39 (1984), the Court held that a trial court could not close a preliminary hearing when the defendant objected to closure. Finally, in *Press-Enterprise Co. v. Superior Court*, 478 U.S. 1 (1986), the Court held that the press and public have a right of access to some pretrial hearings. To decide whether a pretrial hearing may be closed, the trial court must first determine whether the particular process has a tradition of openness. With respect to pretrial hearings, the Court emphasized the need for openness. It concluded that closure was only permissible when there is a substantial probability that fair trial rights will be compromised and there are no reasonable alternatives.

The Media and Fair Trials. Media presence at a criminal trial creates potential tension with a defendant's interest in a trial free of prejudicial publicity. At issue in these circumstances is the right to a fair trial, protected under the Fifth and Fourteenth Amendment due process clauses, and the Sixth Amendment guarantee of a "public trial, by an impartial jury." In *Sheppard v. Maxwell*, 384 U.S. 333 (1966), the Court overturned a murder conviction because it was influenced by massive and prejudicial pretrial publicity and disruptive media conduct during the trial. Not only did the press publish extra-judicial evidence (suggestive of defendant's guilt), it also published the juror's identities. In addition, the judge did not sequester the jury until deliberations began. Even then the jurors were given great freedom. Reporters were given ready access to the courtroom, and the judge took few steps to control pretrial publicity. Although the Court recognized the importance of First Amendment interests, it held that the trial judge was required to take steps to ensure defendant's right to a fair trial. It reversed the defendant's conviction because he had been denied due process.

Although *Sheppard* holds that courts must take steps as needed to ensure a fair trial, the balance cuts in favor of the public's right to be informed regarding those proceedings. Even though a trial may be open, the trial court judge can limit the number of media representatives present in the courtroom and can establish rules for press decorum. The judge can also use the *voir dire* process to screen out jurors who have been unfairly influenced by prejudicial pretrial publicity, and can sequester jurors to limit their exposure to external influences, including the press. Other possible actions include a change of venue or a continuance, or even a gag order directed at parties, witnesses, counsel, police, or other participants. A trial judge must be active in terms of protecting the integrity of the trial process, while maintaining a proceeding that is open to the press and public.

In *Nebraska Press Association v. Stuart*, 427 U.S. 539 (1976), the Court struck down a pretrial order that prohibited the media from publishing confessions made to police. The gag order also barred the media from reporting information obtained during a preliminary hearing, as well as from disseminating any information that strongly implicated the defendant. The Court emphasized that prior restraints are the "most serious and the least tolerable infringement on First Amendment rights." They are subject to a strong presumption of unconstitutionality and are subject to a heavy burden of justification. Although the case involved a substantial risk of prejudicial publicity, the Court concluded that the trial judge had less drastic means at his disposal.

The Court has been more willing to uphold speech restrictions imposed upon parties to a judicial proceeding and their attorneys. In *Gentile v. State Bar of Nevada*, 501 U.S. 1030 (1991), the Court held that restrictions could be imposed on the parties and their attorneys when there is a "substantial likelihood of material prejudice." Although *Stuart* did not completely reject the possibility of a gag order, it did suggest that several requirements must be satisfied before one could be imposed. First, the trial court must determine that there is a clear and present danger (as opposed to a simple "possibility") that pretrial publicity will undermine the defendant's right to a fair trial. Second, even if a clear and present danger exists, the trial judge must find that alternatives to a gag order (*e.g.*, continuance or change of venue) are inadequate. Third, the trial court must determine that the gag order will actually be effective. Finally, the trial court may not restrain the media from accurately reporting information acquired in open court.

In 2019, Roger Stone, a special adviser to President Trump, was indicted for lying to Congress regarding his communications with WikiLeaks and its founder, Julian Assange, as well as for witness tampering and obstruction of an investigation. The judge entered an order prohibiting Stone, his attorneys, and attorneys working for Special Counsel Robert Mueller, from making public statements that could bias any jurors who might be selected to hear the case. The judge tightened the gag order after Stone published a picture of her in the sights of a rifle, and she prohibited Stone from doing media interviews and social media posts related to the case. She did allow Stone to claim his innocence in emails seeking contributions for his defense fund.

Cameras in the Courtroom. The Court's attitude towards video coverage has changed over time. Because of due process concerns, early decisions disfavored cameras in the courtroom. In *Estes v. Texas,* 381 U.S. 532 (1965), the Court found a due process violation based on the presence of television cameras in the courtroom. The Court expressed fear that their presence might distract jurors, parties, witnesses, lawyers, and judges, as well as diminish the quality of legal representation. However, in *Chandler v. Florida*, 449 U.S. 560 (1981), the Court held that the mere presence of cameras in the courtroom did not automatically violate due process. It held that a defendant must prove actual prejudice (in the sense that the presence of cameras impaired the jurors' ability to decide the case based on the evidence presented, or that their presence adversely affected the trial) in order to establish a due process claim.

Because of the coronavirus pandemic, which required closure of the Supreme Court building, for the first time, the Court heard oral arguments by telephone and allowed the audio to be streamed online and on C-Span. Nina Totenberg, *Supreme Court Arguments Resume, But with a Twist*, NPR, May 4, 2020, https://www.npr.org/2020/05/04/847785015/supreme-court-arguments-resume-but-with-a-twist.

Media, Technology and the First Amendment. Over the centuries, media technology has changed dramatically. When the First Amendment was framed and ratified, the dominant technology was the printing press which could be used to create newspapers, pamphlets and letters. Over time, the printing press was supplemented by other technologies, including the telegraph, radio, television and movies. Newer technologies include cable, satellite radio and television, cell phone text messaging, blogs, and the internet. Moreover, the nature of press ownership has changed as large media corporations have come into existence and altered the media landscape with mass produced information.

As technology has evolved, the courts have expanded the reach of the First Amendment. The Court, in *Mutual Film Corporation v. Industrial Commission of Ohio*, 236 U.S. 230 (1915), found that motion pictures did not come within the definition of the press. Later, the Court reversed itself and held that motion pictures qualify as the "press" and are therefore protected under the First Amendment. *Joseph Burstyn, Inc. v. Wilson*, 343 U.S. 495 (1952); *United States v. Paramount Pictures, Inc.,* 334 U.S. 131 (1948). And the Court has developed medium specific standards for evaluating different types of technology. As the Court recognized, in *Joseph Burstyn, Inc. v.*

Wilson, 343 U.S. 495 (1952), "each [medium] tends to present its own peculiar problems."

The Print Media. The print media existed when the First Amendment was ratified and clearly was within the contemplation of the Framers. Courts historically have applied the highest level of scrutiny to governmental efforts to regulate press content. For example, in *Miami Herald Publishing Co. v. Tornillo,* 418 U.S. 241 (1974), the Court struck down a state law that required newspapers to provide equal space for political candidates who they attacked editorially. The Court was concerned that, if newspapers were required to grant individuals a right of reply, editors might be reluctant to publish attacks for fear that they would have to create space for the reply.

Broadcasting. The Court generally has provided less protection to the broadcast media. As the Court indicated in *Federal Communications Commission v. Pacifica Foundation*, 438 U.S. 726 (1978), "of all forms of communication, it is broadcasting that has received the most limited First Amendment protection." In *Red Lion Broadcasting Co. v. Federal Communications Commission*, 395 U.S. 367 (1969), the Court thus upheld the Federal Communication Commission's "Fairness Doctrine." This rule required broadcasters to provide balanced coverage of controversial issues. The Court held that broadcasters have diminished First Amendment protection because they use a scarce resource (i.e., the broadcast spectrum). The Fairness Doctrine thus established the public's right "to receive suitable access to social, political, esthetic, moral, and other ideas." Ultimately, the Federal Communications Commission (FCC) reconsidered and abandoned the Fairness Doctrine.

Despite the *Red Lion* decision, the Court has recognized that the broadcast media is entitled to exercise some control over broadcasting content. In *Columbia Broadcasting System, Inc. v. Democratic National Committee,* 412 U.S. 94 (1973), the Court held that broadcasters retain editorial freedom regarding whether to accept political advertisements from the public. Thus, broadcasters are not required to function like common carriers and accept all comers (advertisements).

Although the Fairness Doctrine required broadcasters to provide fair and balanced coverage of important public issues, the Court emphasized that broadcasters could determine the method of coverage. The Court, in *Federal Communications Commission v. League of Women Voters,* 468 U.S. 364 (1984), struck down a law that prohibited public broadcasters from editorializing or endorsing political candidates. It introduced a standard of review that requires government to demonstrate the existence of an important government interest and the law must be narrowly tailored to achieve that interest. Although the Court identified an important governmental interest (shielding public broadcasters from funding cutbacks imposed as political retaliation for their expressed views), the Court held that there were less speech restrictive means of pursuing this interest (*e.g.*, providing opportunities for competing viewpoints).

The Court has generally provided less protection to sexually explicit but non-obscene expression in the broadcast format. At issue in *Federal Communications Commission v. Pacifica Foundation*, 438 U.S. 726 (1978), was a mid-afternoon broadcast of a famous comedian's monologue entitled "Filthy Words." The broadcast was aired as part of a program on contemporary attitudes towards speech, and was preceded by warnings that it might offend some viewers. In upholding the FCC's determination, the Court concluded that the scarcity rationale was not implicated. It identified two other aspects of broadcasting that warrant special restrictions: broadcasting's "uniquely pervasive presence in the lives of all Americans" and the fact that the broadcast medium is "uniquely accessible to children, even those too young to read." The Court's concerns regarding pervasiveness reflected a privacy concern insofar as individuals were exposed to unwanted expression in their homes or in public. The Court suggested that a program of this nature might be permissible if it were confined to late night hours when children were less likely to be listening.

In *Federal Communications Commission v. Fox Television Stations, Inc.*, 556 U.S. 502 (2009), the Court upheld the FCC's ban on fleeting expletives. Historically, the FCC had maintained that the fleeting use of expletives weighed against a finding of indecency. In 2004, the FCC concluded that even a fleeting expletive could be regarded as indecent even though the word was used as an intensifier (*e.g.*, this is "f_______ brilliant") rather than as a literal descriptor. The FCC concluded that "the F-Word is one of the most vulgar, graphic and explicit descriptions of sexual activity in the English language, because its use invariably invokes a coarse sexual image, as well as because the Court viewed the language as entirely shocking and gratuitous" The "Commission could reasonably conclude that the pervasiveness of foul language, and the coarsening of public entertainment in other media such as cable, justify more stringent regulation of broadcast programs so as to give conscientious parents a relatively safe haven for their children."

In *FCC v. Fox Television Stations, Inc.*, 567 U.S. 239 (2012) (Fox II), the Court issued a narrow ruling that the FCC had violated due process by its lack of fair notice to Fox and ABC "that a fleeting expletive or a brief shot of nudity could be actionably indecent." With regard to Fox, the FCC did not impose a fine for the two offending broadcasts, and therefore the FCC argued that Fox could not bring a vagueness challenge. However, the Court rejected that argument because the FCC possessed the authority to take the history of the violation into account when setting future penalties, and because the wide publicity of FCC sanctions would cause reputational injury to Fox. As for ABC, which was penalized $1.4 million dollars for the fleeting nudity broadcast, the Court pointed to FCC rulings that found 30 seconds of nudity to be nonactionable, echoing the pre-Golden Globes rulings that treated Fox's type of fleeting expletives as nonactionable. The *Fox II* Court observed that because it "resolves these cases on fair notice grounds under the Due Process Clause, it need not address the First Amendment implications of the FCC's indecency policy." After noting the vagueness issue, the Court concluded by saying, "This opinion leaves the Commission free to modify its current indecency policy in light of its determination of the public interest and applicable legal requirements. And it leaves the courts free to review the current policy or any modified policy in light of its content and application."

Cable Television. The development of cable television facilitated the retransmission of broadcast signals to remote areas that could not easily receive broadcast signals. Cable television as it developed, became distinguishable from broadcasting because it had far more channels and programming options. Broadcast signals are distinguishable from cable by the fact that they are transmitted through the air, whereas cable signals travel through coaxial cable or fiber optic lines. Broadcasters also are licensed by the FCC, whereas cable operators receive franchises from local governments. Unlike broadcasting, spectrum scarcity is not a problem with cable television. Most cable companies offer dozens, if not hundreds, of channels. Most communities, however, are served by a single cable operator who can control content. Despite this gatekeeper function, the Court has differentiated cable from broadcasting.

In *City of Los Angeles v. Preferred Communications, Inc.*, 476 U.S. 488 (1986), the Court held that cable is entitled to First Amendment protection. It did not indicate, however, whether cable should receive the lesser level of protection provided to broadcasters or the higher level of protection accorded to the print media. Although the Court stated that cable television "partakes of some of the aspects of speech and the communication of ideas as do the traditional enterprises of newspaper and book publishers, public speakers, and pamphleteers," it also stated that the cable industry appears to "implicate First Amendment interests as do the activities of wireless broadcasters."

The Court, in *Turner Broadcasting System, Inc. v. Federal Communications Commission*, 512 U.S. 622 (1994), upheld federal rules that required cable operators to carry the signals of local broadcasters ("must carry rules") despite claims that they interfered with editorial discretion. Having found that they were not content-based, the Court did not view the must carry rules as an invasion of editorial freedom. As a result, the Court applied the content-neutral analysis and lower standard of review articulated in *United States v. O'Brien*, 391 U.S. 367 (1968). The government thus was required to show an important or substantial governmental interest, that is unrelated to suppression of expression and restricts speech no more extensively than necessary to further its interest. The Court found substantial governmental interests (preservation of free local broadcasting, preservation of diverse information sources, and maintenance of fair competition in television programming). Following a remand of the case to the lower court, the Court found that the rules directly advanced those concerns. It noted that the cable industry had an interest in minimizing broadcasting's status as a competitor. The narrowly tailored requirement was satisfied because the number of broadcast signals being carried did not exceed the number of cable channels that were displaced. The Court thus concluded that the must carry rules did not implicate editorial freedom issues.

Problems with "indecent" programming have also arisen with regard to cable television. Congress in 1992 enacted legislation requiring the FCC to implement indecency controls for leased access channels and public access channels. Under this law, cable television operators were (1) allowed to prohibit patently offensive programming from leased access channels; (2) required to segregate such programming on a single channel and block it or unblock it upon the subscriber's written request; and (3) allowed to prohibit patently offensive programming from public, educational, and government access channels.

In *Denver Area Educational Telecommunications Consortium, Inc. v. Federal Communications Commission*, 518 U.S. 727 (1996), the Court upheld the authority of cable operators to prohibit patently offensive programming on leased channels but struck down the block and segregate provisions and a prohibition on public, educational, and government access channels. A plurality of four justices applied strict scrutiny. In so doing, they found that the content restrictions for leased access channels were justified by a compelling state interest in protecting children and were narrowly tailored. The plurality also suggested that cable operators had historically exercised editorial control over leased access channels. A majority of the Court struck down the segregate and block requirement on grounds it was not the least restrictive alternative. The blocking and unblocking requirement entailed a 30 day notice from subscribers. The Court concluded that this requirement imposed a planning burden upon subscribers, and exposed them to potential embarrassment if their names were disclosed. It suggested that blocking devices might serve the government's interest in protecting children without excessively burdening speech. In regard to the public access provision, the Court concluded that it did not represent the least restrictive alternative. A three-justice plurality concluded that public access channels typically are subject to more extensive self-policing controls. Unlike leased access channels, that draw programming from a multiplicity of sources, public access channels typically are overseen by a government unit or entity that has mainstream orientations.

The Court reviewed a federal law in *United States v. Playboy Entertainment Group*, 529 U.S. 803 (2000), requiring cable and direct broadcast satellite operators to scramble audio and video signals for channels dedicated to sexually explicit programs. The law was designed to shield non-subscribers from program bleed. It also prohibited unscrambled signals except between 10:00pm and 6:00am. The Court adopted strict scrutiny as the standard of review for content regulation in the context of cable, and found a compelling state interest related to the protection of children. It concluded, however, that there was insufficient evidence that children are likely to be exposed, and therefore that a less restrictive alternative existed in the ability of parents to block certain channels.

Telephone. Telephones constitute one of the older electronic communication devices, and providers of telephone service historically have been regarded as common carriers. Since common carriers must provide access to anyone who can pay for the service, telephone providers do not have editorial discretion. Originators of content provided by telephone, however, have a First Amendment interest. In *Sable Broadcasting, Inc. v. Federal Communications Commission*, 492 U.S. 115 (1989), the Court struck down a law that banned obscene communications and indecent dial-a-porn services. The Court distinguished broadcasting regulation from telephonic communications on the basis that they involve significantly different risks. Telephone communications are not as "uniquely pervasive", insofar as individuals must take affirmative steps to access the content. The Court applied strict scrutiny and concluded that the government's interest in protecting children was compelling.

However, it held that the government had alternatives available to it that were less restrictive than a ban on indecent communications (*e.g.*, credit cards and access codes).

Internet. The internet has emerged as perhaps the most significant communications medium in recent decades. Its impact has been so profound that the internet ultimately may force the Court to reassess its medium-specific analytical model. The internet does not exist in isolation, but in conjunction with other media. Most newspapers and magazines offer their content online. In addition, they use over-the-air signals, telephone lines, and satellite transmissions to transport content from editorial rooms to printing and distribution centers. These developments challenge the logic of medium-specific analysis.

Citing the pervasive nature of the internet and its availability to children, Congress enacted the Communications Decency Act of 1996 (CDA). The CDA prohibited the knowing dissemination of indecent messages to persons under the age of 18 and the knowing dissemination of "patently offensive" messages that would be available to persons under this age. In *Reno v. American Civil Liberties Union*, 521 U.S. 844 (1997), the Court struck down the law. It equated the internet with print media and thus accorded it the highest level of constitutional protection. Unlike broadcasting, which is characterized by spectrum limitations, the internet is almost universally accessible through personal computers, libraries and cyber-cafes. Moreover, the Court noted a historical absence of governmental regulation and lack of intrusiveness.

Applying strict scrutiny, the Court found a compelling governmental interest in the desire to protect children from exposure to indecent material. However, because the CDA could not be enforced against foreign sites, and age is difficult to verify, the Court concluded that the regulatory means could not effectively achieve their purpose. Moreover, the CDA imposed a significant burden on adult users by limiting their right to receive information unsuitable for children. The Court concluded that Congress could use less constitutionally restrictive means, including blocking or filtering software, to achieve its objectives. Justice O'Connor would have upheld provisions of the legislation that prohibited knowing transmission, such as emails, of indecent materials to minors.

TikTok Inc. v. Garland, 604 U.S. 56 (2025), involved national security issues. In that case, Congress required that TikTok (an app which allows users to create and post short videos) be severed from the control of ByteDance Ltd., or it would be forced to cease operations in the U.S. At the time, TikTok was an American company that was owned by ByteDance Ltd., a privately held Chinese company. The law was challenged by TikTok as well as by users and content creators on the platform. The government sought to support the law on national security grounds, claiming that TikTok can access "any data stored in the user's contact list," including names, contact information, contact photos, job titles. Access to such detailed information about U. S. users, the Government worried, may enable "China to track the locations of Federal employees and contractors, build dossiers of personal information for blackmail, and conduct corporate espionage." Moreover, Chinese law required ByteDance to surrender data to the Chinese government, "making companies headquartered there an espionage tool" of China. Since the Act did not limit the free speech rights of those who post videos on TikTok, in that they could post elsewhere, the real impact of the Act was to require ByteDance to divest. The Court treated the law as content-neutral, applied intermediate scrutiny, and upheld the law. The Court applied intermediate scrutiny, and held that the government interest in preventing China—a designated foreign adversary—from leveraging its control over ByteDance Ltd. to capture the personal data of U.S. TikTok users qualified as an important Government interest. In addition, the Court deferred to Congress' conclusion that there was a sufficient probability that China would compel TikTok to turn over user data for intelligence-gathering purposes, and the Court held that the Act was sufficiently tailored to address the Government's interest in preventing a foreign adversary from collecting vast swaths of sensitive data about the 170 million U. S. persons who use TikTok.

Twitter, Inc. v. Taameh, 598 U.S. 471 (2023), involved a suit under 18 U. S. C. § 2333, which gives those who have been "injured by reason of an act of international terrorism" the right to sue for damages. Plaintiffs, who were injured by a ISIS terrorist attack in Turkey, sued three large social-media companies (Facebook, Twitter and Google) for allegedly aiding and abetting the ISIS attacks. Plaintiffs alleged that the companies knew that ISIS was using their platforms to recruit terrorists and raise funds, but failed to stop it. Of course, the platforms function by allowing users to post content and then using algorithms to match users with content similar to what they have previously viewed. In addition, the platforms sometimes made income from advertisements displayed with the content.

The Court held that the platforms could not be held liable as an aiders and abettors unless they consciously and culpably "participated in" a tortious act in such a way as to help "it succeed." The Court noted that the platforms' "recommendation" algorithms [which funnel information to platform users based on their browsing history] are merely part of their infrastructure and are used in conjunction with all content on their sites (and not just terrorist content). In addition, the algorithms are agnostic as to the nature of the content, matching any content (including ISIS' content) with any user who is more likely to view that content. In the Court's view, the mere fact that the algorithms matched ISIS content with some users does not convert defendants' passive assistance into active abetting." The Court viewed any connection between the platforms and the terrorist act as "highly attenuated": "Plaintiffs point to no act of encouraging, soliciting, or advising the commission of the attack that would normally support an aiding-and-abetting claim." Rather, they essentially portray defendants as bystanders, watching passively as ISIS carried out its nefarious schemes. Such allegations do not state a claim for culpable assistance or participation in the attack. "Plaintiffs have failed to allege that defendants intentionally provided any substantial aid to the attack or otherwise consciously participated in the attack—much less that defendants so pervasively and systemically assisted ISIS as to render them liable for every ISIS attack."

Moody v. Netchoice, LLC, 603 U.S. 707 (2024), involved Texas and Florida laws which sought to limit the ability of social media platforms to moderate content on their platforms. Both states expressed concern that social media platforms were discriminating against conservative viewpoints and sought to prohibit that discrimination. Although the case involved a facial challenge, and the Court ultimately remanded the case to the lower courts, the Court articulated the principle that "a State may not interfere with private actors' speech to advance its own vision of ideological balance." The Court noted that social media platforms are entitled to control their content decisions even when social media content comes from third parties. "Like the editors, cable operators, and parade organizers, the major social-media platforms are in the business, when curating their feeds, of combining "multifarious voices" to create a distinctive expressive offering. The individual messages may originate with third parties, but the larger offering is the platform's. It is the product of a wealth of choices about whether—and, if so, how—to convey posts having a certain content or viewpoint. Those choices rest on a set of beliefs about which messages are appropriate and which are not (or which are more appropriate and which less so). In the aggregate they give the feed a particular expressive quality." "When the government interferes with such editorial choices—say, by ordering the excluded to be included—it alters the content of the compilation. In overriding a private party's expressive choices, the government confronts the First Amendment." "The Court has barred the government from forcing a private speaker to present views it wished to spurn in order to rejigger the expressive realm." "If Texas's law is enforced, the platforms could not—as they do now—disfavor posts because they: support Nazi ideology; advocate for terrorism; espouse racism, Islamophobia, or anti-Semitism; glorify rape or other gender-based violence; encourage teenage suicide and self-injury; discourage the use of vaccines; advise phony treatments for diseases; advance false claims of election fraud. Texas's law profoundly alters the platforms' choices about the views they will, and will not, convey."

In *Free Speech Coalition, Inc. v. Paxton*, 606 U.S. 461 (2025), the Court returned to the question of age verification. Texas enacted a law that required commercial websites that publish sexually explicit content to verify the age of their visitors. In upholding the law, the Court noted that the law furthered the lawful end of preventing children from accessing sexually explicit content. Although the law also burdened adults who might want to access some of the content, and who would also have to provide age verification, the Court emphasized that many states require age verification to obtain alcohol, tobacco, a lottery ticket; a tattoo, a body piercing, fireworks, and a driver's license. The Court ultimately held that Texas could require age verification based on its authority to prevent children from accessing sexually explicit content. Although the law might burden the ability of adults to view sexually explicit content, the Court applied intermediate scrutiny and held that the requirement did not unduly burden the ability of adults to visit the websites.

Following the decision in *Reno*, Congress enacted the Child On Line Pornography Act (COPA) which was designed to protect children from exposure to indecent materials on the World Wide Web. The Child On Line Pornography Act (COPA) prohibited knowing communication for commercial purposes of any material that is harmful to minors. In *Ashcroft v. Free Speech Coalition*, 535 U.S. 234 (2002), the Court addressed the question of whether COPA's use of the term "community standards," as the basis for determining whether material was harmful, created a problem of substantial overbreadth. It concluded that, because COPA applies to significantly less material than the CDA and defines harmful-to-minors by reference to well-established obscenity criteria, the community standards provision was not overbroad.

In *American Civil Liberties Union v. Mukasey*, 534 F.3d 181 (3rd Cir. 2008), *cert. denied*, 555 U.S. 1137 (2009), the court of appeals upheld a lower court order holding that the COPA violated the First and Fifth Amendments of the Constitution. Noting that the COPA criminalized a category of speech that was harmful to minors, but which was constitutionally protected for adults, the court applied strict scrutiny. Although the court held that the state had a compelling interest in protecting the physical and psychological well-being of minors, and in protecting minors from exposure to harmful material on the Web, it concluded that COPA was not narrowly tailored to effectuate its purpose. In particular, "COPA endangers a wide range of communications, exhibits, and speakers whose messages do not comport with the type of harmful materials legitimately targeted under COPA, i.e., material that is obscene as to minors." Moreover, COPA defined the term "minor" so broadly as to encompass "an infant, a five-year old, or a person just shy of age seventeen."

In *Ashcroft v. Free Speech Coalition*, 535 U.S. 234 (2002), the Court struck down the Child Pornography Prevention Act (CPPA) which prohibited the visual depiction, including computer or computer-generated images, of a minor engaged in sexually explicit conduct. In striking down the law, the Court noted that CPPA did not merely prohibit images that appealed to a prurient interest or that were patently offensive. It also prohibited speech that had serious literary, artistic, political, or scientific value. The Court rejected the government's concern that pedophiles might use virtual child pornography to seduce children. In this regard, it noted that many innocent materials can be used for immoral purposes, including candy, video games, and cartoons, but those materials are not prohibited. The Court also rejected the argument that virtual child pornography whets the appetites of pedophiles and encourages pedophilia, noting that speech cannot be banned merely for its bad tendency. Nor can speech that is protected for adults be silenced totally in an effort to protect children. The Court also was unmoved by the argument that allowing virtual child pornography makes it difficult to prosecute persons who use real children to produce pornography. The Court found that this argument "turned the First Amendment upside down", insofar as it would suppress lawful speech as a means of regulating unlawful speech.

A recent decision focused on whether the government may prohibit registered sex offenders from accessing the internet. *Packingham v. North Carolina*, 582 U.S. 98 (2017), involved a North Carolina law that made it a felony for a registered sex offender "to access a commercial social networking Web site where the sex offender knows that the site permits minor children to become members or to create or maintain personal Web pages." Packingham—a 21-year-old student—had sex with a 13-year-old girl, pleaded guilty to taking indecent liberties with her, and was required to register as a sex offender which barred him from accessing commercial social networking sites. After a state court dismissed a traffic ticket against Packingham, he went on Facebook to thank and praise God for the dismissal. A police officer, who realized that petitioner was a convicted sex offender, charged him with violating the ban. In striking down the law, the Court emphasized that the internet has become a "vast democratic forum," noting that Facebook is used by some 1.79 billion active users and offers "relatively unlimited, low-cost capacity for communication of all kinds." Even though the Court viewed the statute as content-neutral and subject to intermediate scrutiny, the Court emphasized that the law must nonetheless be "narrowly tailored to serve a significant governmental interest" and cannot "burden substantially more speech than is necessary to further the government's legitimate interests." At the same time, the court recognized that the internet and social media can be used to commit crimes, and in particular to approach children. The difficulty with the North Carolina law was that it was so broadly worded that it would have prohibited most access to the internet, including such websites as Amazon.com, Washingtonpost.com, and Webmd.com, as well as social networking sites such as Facebook, LinkedIn, and Twitter. As a result, the Court concluded that the law was not narrowly tailored to prohibit a sex offender from engaging in conduct that might presage a sexual crime, like contacting a minor or using a website to gather information about a minor.

The Court emphasized the importance of the internet to modern life, noting that the law precluded sex offenders from accessing "the principal sources for knowing current events, checking ads for employment, speaking and listening in the modern public square, and otherwise exploring the vast realms of human thought and knowledge." Since those sites "provide perhaps the most powerful mechanisms available to a private citizen to make his or her voice heard," the Court was concerned about depriving even convicted criminals off from such sites as they seek "access to the world of ideas, in particular if they seek to reform and to pursue lawful and rewarding lives." As a result, the Court invalidated the law.

By contrast, in *United States v. Egli*, 13 F.4th 1139 (10th Cir. 2021), the court upheld a total internet ban as a condition of a child pornography defendant's supervised release. The court emphasized that defendant had ignored previously-imposed partial internet bans

CHECKLIST

A. What were the origins of the First Amendment? The origins are rooted in a history of free speech repression.

1. **What types of restrictions on speech were imposed in the American colonies?** A variety of restrictions, including licensing, were imposed. In other words, if citizens wanted to print written material, they had to obtain the permission of governmental officials.

2. **Why were licensing restrictions objectionable?** Because licensing could be used to impose censorship on speech. If government officials did not like the material, they would withhold permission to print.

3. **Were there other restrictions on speech?** In England and in the colonies, governmental officials imposed the crime of seditious libel which made it a crime to criticize government officials (and, early on, high clergy).

4. **Why was the crime of seditious libel objectionable?** Because criticism was prohibited whether it was true or false. Indeed, truthful criticisms were punished more severely because it was assumed that true criticisms were more likely to undermine the government.

B. **What does the First Amendment provide and to whom does it apply? It was designed to achieve a variety of objectives.**

1. **What does the First Amendment provide?** The First Amendment states that "Congress shall make no law . . . abridging the freedom of speech, or of the press."

2. **So, the First Amendment applies only to Congress?** Not only does it apply to Congress, the U.S. Supreme Court has interpreted it as applying to all branches of the federal government.

3. **Does the First Amendment also apply to the states?** Although the First Amendment was not initially interpreted as applying to the states, almost the entire Bill of Rights was eventually incorporated into the Fourteenth Amendment and applied to the states.

C. **What was the First Amendment designed to accomplish?** The Framers of the First Amendment did not clearly state their goals and objectives, but various theories have been advanced regarding the Amendment's meaning and application.

1. The "marketplace of ideas" theory provides that "the ultimate good is better reached by free trade in ideas and the best test of truth is the power of thought to get itself accepted in the marketplace of ideas."

2. The "self-fulfillment" theory focuses on the fact that freedom of speech helps facilitate personal development and self-fulfillment.

3. The "democratic process theory" posits that free speech has inherent value for promoting participatory decision-making in a democracy.

4. The "safety valve" theory provides that free expression provides a way to let off steam and advance one's ideas and agenda without the need to resort to violence.

D. **Does the First Amendment protect even speech that advocates violent or illegal action?** Yes, but the Court took a while to reach that conclusion.

1. Early decisions applied the "clear and present" danger test, but did not really require that the danger be so "clear" or so "present."

2. Justice Holmes, dissenting in *Abrams v. United States*, 250 U.S. 616 (1919), laid the framework for the modern approach when he argued that illegal advocacy should not be punished unless it "so imminently threatens immediate interference with the lawful and pressing purpose of the law that an immediate check is required to save the country."

3. The Court's current approach, articulated in *Brandenburg v. Ohio*, 395 U.S. 444 (1969), provides that such speech can only be prosecuted when it "is directed to inciting or producing imminent lawless action and is likely to incite or produce such action."

E. **Are the protections provided by the First Amendment absolute?** No, the protections are not absolute.

1. In general, the Court had held that content-based and viewpoint-based restrictions on speech are presumptively unconstitutional and are therefore subject to strict scrutiny.

2. However, in *Chaplinsky v. New Hampshire*, 315 U.S. 568 (1942), the Court suggested that there are certain categories of speech that are not entitled to constitutional protection.

3. *Chaplinsky* held that there are "certain well-defined and narrowly limited classes of speech, the prevention and punishment of which have never been thought to raise any Constitutional problem."

4. The Court included within these categories, the lewd and obscene, the profane, the libelous, and insulting or "fighting words."

F. **Are "fighting words" protected under the First Amendment?** No, they are a category of speech that is unprotected.

1. "Fighting Words" are words "which by their very utterance inflict injury or tend to incite an immediate breach of the peace."

2. "The test is what men of common intelligence would understand would be words likely to cause an average addressee to fight."

3. Many "fighting words" convictions are reversed on vagueness or overbreadth grounds because the convictions are based on statutes that are phrased in very broad terms, or that use terms that suffer from vagueness or ambiguity (*e.g.*, prohibiting the use of "opprobrious" or "abusive" language).

G. **Is defamatory speech protected under the First Amendment?** Yes, with some limitations.

1. A category of speech that *Chaplinsky* identified as unprotected was defamatory speech.

2. In *New York Times Co. v. Sullivan*, 376 U.S. 254 (1964), the Court reversed and held that defamatory speech is protected under the First Amendment.

3. In extending protection to defamatory speech, the Court recognized the citizenry's interest in governmental processes in a democracy, as well as the potential chilling effect of defamation judgments.

4. Under the *New York Times* decision, a public official cannot recover for defamation unless plaintiff can prove by clear and convincing evidence that the defendant made the defamatory statements with "actual malice."

5. The term *"actual malice"* requires that defendant must have acted with "knowledge that [the allegedly defamatory statement] was false or in reckless disregard of whether it was false or malicious."

6. In later cases, the Court extended the actual malice standard to defamation suits brought by so-called "public figures." Like public officials, public figures are "intimately involved in the resolution of important public questions or,

by reason of their fame, shape events in areas of concern to society at large," and they have access to the media to respond.

7. However, the Court has refused to extend the actual malice standard to defamation actions brought by private individuals who do not invite public attention to themselves, have not voluntarily exposed themselves to a higher risk of reputational harm, and do not command access to the media and possess an ability to undo or mitigate reputational injury.

8. In a suit by a private individual, a state cannot subject the defendant to strict liability, and cannot impose presumed or punitive damages absent a showing of actual malice. These include "out-of-pocket loss" for "impairment of reputation and standing in the community, personal humiliation, and mental anguish and suffering."

9. The Court distinguishes between private individuals based on whether the matter involves the public interest as opposed to matters of "purely private interest," and allows the states broader authority to impose liability in cases brought by such individuals.

H. Does constitutional protection extend to individuals who intentionally inflict mental and emotional distress with their speech? Yes.

1. The Court has held that parody is entitled to First Amendment protection, noting that even depictions that cause distress can have speech value, and noting further that political cartoonists and satirists often make insulting or upsetting commentary.

2. A public figure cannot recover for mental and emotional distress without showing that the material was published with actual malice (as defined in the *New York Times* case).

3. When mental distress is caused by protests that relate to matters of public interest, constitutional protections apply.

I. Does the tort of privacy have a constitutional dimension? Yes.

1. In general, the Court has been reluctant to impose liability for publication of truthful information even when there are privacy implications.

2. A newspaper cannot be held liable under a state law prohibiting publication of a rape victim's name if the victim's identity was obtained legally from a public record.

3. In *Time, Inc. v. Hill*, 385 U.S. 374 (1967), the Court held that a magazine cannot be held liable in a false light privacy case absent proof that defendant published the false light information with knowledge of falsehood or reckless disregard of the truth.

4. Courts are more inclined to impose liable when a publication has misappropriated an individual's name, image, talent.

J. In *Chaplinsky v. New Hampshire*, 315 U.S. 568, 572 (1942), the Court noted, in dicta, that obscenity is a category of speech that is not protected under the First Amendment, noting that obscenity plays "no essential part of any exposition of ideas, and [has] slight social value as a step to the truth." In *Roth v. United States,* 354 U.S. 476, 484 (1957), the Court reinforced that idea by stating that obscenity is "utterly without redeeming social importance."

1. The Court has acknowledged that sex and obscenity are not synonymous terms, and has stated that obscenity involves material that "deals with sex in a manner appealing to the *prurient interest.*"

2. Most obscenity cases focus on the definitional question of whether a particular publication is obscene.

3. In *Miller v. California*, 413 U.S. 15 (1973), the Court held that, in order to be obscene, the following questions must be asked: "(1) whether the average person applying contemporary community standards would find that the work, taken as a whole, appeals to the prurient interest, (2) whether it depicts or describes, in a patently offensive way, sexual conduct specifically defined by the applicable state law, and (3) whether the work taken as a whole, lacks serious literary, artistic, political, or scientific value."

4. The Court rejected the requirement of a national standard, in favor of a local standard. While those local standards could be out of the mainstream, the Court has held that appellate courts must independently review constitutional claims in obscenity cases.

5. In determining whether a publication has serious literary, artistic, political, or scientific value, courts need not use "contemporary community standards" to assess whether

material lacks the required social value, but instead should focus on whether a "reasonable person" would find the material so lacking.

6. Appellate courts must independently review constitutional claims in obscenity cases. As a result, even if a jury concludes that a publication is inconsistent with contemporary community standards, the Court can review and reverse for constitutional deficiencies.

7. Even though obscenity is outside constitutional protection, the Court has held that citizens have the right to possess obscene materials in the privacy of their homes.

8. Subsequent decisions refused to provide homeowners with the right to purchase child pornography, or to view it outside of the home.

K. **The Court has also held that local governments may create zoning laws that restrict the location of adult entertainment enterprises based on the secondary effects of those businesses.**

L. **In general, the Court has been reluctant to hold that speech can be banned simply because it is "offensive."**

1. Even though it may be possible for someone to state their protest less offensively, government cannot force people to say things in inoffensive ways. Indeed, in some instances, more emotive language is more powerful, and speakers have the option to use the more offensive language unless the speech fits within some unprotected category of speech.

2. In many offensive speech cases, the Court applies "vagueness" and "overbreadth" principles to overturn convictions.

3. In a few (limited) contexts, offensive speech is subject to governmental regulation. For example, the Court upheld the FCC's decision to place restrictions on offensive speech (the seven "filthy" words) by limiting such broadcasts to late night hours when children would be less likely to be listening.

4. The Court has also upheld limitations on offensive speech when the government is financing the speech in the sense that Congress direct agencies to consider "general standards of decency and respect for the diverse beliefs and values of the American public" in making art awards.

M. Child pornography is a category of speech that the Court has recently recognized is unprotected.

1. In placing depictions of child sexuality outside of constitutional protection, the Court has emphasized that the state has a compelling interest in protecting the physical and psychological well-being of minors, that depictions of child sex abuse create a permanent record of a child's participation, and that the state can dry up the market for child pornography only by imposing criminal penalties on those who sell, advertise or promote it.

2. In addition, the Court regards the speech value of child pornography as "exceedingly modest, if not *de minimis*."

3. The Court offered several justifications for giving states greater leeway to ban child pornography: states have a "compelling" interest in "safeguarding the physical and psychological well-being" of minors, and the Court indicated that it would be deferential to legislature's conclusion that suppression of child pornography is necessary to achieve this objective; that the distribution of photographs and films depicting sexual activity by juveniles is intrinsically related to the sexual abuse of children because it creates a permanent record of a child's participation and the harm is reinforced by circulation.

4. Unlike obscenity, the Court has held that individuals do not have a constitutional right to possess child pornography in their homes.

5. Government cannot prohibit virtual (as opposed to actual) depictions of child pornography since no children are actually abused.

6. Some virtual child pornography laws are so broad that they could apply to a broad range of pictures, including pictures in psychology manuals, as well as images that are not "patently offensive," that did not "contravene community standards," and that could have "serious literary, artistic, political, or scientific value."

7. Youth sexuality has been a theme in art and literature "throughout the ages" in such works as Romeo and Juliet (in which one of the lovers was only 13 years old), as well as in recent prominent movies.

8. The Court has rejected the argument that virtual child pornography might lead to actual child abuse. Even though pedophiles can use virtual child pornography to seduce

children, the Court has noted that many "innocent" things can be abused—including cartoons, video games, and candy—but government cannot prohibit such items merely "because they can be misused."

9. The Court has rejected the argument that virtual child pornography can be prohibited in order to help eliminate the market for pornography that uses real children, noting that pornographers would be more likely to use virtual images than real ones if there were no criminal penalties for using virtual pictures.

10. The Court left open the question of whether the state can (someday) prohibit virtual child pornography if technology advances to the point where it is impossible to distinguish virtual child pornography from actual child pornography.

N. Can governments prohibit pornography that degrades or portrays women in objectionable or subordinate ways? No.

1. In *American Booksellers Association, Inc. v. Hudnut*, 771 F.2d 323 (7th Cir. 1985), the court held that the state "may not ordain preferred viewpoints" and may not "declare one perspective right and silence opponents."

2. "If there is any fixed star in our constitutional constellation, it is that no official, high or petty, can prescribe what shall be orthodox in politics, nationalism, religion, or other matters of opinion or force citizens to confess by word or act their faith therein."

3. If some pornographers depict torture of women, and some pornographers use fraud, trickery, or force to compel women to perform, the state can prohibit such conduct without prohibiting the ideas conveyed by the pornographers.

4. The Court has also rejected the argument that speech can be prohibited because the speech is "unanswerable" and therefore the "marketplace of ideas" metaphor is inapplicable: "the Constitution does not make the dominance of truth a necessary condition of freedom of speech," and he rejected the argument that government has the power to declare "truth."

5. The court also rejected the argument that pornography is "low value" speech because the government is not allowed to choose among viewpoints, and questioned whether such speech is "low value" because Indianapolis (which passed

the law in question) chose to prohibit this speech because it "influences social relations and politics on a grand scale, that it controls attitudes at home and in the legislature."

O. Can hate speech be prohibited without running afoul of the First Amendment? No.

1. "Hate speech" refers to expression that derogatorily targets individuals or groups by reason of their race, ethnicity, sex, or sexual preference.
2. Courts have generally held that government does not have the power to prohibit hate speech (assuming, of course, that it does not fit into an unprotected category of speech such as fighting words).
3. The Court has generally concluded that such statutes contain "content discrimination" or "viewpoint discrimination," and the Court has rejected the idea that government may "regulate speech based on hostility—or favoritism—towards the underlying message."
4. The Court has also rejected the idea that hate speech ordinances can be upheld as a way of ensuring the "basic human rights of members of groups that have historically been subjected to discrimination, including the right of such group members to live in peace where they wish."
5. Note that the Court has not held that government is precluded from imposing any content-based or viewpoint-based restrictions on speech. Indeed, as we have seen, the Court's First Amendment jurisprudence is based on the notion some categories of speech may be treated differently than other categories (*e.g.*, obscenity is not constitutionally protected). However, the Court has held that political ideas cannot be prohibited based on their content or viewpoint.
6. The Court has also rejected the idea that one's ideas can be considered in a sentencing hearing when they bear no relationship to the crime, and are introduced simply to prejudice the defendant.
7. However, when there is a correlation between the crime and the belief, and the racial belief motivated the crime, the Court has held that the belief can be considered for sentence enhancement purposes on the theory that judges have historically considered a range of factors in deciding on the appropriate punishment.

P. **Can true threats be prohibited consistently with the First Amendment?** Yes, depending on circumstances.

1. In one decision, the Court struck down a cross burning ordinance because it involved content-based and viewpoint-based discrimination against speech. *See R.A.V. v. City of St. Paul*, 505 U.S. 377 (1992).
2. In *Virginia v. Black*, 538 U.S. 343 (2003), the Court suggested that it would uphold a cross burning statute when the cross is burned with the intent to make a true threat designed to intimidate another person or group of persons.
3. The Court based its conclusion on the fact that cross burning in the United States has been used by the Ku Klux Klan (KKK) as a "tool of intimidation and as a threat of impending violence" against the targets of the cross-burning. Because of this history, the Court concluded that a burning cross can be used to convey a very serious threat of future bodily harm.
4. As a result, cross burning could be regarded as a "true threat" which the Court defined as "those statements where the speaker means to communicate a serious expression of an intent to commit an act of unlawful violence to a particular individual or group of individuals."
5. The Court held that such threats could be prohibited whether or not the speaker actually intends to carry out the threat, because the doctrine is designed to protect individuals from the fear of violence as well as the possibility of violence.
6. Even though Virginia could prohibit true threats, the Court concluded that the statute was unconstitutional because it contained a *prima facie* evidence provision which allowed a court to presume that a cross burning was undertaken with the intent to intimidate.
7. The Court noted that "burning a cross at a political rally would almost certainly be protected expression" and might not involve an attempt at intimidation.

Q. **Is commercial speech entitled to any constitutional protection?** While commercial speech may receive less protection than political speech, it is not unprotected.

1. Historically, the Court did not protect so-called "commercial expression" (speech that proposes an economic transaction

or that pertains "solely to the economic interests of the speaker and audience").

2. The Court reversed its earlier precedent in *Virginia State Board of Pharmacy v. Virginia Citizens Consumer Council*, 425 U.S. 748 (1976), and extended constitutional protection to commercial speech in striking down a Virginia law that banned the advertisement of prescription drugs.

3. The Court concluded that advertising has speech value because it provides increased information to the public, thereby facilitating competition and informed consumer choices. The Court rejected Virginia's claim that it had the right to protect consumers against advertising.

4. The Court does not accord commercial speech as much protection as political speech, and has suggested that advertising could more readily be subjected to prior restraints, as well as disclaimers, disclosures, and warnings.

5. The Court tends to apply the *Central Hudson Gas & Electric Co. v. Public Service Commission*, 447 U.S. 557 (1980) test to evaluate restrictions on commercial speech: 1) whether the regulated speech is misleading or related to an unlawful transaction in which case regulation is permissible; 2) if the speech is not misleading or related to an unlawful activity, whether the regulation is supported by a substantial government interest; 3) whether the regulation directly advances the interest; 4) whether the governmental interest can be achieved by a more limited restriction on commercial speech.

6. In recent years, the justices have sometimes disagreed regarding the standard of review to be applied in commercial speech cases with a plurality of the Court stating that the Court should apply a *"rigorous" standard of review* for total bans on "truthful nonmisleading commercial messages for reasons unrelated to the preservation of a fair bargaining process."

7. In *Bates v. State Bar of Arizona*, 433 U.S. 350 (1977), the Court struck down a disciplinary decision prohibiting a newspaper from carrying an advertisement listing a law clinic's fees, and from making representations regarding the quality of the clinic's service or the results it could achieve.

8. In *In re R.M.J.*, 455 U.S. 191 (1982), the Court held that a lawyer was improperly disciplined for advertising areas of practice and qualifications not permitted under state rules, noting that the advertisement was not deceptive, and that the state had offered no substantial justification for limiting the content of the advertisement.

R. What do the overbreadth and vagueness doctrines provide?

1. In overbreadth cases, plaintiffs claim that an overbroad law "chills" their expression by causing "persons whose expression is constitutionally protected to refrain from exercising their rights for fear of criminal sanctions by a statute susceptible of application to protected expression."
2. Because of this chilling effect, the Court has allowed individuals to attack overbroad laws, even though the conduct of those individuals is clearly unprotected by the First Amendment, and even though their conduct could have been proscribed by a narrowly drawn law.
3. Both the vagueness and overbreadth doctrines can involve either a "facial" challenge to a law (a suit which alleges that a law is facially unconstitutional and should be struck down in its entirety) or an "as applied" challenge (alleging that the law is invalid as applied to the facts of a particular case).
4. Facial challenges are controversial because the party before the court may not be arguing that a particular law is "vague" or "overbroad" as to her (or her conduct), but may be asking the court to strike down a law because it is overbroad or vague as applied to others.
5. The Court tends to be restrictive in its application of the vagueness and overbreadth doctrines. The Court has stated that facial challenges involve "strong medicine" because they allow "a defendant whose speech may be outside the scope of constitutional protection to escape punishment because the state failed to draft its law with sufficient precision." *Gooding v. Wilson,* 405 U.S. 518 (1972).
6. The Court has tended to apply the overbreadth doctrine "only as a last resort," and has generally required that the overbreadth be "substantial" before a law will be invalidated on its face.
7. The "vagueness" doctrine is grounded in the due process clause.

8. As the Court stated in *Connally v. General Construction Co.*, 269 U.S. 385, 391 (1926), "a statute which either forbids or requires the doing of an act in terms so vague that men of common intelligence must necessarily guess at its meaning and differ as to its application violates the first essential of due process of law."

9. There are various justifications underlying the vagueness doctrine. "First, vague laws may trap the innocent by not providing fair warning. Second, if arbitrary and discriminatory enforcement is to be prevented, laws must provide explicit standards for those who apply them. A vague law impermissibly delegates basic policy matters to policemen, judges, and juries for resolution on an *ad hoc* and subjective basis, with the attendant dangers of arbitrary and discriminatory application."

10. In addition, as the Court noted in *Grayned v. City of Rockford*, "uncertain meanings inevitably lead citizens to steer far wider of the unlawful zone than if the boundaries of the forbidden areas were clearly marked." This so-called "chilling effect" is particularly objectionable when citizen's speech rights are implicated.

S. In general, the First Amendment imposes a very strong presumption against the validity of "prior restraints"—restrictions on speech that are imposed prior to its dissemination.

1. In *Lovell v. City of Griffin*, 303 U.S. 444 (1938), the Court emphasized that the "struggle for the freedom of the press was primarily directed against the power of the licensor".

2. The Court has been more lax in applying the prohibition against prior restraints to motion picture licensing schemes provided that these schemes contain a number of components: 1) the burden of proving that a film is unprotected expression must rest on the censor; 2) while the State may require advance submission of a film, the censor must, within a specified brief period, either issue a license or go to court to restrain showing the film; 3) the procedure must also assure a prompt final judicial decision, to minimize the deterrent effect of an interim and possibly erroneous denial of a license.

3. Courts have also upheld content neutral time, place, and manner licensing restrictions for parades and other public events. Such restrictions are deemed essential to "prevent confusion by overlapping parades or processions, to secure

convenient use of the streets by other travelers, and to minimize the risk of disorder."

4. The rule against prior restraints has also been applied to injunctions against expression.
5. In *New York Times Co. v. United States*, 403 U.S. 713 (1971), also known as the *Pentagon Papers* case, the Court extended the prohibition against prior restraints to publications that implicate national security interests.
6. In *Madsen v. Women's Health Center, Inc.*, 512 U.S. 753 (1994), the Court held that an injunction against abortion protest activities would not be viewed as imposing "content based" or "viewpoint based" restrictions on speech. The injunction was not viewpoint-based, even though it restricted only abortion protestors and not those who protested in favor of abortion, because of the "lack of any similar demonstrations by those in favor of abortion, and of any consequent request that their demonstrations be regulated by injunction."
7. Nevertheless, the Court decided that a simple rational basis standard was too low, and that injunctions should still be subject to a "more stringent" standard of review that focuses on whether there is a "fit between the objectives of an injunction and the restrictions it imposes on speech" so that the relief is "no more burdensome to the defendants than necessary to provide complete relief to the plaintiffs."

T. The Court has also held that "symbolic speech" (speech that expresses ideas through symbols rather than spoken or written words) is protected under the First Amendment.

1. However, symbolic speech can involve either pure speech or conduct. When conduct is involved, the Court has been less inclined to provide as much protection as it does for pure speech.
2. The Court's current approach to symbolic speech was articulated in *United States v. O'Brien,* 391 U.S. 367 (1968), in which the Court articulated a four-part test for evaluating restrictions on symbolic speech. In general, such restrictions are permissible provided that four requirements are met: 1) government must have the power to regulate in the field; 2) the regulation must advance a substantial or important government interest; 3) the interest must be unrelated to the suppression of free

expression; & 4) the incidental burden on speech must be no greater than necessary to achieve the governmental interest.

3. Flag desecration statutes fail the *O'Brien* test because they are focused on prohibiting the message of the flag burner.

U. The Court has applied special rules that apply when individuals attempt to use public places for speech purposes.

1. Historically, certain public venues (*e.g.*, streets, sidewalks and parks) have been available for expressive activity. These are called "traditional public fora."

2. There are also "designated public fora" which are places that have not traditionally been made available for expressive activities, but which the state has chosen to make available for those purposes.

3. Some venues (*e.g.*, jails and defense facilities) are treated as "nonpublic" in the sense that they have traditionally been closed to most expressive activities.

4. Modern public forum doctrine recognizes that governments may have legitimate non-content-based reasons for restricting access to fora, including the protection of governmental property, the management of competing uses, efficient traffic flow, public safety, and other considerations.

5. As a result, the courts have upheld content-neutral restrictions that relate to the time, place, or manner of expression. For example, government might justifiably require those who wish to hold a parade to obtain a permit so that government can anticipate and deal with possible traffic disruptions.

6. Because of the higher level of scrutiny, content-based restrictions on public fora have generally been struck down unless they are supported by a compelling or overriding governmental interest, are "narrowly tailored," and impose the least restrictive imposition on speech.

7. Government ownership of property by itself does not give the public a right to access the property for speech and assembly purposes. Like a private property owner, federal, state and local governments have an interest in using the property under their control for the uses to which they are lawfully dedicated.

V. Religious speech may be entitled to protection under the First Amendment.

1. The Court has held that government cannot discriminate against religious speech in public forums, and must (in some instances) allow religious groups to use school premises on the same basis as other groups.

2. In *Rosenberger v. Rector and Visitors of the University of Virginia*, 515 U.S. 819 (1995), the Court struck down a university policy that funded the publications of registered student organizations, but specifically excluded the publications of religious groups.

W. The Court has also held that campaign finance—the raising and spending of money for political campaign purposes—is entitled to constitutional protection.

1. In *Buckley v. Valeo*, 424 U.S. 1 (1976), the Court held that both campaign donations and campaign expenditures constitute protected speech because they involve discussions regarding public issues and the qualifications of candidates.

2. Although campaign contributions are entitled to protection, the Court has viewed contribution limitations as having less impact on free expression because they reflect support for a candidate, but do not convey the underlying basis for support.

3. Restrictions on campaign contributions can be justified by the interest in prohibiting corruption or the appearance of corruption.

4. Government may not justify campaign finance restrictions as an attempt to equalize the resources of individuals and groups and their ability "to influence the outcome of elections."

5. Government may not place limitations on expenditures by candidates from personal or family resources, holding that a candidate has the right to "vigorously and tirelessly to advocate his own election and the election of other candidates."

6. The Court has upheld disclosure provisions that require candidates to publicly disclose the names of their donors because disclosure laws provide the electorate with information as to where political campaigns are receiving

their money, and provide an indication of the interests to which a candidate is likely to be responsive.

7. The Court has also upheld provisions allowing presidential candidates to opt for public financing of their presidential election campaigns.

8. In *Austin v. Michigan Chamber of Commerce*, 494 U.S. 652 (1990), the Court held that the states could treat corporations differently than individuals for purposes of campaign finance (*e.g.*, upholding the Michigan Campaign Finance Act that prohibited corporations from making contributions and "independent expenditures" in connection with state candidate elections except from "segregated" funds).

9. The Court found a compelling state interest in the fact that state law grants corporations "special advantages (*e.g.*, limited liability, perpetual life, and favorable treatment of the accumulation and distribution of assets) that help them attract capital and allow them to obtain "an unfair advantage in the political marketplace." The Court concluded that this advantage can be unfair because: "the resources in the treasury of a business corporation [are] not an indication of popular support for the corporation's political ideas." They reflect instead the economically motivated decisions of investors and customers.

10. The Court expressed concern that corporations may have a "formidable political presence, even though the power of the corporation may be no reflection of the power of its ideas." The Court also focused on "the corrosive and distorting effects of immense aggregations of wealth that are accumulated with the help of the corporate form and that have little or no correlation to the public's support for the corporation's political ideas."

11. Despite *Austin's* holding, *First National Bank of Boston v. Bellotti*, 435 U.S. 765 (1978), struck down a criminal statute that prohibited expenditures by banks and business corporations for the purpose of influencing the vote on referendum proposals except for matters "materially affecting any of the property, business or assets of the corporation." In addition, *Citizens United v. Federal Elections Commission*, 558 U.S. 310 (2010), expanded the ability of corporations to participate in the political process.

12. In *FEC v. National Conservative Political Action Committee*, 470 U.S. 480 (1985), the Court struck down

portions of the Presidential Election Campaign Fund Act which made it a crime for independent "political committees" to spend more than $1,000 in support of a candidate who accepted the financing.

13. In *McConnell v. Federal Election Commission,* 540 U.S. 93 (2003), the Court upheld Section I and Section II of BCRA. The Court viewed BCRA as designed to deal with flaws in the prior campaign finance scheme.

14. Among other things, BCRA subjected *all* funds raised and spent by national parties to FECA's hard-money source and amount limits, including funds spent on purely state and local elections in which no federal office was at stake.

15. In addition, BCRA required that "electioneering communications" clearly identify the candidate or committee or, if not so authorized, identify the payor and announce the lack of authorization.

16. In *Randall v. Sorrell,* 548 U.S. 230 (2006), the Court struck down a law that controlled the total amount a candidate for state office could raise and spend during a "two-year general election cycle" that included the primary election and the general election because they were so low as to prevent candidates from "amassing the resources necessary for effective [campaign] advocacy" and can place challengers (who may need to raise and spend more money) at a significant disadvantage.

17. Portions of the *McConnell* decision were effectively overruled in *Federal Election Commission v. Wisconsin Right to Life, Inc.*, 551 U.S. 449 (2007), which held that: "A court should find that an ad is the functional equivalent of express advocacy [and, therefore, subject to campaign finance restrictions] only if the ad is susceptible of no reasonable interpretation other than as an appeal to vote for or against a specific candidate."

18. In *Caperton v. Massey*, 556 U.S. 868 (2009), the Court found that a state supreme court justice who received substantial campaign contributions from a corporate executive should have recused himself from a lawsuit concerning his company.

X. Since the Constitution protects "speech," it implicitly protects the right of association since people can speak more effectively when they join together to speak with a common voice.

1. *NAACP v. Alabama*, 357 U.S. 449 (1958), held that an association could shield its membership lists from disclosure when the members would be subject to retaliation, and the association would have difficulty obtaining/retaining members if disclosure were required.

2. Many modern freedom of association cases focus not on whether the government can compel an organization to disclose the names of its members, but on whether government can force organizations to accept members that they do not want.

3. In *Roberts v. United States Jaycees*, 468 U.S. 609 (1984), the Court held that Minnesota could force the United States Jaycees to admit women as regular members.

4. The Court has distinguished between the right to "intimate" association and the right to associate for speech purposes.

5. Association of an "intimate nature" involves "highly personal relationships" such as the "creation and sustenance of a family," including marriage, childbirth, the raising and education of children, and cohabitation with one's relatives. These "relationships, by their nature, involve deep attachments and commitments to the necessarily few other individuals with whom one shares not only a special community of thoughts, experiences, and beliefs but also distinctively personal aspects of one's life. These relationships are distinguished by relative smallness, a high degree of selectivity in decisions to begin and maintain the affiliation, and seclusion from others in critical aspects of the relationship."

6. The Court found that such "intimate" relationships "must be secured against undue intrusion by the State because of the role of such relationships in safeguarding the individual freedom that is central to our constitutional scheme" and which are "a fundamental element of personal liberty."

7. The Jaycees associative relationship could not qualify as "intimate" because the organization was "large and basically unselective."

8. The right to speak, to worship, and to petition the government for the redress of grievances "could not be vigorously protected from interference by the State unless a correlative freedom to engage in group effort toward those ends were not also guaranteed."

9. After finding a compelling governmental interest underlying the Minnesota law (the prevention of discrimination), the Court concluded that the Jaycees could be forced to admit women because the Jaycees were more involved in the equivalent of commercial or quasi-commercial conduct than pure speech. To the extent that the Jaycees were engaged in expression, it held that the admission of women as full voting members would not "impede the organization's ability to engage in these protected activities or to disseminate its preferred views."

10. In *Boy Scouts of America v. Dale*, 530 U.S. 640 (2000), the Court held that the Boy Scouts could exclude individuals based on their sexual orientation, despite a local law requiring non-discrimination when the Boy Scouts regarded homosexual conduct, as inconsistent with its message.

11. One component of the right to associate is the right not to be forced to be associated with ideas or principles with which one disagrees.

12. In *West Virginia State Board of Education v. Barnette,* 319 U.S. 624 (1943), the Court struck down a state law that required students to salute the United States flag. The Court held that a flag salute is a "form of utterance" and that the First Amendment protects an individual from being forced to "utter what is not in his mind."

13. In *Wooley v. Maynard,* 430 U.S. 705 (1977), the Court struck down a state law that required motor vehicle owners to display license plates with the motto "Live Free or Die" in response to a challenge by a Jehovah's Witness who found the motto morally and religiously objectionable.

14. In *Rumsfeld v. Forum for Academic and Institutional Rights, Inc.*, 547 U.S. 47 (2006), the Court upheld the Solomon Amendment that required law schools to admit military recruiters on the same basis as other employers. *Rumsfeld* rejected the law schools' argument that the statute forced them to engage in speech in violation of the compelled speech doctrine, or violated their right of association.

15. In *Hurley v. Irish-American Gay, Lesbian and Bisexual Group of Boston*, 515 U.S. 557 (1995), the Court held that parade organizers could not be forced to include a message that they did not want to convey in a St. Patrick's

day/Evacuation day (which marked the date when royal troops and loyalists "evacuated" from the city) parade.

16. In *Abood v. Detroit Board of Education*, 431 U.S. 209 (1977), the Court held that non-union public school teachers could not be required to pay that portion of a "service fee" that included political speech to which they objected.

17. In subsequent cases, the Court has upheld some assessments (even though the assessments paid for speech to which someone objected), and in other cases the Court has struck them down.

Y. The "unconstitutional conditions" doctrine provides that states that, while government may distribute benefits, it may not condition their receipt upon waiver of a basic right or liberty.

1. In *Regan v. Taxation With Representation of Washington*, 461 U.S. 540 (1983), the Court held that Congress may choose to make contributions to nonprofit organizations deductible only if those organizations do not engage in lobbying activities.

2. In *Rosenberger v. University of Virginia*, 515 U.S. 819 (1995), the Court held that a university could not choose to fund most publications, but exclude publications by religious groups. In reaching its conclusion, the Court held that viewpoint discrimination is impermissible when, instead of conveying its own message, government has chosen to expend "to encourage a diversity of views from private speakers."

3. In *Legal Services Corp. v. Velazquez*, 531 U.S. 533 (2001), the Court struck down a federal law that prohibited federally funded legal services offices from challenging the constitutional or statutory validity of welfare laws. To the extent that Congress precluded legal services offices from pursuing theories that may be critical to effective litigation, the law was invalid.

4. In *Rumsfeld v. Forum for Academic and Institutional Rights, Inc.*, 547 U.S. 47 (2006), the Court upheld a federal statute requiring law schools to admit military recruiters on the same basis as other recruiters on pain of losing federal funds.

Z. In some instances, government employees can be treated quite differently than other citizens for free speech purposes.

1. In *United Public Workers of America v. Mitchell*, 330 U.S. 75 (1947), the Court upheld § 9(a) of the Hatch Act which prohibited federal employees from taking "any active part in political management or in political campaigns." The Court concluded that an "actively partisan governmental personnel threatens good administration" in that "political rather than official effort may earn advancement and to the public in that governmental favor may be channeled through political connections."

2. In *United States v. National Treasury Employees Union*, 513 U.S. 454 (1995), the Court struck down a criminal statute that prohibited federal employees from accepting any compensation for making speeches or writing articles which applied whether or not the subject had any relationship to the employee's official duties.

3. In *Wieman v. Updegraff*, 344 U.S. 183 (1952), the Court held that public school teachers could not be required to swear an oath of loyalty to the state and to reveal the groups with which they were associated.

4. In *Pickering v. Board of Education*, 391 U.S. 563 (1968), the Court articulated a balancing test for considering restrictions on employee free speech rights that sought to strike a balance "between the interests of the employee, as a citizen, in commenting upon matters of public concern and the interest of the State, as an employer, in promoting the efficiency of the public services it performs through its employees."

5. Applying *Pickering*, in *City of San Diego v. Roe*, 543 U.S. 77 (2004), the Court held that a police officer could be terminated for off-duty speech (selling videotapes depicting himself engaged in sexually explicit acts while wearing a police uniform, and one which depicted a police officer engaged in sex acts while issuing a citation), concluding that he had violated specific police department policies, including engaging in conduct unbecoming of an officer and immoral conduct.

6. In *Garcetti v. Ceballos*, 547 U.S. 410 (2006), the Court held that the First Amendment does not protect a government employee from discipline based on speech made pursuant to the employee's "official duties."

7. In *Keyishian v. Board of Regents*, 385 U.S. 589 (1967), the Court invalidated New York statutes barring employment on the basis of membership in "subversive" organizations on

the theory that political associations, by themselves, do not constitute an adequate ground for denying public employment.

8. In *Elrod v. Burns*, 427 U.S. 347 (1976), the Court held that an employee had been improperly discharged because of his party affiliation.

AA. While the Court has recognized in a number of cases that students do not relinquish their First Amendment rights at the schoolhouse door, the Court has been reluctant to hold that student speech rights are co-extensive with those of adults.

1. In *Tinker v. Des Moines Independent School District*, 393 U.S. 503 (1969), the Court recognized that high school students have a First Amendment right of expression that includes the right to wear black arm bands.

2. In *Bethel School District No. 403 v. Fraser*, 478 U.S. 675 (1986), the Court upheld a disciplinary action against a high school student who delivered a sexually explicit speech at a school assembly during the nomination of a fellow student for student elective office.

3. In *Morse v. Frederick,* 551 U.S. 393 (2007), the Court upheld a principal's decision to suspend a student who displayed a banner with the words "Bong Hits for Jesus" at a school event (students had gone outside of the school, during the school day, to witness a runner bearing the Olympic torch pass by). The Court viewed the banner as inappropriately encouraging drug use.

4. In *Hazelwood School District v. Kuhlmeier*, 484 U.S. 260 (1988), the Court upheld a high school principal's decision to require students to delete two pages from the school's newspaper because it contained inappropriate content (in appropriate for children of that age).

5. A school's authority to regulate student speech may be less compelling when it occurs off-campus outside of school hours. In *Mahanoy Area School District v. B.L.*, 594 U.S. 180 (2021), the Court held that a student could not be sanctioned for a vulgar video that she posted online during non-school hours. A school's authority to regulate in this context depends on whether the student's speech is disruptive to the school environment.

AB. In some instances, the government provides financial support for speech, and questions have arisen regarding

the government's right to dictate the message for which it pays.

1. When the government is financing speech, the Court has been more willing to allow the government to impose restrictions on that speech.

2. In *Rust v. Sullivan*, 500 U.S. 173 (1991), the Court upheld a federal statute that provided funding for "preventive family planning services, population research, infertility services, and other related medical, informational, and educational activities," but specifically precluded the use of funds for "programs where abortion is a method of family planning."

3. In *National Endowment for the Arts v. Finley*, 524 U.S. 569 (1998), the Court upheld a law requiring the National Endowment of the Arts to consider "artistic excellence and artistic merit as the criteria by which [grant] applications are judged, taking into consideration general standards of decency and respect for the diverse beliefs and values of the American public" in making arts grants.

4. In *Legal Services Corp. v. Velazquez,* 531 U.S. 533 (2001), the Court struck down restrictions imposed on governmentally funded lawyers.

AC. The press clause was specifically incorporated into the First Amendment to the United States Constitution.

1. In general, the Court has rejected the notion that the press has a special status that provides it with special rights over and above the speech rights of citizens.

2. Case law suggests that the Court does not view the press as an institution, but as part of an overall process that is critical to informed self-governance.

3. In *Branzburg v. Hayes*, 408 U.S. 665, 704 (1972), the Court rejected the notion that reporters have a First Amendment privilege that shields them from being forced to testify before grand juries regarding their sources.

4. In *Zurcher v. Stanford Daily*, 436 U.S. 547 (1978), the Court held that a newsroom search did not violate the First Amendment.

5. The courts have upheld limitations on the media's access to prison to interview inmates and investigate conditions.

6. Generally, the courts have held that the public has a right to information regarding judicial proceedings, especially

criminal proceedings, and that the press and the public have a right of access to such proceedings.

7. The Court has been protective of the right of access to judicial proceedings as applied to preliminary hearings, *voir dire*, and other pretrial proceedings.

8. The right of press access to judicial proceedings creates the possibility for tension with a defendant's right to a trial free of prejudicial publicity which is protected under the Fifth and Fourteenth Amendment due process clauses, and the Sixth Amendment guarantee of a "public trial, by an impartial jury."

9. In *Sheppard v. Maxwell*, 384 U.S. 333 (1966), the Court overturned a murder conviction because it was influenced by massive and prejudicial pretrial publicity, and disruptive media conduct during the trial.

10. Although *Sheppard* held that courts must take steps to ensure defendants a fair trial, the balance cuts in favor of the public's right to be informed regarding those proceedings.

11. Judges can protect a defendant's rights by limiting the number of media representatives present at a trial, establishing rules for press decorum, using the *voir dire* process to screen out jurors who have been unfairly influenced by prejudicial pretrial publicity, and sequestering jurors to limit their exposure to external influences, including the press.

12. In *Nebraska Press Association v. Stuart*, 427 U.S. 539 (1976), the Court held that gag orders are prior restraints and thus presumptively unconstitutional.

13. The Court has been more willing to uphold speech restrictions imposed upon parties to a proceeding and their attorneys when there is a "substantial likelihood of material prejudice."

14. In *Chandler v. Florida*, 449 U.S. 560 (1981), the Court held that the mere presence of cameras in the courtroom did not automatically violate due process, and that a defendant must prove actual prejudice to establish a due process claim.

AD. First Amendment analysis of media is medium-specific, so laws governing one medium may be impermissible in another.

1. Medium-specific analysis assumes that, "each [medium] tends to present its own peculiar problems," *Joseph Burstyn, Inc. v. Wilson*, 343 U.S. 495 (1952).
2. The courts historically have applied the highest level of scrutiny to governmental efforts to regulate press content.
3. In *Miami Herald Publishing Co. v. Tornillo,* 418 U.S. 241 (1974), the Court struck down a state law that required newspapers to provide equal space for political candidates whom they attack editorially.
4. The Court generally has provided less protection to the broadcast media as the Court suggested in *Federal Communications Commission v. Pacifica Foundation*, 438 U.S. 726 (1978).
5. The Court has recognized that the broadcast media is entitled to exercise some control over broadcasting content in the sense of retaining the freedom to decide whether to accept political advertisements from the public.
6. The Court generally has provided less protection to sexually explicit but non-obscene expression in the broadcast format, holding that it can be zoned to late night hours when children are less likely to be listening or watching.
7. In *Turner Broadcasting System, Inc. v. Federal Communications Commission*, 512 U.S. 622 (1994), the Court upheld federal rules that required cable operators to carry the signals of local broadcasters (a/k/a "must carry rules") despite claims that the rules interfered with editorial discretion.
8. In *City of Los Angeles v. Preferred Communications, Inc.*, 476 U.S. 488 (1986), the Court held that the cable industry is entitled to First Amendment protection.
9. The Court since has determined that content regulation of cable is subject to strict scrutiny.
10. In *Sable Broadcasting, Inc. v. Federal Communications Commission*, 492 U.S. 115 (1989), the Court struck down a law that banned obscene telephonic communications and indecent dial-a-porn services.

AE. The Court has provided a significant level of free speech protection to the internet.

1. In *Reno v. American Civil Liberties Union*, 521 U.S. 844 (1997), the Court struck down the Communications

Decency Act, which prohibited indecent communications on the internet.

2. The Court has equated the internet with print media, and thus given it the highest level of First Amendment protection.

3. Unlike broadcasting, in which only a few broadcast spectrum are available, the internet is almost universally accessible through personal computers, libraries and cyber-cafes.

4. In *Ashcroft v. Free Speech Coalition*, 535 U.S. 234 (2002), the Court struck down the Child Pornography Prevention Act (CPPA) which prohibited the visual depiction, including computer or computer-generated images, of a minor engaged in sexually explicit conduct.

■ PROBLEMS ■

Problem #1: The University of Glenview Hills (GHU) decides to ban "racist" and "hate" speech on the theory that it is offensive, and is inconsistent with the "marketplace of ideas." The ban applies to all speech, including both fighting words and speech that does not qualify as fighting words. In announcing the ban, GHU's President, Corey Williams, stated that: "Neither racist speech nor hate speech advances the marketplace of ideas. It conveys unfair and inaccurate views regarding certain groups or categories of people, and it lets hate flourish. At a University, which is dedicated to open and free expression, we should never let anyone shut down the marketplace." Is GHU's ban constitutional?

Answer: No, the ban would be unconstitutional. The First Amendment prohibits governmental censorship of speech. Moreover, government may not prohibit speech simply because it regards that speech as offensive or wrong, and it cannot bar ideas based on its own views of that speech. In a democracy, the people have the right to articulate their ideas, and to enter those ideas into the marketplace of ideas.

Problem #2: Invoking its power to legislate in order to protect the health, welfare and morals of society, the City of Seneca Gardens passes an ordinance prohibiting the display of "signs" within the city limits. Mabel McCown, a long-time resident, is opposed to the war in Afghanistan. In protest, she flies a United States flag upside down. The City, which views her flag as a "sign," seeks to prosecute Mabel for violating the ordinance. Does the First Amendment protect Mabel in flying her flag upside down?

Answer: Yes. While the City may have some leeway to prohibit "signs" (*e.g.*, commercial yard signs placed by real estate brokers), it has more limited authority to prohibit political signs. In this case, the governmental interest is not sufficient to protect the ordinance against running afoul of the First Amendment.

Problem #3: The City of Louisville, Kentucky, establishes a permit system for public events. Under this system, anyone who wants to conduct a parade must apply for and obtain a permit to march on a public street. Under this ordinance, the Ku Klux Klan (KKK) applies for a permit to march on one of the main thoroughfares on a Saturday afternoon. The City rejects the request on the theory that many citizens object to the KKK and its ideas. Did the City act constitutionally in rejecting the KKK's request for a permit?

Answer: No. In order to be valid, a parade permit ordinance cannot discriminate based on content or viewpoint, and may impose only content neutral time, place and manner restrictions. In this case, the City rejected the KKK's application on the theory that many people object to the KKK and its ideas rather than because of content-neutral time, place and manner considerations. Accordingly, the city acted unconstitutionally because it did not act in a content neutral manner.

Problem #4: In the prior problem, suppose again that the KKK has applied for a permit to march in Louisville on the same street. However, this time, the KKK has applied to march on Derby Day (the first Saturday in May when the Kentucky Derby is held in Louisville at Churchill Downs). The City rejects the request on the theory that the Derby attracts more than one hundred thousand people, and that the police will already be devoting substantial police resources to Derby activities (and associated parties and other events). The City's reply suggests that it is willing to allow the KKK to march on city streets on another day, even a day close to the Derby, but that it will not grant a permit for Derby Day. Did the City act constitutionally in denying the parade request?

Answer: The denial was probably appropriate. In deciding whether to grant or deny a parade permit, a city can appropriately consider the scope of other events already occurring on city streets, and anticipated demands on police resources. Indeed, that is the very reason why the U.S. Supreme Court allows cities to impose content neutral time, place and manner restrictions. For example, a city can deny a parade request if two rival groups want to hold parades on the same street at the same time, and it is physically impossible to hold both parades simultaneously. In this case, it is probably appropriate for the City to refuse a request to hold a controversial parade on a day when the police are already running at full capacity.

Problem #5: Congress is worried about the potential impact of internet content on children. As a result, Congress passes a law that "zones" sexually-related speech (whether or not it is obscene) to late night hours when it can be accessed only by adults. An organization of web site providers that deal in sexually-related (but not obscene) speech seek to challenge the law. Did Congress act constitutionally in imposing this "zoning" ban?

Answer: While such a law might be constitutional as applied to radio or television broadcasts, the Court has provided a higher level of protection for internet communications. As a result, even though the societal interest in protecting children might be regarded as compelling, there are probably less restrictive means available for effectuating that interest. Moreover, since internet communications come from all over the world, and it is always night somewhere and always day somewhere, and the internet is always "on," it is not realistic to think that internet communications can be zoned to late night hours.

POINTS TO REMEMBER

- Under the First Amendment to the U.S. Constitution, freedom of speech receives a high level of protection.
- Although the First Amendment is explicitly applicable only to Congress, it has been interpreted as applying to all of the federal government as well as to the actions of state and local governments.
- Courts and commentators have offered various justifications for according freedom of expression a preferred position in the constitutional structure, including the "marketplace of ideas" theory (which provides that "the ultimate good is better reached by free trade in ideas and . . . the best test of truth is the power of thought to get itself accepted in the marketplace of ideas").
- Other justifications have been offered, including the notion that speech helps facilitate personal development and self-fulfillment, has inherent value for purposes of promoting participatory decision-making in a democracy, as well as for providing a social safety value (a way to let off steam and advance one's ideas and agenda) through speech rather than through violence.
- The Court does not treat the First Amendment free speech rights as absolute.
- Instead, the Court generally applies strict scrutiny to content-based or viewpoint-based restrictions on speech. However, the

Court has concluded that certain categories of speech (*e.g.*, obscenity, child pornography and fighting words) are entitled to less protection, or no protection, under the First Amendment. By contrast, political speech receives the highest level of protection.

- Even speech that advocates violence or illegal action is constitutionally protected provided that the speaker does not seek to incite imminent lawless action and provided that such lawless action is not likely to result.
- Fighting Words—words "which by their very utterance inflict injury or tend to incite an immediate breach of the peace"—are not protected under the First Amendment.
- Although defamatory speech did not initially receive constitutional protection, it now does on the theory that a certain amount of error is inevitable in the political process, and defamatory speech must be protected to avoid having a chilling effect on speech.
- Public officials and public figures cannot recover for defamation unless they satisfy the "actual malice" standard (in other words, they must show that defendant knew that the statement was false or acted in reckless disregard for truth or falsity).
- The states are free to permit private individuals, especially private individuals involved in matters of purely private interest, to recover based on lesser standards.
- Even speech that inflicts mental or emotional distress is constitutionally protected when the plaintiff is a public official or a public figure.
- Speech that invades personal privacy may receive a degree of constitutional protection when the subject is a public official or a public figure.
- Obscenity receives no constitutional protection.
- A publication is obscene when "(1) the average person applying contemporary community standards would find that the work, taken as a whole, appeals to the prurient interest, (2) it depicts or describes, in a patently offensive way, sexual conduct specifically defined by the applicable state law, and (3) the work taken as a whole, lacks serious literary, artistic, political, or scientific value." In *Miller*, the Court rejected the requirement of a national standard, in favor of a local standard.
- Even though obscenity is outside constitutional protection, the Court has held that citizens have the right to possess obscene materials in the privacy of their homes.

- Local governments may create zoning laws that restrict the location of adult entertainment enterprises based on the secondary effects of those businesses.
- In general, the Court has been reluctant to hold that speech can be banned simply because it is "offensive."
- In a few (limited) contexts, offensive speech is subject to governmental regulation. For example, the FCC can limit sexually explicit broadcasts to late night hours when children are less likely to be listening.
- Child pornography is a category of speech that the Court has recently recognized is unprotected because of the potential harm inflicted on children who are the subjects of the pornography.
- Unlike obscenity, which the Court has held that individuals may possess in the privacy of their homes (even if they cannot make, buy or distribute it), the Court has held that individuals do not have a constitutional right to possess child pornography in their homes.
- The Court has held that government cannot prohibit virtual (as opposed to actual) depictions of child pornography when actual children are not used or harmed in the production process.
- The government cannot prohibit depictions of women that it regards as inconsistent with its preferred view of women.
- As with other speech, hate speech is generally protected under the First Amendment (unless, of course, it involves fighting words or some other category of unprotected speech such as a true threat).
- Government cannot ban speech simply because it disagrees with the underlying message.
- Government can prohibit cross-burnings that convey a true threat of impending violence.
- Commercial speech is constitutionally protected, but generally receives less protection than political speech.
- Under the *Central Hudson* test, the Court applies a four part test in evaluating regulations of commercial speech: 1) whether the regulated speech is misleading or relates to an unlawful transaction in which case regulation is permissible; 2) if the speech is not misleading or related to an unlawful activity, whether the regulation is supported by a substantial government interest; 3) whether the regulation directly advances the interest; 4) whether the governmental interest can be achieved by a more limited restriction on commercial speech.

- In recent years, the justices have sometimes disagreed regarding the standard of review to be applied in commercial speech cases with some justices arguing for a more rigorous standard of review.
- In overbreadth cases, plaintiffs claim that an overbroad law "chills" their expression by causing "persons whose expression is constitutionally protected to refrain from exercising their rights for fear of criminal sanctions by a statute susceptible of application to protected expression."
- Both the vagueness and overbreadth doctrines can involve either a "facial" challenge to a law (a suit which alleges that a law is facially unconstitutional and should be struck down in its entirety) or an "as applied" challenge (alleging that the law is invalid as applied to the facts of a particular case).
- The Court has tended to apply the overbreadth doctrine "only as a last resort," and has generally required that the overbreadth be "substantial" before a law will be invalidated on its face.
- The vagueness doctrine provides that "a statute which either forbids or requires the doing of an act in terms so vague that men of common intelligence must necessarily guess at its meaning and differ as to its application violates the first essential of due process of law."
- The vagueness doctrine is grounded in several ideas: "First, vague laws may trap the innocent by not providing fair warning. Second, if arbitrary and discriminatory enforcement is to be prevented, laws must provide explicit standards for those who apply them. A vague law impermissibly delegates basic policy matters to policemen, judges, and juries for resolution on an ad hoc and subjective basis, with the attendant dangers of arbitrary and discriminatory application."
- In general, the First Amendment imposes a very strong presumption against the validity of "prior restraints"—restrictions on speech that are imposed prior to its dissemination.
- The Court has been more lax in applying the prohibition against prior restraints to motion picture licensing schemes provided that the scheme contains appropriate protections for speech.
- Courts have also upheld content neutral time, place, and manner licensing restrictions for parades and other public events.

- The rule against prior restraints has also been applied to injunctions against expression, including defamatory speech and speech relating to matters of national security.
- In more recent cases, the Court has suggested that injunctions should be subject to a different standard of review that focuses on whether there is a "fit between the objectives of an injunction and the restrictions it imposes on speech" so that the relief is "no more burdensome to the defendants than necessary to provide complete relief to the plaintiffs."
- The Court has also held that "symbolic speech" (speech that expresses ideas through symbols rather than spoken or written words) is protected under the First Amendment.
- Symbolic speech can involve either pure speech (as when an individual wears a black armband to protest a war) or can involve conduct. When conduct is involved, the Court has been less inclined to provide as much protection as it does for pure speech.
- In order for a restriction on symbolic speech to be upheld, four requirements must be met: 1) government must have the power to regulate in the field; 2) the regulation must advance a substantial or important government interest; 3) the interest must be unrelated to the suppression of free expression; & 4) the incidental burden on speech must be no greater than necessary to achieve the governmental interest.
- If the government has targeted symbolic speech because of its content, and assuming that the speech is not low or no value (*e.g.*, obscenity), the *O'Brien* test will not apply (because part three of the test is not satisfied) and the Court will instead apply strict scrutiny.
- Historically, certain public venues (*e.g.*, streets, sidewalks and parks) have been available for expressive activity. These are called "traditional public fora."
- There are also "designated public fora" which are places that have not traditionally been made available for expressive activities, but which the state has chosen to make available for those purposes.
- Modern public forum doctrine recognizes that governments may have legitimate non-content-based reasons for restricting access to fora based on the time, place and manner of the expression.
- The Court has held that government cannot discriminate against religious speech in public forums, and must (in some

instances) allow religious groups to use school premises on the same basis as other groups.

- The Court has also held that campaign finance—the raising and spending of money for political campaign purposes—is entitled to constitutional protection.
- Both campaign donations and campaign expenditures constitute protected speech because they relate to discussions regarding public issues and the qualifications of candidates.
- Although campaign contributions are entitled to protection, they are entitled to less protection than campaign expenditures because they do not convey the underlying basis for support.
- The Court has rejected the argument that government may try to equalize the resources of individuals and groups, as well as their ability "to influence the outcome of elections."
- Since the Constitution protects "speech," it implicitly protects the right of association since people can speak more effectively when they join together to speak with a common voice.
- The right of association protects interests of an "intimate nature" that involve "highly personal relationships" such as the "creation and sustenance of a family," including marriage, childbirth, the raising and education of children, and cohabitation with one's relatives.
- The right of association also protects relations developed for speech purposes.
- When a group is large and unselective, and primarily of a commercial (rather than a speech) nature, the government may limit the group's right to associate in order to further a compelling governmental interest.
- A component of the right to associate is the right not to be forced to associate with ideas or principles with which one disagrees.
- There are also limits on government's ability to force individuals to provide financial contributions to causes or ideas with which they disagree.
- The "unconstitutional conditions" doctrine suggests that, in some instances, the nature or level of governmental encouragement or incentives transcends constitutional bounds.
- A university may not choose to fund most publications, but exclude publications by religious groups, when it has created a forum "to encourage a diversity of views from private speakers."

- While Congress is not obligated to fund legal services or to fund the entire range of legal claims, it may not preclude legal services offices from pursuing theories that may be critical to effective litigation (*e.g.*, insulating the government's interpretation of the Constitution from challenge by legal services attorneys).
- The government may require law schools to admit military recruiters on the same basis as other recruiters on pain of losing federal funds.
- While governmental employees have First Amendment rights, those rights are not co-extensive with those of other citizens.
- Federal employees can be prohibited from taking "any active part in political management or in political campaigns."
- The federal government cannot prohibit its employees from accepting any compensation for making speeches or writing articles when the subject has no relationship to the employee's official duties.
- Public school teachers cannot be required to swear an oath of loyalty to the state and to reveal the groups with which they associate.
- Governmental employees do not relinquish their right to comment on matters of public interest simply because of their status as government employees.
- In evaluating governmental restrictions on the rights of public employees, the Court usually balances "the interests of the employee, as a citizen, in commenting upon matters of public concern and the interest of the State, as an employer, in promoting the efficiency of the public services it performs through its employees."
- A police officer may be terminated for off-duty speech (selling videotapes depicting himself engaged in sexually explicit acts while wearing a police uniform, and one which depicted a police engaged in sex acts while issuing a citation) when that speech violate specific police department policies, including engaging in conduct unbecoming of an officer and immoral conduct.
- A state cannot force its employees to recite a loyalty oath denying their past affiliation with Communists, and cannot bar employment on the basis of membership in "subversive" organizations.
- While the Court has recognized that students do not relinquish their First Amendment rights at the schoolhouse door, the Court

has been reluctant to hold that student speech rights are co-extensive with those of adults.

- Because of the special characteristics of the school environment, the Court has upheld some restrictions on student speech (*e.g.*, it can prohibit sexually explicit and drug-related speech).
- School officials may control the content of a student publication in order to make sure that the paper's content is consistent with the school's "basic educational mission," and is otherwise appropriate for the student audience.
- School officials have less authority to regulate off-campus student speech during non-school hours unless that speech constitutes a material disruption to the school environment.
- When the government is financing speech, the Court has been more willing to allow the government to impose restrictions on that speech to ensure that the speech accords with the government's wishes.
- If government chooses to fund preventive family planning services, population research, infertility services, and other related medical, informational, and educational activities, it can preclude the use of funds for "programs where abortion is a method of family planning."
- In providing funding for the arts, the federal government can require the funding agency to consider "general standards of decency and respect for the diverse beliefs and values of the American public."
- The Court has rejected the notion that the press has a special status that provides it with special rights over and above the speech rights of other citizens.
- The Court does not view the press as an institution that gives it speaking rights superior to those accorded to the public.
- Reporters do not have a First Amendment privilege that shields them from being forced to testify before grand juries regarding their sources.
- The police can obtain a search warrant for a newsroom without violating the First Amendment.
- The Court has upheld state and federal prison regulations prohibiting media interviews with inmates, and limiting media access to prisons, in deference to the security concerns of prison officials.

- There is a right of access to judicial proceedings, especially criminal proceedings.
- The press' right of access to proceedings extends to *voir dire*, preliminary hearings, and other pretrial hearings.
- The right of access to judicial proceedings may conflict with a defendant's right to a trial free of prejudicial publicity and the Sixth Amendment guarantee of a "public trial, by an impartial jury."
- Although the Court has held that a trial judge must take various steps designed to ensure defendants a fair trial, the balance cuts in favor of the public's right to be informed regarding those proceedings.
- Judges can take various steps to ensure a defendant's right to a fair trial: establish rules for press decorum; use the *voir dire* process to screen out jurors who have been unfairly influenced by prejudicial pretrial publicity; sequester jurors to limit their exposure to external influences, including the press; entertain the possibility of a change of venue or a continuance; or possibly enter a gag order directed at parties, witnesses, counsel, police, or other participants.
- Absent extraordinary circumstances, courts may not impose gag orders that prevent the press from reporting on trials or other public judicial proceedings.
- The Court has been more willing to uphold speech restrictions imposed upon parties to a proceeding and their attorneys when there is a "substantial likelihood of material prejudice."
- The Court has held that the mere presence of cameras in the courtroom does not automatically violate due process, and that a defendant must prove actual prejudice (in the sense that the presence of cameras impairs the jurors' ability to decide the case based on the evidence presented, or that their presence adversely affected the trial) in order to establish a due process claim.
- The First Amendment applies to many media, including movies, broadcasting, cable, and the internet.
- The Court views each medium differently for First Amendment purposes, based upon the unique problems it presents.
- The Court generally has been most protective of the print media.
- The Court has provided less protection to the broadcast media, because of spectrum scarcity (only a relative few can have

broadcast licenses), their uniquely pervasive presence, and their easy access by children.

- The Court has recognized that broadcasters have editorial discretion over broadcasting content (*e.g.*, to choose which advertisements to accept).
- The Court has provided less protection to sexually explicit but non-obscene expression in the broadcast format.
- The Court has upheld federal rules that require cable operators to carry the signals of local broadcasters ("must carry rules") despite claims that the rules interfere with editorial discretion.
- Content regulation of broadcasting is subject to strict scrutiny.
- Telephone and accessibility to children may be blocked so indecent expression may not be regulated.
- The Court has held that Congress cannot ban all "indecent" material from the internet and has equated this medium with print for First Amendment purposes.

CHAPTER 11

The Establishment Clause

The Establishment Clause provides that "Congress shall make no law respecting an establishment of religion." Although the Clause explicitly applies only to Congress, it has been interpreted as applying to both the federal government and the states by virtue of the Fourteenth Amendment due process clause.

Even though there is disagreement about what the Clause means, most commentators agree that it (at least) prohibits the establishment of a governmentally endorsed church, the requiring of individuals to go to or remain away from church against their will, as well as forcing individuals to believe or disbelieve a particular religion. However, most Establishment Clause litigation does not fall into these categories, and instead focuses on whether other lesser governmental acts (*e.g.*, providing financial aid to religion) constitutes an establishment of religion.

In addition to the Establishment Clause, the First Amendment also contains the Free Exercise Clause, and there are inevitable conflicts between the two clauses. These tensions are revealed in *Everson v. Board of Education,* 330 U.S. 1 (1947), which involved a decision by the New Jersey board of education to reimburse parents for money spent to transport their children to school (including religious schools) on public buses. The Court recognized that the state should not hamper citizens in the free exercise of their religion, and should not prohibit members of any faith, "*because of their faith, or lack of it,* from receiving the benefits of public welfare legislation." However, the Court concluded that the Establishment Clause did not require the state to cut schools off from ordinary benefits, but simply "requires the state to be a neutral in its relations with groups of religious believers and non-believers; it does not require the state to be their adversary. State power is no more to be used so as to handicap religions, than it is to favor them." As a result, the Court upheld the reimbursements.

Everson is a famous decision because it is the case in which Justice Black articulated his metaphor regarding a "wall" between church and state: "The First Amendment has erected a *wall between church and state.* That wall must be kept high and impregnable. We could not approve the slightest breach. New Jersey has not breached it here." Some justices disagree and question whether the Establishment Clause really was intended to create a "wall of separation." Indeed, as the decision in *Everson* suggests, it is not so clear that a "wall" does exist.

Financial Aid to Religious Schools. Beginning in 1971, and continuing for half-a-century, the Court has analyzed Establishment Clause cases using the so-called *Lemon* test. That test, articulated in *Lemon v. Kurtzman*, 403 U.S. 602 (1971), established a three-prong test for evaluating the validity of establishment clause issues: "First, the statute must have a secular legislative purpose; second, its principal or primary effect must be one that neither advances nor inhibits religion; finally, the statute must not foster 'an excessive government entanglement with religion.' " *Lemon* itself involved a Rhode Island law that authorized state officials to supplement the salaries of teachers of secular subjects in private schools by 15%, and Pennsylvania's Nonpublic Elementary and Secondary Education Act which authorized direct payments to nonpublic schools for the actual cost of teachers' salaries, textbooks, and instructional materials. However, secular costs were required to be segregated from religious costs, and monies could only be spent for courses in mathematics, modern foreign languages, physical science, and physical education using state provided textbooks and instructional materials, and the courses must be free of religious teaching, morals or forms of worship. The Court struck both laws down. Even though their purpose and effect were secular (to make sure that all children were educated in secular subjects), the Court found an excessive entanglement between church and state. In order to ensure that teachers did not infuse religious doctrine into their classes, the state would be required to monitor their teachings. The Court also emphasized the tendency of both the Rhode Island and Pennsylvania programs to create "political divisiveness" because "partisans of parochial schools, understandably concerned with rising costs and sincerely dedicated to both the religious and secular educational missions of their schools, will inevitably promote political action to achieve their goals. Those who oppose state aid, whether for constitutional, religious, or fiscal reasons, will inevitably respond and employ all of the usual political campaign techniques to prevail. Candidates will be forced to declare and voters to choose."

After 1971, the *Lemon* test was applied in many cases, but not always with satisfactory or consistent results. For example, in *Board of Education v. Allen*, 392 U.S. 236 (1968), the Court upheld a state program that provided textbooks (the same ones used in the public schools) to parochial schools for the teaching of secular subjects. Nevertheless, in *Meek v. Pittenger*, 421 U.S. 349 (1975), and *Wolman v. Walter*, 433 U.S. 229 (1977), the Court held that a state could not loan "instructional material and equipment" to parochial schools because the Court believed that such aid would have the impermissible effect of advancing religion by aiding "the sectarian school enterprise as a whole." In *Wolman*, the Court held that the state may provide speech and hearing diagnostic services, and diagnostic psychological services, to pupils attending nonpublic schools, because they "have little or no educational content and are not closely associated with the educational mission of the nonpublic school."

In *Wolman*, the Court also held that the state may pay for therapeutic, guidance, and remedial services for students who have been identified as having a need for specialized attention at neutral sites away from the parochial schools. However, *Wolman* also held that the state may not spend funds for student field trips "to governmental, industrial, cultural, and scientific centers designed to enrich the secular studies of students" without implicating "direct aid to sectarian education" and creating the need for "close supervision [and] excessive entanglement." Finally, in *Committee for Public Education and Religious Liberty v. Nyquist*, 413 U.S. 756 (1973), the Court held that the state may not provide direct money grants to "qualifying" nonpublic schools for the "maintenance and repair [of] school facilities and equipment to ensure the health, welfare and safety of enrolled pupils" when payments were not restricted facilities used exclusively for secular purposes.

Because of these inconsistent results, a number of U.S. Supreme Court justices criticized the *Lemon* test, arguing that the test has proven inadequate for resolving Establishment Clause issues. *See Wallace v. Jaffree*, 472 U.S. 38, 111 (1985) (Rehnquist, J., dissenting). In *Shurtleff v. City of Boston*, 596 U.S. 243 (2022), a concurring Justice Gorsuch leveled his own criticisms of the *Lemon* test:

> *Lemon* held out the promise that any Establishment Clause dispute could be resolved by following a neat checklist focused on three questions. The only sure thing *Lemon* yielded was new business for lawyers and judges. Faced with such a malleable test, risk-averse local officials found themselves in an ironic bind. To avoid Establishment Clause liability, they sometimes felt they had to discriminate against religious speech and suppress religious exercises. But those actions only invited liability under other provisions of the First Amendment. *Lemon*'s

abstract and ahistoric test put "policymakers in a vise between the Establishment Clause and the Free Speech and Free Exercise Clauses." *Capitol Square Review and Advisory Bd. v. Pinette*, 515 U.S. 753, 767 (1995) (plurality opinion). It is less clear is why this state of affairs still persists. *Lemon* has long since been exposed as an anomaly and a mistake.

From the birth of modern Establishment Clause litigation in *Everson v. Board of Ed. of Ewing*, this Court looked primarily to historical practices and analogues to guide its analysis. 330 U.S. 1 (1947). *Lemon* interrupted this long line of precedent. It offered no plausible reason. And the ahistoric alternative it offered quickly proved both unworkable in practice and unsound in its results. Several early decisions applying *Lemon* were rapidly overruled. All of which led Justice after Justice to conclude that *Lemon* was "flawed in its fundamentals," "unworkable in practice," and "inconsistent with our history and precedents." *County of Allegheny v. American Civil Liberties Union*, 492 U.S. 573, 355, 669 (1989) (Kennedy, J., concurring and dissenting). Recognizing *Lemon*'s flaws, this Court has not applied its test for nearly two decades.

It's hard not to wonder whether some simply prefer the policy outcomes *Lemon* can be manipulated to produce. The test is guaranteed to spit out results more hostile to religion than anything a careful inquiry into the original understanding of the Constitution could sustain. *Lemon* may promote an unserious, results-oriented approach to constitutional interpretation. But for some, that may be more a virtue than a vice. If your policy goal is to lump in religious speech with fighting words and obscenity, if it is to celebrate only a "particular" type of diversity consistent with popular ideology, the First Amendment is not exactly your friend. Dragging *Lemon* from its grave may be your only chance.

After significant doctrinal consternation, the Court modified the *Lemon* test in important respects in *Agostini v. Felton*, 521 U.S. 203 (1997). The Court continued to apply the purpose prong of the *Lemon* test, but altered the effect prong to abandon the presumption that "the placement of public employees on parochial school grounds inevitably results in the impermissible effect of state-sponsored indoctrination or constitutes a symbolic union between government and religion." In addition, the Court was willing to assume that program participants would dutifully perform their tasks, and therefore did not have to be monitored (with the attendant entanglement that would occur from that monitoring), and the Court rejected the idea that any "government aid that directly aids the educational function of religious schools is invalid." The Court's revised approach opened up the possibility that states could provide significantly increased aid to religious organizations.

In *Mitchell v. Helms*, 530 U.S. 793 (2000), a plurality of the Court sought to revive the "neutrality" test in a case that allocated federal funds for instructional and educational materials, including library services and materials, assessments, reference materials, computer software and hardware for instructional use, and other curricular materials. The funds could be used to "supplement," but could not "supplant" funds from non-Federal sources, and the "services, materials, and equipment" must be "secular, neutral, and nonideological," and private schools could not acquire control of the service, materials or equipment. In upholding the law, the plurality applied the neutrality principle: "If the government, seeking to further some legitimate secular purpose, offers aid on the same terms, without regard to religion, to all who adequately further that purpose, then it is fair to say that any aid going to a religious recipient only has the effect of furthering that secular purpose." The plurality emphasized that the statute did not define "recipients by reference to religion," and concluded that the fact that the program provided religious schools "a benefit that they did not previously receive does not mean that the program, by reducing the cost of securing a religious education, creates an 'incentive' for parents to choose such an education for their children. *Any* aid will have some such effect." The plurality opinion rejected any distinction between "direct" and "indirect" aid to religion, including the argument that any aid to religious schools must not be divertible to religious use, and held that a school could receive aid even though the school was "pervasively sectarian." On the latter point, the Court noted: "it is bizarre that the Court would reserve special hostility for those who take their religion seriously." Under *Mitchell's* "neutrality" test, and even under *Agostini's* modified three-part test, one can justify far more support to parochial schools than would have been permissible under prior decisions.

Finally, in *Kennedy v. Bremerton School District*, 597 U.S. 507 (2022), the Court effectively overruled *Lemon*. The case involved a high school football coach who prayed at the 50-yard line after every game. After repeated demands to stop, the school district took disciplinary action against him, arguing that it could not permit the prayers without running afoul of the Establishment Clause. In concluding that the coach's prayers were protected under the Free

Exercise Clause, and rejecting the District's Establishment Clause claim, the Court overruled the *Lemon* decision. The Court noted that it had attempted in *Lemon* to create a "grand unified theory" for assessing Establishment Clause claims. "In time, the approach also came to involve estimations about whether a 'reasonable observer' would consider the government's challenged action an 'endorsement' of religion." However, the Court believed that the "shortcomings" associated with this "ambitious," abstract, and ahistorical approach to the Establishment Clause became so "apparent" that this Court "long ago abandoned *Lemon* and its endorsement test offshoot." The tests "invited chaos," led to "differing results" in materially identical cases and created a "minefield" for legislators. In the Court's view, the Establishment Clause does not include anything like a "modified heckler's veto, in which religious activity can be proscribed" based on "perceptions" or "discomfort." It concluded that an "Establishment Clause violation does not automatically follow whenever a public school or other government entity 'fails to censor' private religious speech. Nor does the Establishment Clause "compel the government to purge from the public sphere" anything an objective observer could reasonably infer endorses or "partakes of the religious." The Court held that the *Lemon* test should be replaced with a new test: "the Establishment Clause must be interpreted by 'reference to historical practices and understandings.' *Town of Greece v. Galloway*, 572 U.S. 565, 576 (2014)." The Court suggested that the line between "the permissible and the impermissible" must "accord with history and faithfully reflect the understanding of the Founding Fathers."

Justice Sotomayor, joined by Justice Breyer and Justice Kagan, dissented, arguing that the Court should apply the endorsement test which had been applied in governmental acknowledgement of religion cases, and "one of the relevant questions is whether an objective observer, acquainted with the text, legislative history, and implementation of the practice, would perceive it as a state endorsement of prayer in public schools." She rejected the idea that the test involved a "modified heckler's veto, in which religious activity can be proscribed" based on "perceptions" or "discomfort." On the contrary, she argued, "The endorsement inquiry considers the perspective not of just any hypothetical or uninformed observer experiencing subjective discomfort, but of 'the reasonable observer' who is 'aware of the history and context of the community and forum in which the religious speech takes place.' " She argued that the proper approach is to accommodate "religious practices to the degree possible while respecting the Establishment Clause." As a result, she believed that the Court was wrong to overrule the *Lemon* test: "*Lemon* summarized 'the cumulative criteria developed by the Court over many years' of experience 'drawing lines' as to when government engagement with religion violated the Establishment Clause." While she agreed "that the *Lemon* test does not solve every Establishment Clause problem," she believed that the "purposes and effects of a government action matter in evaluating whether that action violates the Establishment Clause."

Justice Sotomayor also questioned the wisdom of the Court's new Establishment Clause test. While she recognized that the "Court has long referred to historical practice as one element of the analysis in Establishment Clause cases, the Court has never announced this as a general test or exclusive focus." In addition, she worried that the test did not provide sufficient guidance for school administrators: "If even judges and Justices, with full adversarial briefing and argument tailored to precise legal issues, regularly disagree (and err) in their amateur efforts at history, how are school administrators, faculty, and staff supposed to adapt? How will school administrators exercise their responsibilities to manage school curriculum and events when the Court elevates individuals' rights to religious exercise above all else? Today's opinion provides little in the way of answers."

School Vouchers. School voucher programs have constituted a more controversial form of aid to parochial schools. Under these programs, government provides vouchers to every parent that can be used to purchase education at public or private schools (including parochial). The vouchers help parents send their children to the school of their choice, be it private, public, or parochial. By introducing choice into the system, vouchers force schools to compete with each other, and hopefully lead to a better educational system.

A number of early cases dealt with tuition reimbursement schemes without definitively resolving questions relating to their validity. For example, in *Committee for Public Education and Religious Liberty v. Nyquist*, 413 U.S. 756 (1973), the Court struck down a law that provided partial tuition reimbursements and tax benefits to the parents of elementary and secondary non-public school students. The Court held that the reimbursement plan violated the effects prong of the *Lemon* test because there was no mechanism to ensure that "the state aid derived from public funds will be used exclusively for secular, neutral, and nonideological purposes," and the Court noted that "direct aid in whatever form is invalid." Likewise, in *Sloan v. Lemon*, 413 U.S. 825 (1973), the Court struck down Pennsylvania's "Parent Reimbursement Act for Nonpublic Education," which reimbursed parents for a portion of tuition expenses incurred at nonpublic schools, finding "no constitutionally significant distinctions between this law and the one declared invalid [in] *Nyquist*."

In *Mueller v. Allen*, 463 U.S. 388 (1983), the Court departed from *Nyquist* and *Sloan* in upholding a Minnesota law that allowed taxpayers to deduct certain expenses incurred in educating their children from state income taxes. The deduction was limited to actual expenses incurred for "tuition, textbooks and transportation" of dependents attending elementary or secondary schools, and could not exceed $500 per dependent in grades K through six and $700 per dependent in grades seven through twelve. In upholding the law, the Court applied *Lemon's* three-part test and emphasized that the program was not invalid simply because it provided aid to a religious institution. The Court emphasized that the law had a "secular" purpose (defraying the cost of educational expenses incurred by parents, and helping to create an educated populace), and its "primary effect" did not advance religion. Indeed, the deduction was only one of many deductions provided by the state, including deductions for such things as medical expenses, and charitable contributions, and was allowed for all parents including those with children in public schools, and therefore "neutrally" provided state assistance to a broad spectrum of citizens. Finally, all aid to parochial schools came through individual parents, and as a result of their choice to send their children to private schools, rather than as direct payments to religious institutions. The Court noted that private schools provide alternatives to public schools, thereby promoting competition, and thereby relieving the tax burden on public schools by diverting students. The Court found that there was no "excessive entanglement" because financial aid came to religious institutions only as a result of the individual decisions of parents rather than because of a governmental decision to fund religious schools.

In *Zelman v. Simmons-Harris*, 536 U.S. 639 (2002), the Court extended *Mueller* in upholding a voucher program. *Zelman* involved an Ohio program for low-income and minority school districts that were in crisis, and that was designed to provide educational choices to parents who could send their children to public schools or to participating schools, religious or nonreligious. Participating private schools were required to agree not to discriminate on the basis of race, religion, or ethnic background, or to "advocate or foster unlawful behavior or teach hatred of any person or group on the basis of race, ethnicity, national origin, or religion." Public schools located in adjacent school districts could also participate in the program and receive a $2,250 tuition grant for each student accepted in addition to the full amount of per-pupil state funding attributable to each student. The tuition involved differential payments and co-payments based on need. However, religious institutions received funds only when parents chose to endorse the voucher to the school. During the 1999–2000 school year, 56 private schools participated in the program, 46 (or 82%) of which had a religious affiliation. None of the public schools in districts adjacent to Cleveland elected to participate. Of the 3,700 students who participated in the program, 96% enrolled in religiously affiliated schools. Also included in the program were 10 community schools that were funded by the state but were run by independent school boards, with the authority to hire their own teachers and determine their own curriculum, and who enrolled more than 1,900 students and received $4,518 per student under the tuition assistance program. Magnet schools were public schools that emphasized a particular subject area, teaching method, or service to students, and they received $7,746 per student and enrolled more than 13,000 students in 1999.

The Court upheld the voucher program, finding a valid secular purpose (of providing educational assistance to poor children in a demonstrably failing public school system), and concluding that the program did not have an impermissible effect (because it provided aid to religious schools only as the "result of the genuine and independent choices of private individuals"). In addition, the program was neutral in that it conferred educational assistance without regard to religion, and permitted all schools, religious and nonreligious to participate. The only preference was for low-income families, and the Court found no financial incentives that skewed the program in favor of religious schools. The Court rejected the argument that the Cleveland program created "a public perception that the State is endorsing religious practices and beliefs" because aid reached public schools only a result of the independent decisions of private individuals, as well as because a "reasonable observer" would realize that the program is part of a broader plan to assist poor children in failed schools. The Court emphasized that the program provided a "range" of educational choices to Cleveland children. The Court refused to attach significance to the fact that 96% of the students, who enrolled in private schools, attended religious schools: "the constitutionality of a neutral educational aid program simply does not turn on whether and why, in a particular area, at a particular time, most private schools are run by religious organizations, or most recipients choose to use the aid at a religious school."

Espinoza v. Montana Department of Revenue, 591 U.S. 464 (2020), broke new ground on the question of governmental support for parochial schools. *Espinoza* involved a Montana law which sought to create parental and student choice through a scholarship program for students who attended private schools. The program created a tax credit of up to $150 to any taxpayer who donates to a participating "student scholarship organization" which, in turn, passed the money on as scholarships to students who attended private schools. However, the legislature directed that the aid program be administered consistently with Article X, section 6, of the Montana Constitution, which contains a "no-aid" provision that barred direct or indirect governmental aid to sectarian schools. In order to comply with the no aid provision, the Montana Supreme Court terminated the aid program for all students whether enrolled in sectarian or secular schools.

The Court held that Montana acted improperly in terminating the program and in denying aid to sectarian schools: "Montana's no-aid provision bars religious schools from public benefits solely because of the religious character of the schools," and it denies "parents who wish to send their children to a religious school from those same benefits, again solely because of the religious character of the school." As applied, Montana's no-aid (to religious schools) provision "imposes special disabilities on the basis of religious status" and "conditions the availability of benefits upon a recipient's willingness to surrender its religiously impelled status." Since placing such a condition on benefits or privileges "inevitably deters or discourages the exercise of First Amendment rights," the Court held that it "is enough to conclude that strict scrutiny applies under *Trinity Lutheran* because Montana's no-aid provision discriminates based on religious status."

Espinoza was extended by the holding in *Carson v. Makin*, 596 U.S. 767 (2022). *Carson* involved a Maine law requiring local towns to provide every child with the benefits of a free public education. For cities that were too rural or too small to maintain their own schools, Maine created a tuition assistance program that provided for the payment of "the tuition at the public school or the approved private school of the parent's choice at which the student is accepted." "Approved" schools included those that were "currently accredited by a New England association of schools and colleges" or separately "approved for attendance purposes" by the Department, and which met certain curricular requirements (e.g., using English as the language of instruction, offering a course in "Maine history, including the Constitution of Maine and Maine's cultural and ethnic heritage," and maintaining a student-teacher ratio of not more than 30 to 1). Thus, the program provided for parental choice with one restriction: even though parents could send their children to schools inside or outside the state, or even in foreign countries, Maine precluded religious schools from participating in the program if they infused religion into their classes. The Court struck down the Maine prohibition on the inclusion of religious schools as involving discrimination against those schools.

School Prayer. In *Engel v. Vitale,* 370 U.S. 421 (1962), the Court struck down a state-initiated prayer that was to be read aloud at the beginning of each school day. In doing so, the Court held that: "It is no part of the business of government to compose official prayers for any group of people to recite as part of a religious program carried on by government." The Court emphasized the history of the Establishment Clause, and the fact that many colonists left Europe to escape state-imposed religions. The Court regarded the prayer as an establishment even though it was denominationally neutral: "When the power, prestige and financial support of government is placed behind a particular religious belief, the indirect coercive pressure upon religious minorities to conform to the prevailing officially approved religion is plain." The Court expressed concern that "a union of government and religion tends to destroy government and to degrade religion. Religion is too personal, too sacred, too holy, to permit its 'unhallowed perversion' by a civil magistrate." The Court rejected the idea that, by prohibiting the prayer, the Court was "anti-religious": "It is neither sacrilegious nor antireligious to say that [government] should stay out of the business of writing or sanctioning official prayers and leave that purely religious function to the people themselves and to those the people choose to look to for religious guidance."

Although the Establishment Clause prohibits official prayer at schools, either as part of the school curriculum or at football games or graduation, questions have arisen regarding whether government officials have the right to engage in private prayer in relation to school activities. That issue was presented in *Kennedy v. Bremerton School District,* 597 U.S. 507 (2022), a case in which a high school football coach had a practice of praying at midfield following the conclusion of every football game. Sometimes, players chose to join him. Sometimes not. For a while, he also conducted pregame and postgame prayers in the locker room, but he discontinued that practice after school officials objected on Establishment Clause grounds. School officials also ordered Kennedy to discontinue his mid-field post-game prayers, viewing those prayers as a violation of the Establishment Clause as well, but he refused to stop. Instead, Kennedy requested an accommodation that would have allowed him to continue the prayers while students were otherwise engaged (e.g., heading to the locker room, boarding the bus, or singing the school fight song), but his request was denied. He was ultimately disciplined for praying on three occasions, all of which were relatively private. For example, he was disciplined for praying following the October 16 game while most players were singing the school fight song. On October 23, after the game, Kennedy knelt at the 50-yard line, where "no one joined him," and bowed his head for a "brief, quiet prayer."

After the football game on October 26, Kennedy knelt alone to offer a brief prayer as the players engaged in postgame traditions, although some other adults gathered around him. Following that game, the district placed Kennedy on administrative leave for engaging in "public and demonstrative religious conduct while on duty as an assistant coach" by offering a prayer following the games on October 16, 23, and 26, and suggested that he should have prayed behind closed doors. He was not rehired for the following season. Kennedy filed suit against the school district, claiming that it had unconstitutionally infringed his rights to engage in free speech and to freely exercise his religion.

In analyzing the case, the Court indicated that Kennedy bore the initial burden of proving an infringement of his rights under the Free Exercise and Free Speech Clauses. Kennedy could satisfy that burden by showing that a government entity has burdened his sincere religious practice pursuant to a policy that is not "neutral" or "generally applicable." If plaintiff satisfies that burden, the governmental action is subject to "strict scrutiny" in that the school district must show that its action was justified by a compelling state interest and was narrowly tailored to further that interest. The Court held that Kennedy had discharged his burden. He sought to engage in a sincerely motivated religious exercise, and the school district disciplined him *only* for his decision to persist in praying quietly without his players after three games in October 2015. The school district's performance evaluation after the 2015 football season advised against rehiring Kennedy on the ground that he "failed to supervise student athletes after games." In fact, this requirement was based on Kennedy's religious exercise. The school district permitted other members of the coaching staff to forgo supervising students briefly after the game to do things like visit with friends or take personal phone calls. Thus, any postgame supervisory requirement was not applied in an evenhanded way.

While the Court recognized that government employees are entitled to speak as private citizens, "teachers and coaches are government employees paid in part to speak on the government's behalf and convey its intended messages." Accordingly, the Court held that his free speech rights should be evaluated using the two-part test articulated in *Pickering v. Board of Ed. of Township High School Dist. 205, Will Cty.*, 391 U.S. 563 (1968), and *Garcetti v. Ceballos*, 547 U.S. 410 (2006) (discussed in Chapter 9). Under the first step of this test, if a public employee speaks "pursuant to official duties," the Free Speech Clause generally will not shield the individual from an employer's control and discipline, because that kind of speech is — for constitutional purposes — the government's own speech. However, when an employee "speaks as a citizen addressing a matter of public concern," the First Amendment may be implicated, and courts should proceed to a second step. At that step, courts engage in "a delicate balancing of the competing interests surrounding the speech and its consequences." Even then, courts will consider whether an employee's speech interests are outweighed by "the interest of the State, as an employer, in promoting the efficiency of the public services it performs through its employees."

In applying the two-part test, the Court held that Kennedy was engaged in private speech, not government speech because he was not engaged in speech "within the scope" of his duties as a coach: "He was not instructing players, discussing strategy, encouraging better on-field performance, or engaged in any speech the school district paid him to produce as a coach." Although Kennedy was working for the school district, he gave the prayer "during a time when coaches were free to attend briefly to personal matters — everything from checking sports scores on their phones to greeting friends and family in the stands." As a result, the Court concluded that he was not "fulfilling a responsibility imposed by his employment" during that time, especially since the students were engaged in other activities like singing the school fight song"; "both the substance of Kennedy's speech and the circumstances suggested that he was engaged in private speech." Thus, according to the Court, whether the case was decided under Free Exercise Clause or under the Free Speech Clause, the Court suggested that it would apply "strict scrutiny," meaning that any restrictions must serve a compelling interest and be narrowly tailored to achieve that interest. The Court indicated that whether it applied strict scrutiny, or the intermediate standard mandated by *Pickering-Garcetti*, the District could not satisfy the standard.

An important part of the decision involved the Court's refusal to apply the *Lemon* test, or *Lemon*'s focus on whether a "reasonable observer" would view the government's challenged action as an "endorsement" of religion. The Court indicated that the *Lemon* test had " 'invited chaos,' led to 'differing results' in materially identical cases and created a 'minefield' for legislators." In rejecting the "reasonable observer" test, the Court emphasized that the Establishment Clause does not include anything like a " 'modified heckler's veto, in which religious activity can be proscribed' based on 'perceptions' or 'discomfort.' " The Court decreed that the Establishment Clause should instead be interpreted by "reference to historical practices and understandings."

The Court also rejected the idea that the district would be regarded as "endorsing" Kennedy's prayer by refusing to suppress it, or that students would have felt compelled to participate in Kennedy's prayers: "There is no indication that anyone expressed any coercion concerns about the quiet, postgame prayers that Kennedy asked to continue and that led to his suspension. Nor is there any evidence that students felt pressured to participate in these prayers." Not only did the students not feel coerced, nobody joined Kennedy for some of the prayers in question, and only members of the public joined for the third one. The Court also rejected the idea "that *any* visible religious conduct by a teacher or coach should be deemed — without more and as a matter of law — impermissibly coercive on students." The Court was concerned by the impact of this approach: "Rather than respect the First Amendment's double protection for religious expression, it would have us prefer secular activity. Schools could fire teachers for praying quietly over their lunch, for wearing a yarmulke to school, or for offering a midday prayer during a break before practice." The Court concluded that the "prayers for which Kennedy was disciplined were not publicly broadcast or recited to a captive audience. Students were not required or expected to participate and were engaged in other activities. And none of Kennedy's students did participate in any of the October 2015 prayers that resulted in Kennedy's discipline. As a result, there was no coercion." The Court ultimately concluded that the district's action was impermissible because it "sought to punish an individual for engaging in a brief, quiet, personal religious observance doubly protected by the Free Exercise and Free Speech Clauses of the First Amendment."

Justice Thomas, concurred, arguing that "the district had no constitutional basis for reprimanding Kennedy under any possibly applicable standard of scrutiny." Justice Alito concurred, arguing that Kennedy's prayer occurred "during a time when a brief lull in his duties gave him a few free moments to engage in private activities."

Justice Sotomayor dissented, arguing that *Engel v. Vitale*, 370 U.S. 421 (1962), prohibited school officials from leading prayer. She emphasized his prior conduct of leading student prayer prior to and after football games and noted that Kennedy had invited others to join his prayers, including attracting media attention, and that his activities had led to significant disruptions. As a result, she did not view the case as being about "an individual's ability to engage in private prayer at work," but rather as "about whether a school district is required to allow one of its employees to incorporate a public, communicative display of the employee's personal religious beliefs into a school event, where that display is recognizable as part of a longstanding practice of the employee ministering religion to students as the public watched." She would have answered the latter question in the negative, emphasizing that "neutrality toward religion is particularly important in the public school" given that parents "entrust public schools with the education of their children on the understanding that the classroom will not purposely be used to advance religious views that may conflict with the private beliefs of the student and his or her family," and that children are particularly vulnerable to coercion because of their "emulation of teachers as role models" and "susceptibility to peer pressure." In her view, since Kennedy was the face of the football program, his "prayer practice implicated the coercion concerns at the center of Establishment Clause jurisprudence." She emphasized that Kennedy served as a role model for students, had the power to affect students in various ways, and worried that a reasonable observer might have viewed Kennedy's prayers as representing the district's official position. In her view, Kennedy "accepted certain limitations" on his freedom of speech when he accepted government employment, and she believed that the school district's responsibilities under the Establishment Clause provided "adequate justification" for restricting his speech.

Moment of Silence Laws. Following *Engel*, some states moved to adopt "moment of silence" laws. Under those laws, schools could impose a "moment of silence" during which children could choose to mediate, pray, or think what they wish as long as they are silent. In *Wallace v. Jaffree,* 472 U.S. 38 (1985), the Court struck down Alabama's moment of silence laws on the theory that they were adopted with the purpose of promoting religion. In reaching this conclusion, the Court emphasized that the bill's sponsor stated in the legislative record, as well as in testimony before the trial court, that his motive for promoting the laws was to return voluntary prayer to the public schools. The Court noted that one of the earlier laws referred only to "meditation" and allowed students to meditate or to pray during the meditation period. The Court concluded that the "addition of 'or voluntary prayer' to the language of the statute" suggested that the State intended to characterize prayer as a favored practice, and therefore violated the requirement of "complete neutrality toward religion." Even though *Wallace* struck down Alabama's moment of silence law, the decision does not necessarily require invalidation of all moment of silence laws—at least, not those enacted for a purely secular purpose (*e.g.*, to solemnize the opening of the school day).

Legislative Prayer. In *Marsh v. Chambers*, 463 U.S. 783 (1983), the Court upheld the Nebraska legislature's practice of beginning each day with a prayer by a chaplain paid out of public funds. The

Court upheld the practice pointing to the history of the Establishment Clause, and noting that the practice of legislative prayer has existed since the nation's beginning. While the Court recognized that "historical patterns" and practices cannot justify an unconstitutional act, the Court viewed the historical evidence as shedding light on "what the draftsmen intended the Establishment Clause to mean" and "how they thought that Clause applied to the practice authorized by the First Congress." The Court concluded: "It can hardly be thought that in the same week Members of the First Congress voted to appoint and to pay a Chaplain for each House and also voted to approve the draft of the First Amendment for submission to the States, they intended the Establishment Clause of the Amendment to forbid what they had just declared acceptable." Mr. Justice Brennan dissented, applying the *Lemon* test and arguing that the " 'purpose' of legislative prayer is preeminently religious" and the " 'primary effect' of legislative prayer is also clearly religious."

Graduation Prayer. In *Lee v. Weisman,* 505 U.S. 577 (1992), the Court struck down the practice of school sponsored prayers at middle schools and high school graduations. The prayers were supposed to be non-sectarian, and the clergy were given instructions about what not to say. In striking down the prayers, the Court expressed concern about the potential for divisiveness regarding a variety of issues, including the choice of the clergy member. The Court also expressed concern about the "guidelines" given to clergy. While the Court recognized that the guidelines constituted an effort to avoid sectarian prayers, it questioned whether the government had any business intruding in this area—even if the instructions constituted a good faith attempt to avoid sectarianism. The Court rejected the notion that a "practice of nonsectarian prayer" existed, as held that the "First Amendment's Religion Clauses mean that religious beliefs and religious expression are too precious to be prescribed by the State." The Court also rejected the idea that the prayer could be regarded as an accommodation of religion: "Psychology supports the assumption that adolescents are susceptible to pressure from their peers towards conformity, and that the influence is strongest in matters of social convention. The government may no more use social pressure to enforce orthodoxy than it may use more direct means." The Court was unpersuaded by the fact that attendance at graduation ceremonies was voluntary: "In our society and in our culture high school graduation is one of life's most significant occasions." The Court distinguished *Marsh,* noting that "At a high school graduation, teachers and principals must and do retain a high degree of control over the precise contents of the program. In this atmosphere the state-imposed character of an invocation and benediction by clergy selected by the school combine to make the prayer a state-sanctioned religious exercise in which the student was left with no alternative but to submit."

Prayer at Football Games. In *Santa Fe Independent School District v. Doe*, 530 U.S. 290 (2000), the Court struck down a school district policy allowing non-denominational prayer at football games. Students were allowed to vote on whether to have a prayer, and to select the student who would give it. The Court applied the so-called "endorsement" test and concluded that an "objective Santa Fe High School student will unquestionably perceive the inevitable pregame prayer as stamped with her school's seal of approval." In addition, because the policy allowed students to veto certain prayer speakers through elections, the Court was concerned about discrimination: "Because" fundamental rights may not be submitted to vote; they depend on the outcome of no elections, "the District's elections are insufficient safeguards of diverse student speech." In addition the Court found that the policy "invites and encourages religious messages" at school sponsored events.

School Curricula. In *School District of Abington Township v. Schempp*, 374 U.S. 203 (1963), the Court struck down a Baltimore, Maryland, law that required the reading of a chapter from the Holy Bible and/or the use of the Lord's Prayer in public school classes. Also at issue was a Pennsylvania law which required that "At least ten verses from the Holy Bible be read, without comment, at the opening of each public school on each school day" In Abington, Pennsylvania, the verses were followed by recitation of the Lord's Prayer. The students reading the Bible verses were allowed to select passages and read from any version they chose, although the school furnished only the King James version. Students actually used various versions of the Bible and the Jewish Holy Scriptures. Students were allowed to absent themselves from the classroom or elect not to participate in the exercises. Even though the states articulated secular purposes for the readings (*e.g.*, the promotion of moral values, contradiction of the materialistic trends of our times, the perpetuation of our institutions and the teaching of literature), the Court found that the purpose was primarily religious: "The place of the Bible as an instrument of religion cannot be gainsaid, and the State's recognition of the pervading religious character of the ceremony is evident from the rule's specific permission of the alternative use of the Catholic Douay version as well as the recent amendment permitting nonattendance at the exercises. None of these factors is consistent with the contention that the Bible is used either as an instrument for nonreligious moral inspiration or as a reference for the teaching of secular subjects."

Over the years, some have argued that, because schools teach values and at the same time have banished prayer and religious teachings from the classrooms, that schools are essentially teaching a "religion of secular humanism." In *Schempp*, the Court agreed that the states "may not establish a 'religion of secularism,' in the sense of affirmatively opposing or showing hostility to religion, thus 'preferring those who believe in no religion over those who do believe.' "

Evolution. There has been considerable litigation regarding the teaching of evolution (the idea that man evolved from lower-human forms) in public schools. The idea of evolution is inconsistent with the biblical notion of creationism—the idea that God created man in his present form. The landmark decision is *Epperson v. Arkansas*, 393 U.S. 97 (1968), which struck down Arkansas' 1928 "anti-evolution" statute that made it illegal for teachers in state-supported schools or universities "to teach the theory or doctrine that mankind ascended or descended from a lower order of animals," or "to adopt or use in any such institution a textbook that teaches" the theory. A violation of the Arkansas law was punishable only as a misdemeanor, but could lead to dismissal of the teacher. When the district adopted a textbook that discussed evolution, Epperson was faced with a choice between using the textbook, and teaching evolution, or following the Arkansas law. While the Court recognized that the State of Arkansas was generally free to stipulate the curriculum for its public schools, the Court concluded that the anti-evolution statute was religiously motivated "because it is contrary to the belief of some that the Book of Genesis must be the exclusive source of doctrine as to the origin of man."

Edwards v. Aguillard, 482 U.S. 578 (1987), dealt with the question of whether a state could pass a statute that did not require schools to teach either evolution or creation science, but did prohibit the teaching of evolution in public schools unless it was accompanied by instruction in "creation science." Applying the *Lemon* test, the Court noted that, while it is normally deferential when a state articulates a secular purpose, the Court found that the Act's stated purpose (academic freedom) was a sham: "Before the passage of the Act, there was no law that prohibited Louisiana public school teachers from teaching any scientific theory. After passage of the law, teachers could only teach evolution if they also taught creation science. Thus, the purpose was to restrict rather than to expand academic freedom." The Court also found a religious purpose in that the law discriminated in favor of creation science and against evolution by requiring that creation science be taught without requiring that evolution be taught. So, the Court held that the "preeminent purpose of the Louisiana Legislature was clearly to advance the religious viewpoint that a supernatural being created humankind." The Court noted that the sponsor of the bill had emphasized his "disdain" for the theory of evolution which was contrary to his religious beliefs. While the Court did not rule out the possibility that a legislature could validly require "scientific critiques of prevailing scientific theories," if done "with the clear secular intent of enhancing the effectiveness of science instruction," this statute was invalid because it was motivated by religious purpose.

Governmental Acknowledgement of Religion. There has been considerable disagreement about whether, and to what extent, the government may acknowledge the existence of religion. This issue has arise in various contexts.

The Ten Commandments. Stone v. Graham, 449 U.S. 39 (1980), struck down a Kentucky statute that required the posting of a copy of the Ten Commandments on the wall of each public classroom in the State. Although the Commonwealth argued that the law was supported by a secular purpose (*e.g.*, the state argued that the Ten Commandments is the fundamental legal code of Western Civilization and the Common Law of the United States), the Court found a religious purpose: "The Commandments do not confine themselves to arguably secular matters. Rather, the first part of the Commandments concerns the religious duties of believers: worshipping the Lord God alone, avoiding idolatry, not using the Lord's name in vain, and observing the Sabbath Day." The Court held that the Ten Commandments need not be barred from the public schools because they might be "integrated into the school curriculum, where the Bible may constitutionally be used in an appropriate study of history, civilization, ethics, comparative religion, or the like." However, the Court concluded that it was inappropriate to post the Ten Commandments in such a way as "to induce the schoolchildren to read, meditate upon, perhaps to venerate and obey, the Commandments" when there was no educational function.

Stone was followed by *Van Orden v. Perry*, 545 U.S. 677 (2005), in which the Court upheld the constitutionality of a Ten Commandments display on the grounds of the Texas State Capitol. In upholding the display, a plurality of the Court concluded that the Court's precedent regarding the Establishment Clause points "Januslike" in opposite directions. "One face recognizes and respects the strong role that religion and religious traditions have played in United States history. The other face recognizes that governmental intrusion into religious matters can endanger religious freedom." The plurality concluded that it was required to respect both faces of this tradition and that government must not "evince a hostility to religion by disabling the government from in some ways recognizing our religious heritage." In upholding the display, the plurality emphasized historical evidence which showed that all three branches of the federal government had recognized religion from the beginning of the nation. Both Houses of Congress had passed resolutions urging President George Washington to issue a Thanksgiving Day Proclamation "acknowledging, with grateful hearts, the many and signal favors of Almighty God." President Washington complied by issuing a proclamation which "attributed to the Supreme Being the foundations and successes of our young Nation." The plurality also recognized that the Court's own decisions had allowed a state legislature to open its daily sessions with a prayer by a state-paid chaplain.

The plurality emphasized that religious displays were common throughout the United States, including at the U.S. Supreme Court which displays a frieze of Moses holding two tablets that reveal portions of the Ten Commandments written in Hebrew, displayed along with other lawgivers. On the metal gates lining the courtroom, as well as on the doors, there is a representation of the decalogue. The plurality noted that there were similar depictions throughout Washington, D.C., including at the Great Reading Room and the rotunda of the Library of Congress' Jefferson Building, and that a medallion with two tablets depicting the Ten Commandments decorates the floor of the National Archives. Inside the Department of Justice, a statue entitled "The Spirit of Law" includes two tablets representing the Ten Commandments lying at its feet. In addition, the Chamber of the U.S. House of Representatives prominently features Moses, and God is reflected in various monuments and buildings including the Washington, Jefferson, and Lincoln Memorials (with phrases such as "Laus Deo" ("Praise be to God") and various Biblical citations).

While the plurality acknowledged that the Ten Commandments have religious significance, it found that they have dual meaning since Moses was both a lawgiver and a religious leader. While the Court suggested that it might be less inclined to sustain a display in an elementary or secondary school context where it might be viewed by impressionable children, the plurality was more willing to sustain religious displays in legislative chambers or capitol grounds. The Court also emphasized that the Texas display was only one of 17 monuments and 21 historical markers that "represented various strands in the State's political and legal history," and the plurality concluded that inclusion of the Ten Commandments monument in this group has a dual significance, partaking of both religion and government.

On the same day that the Court decided *Van Orden*, it struck down courthouse displays in *McCreary County v. American Civil Liberties Union of Kentucky*, 545 U.S. 844 (2005). *McCreary County* involved Ten Commandments displays in two Kentucky courthouses both of which included the King James version of the Ten Commandments with a citation to the Book of Exodus. In response to litigation, the counties posted several different displays, and the final display described the Ten Commandments as "the precedent legal code upon which the civil and criminal codes of Kentucky are founded," and stated that "the Ten Commandments are codified in Kentucky's civil and criminal laws." Although the initial display involved a large framed copy of the edited King James version of the Commandments, later displays included other documents in smaller frames with religious themes, including the "endowed by their Creator" passage from the Declaration of Independence, the Preamble to the Constitution of Kentucky, the national motto ("In God We Trust"), a page from the Congressional Record . . . proclaiming the Year of the Bible and including a statement of the Ten Commandments, a proclamation by President Abraham Lincoln designating April 30, 1863 as a National Day of Prayer and Humiliation, an excerpt from President Lincoln's "Reply to Loyal Colored People of Baltimore upon Presentation of a Bible," reading that "the Bible is the best gift God has ever given to man", a proclamation by President Reagan marking 1983 the Year of the Bible, and the Mayflower Compact. Assembled with the Commandments were framed copies of the Magna Carta, the Declaration of Independence, the Bill of Rights, the lyrics of the Star Spangled Banner, the Mayflower Compact, the National Motto, the Preamble to the Kentucky Constitution, and a picture of Lady Justice. The collection, eventually entitled "The Foundations of American Law and Government Display," came with a statement of historical and legal significance. The comment on the Ten Commandments read: "The Ten Commandments have profoundly influenced the formation of Western legal thought and the formation of our country. That influence is clearly seen in the Declaration of Independence, which declared that 'We hold these truths to be self-evident, that all men are created equal, that they are endowed by their Creator with certain unalienable Rights, that among these are Life, Liberty, and the pursuit of Happiness.' The Ten Commandments provide the moral background of the Declaration of Independence and the foundation of our legal tradition." The Counties offered various explanations for the new display, including a desire "to demonstrate that the Ten Commandments were part of the foundation of American Law and Government," and "to educate the citizens of the county regarding some of the documents that played a significant role in the foundation of our system of law and government."

Relying on its holding in *Stone,* the Court noted that the second McCreary County display was distinguishable from the *Van Orden* display because of its "predominantly religious purpose" and lack of neutrality between religions and between religion and nonreligion. The Court felt that the display "sends the message to nonadherents that they are outsiders, not full members of the political community, and an accompanying message to adherents that they are insiders, favored members." The Court emphasized that the second of the county's displays had an "unstinting focus" on religious passages, and that the Ten Commandments were posted "precisely because of their sectarian content." The religious theme was reinforced by "serial religious references and the accompanying resolution's claim about the embodiment of ethics in Christ." The Court concluded that the third display was invalid even though it included secular documents, focused on documents thought especially significant in the historical foundation of American government, and expressed a desire "to educate the citizens of the county regarding some of the documents that played a significant role in the foundation of our system of law and government." Although the Court accepted the proposition that a sacred text can be integrated into a constitutionally permissible governmental display on the subject of law, or American history, the Court concluded that a "*reasonable observer*" would not believe that the counties "had cast off the religious objective so unmistakable in the earlier displays." The Court distinguished the frieze displayed in the U.S. Supreme Court (depicting Moses along with 17 other lawgivers, most of whom are secular figures) on the basis that "there is no risk that Moses would strike an observer as evidence that the National Government was violating neutrality in religion."

Since the Court's attitude towards the Establishment Clause and the Free Exercise Clause seems to have changed in recent years, some believe that the *Stone* decision might be overturned. In 2024, Louisiana's legislature adopted a law requiring that a poster-size version of the Ten Commandments be posted in all public school classrooms. Texas adopted a similar law. The Louisiana law specified the exact language that must be printed on the displays, and provided that the text of Ten Commandments must be the focus of the display. The bill's sponsor stated that the Ten Commandments are rooted in legal history, and that the displays place a moral code in the classroom. In signing the law, Louisiana's governor declared that "If you want to respect the rule of law, you must start from the original law which was given to Moses. He received his commandments from God." Of course, one issue is whether this law is sufficiently distinguishable from the McCreary County displays so that it is constitutional. Or whether the law has changed. The law is being challenged and is working its way through the lower courts. *See Roake v. Brumley*, 141 F.4th 614, 2025 WL 1719978 (5th Cir.).

Church Vetoes. In *Larkin v. Grendel's Den, Inc.,* 459 U.S. 116 (1982), the Court struck down a Massachusetts law that gave the governing bodies of churches and schools the power to veto applications to sell liquor within a five hundred foot radius of the church or school. Although the Court recognized that schools and churches have an interest in being insulated from businesses that serve liquor, the Court found that the state had impermissibly delegated zoning power to a religious institution in violation of the Establishment Clause. The Court was concerned about the fact that the law contained a "standardless" delegation "calling for no reasons, findings, or reasoned conclusions," and therefore might be used "for explicitly religious goals, for example, favoring liquor licenses for members of that congregation or adherents of that faith." In addition, "the mere appearance of a joint exercise of legislative authority by Church and State provides a significant symbolic benefit to religion in the minds of some by reason of the power conferred."

Holiday Displays. There has been considerable litigation regarding the constitutionality of holiday displays, particularly Christmas and Chanukah displays. One of the more important recent decisions was *Lynch v. Donnelly*, 465 U.S. 668 (1984), which upheld a Christmas display in a city park in Pawtucket, Rhode Island that included, in addition to a creche, a Santa Claus house, reindeer pulling Santa's sleigh, candy-striped poles, a Christmas tree, carolers, cutout figures representing such characters as a clown, an elephant, and a teddy bear, hundreds of colored lights, and a large banner that read "SEASONS GREETINGS." The Court found that the creche did not have the impermissible effect of advancing or promoting religion. In addition, the Court regarded any benefits the government's display gave religion as "no more than 'indirect, remote, and incidental.' "

Perhaps the most important part of *Lynch* was Justice O'Connor's concurrence. She argued that government is not allowed to "endorse" religion because it "sends a message to nonadherents that they are outsiders, not full members of the political community, and an accompanying message to adherents that they are insiders, favored members of the political community." In evaluating a "message" to see whether it constitutes an "endorsement," she argued that the focus should be on the message that the government's practice communicates based on the context in which it appears: In analyzing the Pawtucket display, Justice O'Connor felt that the overall display did not convey a message of endorsement. In addition to the creche, the display contained "a Santa Claus house with a live Santa distributing candy; reindeer pulling Santa's sleigh; a live 40-foot Christmas tree strung with lights; statues of carolers in old-fashioned dress; candy-striped poles; a 'talking' wishing well; a large banner proclaiming 'SEASONS GREETINGS'; a miniature 'village' with several houses and a church; and various 'cut-out' figures, including those of a clown, a dancing elephant, a robot, and a teddy bear." Justice O'Connor felt that because the creche is 'a traditional symbol' of Christmas, a holiday with strong secular elements, and because the creche was 'displayed along with purely secular symbols,' the creche's setting affected how the entire display was viewed." She found that the overall display would fairly be understood to negate "any message of endorsement" of Christian beliefs.

Four justices dissented, agreeing that the issue was whether the city had endorsed religion, but they felt that the display contained a message of endorsement: the creche placed "the government's imprimatur of approval on the particular religious beliefs exemplified by the creche." In their view, the effect of the display on "minority religious groups [was] to convey the message that their views are not similarly worthy of public recognition nor entitled to public support."

Lynch was followed by *County of Allegheny v. American Civil Liberties Union*, 492 U.S. 573 (1989), which involved two separate holiday displays. The first was a creche placed by a Roman Catholic group next to the Grand Staircase inside a county courthouse. The creche was surrounded by a wooden fence which bore a plaque stating: "Donated by the Holy Name Society." The county government placed poinsettia plants around the fence, and a small evergreen tree, decorated with a red bow, behind each of the two endposts of the fence. At the apex of the creche display was an angel. Unlike the Pawtucket display upheld in *Lynch*, the County of Allegheny display did not include any "secular Christmas symbols" such as Santa Claus. The county held its annual Christmas-carol program at the site of the creche, and invited high school choirs and other musical groups to perform at the creche during weekday lunch hours. The county dedicated these musical programs to world peace and to the families of prisoners-of-war and of persons missing in action in Southeast Asia. The second display was erected at the City-County Building about a block away from the county courthouse, and involved a large Christmas tree under the middle arch outside the Grant Street entrance. At the foot of the tree was a sign bearing the mayor's name and the words "Salute to Liberty," and additional words which stated: "During this holiday season, the city of Pittsburgh salutes liberty. Let these festive lights remind us that we are the keepers of the flame of liberty and our legacy of freedom." The display also included an 18-foot Chanukah menorah of an abstract tree-and-branch design that was placed next to the Christmas tree. The menorah was owned by a Jewish group, but was stored, erected, and removed each year by the city.

A majority of the justices who participated in the *Lynch* case applied the endorsement test and held that the creche display violated the endorsement test because of its unmistakably religious message. It used the creche display, as well as religious words "Glory to God in the Highest!" to convey an unmistakable religious meaning. Unlike the *Lynch* display, the creche stood alone and was the single element in the display. In addition, the creche was placed on the grand staircase, and the Court concluded that: "No viewer could reasonably think that it occupies this location without the support and approval of the government." As a result, the "county sends an unmistakable message that it supports and promotes the Christian praise to God that is the creche's religious message" notwithstanding the sign suggesting that the display is owned by a Roman Catholic organization. Indeed, the private sign suggested to the Court that the city was endorsing the religious message.

The Court upheld the display at the City-County building. While the Court conceded that the Menorah is a religious symbol, the Court recognized that the Menorah has both religious and secular dimensions. In addition, the Court emphasized that the Menorah was accompanied by a Christmas tree and a sign saluting liberty which created an "overall holiday setting" that represented both Christmas and Chanukah. Because "government may celebrate Christmas as a secular holiday," it may also celebrate Chanukah in a similar manner. The Court found that the combined displays did not endorse either religious faiths, but instead simply recognized that "both Christmas and Chanukah are part of the same winter-holiday season, which has attained a secular status in our society." Although Christmas trees once carried religious connotations, they now "typify the secular celebration of Christmas." Moreover, the tree was the predominant element in the display because of its 45-foot size, and the smaller Menorah was at its side, with the two suggesting a secular celebration of Christmas. Although the menorah is a religious symbol, it was "difficult to imagine a predominantly secular symbol of Chanukah that the city could place next to its Christmas tree." In addition, the Court concluded that the mayor's sign diminished the possibility that the tree and the menorah would be "interpreted as [an] endorsement of Christianity and Judaism." As a result, the Court concluded that it was not "sufficiently likely" that reasonable observers would "perceive the combined display of the tree, the sign, and the menorah as an 'endorsement' or 'disapproval [of] their individual religious choices.' " The Court remanded for consideration of whether the display might violate either the "purpose" or "entanglement" prongs of the *Lemon* analysis.

Lynch and *County of Allegheny* illustrate the importance of context to the Court's evaluation of a religious display. In deciding whether a display sends a message of endorsement, the Court will consider not only the display itself, but its setting and other items displayed along with it. As a result, the same display (*e.g.*, a creche) may be impermissible in one context (beside the grand staircase where it is framed by a floral display and a statement of "Glory to God in the highest"), but permissible in another context (*e.g.*, a park where it is surrounded by secular symbols such as Rudolph the Red Nosed Reindeer).

Other Acknowledgements of Religion. Numerous other cases have held that government may (or may not) acknowledge religion in one respect or another. For example, in *Torcaso v. Watkins*, 367 U.S. 488 (1961), the Court held that a State may not constitutionally require an applicant for the office of Notary Public to swear or affirm that he believes in God. In *McGowan v. Maryland*, 366 U.S. 420 (1961), the Court held that state laws compelling a uniform day of rest from worldly labor do not violate the Establishment Clause even though Sunday was chosen as the day of rest. Although the Sunday Laws were first enacted for religious ends, they were continued for reasons wholly secular—to provide a universal day of rest and ensure the health and tranquility of the community. Likewise, in *Estate of Thornton v. Caldor, Inc.*, 472 U.S. 703, 709–710 (1985), the Court upheld a law that granted employees the right not to work on their sabbaths.

The question of symbolism also arose in the *American Legion v. American Humanist Association*, 588 U.S. 29 (2019). That case involved the Bladensburg Peace Cross which was erected as a tribute to soldiers who gave their lives in the First World War. The cross was erected on public land near a busy intersection. In upholding the statue, the Court emphasized that the cross assumed special significance following World War I because "the picture of row after row of plain white crosses marking the overseas graves of soldiers who had lost their lives in that horrible conflict was emblazoned on the minds of Americans," and "the Cross has expressed the community's grief at the loss of the young men who perished, its thanks for their sacrifice, and its dedication to the ideals for which they fought."

The Court found no violation of the Establishment Clause, noting that the "Religion Clauses of the Constitutionalism foster a society in which people of all beliefs can live together harmoniously, and the presence of the Cross on the land where it has stood for so many years is fully consistent with that aim." The Court emphasized that the Bladensburg Cross carries special significance in commemorating World War I, especially given that it symbolizes the simple wooden crosses that originally marked the graves of American soldiers killed in the war. As a result, the cross symbolizes their sacrifice. Even though the cross originated as a Christian symbol, and retains that meaning in many contexts, the symbol took on an added secular meaning when it was used on graves in World War I memorials. In addition, the Court believed that the cross had gained historical importance with time in that it "reminds the people of Bladensburg and surrounding areas of the deeds of their predecessors and of the sacrifices they made in a war fought in the name of democracy." Finally, the Court remarked on the length of time that the memorial had been in existence, and noted that it had "acquired additional layers of historical meaning in subsequent years." "The cross is undoubtedly a Christian symbol, but that fact should not blind us to everything else that the Bladensburg Cross has come to represent. For some, that monument is a symbolic resting place for ancestors who never returned home. For others, it is a place for the community to gather and honor all veterans and their sacrifices for our Nation. For others still, it is a historical landmark. For many of these people, destroying or defacing the Cross that has stood undisturbed for nearly a century would not be neutral and would not further the ideals of respect and tolerance embodied in the First Amendment."

Establishment-Free Exercise Tension. Board of Education of Kiryas Joel Village School District v. Grumet, 512 U.S. 687 (1994), illustrates the conflict between the two religion clauses. In that case, the Court held that the State of New York could not establish a special school district that was co-extensive with the boundaries of a village owned by members of a Satmaar Hasidic Jewish sect. The Satmars were "vigorously religious people who make few concessions to the modern world and go to great lengths to avoid [assimilation]. They interpret the Torah strictly; segregate the sexes outside the home; speak Yiddish as their primary language; eschew television, radio, and English-language publications; and dress in distinctive ways that include headcoverings and special garments for boys and modest dresses for girls. Children are educated in private religious schools, most boys at the United Talmudic Academy, [and] girls at [an] affiliated school with a curriculum designed to prepare girls for their roles as wives and mothers."

Because the religious schools did not offer special services to handicapped children, the Monroe-Woodbury Central School District provided such services for the children of Kiryas Joel at an annex. This program was terminated following the decisions in *Aguilar v. Felton* and *School Dist. of Grand Rapids v. Ball*. As a result, Kiryas Joel children who needed special education (including the deaf, the mentally retarded, and others suffering from a range of physical, mental, or emotional disorders) were forced to attend public schools outside the village. Because the Satmars were so different, they encountered "the panic, fear and trauma [suffered] in [being] with people whose ways were so different." By 1989, only one Kiryas Joel child was attending Monroe-Woodbury's public schools. The village's other handicapped children received privately funded special services or received no education at all. The New York Legislature then enacted a statute which provided that the village of Kiryas Joel "is constituted a separate school district." New York Governor Mario Cuomo stated that he viewed the bill as "a good faith effort to solve the unique problem" of providing special education services to handicapped children in the village. Although the statute gave the school district plenary legal authority over the elementary and secondary education of all school-aged children in the village, the district ran only a special education program for handicapped children. The village's other children attended parochial schools, and received only transportation, remedial education, and health and welfare services from the public school district. If a non-handicapped student had sought a public education, the district would have sent the child to a nearby school district and paid the tuition. In addition, several neighboring school districts sent their handicapped Hasidic children to the Kiryas Joel school.

The Court struck down the law creating the special school district, finding that the State was required to be neutral towards religion, and holding that New York had crossed the line by delegating its authority to a religious community with "no assurance that governmental power has been or will be exercised neutrally." While the Court recognized that religious officials could not be denied the right to hold public office, the Court held the Kiryas Joel district unconstitutional because of the "government's purposeful delegation on the basis of religion and a delegation on principles neutral to religion, to individuals whose religious identities are incidental to their receipt of civic authority." Even though New York did not delegate power with express reference to the religious beliefs of the Satmars, the Court concluded that New York had effectively delegated power "by reference to doctrinal adherence." The Court emphasized that the district originated in a special act of the legislature, "the only district ever created that way," and noted that "those who negotiated the village boundaries excluded all but Satmars, and the New York Legislature was well aware that the village remained exclusively Satmar."

The Court rejected the argument that the state's decision to create the special district constituted an accommodation of religion. Although the state can "accommodate religious needs by alleviating special burdens," the Court found this law invalid because the "proposed accommodation singles out a particular religious sect for special treatment." The Court suggested that it would be permissible for the district to provide bilingual and bicultural special education to Satmar children at a neutral site near one of the village's parochial schools. The Court also noted that it would "not disable a religiously homogeneous group from exercising political power conferred on it without regard to religion" (*e.g.*, Mormons in Utah), but it concluded that this school district was created "to separate Satmars from non-Satmars" and therefore fails the neutrality requirement. "It therefore crosses the line from permissible accommodation to impermissible establishment."

In the Court's recent decisions, it has struggled to find the dividing line between an establishment of religion and an accommodation. As in *Kiryas Joel*, the cases seem to suggest that government can, and indeed should, attempt to "accommodate" religious beliefs when possible. Difficulties arise when, in accommodating religion, government appears to be endorsing particular religious beliefs or the accommodation appears to be designed to promote those beliefs. In *Locke v. Davey*, 540 U.S. 712 (2004), the Court upheld the State of Washington's scholarship program that paid for post-secondary education expenses. While students could use PSP scholarships at either public or private institutions, including religious institutions, the scholarships could not be used to pursue a degree in theology. In upholding the exclusion, the Court rejected the argument that its prior decision in *Church of Lukumi Babalu Aye v. Hialeah*, 508 U.S. 520 (1993), required invalidation of the exclusion on the basis that the PSP was not facially neutral with respect to religion. The Court noted that the State of Washington did not impose criminal or civil sanctions on any type of religious service or rite, did not deny ministers the right to participate in political affairs, and did not require students to choose between their religious beliefs and receiving a government benefit. Instead, the State had merely chosen not to fund a distinct category of degree and the Court recognized that "majoring in devotional theology is akin to a religious calling as well as an academic pursuit." Given that the First Amendment protects free exercise, as well as prohibits establishments, the Court concluded that it might be appropriate for a court to "deal differently with religious education for the ministry than with education for other callings," and that this difference in treatment simply reflects the tension between the religion clauses rather than "hostility toward religion." Moreover, the Court emphasized that most "States that sought to avoid an establishment of religion around the time of the founding placed in their constitutions formal prohibitions against using tax funds to support the ministry."

In *Illinois ex rel. McCollum v. Board of Education*, 333 U.S. 203 (1948), the Court struck down an Illinois law that allowed religious teachers employed by private religious groups to enter public school buildings during the regular hours set apart for secular teaching, and substitute their religious teaching for the secular education provided under the compulsory education law. The Court held that the religious organization was using "the tax-established and tax-supported public school system to aid religious groups to spread their faith which falls squarely under the ban of the First Amendment."

In some contexts, the Court has sustained accommodations of religion as not creating and establishing religion. In *Corporation of Presiding Bishop v. Amos*, 483 U.S. 327 (1987), the Court upheld Title VII of the Civil Rights Act of 1964 even though it exempted religious organizations from Title VII's prohibition against discrimination in employment on the basis of religion. Applying the *Lemon* test, the Court recognized that government may lift the burdens of regulation on the exercise of religion. Likewise, in *Zorach v. Clauson*, 343 U.S. 306 (1952), the Court upheld an arrangement whereby students are released from public school classes so that they may attend religious classes offsite. Nevertheless, in *Witters v. Washington Department of Services for the Blind*, 474 U.S. 481 (1986), the Court invalidated parts of a State of Washington statute. The law provided funds authorized to "provide for special education and/or training in the professions, business or trades" as well as to "assist visually handicapped persons to overcome vocational handicaps and to obtain the maximum degree of self-support and self-care." When the state denied assistance to a blind person who was studying at a Christian college to become a pastor, missionary, or youth director, the Court held that he was entitled to assistance noting that the aid went to the student who choose to give it to the educational institution. As a result, any "aid that flows to religious institutions does so only as a result of the independent and private choices of aid recipients." In addition, the Court emphasized that the program is "made available generally without regard to the sectarian-nonsectarian, or public-nonpublic nature of the institution benefited, and is in no way skewed towards religion."

In *Bowen v. Kendrick,* 487 U.S. 589 (1988), the Court upheld a federal grant program, the Adolescent Family Life Act (AFLA or Act), that provided funding to public or nonprofit private organizations addressing problems relating to pregnancy and childbirth among unmarried adolescents. The grants were intended to promote "self discipline and other prudent approaches to the problem of adolescent premarital sexual relations," to promote adoption as an alternative for adolescent parents, to establish new approaches for the delivery of care services for pregnant adolescents, and to support research and demonstration projects "concerning the societal causes and consequences of adolescent premarital sexual relations, contraceptive use, pregnancy, and child rearing."

An Establishment Clause challenged was brought when Congress specifically amended the Act to require grant applicants to describe how they would involve religious organizations in the programs funded by AFLA. In rejecting the challenge, the Court emphasized that grantees need not be affiliated with any particular religious denomination. Moreover, the services provided were not religious in character, and there was nothing indicating that the program had the effect of advancing religion. The Court noted that it was "Congress' considered judgment that religious organizations can help solve the problems" to which the Act was addressed, and the Court held that nothing "prevents Congress from making such a judgment or from recognizing the important part that religion or religious organizations may play in resolving certain secular problems." Moreover, there was no indication that "a significant proportion of the federal funds were being disbursed to 'pervasively sectarian' institutions." The program was not unconstitutional simply because of a potential overlap between the government's secular concerns and the religious groups' interest in the subject of the funding. "But the possibility or even the likelihood that some of the religious institutions who receive AFLA funding will agree with the message that Congress intended to deliver to adolescents through the AFLA is insufficient to warrant a finding that the statute on its face has the primary effect of advancing religion." The Court also rejected the argument that AFLA excessively entangled government with religion: "There is no reason to fear that the less intensive monitoring involved here will cause the Government to intrude unduly in the day-to-day operation of the religiously affiliated AFLA grantees."

The tension between accommodation and establishment is illustrated by the holding in *Rosenberger v. Rector and Visitors of the University of Virginia*, 515 U.S. 819 (1995). In that case, the Court held that the free speech clause entitled a religious publication to state funding. The University of Virginia's Student Activities Fund (SAF) provided funding to an array of student publications, including publications focused on "student news, information, opinion, entertainment and academic communications media groups," but specifically excluded funding for religious publications. The University was concerned that inclusion of religious organizations in the funding program would violate the Establishment Clause. The Court disagreed, noting that the University provides printing services to a "broad spectrum of student newspapers" so that any "benefit to religion is incidental to the government's provision of secular services for secular purposes on a religion-neutral basis." The Court concluded that the Establishment Clause did not require the University to deny funding to Wide Awake. On the contrary, the Court held that the University had unconstitutionally discriminated against Wide Awake's religious speech by denying it funding.

Likewise, in *Widmar v. Vincent,* 454 U.S. 263 (1981), the Court held that a state university that made its facilities generally available to registered student groups could not close those facilities to groups desiring to use them for religious worship and religious discussion. "Having created a forum generally open to student groups, the University seeks to enforce a content-based exclusion of religious speech. Its exclusionary policy violates the fundamental principle that a state regulation of speech should be content-neutral." In *Good News Club v. Milford Central School,* 533 U.S. 98 (2001), the Court rendered a similar holding in the context of an elementary school which had a community use policy governing the use of its building after school hours, but denied the use of those facilities to a religious organization. When the Good News Club, a private Christian organization for children ages 6 to 12, sought permission to meet in the cafeteria to recite Bible verses, pray, sings songs, and engage in games involving Bible verses, the school district rejected the Club's request because it involved "religious instruction and Bible study." The Court found that Milford was operating a "limited public forum"—a forum in which the state was permitted to reserve the forum for certain groups or for the discussion of certain topics-and concluded that it had improperly excluded the Good News Club based on viewpoint discrimination: "The Club seeks to address a subject otherwise permitted under the rule, the teaching of morals and character, from a religious standpoint. The only apparent difference is that the Club chooses to teach moral lessons from a Christian perspective through live storytelling and prayer."

CHECKLIST

A. The Establishment Clause of the First Amendment was included in the First Amendment as a response to an extensive history of religious persecution in both Europe and the American colonies.

1. The Establishment Clause provides that "Congress shall make no law respecting an establishment of religion."
2. The Clause explicitly applies to Congress, but has been interpreted as applying to the entire the entire federal government and to the states by virtue of Fourteenth Amendment.
3. In modern history, there have been no attempts to establish an official religion in the United States although there were establishments in the colonies.
4. In modern times, most establishment clause cases focus on whether certain lesser acts constitute the functional equivalent of an establishment of religion.
5. It is clear that the Establishment Clause prohibits certain governmental activities that had been commonplace in Europe: laws requiring individuals to go to or remain away from church against their will; laws forcing individuals to believe or disbelieve a particular religion.
6. Modern cases focus on whether particular governmental actions constitute an establishment of religion, including the provision of financial aid to religious schools, the conduct Bible readings in public schools, or the posting of religious displays in public places.

B. Although the Court sometimes uses the metaphor of a wall between church and state, most cases are more nuanced.

1. Justice Black ended the *Everson* opinion with the following rhetorical flourish: "The First Amendment has erected a *wall between church and state.* That wall must be kept high and impregnable. We could not approve the slightest breach. New Jersey has not breached it here."
2. Many Establishment Clause cases focus on the conflict between that clause and the Free Exercise Clause. In other words, if government tries to accommodate religion and

religious beliefs, is there a risk that it will establish religion.

3. In *Everson v. Board of Education,* 330 U.S. 1 (1947), the Court held that a New Jersey board of education could reimburse parents for money spent to transport their children to school on public buses, including parents who sent their children to religious schools. In other words, there is no wall of separation that prevented the payments.

4. In *Everson,* plaintiffs argued that the state could not use taxpayer-raised funds to support an institution that teaches the tenets and faith of a religion, and that it might enable some children to attend those schools who might not otherwise be able to do so, constitutes an establishment of religion.

5. *Everson* held that, not only must government not establish a religion, it must not express hostility towards religion. As the Court noted, parents might be reluctant to send their children to parochial schools that are cut-off from "such general government services as ordinary police and fire protection, connections for sewage disposal, public highways and sidewalks." The Court concluded that the First Amendment "requires the state to be neutral in its relations with groups of religious believers and non-believers; it does not require the state to be their adversary."

C. **Many Establishment Clause cases have involved claims that government impermissibly provided financial aid to religious organizations, including churches and parochial schools.**

1. Like *Everson,* many early decisions focused on whether financial aid was "neutrally" available. In other words, was the aid available equally to all individuals regardless of their religious beliefs.

2. Some commentators have expressed support for the idea of allowing aid to religion under a "neutrality" standard, but such a standard is broad and could be used to sustain large payments to religious organizations and religious schools. *See* Douglas Laycock, *Formal, Substantive and Disaggregated Neutrality Toward Religion,* 39 DEPAUL L. REV. 993, 1000–1003 (1990).

3. For nearly half-a-century, the Court analyzed Establishment Clause cases using the so-called *Lemon* test.

That test, articulated in *Lemon v. Kurtzman*, 403 U.S. 602 (1971), established a three-prong test for evaluating the validity of establishment clause issues: "First, the statute must have a secular legislative purpose (in other words, the purpose must not be designed to enhance of promote religion); second, its principal or primary effect must be one that neither advances nor inhibits religion; finally, the statute must not foster 'an excessive government entanglement with religion.' "

4. *Lemon* involved a Rhode Island law that authorized state officials to supplement the salaries of teachers of secular subjects in private schools by paying the teachers an amount not exceeding 15% of their annual salary, and also involved Pennsylvania's Nonpublic Elementary and Secondary Education Act which authorized direct payments to nonpublic schools for the actual cost of teachers' salaries, textbooks, and instructional materials.

5. In *Lemon*, even though the Court found a secular purpose and effect (to enhance the quality of education), the Court struck the laws down as creating an excessive entanglement between church and state. In order to make sure that teachers do not infuse religion into secular courses, the state would have needed to engage in a "comprehensive, discriminating, and continuing state surveillance will inevitably be required to ensure that these restrictions are obeyed and the First Amendment otherwise respected."

6. The Court also emphasized the tendency of both the Rhode Island and Pennsylvania programs to create "political divisiveness" because "partisans of parochial schools, understandably concerned with rising costs and sincerely dedicated to both the religious and secular educational missions of their schools, will inevitably promote political action to achieve their goals."

7. The *Lemon* test has been applied in a variety of contexts, including decisions regarding whether states can provide the following types of aid to religious schools: textbooks for the teaching of secular subjects; "instructional material and equipment" (*i.e.*, maps, charts, periodicals, photographs, sound recordings, films and laboratory equipment); standardized testing; special services for school children with special needs (*e.g.*, speech and hearing diagnostic services, and diagnostic psychological services); state

funding for student field trips to non-religious sites; and maintenance and repair of religious schools.

8. In *Tilton v. Richardson*, 403 U.S. 672 (1971), the Court suggested that college "students are less impressionable and less susceptible to religious indoctrination," noted that many "church-related colleges and universities are characterized by a high degree of academic freedom and seek to evoke free and critical responses," and are not primarily concerned with religious indoctrination. Likewise, in *Roemer v. Board of Public Works*, 426 U.S. 736 (1976), the Court upheld a Maryland law that provided annual grants (15% of per pupil appropriation in the state system) to private colleges subject to the restriction that the funds not be used for "sectarian purposes."

9. A number of justices have suggested that *Lemon* has not produced a workable Establishment Clause theory or sound results.

10. In fact, the justices have experimented with different approaches for evaluating alleged establishments of religion.

11. In *Aguilar v. Felton*, 473 U.S. 402 (1985), the Court suggested that it would no longer presume that public school employees who teach secular subjects in religious schools would depart from their obligations and attempt to inculcate religion. As a result, there was no need to monitor their activities and no excessive entanglement between church and state in placing them there.

12. In *Mitchell v. Helms*, 530 U.S. 793 (2000), a plurality applied a "neutrality" test which allowed government to provide aid to religious schools and organizations provided it did so on a neutral basis that neither favored nor disfavored religion.

13. The decisions in *Agostini* and *Mitchell* have raised questions regarding the continuing vitality of a number of cases decided under the *Lemon* three-part test, and suggested that the Court might permit greater assistance to religious schools or organizations.

D. There has been much litigation about whether government can provide school vouchers to students to allow them to attend the school of their choice.

1. School vouchers raise Establishment Clause issues because, through the vouchers, the state can end up paying the cost of a religious education.

2. The vouchers allow parents to send their children to the school of their choice, be it private, public, or parochial. By introducing choice into the system, vouchers force schools to compete with each other, and hopefully lead to a better educational system.

3. In *Committee for Public Education and Religious Liberty v. Nyquist*, 413 U.S. 756 (1973), the Court struck down a law that provided for partial tuition reimbursements and tax benefits to the parents of elementary and secondary non-public school students. The Court concluded that the reimbursement plan violated the effects prong of the *Lemon* test because there was no mechanism to ensure that "the state aid derived from public funds will be used exclusively for secular, neutral, and nonideological purposes, [direct] aid in whatever form is invalid. . . ."

4. In *Sloan v. Lemon*, 413 U.S. 825 (1973), the Court struck down Pennsylvania's "Parent Reimbursement Act for Nonpublic Education," which reimbursed parents for a portion of tuition expenses incurred at nonpublic schools. The Court found "no constitutionally significant distinctions between that law and the one declared invalid [in] *Nyquist*."

5. In *Mueller v. Allen*, 463 U.S. 388 (1983), the Court upheld a Minnesota law that allowed taxpayers, in computing their state income tax, to deduct certain expenses incurred in providing for the education of their children. The Court noted that the law had a "secular" purpose (defraying the cost of educational expenses incurred by parents, regardless of the type of schools their children attended, and helping to create an educated populace), and its "primary effect" did not advance religion. The deduction was only one of many deductions provided by the state. Finally, all aid to parochial schools came through individual parents, and as a result of their choice to send their children to private schools, rather than as direct payments to religious institutions.

6. In *Zelman v. Simmons-Harris,* 536 U.S. 639 (2002), the Court upheld a Cleveland, Ohio, school voucher program designed primarily for low-income and minority students enrolled in a school district that was in crisis. The program provided two kinds of assistance to parents in a covered district: tuition aid and tutorial aid for students who remained in public school. The Court concluded that the program had a secular purpose and effect, was neutral towards religion (all schools, religious and non-religious, private and public, could participate), and did not involve excessive entanglement because the parents chose to use the vouchers at religious schools (rather than the state deciding to send public aid directly to those schools).

E. There has been considerable litigation regarding the permissibility of government sponsored prayer.

1. In *Engel v. Vitale,* 370 U.S. 421 (1962), the Court struck down a prayer written and imposed by a local school board under the authority of state law. The Court held that the prayer had both a religious purpose and effect, and concluded: "The constitutional prohibition against laws respecting an establishment of religion must at least mean that it is no part of the business of government to compose official prayers for any group of people to recite as part of a religious program carried on by government."

2. In *Engel,* the Court regarded the prayer as an establishment even though it was denominationally neutral. The Court expressed concern that "a union of government and religion tends to destroy government and to degrade religion. Religion is too personal, too sacred, too holy, to permit its 'unhallowed perversion' by a civil magistrate."

3. Some legislators have unsuccessfully tried to amend the Constitution to permit prayer in public schools.

4. In *Wallace v. Jaffree,* 472 U.S. 38 (1985), the Court struck down Alabama's moment of silence law on the basis that it was religiously motivated and involved simply an effort to re-introduce prayer into the public schools.

5. In *Marsh v. Chambers*, 463 U.S. 783 (1983), which involved the Nebraska legislature's practice of beginning each day with a prayer by a chaplain, the Court held that legislative prayer is constitutional. In upholding the constitutionality of legislative prayer, the Court emphasized the history of the First Amendment, and noted that even the Continental

Congress had begun its sessions with prayer. As a result, the Court concluded that such prayer was not constitutionally prohibited.

6. In *Lee v. Weisman*, 505 U.S. 577 (1992), the Court struck down the practice of having state sponsored prayer at middle school and high school graduation ceremonies. The Court expressed concern regarding the potential for divisiveness (both as to the content of the prayer and who delivers it), and expressed concern that state sponsorship might be interpreted as coercing attendees to participate in the prayer.

7. In *Santa Fe Independent School District v. Doe*, 530 U.S. 290 (2000), the Court struck down a school district policy allowing non-denominational prayer at football games based on a student referendum. The Court applied the "endorsement" test (which focuses on whether it appears that the state has endorsed religion), and concluded that an "objective Santa Fe High School student will unquestionably perceive the inevitable pregame prayer as stamped with her school's seal of approval."

8. In the *Santa Fe* case, the Court was concerned about submitting the question of who gives the prayer to a vote. Because "fundamental rights may not be submitted to vote; they depend on the outcome of no elections," the District's elections are "insufficient safeguards of diverse student speech." In addition, the Court found that the policy "invites and encourages religious messages" at school sponsored events.

F. A number of cases have dealt with the question of whether public schools can include Bible readings in their studies, or ban views inconsistent with particular religious beliefs.

1. In *School District of Abington Township v. Schempp*, 374 U.S. 203 (1963), the Court struck down a Baltimore, Maryland, law that required the reading of a chapter in the Holy Bible and/or the use of the Lord's Prayer in public school classes. Also struck down was a Pennsylvania law which required that "At least ten verses from the Holy Bible be read, without comment, at the opening of each public school on each school day"

2. In *Schempp*, the district argued that there were secular purposes, including the promotion of moral values, the contradiction to the materialistic trends of our times, the

perpetuation of our institutions and the teaching of literature.

3. The Court found that: "Even if its purpose is not strictly religious, [the] place of the Bible as an instrument of religion cannot be gainsaid, and the State's recognition of the pervading religious character of the ceremony is evident from the rule's specific permission of the alternative use of the Catholic Douay version as well as the recent amendment permitting nonattendance at the exercises. None of these factors is consistent with the contention that the Bible is used either as an instrument for nonreligious moral inspiration or as a reference for the teaching of secular subjects."

4. In *Epperson v. Arkansas*, 393 U.S. 97 (1968), the Court struck down Arkansas' "anti-evolution" statute that made it illegal for teachers in state-supported schools or universities "to teach the theory or doctrine that mankind ascended or descended from a lower order of animals." The law also made it illegal "to adopt or use in any such institution a textbook that teaches" that theory. The Court found that the law was religiously motivated: "There can be no doubt that Arkansas has sought to prevent its teachers from discussing the theory of evolution because it is contrary to the belief of some that the Book of Genesis must be the exclusive source of doctrine as to the origin of man."

5. In *Edwards v. Aguillard*, 482 U.S. 578 (1987), the Court struck down a statute requiring a "Balanced Treatment for Creation-Science and Evolution-Science in Public School Instruction" Act. In striking down the law, the Court applied the *Lemon* test and concluded that the law was religiously motivated (to re-introduce the theory of creationism into the public schools).

G. There has been considerable litigation about the extent to which the government may post copies of the Ten Commandments in various public places.

1. In *Stone v. Graham*, 449 U.S. 39 (1980), the Court struck down a Kentucky statute that required the posting of a copy of the Ten Commandments on the wall of each public classroom in the State.

2. Although the Commonwealth argued that the law was supported by a secular purpose (*e.g.*, the state argued that the Ten Commandments is the fundamental legal code of

Western Civilization and the Common Law of the United States).

3. The Court invalidated the display, noting that the "pre-eminent purpose for posting the Ten Commandments on schoolroom walls is plainly religious in nature. The Ten Commandments are a sacred text in the Jewish and Christian faiths, and no legislative recitation of a supposed secular purpose can blind us to that fact."

4. In *Van Orden v. Perry*, 545 U.S. 677 (2005), a plurality of the Court upheld the constitutionality of a Ten Commandments display on the grounds of the Texas State Capitol. The plurality noted that our history "recognizes and respects the strong role that religion and religious traditions have played in United States history," and noted that there are lots of other similar displays. The Court also emphasized that the Ten Commandments also have secular significance because Moses was a lawgiver, and the Court emphasized that this monument was only one of 17 monuments and 21 historical markers on the grounds.

5. On the same day that the Court decided *Van Orden*, it struck down courthouse displays of the Ten Commandments in *McCreary County v. American Civil Liberties Union of Kentucky*, 545 U.S. 844 (2005). That display involved various other documents, including: the "endowed by their Creator" passage from the Declaration of Independence; the Preamble to the Constitution of Kentucky; the national motto, "In God We Trust"; a page from the Congressional Record proclaiming the Year of the Bible and including a statement of the Ten Commandments; a proclamation by President Abraham Lincoln designating April 30, 1863, a National Day of Prayer and Humiliation; an excerpt from President Lincoln's "Reply to Loyal Colored People of Baltimore upon Presentation of a Bible," reading that "the Bible is the best gift God has ever given to man"; a proclamation by President Reagan marking 1983 the Year of the Bible; and the Mayflower Compact. Assembled with the Commandments were framed copies of the Magna Carta, the Declaration of Independence, the Bill of Rights, the lyrics of the Star Spangled Banner, the Mayflower Compact, the National Motto, the Preamble to the Kentucky Constitution, and a picture of Lady Justice.

6. The Court held that the *McCreary County* display was distinguishable from the *Van Orden* display because of its

"predominantly religious purpose" and lack of neutrality between religions and between religion and nonreligion. The Court felt that the display "sends the message to nonadherents that they are outsiders, not full members of the political community, and an accompanying message to adherents that they are insiders, favored members."

H. There has been much litigation over whether it is permissible for a city to erect a holiday Christmas display that includes a creche with baby Jesus.

1. In *Lynch v. Donnelly*, 465 U.S. 668 (1984), the Court upheld a Christmas display in Pawtucket, Rhode Island. The display was erected by the city in a private park in a downtown shopping district, and included a Santa Claus house, reindeer pulling Santa's sleigh, candy-striped poles, a Christmas tree, carolers, cutout figures representing such characters as a clown, an elephant, and a teddy bear, hundreds of colored lights, a large banner that read "SEASONS GREETINGS," and a creche.

2. The Court found that the creche did not have the impermissible effect of advancing or promoting religion. In addition, the Court regarded any benefits the government's display gave religion as "no more than 'indirect, remote, and incidental.' "

3. In *Lynch*, the Court applied Justice O'Connor's endorsement test which suggests that government is not allowed to "endorse" religion because it "sends a message to nonadherents that they are outsiders, not full members of the political community, and an accompanying message to adherents that they are insiders, favored members of the political community." In evaluating a "message" to see whether it constitutes an "endorsement," the focus should be on the message that the government's practice communicates based on the context in which it appears.

4. Justice O'Connor, concurring, felt that the overall display did not convey a message of endorsement. In addition to the creche, the display contained "a Santa Claus house with a live Santa distributing candy"; reindeer pulling Santa's sleigh; a live 40-foot Christmas tree strung with lights; statues of carolers in old-fashioned dress; candy-striped poles; a 'talking' wishing well; a large banner proclaiming 'SEASONS GREETINGS'; a miniature 'village' with several houses and a church; and various 'cut-out' figures, including those of a clown, a dancing elephant, a robot, and a teddy

bear." She found that the overall display would fairly be understood to negate "any message of endorsement" of Christian beliefs.

5. The endorsement test is an alternate test that the Court has sometimes used to evaluate establishment claims, especially in the context of displays like the one involved in *Lynch*. However, in recent decisions, the Court has repudiated that test.

6. The Court now decides Establishment Clause cases by reference to historical practices and understandings.'

7. In *County of Allegheny v. American Civil Liberties Union*, 492 U.S. 573 (1989), the Court used the endorsement test to strike down one of two holiday displays.

8. In *County of Allegheny*, one display involved a creche, placed by a Roman Catholic group next to the Grand Staircase inside the county courthouse, that was surrounded by a wooden fence, poinsettia plants, a small evergreen tree, decorated with a red bow, and a statement Glory to God in the Highest. The Court viewed the display as containing a religious message that was not muted by any of the secular symbols evident in *Lynch*. The Court held that the creche display violated the endorsement test because of its unmistakably religious message: "the creche sits on the Grand Staircase, the 'main' and 'most beautiful part' of the building that is the seat of county government. No viewer could reasonably think that it occupies this location without the support and approval of the government." As a result, the "county sends an unmistakable message that it supports and promotes the Christian praise to God that is the creche's religious message."

9. In *County of Allegheny*, the second display was erected at the City-County Building about a block away from the county courthouse, and involved a large Christmas tree under the middle arch outside the Grant Street entrance. At the foot of the tree was a sign bearing the mayor's name and the words "Salute to Liberty," and additional words which stated: "During this holiday season, the city of Pittsburgh salutes liberty. Let these festive lights remind us that we are the keepers of the flame of liberty and our legacy of freedom." The display also included an 18-foot Chanukah menorah of an abstract tree-and-branch design that was placed next to the Christmas tree. The menorah

was owned by a Jewish group, but was stored, erected, and removed each year by the city.

10. In *County of Allegheny*, while the Court conceded that the Menorah is a religious symbol, the Court also recognized that the Menorah has both religious and secular dimensions. In addition, the Menorah in that case was accompanied by a Christmas tree and a sign saluting liberty which creates an "overall holiday setting" that represented both Christmas and Chanukah. The Court found that the combined displays did not endorse either religious faith, but instead simply recognized that "both Christmas and Chanukah are part of the same winter-holiday season, which has attained a secular status in our society." Although Christmas trees once carried religious connotations, they now "typify the secular celebration of Christmas." Moreover, the tree was the predominant element in the display because of its 45-foot size, and the smaller Menorah was at its side. As a result, the Court concluded that it was not "sufficiently likely" that reasonable observers would "perceive the combined display of the tree, the sign, and the menorah as an 'endorsement' or 'disapproval of their individual religious choices.'" The Court remanded for consideration of whether the display might violate either the "purpose" or "entanglement" prongs of the *Lemon* analysis.

11. In *Torcaso v. Watkins*, 367 U.S. 488 (1961), the Court held that a State may not constitutionally require an applicant for the office of Notary Public to swear or affirm that he believes in God. In *McGowan v. Maryland*, 366 U.S. 420 (1961), the Court held that state laws compelling a uniform day of rest from worldly labor do not violate the Establishment Clause even though Sunday was chosen as the day of rest. The Court concluded that, although the Sunday Laws were first enacted for religious ends, they were continued for reasons wholly secular—to provide a universal day of rest and ensure the health and tranquility of the community.

I. Other decisions also reveal the tension between the Establishment Clause and the Free Exercise Clause.

1. In *Board of Education of Kiryas Joel Village School District v. Grumet*, 512 U.S. 687 (1994), the Court held that the State of New York could not establish a special school district co-extensive with the boundaries of a village owned by members of Satmaar Hasidic Jewish sect.

2. In *Locke v. Davey*, 540 U.S. 712 (2004), the Court upheld the State of Washington's Promise Scholarship Program (PSP) which provided renewable one year scholarships for the payment of post-secondary education expenses, but which could not be used to pursue a degree in theology.

3. In *Locke*, the Court rejected the argument that the exclusion was invalid because it was not facially neutral with respect to religion. The Court noted that the State of Washington did not impose criminal or civil sanctions on any type of religious service or rite, did not deny ministers the right to participate in political affairs, and did not require students to choose between their religious beliefs and receiving a government benefit. Instead, the State had merely chosen not to fund a distinct category of degree and the Court recognized that "majoring in devotional theology is akin to a religious calling as well as an academic pursuit."

4. In *Corporation of Presiding Bishop v. Amos*, 483 U.S. 327 (1987), the Court upheld Title VII of the Civil Rights Act of 1964 even though it exempted religious organizations from Title VII's prohibition against discrimination in employment on the basis of religion.

5. In *Katcoff v. Marsh*, 755 F.2d 223 (2d Cir. 1985), the court held that the Armed Forces could hire chaplains to enable soldiers to practice the religion of their choice, and could appoint the chaplains as commissioned officers with rank and uniform but without command. In upholding the practice, the Court emphasized that the provision of chaplains began during the Revolutionary War and "has continued ever since then."

6. In *Illinois ex rel. McCollum v. Board of Education*, 333 U.S. 203 (1948), the Court struck down an Illinois law that allowed religious teachers employed by private religious groups to enter public school buildings during hours set apart for secular teaching, and substitute their religious teaching for the secular education provided under the compulsory education law.

7. In *Zorach v. Clauson*, 343 U.S. 306 (1952), the Court upheld an arrangement whereby students were released from public school classes so that they may attend religious classes offsite.

8. In *Witters v. Washington Department of Services for the Blind*, 474 U.S. 481 (1986), the Court invalidated parts of a Washington statute that authorized payments to "provide

for special education and/or training in the professions, business or trades" to "assist visually handicapped persons to overcome vocational handicaps and to obtain the maximum degree of self-support and self-care," but excluded such support for students pursuing religious degree.

9. In *Bowen v. Kendrick,* 487 U.S. 589 (1988), the Court upheld a federal grant program, the Adolescent Family Life Act (AFLA or Act), that provided funding to public or nonprofit private organizations addressing problems relating to pregnancy and childbirth among unmarried adolescents even though some grants went to religious organizations.

J. A significant amount of Establishment Clause litigation has focused on the interplay between the Establishment Clause, the Free Exercise Clause and the Speech Clause

1. In *Rosenberger v. Rector and Visitors of the University of Virginia,* 515 U.S. 819 (1995), the Court held that the free speech clause entitled a religious publication to state funding when funding was provided for all other types of publications.

2. In *Widmar v. Vincent,* 454 U.S. 263 (1981), the Court held that a state university that makes its facilities generally available to registered student groups could not close those facilities to groups desiring to use them for religious worship and religious discussion.

3. In *Good News Club v. Milford Central School,* 533 U.S. 98 (2001), the Court held that an elementary school acted improperly when it enacted a community use policy governing the use of its building after school hours, but denied the use of those facilities to a religious organization.

■ PROBLEMS ■

Problem #1: The Commonwealth of Kentucky, anxious to promote the education of Kentucky's children, enacts a law providing for financial subsidies for parochial schools. In enacting the law, the legislature states that: "By educating children outside the public school system, Kentucky's parochial schools provide a financial benefit to Kentucky's taxpayers. It is only fitting that Kentucky contribute to the cost of operating those schools." The legislation provides a 10% salary supplement to all teachers in parochial schools. No similar funding is available for other private schools. Is the financial subsidy constitutional?

Answer: No. In earlier decisions, such as *Lemon*, the Court struck down comparable financial assistance programs. In later decisions, the Court has suggested that its approach to school funding has changed. Nevertheless, this program is unlikely to survive constitutional review. The Commonwealth is discriminating in favor of some private schools (*e.g.*, parochial) and the remaining private schools, and certainly is not treating all schools equally or neutrally.

Problem #2: Based on research which shows that students perform better if they can be encouraged to calm down for a few minutes at the beginning of the school day, Kentucky passes a law providing for a "moment of silence" at the beginning of each school day. Under the law, teachers are specifically prohibited from encouraging or instructing children to pray. If teachers are asked what children may think about during the moment of silence, they are instructed to respond only that the children may meditate or pray about things that are meaningful to them. Might this moment of silence law be constitutionally valid?

Answer: Perhaps. Although the U.S. Supreme Court struck down a prior moment of silence law, it did so because it was motivated by a religious purpose. This moment of silence law is arguably different because the legislature claims a secular motivation. In addition, in an effort to maintain secularity, the legislature has built in a number of safeguards. It's still possible that the law may require monitoring—in order to make sure that teachers comply with the requirements—and therefore may create an excessive entanglement between church and state and be unconstitutional. However, the Court has been less focused on monitoring and entanglement issues in recent years.

Problem #3: The University of Louisville seeks to create a "holiday" display in December. The display includes religious displays from a number of religious traditions. It also contains secular objects such as Rudolf the Red Nosed Reindeer, Frosty the Snowman, etc. Is it permissible for the University (a state university) to erect such a display?

Answer: Probably. Since the display includes various religions, as well as various secular symbols of the season, it will probably not be regarded as an "endorsement" of religion. Instead, it may be regarded as simply a salute to religions and the holiday season. Such a salute is permissible.

POINTS TO REMEMBER

- The Establishment Clause was premised upon a history of established religions in Europe:

- In early Europe, both adherents and non-adherents were taxed to support state religions.
- In Europe, non-adherents might have been persecuted (indeed, jailed or imprisoned) for practicing other religions.
- In the U.S., there have been no modern attempts to establishment religion in the historical sense that government decrees that one religion as the "official" or state-sanctioned religion.

- Today, most claimed establishments of religion involve something far less dramatic than the declaration of an official religion. They often involve questions relating to financial aid to parochial schools, Bible readings in public schools, prayer and curricular issues in public schools, and questions regarding the validity of religious or holiday displays.
- Historically, the U.S. Supreme Court has analyzed establishment clause issues under the so-called *Lemon* test. In other words, the Court applies a three prong test in which it inquires whether the action in question was motivated by a secular or a religious purpose, whether the action has a secular or religious effect, and whether the action promotes excessive entanglement between religion and governmental officials. However, the *Lemon* decision has now been overruled.
- The Court also sometimes applies the "endorsement" test (which has also been overruled) in which the Court asks whether the governmental action has the effect of endorsing religion in general or one religion in particular. If so, the action is invalid.
- As a general rule, governmental attempts to impose prayer in public schools have been invalidated, as have governmental attempts to post the Ten Commandments in public schools or to impose religious curricula.
- However, each Establishment Clause turns on the context in which the case arises (*e.g.*, some Ten Commandments displays and some religious holiday displays have been upheld against Establishment Clause challenges).
- In some cases, the Court has focused on whether the state has acted with "neutrality" towards religion.
- School voucher programs can be constitutional if they are not skewed in favor of religious schools and so long as the aid that goes to religious schools arrives as a result of private (parental) choices.

- Although the Court struck down a moment of silence law (because of a religious motivation), such laws might be permissible depending on whether they are created for a secular reason and carried out in a way that does not promote religion.
- Because of a supportive history, the Court has upheld legislative prayer as a permissible practice.
- The Court has struck down efforts to have prayer at middle school and high school graduations and high school football games. The prayers were religiously motivated.
- The Court invalidated as religiously motivated a state law that required the reading of a chapter from the Holy Bible and/or the use of the Lord's Prayer in public school classes.
- States cannot prohibit the teaching of evolution (the idea that man evolved from lower-human forms) in public schools. Anti-evolution laws are religiously motivated.
- There has been considerable disagreement about whether, and to what extent, the government may acknowledge the existence of religion.
- The Court struck down a Kentucky statute that required the posting of a copy of the Ten Commandments on the wall of each public classroom in a state because it was motivated by a religious purpose.
- The Court upheld a Ten Commandments display on the Texas State Capitol grounds when it was one of many (different) displays. The Court regarded the display as a permissible recognition and accommodation of religion.
- However, the Court struck down a Ten Commandments display in a Kentucky courthouse (that was surrounded by various other legal documents) because of a religious motivation.
- The Court struck down a Massachusetts law that vested in the governing bodies of churches and schools the power to veto applications for liquor licenses within a five-hundred foot radius of the church or school. The state cannot delegate its veto power in a religious organization.
- Christmas and Chanukah displays that do not convey the message that the government is "endorsing" religion can be constitutional.
- A Pawtucket, Rhode Island display, that included a Santa Claus house, reindeer pulling Santa's sleigh, candy-striped poles, a Christmas tree, carolers, cutout figures representing such characters as a clown, an elephant, and a teddy bear, hundreds

of colored lights, a large banner that reads "SEASONS GREETINGS," and a creche, was held to be constitutional.

- A creche that was placed by a Roman Catholic group next to the Grand Staircase in a county courthouse, that was surrounded by a wooden fence, poinsettia plants, a small evergreen tree, and a sign saying "Glory to God in the Highest" was unconstitutional because it conveyed a message of endorsement of religion.
- The Court upheld a Christmas tree display that included a large Chanukah menorah of an abstract design, the words "Salute to Liberty," and additional words which stated: "During this holiday season, the city of Pittsburgh salutes liberty. Let these festive lights remind us that we are the keepers of the flame of liberty and our legacy of freedom." The display did not reflect an endorsement of religion.
- The Court held that the State of New York could not establish a special school district co-extensive with the boundaries of a village owned by members of Satmaar Hasidic Jewish sect. The Court held that New York had delegated its authority to a religious community with "no assurance that governmental power has been or will be exercised neutrally."
- The Court upheld a State of Washington scholarship program that paid for post-secondary education expenses, but could not be used to pursue a degree in theology on the theory that the state could choose not to pay for religious degrees.

CHAPTER 12

The Free Exercise Clause

In addition to providing protection against governmental attempts to establish religion, the First Amendment provides protections for religious freedom. *See Everson v. Board of Education*, 330 U.S. 1 (1947). As with other provisions of the Bill of Rights, the Free Exercise Clause has been incorporated into the Fourteenth Amendment due process clause, and therefore applies to the states.

A. BURDENS ON RELIGION

Unquestionably, the Free Exercise Clause protects religious *belief* and *thought*, but there is less agreement about the extent to which the Clause protects religious *conduct*. Most free exercise cases involve claims that an individual, or group of individuals, should be exempt from laws that "burden" their religion either by prohibiting them from engaging in conduct required by their religious beliefs, or by requiring conduct prohibited by their religious beliefs. Usually, these laws are not directed at religion or religious practices *per se*, but are designed to deal with some unrelated societal ill. Litigation usually focuses on whether the individual's interest in free exercise must give way in face of the societal interest, or whether the state interest must give way to accommodate the individual's free exercise interests, and more particularly on the standard of review to be applied in deciding that issue. As with the right to free speech, the Free Exercise Clause does not provide absolute protection for all religious practices, and instead has involved some balancing of the state interest against the religious interest.

1. Early Precedent

In some early decisions, the Court distinguished between "belief" and "conduct." For example, in *Reynolds v. United States,* 98 U.S. (8 Otto) 145 (1878), the Court upheld a federal law prohibiting polygamy as applied to a Mormon whose religion required him to engage in that practice. The Court held that the government has broad authority to prohibit religious conduct, and rejected the argument that a religious exemption was required. *See also Davis v. Beason*, 133 U.S. 333 (1890).

Reynolds' distinction between "belief" and "conduct" was partially rejected in *Cantwell v. Connecticut*, 310 U.S. 296 (1940). In that case, the Court overturned the conviction of a Jehovah's witness and his sons for attempting to sell religious magazines without a permit and disorderly conduct. The Court emphasized that the Free Exercise Clause protects both the freedom to believe *and* the freedom to act. While the Court regarded the freedom to believe as absolute, it held that religious conduct "remains subject to regulation for the protection of society." However, the Court overturned Cantwell's conviction, noting that individuals have the right to preach and to disseminate their religious views.

2. From *Sherbert* to *Smith*

In a number of later cases, the Court has struck down laws that infringed religious beliefs. Indeed, for a three-decade period, the Court overrode a number of laws based on religious objections. For example, in *Torcaso v. Watkins*, 367 U.S. 488 (1961), the Court struck down a state constitutional provision that required public officials to declare a belief in God as a prerequisite to assuming office. The Court held that the government may not compel anyone to affirm or deny a religious belief.

In a number of Free Exercise cases, the Court has applied strict scrutiny analysis to laws burdening religion. For example, in *Sherbert v. Verner*, 374 U.S. 398 (1963), the Court held that a Seventh-day Adventist adherent was entitled to unemployment benefits when she was discharged by her employer for refusing to work on Saturday, her Sabbath. In upholding her demand for benefits, despite a law that effectively required her to accept available work on her Sabbath, the Court held that the law burdened the exercise of her religion because it forced her to choose between her religious beliefs (which precluded her from accepting Saturday employment) and the right to receive unemployment benefits. The Court rejected the state's argument that unemployment compensation benefits constitute a "privilege" rather than a "right," and struck down the law concluding that the asserted state interest (fraudulent claims by unscrupulous claimants claiming religious objections to Saturday work) was insufficient, and could be satisfied without denying Sabbatarians unemployment benefits.

A common problem in cases like *Sherbert* is whether, by granting a religious exemption to a law that is applicable to everyone else, the state fosters an "establishment" of religion. In *Sherbert*, the Court found no establishment because the exemption "reflects nothing more than the governmental obligation of neutrality in the face of religious differences, and does not represent that level of governmental involvement of religious with secular institutions which is the object of the Establishment Clause to forestall."

In general, the Court has been unwilling to delve into the sincerity of an individual's religious beliefs, or to determine whether these beliefs are "genuine" or "valid." As the Court concluded in *Thomas*, the Court is "singularly ill equipped to resolve" differences of opinion regarding a particular religion's requirements or beliefs.

The Court also applied strict scrutiny in *Wisconsin v. Yoder*, 406 U.S. 205 (1972). *Yoder* involved members of the Old Order Amish religion who were criminally prosecuted for refusing to send their children to school after the eighth grade in violation of Wisconsin's compulsory school-attendance law (that required them to send their children to school until age 16). The Amish believed that their salvation requires life in a church community separate from the world and worldly influences, and in harmony with nature and the soil by making their living through farming or closely related activities. The Amish did not object to formal schooling through the eighth grade because they believed that children needed to learn basic reading and writing skills, and elementary mathematics. However, they viewed formal education beyond the eighth grade as inconsistent with their central religious concepts because it prevented their children from learning manual work and self-reliance, and from acquiring the specific skills needed to perform the adult role of an Amish farmer or housewife. The Amish also objected because high schools teach values that conflict with Amish values and the Amish way of life exposes children to "worldly" influences, and emphasizes intellectual and scientific accomplishments, self-distinction, competitiveness, worldly success, and social life with other students. As a result, the Amish believed that high school attendance could result in psychological harm to Amish children, because of the conflicts it would produce, and might result in destruction of the Old Order Amish church community. In overturning the conviction, the Court held that the Free Exercise Clause gives parents the right to control the religious upbringing of their children. After balancing the competing interests, the Court concluded that state educational requirements must yield to the rights of parents to choose how to educate their children. The Court found that the state interest in educating its citizenry was adequately protected by the alternate way in which the Amish educated their children.

Even during this three-decade period during which cases like *Sherbert* and *Yoder* were decided, the Court upheld some burdens on religion. For example, in *United States v. Lee*, 455 U.S. 252 (1982), the Court held that a member of the Old Order Amish could be required to pay Social Security taxes despite his religious objections to the receipt of public insurance benefits as well as to the payment of taxes to support public insurance funds. The Court held that the "social security system serves the public interest by providing a comprehensive insurance system with a variety of benefits available to all participants, with costs shared by employers and employees," and that mandatory participation is necessary for a viable system. Likewise, in *Jimmy Swaggart Ministries v. Board of Equalization*, 493 U.S. 378 (1990), the Court held that a sales and use tax that applied to the sale of all goods and services could be applied to the sale of religious literature. Finally, in *Goldman v. Weinberger,* 475 U.S. 503 (1986), the Court held that a service person did not have a Free Exercise right to wear a yarmulke in conjunction with his military uniform in contravention of an Air Force regulation mandating uniform dress.

3. The *Smith* Approach

Beginning in 1990, the Court became less willing to accommodate religious claims. *Employment Division v. Smith,* 494 U.S. 872 (1990), involved an Oregon law that provided criminal penalties for the knowing or intentional possession of a "controlled substance" (unless the substance has been prescribed by a medical practitioner). Several Native Americans who wanted to use peyote (a controlled substance used for hallucinogenic purposes) for religious reasons raised religious claims when they were fired from their jobs with a private drug rehabilitation organization because of work-related "misconduct" (using peyote). The Court held that the Free Exercise Clause clearly protects the "right to believe and profess whatever religious doctrine one desires," as well as the right to perform religious acts such as "assembling with others for a worship service, participating in sacramental use of bread and wine, proselytizing, abstaining from certain foods or certain modes of transportation." However, the Court rejected the idea that respondents' religious motivation for using peyote provided an exemption from an otherwise valid criminal law that does not discriminate against religion. The Court concluded that states were not required to create exceptions for "generally applicable and otherwise valid" laws that have the "incidental" effect of burdening religion. *Smith* specifically rejected *Sherbert's* "compelling government interest" test, viewing *Sherbert* as applicable only in the unemployment compensation field, and only then when a "generally applicable criminal law" is absent. The Court feared that, to create exemptions under such circumstances, would be to allow a religious objector "to become a law unto himself."

Smith did suggest that the Court might strike down a law that burdens religion when it implicates other constitutional rights, particularly free speech rights. For example, in an earlier case, *Wooley v. Maynard*, 430 U.S. 705 (1977), the Court held that a state could not compel an individual to display a license plate containing a slogan that offended his religious beliefs. However, that case involved free speech and the concept that an individual could not be forced to associate with beliefs that he found repugnant (on religious grounds or otherwise). In *West Virginia Bd. of Education v. Barnette*, 319 U.S. 624 (1943), the Court struck down a state statute requiring a flag salute. Once again, the Court relied heavily on free speech principles. In *Smith,* the Court found that the Oregon law did not discriminate against religion and did not present a combination of constitutional claims.

In *Smith*, respondents argued that, even if the "compelling state interest" is not applied to all free exercise claims, it should apply to religious conduct that is "central" to the individual's religion. The Court rejected that argument, noting that it is not the court's job to determine whether a particular belief is "central" to an individual's religious beliefs. Moreover, the Court expressed concern that respondents' position "would open the prospect of constitutionally required religious exemptions from civic obligations of almost every conceivable kind."

In response to the holding in *Smith,* Congress passed the Religious Freedom Restoration Act (RFRA). 42 U.S.C. § 2000bb, et seq. In enacting RFRA, Congress declared that the Framers of the Constitution viewed the free exercise of religion as an "unalienable right," and that *Smith* had "virtually eliminated the requirement that the government justify burdens on religious exercise imposed by laws neutral toward religion." Instead of the *Smith* test, RFRA provided that the government could not "substantially burden a person's exercise of religion even if the burden results from a rule of general applicability," unless it demonstrates that the burden to the person—(1) is in furtherance of a compelling governmental interest; and (2) is the least restrictive means of furthering that compelling governmental interest. RFRA further stated that its provisions should not be construed as affecting the court's interpretation of the Establishment Clause.

In *City of Boerne v. Flores*, 521 U.S. 507 (1997), the Court struck down RFRA as applied to the states concluding that, as broad "as the power of Congress is under the Enforcement Clause of the Fourteenth Amendment, RFRA contradicts vital principles necessary to maintain separation of powers and the federal balance." Likewise, in *Sossamon v. Texas*, 563 U.S. 277 (2011), the Court held that a state which accepts federal funds does not (by virtue of the acceptance of federal funds) consent to waive its sovereign immunity to suits for money damages under the Religious Land Use and Institutionalized Persons Act of 2000 (RLUIPA).

However, it is important to realize that *City of Boerne* does not preclude all applications of RFRA or other congressional enactments mandating a higher level of review in free exercise cases. In *Gonzales v. O Centro Espirita Beneficente Uniao Do Vegetal*, 546 U.S. 418 (2006), a unanimous Court used RFRA to strike down a federal ban on the use of sacramental tea by a religious organization. The Court applied RFRA to the federal law and concluded that the federal interest was insufficient to show that the government had adopted the least restrictive means of advancing a compelling interest. The government had offered three interests in support of the law: protecting the health and safety of church members, preventing the diversion of *hoasca* from the church to recreational users, and complying with the 1971 United Nations Convention on Psychotropic Substances (a treaty signed by the United States and implemented by the Act). Although both parties presented evidence regarding the health effects of *hoasca*, the trial court found that the evidence was in equilibrium. The Government contended that the CSA established a "closed" system that prohibits all use of controlled substances except as authorized by the Act itself, and "cannot function with its necessary rigor and comprehensiveness if subjected to judicial exemptions." In rejecting the United States' position, the Court noted that federal law has contained an exception for peyote use for the last 35 years, and that Congress extended this exemption in 1994 to every recognized Indian tribe. Moreover, the Court noted that all of the government's arguments regarding *hoasca—e.g.*, that it "has a high potential for abuse," "has no currently accepted medical use," and has "a lack of accepted safety for use [under] medical supervision"—applied as well to the use of peyote. Given the peyote exception, the Court was reluctant to conclude that the government had a compelling interest in prohibiting *hoasca*.

Likewise, in *Burwell v. Hobby Lobby Stores, Inc.*, 573 U.S. 682 (2014), the Court held that RFRA precluded the U.S. Department of Health and Human Services (HHS) from requiring three closely held corporations to provide health-insurance coverage for methods of contraception that violate the sincerely held religious beliefs of the companies' owners. The Court rejected the argument that the owners of the corporations forfeited all RFRA protection when they organized their businesses as corporations, rather than as sole proprietorships or general partnerships, and the Court found a substantial burden on the owners' religious beliefs. In addition, although the Court determined that Congress had a "compelling" governmental interest in mandating contraceptive coverage, the Court concluded that there were less restrictive means for achieving that objective. Indeed, the Court noted that HHS had already devised and implemented a system that sought to provide contraceptive coverage while respecting the religious liberty of religious nonprofit corporations. However, the courts have generally rejected other religiously based challenges to the ACA.

The Court also sustained heightened legislative protection in *Cutter v. Wilkinson*, 544 U.S. 709 (2005). That case involved Section 3 of the Religious Land Use and Institutionalized Persons Act of 2000 (RLUIPA), 42 U.S.C. § 2000cc–1(a)(1)–(2), which provided in part: "No government shall impose a substantial burden on the religious exercise of a person residing in or confined to an institution," unless the burden furthers "a compelling governmental interest," and does so by "the least restrictive means." Plaintiffs were current and former inmates of the Ohio Department of Rehabilitation and Correction who asserted that they were adherents of "non-mainstream" religions (*e.g.*, Satanist, Wicca, and Asatru religions, and the Church of Jesus Christ Christian), and who complained that prison officials violated RLUIPA by failing to accommodate their religious exercise in various ways: "retaliating and discriminating against them for exercising their nontraditional faiths, denying them access to religious literature, denying them the same opportunities for group worship that are granted to adherents of mainstream religions, forbidding them from adhering to the dress and appearance mandates of their religions, withholding religious ceremonial items that are substantially identical to those that the adherents of mainstream religions are permitted, and failing to provide a chaplain trained in their faith." The Court rejected plaintiffs' challenges against RLUIPA. The Court distinguished RFRA on the basis that the jurisdictional scope of RLUIPA was more limited. It applied only when a "substantial burden" on religious exercise is imposed by a program or activity that receives Federal financial assistance, or "the substantial burden affects, or removal of that substantial burden would affect, commerce with foreign nations, among the several States, or with Indian tribes." The Court also rejected the argument that RLUIPA improperly advanced religion in violation of the Establishment Clause, noting that RLUIPA involved a permissible legislative accommodation of religion.

In other instances, government has chosen to accommodate religion by granting exemptions to regulatory requirements, and a number of those exemptions have been upheld. In *Little Sisters of the Poor Saints Peter and Paul Home v. Pennsylvania*, 591 U.S. 657 (2020), relying on RFRA, the Court held that the Government had created lawful exemptions from a regulatory requirement implementing the Patient Protection and Affordable Care Act of 2010 (ACA). The requirement at issue obligated certain employers to provide contraceptive coverage to their employees through their group health plans. Though contraceptive coverage was not required by (or even mentioned in) the ACA, the Government mandated such coverage by promulgating interim final rules (IFRs) shortly after the ACA's passage. After six years of protracted litigation, the Departments of Health and Human Services, Labor, and the Treasury (Departments)—which jointly administer the relevant ACA provision—exempted certain employers who have religious and conscientious objections from this agency-created mandate. The Court held that the Departments had the authority to provide exemptions from the regulatory contraceptive requirements for employers with religious and conscientious objections. In 2019, the Trump administration enacted a new regulation designed to protect workers who oppose abortion, sterilization, or assisted suicide on religious or moral grounds from being forced to participate in those procedures. The rule is enforceable through the loss of federal funding to health care institutions. Opponents expressed concern that the rule might lead to discrimination against transgender or homosexual individuals.

Although *Smith* is the most important recent decision, another significant pre-*Smith* decision is *Lyng v. Northwest Indian Cemetery Protective Association*, 485 U.S. 439 (1988), in which the Court refused to stop the U.S. Forest Service from building a road through the Chimney Rock section of the Six Rivers National Forest. The road project was challenged by Indians who claimed that the area was part of "an integral and indispensable part of Indian religious conceptualization and practice," and that "successful use of the area is dependent upon and facilitated by certain qualities of the physical environment, the most important of which are privacy, silence, and an undisturbed natural setting." They alleged that the new road would cause serious and irreparable damage to the sacred areas. After the Forest Service rejected alternative sites as unfeasible, the Court held that an accommodation was not required. While the Court acknowledged that respondents' beliefs were "sincere," and that the proposed road would adversely affect the practice of their religion, the Court held that the "Free Exercise Clause claim simply cannot be understood to require the Government to conduct its own internal affairs in ways that comport with the religious beliefs of particular citizens." While the Free Exercise Clause might provide an individual some protection against governmental compulsion, it does not give that individual the right to "dictate the conduct of the Government's internal procedures." Justice Brennan, joined by justices Marshall and Blackmun, dissented, arguing that respondents "have demonstrated that the Government's proposed activities will completely prevent them from practicing their religion, and such a showing [entitles] them to the protections of the Free Exercise Clause."

Although Smith imposed a new approach to free exercise claims, the Court has not strictly adhered to the *Smith* approach. As we shall see, in a number of cases, the Court has required exemptions to neutral, generally applicable, laws because the Court concluded that there was discrimination against religion. In addition, the Court carved out an exception to *Smith* in *Mahmoud v. Taylor*, 606 U.S. 522 (2025), involved a board of education's decision to introduce books on same-sex marriage and transgenderism into its elementary school curriculum in an effort to "disrupt" children's thinking about sexuality and gender. Some of the children were as young as five years old. The books celebrated same-sex marriage and transgenderism. When parents raised religious objections to the material (some believing that marriage can only involve a union between a man and a woman, and some believing one's sex and gender are God given and are established at birth), the Board refused to allow them to opt their children out of instruction regarding the books. Even though the Board policy appeared to be neutral and generally applicable, the Court refused to apply *Smith* because it viewed the curriculum requirement as imposing a burden similar to the one imposed in Yoder. In other words, the school district had burdened on the parents' ability to raise their children in accordance with their religious beliefs. The Court held that the Board was required to give parents notice when the material would be discussed and allow them to opt their children out of the instruction. The Court noted that the Board policy posed "a very real threat of undermining the religious beliefs and practices that the parents wish to instill in their children," and therefore imposed an unconstitutional burden on the parents ability to raise their children consistently with their religious beliefs: "A government burdens the religious exercise of parents when it requires them to submit their children to instruction that poses 'a very real threat of undermining' the religious beliefs and practices that the parents wish to instill. A government cannot condition the benefit of free public education on parents' acceptance of such instruction." In response to the Board's objection that opt outs would cause significant disruptions, the Court noted that the Board was able to offer opt outs for other types of material.

B. DISCRIMINATION AGAINST RELIGION

In a number of cases, the Court has held that laws that discriminate against religion should be subjected to heightened scrutiny. For example, in *McDaniel v. Paty*, 435 U.S. 618 (1978), the Court struck down a statute that prohibited ministers or members of religious orders from being state legislators. Likewise, in *Fowler v. Rhode Island*, 345 U.S. 67 (1953), the Court struck down a municipal ordinance that had been construed as prohibiting preaching in a public park by a Jehovah's Witness, but as allowing a Catholic mass or Protestant church service.

Smith reaffirmed the anti-discrimination principle, as did the Court's subsequent decision in *Church of the Lukumi Babalu Aye, Inc. v. City of Hialeah*, 508 U.S. 520 (1993), which struck down a local law prohibiting the religious sacrifice of animals. That case involved the Santeria religion which believes in spirits ("orishas") which help people fulfill their destinies, but which survive based on animal sacrifices made at birth, marriage, and death rituals, as well as at ceremonies designed to heal the sick and at various initiation and annual celebrations. When the Santerias opened the Church of the Lukumi Babalu Aye, Inc. (Church) in Hialeah, Florida, the city passed a series of ordinances prohibiting animal sacrifice. Although the City couched the ordinances in notions of "public morals, peace or safety," the Court concluded that the primary objective was to prohibit Santeria sacrifice. In striking down the ordinances, the Court recognized that animal sacrifice can constitute a religious practice, and distinguished *Smith* noting that the Free Exercise Clause was included in the First Amendment because of "historical instances of religious persecution and intolerance." The Court held that a law that discriminates on the basis of religion is "invalid unless it is justified by a compelling interest and is narrowly tailored to advance that interest." In concluding that the Hialeah law discriminated against religion, the Court's examination began with the text of the law, including the wording, background and function of the ordinance. In applying those criteria, the Court held that the Hialeah ordinances were facially neutral, but that the city's purpose was to discriminate against religion based on citizen objections to Santeria practices which led to enactment of the ordinances.

In *Church of the Lukumi,* while the Court concluded that the City had "legitimate governmental interests in protecting the public health and preventing cruelty to animals," the Court concluded that those interests could be addressed by restrictions stopping far short of a flat prohibition of all Santeria sacrificial practice." For example, if the city was concerned about the proper disposal of carcasses, "the city could have imposed a general regulation on the disposal of organic garbage." The Court also found that a "narrower regulation would achieve the city's interest in preventing cruelty to animals." While the narrower regulation would not prevent the sacrifice, it would ensure that animals were killed humanely by the simultaneous and instantaneous severance of the carotid arteries.

Ultimately, *Church of the Lukumi* is distinguishable from *Smith*. Because *Smith* involved a neutral generally applicable law, that was not directed at religion, the Court was deferential and more inclined to uphold the statute. By contrast, *Church of the Lukumi* involved a law that was directed at, and involved discrimination against, religion, and therefore the Court applied strict scrutiny and struck the law down.

Church of the Lukumi was affirmed and followed in *Masterpiece Cakeshop, Ltd. v. Colorado Civil Rights Commission*, 584 U.S. 617 (2019). That case involved a bakery which made elaborate custom-designed cakes for birthday parties, weddings, and other events. The owner, Jack Phillips, an expert baker, was a devout Christian whose "main goal in life is to be obedient to" Jesus Christ and Christ's "teachings in all aspects of his life." He sought to "honor God through his work at Masterpiece Cakeshop." One of Phillips' religious beliefs was that "God's intention for marriage is that it is and should be the union of one man and one woman." To Phillips, creating a wedding cake for a same-sex wedding would have been equivalent to participating in a celebration that is contrary to his own most deeply held beliefs. As a result, he refused to create a wedding cake for same-sex couples. He stated that he would make birthday cakes for them and sell them cookies or brownies, but he would not create wedding cakes because of his religious opposition to same-sex marriage. When Phillips was charged under the Colorado Anti-Discrimination Act (CADA) with discriminating on the basis of sexual orientation, he challenged the law on two grounds. First, he claimed that being compelled to exercise his artistic talents to express a message with which he disagreed was a violation of his First Amendment right to free speech. Second, Phillips claimed that requiring him to create cakes for same-sex weddings would violate his right to the free exercise of religion, also protected by the First Amendment. The ALJ determined that CADA is a "valid and neutral law of general applicability" and therefore ruled against Phillips and the cakeshop on both constitutional claims. The Colorado Civil Rights Commission (CCRV) concluded that Phillips was in violation of CADA and entered a cease-and-desist order, as well as various remedial actions.

The U.S. Supreme Court reversed, concluding that the CCRV had discriminated against Phillips on the basis of religion. While recognizing that gay persons and gay couples cannot be treated as social outcasts or as inferior in dignity and worth, the Court held that "religious and philosophical objections to gay marriage are protected views and in some instances protected forms of expression." As a result, "a member of the clergy who objects to gay marriage on moral and religious grounds cannot be compelled to perform the ceremony without denial of his or her right to the free exercise of religion." But, ordinarily, a business might be required by law to offer its goods and services to same-sex couples "on the same terms and conditions offered to other members of the public."

Nevertheless, the Court overturned the CCRV's decision because the CCRV did not provide Phillips with a "neutral and respectful consideration" of his challenges. On the contrary, the CCRV had evinced "a clear and impermissible hostility toward the sincere religious beliefs" that motivated Phillip's objection. At several points, commissioners had endorsed the view that religious beliefs cannot legitimately be carried into the public sphere or commercial domain, implying that religious beliefs and persons are less than fully welcome in Colorado's business community. One commissioner stated that Phillips can believe "what he wants to believe," but cannot act on his religious beliefs "if he decides to do business in the state." Another commissioner stated: "Freedom of religion and religion has been used to justify all kinds of discrimination throughout history, whether it be slavery, whether it be the holocaust, whether it be—we can list hundreds of situations where freedom of religion has been used to justify discrimination. To me it is one of the most despicable pieces of rhetoric that people can use to—to use their religion to hurt others." The Court concluded that, to "describe a man's faith as "one of the most despicable pieces of rhetoric that people can use" is to disparage his religion in at least two distinct ways: by describing it as despicable, and also by characterizing it as merely rhetorical—something insubstantial and even insincere. The commissioner went so far as to compare Phillips' invocation of his sincerely held religious beliefs to defenses of slavery and the Holocaust. The Court concluded that this "sentiment is inappropriate for a Commission charged with the solemn responsibility of fair and neutral enforcement of Colorado's antidiscrimination law—a law that protects discrimination on the basis of religion as well as sexual orientation." The Court emphasized that the record showed no objection to these comments from other commissioners, and the state-court that reviewed the case did not express concern either. The Court concluded that the Commission's actions "cast doubt on the fairness and impartiality of the Commission's adjudication of Phillips' case."

In addition, the Court concluded that the CCRV had treated Phillips differently than other bakers who had objected to a requested cake on the basis of conscience. In each of those cases, the bakers had prevailed before the Commission, but each of those cases involved customers who had requested cakes "that conveyed disapproval of same-sex marriage, along with religious text." In each of those cases, the CCRV, found that the baker acted lawfully in refusing service. It made those determinations because the requested cakes included "wording and images the baker deemed derogatory," featured "language and images the baker deemed hateful," or displayed a message the baker "deemed as discriminatory. The treatment of the conscience-based objections in those cases contrasted with the Commission's treatment of Phillips. The Commission ruled against Phillips in part on the theory that any message the requested wedding cake would carry would be attributed to the customer, not to the baker. Yet the Division did not address this point in any of the other cases. The Division found no violation of CADA in the other cases in part because each bakery was willing to sell other products, including those depicting Christian themes, to the prospective customers. But the Commission dismissed Phillips' willingness to sell "birthday cakes, shower cakes, and cookies and brownies," to gay and lesbian customers as irrelevant. The treatment of the other cases and Phillips' case could reasonably be interpreted as being inconsistent as to whether speech is involved, quite apart from whether the cases should ultimately be distinguished. "In short, the Commission's consideration of Phillips' religious objection did not accord with its treatment of these other objections."

The Court therefore held that the CCRV's "treatment of [Phillips] violated the State's duty under the First Amendment not to base laws or regulations on hostility to a religion or religious viewpoint." The decision was important because the Court identified factors that it deemed relevant to the assessment of governmental neutrality, including "the historical background of the decision under challenge, the specific series of events leading to the enactment or official policy, and the legislative or administrative history, including contemporaneous statements made by members of the decisionmaking body." The Court concluded that the "Commission's consideration of Phillips' case was neither tolerant nor respectful of Phillips' religious beliefs." In regard to CCRV's negative "evaluation of the particular justification" for Phillip's objection and the religious grounds for it, the Court decreed that government "has no role in deciding or even suggesting whether the religious ground for Phillips' conscience-based objection is legitimate or illegitimate" and it concluded that "Phillips' religious objection was not considered with the neutrality that the Free Exercise Clause requires." Justice Kagan concurred, agreeing that state officials "cannot show hostility to religious views; rather, they must give those views 'neutral and respectful consideration,'" and that the CCRV "did not satisfy that obligation." However, she felt that Phillips did not treat same-sex customers in the same way that he would have treated opposite sex couples. Justice Gorsuch also concurred because the CCRV "failed to act neutrally by applying a consistent legal rule." "The Commission's decisions presumed that Phillip harbored.

The pandemic produced a number of cases alleging discrimination against religion. For example, in *Roman Catholic Diocese of Brooklyn v. Cuomo*, 592 U.S. 14 (2020), the Court granted an application for injunctive relief against New York Governor Mario Cuomo's order limiting attendance at religious services held in "red" zones (zones where Covid infection rates were highest) to 10 people, and in "orange" zones to 25 people. Under the order, so-called "essential" businesses in red zones (which included things such as acupuncture facilities, camp grounds, garages, as well as all plants manufacturing chemicals and microelectronics and all transportation facilities) were not subject to occupancy limits. In orange zones, while attendance at houses of worship was limited to 25 persons, non-essential businesses could decide for themselves how many persons to admit. The Court concluded that the Governor's order was not neutral towards religion because it targeted the "ultra-Orthodox Jewish community" and in any event discriminated against houses of worship. The Court noted that a nearby store could "literally have hundreds of people shopping there on any given day" whereas attendance at church or synagogue services were dramatically limited. And, although "factories and schools have contributed to the spread of COVID-19, they are treated less harshly than the Diocese's churches and Agudath Israel's synagogues, which have admirable safety records." The Court found irreparable harm because "remote viewing is not the same as personal attendance. Catholics who watch a Mass at home cannot receive communion, and there are important religious traditions in the Orthodox Jewish faith that require personal attendance." *See also Tandon v. Newsom*, 593 U.S. 61 (2021) (striking down an executive order limiting attendance at in-home religious services while permitting secular activities under similar circumstances); *Gateway City Church v. Newsom*, 141 S.Ct. 1460 (2021); *but see Calvary Chapel v. Sisolak*, 140 S.Ct. 2603 (2020).

Another important discrimination decision was rendered in *Fulton v. City of Philadelphia*, 593 U.S. 522 (2021), a case involving CSS (Catholic Social Services) which participated in Philadelphia's foster care system. CSS believes that "marriage is a sacred bond between a man and a woman." Because the agency understood the certification of prospective foster families to be an endorsement of their relationships, it refused to certify unmarried couples—regardless of their sexual orientation—or same-sex married couples. CSS did not object to certifying gay or lesbian individuals as single foster parents or to placing gay and lesbian children, and no same-sex couple had ever sought certification from CSS. If one did, CSS would have directed the couple to one of the more than 20 other agencies in the City which certified same-sex couples. Because of CSS' policy on same-sex couples, Philadelphia decided that it would no longer refer children to CSS which it regarded as in violation of a non-discrimination provision in its contract, as well as in violation of the city's Fair Practices Ordinance. CSS filed suit, challenging the city's position as a violation of the Free Exercise Clause.

Although the Court was strongly urged to overrule *Smith*, and several justices argued that it should have done so, the Court did not. Instead, although the Court reaffirmed *Smith's* suggestion that no exemption is required for neutral, generally applicable, laws, the Court noted that a "law is not generally applicable if it 'invites' the government to consider the particular reasons for a person's conduct by providing 'a mechanism for individualized exemptions.' " In this case, the city's system included "a system of individual exemptions, made available at the 'sole discretion' of the Commissioner," and the Commissioner made clear that he "has no intention of granting an exception" to CSS. "The inclusion of a formal system of entirely discretionary exceptions in section 3.21 renders the contractual non-discrimination requirement not generally applicable."

An interesting aspect of the case was the city's argument that CSS's refusal to certify same-sex couples constitutes an "Unlawful Public Accommodations Practice" in violation of the Fair Practices Ordinance. That ordinance forbade "denying or interfering with the public accommodations opportunities of an individual or otherwise discriminating based on his or her race, ethnicity, color, sex, sexual orientation, disability, marital status, familial status," or several other protected categories. Phila. Code § 9–1106(1) (2016). However, the Court rejected the idea that a foster care agency is a "public accommodation" because it bears little resemblance to staying in a hotel, eating at a restaurant, or riding a bus.

The Court also rejected the city's argument that it had compelling reasons for requiring CSS to minister to same-sex couples, including maximizing the number of foster parents, protecting the City from liability, and ensuring equal treatment of prospective foster parents and foster children. The Court concluded that, while maximizing the number of foster families and minimizing liability are important goals, "the City failed to show that granting CSS an exception will put those goals at risk. If anything, including CSS in the program seems likely to increase, not reduce, the number of available foster parents." The Court dismissed possible liability claims as "speculative." In addition, even though the Court recognized the state's interest in providing "equal treatment of prospective foster parents and foster children," the Court held that "this interest cannot justify denying CSS an exception for its religious exercise." As a result, the Court concluded that the Philadelphia system failed strict scrutiny.

The Court's most recent decision on discrimination against religion was rendered in *Catholic Charities Bureau, Inc. v. Wisconsin Labor & Industry Review Commission*, 605 U.S. 238 (2025). Wisconsin exempted religious employers from its unemployment compensation scheme. It also exempted nonprofit organizations "operated, supervised, controlled, or principally supported by a church or convention or association of churches," but only if they are "operated primarily for religious purposes." The case arose when Wisconsin refused to exempt Catholic Charities Bureau, Inc., a nonprofit organization that served as the social ministry arm of the Roman Catholic Diocese, on the basis that the Bureau was not "operated primarily for religious purposes." Wisconsin concluded that the Bureau's "charitable social services are neither inherently or primarily religious activities." The Bureau's mission was to "carry on the redeeming work of our Lord," and it did so by providing "services to the poor and disadvantaged" and seeking to "be an effective sign of the charity of Christ." But it did not distinguish on the basis of "race, sex, or religion in reference to clients served, staff employed and board members appointed." The Bureau operated several separately incorporated entities which provide a range of charitable services to local communities across the area. However, the Bureau's executive director need not be a Catholic priest. Participants in the Bureau's programs did not receive religious training or orientation, and neither the Bureau nor its subentities "tries to 'inculcate'" participants with the Catholic faith. The Bureau's approach reflected religious doctrine prohibiting Catholic bodies from "misusing works of charity for purposes of proselytism." Catholic teachings distinguish between "evangelization," which involves "sharing one's faith," and "proselytization," which seeks to "influence" or "coerce" others into accepting one's religious views. The former is permitted, the latter is not. Wisconsin denied the Bureau an exemption from the unemployment scheme because it believed that the Bureau was not "operated primarily for religious purposes" since petitioners' "charitable social services are neither inherently or primarily religious activities." The U.S. Supreme Court held that Wisconsin had discriminated against the Bureau, noting that the "clearest command of the Establishment Clause" is that the government may not "officially prefer" one religious denomination over another. "Wisconsin's exemption thus grants a denominational preference by explicitly differentiating between religions based on theological practices."

The prohibition against discrimination also extends to governmental benefits. In *Trinity Lutheran Church of Columbia, Inc. v. Director*, 582 U.S. 449 (2017), a church applied for a government grant that would have allowed it to replace a gravel playground surface at its childcare center with a pour-in-place rubber surface (created with recycled tires) that was safer for children. The State of Missouri offered the grants to nonprofit organizations, and in general, the grants were awarded on a competitive basis looking at several criteria, including the poverty level in the area and the applicant's plan to promote recycling. However, the Department had a strict policy of denying grants to any applicant owned or controlled by a church, sect, or other religious entity. Although the center ranked fifth among 44 applicants, and even though the program awarded 14 grants, the center was denied because of the state's policy of denying grants to religiously affiliated applicants.

The Court held that the state had violated the Free Exercise Clause. After noting that the Establishment Clause does not prevent Missouri from including Trinity Lutheran in its Program, the Court emphasized that the Free Exercise Clause "protects religious observers against unequal treatment" and subjects to the strictest scrutiny laws that target the religious for "special disabilities" based on their "religious status." The Court expressed concern because Missouri's decision to deny "a generally available benefit solely on account of religious identity imposes a penalty on the free exercise of religion that can be justified only by a state interest 'of the highest order.' " Noting that the Department's policy expressly discriminates against otherwise eligible recipients by disqualifying them from a public benefit solely because of their religious character, "the State has punished the free exercise of religion. The express discrimination against religious exercise here is not the denial of a grant, but rather the refusal to allow the Church—solely because it is a church—to compete with secular organizations for a grant."

The Court distinguished *Locke v. Davey*, 540 U.S. 712 (2004), and its denial of a scholarship program to assist high-achieving students with the costs of postsecondary education: "Davey was not denied a scholarship because of who he was; he was denied a scholarship because of what he proposed to do—use the funds to prepare for the ministry. Here Trinity Lutheran was denied a grant simply because of what it is—a church." The Court also distinguished *Locke* on the basis that he sought funding for an "essentially religious endeavor akin to a religious calling as well as an academic pursuit," and opposition to such funding "to support church leaders" lay at the historic core of the Religion Clauses. "Here nothing of the sort can be said about a program to use recycled tires to resurface playgrounds." "In this case, Trinity Lutheran is put to the choice between being a church and receiving a government benefit."

Carson v. Makin, 596 U.S. 767 (2022), *Carson* involved a Maine law that required local towns to provide every child with the benefits of a free public education. For cities that were too rural or too small to maintain their own schools, Maine created a tuition assistance program that provided for the payment of "the tuition at the public school or the approved private school of the parent's choice at which the student is accepted." "Approved" schools included those that were "currently accredited by a New England association of schools and colleges" or separately "approved for attendance purposes" by the Department, and which met certain curricular requirements (e.g., using English as the language of instruction, offering a course in "Maine history, including the Constitution of Maine and Maine's cultural and ethnic heritage," and maintaining a student-teacher ratio of not more than 30 to 1). Parents could send their children to schools inside or outside the state, or even in foreign countries. However, Maine precluded religious schools from participating in the program if they infused religion into their classes.

The Court struck down the Maine prohibition on the inclusion of religious schools on the basis that it involved discrimination against religion. The Court emphasized that Maine offers tuition assistance to any family whose school district does not provide a public secondary school, and a wide range of schools are eligible for the payments, but religious schools are disqualified. "Maine's tuition assistance program—like the program in *Trinity Lutheran* [discussed in Section [G], below]—'effectively penalizes the free exercise' of religion. While the wording of the Montana and Maine provisions is different, their effect is the same: to 'disqualify some private schools' from funding 'solely because they are religious.' " As a result, the Court applied "the strictest scrutiny" and held that the "State's antiestablishment interest does not justify enactments that exclude some members of the community from an otherwise generally available public benefit because of their religious exercise."

Justice Breyer dissented, arguing that "Maine chooses not to fund only those schools that 'promote the faith or belief system with which the schools are associated and/or present the academic material taught through the lens of this faith'—*i.e.*, schools that will use public money for religious purposes. Maine excludes schools not because of the schools' religious character but because the schools will use the funds to teach and promote religious ideals." In his view, "Nothing in our Free Exercise Clause cases *compels* Maine to give tuition aid to private schools that will use the funds to provide a religious education. *Trinity Lutheran* and *Espinoza* prohibit States from denying aid to religious schools solely because of religious *status*. But the Free Exercise Clause does not require Maine to fund schools that will use public money to promote religion. Maine's decision not to fund such schools falls squarely within the play in the joints between those two Clauses."

The Court also applied the non-discrimination principle in *Shurtleff v. City of Boston*, 596 U.S. 243 (2022). That case involved a flagpole outside the Boston City Hall where the city allowed individuals to hold flag-raising ceremonies, at which they raised a flag of their choice, and let it fly for a couple of hours. Although the city allowed individuals and groups to raise flags commemorating numerous and diverse things (e.g., marking the national holidays of Bostonians' many countries of origin, recognizing Pride Week, honoring emergency medical service workers), the city denied a request to raise a Christian flag, fearing a violation of the Establishment Clause. After concluding that the flag raisings did not constitute "government speech," the Court held that the city's action constituted discrimination against religion: "Boston acknowledges that it denied Shurtleff's request because it believed flying a religious flag at City Hall could violate the Establishment Clause. When a government does not speak for itself, it may not exclude speech based on religious viewpoint; doing so constitutes impermissible viewpoint discrimination." Applying that rule, the Court concluded that the City of Boston had discriminated against religion: "Here, Boston concedes that it denied Shurtleff's request solely because the Christian flag he asked to raise 'promoted a specific religion.' That refusal discriminated based on religious viewpoint and violated the Free Speech Clause. We conclude that Boston's flag-raising program does not express government speech. As a result, the city's refusal to let Shurtleff and Camp Constitution fly their flag based on its religious viewpoint violated the Free Speech Clause of the First Amendment."

Justice Kavanaugh concurred, arguing that "government does not violate the Establishment Clause merely because it treats religious persons, organizations, and speech equally with secular persons, organizations, and speech in public programs, benefits, facilities, and the like." In his view, "government *violates* the Constitution when (as here) it *excludes* religious persons, organizations, or speech because of religion from public programs, benefits, facilities, and the like." He concluded that "a government may not treat religious persons, religious organizations, or religious speech as second-class." Justice Alito, joined by Justices Thomas and Gorsuch, concurred: "The flag displays were plainly private speech within a forum created by the city, not government speech. Having created a forum with those characteristics, the city could not reject Shurtleff's application on account of the religious viewpoint he intended to express."

The Ministerial Exception. Smith was further qualified in *Hosanna-Tabor Evangelical Lutheran Church and School v. Equal Employment Opportunity Commission*, 565 U.S. 171 (2012), in which the Court held that the First Amendment religion clauses exempt a church from employment discrimination laws for the termination of an employee who performs ministerial functions. The case involved a "called teacher" in a school that employed both "called" and "lay" teachers. "Called" teachers were regarded as called to their vocation by God through a congregation, and were required to satisfy academic requirements involving theological study, be endorsed by their local Synod, and pass an oral examination. "Called" teachers received the formal title of "Minister of Religion, Commissioned." "Lay" or "contract" teachers need not be trained or even Lutheran. They were appointed by the school board to one-year renewable terms. Although teachers at the school generally performed the same duties regardless of whether they were lay or called, lay teachers were hired only when called teachers were unavailable.

The case arose when a called teacher at the school became sick and went on leave. When she believed that she was ready to return to her work, but the school did not, she protested. The church responded by revoking her "call" and dismissing her. The teacher sued, claiming a violation of the Americans with Disabilities Act, and she sought reinstatement, back pay, compensatory and punitive damages, attorney's fees, and other injunctive relief. The Court concluded that the church's action was protected by the First Amendment's "ministerial exception."

The Court traced the history of governmental attempts to control church appointments and church decisions, and concluded that the exception is premised on both the Establishment Clause and the Free Exercise Clause: "The Establishment Clause prevents the Government from appointing ministers, and the Free Exercise Clause prevents it from interfering with the freedom of religious groups to select their own." The Court emphasized that "members of a religious group put their faith in the hands of their ministers," and that the government cannot force them "to accept or retain an unwanted minister," or punish a church for failing to do so. "Such action interferes with the internal governance of the church, depriving the church of control over the selection of those who will personify its beliefs." The Court distinguished *Smith* on the basis that "a church's selection of its ministers is unlike an individual's ingestion of peyote. *Smith* involved government regulation of only outward physical acts. The present case, in contrast, concerns government interference with an internal church decision that affects the faith and mission of the church itself. The contention that *Smith* forecloses recognition of a ministerial exception rooted in the Religion Clauses has no merit."

The Court ruled against the teacher even though the EEOC and Perich foresaw a parade of horribles that would follow the Court's recognition of a ministerial exception to employment discrimination suits. They argued that such an exception would protect religious organizations from liability for retaliating against employees for reporting criminal misconduct or for testifying before a grand jury or in a criminal trial, and would give religious employers "unfettered discretion" to violate employment laws by, for example, hiring children or aliens. The Court found these arguments unpersuasive, noting that the "ministerial exception has been around in the lower courts for 40 years, and has not given rise to the dire consequences predicted by the EEOC and Perich." The Court declined to hold that the exception would protect religious organizations against liability for retaliating against employees for reporting criminal misconduct or for testifying before a grand jury or in a criminal trial, and also declined to decide whether the exception would exempt churches from other employment laws. Noting that the exception had existed for more than four decades, and had not given rise to such claims, the Court postponed consideration of those issues until they arise in an actual case.

In *Our Lady of Guadalupe School v. Morrisey-Berru*, 591 U.S. 732 (2020), the Court extended the ministerial exception to lay teachers entrusted with responsibility for instructing their students in the faith: "Morrissey-Berru and Biel both performed vital religious duties. Educating and forming students in the Catholic faith lay at the core of the mission of the schools where they taught, and their employment agreements and faculty handbooks specified in no uncertain terms that they were expected to help the schools carry out this mission and that their work would be evaluated to ensure that they were fulfilling that responsibility. They prayed with their students, attended Mass with the students, and prepared the children for their participation in other religious activities."

The Court held that, when "a school with a religious mission entrusts a teacher with the responsibility of educating and forming students in the faith, judicial intervention into disputes between the school and the teacher threatens the school's independence in a way that the First Amendment does not allow." Justice Thomas concurred: "To avoid disadvantaging these minority faiths and interfering in 'a religious group's right to shape its own faith and mission,' courts should defer to a religious organization's sincere determination that a position is 'ministerial.'" Justice Sotomayor dissented: "Neither school publicly represented that either teacher was a Catholic spiritual leader or "minister." Rather, the schools referred to both as "lay" teachers. Neither teacher had a "significant degree of religious training" or underwent a "formal process of commissioning." Nor did either school require such training or commissioning as a prerequisite to gaining (or keeping) employment. Neither held herself out as having a leadership role in the faith community. Neither claimed any benefits (tax, governmental, ceremonial, or administrative) available only to spiritual leaders. Both Biel and Morrissey-Berru had almost exclusively secular duties, making it especially improper to deprive them of all legal protection when their employers have not offered any religious reason for the alleged discrimination. Morrissey-Berru did lead classroom prayers, bring her students to a cathedral once a year, direct the school Easter play, and sign a contract directing her to 'assist with Liturgy Planning.' But these occasional tasks should not trigger as a matter of law the ministerial exception. Morrissey-Berru did not lead mass, deliver sermons, or select hymns. And there is no evidence that Morrissey-Berru led devotional exercises."

In *Fratello v. Archdiocese of New York*, 863 F.3d 190 (2d Cir. 2017), the court held that the ministerial exception applied to a principal at a Roman Catholic elementary school. She was officially labeled as a "lay principal," but she held herself out as a spiritual leader and she performed important religious functions. In addition, she was charged with advancing the school's religious mission. Likewise, in *Lee v. Sixth Mount Zion Baptist Church*, 903 F.3d 113 (3rd Cir. 2018), the court refused to hear a pastor's breach of contract suit against a church that fired him in breach of his written employment agreement. The church fired the pastor for failure to provide "spiritual leadership." The court held that to rule on the adequacy of the pastor's leadership "would impermissibly entangle the court in religious governance and doctrine."

CHECKLIST

A. The scope of the Free Exercise Clause's application.

1. In addition to providing protection against governmental attempts to establish religion, the First Amendment protects religious freedom.

2. As with other provisions of the Bill of Rights, the Free Exercise Clause has been incorporated into the Fourteenth Amendment due process clause, and therefore applies to the states.

3. Unquestionably, the Free Exercise Clause protects religious *belief* and *thought*, but there is less agreement about the extent to which the Clause protects religious *conduct*.

4. Most free exercise cases involve claims that an individual, or group of individuals, should be exempt from laws that "burden" their religion either by prohibiting them from engaging in conduct required by their religious beliefs, or by requiring conduct prohibited by these beliefs.

5. Free exercise litigation usually focuses on whether the individual's interest in free exercise must give way in face of societal interests, or whether the state interest must give way to accommodate the individual's free exercise interests, and more particularly the litigation focuses on the standard of review to be applied in deciding those issues.

6. In *Reynolds v. United States,* 98 U.S. (8 Otto) 145 (1878), the Court held that the government has broad authority to prohibit religious conduct, and rejected the argument that a religious exemption was required.

7. *Reynolds'* distinction between "belief" and "conduct" was partially rejected in *Cantwell v. Connecticut*, 310 U.S. 296 (1940). While the Court regarded the freedom to believe as absolute, it held that religious conduct "remains subject to regulation for the protection of society." However, the Court overturned Cantwell's conviction, noting that individuals have the right to preach and to disseminate their religious views.

B. In a number of later cases decided before *Smith*, the Court has struck down laws that infringed religious beliefs.

1. In *Torcaso v. Watkins*, 367 U.S. 488 (1961), the Court struck down a state constitutional provision that required public officials to declare a belief in God as a prerequisite to assuming office.

2. In a number of Free Exercise cases, the Court has applied strict scrutiny analysis to laws burdening religion.

3. In *Sherbert v. Verner*, 374 U.S. 398 (1963), the Court held that a Seventh-day Adventist adherent was entitled to unemployment benefits when she was discharged by her employer for refusing to work on Saturday, her Sabbath. The Court overrode a state law a law denying benefits to someone who refuses to accept work.

4. In *Wisconsin v. Yoder*, 406 U.S. 205 (1972), the Court held that members of the Old Order Amish religion could be excused from mandatory school attendance laws that conflicted with their religious beliefs (which required "learning by doing" after eighth grade.)

5. However, *United States v. Lee*, 455 U.S. 252 (1982), held that a member of the Old Order Amish could be required to pay Social Security taxes despite his religious objections to the receipt of public insurance benefits and to the payment of taxes to support public insurance funds.

C. The Court has been less willing to accommodate religious claims in recent years.

1. In *Employment Division v. Smith*, 494 U.S. 872 (1990), the Court upheld an Oregon law that prohibited the use of peyote as applied to Native Americans who wanted to use peyote for religious reasons.

2. *Smith* concluded that states were not required to create exceptions for "generally applicable and otherwise valid" laws that have the "incidental" effect of burdening religion.

3. *Smith* did suggest that it might strike down a law that burdens religion when it implicates other constitutional rights, particularly free speech rights.

4. In *Lyng v. Northwest Indian Cemetery Protective Association*, 485 U.S. 439 (1988), the Court refused to stop the U.S. Forest Service from building a road through a forest despite Indian claims that the area was part of "an

integral and indispensable part of Indian religious conceptualization and practice," and that "successful use of the [area] is dependent upon and facilitated by certain qualities of the physical environment, the most important of which are privacy, silence, and an undisturbed natural setting."

5. *Smith* has been qualified in subsequent cases. In some instances, courts have found that facially neutral laws have been applied in a discriminatory manner and therefore are unconstitutional.

6. In *Mahmoud v. Taylor*, 606 U.S. 522 (2025), the Court held that *Smith* would not apply to cases involving injury to parental rights like those presented in *Yoder*.

D. In a number of cases, the Court has held that laws that discriminate against religion should be subjected to heightened scrutiny.

1. In *McDaniel v. Paty*, 435 U.S. 618 (1978), the Court struck down a statute that prohibited ministers or members of religious orders from being state legislators.

2. In *Fowler v. Rhode Island*, 345 U.S. 67 (1953), the Court struck down a municipal ordinance that had been construed as prohibiting preaching in a public park by a Jehovah's Witness, but as allowing a Catholic mass or Protestant church service.

3. In *Church of the Lukumi Babalu Aye, Inc. v. City of Hialeah*, 508 U.S. 520 (1993), the Court struck down a local law prohibiting the religious sacrifice of animals which was based on an intent to discriminate against the Santeria religion. The Court found that the "legitimate governmental interests in protecting the public health and preventing cruelty to animals could be addressed by restrictions stopping far short of a flat prohibition of all Santeria sacrificial practice."

E. The Court has established a "ministerial exception" that exempts religious organizations from discrimination laws.

■ PROBLEMS ■

Problem #1: A group of college students band together to form a new religion. The essence of the religion is that the use of LSD (an hallucinogenic drug) will lead them to a higher state of consciousness and spirituality. Of course, under both federal and state law, it is illegal to use LSD. Accordingly, the students file a declaratory judgment action seeking to have the federal and state laws declared unconstitutional as applied to them. Do the students' religious beliefs entitle them to an exemption from the anti-LSD laws?

Answer: No. The *Smith* decision provides that individuals are not entitled to religious exemptions from neutral, generally applicable, criminal laws. In that case, the law is neutral (it was not created to discriminate against religion) and s applicable to everyone regardless of their religious beliefs. As a result, the law is probably constitutional, and the college students are not entitled to an exemption that would allow them to use LSD or other hallucinogenic drugs.

Problem #2: Congress, after successfully amending the U.S. Constitution to allow it do so, passes a new law prohibiting the manufacture, sale, distribution and use of alcohol. Sensitive to the fact that the Catholic religion uses wine in its sacraments, the law specifically provides an exemption for the use of wine in Catholic services. However, the law does not create a similar exemption for other religions that use wine in their services. The FBI, and other federal agencies, have taken the position that only the Catholic religion may use wine in its services. Is the exclusion of other religions constitutionally permissible?

Answer: No. Congress appears to have discriminated in favor of one religion (Catholicism) and against others. Even though Congress would not ordinarily be required to create an exception from a generally applicable law for a religious practice, it cannot discriminate by creating an exception for one religion and denying other religions a comparable exemption.

Problem #3: An Indian tribe likes to use a particular section of a national park for religious purposes. It views the area as "sacred." By meditating there, members of the tribe enhance their spirituality and help bring themselves to a higher state of consciousness. When the U.S. Forest Service (USFS) announces that it intends to build a road through the area, the Indians object that the road will mar their sacred area, inhibit their religious exercises, and prevent them from satisfactorily practicing their religion. Based on their religious concerns, do the Indians have the right to prevent the USFS from building the road?

Answer: No. While the Indians have the right to practice their religion, they do not have the right to require the USFS to set aside portions of the national parks for their use, and they do not have the right to prohibit the USFS from building a road through the area.

POINTS TO REMEMBER

- In addition to providing protection against governmental attempts to establish religion, the First Amendment protects religious freedom.
- As with other provisions of the Bill of Rights, the Free Exercise Clause has been incorporated into the Fourteenth Amendment due process clause, and therefore applies to the states.
- Unquestionably, the Free Exercise Clause protects religious *belief* and *thought*, but there is less agreement about the extent to which the Clause protects religious *conduct*.
- Most free exercise cases involve claims that an individual, or group of individuals, should be exempt from laws that "burden" their religion either by prohibiting them from engaging in conduct required by their religious beliefs, or by requiring conduct prohibited by those beliefs.
- As with the right to free speech, the Free Exercise Clause does not provide absolute protection for all religious practices, and instead has involved a balancing of the state interest against the religious interest.
- In some early decisions, the Court distinguished between "belief" and "conduct." In *Reynolds v. United States,* 98 U.S. (8 Otto) 145 (1878), the Court held that the government has broad authority to prohibit religious conduct, and rejected the argument that a religious exemption was required.
- In a number of later cases, the Court has struck down laws that infringed religious beliefs. Indeed, for a three-decade period, the Court held that a number of laws must give way to religious objections.
- In a number of early Free Exercise cases, the Court has applied strict scrutiny analysis to laws burdening religion.
- The Court has been less willing to accommodate religious claims in recent years.
- In *Employment Division v. Smith,* 494 U.S. 872 (1990), the Court held that the Free Exercise Clause clearly protects the "right to believe and profess whatever religious doctrine one desires," as well as the right to perform religious acts such as "assembling with others for a worship service, participating in sacramental use of bread and wine, proselytizing, abstaining from certain foods or certain modes of transportation."

- However, *Smith* held that the Free Exercise Clause does not require the state to create exemptions from "generally applicable and otherwise valid" laws that have the "incidental" effect of burdening religion.
- *Smith* suggested that it might strike down a law that burdens religion when the law implicates other constitutional rights, particularly free speech rights.
- The Court qualified *Smith* in *Mahmoud v. Taylor*, 606 U.S. 522 (2025), in regard to parental injuries like that suffered in *Yoder*.
- The Court has held that laws that discriminate against religion should be subjected to heightened scrutiny.
- The Court has established a "ministerial exception" under the First Amendment. That exception exempts religious organizations from certain anti-discrimination laws.

CHAPTER 13

State Action

The Bill of Rights, as well as the fourteenth and fifteenth amendments, are designed to protect individuals against "governmental" action. In other words, before they apply, it must be shown that the state is sufficiently involved in the challenged conduct so that the Bill of Rights (*e.g.*, freedom of speech, free exercise of religion, freedom of the press) or the Fourteenth Amendment apply. Thus, these constitutional provisions (with the exception of the Thirteenth Amendment's prohibition against slavery) do not constrain the actions of private individuals. Private conduct may be actionable under tort or statutory law, but it is not constitutionally prohibited in and of itself.

In the *Civil Rights Cases*, 109 U.S. 3 (1883), the Court struck down portions of the Civil Rights Act of 1875 which prohibited discrimination on the basis of race or color "in the enjoyment of the accommodations and privileges of inns, public conveyances, theaters, and other places of public amusement." The Court held that the Fourteenth Amendment prohibited only "state action," and that Congress could not restrain the conduct of private individuals. The Court also rejected the argument that the legislation was justified by the Thirteenth Amendment, which authorizes Congress to abolish the "badges and incidents of slavery," on the basis that it "would be running the slavery argument into the ground to make it apply to every act of discrimination."

In many cases, when plaintiffs assert a violation of the Bill of Rights or the Fourteenth Amendment, state involvement will be obvious. In other words, Congress or a state legislature will have passed a law, or a governmental agency or government official will have taken action against the citizen. More difficult questions arise when the violation seems to be the result of private action, but there appears to be some governmental involvement in that action. As we shall see, government is involved in virtually all private conduct in one way or another. Thus, the real question is whether the government is sufficiently involved so that the ostensibly private action effectively becomes "state action." Questions about state action present difficult issues for the courts.

A. GOVERNMENT FUNCTION

One situation in which the Court has found state action is when a private entity performs a "traditional governmental function." In other words, the private entity performs functions that are really "governmental" in their function and nature. For example, if a private corporation runs a town which functions like an ordinary public town, the private corporation may be regarded as performing a governmental function in running the town. If a private entity is found to be performing a governmental function, then the protections of the Bill of Rights and the Fourteenth Amendment may apply to that governmental function. The difficulty in these cases is in determining what constitutes a "traditional governmental function."

1. Company Towns

So-called "company towns" provide a classic example of state action. In these cases, a private town is functioning like a public one, and therefore the argument is made that its actions should be treated like a public town for constitutional purposes. In *Marsh v. Alabama*, 326 U.S. 501 (1946), the "town" (Chickasaw), owned by a private company, included residential buildings, streets, a sewer system, a sewage disposal plant, various businesses, a United States post office, a sheriff (paid by the company), and a business block with stores, paved sidewalks, and streets that connected to public highways. The Court treated the town as a municipality for purposes of the First and Fourteenth amendments, concluding that the "more an owner, for his advantage, opens up his property for use by the public[,] the more [his] rights become circumscribed by the statutory and constitutional rights of those who use it." The Court emphasized that Chickasaw functioned like any other town, and the mere fact it was privately owned "is not sufficient to justify the State's permitting a corporation to govern a community of citizens so as to restrict their fundamental liberties and the enforcement of such restraint by the application of a State statute." As a result, in *Marsh*, the Court held that the First Amendment applied to attempts to prevent a woman from engaging in expressive activity in the town on the grounds.

Today, company towns are less common than they were in earlier decades, but there has been considerable litigation about whether modern entities such as private shopping malls should be treated as "state action" for purposes of the Constitution. As in *Marsh*, these issues often arise in the context of individuals who seek to use shopping malls for expressive purposes. In *Amalgamated Food*

Employees Union v. Logan Valley Plaza, Inc., 391 U.S. 308 (1968), union members peacefully picketed a business located in a private shopping center. When the owners of the center sought to enjoin the picketing as a trespass, the Court analogized to *Marsh* and held that the shopping center's actions constituted state action so that the First Amendment applied. The Court viewed the shopping center as the modern equivalent of the business district in company towns. *Logan Valley* was distinguished in *Lloyd Corp., Ltd. v. Tanner*, 407 U.S. 551 (1972), which concluded that a shopping center's actions involved private action: "[*Logan Valley*] was carefully phrased to limit its holding to the picketing involved, where the picketing was 'directly related in its purpose to the use to which the shopping center property was being put,' and where the store was located in the center of a large private enclave with the consequence that no other reasonable opportunities for the pickets to convey their message to their intended audience were available. . . . Neither of these elements is present in the case now before the Court." Finally, in *Hudgens v. NLRB*, 424 U.S. 507 (1976), the Court flatly overruled *Logan Valley* in a case that involved union members who were engaged in peaceful protesting inside a privately owned shopping center. The Court held that picketers did not have a First Amendment right to picket inside the mall: "the constitutional guarantee of free expression has no part to play in a case such as this." As a result, the actions of the owners of private shopping malls are generally not regarded as state action today.

2. Party Primaries

The other context in which "governmental function" issues have arisen is related to the conduct of electoral primaries. In a series of cases decided between 1927 and 1953, the Court was confronted by cases challenging the Democratic Party's efforts to preclude blacks from participating in its party primaries. Since political parties are generally regarded as voluntary associations of private individuals, rather than as governmental entities, plaintiffs sought to use the governmental function doctrine to argue that the party's conduct should be treated as state action. In the party primary cases, the Court agreed.

In *Nixon v. Herndon,* 273 U.S. 536 (1927), the Court struck down a Texas statute that explicitly prohibited blacks from voting in the Democratic Party primary because its mandated discrimination constituted state action. Following *Nixon*, the Texas Legislature passed a law giving the Democratic Party's Executive Committee the right to decide who could vote in its party primaries, and the party passed a resolution allowing only white Democrats to vote. In *Nixon v. Condon*, 286 U.S. 73 (1932), the Court struck this law down, too, finding "state action" on the basis that the "Committee operated as representative of the State in the discharge of the State's authority." After the prior laws were struck down, the Texas Democratic Party passed a resolution limiting membership to white citizens of the State of Texas. In *Smith v. Allwright*, 321 U.S. 649 (1944), the Court held that state action existed. Although the Court was unwilling to hold that the "privilege of membership in a party" is a state concern, the Court held that state action existed since the privilege of membership "is also the essential qualification for voting in a primary to select nominees for a general election."

Following *Smith*, in *Terry v. Adams*, 345 U.S. 461 (1953), the Court struck down a Texas county political organization called the "Jaybird Democratic Association" or "Jaybird Party's" pre-primary that excluded black voters from its "pre-primary" elections on racial grounds. With few exceptions, those who won the Jaybird Party pre-primary subsequently won the general election. The Court recognized that a party may not prohibit voters from participating in a primary on the basis of race, and found that the Jaybird Party was doing nothing more than utilizing the primary to ratify the results of its discriminatory pre-primary. As a result, the pre-primary was the equivalent of a prohibited election. The Court found that the "Jaybird primary has become an integral part, indeed the only effective part, of the elective process that determines who shall rule and govern in the county."

It is difficult to know whether the *Smith* decision was simply a product of its times, or whether it has broader application. The First Amendment protects the right of individuals to associate for expressive purposes, and any group has the power to band together to promote those things in which it believes. The Court probably struck down the Jaybird primary because of the history of excluding blacks from the political process in the State of Texas, and the fact that the Jaybird pre-primary seemed to be just another attempt to end-run the Court's prior decisions.

3. Other Modern Cases

Even though few modern cases involve government towns or party primaries, a number of modern cases apply governmental function principles. In *Edmonson v. Leesville Concrete Co., Inc.*, 500 U.S. 614 (1991), the Court held that state action existed when defendant used peremptory challenges to remove black persons from a prospective jury list. The government had allowed the parties to exercise peremptory challenges, and concluded that defendant had made extensive use of state procedures with "the overt, significant assistance of state officials." Not only did Congress establish the qualifications for jury service and the procedures for juror selection, it also required prospective jurors to complete jury qualification forms, and defendant relied on these forms in exercising its peremptory strikes. In addition, when a party exercised a challenge, the court was asked to exercise its formal authority to "discharge the prospective juror, thus effecting the 'final and practical denial' of the excluded individual's opportunity to serve on the petit jury." As a result, the Court found a "traditional function of government" because of the nature of jury deliberations which result in a verdict that is "incorporated in a judgment enforceable by the court." The Court expressed concern that discriminatory use of peremptory challenges could place potential jurors "at risk of open and public discrimination as a condition of their participation in the justice system. The injury to excluded jurors would be the direct result of governmental delegation and participation."

In *West v. Atkins*, 487 U.S. 42 (1988), the Court held that a private doctor's actions constituted state action when a state prison contracted with the doctor to provide inmate medical care. The Court emphasized that the state had a legal obligation to provide adequate medical care to inmates, that inmates were only allowed to use the prison doctor, and that the state had essentially delegated its obligations by contracting out to a private doctor.

B. STATE INVOLVEMENT OR ENCOURAGEMENT

Although the Court has decided a number of governmental function cases, far more cases involve allegations of "state involvement" or "encouragement." The question is whether government is sufficiently involved in private action, or has sufficiently encouraged private action, so that the actions of private individuals or corporations should be treated as state action. The difficulty with these cases is that government is almost always involved in private action in some way. For example, even if government does not explicitly encourage a particular action (*e.g.*, racial discrimination), government may have enacted laws that permit the individual acts of discrimination, or that fail to prohibit the discrimination. The critical question in each case is whether there is enough state involvement or encouragement in a given case to transform private discrimination into state action.

In *Burton v. Wilmington Parking Authority*, 365 U.S. 715 (1961), the Court held that a private coffee shop located in a public parking garage that refused to serve food or drinks to blacks should be treated as state actor for purposes of the Fourteenth Amendment's Equal Protection Clause. The Court emphasized that the parking garage was created by the city to provide adequate parking facilities for the public, that the land and the building were publicly owned, and that the commercial space was designed to generate revenue so that the facility would be economically viable and self-sustaining. In addition, the Court found a synergy between the parking garage and the shop in that the shop's customers could park in the garage, and the shop helped create demand for the parking facilities. The net effect was that "profits earned by discrimination not only contribute to, but also are indispensable elements in, the financial success of a governmental agency." Finally, the Court emphasized that "the restaurant is operated as an integral part of a public building devoted to a public parking service".

Likewise, in *Peterson v. City of Greenville,* 373 U.S. 244 (1963), the Court found state action when petitioners were refused service at a lunch counter and ultimately convicted of trespass for their failure to leave. The Court emphasized that local law required businesses (like the lunch counter) to discriminate on the basis of race. Although private individuals have the right to discriminate on the basis of race unless some law or other enactment prevents them from doing so, the law involved in *Peterson required* the proprietor to discriminate on the basis of race. This requirement transformed the private action into state action.

Other cases have presented facts that less obviously involve state action, and that require more complex and nuanced judgments by the courts. For example, *Norwood v. Harrison*, 413 U.S. 455 (1973), the Court found state action when the State of Mississippi loaned textbooks to private schools that discriminated on the basis of race even though the decision to discriminate was privately made. The state asserted a non-discriminatory interest in support of the law (*e.g.*, the state's desire to ensure that all of its citizens were well-educated), and the program was available to all schools (discriminatory and non-discriminatory). The Court emphasized that the number of private racially discriminatory schools had increased dramatically in the wake of desegregation efforts, and that the existence of the private schools (and their racially discriminatory policies) was undercutting desegregation efforts. In addition, the Court focused on the fact that the cost of learning materials constituted an "inescapable educational cost" and provides support for discrimination. Finally, the Court emphasized that Mississippi's actions were constitutionally barred, noting that "[a] state may not induce, encourage or promote private persons to accomplish what it is constitutionally forbidden to accomplish."

Not all governmental involvement in private discrimination is sufficient to create state action. For example, in *Moose Lodge v. Irvis*,

407 U.S. 163 (1972), the Court held that a private club's racial discrimination did not constitute state action even though the club held a state liquor license. Given the importance of a liquor license to the survival of a private club, Irvis argued that the state was sufficiently involved in the discrimination to create state action. In reaching its decision, the Court emphasized that some "state-furnished services" qualify as "necessities" *(e.g.*, electricity, water, and police and fire protection), and that these services could not be treated as state action without utterly emasculating the distinction between private and state conduct. In order to constitute state action, the state must have "significantly involved itself with invidious discriminations." The Court found that Pennsylvania's liquor license did not "overtly or covertly encourage discrimination." Moreover, distinguishing *Burton*, the Court emphasized that Moose Lodge operated on private property, and did not hold itself out as a place of public accommodation. However, the Court did strike down a portion of the governing statute that affirmatively required licensees to adhere to their constitutions and by-Laws—in this case, a discriminatory constitution and bylaws. *Moose Lodge* illustrates the notion that, even though the state may have some involvement in private action, the state's involvement may be insufficient to create state action. In *Moose Lodge*, the club's decision to discriminate was a private decision that was not encouraged or mandated the state. As a result, the Court regarded the decision to discriminate as "private."

In *Gilmore v. City of Montgomery*, 417 U.S. 556 (1974), the Court held that racially discriminatory schools could use public park facilities without creating state action, but could not be given exclusive use. Justice Frankfurter dissented: "[T]he city's actions significantly enhanced the attractiveness of segregated private schools, formed in reaction against the federal court school order, by enabling them to offer complete athletic programs. [T]his assistance significantly tended to undermine the federal court order mandating the establishment and maintenance of a unitary school system in Montgomery."

Likewise, in *CBS, Inc. v. Democratic National Committee*, 412 U.S. 94 (1973), the Court found no state action even though a company held a public license to operate a radio station, and functioned under a signification level of governmental regulation, when the station refused to air a series of one-minute spot announcements expressing views on the Vietnam War. The Court emphasized that Congress opted for a system of private broadcasting, although licensed and regulated by the government, but treating license holders as "public trustees" "charged with the duty of fairly and impartially informing the public audience" with the government serving as simply an "overseer" whose task was to ensure fairness, balance, and objectivity. In other words, broadcast licensees retained a measure of journalistic freedom so long as they discharge their duties as a public trustee. The Court also emphasized that the FCC did not create or command the station's editorial policy, but simply left decisions on that issue to "journalistic discretion" so that the government was not a "partner" in the licensee's action.

The mere fact that government fails to prohibit discrimination does not necessarily transform private action into state action. However, in *Reitman v. Mulkey*, 387 U.S. 369 (1967), the Court found state action in a California constitutional amendment that removed the authority of state and local governments to "limit or abridge, directly or indirectly, the right of any person, who is willing or desires to sell, lease or rent any part or all of his real property, to decline to sell, lease or rent such property to such person or persons as he, in his absolute discretion, chooses." The Court viewed the amendment as more than a repeal of existing statutes because it nullified local anti-discrimination policies, and established "a purported constitutional right to privately discriminate on grounds which admittedly would be unavailable under the Fourteenth Amendment should state action be involved." In other words, the "right to discriminate is now one of the basic policies of the State," and there is a risk that the amendment "will significantly encourage and involve the State in private discriminations."

C. JUDICIAL INVOLVEMENT

In *Shelley v. Kraemer*, 334 U.S. 1 (1948), the Court held that judicial enforcement of private racially restrictive covenants involves state action. Although private parties had created the covenants without state support or encouragement, the Court noted that but for the intervention of the state courts, "petitioners would have been free to occupy the properties in question without restraint." This judicial involvement was viewed as state action. It is doubtful that *Shelley* should be read broadly to suggest that judicial enforcement of private rights transforms those rights into state action. A more likely explanation of the decision is that it arose out of the Civil Rights movement of the 1960s and involved an attempt to enforce a racially restrictive covenant.

Nevertheless, there are contexts in which *Shelley* retains validity. In *Barrows v. Jackson*, 346 U.S. 249 (1953), the Court held that state action existed when a court awarded damages (rather than injunctive relief) for violation of a racially restrictive covenant. Although the Court recognized that private individuals could voluntarily follow such agreements, the Court concluded that, if respondent were forced to pay damages, the consequence "of that sanction by the State would be to encourage the use of restrictive covenants."

Shelley and *Barrows* were reinforced by *Evans v. Newton*, 382 U.S. 296 (1966). That case involved a U.S. Senator who willed land to the City of Macon on condition that the land be reserved as a park for white people. While the will stated that the Senator had only the kindest feeling for blacks, he believed that the two races should be kept separate. The City kept the park segregated for years, but then began to integrate the park on the basis that it was constitutionally impermissible to maintain a segregated facility. At that point, the trustees of the will sued to remove the city as trustee and to appoint private trustees. The Court concluded that the park could not be segregated whether or not it was in private hands: "The predominant character and purpose of this park are municipal [and] requires that it be treated as a public institution subject to the command of the Fourteenth Amendment, regardless of who now has title under state law."

The limits of the *Shelley* and *Barrows* judicial involvement concept are revealed by the holding in *Evans v. Abney*, 396 U.S. 435 (1970). Following the decision in *Newton*, the Senator's heirs sued to reclaim the park, claiming that the trust failed since the Senator's intention to provide a park for whites only could not be fulfilled, and therefore the park reverted to them. The Court could have relied on *Shelley* to hold that judicial enforcement of the reverter provision constituted state action. However, the Court upheld the reverter provision, finding no state action, because there was "not the slightest indication that any of the Georgia judges involved were motivated by racial animus or discriminatory intent of any sort in construing and enforcing Senator Bacon's will." The "Senator's will shows that the racial restrictions were solely the product of the testator's own full-blown social philosophy." The Court distinguished *Shelley*, noting that "the effect of the Georgia decision eliminated all discrimination against Negroes in the park by eliminating the park itself, and the termination of the park was a loss shared equally by the white and Negro citizens of Macon since both races would have enjoyed a constitutional right of equal access to the park's facilities had it continued."

In later cases, the Court has applied *Shelley's* holding in the context of judicial actions enforcing creditors' rights. In *Sniadach v. Family Finance Corp.*, 395 U.S. 337 (1969), the Court found state action when creditors invoked state-created garnishment procedures to enforce a debt. In *Mitchell v. W. T. Grant Co.*, 416 U.S. 600 (1974), the Court reached a similar result regarding a vendor's execution of a lien. In both cases, the Court found state action because state officials aided the creditor in securing the disputed property even though the litigation was between creditors and debtors and involved no state officials. The Court emphasized that the deprivation was "caused by the exercise of some right or privilege created by the State or by a rule of conduct imposed by the state or by a person for whom the State is responsible." By finding state action, the Court was able to impose due process requirements on the debt enforcement process, and thereby to protect debtors against possibly predatory creditors.

In recent years, however, the Court has refused to extend the due process decisions. In *Flagg Brothers, Inc. v. Brooks*, 436 U.S. 149 (1978), the Court held that a warehouseman's proposed sale of goods entrusted to him for storage, as permitted by New York's Uniform Commercial Code, did not constitute state action. The challenge was brought by a woman, evicted from her apartment, to prevent the threatened sale as a violation of the Due Process and Equal Protection Clauses of the Fourteenth Amendment. The Court refused to find state action because no public officials were defendants in the suit, as well as because there was a "total absence of overt official involvement." While the Court could have found state action based on the fact that the warehouseman acted pursuant to statutory authorization, the Court rejected the idea that the state had delegated to the warehouseman a power "traditionally exclusively reserved to the State" concluding that few functions traditionally performed by governments have been "exclusively reserved to the State." The Court emphasized that the state's "system of rights and remedies" recognizes "the traditional place of private arrangements in ordering relationships in the commercial world" so that "the settlement of disputes between debtors and creditors is not traditionally an exclusive public function." The Court also rejected the idea that the state had "authorized and encouraged" the warehouseman's action, finding only "mere acquiescence."

In *Lugar v. Edmondson Oil Co., Inc.*, 457 U.S. 922 (1982), the Court held that a creditor's actions pursuant to a prejudgment attachment statute involved state action. The governing statute provided that a creditor could gain an attachment from a court only by alleging, *ex parte*, that the debtor was disposing of or might dispose of his property in an effort to defeat the creditor's rights. In *Lugar*, the Court held that the procedure involved state action within the meaning of the due process clause, noting that the courts had consistently held that a private party's joint participation with state officials in the seizure of disputed property is sufficient to characterize that party as a "state actor" for purposes of the Fourteenth Amendment. The Court found "joint participation" because the State had created a system whereby state officials attached property on the *ex parte* application of one party to a private dispute.

D. MIXED CASES (INVOLVING ALLEGATIONS OF GOVERNMENT FUNCTION AND/OR GOVERNMENTAL INVOLVEMENT OR ENCOURAGEMENT OR SOME OTHER INVOLVEMENT)

Most modern state action cases do not fit neatly into either the governmental function or the governmental involvement/ encouragement category. In many cases, plaintiffs argue not only that defendant's conduct involves a governmental function, but that the government is implicated or involved in some other way. In more modern cases, the Court has been somewhat less willing to find state action even though arguments can be made that there is governmental "involvement" or "encouragement" and even though it can be argued that defendant is performing a "traditional governmental function".

1. Private Corporations

Public Utilities. In *Jackson v. Metropolitan Edison Company*, 419 U.S. 345 (1974), the Court held that a privately owned and operated utility company did not function as a state actor even though it held a certificate of public convenience from a state utility commission that authorized it to deliver electricity in a defined area, and even though the utility was subject to extensive regulation by a state Commission. In addition, under a provision of its general tariff filed with the Commission, the utility had the right to discontinue service to any customer on reasonable notice of nonpayment of bills. As a result, when the company terminated a customer for failure to pay her bills, the termination did not constitute state action requiring application of due process principles. The mere fact that a business is subject to state regulation did not, by itself, convert the company's actions into state action for purposes of the Fourteenth Amendment. In addition, the utility's monopoly status and the fact that it provided an "essential public service" were not enough, by themselves, to create state action. Indeed, the Court concluded that many business (*e.g.*, doctors, optometrists, lawyers, and milk distributors) are all affected with the "public interest." Moreover, the Court rejected the argument that Metropolitan's termination was state action merely because the State had "specifically authorized and approved" the termination practice. The Court concluded that the government's involvement was "not sufficient to connect the State of Pennsylvania with respondent's action so as to make the latter's conduct attributable to the State for purposes of the Fourteenth Amendment."

Public Access Cable Channels. In *Manhattan Community Access Corp. v. Halleck*, 587 U.S. 802 (2019), the Court held that the public access channels on a cable network did not constitute "state action," and therefore the First Amendment did not restrain the network's editorial discretion. In that case, there was some state regulation of public access channels: they were required to offer public access channels, and to do so free of charge and on a first-come, first-served, basis. Although Time Warner owned the network, the agreement with Time Warner allowed the state to designate a private nonprofit corporation to run the public access channels. The city designated Manhattan Neighborhood Network (MNN), and the case arose when MNN suspended two producers from using the channels.

Although the Court recognized that a private entity may qualify as a state actor when it exercises "powers traditionally exclusively reserved to the State," the Court held that the action qualifies as state action only when the government had "traditionally and exclusively performed the function" in question. The Court concluded that very few functions met those requirements. In the case before it, the Court concluded that the relevant function, operation of public access channels on a cable system, is one that "has not traditionally and exclusively been performed by government." The Court also rejected the idea that public access channels constitute public fora for speech: "Merely hosting speech by others is not a traditional, exclusive public function and does not alone transform private entities into state actors subject to First Amendment constraints."

The Court emphasized that MNN had nothing more than a "license" to operate the public access channels, and the mere "fact that the government licenses, contracts with, or grants a monopoly to a private entity does not convert the private entity into a state actor—unless the private entity is performing a traditional, exclusive public function." The City did not own or lease the public access channels, and the City did not possess a formal easement or other property interest in those channels. The only thing that the city did was to designate a private entity to operate the channels. The Court deemed it irrelevant that NYC had authorized Time Warner, to lay cable along public rights-of-way in the City. Although "access to public rights-of-way is essential to lay cable and construct a physical cable infrastructure, the same is true for utility providers" (whose actions are not treated as state action). Justice Sotomayor, joined by three other justices, argued that the cable outlet constituted a public forum.

Amtrak. As *Jackson* implies, the Court's attitude towards state action and the governmental function exception has changed over time. In cases like *Burton*, *Shelley*, *Marsh* and *Terry*, the Court seemed to adopt a more expansive view of state action. Nevertheless, the Court has been willing to find that private corporations are functioning as state actors in some cases. In *Lebron v. National Railroad Passenger Corporation*, 513 U.S. 374 (1995), the Court held that the National Railroad Passenger Corporation (a/k/a, Amtrak) was a state actor for purposes of the Fist Amendment when it rejected a billboard display. Although Amtrak was technically a private corporation, it was government-created and -controlled in the sense that it was created by a special statute and the federal government appointed six of the corporation's eight directors. Moreover, Amtrak was created to further federal governmental goals under the direction and control of federal governmental appointees. As a result, the Court held that Amtrak should be treated differently than the public utility at issue in *Jackson*.

U.S. Olympic Committee. In *San Francisco Arts & Athletics, Inc. v. United States Olympic Committee*, 483 U.S. 522 (1987), the Court refused to hold that the United States Olympic Committee (USOC) was a state actor when it discriminated on the basis of sexual orientation. The Court reached this conclusion even though there was significant governmental involvement in the USOC (which Congress had authorized to coordinate amateur athletics in the United States, had granted a corporate charter, provided funding through direct grants, and given the right to exclusively use the Olympic words and symbols). However, Congress allowed the USOC to function independently of the government even though the International Olympic Committee was "structured according to nations" with athletes being viewed as representing their nations (athletes wear national uniforms, carry national flags, and the IOC keeps a medal count by nation), and the USOC was designated as the United States' representative. As a result, it was possible to argue that the USOC was performing a traditional governmental function. The Court found that the USOC's federal charter did not, by itself, render the USOC a government agent because all "corporations act under charters granted by a government." Likewise, the fact that Congress granted the USOC exclusive use of the word "Olympic" was not dispositive because all "enforceable rights in trademarks are created by some governmental act, usually pursuant to a statute or the common law" even though the actions of the owners "nevertheless remain private." Governmental funding was also not regarded as sufficient because the "Government may subsidize private entities without assuming constitutional responsibility for their actions." Moreover, the Court found that the USOC was not performing a "traditional governmental function" since Congress simply authorized the USOC to "coordinate activities that always have been performed by private entities." In the final analysis, the Court concluded that the USOC's "choice of how to enforce its exclusive right to use the word 'Olympic' simply is not a governmental decision" because the federal government did not try to coerce or encourage the USOC in its decisionmaking, and at most passively acquiesced.

2. School Associations

The Court has been somewhat more inclined to find state action in cases involving school associations, especially when there is significant state involvement in the associations. For example, in *Brentwood Academy v. Tennessee Secondary School Athletic Association*, 531 U.S. 288 (2001), the Court held that a statewide association that regulated interscholastic athletic competition among public and private secondary schools in Tennessee (TSAA) qualified as a state actor. In reaching that conclusion, the Court emphasized that almost all the State's public high schools belonged to the TSAA, that member schools could only play or scrimmage against other members (absent special dispensation), that voting rights were limited to high school principals, assistant principals, and superintendents, and that TSAA staff members were allowed to participate in State's public retirement system (even though they were not state employees). In addition, Tennessee's State Board of Education acknowledged the TSAA as "providing standards, rules and regulations for interscholastic competition in the public schools of Tennessee."

However, in *National Collegiate Athletic Association v. Tarkanian*, 488 U.S. 179 (1988), the Court held that the National Collegiate Athletic Association (NCAA) was not a state actor when it regulated intercollegiate athletics, and in particular when it suggested sanctions to the University of Nevada, Las Vegas, against a coach. The NCAA is a private association that includes virtually all public and private universities that have major athletic programs, and that has adopted "legislation" governing issues such as academic standards for eligibility, admissions, financial aid, and the recruiting of student athletes. NCAA rules are administered by a Committee on Infractions (Committee) which has an investigative staff, makes factual determinations concerning alleged rule violations, and "impose appropriate penalties" for violations which can include suspension or termination of membership. However, the NCAA may not sanction a member institution's employees directly, but the

NCAA's charter provides that member institutions "are expected to cooperate fully" with the administration of the enforcement program. The Court held that, neither "UNLV's decision to adopt the NCAA's standards nor its minor role in their formulation is a sufficient reason for concluding that the NCAA was acting under color of Nevada law when it promulgated standards governing athlete recruitment, eligibility, and academic performance." The Court also rejected the argument that UNLV delegated power to the NCAA. On the contrary, UNLV defended Tarkanian before the NCAA, and functioned more like an adversary than a partner of the NCAA. In addition, the NCAA lacked the power to directly discipline Tarkanian, and it did not request that the University do so, but instead simply issued a "show cause" order against UNLV in case it decided not to suspend. In other words, UNLV had options other than suspension in that it could have risked additional sanctions or could have withdrawn from the NCAA.

3. Other Modern Cases

There are a number of modern cases which suggest that the Court has adopted a more restrictive approach in which it refuses to find state action despite significant evidence of governmental involvement. In *Rendell-Baker v. Kohn*, 457 U.S. 830 (1982), the Court held that a private school did not function as a state actor in discharging employees even though most of the school's income was derived from public sources and even though the school was regulated by public authorities. The school specialized in dealing with students who experienced difficulties in public schools (because of drug, alcohol, or behavioral problems, or other special needs), received virtually all of its students and its funding from public schools or public agencies, and the state imposed various regulations that applied to all schools on issues such as recordkeeping, student-teacher ratios, personnel policies, and requiring written job descriptions and written statements of personnel standards and procedures. However, the contracts under which the private school received employees provided that it was functioning as a "contractor" and that the school's employees were not city employees. The Court concluded that the funding did not transform the school into a state actor. "Here the decisions to discharge the petitioners were not compelled or even influenced by any state regulation," and public officials "showed relatively little interest in the school's personnel matters." The Court also rejected the argument that the school was performing a public function. Even though the Court recognized that the "education of maladjusted high school students is a public function," the Court noted that the state had not until recently "undertaken to provide education for students who could not be served by traditional public schools." Finally, there was no "symbiotic relationship" between the school and the State arising from the fiscal relationship which the Court viewed as "not different from that of many contractors performing services for the government."

Also illustrative of the current approach is *Blum v. Yaretsky*, 457 U.S. 991 (1982), in which the Court refused to find state action in the transfer of Medicaid patients from nursing homes to other facilities without an opportunity for a hearing. New York directly reimbursed nursing homes for the reasonable cost of health care services provided that the patient satisfies income and resource standards, and is seeking medically necessary services. However, federal regulations required nursing homes to establish utilization review committees (URC) of physicians which were required to periodically assess whether patients were receiving the appropriate level of care, and whether the patient's continued stay in the facility was justified. The case arose when a URC decided that respondents did not need the care they were receiving and should be transferred to a lower level of care. The Court refused to find state action, noting that there must be a "sufficiently close nexus between the State and the challenged action of the regulated entity so that the action of the latter may be fairly treated as that of the State itself." The Court failed to find that nexus, noting that a state is "responsible for a private decision only when it has exercised coercive power or has provided such significant encouragement, either overt or covert, that the choice must in law be deemed to be that of the State. Mere approval of or acquiescence" is insufficient even if the state responds to the actions by adjusting benefit levels. "The decisions [are] made by physicians and nursing home administrators, all of whom are concededly private parties." Even though the regulations require nursing home action for patients that are inappropriately placed, the decision to transfer ultimately turns "on medical judgments made by private parties according to professional standards that are not established by the State." Moreover, even though the state provided more than 90% of the funding for the facilities, the Court refused to find state action because privately owned enterprises were "providing services that the State would not necessarily provide, even though they are extensively regulated." Finally, the Court concluded that the nursing homes perform a function that has been "traditionally the exclusive prerogative of the State."

Likewise, in *American Manufacturers Mutual Insurance Company v. Sullivan*, 526 U.S. 40 (1999), the Court dealt with a state's compulsory insurance systems which required employers to compensate employees for work-related injuries without regard to fault, as well as a utilization review procedure under which the reasonableness and necessity of an employee's past, ongoing, or prospective medical treatment could be reviewed before a medical bill must be paid. The Court concluded that the actions of these utilization review boards did not constitute state action. Even though the private insurers function under statutory authority, their actions were not "fairly attributable to the State so as to subject insurers to the constraints of the Fourteenth Amendment." The Court failed to find a "sufficiently close nexus" between the state and the challenged action of the regulated entity because there was no state coercion and no evidence of "significant encouragement, either overt or covert," so as to make the insurer's choice that of the state. The mere fact that the private entities acted with the approval or acquiescence of the state was regarded as insufficient. While the Court found some "encouragement" in the fact that state gave insurers "the option of deferring payment for unnecessary and unreasonable treatment pending review," it concluded that "this kind of subtle encouragement is no more significant than that which inheres in the State's creation or modification of any legal remedy." The Court also rejected the argument that the state had delegated to insurers "powers traditionally exclusively reserved to the State." The Court concluded that "Pennsylvania 'has done nothing more than authorize (and indeed limit)—without participation by any public official—what [private insurers] would tend to do, even in the absence of such authorization,' *i.e.*, withhold payment for disputed medical treatment pending a determination that the treatment is, in fact, reasonable and necessary."

In *DeShaney v. Winnebago County*, 489 U.S. 189 (1989), the Court held that the state did not deprive a boy of "liberty" without due process when he was severely beaten by his father and suffered permanent injuries including retardation. Although the boy was removed from by his father by state social workers, they later returned him to the father's care. Petitioner sued the social workers and other local officials claiming that their failure to remove him from a dangerous situation deprived him of his liberty in violation of the Due Process Clause of the Fourteenth Amendment. The Court concluded that the Due Process Clause did not protect individuals against the actions of private individuals, and does not guarantee individuals the right to governmental aid. The Court rejected the idea that a "special relationship" existed between the boy and the state "because the State knew that Joshua faced a special danger of abuse at his father's hands, and specifically proclaimed, by word and by deed, its intention to protect him against that danger," thereby assuming an "affirmative duty" to protect him and creating a substantive due process violation. The Court distinguished a state's obligation to prisoners, noting that the state has an obligation to protect prisoners because it restrains them and thereby prevents them from protecting themselves. The boy was not in state custody, but rather in the custody of his father: "While the State may have been aware of the dangers that Joshua faced in the free world, it played no part in their creation, nor did it do anything to render him any more vulnerable to them." At most, the state had a tort duty to protect the boy, but the present claim could not survive because it was based on the Fourteenth Amendment which required state action.

CHECKLIST

A. The Bill of Rights, as well as the fourteenth and fifteenth amendments, are designed to protect individuals against "governmental" action.

1. In other words, before they apply, it must be shown that the state is sufficiently involved in the challenged conduct so that the Bill of Rights (*e.g.*, freedom of speech, free exercise of religion, freedom of the press) or the Fourteenth Amendment apply.
2. Thus, these constitutional provisions (with the exception of the Thirteenth Amendment's prohibition against slavery) do not constrain the actions of private individuals.
3. Private conduct may be actionable under tort or statutory law, but it is not constitutionally prohibited in and of itself.
4. The seminal cases are the *Civil Rights Cases*, 109 U.S. 3 (1883), in which the Court held that the Fourteenth Amendment prohibited only "state action," and held that Congress could not restrain the conduct of private individuals.

B. Courts engage in a sophisticated process for determining whether state action exists.

1. In many cases, when plaintiffs assert a violation of the Bill of Rights or the Fourteenth Amendment, state involvement will be obvious.
2. In other words, Congress or a state legislature will have passed a law, or a governmental agency or government official will have taken action against the citizen.
3. More difficult questions arise when the violation seems to be the result of private action, but there appears to be some governmental involvement.

4. Government is involved in virtually all private conduct in one way or another.

5. Thus, the real question is whether the government is sufficiently involved so that the ostensibly private action effectively becomes "state action."

C. **One situation in which the Court has found state action is when a private entity performs a "traditional governmental function." In other words, the private entity performs functions that are really "governmental" in their function and nature.**

1. If a private corporation runs a town which functions like an ordinary public town, the private corporation may be regarded as performing a governmental function in running the town.

2. If a private entity is found to be performing a governmental function, then the protections of the Bill of Rights and the Fourteenth Amendment may apply to that governmental function.

3. The difficulty in these cases is in determining what constitutes a "traditional governmental function."

4. So-called "company towns" provide a classic example of state action. In these cases, a private town is functioning like a public one, and therefore the argument is made that its actions should be treated like a public town for constitutional purposes.

5. While the Court has vacillated on the issue, the Court has not held that shopping centers are like company towns.

6. The other context in which "governmental function" issues have arisen is related to the conduct of electoral primaries.

7. In a series of cases decided between 1927 and 1953, the Court held that the Democratic Party's efforts to preclude blacks from participating in its party primaries constituted state action.

8. Even though few modern cases involve government towns or party primaries, a number of modern cases apply governmental function principles.

9. In *Edmonson v. Leesville Concrete Co., Inc.*, 500 U.S. 614 (1991), the Court held that state action existed when defendant used peremptory challenges to remove black persons from a prospective jury list.

10. In *West v. Atkins*, 487 U.S. 42 (1988), the Court held that a private doctor's actions constituted state action when a state prison contracted with the doctor to provide inmate medical care.

D. Although the Court has decided a number of governmental function cases, far more cases involve allegations of "state involvement" or "encouragement."

1. The question is whether government is sufficiently involved in private action, or has sufficiently encouraged private action, so that the actions of private individuals or corporations should be treated as state action.
2. The difficulty with these cases is that government is almost always involved in private action in some way. For example, even if government does not explicitly encourage a particular action (*e.g.*, racial discrimination), government may have enacted laws that permit the individual acts of discrimination, or that fail to prohibit the discrimination.
3. The critical question in each case is whether there is enough involvement or encouragement in a given case to transform private discrimination into state action.
4. In *Burton v. Wilmington Parking Authority*, 365 U.S. 715 (1961), the Court held that a private coffee shop located in a public parking garage that refused to serve food or drinks to blacks should be treated as state actor for purposes of the Fourteenth Amendment's Equal Protection Clause.
5. In *Peterson v. City of Greenville,* 373 U.S. 244 (1963), the Court found state action when petitioners were refused service at a lunch counter and ultimately convicted of trespass for their failure to leave because local law required businesses (like the lunch counter) to discriminate on the basis of race.
6. In *Norwood v. Harrison*, 413 U.S. 455 (1973), the Court found state action when the State of Mississippi loaned textbooks to private schools that discriminated on the basis of race even though the decision to discriminate was privately made, the state asserted a non-discriminatory interest in support of the law (*e.g.*, the state's desire to ensure that all of its citizens were well-educated), and the program was available to all schools (discriminatory and non-discriminatory).

7. In *Moose Lodge v. Irvis*, 407 U.S. 163 (1972), the Court held that a private club's racial discrimination did not constitute state action even though the club held a state liquor license.

8. In *Gilmore v. City of Montgomery*, 417 U.S. 556 (1974), the Court held that racially discriminatory schools could use public park facilities, but could not be given exclusive use.

9. In *CBS, Inc. v. Democratic National Committee*, 412 U.S. 94 (1973), the Court found no state action even though a company held a public license to operate a radio station, and functioned under a significant level of governmental regulation.

10. In *Reitman v. Mulkey*, 387 U.S. 369 (1967), the Court found state action in a California constitutional amendment that removed the authority of state and local governments to "limit or abridge, directly or indirectly, the right of any person, who is willing or desires to sell, lease or rent any part or all of his real property, to decline to sell, lease or rent such property to such person or persons as he, in his absolute discretion, chooses."

E. The Court has sometimes held that judicial involvement in the enforcement of private rights constitutes state action.

1. In *Shelley v. Kraemer*, 334 U.S. 1 (1948), the Court held that judicial enforcement of private racially restrictive covenants involves state action.

2. In *Barrows v. Jackson*, 346 U.S. 249 (1953), the Court held that state action existed when a court awarded damages (rather than injunctive relief) for violation of a racially restrictive covenant.

F. In later cases, the Court has applied *Shelley's* holding in the context of judicial action enforcing creditors' rights.

1. In *Sniadach v. Family Finance Corp.*, 395 U.S. 337 (1969), the Court found state action when creditors invoked state-created garnishment procedures to enforce a debt.

2. In *Mitchell v. W. T. Grant Co.*, 416 U.S. 600 (1974), the Court reached a similar result regarding a vendor's execution of a lien. In both cases, the Court found state action because state officials aided the creditor in securing the disputed property even though the litigation was between creditors and debtors and involved no state officials.

3. In recent years, however, the Court has refused to extend the due process decisions.

4. In *Flagg Brothers, Inc. v. Brooks*, 436 U.S. 149 (1978), the Court held that a warehouseman's proposed sale of goods entrusted to him for storage, as permitted by New York's Uniform Commercial Code, did not constitute state action.

5. In *Lugar v. Edmondson Oil Co., Inc.*, 457 U.S. 922 (1982), the Court held that a creditor's actions pursuant to a prejudgment attachment statute involved state action.

G. Most modern state action cases do not fit neatly into either the governmental function or the governmental involvement/encouragement category. In many cases, plaintiffs argue not only that defendant's conduct involves a governmental function, but that the government is implicated or involved in some way.

1. In more modern cases, the Court has been somewhat less willing to find state action even though arguments can be made that there is governmental "involvement" or "encouragement" and even though it can be argued that defendant is performing a "traditional governmental function".

2. In *Jackson v. Metropolitan Edison Company*, 419 U.S. 345 (1974), the Court held that a privately owned and operated utility company did not function as a state actor even though it held a certificate of public convenience from a state utility commission that authorized it to deliver electricity in a defined area, and even though the utility was subject to extensive regulation by a state commission.

H. The Court's attitude towards state action and the governmental function exception has changed over time.

1. In cases like *Burton, Shelley, Marsh* and *Terry*, the Court seemed to adopt a more expansive view of state action.

2. In *Lebron v. National Railroad Passenger Corporation*, 513 U.S. 374 (1995), the Court held that the National Railroad Passenger Corporation (a/k/a, Amtrak) was a state actor for purposes of the Fist Amendment when it rejected a billboard display.

3. In *San Francisco Arts & Athletics, Inc. v. United States Olympic Committee*, 483 U.S. 522 (1987), the Court refused to hold that the United States Olympic Committee (USOC)

was a state actor when it discriminated on the basis of sexual orientation.

I. The Court has been somewhat more inclined to find state action in cases involving school associations, especially when there is significant state involvement in the association.

1. In *Brentwood Academy v. Tennessee Secondary School Athletic Association*, 531 U.S. 288 (2001), the Court held that a statewide association that regulated interscholastic athletic competition among public and private secondary schools in Tennessee (TSAA) qualified as a state actor.
2. However, in *National Collegiate Athletic Association v. Tarkanian*, 488 U.S. 179 (1988), the Court held that the National Collegiate Athletic Association (NCAA) was not a state actor when it regulated intercollegiate athletics, and in particular when it suggested sanctions to the University of Nevada, Las Vegas, against a coach.

J. There are a number of modern cases which suggest that the Court has adopted a more restrictive approach to standing in which it refuses to find state action despite significant evidence of governmental involvement.

1. In *Rendell-Baker v. Kohn*, 457 U.S. 830 (1982), the Court held that a private school did not function as a state actor in discharging employees even though most of the school's income was derived from public sources and even though the school was regulated by public authorities.
2. In *Blum v. Yaretsky*, 457 U.S. 991 (1982), the Court refused to find state action in the transfer of Medicaid patients from nursing homes to other facilities without an opportunity for a hearing even though New York directly reimbursed nursing homes for the reasonable cost of health care services provided that the patient satisfies income and resource standards, and was seeking medically necessary services.
3. In *DeShaney v. Winnebago County*, 489 U.S. 189 (1989), the Court held that the state did not deprive a boy of "liberty" without due process when he was severely beaten by his father and suffered permanent injuries even though the boy was removed from by his father by state social workers who later returned him to the father's care.

■ PROBLEMS ■

Problem #1: A city passes a housing law that requires landlords to maintain rental property in a clean, healthy and safe condition, and requires that all landlords treat tenants "fairly." In addition, the city requires that all landlords hold a license to rent property. Following a dispute, a landlord summarily evicts a tenant from his apartment. The tenant sues the landlord claiming that the landlord failed to provide him with due process of law during the eviction process. Is the landlord subject to the constitutional requirement of due process?

Answer: No. Even though the city regulates landlords, and even though it requires them to have a license, the existence of a license and regulation are not sufficient (by themselves) to create state action. The landlord is a private individual who was acting for private motives without state encouragement or support. As a result, the landlord is not subject to the due process clause.

Problem #2: In addition to regulating private landlords and their rental properties, the city decides to create a public housing project. Although the city pays to construct the housing, the city does not want to manage the housing itself. Accordingly, it creates a separate corporation (The Public Housing Management Authority (PHMA)). The PHMA functions independently of the city, but the city council appoints all of its members. When the PHMA evicts a tenant, the tenant sues claiming that he was denied due process of law. Is the PHMA subject to the constitutional requirement of due process?

Answer: Because of the circumstances, the PHMA would not be regarded as a private entity, but rather a public one, and therefore would be subject to the constitutional requirement of due process. The housing project was financed entirely out of public monies. In addition, although the PHMA is a separate corporation, it was created by the city which appoints all of its members. Under the circumstances, the PHMA's actions would be regarded as state action for purposes of the due process clause.

Problem #3: In the prior problem, rather than create the PHMA and finance a public housing project, the city decides to provide housing subsidies to low-income residents. The subsidies come in the form of "housing vouchers" that can be given to landlords to pay rent. Zeon takes his voucher to a private landlord who agrees to accept it in exchange for rent. When the landlord later tries to evict Zeon for misconduct, Zeon sues claiming a denial of due process. Under these circumstances, is the landlord engaged in state action so that his conduct is subject to the constitutional requirements of the due process clause?

Answer: No. Unlike the prior problem, the present landlord is a private entity that generally functions independently of the state, and therefore would ordinarily be regarded as a private actor. The only question is whether the landlord's acceptance of the voucher is sufficient to transform his conduct from private action to state action. In a number of cases, the Court has suggested that the mere fact that a state provides some financial support to private actors does not necessarily transform their actions into state actions. In this case, the critical actions were private actions that were not coerced, encouraged or controlled by the state.

POINTS TO REMEMBER

- The Bill of Rights, as well as the fourteenth and fifteenth amendments, are designed to protect individuals against "governmental" action.
- In other words, before they apply, it must be shown that the state is sufficiently involved in the challenged conduct so that the Bill of Rights (*e.g.*, freedom of speech, free exercise of religion, freedom of the press) or the Fourteenth Amendment apply.
- Thus, these constitutional provisions (with the exception of the Thirteenth Amendment's prohibition against slavery) do not constrain the actions of private individuals.
- Private conduct may be actionable under tort or statutory law, but it is not constitutionally prohibited in and of itself.
- In the *Civil Rights Cases*, 109 U.S. 3 (1883), the Court held that the Fourteenth Amendment prohibited only "state action," and that Congress could not restrain the conduct of private individuals.
- In many cases, when plaintiffs assert a violation of the Bill of Rights or the Fourteenth Amendment, state involvement will be obvious. In other words, Congress or a state legislature will have passed a law, or a governmental agency or government official will have taken action against the citizen.
- More difficult questions arise when the violation seems to be the result of private action, but there appears to be some governmental involvement.
- As we shall see, government is involved in virtually all private conduct in one way or another. Thus, the real question is whether the government is sufficiently involved so that the ostensibly private action effectively becomes "state action."

- One situation in which the Court has found state action is when a private entity performs a "traditional governmental function." In other words, the private entity performs functions that are really "governmental" in their function and nature.
- For example, if a private corporation runs a town which functions like an ordinary public town, the private corporation may be regarded as performing a governmental function in running the town.
- In *Marsh v. Alabama*, 326 U.S. 501 (1946), a "town" owned by a private company, included residential buildings, streets, a sewer system, a sewage disposal plant, various businesses, a United States post office, a sheriff (paid by the company), and a business block with stores, paved sidewalks, and streets that connected to public highways, and was treated as subject to the First Amendment's protections for speech.
- In *Hudgens v. NLRB*, 424 U.S. 507 (1976), the Court held that picketers did not have a First Amendment right to picket inside a shopping mall: "the constitutional guarantee of free expression has no part to play in a case such as this." As a result, the actions of the owners of private shopping malls are generally not regarded as state action today.
- In a variety of cases, the Court has found state action in cases involving political party primaries (even though political parties are regarded as voluntary associations of individuals).
- Even though few modern cases involve government towns or party primaries, a number of modern cases apply governmental function principles.
- In *Edmonson v. Leesville Concrete Co., Inc.*, 500 U.S. 614 (1991), the Court held that state action existed when defendant used peremptory challenges to remove black persons from a prospective jury list.
- In *West v. Atkins*, 487 U.S. 42 (1988), the Court held that a private doctor's actions constituted state action when a state prison contracted with the doctor to provide inmate medical care.
- Although the Court has decided a number of governmental function cases, far more cases involve allegations of "state involvement" or "encouragement." The question is whether government is sufficiently involved in private action, or has sufficiently encouraged private action, so that the actions of private individuals or corporations should be treated as state action.

- The difficulty with these cases is that government is almost always involved in private action in some way. For example, even if government does not explicitly encourage a particular action (*e.g.*, racial discrimination), government may have enacted laws that permit the individual acts of discrimination, or that fail to prohibit the discrimination.
- The critical question in each case is whether there is enough governmental involvement or encouragement in a given case to transform private discrimination into state action.
- In *Burton v. Wilmington Parking Authority*, 365 U.S. 715 (1961), the Court held that a private coffee shop located in a public parking garage that refused to serve food or drinks to blacks should be treated as state actor for purposes of the Fourteenth Amendment's Equal Protection Clause.
- In *Peterson v. City of Greenville,* 373 U.S. 244 (1963), the Court found state action when petitioners were refused service at a lunch counter and ultimately convicted of trespass for their failure to leave. The Court emphasized that local law required businesses (like the lunch counter) to discriminate on the basis of race.
- In *Norwood v. Harrison*, 413 U.S. 455 (1973), the Court found state action when the State of Mississippi loaned textbooks to private schools that discriminated on the basis of race.
- However, in *Moose Lodge v. Irvis*, 407 U.S. 163 (1972), the Court held that a private club's racial discrimination did not constitute state action even though the club held a state liquor license.
- In *CBS, Inc. v. Democratic National Committee*, 412 U.S. 94 (1973), the Court found no state action even though a company held a public license to operate a radio station, and functioned under a significant level of governmental regulation.
- The mere fact that government fails to prohibit discrimination does not necessarily transform private action into state action.
- In *Reitman v. Mulkey*, 387 U.S. 369 (1967), the Court found state action in a California constitutional amendment that removed the authority of state and local governments to "limit or abridge, directly or indirectly, the right of any person, who is willing or desires to sell, lease or rent any part or all of his real property, to decline to sell, lease or rent such property to such person or persons as he, in his absolute discretion, chooses."
- In *Shelley v. Kraemer*, 334 U.S. 1 (1948), the Court held that judicial enforcement of private racially restrictive covenants

involves state action. Although private parties had created the covenants without state support or encouragement, the Court noted that but for the intervention of the state courts, "petitioners would have been free to occupy the properties in question without restraint."

- In *Barrows v. Jackson*, 346 U.S. 249 (1953), the Court held that state action existed when a court awarded damages (rather than injunctive relief) for violation of a racially restrictive covenant.
- In *Evans v. Newton*, 382 U.S. 296 (1966), the Court found that a city could not maintain a segregated park even though the park had been willed to the city on condition that it remain segregated.
- In *Evans v. Abney*, 396 U.S. 435 (1970), following the decision in *Newton*. The Court held that the park could revert to the testator's heirs under a provision of its will when it was no longer maintained as a segregated entity.
- In *Sniadach v. Family Finance Corp.*, 395 U.S. 337 (1969), the Court found state action when creditors invoked state-created garnishment procedures to enforce a debt.
- In *Mitchell v. W. T. Grant Co.*, 416 U.S. 600 (1974), the Court reached a similar result regarding a vendor's execution of a lien because state officials aided the creditor in securing the disputed property even though the litigation was between creditors and debtors and involved no state officials.
- However, in *Flagg Brothers, Inc. v. Brooks*, 436 U.S. 149 (1978), the Court held that a warehouseman's proposed sale of goods entrusted to him for storage, as permitted by New York's Uniform Commercial Code, did not constitute state action.
- In *Lugar v. Edmondson Oil Co., Inc.*, 457 U.S. 922 (1982), the Court held that a creditor's actions pursuant to a prejudgment attachment statute involved state action.
- Most modern state action cases do not fit neatly into either the governmental function or the governmental involvement/ encouragement category. In many cases, plaintiffs argue not only that defendant's conduct involves a governmental function, but that the government is implicated or involved in some way.
- In more modern cases, the Court has been somewhat less willing to find state action even though arguments can be made that there is governmental "involvement" or "encouragement" and even though it can be argued that a party is performing a "traditional governmental function".

- In *Jackson v. Metropolitan Edison Company*, 419 U.S. 345 (1974), the Court held that a privately owned and operated utility company did not function as a state actor even though it held a certificate of public convenience from a state utility commission that authorized it to deliver electricity in a defined area, and even though the utility was subject to extensive regulation by a state commission.
- In *Lebron v. National Railroad Passenger Corporation*, 513 U.S. 374 (1995), the Court held that the National Railroad Passenger Corporation (a/k/a, Amtrak) was a state actor for purposes of the First Amendment when it rejected a billboard display.
- In *San Francisco Arts & Athletics, Inc. v. United States Olympic Committee*, 483 U.S. 522 (1987), the Court refused to hold that the United States Olympic Committee (USOC) was a state actor when it discriminated on the basis of sexual orientation.
- The Court has been somewhat more inclined to find state action in cases involving school associations, especially when there is significant state involvement in the association.
- In *Brentwood Academy v. Tennessee Secondary School Athletic Association*, 531 U.S. 288 (2001), the Court held that a statewide association that regulated interscholastic athletic competition among public and private secondary schools in Tennessee (TSAA) qualified as a state actor.
- However, in *National Collegiate Athletic Association v. Tarkanian*, 488 U.S. 179 (1988), the Court held that the National Collegiate Athletic Association (NCAA) was not a state actor when it regulated intercollegiate athletics, and in particular when it suggested sanctions to the University of Nevada, Las Vegas, against a coach.
- In *Rendell-Baker v. Kohn*, 457 U.S. 830 (1982), the Court held that a private school did not function as a state actor in discharging employees even though most of the school's income was derived from public sources and even though the school was regulated by public authorities (but not as to the dismissals).
- In *Blum v. Yaretsky*, 457 U.S. 991 (1982), the Court refused to find state action in the transfer of Medicaid patients from nursing homes to other facilities without an opportunity for a hearing.
- In *DeShaney v. Winnebago County*, 489 U.S. 189 (1989), the Court found no state action when a boy was severely beaten by his father and suffered permanent injuries, including retardation, even though the boy was removed from by his father

by state social workers, but later returned by them to the father's care.